ATLAS *of* IRISH HISTORY

Second Edition

ATLAS *of* IRISH HISTORY

Second Edition

Seán Duffy

Gabriel Doherty

Raymond Gillespie

James Kelly

Colm Lennon

Brendan Smith

GILL & MACMILLAN

Published in Ireland by
Gill & Macmillan
Hume Avenue, Park West, Dublin 12
with associated companies throughout the world
www.gillmacmillan.ie

© 1997, 2000 Arcadia Editions Limited
Derbyshire, England

978 07171 3093 1

Printed in Malaysia

*The paper used in this book is made from the wood pulp
of managed forests. For every tree felled, at least one tree
is planted, thereby renewing natural resources.*

A catalogue record is available for this book
from the British Library.

10 9 8

Contributors

Seán Duffy lectures in Medieval Irish and British history in Trinity College, Dublin.

Gabriel Doherty teaches in the Department of History, University College, Cork.

Raymond Gillespie teaches in the Department of History at St Patrick's College, Maynooth.

James Kelly teaches in the Department of History at St Patrick's College, Drumcondra, Dublin.

Colm Lennon teaches in the Department of History at St Patrick's College, Maynooth.

Brendan Smith teaches history in the Department of Historical Studies at the University of Bristol.

Foreword

OUT ON THE WESTERN EDGE of Europe, a first glance at the map makes Ireland seem a small and isolated place. However, many peoples have by turns established themselves on this remote island, creating an historical dynamic whose dispersed voices are now heard in almost every major city of the globe, in accents unmistakably from Cork or Connemara, Donegal or Dublin. This atlas attempts to explain in a visual, accessible way Ireland's unfolding story, and how this small country's remarkable worldwide impact has come about.

Some ten millennia ago, the first people arrived in Ireland, perhaps across the land bridge that once linked Ireland to Scotland, and began the region's human story. Not much more than two millennia ago arrived the ancestors of the Gaels, who after hundreds of years of assimilation and adaptation gave and continue to give the island its distinct identity.

Over the past thousand years, the Vikings, Normans, English and Scots have all left their mark on Ireland's culture, religion, language and landscape. They have also left schisms which survive to this day. For more than 800 years, Ireland's history was by degrees tied to that of England, moving from the margins of English royal interests to the status of a colony. From 1800 the island was governed directly from Westminster, with Irish soldiers guarding the Asian frontiers of Britain's global empire, Irish workers building bridges in Africa, and Irish settlers roaming the Canadian prairies. While the Irishman's wanderlust has never been in doubt, not all of this dispersion, however, was of Ireland's choosing.

Ireland's desire to set its own direction surfaced many times, and by the 1920s most of the island had secured its independence, with the exception of the north-east corner which remained within the United Kingdom. This partition, and its ramifications for both the southern state and Great Britain, continue to be hotly contested and debated, as the newspapers daily and often tragically remind us.

The maps and texts of this atlas are intended to spotlight the movements of Ireland's long and multi-layered history and to explain how its present circumstances have arisen. Maps tend to show facts rather than influences or ideas, and as such are simply snapshots in time. This collection, however, is accompanied by text written by some of the leading authorities in the field, and it is hoped that, together, these contributions will go some way to explain the story of this unique and fascinating place.

For the authors

Contents

CONTRIBUTORS

FOREWORD

PART I	ORIGINS	10
	Seán Duffy	
	Celtic Ireland	14
	The Arrival of Christianity	16
	Early Peoples and Politics	18
	The Golden Age	20
	Ireland and Europe	22
	The Viking Wars	24
	The Age of Brian Boru	26
	Reform of the Church	28
	Ireland before the Normans	30
PART II	THE CONQUEST OF IRELAND	32
	Brendan Smith	
	The English Invasion	36
	Expansion of the Colony	38
	Irish Resistance	40
	The Decline of English Power	42
	The Gaelic Revival	44
	The Late Middle Ages	46
	The Growth of Dublin	48
PART III	REFORMATION TO RESTORATION	50
	Colm Lennon and Raymond Gillespie	
	The Protestant Reformation	54
	Elizabethan Administration	56
	Plantation and Resistance	58
	O'Neill's Rising	60
	Jacobean Plantations	62
	The Rising of 1641	64
	Cromwell's Campaigns and Administration	66
	The Williamite Revolution	68

PART IV   FROM SPLENDOUR TO FAMINE   70

James Kelly

The Penal Laws   76

The Georgian Economy   78

The Government of Ireland, 1692–1785   80

The 1798 Rebellion   82

Catholic Emancipation and Repeal   84

Nineteenth-Century Catholicism   86

The Pre-Famine Economy   88

Emigration to 1845   90

The Great Famine   92

The Decline of the Irish Language   94

PART V   MODERN IRELAND   96

Gabriel Doherty

Post-Famine Emigration   102

Economic Development before the Great War   104

The Growth of Irish Nationalism   106

Government Policy   108

The Ulster Question   110

The Great War and the Easter Rising   112

Separation 1916–23   114

Cumann na nGaedheal   116

Fianna Fáil   118

The '40s and '50s: Turmoil and Malaise   120

Northern Ireland   122

The '60s: Economic and Social Change   124

The '70s and the '80s: Political and Social Instability   126

The Northern Crisis   128

Ireland in the '90s   130

CHRONOLOGY   132

FURTHER READING   136

INDEX   138

ACKNOWLEDGEMENTS   144

PART I: ORIGINS

Seán Duffy

FAINT TRACES of human food-gathering and hunting survive in Ireland from the Mesolithic period (perhaps as early as 8,000 BC). These early people may have migrated from Britain though hardly before the land-bridge between the islands was washed away, and such weapons and tools as they have left behind are mostly small flint blades. They lived on wild pig, small mammals, fowl, fish and edible plants, and dwelt in small huts in isolated bands and hunting-camps, perhaps migrating seasonally. The island must have been sparsely inhabited, and has yielded no evidence of artistic activity, or of agriculture.

Above: The chamber of the passage tomb at Newgrange, Co. Meath. The massive uprights are parts of the estimated 200,000 tonnes of stones transported to the site during its construction.

Ireland's first crop-growers and live-stock-breeders were Neolithic peoples who arrived by sea from Britain or the continent about 6,000 years ago. It was they who made the first real impact on Ireland's landscape, building more substantial houses and stone boundary walls. Their pottery and decoration developed, and there is evidence of 'industrial' activity in the form of the large-scale manufacture of axes. They also constructed numerous megalithic monuments such as passage-tombs, court-cairns and dolmens, used for burial and for ritualistic and cultic purposes. These are among the earliest examples of true architecture known anywhere in the world and many survive in the Irish landscape today, some preserving examples of advanced mural art.

During the Bronze Age (*c.* 2,500–600 BC) Ireland's first metal-workers, not necessarily new immigrants, exploited the island's rich copper deposits to produce copper and bronze axe- and spear-heads, and later, shields, cauldrons, sickles and craftsmen's tools. Their legacy includes beautiful personal ornaments, many in gold, such as earrings, fibulae (dress fasteners) and lunulae (an item of neck or hair jewellery, shaped like a half-moon). Later they produced a great variety of highly accomplished neck, arm and waist ornaments, the pre-historic goldsmiths' craft probably reaching its peak at about 700 BC. In fact, more gold-crafted objects survive from this period in Ireland than in any other country in western or northern Europe, and some objects of Irish type have been found in Britain and the continent, suggesting an active export trade. From this period, too, may belong the many stone circles and 'wedge' tombs throughout the countryside. Pottery used for food and funerary urns also reached a high standard.

By about 600 BC iron had come to replace bronze as the main source-material for weapons and tools, and it was during the ensuing Iron Age that the first

Celtic peoples appeared in Ireland. They have left us the Irish language and art-work in the La Tène style associated with the Celts of central Europe. By the beginning of this period great hilltop enclosures like Tara and Emain Macha were in use, sites which sometimes also had an earlier importance. Though evidence is scanty, some cliff-top 'promontory forts' may date from this era, as may some 'crannóg' lake-dwellings. The Roman invasion of Britain affected Ireland to the extent that trading contacts with the Empire were enhanced, and Ireland may have provided a haven for refugees from the conquest, and a base from which to raid western Britain. As the Roman Empire declined, unrelated Irish colonies took root in what are now Wales and Cornwall and in western Scotland, the last being ultimately of greatest influence. It was probably in this period that the 'ring-fort' became established as the home of wealthy farmers, those with earthen banks usually being called 'raths' and those with stone walls, 'cashels'. Thousands of these still dot the countryside and many remained in use well into the historic period.

The historic period begins with the introduction of Christianity in the 5th century, and Ireland first emerges into the light of history in documents ascribed to the British missionary, St Patrick. Thereafter it developed a highly literate society which has left a substantial corpus of literature in both Latin and Irish, allowing us to form a mental picture of Dark-Age Ireland that is clearer and far more detailed than that offered by most other European countries. Using annals, genealogies, king-lists and other sources, we can assemble the names of the many peoples who dominated the island, the territories they held, and the rise and fall of their various dynasties. Other sources allow us to plot the progress of Christianity in the country, in which, by the mid-6th century, monks and monasteries had eclipsed bishops and dioceses, their houses becoming centres not just of piety, but of learning, study and art. The members of the monastic communities studied the Bible, the writings of the early Church Fathers, canon law and Latin grammar. They copied manuscripts, many of them beautifully illuminated, and commissioned masterpieces of metalwork and carved stone. As the monastic ideal flourished, earning Ireland the name 'island of saints', their missionaries spread to Britain and the continent, followed by scholars and teachers in what was truly a 'Golden Age'.

The 7th- and 8th-century law tracts, heavily influenced by the Scriptures, por-tray a society that was intensely hierarchical, where status and honour meant much, and where sharp distinctions were drawn between those regarded as 'sacred' (including kings, clerics and poets) and those who were not, and between the free and the unfree. On the highest rungs of the ladder stood the kings, around whom society revolved. Ireland was a land of many kings, the tracts defining three grades: kings of petty local kingdoms, over-kings ruling several of these, and 'kings of over-kings' who effectively ruled a whole province. Although the laws rarely refer to a high-king of all Ireland, it is clear that for much of the early historic period the leading dynasty, the Uí Néill who were based in the northern half of the country with their ceremonial capital at Tara, did claim, and were occasionally able to enforce, supremacy throughout the island. Their primacy was shattered in the early 11th century, and power then revolved around a half-dozen or so leading province-kings, each of whom sought to force his rivals into submission and make himself high-king.

It is difficult to assess the extent to which these changes were the result of the Viking incursions, which for a time in the 9th century appeared likely to over-whelm the country. The Vikings certainly increased the intensity of warfare in an already violent society, and by developing towns at Dublin, Waterford, Limerick, Wexford and Cork, and trading networks overseas, they added to the wealth of what was otherwise a largely pastoral economy. Their presence in strength in Munster no doubt contributed also to the decline of its reigning dynasty, the Eóganachta, and facilitated the rise of Brian Boru. His later fame was attributed to a notable victory over the Vikings at the Battle of Clontarf in 1014, but his real importance lies in the fact that he ended the monopoly on the high-kingship formerly held by the Uí Néill.

In time, the Viking enclaves were assimilated into the Irish political super-structure, and those Irish kings who succeeded in dominating them, in some cases establishing the Viking town as their capital, gained an advantage over their rivals in the race for the high-kingship. This was especially true in the case of Dublin, overlordship of which was by the late 10th century generally assert-ed by successful claimants to the high-kingship and which, by the mid-11th cen-tury, was directly ruled by Irish kings, effectively becoming the country's capital.

This period saw rapid changes in Ireland in both Church and state. The Gregorian reform movement, which sought to eradicate abuses in the Church throughout western Christendom, spread to Ireland by the early 12th century and, under the patronage of reform-minded Irish province-kings, was responsi-ble for major changes in the organization of the Irish Church, though it was considerably less successful in eradicating abuses in Church practice and moral laxities among the laity. In secular affairs, the same period witnessed what may have been the evolution of a national monarchy, as a series of ambitious province-kings steadily increased their powers, started to act as feudal lords in the European mode, and sought to stamp their authority throughout the island. This, however, was cut short in the late 12th century by the Anglo-Norman inva-sion, spearheaded by men from the Welsh borderlands. They came at the insti-gation of the Leinster king, Diarmait MacMurchada (Dermot MacMurrough), who had been expelled by the reigning high-king, Ruaidrí Ua Conchobair (Rory O'Connor). The invaders were led by Richard de Clare, better known as Strongbow, who married MacMurchada's daughter and later succeeded to Leinster. At this point, late in 1171, Henry II, who had earlier received a papal licence to invade Ireland in order, it was claimed, to aid in the process of Church reform, came to Ireland himself, the first English king ever to do so, and estab-lished the English lordship.

Right: The Book of Kells, 'the Arrest of Christ'. The manuscript is one of the supreme examples of Irish art, drawing on the work and development of earlier monastic art. The use of colour and designs around the strong image of man are some of the qualities which make this work unique.

Celtic Ireland

IN THE SECOND half of the first millennium BC, during what prehistorians call the Iron Age, the first Celtic peoples began to arrive in Ireland, though there is no surviving evidence of a large-scale invasion. The people known to the Greeks as Keltoi or Celts had dominated central and western Europe and spoke an Indo-European language which developed into P-Celtic, the language of Britain and Gaul, ancestor of Welsh and Breton, and Q-Celtic, the language of the Celtic inhabitants of Ireland, ancestor of Gaelic.

Celtic culture of this period is called La Tène after a site in Switzerland, and objects in the La Tène style survive mainly from the north and west of Ireland. Best known are the Turoe Stone in County Galway, and some beautifully crafted war-trumpets, golden collars or *torcs*, and decorated bronze scabbards and horse-bits. These objects seem to have belonged to a warrior society and their prevalence in Connacht and Ulster may be significant, for the latter is the setting of the *Táin Bó Cuailnge* and other great sagas of the Irish heroic age. These tales were written considerably later and should be used with caution, but they do capture something of the society that was thought to exist in Ireland in the immediate prehistoric period, a society not unlike that portrayed by contemporary descriptions of the continental Celts.

The earliest detailed account of Ireland is that by Ptolemy, an Alexandrian Greek geographer writing after AD 100, whose information may have come from Roman or British sailors familiar with the island's east coast and its main rivers, 15 of which Ptolemy notes. Of the peoples whose territories Ptolemy records, we can probably identify Dál Riata of Antrim (who were soon to found a powerful kingdom in Argyll), Dál Fiatach of Down, and Ulaid, who were later confined to Antrim and Down, though Ptolemy has them still ruling much of the north from their cult centre at Emain Macha. Emain Macha was the setting of much of the action of the early saga literature.

As Ptolemy moves from the north-east, it becomes harder to match his territories with known dynasties, and he makes no mention of the massive Iron Age earthworks at Tara, County Meath, perhaps the most important of the early royal and ritual sites. It does seem likely, though, that the *Iverni*, whom Ptolemy places in the south-west, may be the Érainn, who dominated Munster in this period: the Greek name for Ireland, *Ierne*, probably came from them, and is itself a version of the Irish word for the island, *Ériu* (later, *Éire*).

Below: *The Turoe Stone, Co. Galway, is probably of La Tène period. Its purpose is unknown though most likely to be of religious significance.*

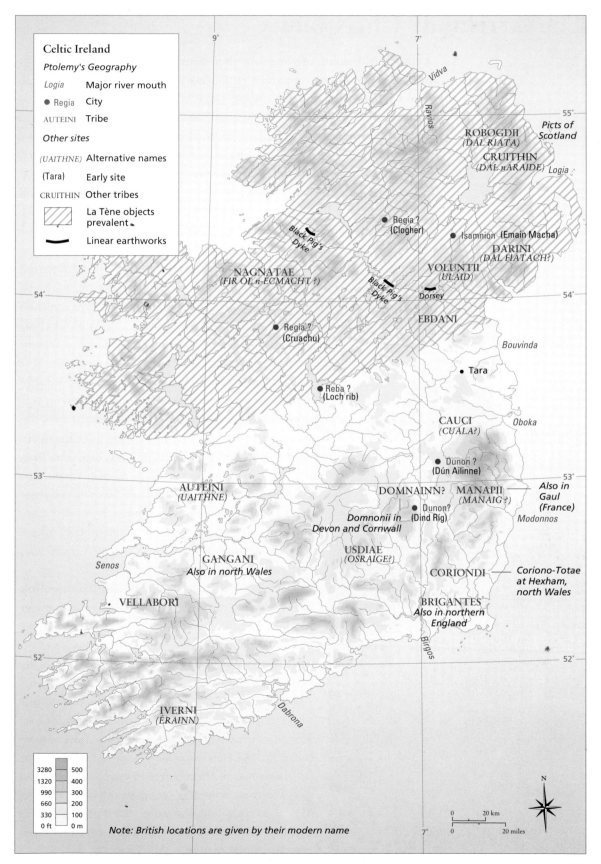

Celtic Ireland

Ptolemy's Geography

Logia	Major river mouth
● *Regia*	City
AUTEINI	Tribe

Other sites

(UAITHNE)	Alternative names
(Tara)	Early site
CRUITHIN	Other tribes
▨	La Tène objects prevalent
◠	Linear earthworks

Vidva

55°

ROBOGDII
(DÁL RIATA)

Picts of Scotland

Ravios

CRUITHIN
(DÁL nARAIDE)

Logia

Regia ?
(Clogher)

Isamnion (Emain Macha)

DARINI
(DÁL FIATACH?)

Black Pig's Dyke

NAGNATAE
(FIR ÓL n-ECMACHT ?)

VOLUNTII
(ULAID)

Black Pig's Dyke

Dorsey

54°

EBDANI

Bouvinda

Regia ?
(Cruachu)

Tara

Reba ?
(Loch rib)

CAUCI
(CUALA?)

Oboka

53°

AUTEINI
(UAITHNE)

Dúnon ?
(Dún Ailinne)

DOMNAINN?

MANAPII
(MANAIG ?)

Also in Gaul
(France)

Dunon?
(Dind Ríg)

Modonnos

Domnonii in Devon and Cornwall

USDIAE
(OSRAIGE?)

CORIONDI

Coriono-Totae at Hexham, north Wales

GANGANI
Also in north Wales

Senos

BRIGANTES
Also in northern England

VELLABORI

Birgos

52°

IVERNI
(ÉRAINN)

Dabrona

3280	500
1320	400
990	300
660	200
330	100
0 ft	0 m

N

0   20 km
0   20 miles

Note: British locations are given by their modern name

The Arrival of Christianity

ALTHOUGH Ireland lay outside the Roman Empire, it was heavily influenced by it, and evidence of trading is considerable. As Roman power in Britain weakened, by the early 5th century the Irish were not only trading and raiding there, but settling along its western coast, most successfully the Dál Riata colony in what became Scotland, but also a Déisi colony in south Wales, a Laigin (Leinster) colony in north Wales, and settlement by the Uí Liatháin in Cornwall and Devon. Such contacts with the Roman world produced the Ogham script, consisting of notches on stone based on the Latin alphabet. No doubt they also produced the first Irish encounters with Christianity.

Below: This stone from Coolmagort, Co. Kerry, displays Ogham inscriptions, the earliest written Irish.

The first Christian missionaries may have come to Ireland from Gaul in the late 4th and early 5th centuries, making it the first country outside the Roman world to be converted. The first exact date is 431, the year in which Palladius, possibly a deacon of Auxerre, was appointed by the Pope as bishop to 'the Irish who believe in Christ'. Gaulish missionaries, whose labours were probably confined largely to the east and south of Ireland, were soon superseded by British, the most famous of whom is the still highly controversial St Patrick. Patrick himself states that he was the son of an official in a city in Roman Britain, and that he was first brought to Ireland as a slave, but later returned as a bishop to preach the gospel. He was most active, it seems, north of a line from Wexford to Galway, and was particularly successful in the north-east; it was a church in this area, Armagh, because of its alleged association with Patrick, that was later to claim primacy over the rest of the Irish Church.

The cult which grew up around Patrick should not mislead us into thinking that the conversion of Ireland was quick, or largely the work of one man. We do not known anything of the activities of Palladius, but later accounts give the names of other bishops active at this period. Auxilius is said to have founded Killashee (*Cill Usailli*) near Naas, one of the royal sites associated with the kings of Leinster, while Dunshaughlin, not far from Tara, is attributed to Secundinus: in Irish it is *Domnach Sechnaill*, and sites with the element *domnach* (from Latin *dominicum*) are known to be early. Like these other early churches, Armagh is near the revered site at Emain Macha, in each case suggesting a deliberate policy of locating the new Christian churches beside old pre-Christian power-centres.

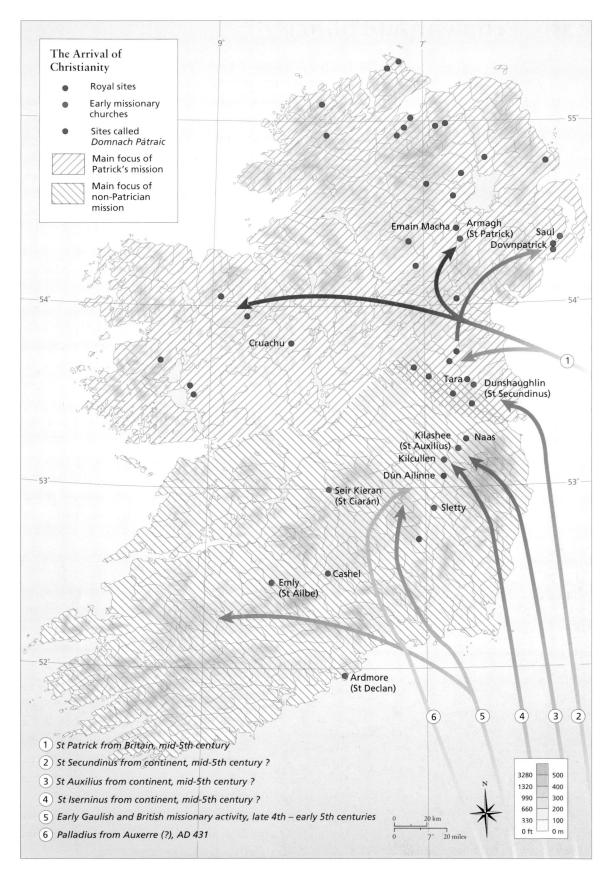

The Arrival of Christianity

- ● Royal sites
- ● Early missionary churches
- ● Sites called *Domnach Pátraic*
- ▨ Main focus of Patrick's mission
- ▨ Main focus of non-Patrician mission

Emain Macha
Armagh (St Patrick)
Saul
Downpatrick
Cruachu
Tara
Dunshaughlin (St Secundinus)
Kilashee (St Auxilius)
Naas
Kilcullen
Dún Ailinne
Seir Kieran (St Ciarán)
Sletty
Cashel
Emly (St Ailbe)
Ardmore (St Declan)

① St Patrick from Britain, mid-5th century
② St Secundinus from continent, mid-5th century ?
③ St Auxilius from continent, mid-5th century ?
④ St Iserninus from continent, mid-5th century ?
⑤ Early Gaulish and British missionary activity, late 4th – early 5th centuries
⑥ Palladius from Auxerre (?), AD 431

3280	500
1320	400
990	300
660	200
330	100
0 ft	0 m

0   20 km
0   20 miles

N

Early Peoples and Politics

Above: Detail of a bearded warrior with spear and shield, from The Book of Kells.

WITH THE introduction of Christianity in the 5th century came the Latin language, and with Latin came learning and literature, both in Latin and, increasingly, in the vernacular. This material, the most comprehensive to survive in any country of Dark-Age Europe, enables us to reconstruct the political map of Ireland even at this early period. The first thing that emerges is the extent to which political divisions had changed since Ptolemy's time. By the 7th century, the Érainn peoples in Munster were eclipsed by a federation of dynasties known as the Eóganachta who traced their descent from the eponymous Eógan, and who may, as their later origin-legend claimed, have been Irish colonists returned from Britain: their capital was at Cashel, which is a borrowing of the Latin castellum. To their east lay the over-kingdom of Laigin (Leinster), bounded on the west by the Barrow. Leinster originally stretched north to the Boyne, but it was pushed back to the Liffey after the 6th century, and was dominated by two dynasties, Uí Dúnlainge, centred on Kildare, and Uí Chennselaig, associated with Ferns.

The Laigin lost their lands in Meath to the Uí Néill, whose origins may lie to the west of the Shannon and who claimed descent from Niall Noígiallach ('Niall of the nine hostages'), a quasi-historical 5th-century figure. Connacht takes its name from a mythical ancestor of Niall, Conn Cétchathach ('Conn of the hundred battles'), and by the 8th century was dominated by two dynasties, Uí Briúin and Uí Fiachrach, allegedly descended from Bríon and Fiachra, brothers of Niall. By this period, Niall's reputed descendants held power in the north-west of Ireland, where they were known as the Northern Uí Néill, with a focal point at Ailech, and also in the midlands, where they are known as the Southern Uí Néill. Tara had been wrested by them from the Laigin, and the over-king of the Uí Néill bore the title 'King of Tara', which in time came to denote the high-kingship of Ireland.

Below: Tara, perhaps the most important site in Ireland archeologically, historically and symbolically, went through many phases of occupation over many centuries, and has yet to yield up many of its secrets.

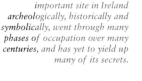

As the Uí Néill and their subjects the Airgialla pushed north, they circumscribed the power of the Ulaid, who had earlier ruled as far south as the Boyne, defending the boundaries of their kingdom with massive linear earthworks, traces of which still survive. We do not know precisely when Emain Macha fell, but for most of the historic period the Ulaid's power was confined to the area east of the Bann, and their most important dynasty was Dál Fiatach, who ruled the Mournes from their capital at Downpatrick.

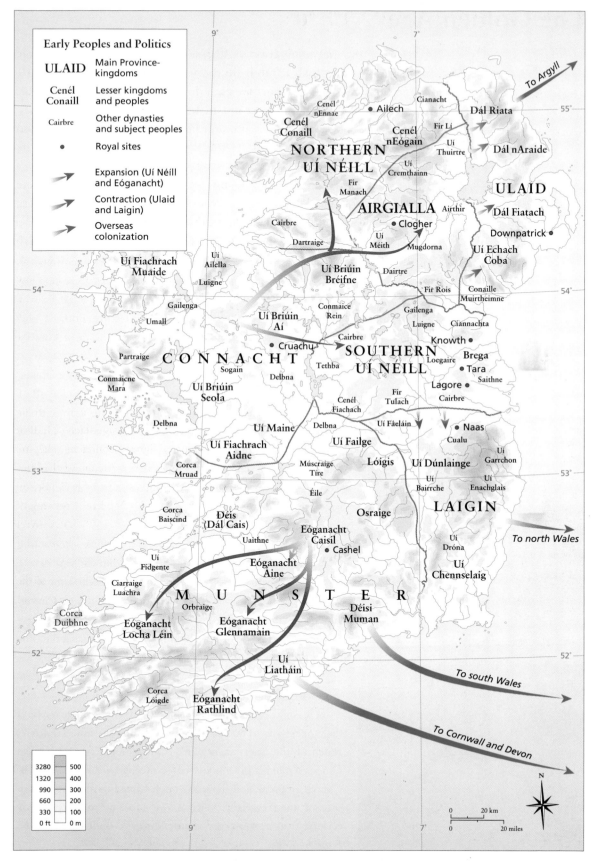

Early Peoples and Politics

ULAID   Main Province-kingdoms

Cenél Conaill   Lesser kingdoms and peoples

Cairbre   Other dynasties and subject peoples

•   Royal sites

→   Expansion (Uí Néill and Eóganacht)

→   Contraction (Ulaid and Laigin)

→   Overseas colonization

To Argyll

Cianacht

Cenél nEnnae • Ailech

Cenél Conaill

Cenél nEógain

Dál Riata

Fir Lí

Uí Thuirtre

Dál nAraide

NORTHERN UÍ NÉILL

Uí Cremthainn

ULAID

Fir Manach

AIRGIALLA

Airthir

Dál Fiatach

Cairbre

• Clogher

Uí Méith

Mugdorna

Downpatrick •

Dartraige

Uí Echach Coba

Uí Fiachrach Muaide

Uí Ailella

Uí Briúin Bréifne

Dairtre

Conaille Muirtheimne

Luigne

Fir Rois

Gailenga

Gailenga

Conmaice Rein

Luigne

Ciannachta

Umall

Uí Briúin Aí

Cairbre

Knowth •

Partraige

C O N N A C H T

• Cruachu

SOUTHERN UÍ NÉILL

Loegaire

Brega

Conmaicne Mara

Sogain

Tethba

Fir Tulach

• Tara

Saithne

Delbna

Uí Briúin Seola

Delbna

Cenél Fiachach

Cairbre

Lagore •

Delbna

Uí Maine

Delbna

Uí Fáeláin

Naas •

Uí Garrchon

Uí Fiachrach Aidne

Uí Failge

Cualu

Corca Mruad

Múscraige Tíre

Lóigis

Uí Dúnlainge

Uí Bairrche

Uí Enachglais

Éile

Osraige

LAIGIN

Corca Baiscind

Déis (Dál Cais)

Uí Dróna

Uaithne

Eóganacht Caisil

Uí Fidgente

Eóganacht Áine

• Cashel

Uí Chennselaig

Ciarraige Luachra

M U N S T E R

Déisi Muman

Orbraige

Corca Duibhne

Eóganacht Locha Léin

Eóganacht Glennamain

To north Wales

Uí Liatháin

To south Wales

Corca Lóigde

Eóganacht Rathlind

To Cornwall and Devon

N

3280   500
1320   400
990   300
660   200
330   100
0 ft   0 m

0   20 km
0   20 miles

The Golden Age

ALTHOUGH the beginnings of a diocesan structure may have been bequeathed to the Irish Church by the early missionaries, by the 6th century Ireland's most important churches were ruled by a monastic hierarchy, many of whom were not bishops, and certain monasteries which were believed to share a common founder were grouped together in what is known as a paruchia.

The original impetus for this wave of monasticism came partly from Britain. St Enda, founder of Inis Mór, studied with St Ninian in Galloway. The Welsh saints, David and Cadoc, were the inspiration for Máedóc of Ferns and Finnian of Clonard. Finnian then taught men who became important monastic founders in their own right, including Brendan (Clonfert), Ciarán (Clonmacnoise), and Colum Cille (Durrow, Derry and Iona). The monastic centres were not the exclusive preserve of men, the most famous house of nuns being St Brigid's at Kildare, and while some churches were easily accessible and richly endowed, and undoubtedly places as much of commerce as of prayer, others, most notably Sceilg Mhicíl off the Kerry coast, were retreats from the world.

This newly Christianized and literate society soon began to display evidence of a high level of scholarship, both in Latin and Irish, clerical and secular, all of it heavily influenced by the Church. By the 7th century, Ireland's monastic schools and libraries were well-stocked with the writings of the early Church Fathers, and were beginning to produce scholars and holy men of their own, whose work was comparable with that emanating from anywhere in contemporary Christendom, and which would soon be widely disseminated throughout western Europe.

In these ecclesiastical centres, the monks themselves undoubtedly participated in manual work, but the vast extent of some monastic estates meant that the great bulk of the work was done by tenants who lived, with their families, on Church lands. This provided the monastic tenants with access to pastoral care, and the Church with a means of exploiting the economic potential of its estates. The consequence was that in this as yet pre-urban society many of the great ecclesiastical centres must have become essential hubs of economic activity.

Increasing secularization, wealth and lay-patronage enabled the monasteries to make an important contribution to the arts. Much of the finest metalwork of the period, including the famous Ardagh and Derrynaflan chalices, was produced under Church auspices, and the stone High Crosses still testify to the skill of their craftsmen, while the supreme masterpiece of ecclesiastical manuscript illumination is undoubtedly *The Book of Kells.*

Below: *Muiredach's Cross at Monasterboice, Co. Louth, is among the most superb examples of the art-form. The biblical scenes carved on the east side here include Adam and Eve, the Murder of Abel, David and Goliath, Moses striking the Rock, and the Adoration of the Kings.*

The Golden Age

- Paruchia of Patrick (churches linked to Armagh)
- Paruchia of Colum Cille
- Other principal monasteries and churches
- ✝ High Crosses
- Illuminated Manuscripts
- ➤ Saints trained in Britain
- ➤ Missionaries abroad

St Enda from Whithorn, early 6th century

St Colum Cille to Iona 563

St Aidan to Iona and Northumbria, 635

St Fursa to East Anglia, 633

St Finnian, from Llancarfan, c. 500

St Máedóc from St Davids, c. 600

St Columbanus to Gaul, 591

Irish missionaries active in Britain and continent from mid-6th century

Irish scholars prevalent on the continent from early 9th century

NORTHERN UÍ NÉILL

ULAID

AIRGIALLA

CONNACHT

SOUTHERN UÍ NÉILL

LAIGIN

MUNSTER

Tory
Fahan
Derry
Raphoe
Coleraine
Camus
Armoy
Rathlin
Connor
Antrim
Bodoney
Ardstraw
Ardboe ✝
Donaghmore ✝
Tynan
Clogher
Armagh
Bangor
Moville
Nendrum
Dromore
Saul
Downpatrick
Inishmurray
Devenish
Boho ✝
Drumcliff ✝
Killevy
Clones ✝
Killala
Achonry
Fenagh
Donaghmoyne
Dromiskin ✝
Louth
Linns
Kilmore
Granard
Monasterboice ✝
Termonfeckin ✝
Elphin
Achagower
Mayo Baslick
Ardagh
Kells (Iona?)
Fore
Ardbraccan
Slane ✝
Duleek ✝
Inishbofin
Roscommon
Trim
Holmpatrick
Cong
Inchcleraun
Tuam
Clonard
Dunshaughlin
Finglas
Swords
Glasnevin
Annaghdown
Clonmacnoise ✝
Durrow ✝
Clondalkin
Tallaght
Roscam
Tihilly ✝
Killashee
Kildare
Clonfert
Inís Mór
Kinnitty ✝
Seir Kieran
Kilcullen
Moone ✝
Glendalough
Kilmacduagh
Lorrha ✝
Birr
Castledermot ✝
Kilfenora
Terryglass
Roscrea
Killeshin
Sletty
Inishcaltra
Leighlin
Aghade
Killaloe
Inis Cathaig
Mungret
Derrynaflan
Kilree ✝
Graigue-namanagh ✝
Ferns
Cashel
Kilkeeran ✝
St Mullins ✝
Killamery ✝
Begerin
Emly
Ahenny ✝
Taghmon
Ardfert
Ardfinnan
Inisfallen
Lismore
Ardmore
Cork
Cloyne
Sceilg Mhicíl
Ross Carbery

ft	m
3280	500
1320	400
990	300
660	200
330	100
0 ft	0 m

0   20 km
0   20 miles

N

21

Ireland and Europe

Above: A carpet-page from the Evangeliary 51, an abundantly decorated book from the library of the monastery founded by St Gall, companion of St Columbanus. This volume, like others, was probably brought from Ireland, but the library also includes manuscripts written by Irish monks at St Gall.

HAVING EARLIER witnessed the evangelizing efforts of men from Britain and mainland Europe, by the mid-6th century Ireland began to repay the debt. Although a hermit's desire to renounce home and family brought Colum Cille (Columba) to the remote Hebridean island of Iona in 563, his efforts were soon channelled into the conversion of the Picts, and his monastery, far from providing a retreat from the world, in time became the ecclesiastical capital of the Scottish kingdom of Dál Riata.

Iona monks preached the faith throughout Scotland and they later led in spreading Christianity into the Anglo-Saxon kingdom of Northumbria, their most charismatic figure being St Aidan, the first bishop of Lindisfarne, whose activities were immortalized by Bede. Other Irish *peregrini pro Christo* ('pilgrims for Christ'), like St Fursa, went further south to preach in East Anglia, having been granted as a monastic site the fortress of Cnobesburh (Burgh Castle, Suffolk). Fursa later turned his attentions towards France, where he and his brothers again became church-builders, and he was buried in the town of Péronne in Picardy which, because of its long association with Irish clerics and pilgrims, became known as *Peronna Scottorum* ('Péronne of the Irish').

In time the trickle of Irish missionary activity on the Continent became a flood, the lead being taken by Columbanus of Bangor. He and twelve disciples are said to have left Ireland for France in 591, founding the monastery of Annegray in a disused Roman fort. Having attracted numerous followers to his austere Rule, Columbanus built a new monastery at Luxeuil nearby, which became a training ground for later monastic founders. Forced out of France, Columbanus sailed up the Rhine to Lake Constance, ending up in Lombardy, where he died in his monastery of Bobbio in 615. He ranks alongside St Benedict as the 'founder of western monasticism'.

Though Irish missionaries continued to found monasteries on the Continent into the 12th century (known as *Schottenklöster*), by the 9th century they were being followed to Europe by scholars, whose learning won them positions as masters in the imperial schools of Charlemagne and his successors. The Irishman Dicuil wrote tracts on geography, grammar and astronomy. Slightly later, at Liège, Sedulius Scottus was the leading scholar-courtier, whose works of grammar, philosophy and theology are complemented by over 80 extant Latin poems. Meanwhile, at Laon, in the palace of Charles the Bald, another group of Irish scholars gathered around Ireland's brightest star in terms of European scholasticism, Johannes Scottus Eriugena.

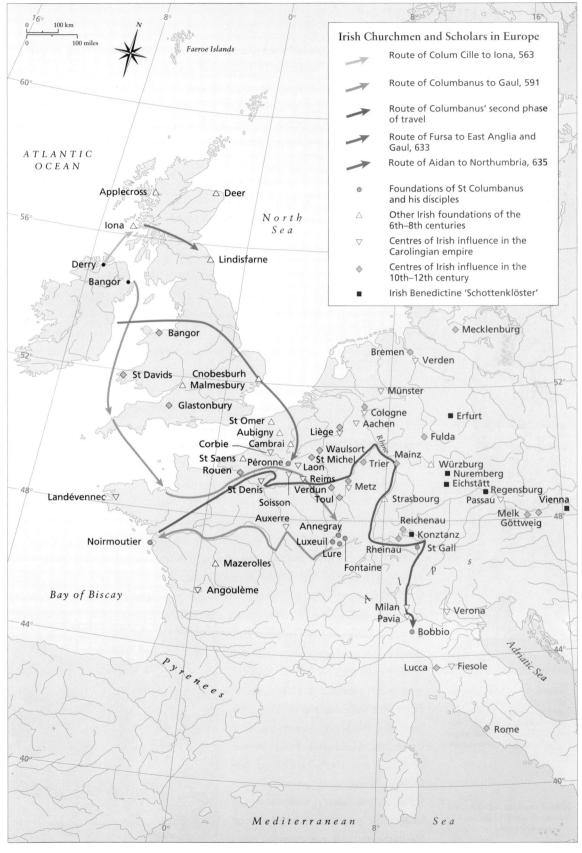

Irish Churchmen and Scholars in Europe

Route of Colum Cille to Iona, 563

Route of Columbanus to Gaul, 591

Route of Columbanus' second phase of travel

Route of Fursa to East Anglia and Gaul, 633

Route of Aidan to Northumbria, 635

● Foundations of St Columbanus and his disciples

△ Other Irish foundations of the 6th–8th centuries

▽ Centres of Irish influence in the Carolingian empire

◆ Centres of Irish influence in the 10th–12th century

■ Irish Benedictine 'Schottenklöster'

ATLANTIC OCEAN

Faeroe Islands

North Sea

Applecross △   △ Deer

Iona △

Derry ●   △ Lindisfarne

Bangor ●

◆ Bangor

◆ St Davids   Cnobesburh △
                Malmesbury △

◆ Glastonbury

St Omer △
Aubigny △
Corbie — Cambrai △
St Saens △ Péronne ●   Liège ▽
Rouen ▽   Waulsort ●
St Denis ▽   Laon ▽   St Michel ◆   Trier ●   Mainz ●
             Reims ▽
             Verdun ▽ Metz ▽
             Toul ▽
Soisson
Auxerre   Annegray ●
               Luxeuil ● ●
               Lure ●
               Fontaine ●

Landévennec ▽

Noirmoutier ●

△ Mazerolles

▽ Angoulème

Bay of Biscay

Mecklenburg ◆

Bremen ◆   ▽ Verden

▽ Münster

Cologne ▽   ■ Erfurt
Aachen ▽
                ◆ Fulda

                Würzburg ◆
                ■ Nuremberg
                ■ Eichstätt
Strasbourg ◆   Regensburg ◆
                Passau   Vienna ■
                Melk ◆ ◆
Reichenau ◆   Göttweig
Konztanz ■
Rheinau ◆ St Gall

Milan ▽   ▽ Verona
Pavia
        ● Bobbio

Lucca ◆ ▽ Fiesole

Rome ◆

Pyrenees

Adriatic Sea

Mediterranean   Sea

23

The Viking Wars

WHATEVER THE underlying causes, bands of Scandinavian warriors, manning fleets of technically advanced warships, began raiding western Europe in the dying years of the 8th century. The first recorded Viking attack on Ireland took place in 795 when Norse raiders assaulted several island monasteries off Ireland's coast. Raids at first tended to be confined to the northern and western seaboards, though by 824 even Sceilg in the far south-west fell victim.

In these first four decades of their campaigns, the Vikings rarely penetrated further than 20 miles inland and were still merely sea-borne raiders based elsewhere. Periodically they plundered Irish churches, not simply because Christian targets made suitable pagan prey, but because the monasteries were important focal points of economic activity, storehouses of moveable goods which were inhabited by potential captives. During the next 20 years the raids intensified and the Vikings began attacking further inland. Throughout the winter of 840–841 they stayed moored on Lough Neagh and then set up a permanent *longphort* ('ship-camp') at Dublin, which in time became their chief settlement in Ireland, a secure base from which to launch extensive plunderings into the surrounding territories.

With permanent bases in Ireland, the Vikings themselves became vulnerable to attack, and from the mid-9th century, although they still threatened to overwhelm the country, one finds Irish kings successfully defeating them in battle. In the second half of the century the Vikings not only attacked Irish targets, but even took part in Irish warfare, allying with one Irish king in opposition to another. Danes competed with Norsemen for power over the Irish enclaves.

By the mid-850s great raids were on the decline, and the Vikings turned their attention further afield, to northern Britain and Iceland. Divisions within the Norse communities in Ireland, and more effective Irish opposition, led to their expulsion from Dublin in 902, and no further Irish Viking activity is recorded until 914, when Viking fleets reappeared in Waterford harbour, attacked Munster and Leinster, re-occupied Dublin and scored some notable victories against the Irish kings. For the next two decades the Dublin Vikings were very powerful and sought to reign over the kingdom of York and over the Norse of Waterford and Limerick. Thereafter their power declined, and the activities of the Dublin Norse were generally confined to the town's hinterland. By about 950 this last great phase of Viking warfare was at an end.

Above: *Round towers, though primarily bell-towers, perhaps served as lookouts and refuges. This fine example at Devenish shows the entrance well above ground and easy to defend.*

Right: *Unearthed in Dublin, this drawing on a ship plank shows a man high in the rigging of a Viking ship.*

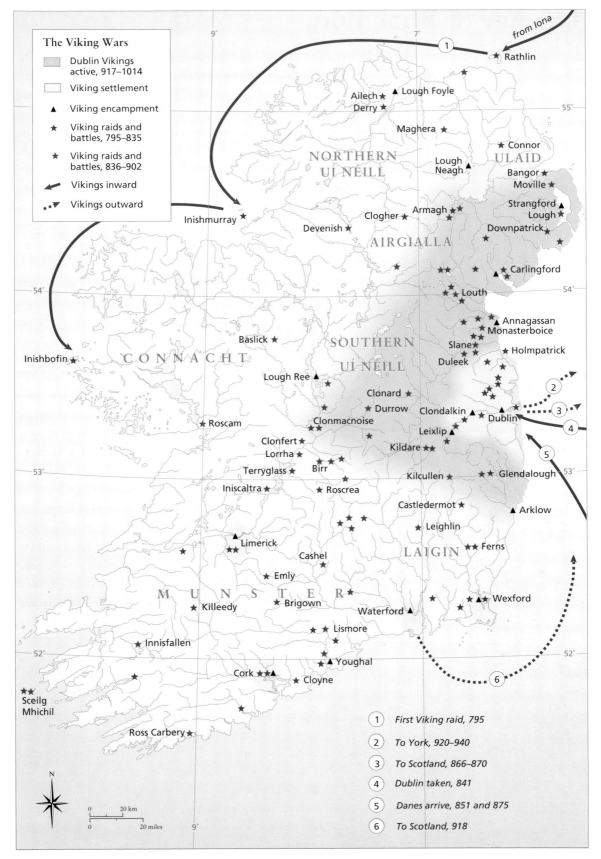

from Iona

The Viking Wars

- Dublin Vikings active, 917–1014
- Viking settlement
- ▲ Viking encampment
- ★ Viking raids and battles, 795–835
- ★ Viking raids and battles, 836–902
- → Vikings inward
- ⋯▶ Vikings outward

Rathlin

Ailech ★   ▲ Lough Foyle
Derry ★

Maghera ★

NORTHERN
UÍ NÉILL

Lough
Neagh ▲

★ Connor   ULAID

Bangor ★
Moville ★

Strangford ▲
Lough ★

Clogher ★   Armagh ★★

Downpatrick ★

Inishmurray ★

Devenish ★

AIRGIALLA

Carlingford

Louth

Baslick ★

CONNACHT

SOUTHERN
UÍ NÉILL

Slane
Duleek

Annagassan
Monasterboice

Holmpatrick

Inishbofin ★

Lough Ree ▲

Clonard ★

★ Durrow

Clondalkin ▲

Dublin

Roscam ★

Clonmacnoise ★★

Leixlip ▲

Clonfert ★
Lorrha ★

Kildare ★★

Birr

Terryglass ★

Kilcullen ★

★★ Glendalough

Iniscaltra ★   ★ Roscrea

Castledermot ★

▲ Arklow

Leighlin

LAIGIN

★★ Ferns

Limerick ▲

Cashel

★ Emly

MUNSTER

★ Killeedy   ★ Brigown

Waterford ▲

Wexford

Lismore

Innisfallen ★

Youghal ▲

Cork ★★▲   ★ Cloyne

★★
Sceilg
Mhichil

Ross Carbery ★

N

0   20 km
0   20 miles

1. First Viking raid, 795
2. To York, 920–940
3. To Scotland, 866–870
4. Dublin taken, 841
5. Danes arrive, 851 and 875
6. To Scotland, 918

The Age of Brian Boru

IT WOULD BE wrong to exaggerate the ill-effects of Viking attacks on the Irish Church, since the latter was already highly politicized, and monastic centres sometimes suffered as much from the depredations of rival Irish rulers as from Viking assaults. The Ostmen, as they called themselves, made many positive contributions to Irish life. They gave the country its first towns, its first coinage and more advanced naval technology. As some of their settlements grew into towns, they expanded Ireland's trading contacts and introduced its artists and craftsmen to new styles and motifs. Dublin became one of the wealthiest ports in western Europe.

The Ostmen generally governed large areas of their towns' hinterland, and in so doing displaced some minor local kingdoms. Their strength in Munster may have contributed to the decline of the reigning Eóganachta kings and to the ascendancy of the rulers of Dál Cais, who controlled the strategic lower Shannon basin. The first of their kings to attain real power was Cennétig mac Lorcáin who died as king of Thomond (north Munster) in 951, to be succeeded by his son, Mathgamain, who brought east Munster, and the Ostmen of Limerick and Waterford, under his sway. After Mathgamain's death in 976, his brother Brian Boru succeeded. He is usually regarded as the greatest of Ireland's high-kings.

Below: *Brian Boru, high-king of Ireland. This fanciful image, made many hundreds of years after his death, indicates a fond folk memory of this king who is popularly thought to have banished the Vikings from Ireland.*

Brian quickly rose to power, overshadowing his Eóganachta rivals to make himself king of all Munster. At this point he emerged as a challenge to the reigning high-king of Ireland, Máel Sechnaill mac Domnaill of the Southern Uí Néill, who in 997 acknowledged Brian as king over the southern half of Ireland (*Leth Moga*) and who finally submitted to Brian as high-king in 1002. In 1005, Brian set about asserting his dominance throughout the island, using the title 'Emperor of the Irish'. A revolt by the Leinstermen and the Ostmen of Dublin, who also raised Viking aid from Man and the Western Isles, led to Brian's great victory over them in the battle of Clóntarf in 1014, at which, however, Brian himself was slain.

Brian's achievement was considerable. Early medieval Ireland did not possess a monarch whose rule was effective over the entire island, but the Uí Néill, who dominated the northern half of the island (*Leth Cuinn*), were often able to compel most, if not all, of the other province-kings to submit to them as high-king. Brian Boru, however, by making himself high-king of all Ireland, ended the Uí Néill monopoly of the title. Others in subsequent generations attempted to emulate him but none was as successful.

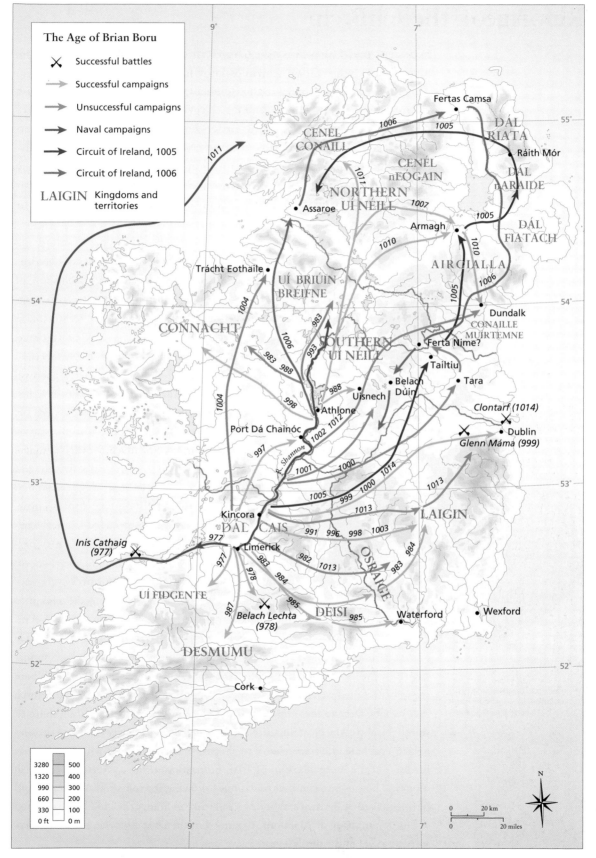

The Age of Brian Boru

✗ Successful battles

Successful campaigns

Unsuccessful campaigns

Naval campaigns

Circuit of Ireland, 1005

Circuit of Ireland, 1006

LAIGIN Kingdoms and territories

Fertas Camsa

DÁL RIATA

Ráith Mór

DÁL nARAIDE

CENEL CONAILL

CENEL nEOGAIN

NORTHERN UÍ NÉILL

Assaroe

Armagh

DÁL FIATACH

AIRGIALLA

Tracht Eothaile

UÍ BRIÚIN BREIFNE

Dundalk

CONAILLE MUÍRTEMNE

CONNACHT

Ferta Nime?

SOUTHERN UÍ NÉILL

Tailtiu

Tara

Belach Dúin

Uisnech

Clontarf (1014)

Dublin

Glenn Máma (999)

Athlone

Port Dá Chainóc

R. Shannon

Kincora

DÁL CAIS

LAIGIN

Inis Cathaig (977)

Limerick

UÍ FIDGENTE

OSRAIGE

Belach Lechta (978)

DÉISI

Waterford

Wexford

DESMUMU

Cork

3280   500
1320   400
990   300
660   200
330   100
0 ft   0 m

N

0   20 km
0   20 miles

Reform of the Church

FROM THE mid-11th century the Church throughout western Christendom underwent a reformation generally known as the Gregorian movement. The abuses afflicting the Church elsewhere were not absent from the Irish Church, which by then had a largely married and hereditary clergy, with individuals not in holy orders holding high office. Abbots exercised more power than bishops, and there was an absence of territorially-based dioceses and parishes. The morals of the laity were also thought in need of reform since Irish (Brehon) law allowed divorce and tolerated marriage within the Church's forbidden degrees of consanguinity.

Above: A reliquary, the shrine of St Patrick's bell, made around the beginning of the 12th century to house an iron bell, traditionally believed to have belonged to the Saint.

The reforms first affected the Ostman towns of Dublin, Waterford and Limerick, which, by the early 12th century, became organized dioceses, whose bishops swore canonical obedience to the archbishop of Canterbury. More than one English primate wrote to Irish kings urging them to initiate programmes of Church reform. This began in earnest when the Munster king, Muirchertach Ua Briain, presided over two synods, that of Cashel (1101), which passed decrees forbidding simony, lay abbots, clerical marriage, and incest, and that of Ráith Bressail (1111), which introduced a diocesan system for the rest of the country, dividing it into two ecclesiastical provinces, Armagh and Cashel, each with 12 dioceses reflecting local territorial boundaries. This system was later modified at the Synod of Kells-Mellifont (1152), at which Tuam and Dublin were elevated to archbishoprics. Armagh, however, held the primacy and thereby ended Canterbury's involvement in the Irish Church, a situation which pertains to this day.

Organizationally, the Church reformers were successful, though the process of dividing dioceses into parishes was protracted. The reformers also made a visual impact: Cormac's Chapel at Cashel, for example, is a notable example of the new style of Irish Romanesque architecture, and was commissioned by the king of South Munster (Desmond), Cormac MacCarthaig. Where the reforms failed were in their attempts to eradicate abuses in both the Church and society. Despite these failures, the Irish Church produced its fair share of saintly bishops, the most illustrious of whom was St Malachy Ua Morgair, who helped end hereditary succession to the see of Armagh, and who was heavily involved in the reorganization of Irish monasticism. He converted older Irish monastic houses into convents of canons following the rule of St Augustine, and having visited St Bernard's abbey of Clairvaux in France, in 1142 he established a Cistercian abbey at Mellifont, County Louth. Over a dozen similar abbeys were founded in the next 20 years.

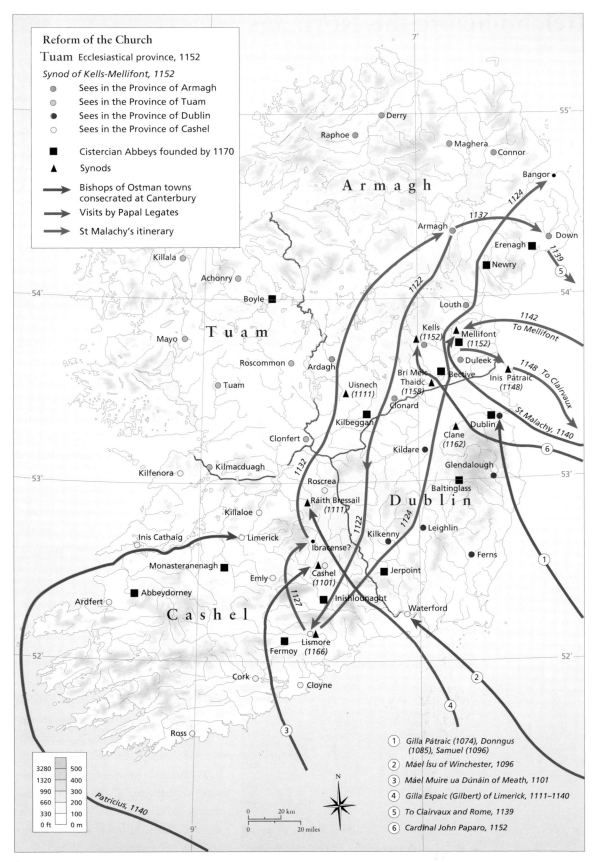

Reform of the Church

Tuam Ecclesiastical province, 1152

Synod of Kells-Mellifont, 1152

- ● Sees in the Province of Armagh
- ● Sees in the Province of Tuam
- ● Sees in the Province of Dublin
- ○ Sees in the Province of Cashel

- ■ Cistercian Abbeys founded by 1170
- ▲ Synods

→ Bishops of Ostman towns consecrated at Canterbury

→ Visits by Papal Legates

→ St Malachy's itinerary

Derry

Raphoe

Maghera

Connor

Bangor

A r m a g h

Armagh

1124

1137

Down

Erenagh

1139

Newry

5

1122

Louth

1142
To Mellifont

Killala

Achonry

Boyle

Kells
(1152)

Mellifont
(1152)

T u a m

Mayo

Roscommon

Ardagh

Uisnech
(1111)

Duleek

Bri Meic
Thaidc
(1158)

Bective

Inis Pátraic
(1148)

1148 To Clairvaux

Tuam

Clonard

St Malachy, 1140

Clonfert

Kilbeggan

Dublin

Clane
(1162)

Kilfenora

Kilmacduagh

Roscrea

Kildare

Glendalough

Killaloe

Ráith Bressail
(1111)

D u b l i n

Baltinglass

6

1132

1122

1124

Kilkenny

Leighlin

Inis Cathaig

Limerick

Ibracense?

Ferns

Monasteranenagh

Emly

Cashel
(1101)

Jerpoint

1127

Ardfert

Abbeydorney

Inishlounaght

Waterford

1

C a s h e l

Lismore
Fermoy (1166)

2

Cork

Cloyne

4

Ross

3

3280	500
1320	400
990	300
660	200
330	100
0 ft	0 m

Patricius, 1140

N

0   20 km

0   20 miles

1 Gilla Pátraic (1074), Donngus
   (1085), Samuel (1096)

2 Máel Ísu of Winchester, 1096

3 Máel Muire ua Dúnáin of Meath, 1101

4 Gilla Espaic (Gilbert) of Limerick, 1111–1140

5 To Clairvaux and Rome, 1139

6 Cardinal John Paparo, 1152

Ireland before the Normans

BRIAN BORU'S lasting achievement was his demonstration that any province-king could make himself master of the whole island, provided his armies were strong enough. The Uí Néill, in the person of Máel Sechnaill mac Domnaill, retook the high-kingship after 1014, but with the latter's death in 1022, the title lay in abeyance. For 50 years no province-king emerged powerful enough to force his enemies into submission and make the title effective.

For most of the middle years of the 11th century, the leading contender for the high-kingship was the Leinster king, Diarmait MacMáil na mBó, who involved himself in the affairs of England and Wales, and whose power was greatly increased in 1052 when he assumed the kingship of Dublin, the first Irish king ever to do so. The practice was repeated by later claimants to the high-kingship, who sometimes appointed their intended heir king of Dublin, which in the process came to replace Tara as symbolic capital of the country.

During this twilight period Irish kingship underwent considerable changes. Wars lasted longer and were more frequent. Kings exercised more power, promulgating laws and imposing taxes, and employing an increasing variety of officials. Besides being the chosen leader of a people, kings became owners of the land, which they could grant by charter to the Church or to their vassals in return for military service, rather like feudal kings elsewhere. They invaded and conquered neighbouring kingdoms, dividing them among their allies or appointing puppet-rulers to govern them under their overlordship.

From 1072 until 1086, Brian Boru's grandson Tairdelbach Ua Briain claimed the high-kingship, though his son Muirchertach (1086–1119) was a more effective ruler, famous for his marriage-alliances with the king of Norway and the Normans of South Wales, and a leading patron of Church reform. Subsequently, the power of the Uí Briain (O'Briens) waned and shifted northwards. The Connacht king, Tairdelbach Ua Conchobhair (O'Connor) was probably the most effective 12th-century high-king, a prodigious builder of fortresses and bridges and master of an effective army and fleet. A declining force in his latter years, he was succeeded in 1156 by the king of the Northern Uí Néill, Muirchertach Mac Lochlainn, whose leading ally was the Leinster King, Diarmait MacMurchada (Dermot MacMurrough). Mac Lochlainn's death in 1166 led to MacMurchada's expulsion overseas by the allies of the new high-King Ruaidrí Ua Conchobhair (Rory O'Connor), and ultimately to the Anglo-Norman invasion of Ireland.

Below: Excavations at Fishamble Street and Wood Quay in Dublin revealed the wealth and significance of pre-Norman Dublin, which by the 12th century had become the capital of Ireland in everything but name. This photograph shows a good example of a fairly typical Hiberno-Scandinavian house.

PART II: THE CONQUEST OF IRELAND

Brendan Smith

THE ELEVENTH and twelfth centuries were a time of expansion throughout western Europe typified by a growth in population and an upturn in economic activity which resulted in a dramatic increase in the number and size of towns. Another consequence of this pressure of population was a colonial movement which saw lords and peasants from Europe's central zone settling in peripheral regions such as the Slav lands of eastern Germany and the Celtic lands of the British Isles. This was also an era of tremendous intellectual advance as ancient disciplines such as law, philosophy and theology came under vigorous re-examination, a process which gave rise to the earliest universities in western Europe at Paris and Bologna. Religious reform was also in the air as the Church sought to meet popular demands for higher standards among the clergy and began to emphasize a more personal approach to spirituality which stressed the individual's relationship to God. New religious orders such as the Augustinians and Cistercians offered a communal existence distant from the world, while the papacy embarked on a campaign to strengthen its authority within society as a whole. With the launching of the First Crusade, aimed at liberating Jerusalem, in 1095 by Pope Urban II, western Europe declared to the wider world a new-found energy and sense of purpose.

Below: *This illustration features Diarmait MacMurchada from a manuscript of* Topographia Hiberniae *by Giraldus Cambrensis, copied c. 1200. Diarmait was instrumental in initiating the English invasion and has a reputation as a ruthless warlord. Hence his depiction bearing the archetypal long axe borrowed by the Irish from the Vikings.*

Intimately involved in all these developments were the Normans, a people descended from Viking raiders who had settled in north-west France in the 9th century. By 1100 the Normans controlled both southern Italy and England and were helping to establish the new Crusader states in Palestine. In the short term their success rested on their martial prowess, but in the long term it was their adaptability and readiness to integrate with the peoples they conquered which secured their achievements. In England, for instance, in the years after the victory at Hastings in 1066 they formed a small ruling élite, fearful of the conquered population which surrounded them, but within a century they ceased to see themselves as foreigners and, although they remained largely French in speech and culture, were happy to be called — and to call themselves — English.

Below: *Carrickfergus castle, Co. Antrim, built by John de Courcy, was among the first stone castles to dominate the local population.*

Kings of England since 1066 had expressed occasional interest in dominating Ireland, and it was no surprise that the English should have become involved there in the 12th century. It was far from inevitable, however, that such involvement would take the form it did, that of conquest. In Scotland, Normans from England were introduced in the early 12th century under the controlling hand of the Scots king himself, and a successful blending of old and new aristocratic elements allowed Scotland to retain its position as an independent kingdom for the rest of the Middle Ages.

In Ireland, however, the existence of competing dynasties such as the Uí Néill, Uí Chonchobhair and MacMurchada on the one hand, and the failure to establish a system of succession to kingship which prevented internecine strife on the other, meant that once the English arrived in the country they were able to play different factions off against each other and to secure their own independence from the native kings.

The attitude of King Henry II was crucial in determining the character of English intervention in Ireland. He might have been reluctant to become involved, but once Strongbow had proved successful, Henry took control of the operation, thereby ensuring both that Ireland would pose no threat to England and that its rich lands would be his alone to bestow upon his favourites. Although only two kings, John and Richard II, visited Ireland in the rest of the Middle Ages, the precedent of direct royal control over Irish affairs had been set.

It soon became clear that not all the native ruling families in Ireland could be displaced and that English settlers would not come in sufficient numbers to turn the island into a 'little England'. Even the most independent Irish kings recognized the English King as their overlord, but at a local level they acknowledged the authority of a neighbouring English lord only if he was strong enough to enforce their compliance. The English did not extend to the Irish their own laws, an omission which worked to the disadvantage of the native population and served to heighten ill-feeling between the two peoples. Many of the settlers assimilated culturally with their Irish neighbours over time, but this provoked harsh condemnation from the more conservative elements in colonial society, who passed

Below: *This effigy of Thomas de Cantwell in Kilfane Church, Co. Kilkenny, shows a stylized image of an Anglo-Norman knight.*

legislation, such as the Statutes of Kilkenny of 1366, to prevent the English from adopting Irish ways. Over time the settler community began to identify increasingly with Ireland and to resent the men from England who were commissioned to rule them, and the policies of the 15th century were dominated by the great settler families of Butler and FitzGerald.

The equilibrium between the two nations in Ireland could not withstand the reinvigoration of English government under Henry VII and Henry VIII, and the destruction of the ruling magnates propelled Ireland into the disastrous chaos of the 16th century.

Below: Richard II, the last English King to visit Ireland before 1689, made two expeditions to the country, in 1394-5 and 1399. The illustration shows a meeting between Richard's representative the Earl of Gloucester, and Diarmait MacMurchada's descendant, the reigning King of Leinster, Art MacMurchada Caomhánach. The English cavalry are depicted heavily armoured, the redoubtable Art considerably less so and riding without stirrups in the usual Irish fashion.

The English Invasion

DIARMAIT MacMurchada's expulsion from Ireland in 1166 set in train a series of events which within ten years saw the kings of Ireland accept the king of England as their lord and saw vast parts of the island fall into the hands of English barons.

MacMurchada travelled first to Bristol, with whose merchants he already had contacts, and from there made his way to France to find Henry II. After acknowledging Henry as his lord, Diarmait was given permission to recruit fighting men in England to help him recover his position in Ireland. It was among the marcher lords of south Wales that he found his first recruits.

A century of conflict with the Welsh had made these men particularly receptive to his promises of new lands waiting to be won by the sword, and their enthusiasm was sharpened by the knowledge that they did not enjoy the favour of their king. Their leader, Richard FitzGilbert, better known as Strongbow, had supported Henry's opponent, King Stephen, in the civil war which troubled England in the 1130s and 1140s, and he and his followers received no patronage from Henry after he become king in 1154.

MacMurchada returned to Ireland in 1167 and quickly re-established his position with the help of a small body of foreign knights. Strongbow arrived with a larger force in August 1170 and, with much bloodshed, he and Diarmait together took the Ostman city of Waterford. At this point Strongbow received his reward from Diarmait by marrying MacMurchada's daughter, Aoife. Dublin was taken a few weeks later, the province of Meath was invaded, and English forces raided the kingdom of Bréifne. Diarmait's death in May 1171, without legitimate male heirs, meant that his kingdom of Leinster came into Strongbow's possession through Aoife.

Below: The seal of Richard FitzGilbert de Clare, lord of Pembroke, alias Strongbow, the Norman marcher lord and leader of a group of Norman warrior lords based in the Welsh border lands.

This was the signal for Henry II to intervene. He was already suspicious of Strongbow. Although he had given Strongbow permission to go to Ireland, Henry was determined to stop an independent kingdom emerging under his rule. The king landed at Waterford with a large force in October 1171 and received acknowledgement of his position as lord of Ireland from both the new conquerors and several of the native kings, though probably not the high-king, Ruaidrí Ua Conchobhair (Rory O'Connor). Strongbow had already offered his subjugation to the King and, having made his royal progress from his landing place to the city of Dublin, Henry II formally granted Leinster to Strongbow in return for homage and performance of military service.

At a stroke Ireland had been added to the lands of the king of England, lands which stretched from the Scottish border to the Pyrenees. Ireland had been brought into the European mainstream, but on terms which were not its own.

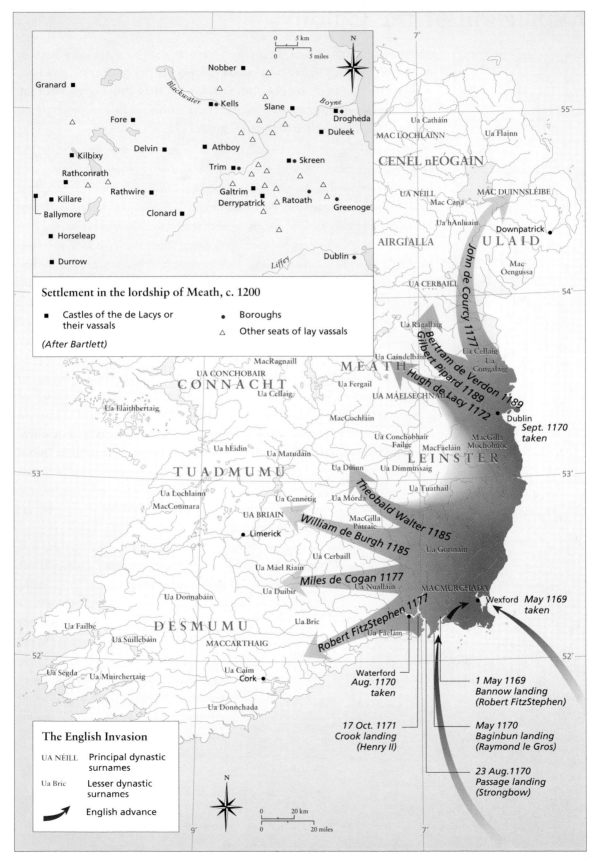

Settlement in the lordship of Meath, c. 1200

- ■ Castles of the de Lacys or their vassals
- ● Boroughs
- △ Other seats of lay vassals

(After Bartlett)

Inset map labels:

Granard
Nobber
Blackwater
Kells
Fore
Slane
Boyne
Drogheda
Delvin
Athboy
Duleek
Kilbixy
Rathconrath
Trim
Skreen
Rathwire
Galtrim
Killare
Derrypatrick
Ratoath
Ballymore
Clonard
Greenoge
Horseleap
Liffey
Dublin
Durrow

Main map labels:

MAC LOCHLAINN
Ua Catháin
Ua Flainn
CENÉL nEOGAIN
MAC DUINNSLÉIBE
UA NÉILL
Mac Cana
Downpatrick
Ua hAnluain
ULAID
AIRGIALLA
Mac Oengussa
UA CERBAILL

John de Courcy 1177
Bertram de Verdon 1189
Gilbert Pipard 1189
Hugh de Lacy 1172

Ua Ragallaig
Ua Cellaig
Ua Congalaig
Ua Gaindelbáin
MacRagnaill
MEATH
Dublin
UA CONCHOBAIR
Ua Fergail
Sept. 1170 taken
CONNACHT
Ua Cellaig
UA MÁELSECHNAILL
MacCochláin
Ua Flaithbertaig
Ua Conchobair Failge
MacGilla Mocholmóc
Ua hÉidin
Ua Matudáin
MacFáeláin
LEINSTER
Ua Dúinn
Ua Dímmussaig
TUADMUMU
Ua Cennétig
Ua Mórda
Ua Tuathail
Ua Lochlainn
MacGilla Pátraic
MacConmara
UA BRIAIN
Theobald Walter 1185
Limerick
William de Burgh 1185
Ua Cerbaill
Ua Gormáin
Ua Máel Riain
Miles de Cogan 1177
Ua Duibir
Ua Nualláin
MACMURCHADA
Ua Donnabáin
Wexford *May 1169 taken*
Ua Failbe
DESMUMU
Ua Bric
Robert FitzStephen 1177
Ua Ségda
MACCARTHAIG
Ua Fáeláin
Ua Súillebáin
Ua Caim
Cork
Ua Muirchertaig
Ua Donnchada

Waterford *Aug. 1170 taken*

1 May 1169 Bannow landing (Robert FitzStephen)

17 Oct. 1171 Crook landing (Henry II)

May 1170 Baginbun landing (Raymond le Gros)

23 Aug.1170 Passage landing (Strongbow)

The English Invasion

UA NÉILL — Principal dynastic surnames

Ua Bric — Lesser dynastic surnames

→ English advance

0 — 5 km
0 — 5 miles

0 — 20 km
0 — 20 miles

Expansion of the Colony

Above: *A carving representing an Anglo-Irish noblewoman, believed to be the first Countess of Ormond, in St Mary's Church at Gowran, near Kilkenny.*

THE CONQUERORS found it relatively easy at first to defeat the Irish in battle. What made their involvement in Irish history so crucial, however, was not their military success, but rather what they chose to do with the lands they had won. It was colonization rather than conquest which changed the course of Irish history after 1171.

Upon entering enemy territory the invaders would first construct a large mound of raised earth with a flat top surrounded by a fence, and would then build a wooden tower on its summit. This primitive castle, known as a 'motte', could be defended with ease and provided a base from which cattle raids could be launched into the lands of the local Irish king. When the local king had been subdued, the leader of the invading force would divide the best land in the territory among his supporters, a process known as subinfeudation.

At this point the emphasis changed from military conquest to economic exploitation. The conquerors had made a long-term investment in Ireland and expected wealth in return. To achieve this they imported the agricultural system, based on the manor and on a mixture of arable and pastoral farming techniques, with which they were familiar in England. Irish peasants were not removed from the land but there was a need for more labourers and so the recruitment of English peasants and artisans began. Land was scarce in England at the time and the promise of new farmland and improved conditions of tenure attracted many settlers. The ports of Bristol and Chester served as points of departure for migrants who, for the most part, came from the west midlands and south-west of England. The legacy of this movement of people is seen in Ireland today in common surnames such as Bermingham, Stafford, Dowdall (Dovedale, Derbyshire) and Bruton (Somerset).

As a result of this colonial movement the landscape of much of Ireland was dramatically transformed in the space of a few generations. New towns such as Drogheda, Dundalk, Carrickfergus, Sligo, Athenry, Nenagh, New Ross, Kilkenny and Trim sprang up, their city walls and impressive castles a reminder that this was a land of conquest. In the countryside woods were cleared, arable cultivation expanded and the volume of internal and foreign trade soared. In all its history Ireland has never experienced an economic boom quite like that of the 13th century.

Left: *In many parts of Ireland the English raised mottes to defend their newly acquired territories. They were often constructed in or near an existing population site in order to exploit the maximum economic potential. This motte is at Clonard, close to the early Christian monastic settlement.*

The English hold on Ireland

▨	English settlers
Sligo	Towns founded by the English
Ó Néill	Gaelic lordship
▲	Cistercian monasteries
▽	Benedictine monasteries
●	Houses of Augustinian Canons Regular
■	Stone castles
▪	Mottes

Greencastle
Coleraine
Carrickfergus
Black Abbey
Grey Abbey
Ó Domhnaill
Ó Néill
MacArtáin
Inch
Down
Dundrum
Sligo
Ó Ruairc
MacUidhir
Ó hAnluain
MacMathghamhna
Greencastle
Ó Conchobhair
Ó Raghailligh
Castleroche
Carlingford
Donaghmoyne
Dundalk
Abbeylara
Fore
Ardee
Ó Conchobhair
Tristernagh
Drogheda
Ó Fearghail
Mullingar
Kilkenny West
Newtown Trim
Roscommon
Trim
Rindown
Ballyboggan
Athlone
Maynooth
Dublin
Galway
Athenry
Ó Conchobair
Failghe
Naas
Ó Briain
Athy
Castledermot
Carlow
MacMurchada
Nenagh
Kilkenny
Limerick
Graiguenamanagh
Abington
(Duiske)
Enniscorthy
Kells
Athassel
New Ross
Tralee
Clonmel
Dunbrody
Wexford
Cahir
Carrick
Ballybeg
Waterford
Killagh
Tintern
MacCarthaigh
Youghal
Tracton
Kinsale

0   20 km
0   20 miles

N

39

Irish Resistance

RORY O'CONNOR was sufficiently powerful to force most of the important Irish kings to join him in an attack on Dublin after its capture by Strongbow, but he proved an inept military commander and his army was scattered with heavy losses. Upon the arrival of Henry II many native kings rushed to submit to him, following the advice of their bishops who saw Henry as the man to bring the Irish Church into line with the rest of Europe.

Armed resistance to the invaders did not, of course, cease completely, but the brutal treatment of those who did continue to oppose the new regime served as a powerful disincentive to others contemplating raiding the new towns and settlements or planning other forms of rebellion. Tigernán O'Rourke, king of Breifne, was treacherously slain on his way to a parley in 1172, and his head and decapitated corpse displayed at various points on the walls of Dublin after the deed.

For those kings who survived the initial English onslaught, the path of survival lay in accommodation with the new regime and in the consolidation of local power.

Below: *A galloglass (gall-óglach, 'foreign warrior'), imported from the west of Scotland. These heavily armoured and well-equipped fighters affected the balance of power.*

The way of compromise, however, was not to last. Piecemeal English advance continued throughout the 13th century, and even the most compliant kings such as Feidlim O'Connor — who fought for the English in Wales in 1245 — found they could not trust the king of England to keep his promises. By the 1250s a reaction had set in and, in 1258, the most important native rulers challenged the English by recognizing Brian O'Neill as high-king of Ireland. Two years later O'Neill's forces were defeated by the colonists at the battle of Down, and his severed head was sent to England for public display at the Tower of London.

With O'Neill died the last attempt to revive the high-kingship of Ireland for a native claimant, but the whole episode was not without future significance. In 1259 Aed O'Connor, son of the king of Connacht, who was with Brian at Down, had married a princess from the west of Scotland who brought back with her to Ireland a force of 160 'galloglass', the fierce mercenary soldiers from the Hebrides. The subsequent employment of galloglass by other Irish kings reduced the military advantage which the English had previously enjoyed.

Irish resistance in the century after the English arrived was, generally speaking, sporadic, uncoordinated and prompted by local rather than national concerns, but it did ensure the survival of the most important native dynasties and guaranteed that the English settlers could never rest easy in Ireland.

Irish Dynasties and
English Settlement, *c.* 1300

Counties and liberties
Irish chiefdoms

Allegiance of Irish chiefdoms

The King of England
The Earl of Ulster
The lord of Connacht
The lord of Trim
The lord of Thomond

*The lordship of Meath was
partitioned in 1244 into two
estates, one administrated
from Trim, the other from Kells*

U l s t e r

O'Donnell

Carrickfergus

O'Neill

*Lough
Neagh*

MacCartan

Downpatrick
*Down
1260*

Maguire

O'Hanlon

O'Connor
of Sligo

O'Rourke

MacMahon

Louth

O'Reilly

Meath
Kells
Drogheda

C o n n a c h t

O'Connor

T

Trim
Trim

O'Farrell

Meath

R
o
s
c
o
m
m
o
n

Dublin

Galway

Athenry

O'Connor
Faly

K i l d a r e

Dublin

to Kildare

O'Brien

MacMurrough

T h o m o n d

Kilkenny

Carlow

Limerick

Limerick

T i p p e r a r y

Kilkenny
Kilkenny

L i m e r i c k

Cashel

Wexford

K e r r y

Waterford

Wexford
Wexford

Waterford

C o r k

MacCarthy

Cork

N

0   20 km

0   20 miles

41

The Decline of English Power

THE INABILITY of the newcomers to uproot the most powerful Irish kings and the failure of greater numbers of English colonists to settle in Ireland ensured that a complete conquest of the island could not be speedily achieved.

However, the flame of ambition which had brought Strongbow and his kind to Ireland in 1170 continued to burn brightly, and as late as the 1230s a full-scale invasion of Connacht was launched which resulted in English colonies being established in places as remote as north Mayo.

That this impetus was not sustained was partly the consequence of many able English leaders in Ireland dying in the 1240s without leaving sons to succeed them. As a result, their estates were divided among daughters whose husbands often had no interest in Ireland and spent no time supporting or defending their holdings in the country. Violent quarrels broke out between the FitzGeralds and the de Burghs, the most important colonial families in the country, and even the suburbs of Dublin, the centre of the king of England's government in Ireland, was regularly attacked, from the 1270s onwards, by the MacMurroughs of the Wicklow Mountains. The colonial parliament of 1297 painted a gloomy picture of the situation and explicitly acknowledged, for the first time, that some of the settlers had begun to abandon their own culture and instead to embrace that of the native Irish.

The weaknesses of the colonial establishment were starkly revealed when Edward Bruce, brother of Robert I, king of Scotland, invaded Ulster in 1315 and joined with O'Neill in attempting to drive out the English settlers. Despite failing to gain unanimous Irish support, Bruce was able to beat English forces on several occasions and came close to capturing Dublin itself. It was not until 1318 that the Scottish menace was finally removed with the defeat and death of Bruce at Fochart near Dundalk.

It might be said, however, that the Bruce invasion also revealed the strength of the English presence in Ireland. The settlers were united in their opposition to the Scottish invaders, despite attempts by Bruce to woo or bully them from their allegiance to the king of England.

The image they had of themselves as a conquering people chosen by God to civilize the barbaric Irish remained as strong in 1320 as it had been a century-and-a-half earlier. If anything, the decline in their fortunes in the intervening period made them even more determined to survive.

Below: The Anglo-Irish victory at the Battle of Athenry in 1316 is commemorated in the seal of the town. The severed heads may represent the vanquished chieftains of Connacht. Five Irish kings are said to have died in this battle.

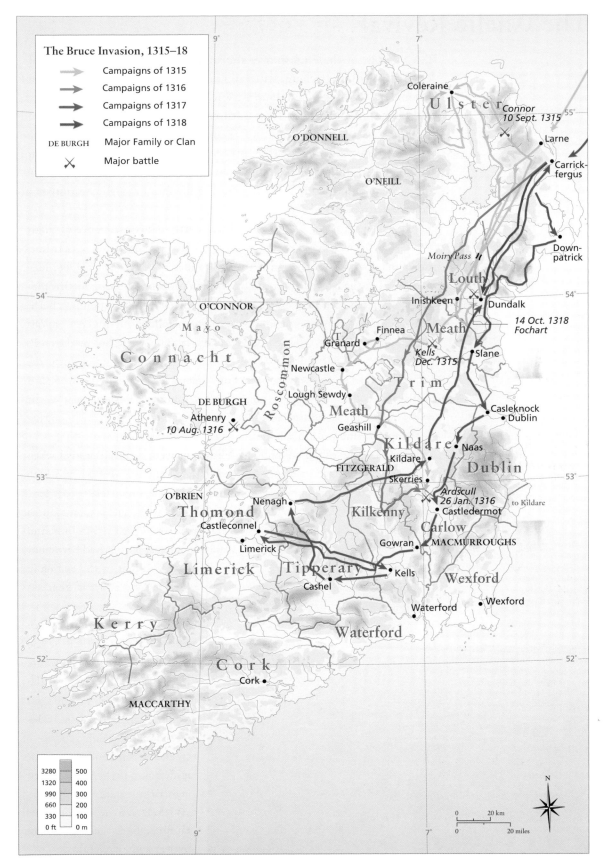

The Bruce Invasion, 1315–18

→ Campaigns of 1315
→ Campaigns of 1316
→ Campaigns of 1317
→ Campaigns of 1318
DE BURGH Major Family or Clan
✕ Major battle

Coleraine
Ulster
Connor
10 Sept. 1315 ✕
Larne
Carrick-fergus
O'DONNELL
O'NEILL
Down-patrick
Moiry Pass
Louth
Inishkeen
Dundalk
14 Oct. 1318
Fochart
O'CONNOR
Mayo
Finnea
Meath
Granard
Kells
Dec. 1315 ✕
Slane
Connacht
Roscommon
Newcastle
Trim
DE BURGH
Lough Sewdy
Caslenock
Dublin
Athenry
10 Aug. 1316 ✕
Meath
Geashill
Kildare
Naas
Kildare
FITZGERALD
Dublin
Skerries
Ardscull
26 Jan. 1316 ✕
to Kildare
O'BRIEN
Nenagh
Kilkenny
Castledermot
Thomond
Carlow
Castleconnel
Gowran
MACMURROUGHS
Limerick
Tipperary
Kells
Wexford
Limerick
Cashel
Wexford
Kerry
Waterford
Cork
Waterford
Cork
MACCARTHY

3280 — 500
1320 — 400
990 — 300
660 — 200
330 — 100
0 ft — 0 m

N

0   20 km
0   20 miles

43

The Gaelic Revival

THE VICTORY of the English over the Scots in 1318 did not end the problems of the colony. Ireland, which had once been an important source of revenue for the king of England was now a heavy drain on his resources, and the natural disasters of the 14th century — famine in 1315–17 and the Black Death in 1348–49 and regularly thereafter — weakened the Irish economy still further. The problems of landlord absenteeism and feuding between nobles increased apace, and large numbers of peasants and artisans migrated back to England in the face of Irish reconquest of frontier settlements.

The greatest threat posed to the English by the Irish, however, was cultural rather than military. Beginning with the Statutes of Kilkenny of 1366, futile attempts were made legally to prohibit the English from speaking the Irish language, marrying Irish partners or fostering children with Irish families. Such a defensive attitude was a testament to the strength and appeal of Gaelic culture. In the century after 1170 this culture had been in full retreat, but by the end of the 13th century confidence had returned and the educated families of Gaelic Ireland embarked on a 300-year period of tremendous energy in the production of poetry, legal commentaries, translations of European medical treatises and works of genealogy and Irish history.

The tone of much of this cultural revival was decidedly archaic. To give but one example, ways of inaugurating Irish kings which had disappeared but 'were remembered by the old men and recorded in the old books' were revived in the early 14th century. This emphasis on continuity with the pre-invasion past could not hide the enormous changes which had occurred in Gaelic society in the meantime. The Irish had not been slow to borrow from the English in matters such as warfare, architecture and law, while Irish kingship itself had become so degraded that by the end of the Middle Ages an Irish 'king' was no longer a law-giver with a public role sanctioned by the Church, but was rather the warrior head of the local dynasty who ensured his authority by billeting his troop of galloglass on the local population. Given the power which the culture of Gaelic Ireland permitted its leaders, it is perhaps not surprising that it should have appealed so strongly to leading colonial families like the de Burghs, Butlers and FitzGeralds.

Below: Rosserk, Co. Mayo, a Franciscan friary of the Third Order Regular, founded in the 15th century. This was a time of religious enthusiasm in Ireland. The Irish founded new monastic houses and went on pilgrimage as far afield as Santiago in Spain. Irish poets also produced quantities of religious verse of great beauty at this time.

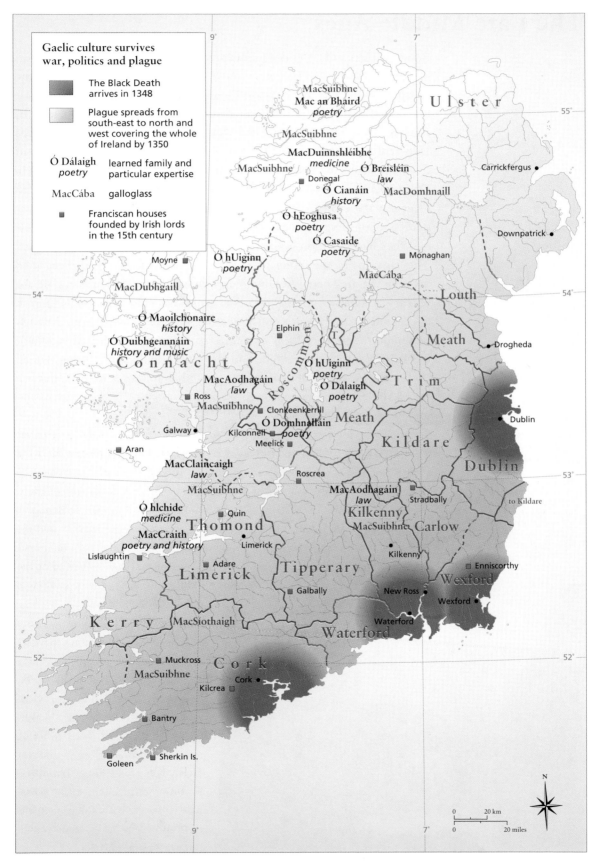

Gaelic culture survives
war, politics and plague

The Black Death
arrives in 1348

Plague spreads from
south-east to north and
west covering the whole
of Ireland by 1350

Ó Dálaigh   learned family and
poetry   particular expertise

MacCába   galloglass

Franciscan houses
founded by Irish lords
in the 15th century

Ulster

MacSuibhne
Mac an Bhaird
poetry

MacSuibhne

MacDuinnshléibhe
medicine

MacSuibhne

Ó Breisléin
law

Donegal

Ó Cianáin
history

MacDomhnaill

Carrickfergus

Ó hEoghusa
poetry

Ó Casaide
poetry

Monaghan

Downpatrick

Moyne

Ó hUiginn
poetry

MacCába

Louth

MacDubhgaill

Meath

Ó Maoilchonaire
history

Elphin

Drogheda

Ó Duibhgeannáin
history and music

C o n n a c h t

Ó hUiginn
poetry

T r i m

MacAodhagáin
law

Ó Dálaigh
poetry

Ross

MacSuibhne

Clonkeenkerrill

Meath

Galway

Ó Domhnalláin
poetry

Kilconnell

Kildare

Meelick

Aran

Dublin

MacClaincaigh
law

Roscrea

MacSuibhne

MacAodhagáin
law

Stradbally

Dublin

to Kildare

Ó hlchide
medicine

Quin

Kilkenny

MacSuibhne

Carlow

Thomond

MacCraith
poetry and history

Limerick

Kilkenny

Lislaughtin

Adare

Tipperary

Enniscorthy

Limerick

Galbally

New Ross

Wexford

K e r r y

MacSíothaigh

Waterford

Wexford

Muckross

Cork

MacSuibhne

Kilcrea

Cork

Bantry

Goleen   Sherkin Is.

Roscommon

0   20 km

0   20 miles

N

The Late Middle Ages

Between 1360 and 1399 the English crown devoted an unusual amount of time and money to Ireland in an effort to shore up the position of the colonists there. Edward III's son Lionel of Clarence was chief governor for five years during the 1360s, and the next king of England, Richard II, came to Ireland twice in the 1390s. Richard was deposed in 1399 and his 15th-century successors were not prepared to throw any more money at the Irish problem. Instead the great magnate families, the Butlers in Ormond and the FitzGeralds in Desmond and Kildare, were expected to represent the crown's interests and defend the settlement. These magnates had long experience of dealing with the Irish of their own districts and they had taken on many of the characteristics of their neighbours. This was not to the liking of the settlers in the towns and those who dwelt in the area between Dublin and Dundalk which by the end of the century was known as the Pale. This group wished to remain as English as possible and they sent a constant stream of complaints about the earls to London. Allowing local magnates to rule, whatever its drawbacks, did bring stability to Ireland, and the amount of new building which took place in the 15th century suggests that it was a time of modest prosperity and economic growth.

When the settlers went to England they found themselves treated as foreigners, and their feeling of resentment showed through in 1460 when they declared in the Irish parliament that they were not bound by laws passed in parliament in England unless they passed them as well. This independent stance became a major problem after the victory of Henry Tudor over Richard III at Bosworth Field in 1485 when the earl of Kildare, who had supported Richard, used the Irish parliament to forward the claim of the pretender Lambert Simnel to the English throne. In 1494 Henry VII dispatched Sir Edward Poynings to bring the settlers to heel and in a parliament held at Drogheda late that year the chief governor pushed through legislation which restated categorically the subordinate position of the Irish to the English parliament. Kildare's stranglehold on real power in Ireland survived this setback, but his actions were in future monitored more closely, and his family was finally driven into rebellion and disgrace in 1534. There was to be no Irish solution to the Irish problem as a new era of English power dawned.

Below: Tower-houses were the most notable development in Irish secular architecture in the late Middle Ages, and were built by both Anglo-Irish and native Irish lords. This one, at Leighlinbridge, Co. Carlow, is a 16th-century device for guarding a vital crossing of the River Barrow.

Late medieval Ireland

O'Brien — Native Irish dynasties
Dalton — English names
▨ — areas obedient to England
▬ — Pale, 1488

O'Doherty
MacDonnell
MacQuillan
MacSweeney
O'Cahan
O'Donnell
O'Neill of Clandeboye
Carrickfergus
The Great O'Neill
O'Rourke
O'Neill of the Fews
MacCartan   Savage
Maguire
MacMahon
Downpatrick
Magennis
O'Dowda   Sligo
Magauran
O'Connor Sligo
MacRannell
O'Hanlon
Barrett
MacDermot
O'Reilly
O'Connor Don and Rua
O'Farrall   Dundalk
MacCostello
MacWilliam Burke
O'Dempsey   Drogheda
O'Malley
Dalton
Bermingham
Dillon
O'Flaherty
O'Kelly
O'Melaghlin   Maynooth
Clanricard Burke
MacGeoghegan   Dublin
Galway
O'Madden   O'Connor Faly   Earldom
Athenry
MacCoghlan   of Kildare
O'More   O'Dempsey   O'Toole
O'Brien
MacGillapatrick   Wicklow
MacNamara   O'Byrne
Earldom of Ormond
Limerick   O'Mulryan   MacMurrough
Clanwilliam Burke   Kilkenny
O'Connor Kerry
Earldom of   Wexford
FitzMaurice   Desmond
Waterford
Roche Condon   Le Poer
MacCarthy Mór
Barry
MacCarthy
Cork
O'Sullivan Mór
O'Sullivan Beare
MacCarthy Reagh
O'Mahony   O'Driscoll

3280	500
1320	400
990	300
660	200
330	100
0 ft	0 m

N

0   20 km
0   20 miles

The Growth of Dublin

Dublin takes its name from the Irish Duibhlinn, 'black pool', which possibly refers to a pool on the Poddle, a tributary of the river Liffey. Duibhlinn was an ecclesiastical centre seized in 841 by Vikings who had been ravaging Ireland for the previous half-century. The alternative Irish name for the city, Áth Cliath, 'the ford of the hurdles', explains its strategic significance, as it was one of the region's most important crossing-points.

Above: St Patrick's Cathedral, Dublin, 1793, by James Malton. The cathedral is shown here from the south-east and it is a valuable historical document as it shows a fine example of Early Gothic architecture in Ireland before the 19th-century restorations. St Patrick's pre-dated the English invasion, but the extant building was erected after it, and elevated to cathedral status c. 1220.

It quickly became the main Viking military base and trading centre in Ireland and its Norse, and sometimes Danish, rulers, involved themselves in raiding and military alliances in Ireland and abroad. In the first half of the 10th century members of its ruling family were also kings of York. In the course of time, though, Dublin became ever more closely integrated into Irish politics, and its Hiberno-Scandinavian rulers exercised power over its hinterland, a trace of which survives today in the area known as Fingal (*Fine Gall*, 'the territory of the foreigners').

Though a powerful military and naval force, the men of Dublin were defeated by the Munster king Brian Boru at the battle of Clontarf in 1014, and thereafter the town was largely an appanage claimed by the contenders for the elusive high-kingship of Ireland. By the time Ireland was invaded by the English in 1169, Dublin had come to replace Tara as the country's symbolic capital, and was also the single greatest concentration of economic wealth, with an extensive network of trading contacts overseas.

It fell to English arms in 1170, and when King Henry II visited the country in the following year he took the city, and what became County Dublin, into his own hands. Dublin remained the headquarters of the new English colony thereafter, Dublin Castle, which underwent many phases of fortification and expansion in the following centuries, coming to represent, in both a practical and symbolic way, the seat of English government in Ireland.

In the aftermath of the English invasion Dublin enjoyed an extended period of physical expansion (including the reclamation of lands from the Liffey), and of economic development and prosperity, as exemplified by the architectural splendour of its two medieval cathedrals, and the foundation of several wealthy religious houses. By the early 14th century, however, the city had begun to decline, in common with the experience elsewhere, though in Dublin's case it lasted until the 17th century. Growth on a considerable scale only gathered pace following the Restoration in 1660, and the 18th century was arguably the most colourful in the city's history, the arts and architecture in particular finding encouragement from the wealthy society of what was now regarded as the second city of the empire.

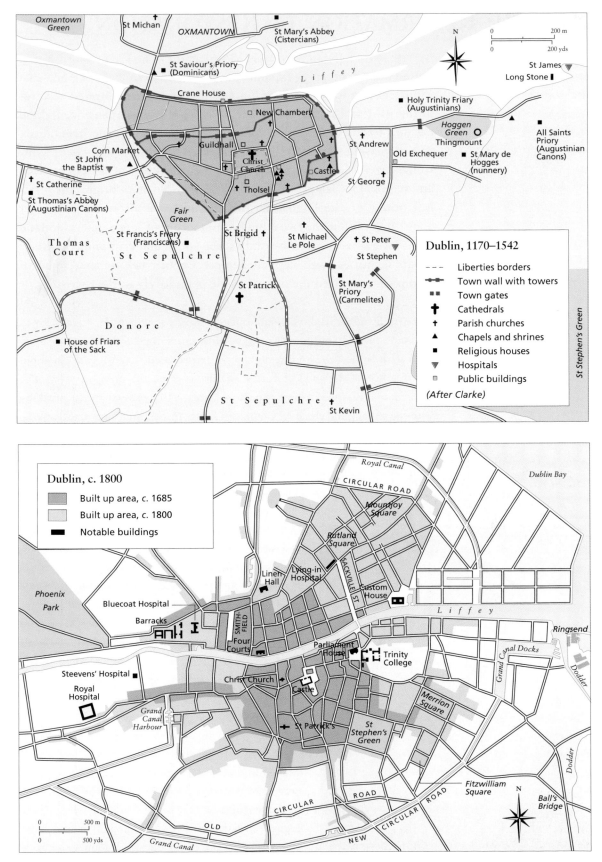

Oxmantown Green

St Michan

OXMANTOWN

St Mary's Abbey
(Cistercians)

N

0   200 m
0   200 yds

St Saviour's Priory
(Dominicans)

St James
Long Stone

L i f f e y

Crane House

New Chambers

Holy Trinity Friary
(Augustinians)

Corn Market
St John
the Baptist

Guildhall

St Andrew

Hoggen Green
Thingmount

All Saints
Priory
(Augustinian
Canons)

Christ
Church

Castle

St George

Old Exchequer

St Mary de
Hogges
(nunnery)

St Catherine

Tholsel

St Thomas's Abbey
(Augustinian Canons)

Fair
Green

St George

Thomas
Court

St Francis's Friary
(Franciscans)

St Brigid

St Michael
Le Pole

St Peter

St Stephen

S t   S e p u l c h r e

St Patrick

St Mary's
Priory
(Carmelites)

Dublin, 1170–1542

- - - Liberties borders
━◆━ Town wall with towers
▪▪ Town gates
✝ Cathedrals
† Parish churches
▲ Chapels and shrines
■ Religious houses
▼ Hospitals
▫ Public buildings

(After Clarke)

D o n o r e

House of Friars
of the Sack

St Stephen's Green

S t   S e p u l c h r e

St Kevin

Dublin, c. 1800

Built up area, *c.* 1685

Built up area, *c.* 1800

Notable buildings

Royal Canal

CIRCULAR ROAD

Dublin Bay

Mountjoy
Square

Rutland
Square

Phoenix
Park

Linen
Hall

Lying-in
Hospital

Custom
House

Bluecoat Hospital

SACKVILLE ST.

L i f f e y

Ringsend

Barracks

SMITHFIELD

Grand Canal Docks

Dodder

Four
Courts

Parliament
House

Trinity
College

Steevens' Hospital

Christ Church

Merrion
Square

Royal
Hospital

Castle

Grand
Canal
Harbour

St Patrick's

St
Stephen's
Green

Fitzwilliam
Square

N

Ball's
Bridge

0   500 m
0   500 yds

CIRCULAR

ROAD

OLD

Grand Canal

NEW

CIRCULAR

ROAD

Dodder

PART III: REFORMATION TO RESTORATION

*Colm Lennon
and
Raymond Gillespie*

BY THE END of Ireland's troubled 15th century, the English lordship of the island in practice extended over the eastern Pale region, east Munster, the towns and their hinterlands, and some scattered enclaves in the west and north. In an age of geographical expansion, Ireland became a zone of English colonial intervention and experimentation. The increasing transatlantic trade affected the thinly populated, lightly urbanized island only slowly. After the overthrow of dozens of local and regional lordships of Gaelic and Anglo-Norman origin, the political power of the English Crown became centralized in Dublin by about 1600. While the two ethnic communities of late medieval Ireland were not mutually exclusive and shared social and economic ties, their group identities were defined against English newcomers, some of whom characterized the native people pejoratively in their writings.

The genesis of the Tudors' commitment to positive policies for Ireland lay in England's increasingly complex entanglement in European diplomacy. As relations with France, the Empire and Spain deteriorated, English concern about the fragility of Ireland's defences against continental invasion grew. The Reformation reached Ireland as part of Henry VIII's programme of breaking with the papacy and chaining Church and state institutions more tightly to the monarchy. In that context the raising of Ireland in 1541 to the constitutional status of a kingdom was another assertion of royal power in the face of Roman claims that the country was a papal fief.

The kingship of Ireland was more importantly the centrepiece of a programme of political and social reform designed to overhaul the Irish adminstration and to restructure the Gaelic and gaelicized lordships, bringing them into line with English norms. Originally conceived as a potential partnership of the communities within a unified constitutional framework, the putative kingdom never became a reality. In the absence of a monarch, the later Tudor viceroys attempted to persuade the native lords to accept English political relationships, common law and land tenure. But persuasion was interspersed with bouts of intimidation and with plantation ventures settling newcomers on lands to which the Crown claimed title. Resistance to English officials' increasingly forceful efforts to impose new institutions resulted in revolts in all provinces, culminating in the struggle of the Nine Years War centred on Ulster. The breakdown of trust between the earl of Tyrone and the English authorities was symptomatic of the tense situation at the end of the century, leading to a hugely

Below: Henry VIII of England during whose reign (1509–47) the Reformation began in Ireland and under whom Ireland was raised to the status of kingdom in 1541.

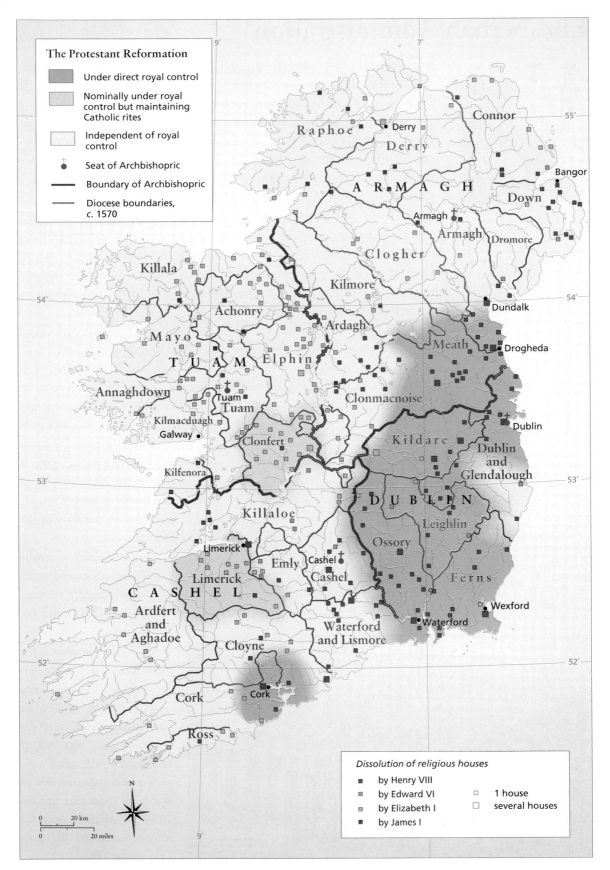

The Protestant Reformation

- Under direct royal control
- Nominally under royal control but maintaining Catholic rites
- Independent of royal control
- ● Seat of Archbishopric
- ━━ Boundary of Archbishopric
- ── Diocese boundaries, c. 1570

Dissolution of religious houses
- ■ by Henry VIII
- ■ by Edward VI
- ■ by Elizabeth I
- ■ by James I
- □ 1 house
- □ several houses

Raphoe
Derry
Connor
Derry
ARMAGH
Down
Bangor
Armagh †
Armagh
Dromore
Clogher
Dundalk
Killala
Kilmore
Achonry
Ardagh
Meath
Drogheda
Mayo
Elphin
TUAM
Annaghdown
Tuam †
Tuam
Clonmacnoise
Kilmacduagh
Galway
Clonfert
Kildare
Dublin
Dublin and Glendalough
Kilfenora
DUBLIN
Killaloe
Leighlin
Limerick
Ossory
Emly
Cashel †
Ferns
Limerick
Cashel
CASHEL
Ardfert and Aghadoe
Wexford
Cloyne
Waterford and Lismore
Waterford
Cork
Cork
Ross

N

0   20 km
0   20 miles

Elizabethan Administration

Above: *Ladies from the region of the Pale are shown here with mercenary soldiers from outside the Pale known as 'Kerns', warriors armed in the traditional Irish fashion. These illustrations were meant to contrast the civilization of the Pale with the supposed barbarism of the Gaelic west.*

THE ELIZABETHAN administration was the principal agency of the anglicization of the newly-constituted kingdom of Ireland. Its central institutions in Dublin underwent reform, although parliament met only three times during the reign. Under a succession of ambitious chief governors, the privy council was streamlined, becoming a more sophisticated and efficient executive body. The judiciary and exchequer were also overhauled, and new prerogative and ecclesiastical courts were established, those of Castle Chamber and High Commission. The huge costs of the reform programme rapidly outstripped available revenues, necessitating heavier taxation of the loyal Old English. Although co-existing uneasily with newly-arrived officials, this community, residing mostly in Leinster, grew increasingly resentful, as attested by its leaders' opposition strategy in parliament over a variety of constitutional, economic and religious issues.

Some progress was made by expanding the administration into the provinces, incorporating presidency councils to foster common law, tenurial reform, abolition of overlordship and of the oppressive and arbitrary taxation known as coign and livery. The key principle was conciliation through composition, a commuting of all levies into a compound tax payable mainly to the Crown, with small residual dues to former overlords. The latter would abandon fiscal and military autonomy, and instead come to rely on the judicial and security powers of the local president. He was to rule in the manner of the lord president of Wales or the Council of the North in England. At the same time, formerly Gaelic territories became shires, leading to the insertion of sheriffs and the establishment of English-style social and landholding structures.

Whereas in Munster the presidency system broke down as a result of revolts caused by displaced Irish swordsmen, aggressive English seneschals and widespread martial law and violence, in Connacht there was attempted a comprehensive settlement known as the Composition of Connacht. This settled the landholding pattern, particularly in the south of the province, establishing an income for the presidents and conciliar courts to redress the grievances of the principal lords. But lack of consistency in English policy was most detrimental in northern Connacht and in Ulster, where peaceful reform collapsed dramatically in the 1590s.

Below: *The citizens of Dublin turn out to greet and pay homage to Sir Henry Sidney, Lord Deputy of Ireland, on his victorious return from his campaigns against the Gaelic Irish in 1575, from John Derricke's* Image of Ireland, *1581.*

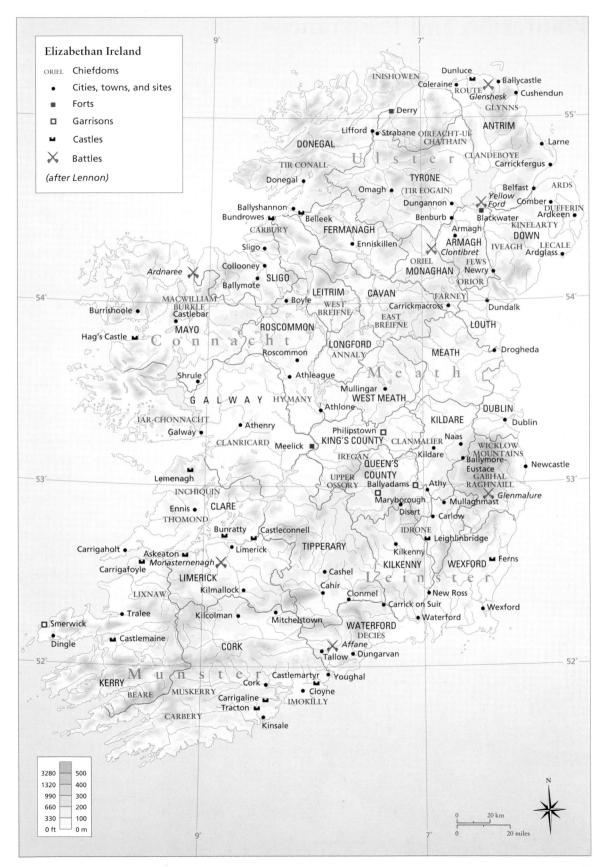

Elizabethan Ireland

ORIEL Chiefdoms

• Cities, towns, and sites

■ Forts

□ Garrisons

⚏ Castles

✕ Battles

(after Lennon)

INISHOWEN

Dunluce
Coleraine   ✕   • Ballycastle
ROUTE   • Cushendun
Glenshesk
GLYNNS

• Derry

Lifford
Strabane •   OIREACHT-UI-
CHATHAIN   ANTRIM
DONEGAL   • Larne
TIR CONALL   U l s t e r   CLANDEBOYE
TYRONE   Carrickfergus •
• Donegal   Omagh   (TIR EOGAIN)   Belfast •   ARDS
Dungannon •   Comber •
Ballyshannon   Benburb •   *Yellow*   DUFFERIN
Bundrowes   • Belleek   Blackwater ■   *Ford*   Ardkeen •
CARBURY   FERMANAGH   • Armagh   KINELARTY
• Sligo   • Enniskillen   ARMAGH   DOWN
Collooney •   ✕   IVEAGH   LECALE
Ardnaree ✕   *Clontibret*   • Ardglass
• Ballymote   SLIGO   ORIEL   FEWS
LEITRIM   CAVAN   MONAGHAN   Newry •
MACWILLIAM   • Boyle   WEST   ORIOR
Burrishoole •   BURKLE   BREIFNE   • Carrickmacross   FARNEY   • Dundalk
Castlebar   EAST   LOUTH
MAYO   ROSCOMMON   BREIFNE   MEATH
Hag's Castle ⚏   C o n n a c h t   LONGFORD   • Drogheda
Roscommon •   ANNALY   M e a t h
Shrule •   • Athleague   Mullingar •
GALWAY   HYMANY   WEST MEATH   DUBLIN
IAR-CHONNACHT   • Athlone   KILDARE   • Dublin
• Athenry   Philipstown □   Naas •
Galway •   CLANRICARD   Meelick •   KING'S COUNTY   CLANMALIER   WICKLOW
IREGAN   • Kildare   Ballymore-   MOUNTAINS
QUEEN'S   Eustace   • Newcastle
UPPER   COUNTY   GABHAL
Lemenagh ⚏   OSSORY   Ballyadams □   • Athy   RAGHNAILL
INCHIQUIN   □ Maryborough   ✕ *Glenmalure*
Ennis •   CLARE   Disert •   Mullaghmast
THOMOND   • Carlow
Bunratty ⚏   Castleconnell   IDRONE
Carrigaholt •   • Limerick   TIPPERARY   • Leighlinbridge
Askeaton ⚏   • Kilkenny   • Ferns
Carrigafoyle   *Monasternenagh* ✕   KILKENNY   WEXFORD
LIMERICK   • Cashel   L e i n s t e r
LIXNAW   Kilmallock •   Cahir •   • New Ross
• Tralee   • Clonmel   • Wexford
Kilcolman •   Carrick on Suir
□ Smerwick   Mitchelstown •   • Waterford
Dingle •   Castlemaine ⚏   WATERFORD   DECIES   *Affane*
CORK   ✕   • Dungarvan
Tallow
KERRY   M u n s t e r   Castlemartyr •   • Youghal
BEARE   MUSKERRY   • Cork   IMOKILLY
Carrigaline •   • Cloyne
Tracton ⚏
CARBERY   • Kinsale

9°   7°   55°

54°

53°

52°

3280   500
1320   400
990   300
660   200
330   100
0 ft   0 m

N

0   20 km

0   20 miles

Plantation and Resistance

ALTHOUGH mooted earlier in the 16th century, plantation of Irish lands by newcomers was not actually attempted until the 1550s in Laois and Offaly. Designed principally to secure the seized estates of the rebellious O'Mores and O'Connors on the Pale borders, the settlement of soldier-farmers in what became Queen's and King's Counties did not effect peaceful agricultural and civic conditions for many years. Some natives received lands in the plantation, but others, excluded from a stake, persisted in raiding the new settlements.

Private plantations were attempted in south-west Munster and parts of Ulster in the mid-Elizabethan years. The Newry settlement by the Bagenals evolved into a sound proprietorship, but the efforts of Sir Thomas Smith in the Ards and of the Earl of Essex in Antrim failed disastrously; they were vigorously opposed by Sir Brian O'Neill of Clandeboye, whose title was overridden by the newly-arrived Englishmen. Ensuing assassinations and massacres reflected the widespread resentment stirred up. In the barony of Idrone in Leinster the Butler family and their allies revolted against the land speculator Sir Peter Carew.

The relative failure of private entrepreneurs ensured a thorough state-planned enterprise in Munster after the collapse of the Earl of Desmond's revolt. After a hasty survey of the escheated estates in five counties, the London government allotted 300,000 acres to 35 undertakers, principally English gentlemen, courtiers and servitors. Recipients of estates of from 4,000 to 12,000 acres, the undertakers were to foster agrarian innovation, exploit natural resources, build substantial residences, encourage crafts and attract up to 90 families to work the land.

Some undertakers became absentees, but those who stayed faced many difficulties. Some lands were not free of putative owners who claimed to be freeholders rather than tenants-at-will of the late Earl, and others were burdened with debts and mortgages. Commissions were established to settle the claims of litigants, but proceedings were complex.

Below: This map shows the Laois-Offaly region in exceptional detail as part of the movement towards its plantation, the first large-scale English settlement in Ireland since the early stages of the Anglo-Norman invasion.

By the time of a major rebellion in 1598 and during the Nine Years War, the number of settlers was only about a third of that anticipated and the tentative roots of the fledgling colony could not withstand the avenging warbands and armies of Gaelic and Old English former landholders.

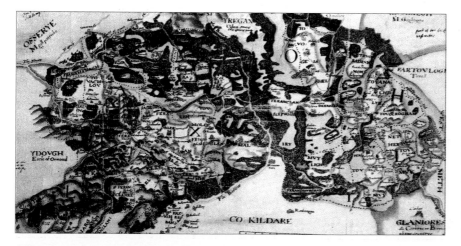

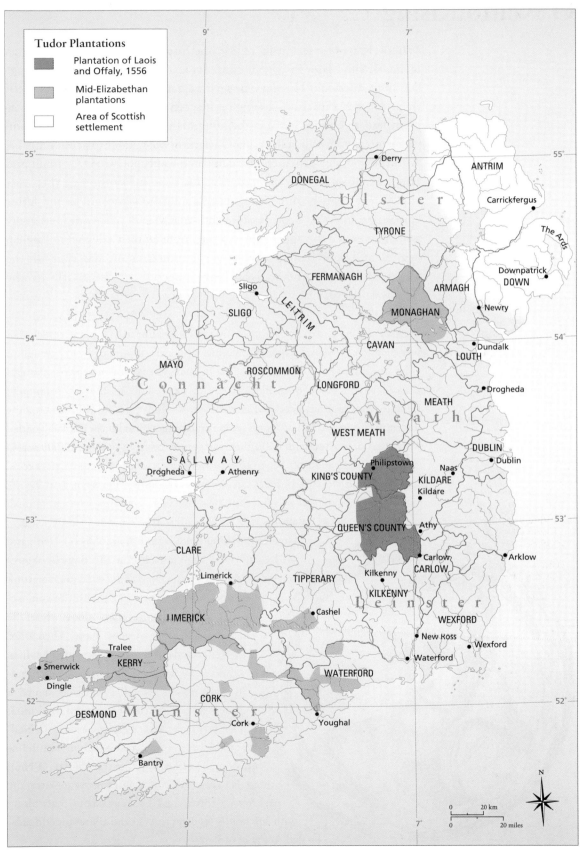

Tudor Plantations

- Plantation of Laois and Offaly, 1556
- Mid-Elizabethan plantations
- Area of Scottish settlement

Derry

DONEGAL

Ulster

ANTRIM

Carrickfergus

TYRONE

The Ards

FERMANAGH

ARMAGH

Downpatrick
DOWN

Sligo

LEITRIM

MONAGHAN

Newry

SLIGO

CAVAN

Dundalk

LOUTH

MAYO

ROSCOMMON

Connacht

LONGFORD

Meath

MEATH

WEST MEATH

Drogheda

G A L W A Y

DUBLIN

Dublin

Drogheda

Athenry

KING'S COUNTY

Philipstown

Naas

KILDARE

Kildare

QUEEN'S COUNTY

Athy

CLARE

Carlow
CARLOW

Arklow

Limerick

TIPPERARY

Kilkenny

Leinster

LIMERICK

Cashel

KILKENNY

WEXFORD

New Ross

Wexford

Tralee

KERRY

Waterford

Smerwick

WATERFORD

Dingle

CORK

DESMOND *Munster*

Cork

Youghal

Bantry

N

0   20 km

0   20 miles

O'Neill's Rising

WHEN HUGH O'NEILL, earl of Tyrone, took the field at Clontibret as leader of the Ulster insurgent confederacy in 1595, he resolved a long-standing dilemma. Having emerged as head of the powerful O'Neill dynasty after a fractious struggle, the erstwhile protégé of the government had to choose between heading an English-style administration in Ulster, thereby alienating his Gaelic kinsfolk, or throwing in his lot with the younger provincial leaders such as Hugh Roe O'Donnell and Hugh Maguire in their campaign against the infiltration of their territories by English officials. Having committed himself to the latter course, he unveiled a professionally-trained and well-equipped army which defended the approaches to the north against advancing English armies and scored many victories, culminating in the rout of the forces of his old antagonist, Henry Bagenal, at the Battle of the Yellow Ford in 1598.

Below: Hugh O'Neill, earl of Tyrone, was brought up among English settlers in the Irish midlands and fought on the side of the English in Munster and Ulster. Aspiring to a leadership role in central Ulster, he realized that the spread of English administration into the province represented a challenge to his position. Eventually he opted to head the confederacy of Ulster chieftains who had begun a major campaign against English garrisons and officials in Ulster in 1594. Aided by a disciplined army, he achieved many successes in the war to 1599. Thereafter the English under Mountjoy asserted their supremacy despite the landing of Spanish troops in Kinsale in 1601. The ensuing treaty of Mellifont guaranteed O'Neill's headship of his clan and his title to the earldom but pressure from officials in Dublin caused him to flee Ireland in 1607.

Now at the height of his success, O'Neill extended the war into the other provinces and renewed a quest for continental aid. As part of his campaign to enlist the support of the Old English in the Pale and in the towns, the earl issued articles demanding liberty of conscience for all the inhabitants of Ireland. Although unsuccessful in this bid, O'Neill and his allies caused the discomfiture of the earl of Essex's huge army in 1599. With the arrival of Lord Mountjoy as governor in 1600, the massive English resources committed to the quelling of the revolt began to bear fruit. By using scorched earth tactics, suborning disaffected confederates, and establishing a garrison near Derry, Mountjoy appeared to be undermining O'Neill's campaign when a Spanish fleet containing 3,500 troops arrived at Kinsale in 1601.

After a gruelling mid-winter march by O'Neill and O'Donnell and their assault on the English armies blockading Kinsale, the fateful engagement took place on Christmas Eve 1601, with the comprehensive defeat of the Irish allies while the Spanish remained at their base. Thereafter, O'Neill, under increasing pressure back in Ulster from Mountjoy's garrisons, eventually gave up his guerrilla war and signed a peace treaty at Mellifont in March 1603. The terms agreed were generous, O'Neill retaining his lands and earldom but relinquishing overlordship of traditional O'Neill vassals except O'Cahan. But four years later, the earl felt so threatened by newcomers that, along with his family and retainers, and like-minded lords, he fled to the continent.

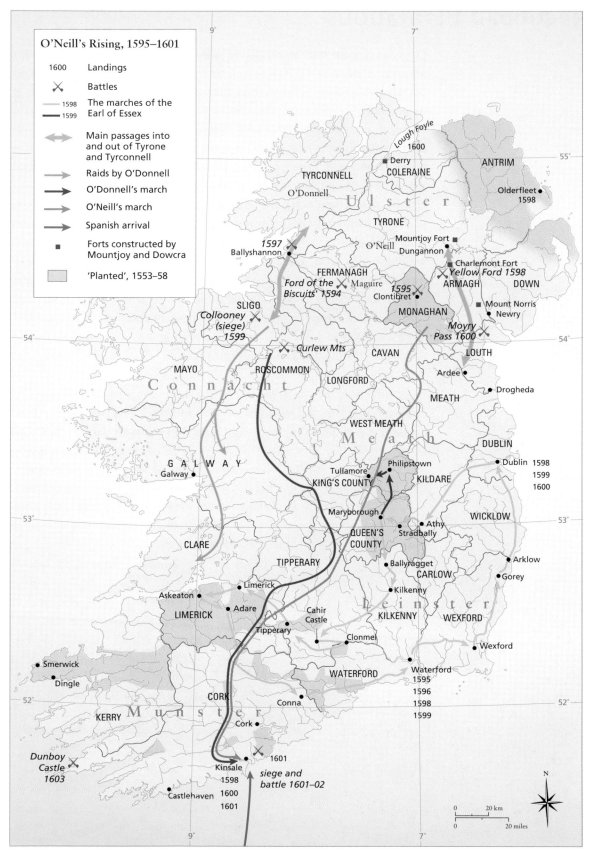

O'Neill's Rising, 1595–1601

1600	Landings
✕	Battles
——1598	The marches of the Earl of Essex
——1599	
⬌	Main passages into and out of Tyrone and Tyrconnell
→	Raids by O'Donnell
→	O'Donnell's march
→	O'Neill's march
→	Spanish arrival
■	Forts constructed by Mountjoy and Dowcra
▨	'Planted', 1553–58

Lough Foyle 1600

Derry
COLERAINE
ANTRIM
Olderfleet 1598

TYRCONNELL
O'Donnell

U l s t e r

TYRONE
O'Neill
Mountjoy Fort
Dungannon
Charlemont Fort
Yellow Ford 1598
ARMAGH
DOWN

1597
Ballyshannon

FERMANAGH
Ford of the ✕ Maguire
Biscuits' 1594
1595
Clontibret
MONAGHAN
Mount Norris
Newry
Moyry
Pass 1600

SLIGO
Collooney ✕
(siege) 1599

✕ Curlew Mts
CAVAN
LOUTH
Ardee
Drogheda

MAYO
ROSCOMMON
LONGFORD
MEATH

C o n n a c h t

WEST MEATH
M e a t h
DUBLIN

GALWAY
Galway

Tullamore
KING'S COUNTY
Philipstown
KILDARE
Dublin 1598
1599
1600

Maryborough
Athy
WICKLOW
Stradbally

CLARE
QUEEN'S COUNTY
Ballyragget
CARLOW
Arklow
Gorey

TIPPERARY
L e i n s t e r
Kilkenny
KILKENNY
WEXFORD

Limerick
Askeaton
Adare
LIMERICK
Cahir Castle
Clonmel
Wexford

Tipperary
Smerwick
Dingle
WATERFORD
Waterford
1595
1596
1598
1599

CORK
Conna
KERRY
M u n s t e r
Cork

Dunboy
Castle
1603

Kinsale
1598 1601
1600
1601
siege and
battle 1601–02

Castlehaven

0   20 km
0   20 miles

N

61

Jacobean Plantations

ON 3 SEPTEMBER 1607 some Ulster lords, recently restored to their lands after the Nine Years War, left Ireland from Lough Swilly without royal permission. Having relinquished their allegiance to the king, James I, their lands, comprising the modern counties of Armagh, Cavan, Donegal, Fermanagh, Derry and Tyrone, were escheated by the Crown. The event was unexpected and it took some time to provide an appropriate response. In January 1608 a plan for these counties was published involving a plantation similar to that of 16th-century Munster. Four groups were eligible for the Ulster lands: Scots and English settlers, servitors (royal officials), 'deserving' Irish and the Church. Baronies were set aside for the first three groups, who were to be granted estates ranging in size from 1,000 to 2,000 acres. The settler landlords were to introduce English and Scottish tenants onto these estates and effect improvements such as the building of towns. In 1610 County Coleraine was exempted from the scheme; the settlement there was to be carried out by a group of London livery companies and as a result the name of the county changed to Londonderry.

In the short term the impact of the plantation was much less than expected by government. Settlers did not arrive in the anticipated numbers and the social backgrounds of the landlords meant they had difficulty raising capital to improve the estates. Surveys in 1611, 1614 and 1622 provided evidence that settlers neither fulfilled their building obligations nor removed the native Irish from their lands. Much of the original settlement was destroyed by the 1641 rising.

In addition to the Ulster plantation there were smaller Jacobean settlements in counties Wexford, Longford and Leitrim, which, being mainly redistributions of land, did not require the introduction of settlers.

Right: The town of Derry was granted to the corporations of the City of London in 1613, as part of the Jacobean plantations becoming, in the process, Londonderry. This drawing was made approximately 70 years later and shows Londonderry around 1680.

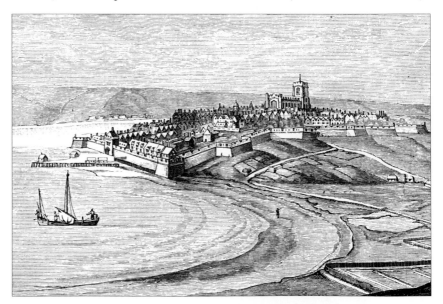

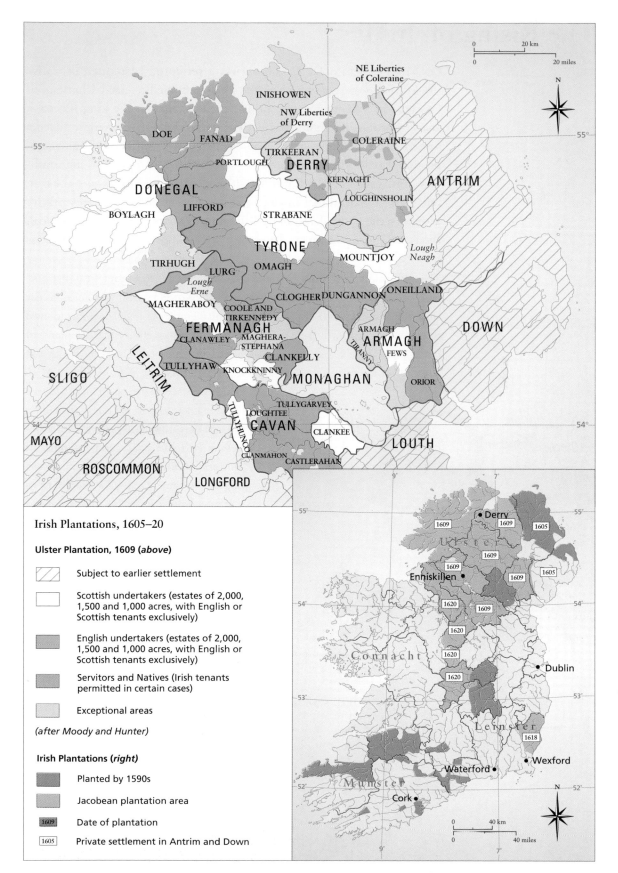

Irish Plantations, 1605–20

Ulster Plantation, 1609 (*above*)

	Subject to earlier settlement
	Scottish undertakers (estates of 2,000, 1,500 and 1,000 acres, with English or Scottish tenants exclusively)
	English undertakers (estates of 2,000, 1,500 and 1,000 acres, with English or Scottish tenants exclusively)
	Servitors and Natives (Irish tenants permitted in certain cases)
	Exceptional areas

(after Moody and Hunter)

Irish Plantations (*right*)

	Planted by 1590s
	Jacobean plantation area
1609	Date of plantation
1605	Private settlement in Antrim and Down

The Rising of 1641

ON THE EVENING of 22 October 1641 a group of Ulstermen of native stock, under the command of Sir Phelim O'Neill, seized Charlemont Castle. They claimed not to be in rebellion against the king but took arms to protect his rights against 'evil counsellors' and even produced a forged royal commission to vindicate their action. The military campaign pushed south, arriving at Drogheda in December 1641. This military pressure forced the Catholic Old English of the Pale to join the war, but their constitutional instinct led them to establish a representative assembly, the Confederation of Kilkenny, to negotiate a settlement with the Dublin government.

The outbreak of civil war in England in 1642 added a further complication to the Irish situation: the king, Charles I, wanted peace in Ireland so that he could use Irish troops in England. The situation was further internalionalized by the arrival of a force of Irishmen from the Spanish Netherlands under the command of Owen Roe O'Neill and Scots commanded by Robert Munroe in 1642. War dragged on for two years until a cessation was declared in September 1643 to enable a peace to be negotiated between the Confederates and the Lord Lieutenant, the earl of Ormond. This proved divisive within the settler camp, and a number of military commanders appealed to the English Parliamentarians for support. The first attempt at a treaty, the Ormond peace of August 1646, proved divisive within the Confederation, the Papal Nuncio Giovanni Rinuccini claiming there were not enough guarantees for the Catholic church. The landing of a Parliamentary force in Ireland in 1647 and plans for the second civil war in England drew together the pro-peace confederates, who negotiated a second treaty in January 1647. After the execution of Charles I on 30 January, this formed the basis of an alliance between the Confederates and the Dublin government against the power of the English Parliamentarians. Thus the Irish civil war became an extension of the English civil war, which was not concluded until 1653.

S:ʳ Phillom O Neale Cheife Traytor of all Ireland

Left: *Sir Phelim O'Neill, leader of a group of Catholic landowners, decided to strengthen their claim to special consideration by armed revolt against the English government of Ireland.*

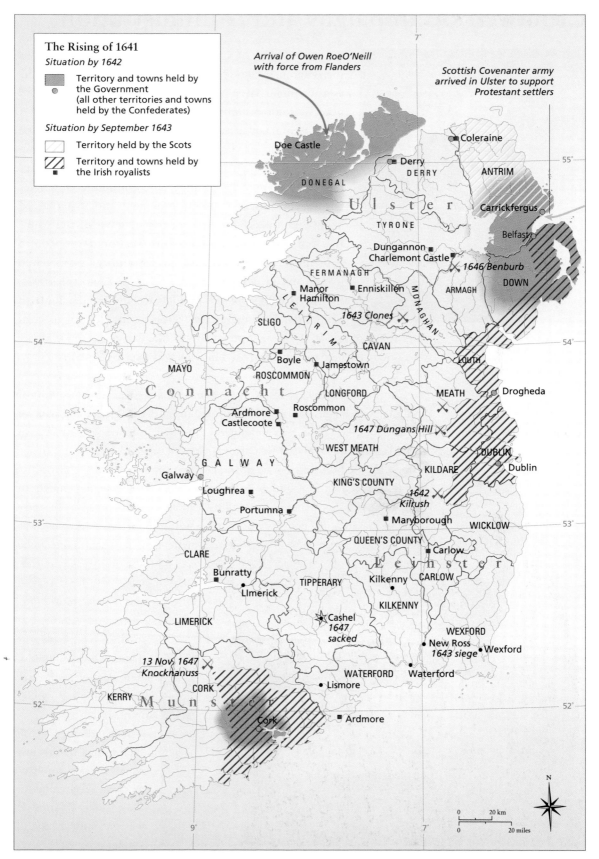

The Rising of 1641

Situation by 1642

Territory and towns held by the Government (all other territories and towns held by the Confederates)

Situation by September 1643

Territory held by the Scots

Territory and towns held by the Irish royalists

Arrival of Owen Roe O'Neill with force from Flanders

Scottish Covenanter army arrived in Ulster to support Protestant settlers

Cromwell's Campaigns and Administration

Above: Oliver Cromwell, ruthless general, country gentleman, devoted father and Puritan zealot. He came to Ireland determined to stamp out military resistance to government authority, to wreak vengeance for the supposed massacres of 1641, and to convert the entire population to the Protestant faith.

Below: The illustration features Burntcourt (Clogheen), Co. Tipperary, a plantation mansion which had only been newly built in 1650 when it was burnt by its owner's wife to deny it to the approaching Cromwellians.

THE EXECUTION of Charles I on 30 January 1649 united the previously divided Irish supporters of the king. The establishment of a Royalist bastion close to England necessitated intervention by the Parliamentary forces. A Parliamentarian army was already in Ireland and had won a significant victory at Baggot Rath (Rathmines) in 1649. That August it was strengthened by a well supplied and trained force under the command of Oliver Cromwell, and this highly-organized and experienced army then quickly gained control of most of the country. Key east-coast walled towns, such as Drogheda in September, and Waterford in December, were taken using cannon, which had been little used in the 1640s. By May 1650 Cromwell had left Ireland for the Scottish campaign, leaving Henry Ireton as his deputy to conclude the war, and by 1651 west-coast towns like Limerick and Galway were under Parliamentary control. The war was over by April 1653.

The government of Ireland between 1651 and 1654 was under the control of Parliamentary commissioners who were also military officers. In 1654 one of these, Charles Fleetwood, was appointed to the civilian office of Lord Deputy, and in 1657 he was replaced by Oliver Cromwell's second son Henry. Henry Cromwell shifted the power-base of the government away from the army and instead conciliated the older political élites, especially the northern Presbyterians and the Munster Protestants.

The 1650s saw a number of significant innovations: the Irish parliament was abolished and replaced by a less than adequate Irish representation at the Westminster parliament; the legal system was made more efficient; and educational institutions such as Trinity College, Dublin were developed to train a reliable and godly ministry.

In December 1659, the Cromwellian regime collapsed as a result of an army coup and in May 1660 Charles II was proclaimed king in Dublin.

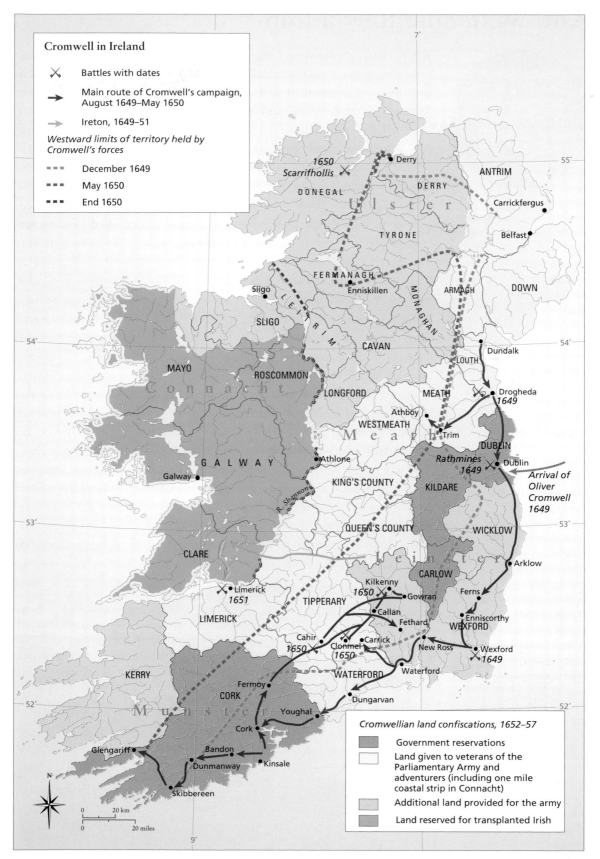

Cromwell in Ireland

- ✗   Battles with dates
- →   Main route of Cromwell's campaign, August 1649–May 1650
- →   Ireton, 1649–51

Westward limits of territory held by Cromwell's forces

- - - -   December 1649
- - - -   May 1650
- - - -   End 1650

Cromwellian land confiscations, 1652–57

-   Government reservations
-   Land given to veterans of the Parliamentary Army and adventurers (including one mile coastal strip in Connacht)
-   Additional land provided for the army
-   Land reserved for transplanted Irish

1650 Scarrifhollis

Derry — ANTRIM — Carrickfergus — Belfast

DONEGAL — DERRY — Ulster — TYRONE — DOWN

FERMANAGH — Enniskillen — MONAGHAN — ARMAGH

Sligo — LEITRIM — SLIGO — CAVAN — Dundalk — LOUTH

MAYO — ROSCOMMON — LONGFORD — Connacht — Athboy — WESTMEATH — Meath — Trim — MEATH — Drogheda *1649*

Galway — GALWAY — Athlone — KING'S COUNTY — *Rathmines 1649* — DUBLIN — Dublin — *Arrival of Oliver Cromwell 1649*

R. Shannon — QUEEN'S COUNTY — KILDARE — WICKLOW

CLARE — Leinster — Arklow

Limerick *1651* — TIPPERARY — Kilkenny *1650* — Gowran — CARLOW — Ferns

LIMERICK — Callan — Fethard — Enniscorthy — WEXFORD

Cahir *1650* — Carrick — Clonmel *1650* — New Ross — Wexford *1649*

KERRY — Munster — WATERFORD — Waterford — Dungarvan

Fermoy — CORK — Youghal

Cork — Bandon — Kinsale

Glengariff — Dunmanway — Skibbereen

N   0   20 km   0   20 miles

The Williamite Revolution

Above: *A medal struck to commemorate the Protestant victories, 1690–91.*

WHEN THE Catholic King James II came to the throne in 1685 there was some nervousness among Irish Protestants. James tried to reassure them with the appointment of a Protestant Lord Deputy, Lord Clarendon. Clarendon's recall in 1687 and the appointment of the earl of Tyrconnell signalled the beginning of a more pro-Catholic policy in Ireland with the Catholicization of the army and local government. While Tyrconnell wished to undo the land settlement of the 1660s, James was more cautious. The birth of a royal heir in June 1688 caused alarm among the English political élite, who invited James's son-in-law William of Orange to take the English throne, whereupon James fled London for France.

The political situation worsened in 1688, when economic difficulties, combined with political opportunism, led to local disturbances. Memories of the 1641 rising were revived and some Protestants fled to England. Most, however, counselled caution, and in December 1688 the closing of the gates of Derry against the army of the Jacobite earl of Antrim was regarded by many as folly. James landed in Ireland with French support in March 1689 and summoned parliament in June. It was this parliament, with its proposal for the dismantling of the Restoration land settlement, which finally alienated James from any residual Protestant support.

William III had been reluctant to come to Ireland, but James's presence and the European implications of the French presence there obligated him. His forces arrived in Ulster in August 1689 and William followed almost a year later. He marched south and engaged James's army at the Boyne on 1 July. Following his defeat, James fled to France while William pushed his campaign west before leaving Ireland in September 1690. The war was concluded by the Treaty of Limerick, after a siege of that city, in October 1691.

Right: *At the end of the second siege of Limerick the Jacobites surrendered, signing the Treaty of Limerick in 1691. As a result of the surrender, many thousands of Catholic officers and soldiers left Ireland to join the armies of France. They became known as the 'wild geese' and were reinforced in the following hundred years by tens of thousands of their countrymen.*

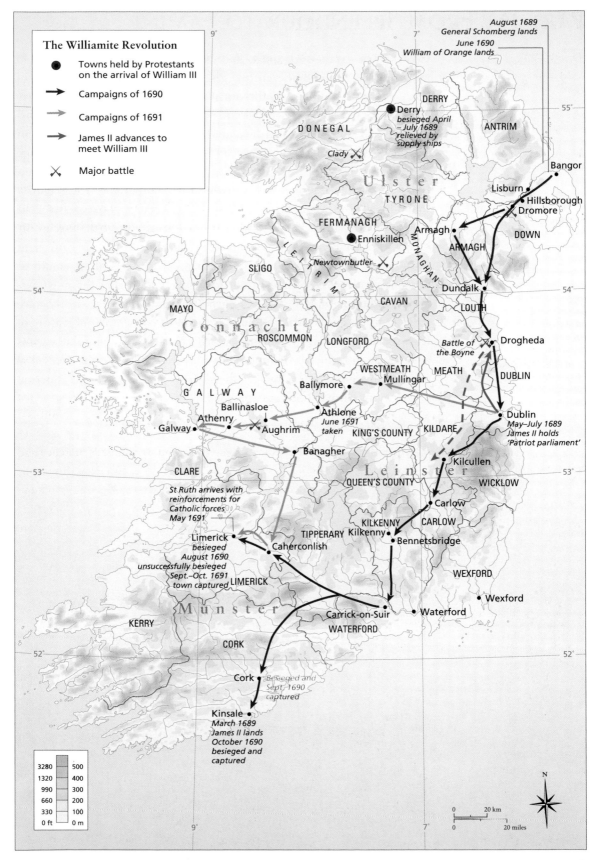

The Williamite Revolution

● Towns held by Protestants on the arrival of William III

→ Campaigns of 1690

→ Campaigns of 1691

→ James II advances to meet William III

✕ Major battle

August 1689
General Schomberg lands

June 1690
William of Orange lands

DONEGAL

DERRY

● Derry
besieged April – July 1689 relieved by supply ships

Clady ✕

ANTRIM

Bangor

Lisburn

● Hillsborough
✕ Dromore

U l s t e r

TYRONE

FERMANAGH

● Enniskillen

MONAGHAN

Armagh

ARMAGH

DOWN

LEITRIM

Newtownbutler ✕

SLIGO

CAVAN

Dundalk

LOUTH

MAYO

C o n n a c h t

ROSCOMMON

LONGFORD

Battle of the Boyne ✕

Drogheda

DUBLIN

WESTMEATH
Mullingar

MEATH

Ballymore

GALWAY

Ballinasloe

Athenry

Athlone
June 1691 taken

KING'S COUNTY

KILDARE

Dublin
May–July 1689 James II holds 'Patriot parliament'

Galway ✕ Aughrim

Banagher

L e i n s t e r

QUEEN'S COUNTY

Kilcullen

CLARE

WICKLOW

St Ruth arrives with reinforcements for Catholic forces May 1691

Carlow

Limerick
besieged August 1690 unsuccessfully besieged Sept.–Oct. 1691 town captured

TIPPERARY

Caherconlish

KILKENNY
Kilkenny

CARLOW

Bennetsbridge

LIMERICK

M u n s t e r

WEXFORD

KERRY

Carrick-on-Suir

Waterford

Wexford

CORK

WATERFORD

Cork
Besieged and Sept. 1690 captured

Kinsale
March 1689 James II lands October 1690 besieged and captured

3280	500
1320	400
990	300
660	200
330	100
0 ft	0 m

0   20 km

0   20 miles

N

PART IV: FROM SPLENDOUR TO FAMINE

James Kelly

COMPARED WITH the 16th and 17th centuries, the 18th century in Ireland appears quiescent and uneventful. There was, it is true, no outbreak of serious religico-political conflict until the 1790s, but both Irish society and politics were less consensual and politics more eventful than the visible absence of civil discord suggests. There is some disagreement between historians as to how we can best interpret Irish society during this period. In his provocative study of 'the making of Protestant Ireland', Sean Connolly has shown how comparable 18th-century Ireland was to other ancien régime societies. From this perspective, the tensions and conflicts that can be identified arose out of the essentially hierarchical character of its social organization, and mirror equivalent phenomena in Britain and on the continent. If this was all, it would be possible to dispense with the traditional perception that the most formative influence on Irish politics during the Georgian era was its colonial subordination to Britain and that the most consequential feature of Irish society was that the preeminently Catholic Gaelic population was ruled by an introduced Anglophone landowning élite, but the two views need not be mutually exclusive. Indeed, Irish history during this period makes more sense if both are appealed to.

Below: In all its glittering finery, a state ball held in Dublin Castle, painted by William van der Hagen in 1731.

There is certainly much to sustain a colonial interpretation from a political perspective. It is significant, for example, that the head of the Irish administration (the Lord Lieutenant) was appointed by the Crown on the recommendation of the British government, and was seldom entrusted to anybody other than Englishmen. This led to the practice for much of the 18th century of lords lieutenant not residing permanently in Ireland for the duration of their posting but, significantly, did not result in a dramatic transfer of power to Irish-born officials. Indeed, successive governments insured against this by determining that the most important offices of state were filled by Englishmen.

Allied with this, the Crown could avail of Poynings' Law (1494), which gave the English (from 1707, the British) Privy Council the power to respite and to amend all legislation emanating from the Irish parliament, and to the Declaratory Act (1719), which made the House of Lords at Westminster the final court of legal appeal in Irish law cases and gave the British parliament the power to make law for Ireland.

If this combination of practices and powers suggest that Ireland's position within the British empire was irrevocably colonial, the emergence of a persuasive Irish Protestant critique of the dependent position to which their kingdom was consigned, defined influentially by J. G. Simms as *colonial nationalism*,

Below: *The Dublin Volunteers saluting the Statue of William III on College Green, 4 November 1779.*

would seem to indicate that this was how Irish Protestants saw it as well. In fact Simms' 'colonial nationalism' can be interpreted equally plausibly as an Irish manifestation of the Europeanwide phenomenon of civic humanism or 'patriotism' because, like its European parallels, the Irish phenomenon placed similar emphasis on political virtue and domestic economic improvement.

More significantly, from the moment it was given political coherency by William Molyneux in his seminal tract *The case of Ireland's being Bound by Acts of Parliament in England Stated* in the late 1690s, equality with Britain was the political *raison d'être* of Irish Protestant Patriots. This is why Molyneux could describe a legislative union as 'an happiness we can hardly hope for', and why the Irish parliament responded to the Anglo-Scottish union of 1707 by appealing to Queen Anne to expedite a similar arrangement with respect to Ireland. However, because neither Queen Anne nor her ministers who, like most English politicians and opinion makers, regarded and treated Ireland as a colony, could perceive any advantage in such an arrangement as long as the Irish parliament continued to vote the revenue needed to fund the Irish army establishment and to pay for the administration of the kingdom, the address was ignored.

This did not please Irish Protestants, and they responded to this and to other manifestations of British unwillingness to acknowledge their equal status under the Crown by asserting their right to govern themselves on the same terms as Englishmen and the equality of the kingdom of Ireland with that of Britain. This is why when, after many decades of pursuing this cause, the Patriots were able to take advantage of the government's difficulties in the American colonies to compel them to repeal the bulk of the laws confining Ireland's freedom to trade in 1779–80 and to accede to the removal or modification of the restrictions on the legislative authority of the Irish parliament, they did not seek to emulate the Americans and achieve independence. Quite the contrary; they did not want separation, just the power to govern. Indeed, so strong was their fear of doing anything that would endanger the Anglo-Irish connection, upon which they realized the security of their ascendant position in Ireland rested, that they made no attempt to challenge the British government's right to nominate the head of the Irish administration and declined an opportunity to reform the Irish legislature to make it more representative of the Protestant population at large.

As this, and the decision of the Irish parliament in 1800 to vote itself out of existence bears witness, a large percentage (probably a majority during the bulk of this era) of Irish Protestants preferred the security of a close (and, if necessary, a dependent) relationship with Britain, because fundamentally the maintenance of what they then termed their ascendancy *vis à vis* the Catholic population was their priority and they perceived its perpetuation as dependent upon the retention of an intimate Anglo-Irish nexus. This is why it is not a coincidence that the decade which saw the advancement by the United Irishmen of the virtues of a republic culminated with the decision of the Irish ruling élite to opt

to govern Ireland from Westminster rather than to continue to do so from College Green.

If this conforms to a colonial pattern, there is also much to sustain Connolly's view that Ireland was an *ancien régime* society. Thus, like most European countries, land was owned by a relatively small number of large landowners and worked by tenant occupiers, who were expected to defer to their social superiors and to assent to their social, economic and political dominance locally as well as nationally. Moreover, as was the case elsewhere, the members of this landed élite were convinced that they were the natural repository of government on the island because only they were equipped economically and intellectually to rule.

The situation in Ireland was complicated by the fact that the religion of the bulk of this élite (the Church of Ireland) differed from that of the majority of the population, but the élite secured itself in this respect by defining itself as the political nation and by implementing a corps of discriminatory legislation (the Penal Laws) which secured them economically, socially and politically against the Catholic majority. For most of the 18th century, indeed, their rule was unchallenged, and the fact that the Irish economy embarked on one of its most sustained periods of growth once it had negotiated poor harvests, famine and

Above: Ireland's ruling élite aristocracy and country landowners embraced the 'Georgian' style with enthusiasm. Many great houses were built or rebuilt. Shown here is Caledon, seat of the Earl of Caledon, Co. Tyrone, completed in 1794.

epidemic disease between 1725 and 1745 seemed to suggest it was advantageous to the country.

The economic, and consequent demographic expansion that was a feature of the second half of the 18th century was not due simply to the guidance of the Protestant élite. But the enthusiasm for improvement manifested by its members, the contributions they made to the success of the linen industry and to advances in internal navigation, to urban development, the enhancement of the road network, land enclosure, demesne development and 'big house' construction all attest to its weighty imprint.

This activity and the rise in population from *c.* 2 million in 1750 to *c.* 4.5 million in 1790 were the most tangible manifestations of the greater prosperity of the Irish economy, but they did not prove equally beneficial to all. Many outside the élite were gravely discommoded by the commercial forces that were released, and this led to a marked upsurge in agrarian unrest from the 1760s. This was essentially conservative in thrust for several decades, but sectarian passions lay just beneath the surface, and when they fused with the reformist and revolutionary doctrines emanating from Britain and France in the 1790s, they facilitated the dissemination of republican ideas, which in the second half of the 1790s posed the confessional *ancien regime* state and colonial Anglo-Irish nexus a formidable challenge that climaxed with the explicitly separatist intent of those who rose in rebellion in 1798.

This was overcome, but the price the Anglo-Irish élite had to pay was high because the Act of Union which followed changed the context within which Irish politics were conducted. If most Irish Protestants had no difficulty accepting this, many Catholics too were content. They believed the abolition of the Irish parliament would pave the way for the repeal of the last major penal disability—the prohibition on Catholics sitting in parliament. However, the united parliament proved less than accommodating.

As a consequence, a more broad-based and assertive Catholic leadership, spearheaded by Daniel O'Connell's Catholic Association, emerged in the 1820s to advance the issue. They eventually obliged ministers to give way in the course of which they shattered the *ancien regime* mould forever. Schooled in

the emerging precepts of democracy by the Association, O'Connell subsequently took up the repeal of the Act of Union in a vain attempt to restore domestic government to Ireland. He was unable to make much progress on the matter, but having transformed Irish politics by creating an active Catholic political interest, he also gave parliamentary politics the key feature of its political agenda for the rest of the century.

At the same time, the priority of the Catholic masses was fixed on the more elemental matter of survival. Following the ending of the Napoleonic wars, the Irish economy embarked on a period of uncertainty. Agricultural exports grew, but the economy was unable to offer security against famine to the rising number of poor and vulnerable among a population which neared 7 million in 1821. Industrialization would have reduced their vulnerability, but the failure of the cotton industry and the mechanization of linen manufacture indicated its limited potential, so that when the country's main staple foodstuff—the potato—was seriously damaged in the late 1840s, a crisis of cataclysmic proportions ensued which changed both Irish society and politics irrevocably.

Below: *Lord Grandison, a landowner concerned with improving his estates, created a carefully designed housing on his estates. Below is an illustration showing a range of houses to be assigned to tradesmen on his Waterford property.*

The Penal Laws

AS A CONSEQUENCE of the military triumph of the Williamites in 1690–91, political authority in Ireland was restored to the Protestant interest, from whom it had been removed during the reign of James II. Convinced by their experiences, and their cultivation of an exaggeratedly baleful memory of the 1641 'massacres', that the Catholics were irrevocably committed to their destruction, many Protestants shared the conclusion of Edward Wetenhall, Church of Ireland bishop of Limerick, that in time there would be a repeat of the events of the 1640s and 1680s if immediate steps were not taken to weaken the Catholic interest. Such conclusions were encouraged by reports in the 1690s that Irish Catholic emigrés were actively pursuing schemes to bring about another French invasion, and by the visible Jacobitism of Catholic priests and ecclesiastics. Indeed, Wetenhall and those of like mind believed that the ratification and enforcement of anti-Catholic law was a matter not of vengeance but of survival.

Percentage of households Catholic – 1732	
Leinster	79%
Ulster	38%
Munster	89%
Connacht	91%
Nationally	73%

Anti-Catholic legislation would serve both to secure the political, economic and social ascendancy of Protestants in Ireland and to increase their number by inducing Catholics to embrace the Protestant religion. Many influential figures in the corridors of power were not convinced of the wisdom of such a course. They sought to honour the spirit of the Treaty of Limerick which offered Catholics an ambiguous promise of toleration, and ensured that no specifically anti-Catholic legislation of Irish origin was ratified in the early 1690s. However, Catholics were precluded by the adoption in 1692 of an English oath from sitting in parliament, and as Dublin Castle struggled in the mid-1690s to win the support of sufficient MPs to ensure the smooth administration of the country, they were obliged to bow to demands for laws to restrict the freedoms of Catholics and the Catholic Church. Thus in 1697, the first of a number of measures, culminating in the 1703 act for registering clergy, was ratified with the purpose of depriving Catholics of ecclesiastical leadership and of limiting the number of clergy in the country. In the years that followed, restrictions were also imposed on the freedom of Catholics to educate their children, to carry arms, inherit, own, lease and work land, to trade and employ, to enter the major professions and, finally in 1728, to vote.

Having already suffered the loss of their lands and traditional leaders to war and to emigration, the Catholics were ill-prepared to resist this legislation. The Penal Laws, as they became known, were not devised systematically to weaken Catholics in every area of life, but they did serve to exclude them from the political process until the 1790s and to hinder their economic advancement.

The Penal Laws were less effective in the religious sphere. The restrictions imposed on the Catholic Church caused serious problems nationally for a number of decades, particularly at times of Jacobite activity, and provided antipathetic landlords with plenty of opportunities to obstruct its mission. But the Church never experienced the shortage of priests or the virulent repression it endured in the early 1650s, and from the mid-1720s it enjoyed a sufficiency of clergy and the freedom to operate competently, if not without difficulty or fear.

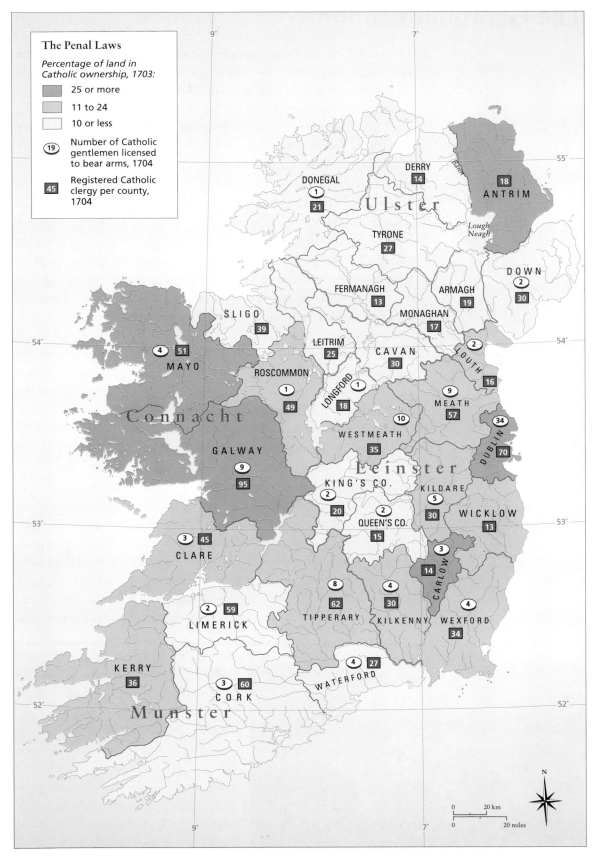

The Penal Laws

*Percentage of land in
Catholic ownership, 1703:*

- 25 or more
- 11 to 24
- 10 or less

(19) Number of Catholic
gentlemen licensed
to bear arms, 1704

[45] Registered Catholic
clergy per county,
1704

DONEGAL
(1)
[21]

DERRY
[14]

ANTRIM
[18]

Ulster

TYRONE
[27]

DOWN
(2)
[30]

Lough
Neagh

FERMANAGH
[13]

ARMAGH
[19]

MONAGHAN
[17]

SLIGO
[39]

LEITRIM
[25]

CAVAN
[30]

LOUTH
(2)
[16]

MAYO
(4) [51]

Connacht

ROSCOMMON
(1)
[49]

LONGFORD
(1)
[18]

MEATH
(9)
[57]

DUBLIN
(34)
[70]

WESTMEATH
(10)
[35]

Leinster

GALWAY
(9)
[95]

KING'S CO.
(2)
[20]

QUEEN'S CO.
(2)
[15]

KILDARE
(5)
[30]

WICKLOW
[13]

CLARE
(3) [45]

CARLOW
(3)
[14]

TIPPERARY
(8)
[62]

KILKENNY
(4)
[30]

WEXFORD
(4)
[34]

LIMERICK
(2) [59]

KERRY
[36]

CORK
(3) [60]

WATERFORD
(4) [27]

Munster

N

0   20 km
0   20 miles

77

The Georgian Economy

THE INFLUENCE of the Protestant interest in Ireland peaked in the 18th century. Politically, this can be pinpointed to the 65 years between 1728 and 1793 when, as well as their exclusion from parliament, Catholics did not possess the franchise. These are the decades commonly regarded as the high-point of Protestant ascendancy, though this term is problematic because of its use by conservative Protestants from the 1780s to justify their undiluted predominance. There was a widespread Protestant perception, articulated in 1781 by Henry Flood, that they were 'the people of Ireland', an exclusive vision, but one softened by their commitment to the island's economic development. This enthusiasm for improvement took many forms, one of the most important of which was the establishment in 1711 of the Linen Board. This body enforced quality controls on the production and sale of exported linens, establishing the industry as the country's leading currency-earner and resulting in the emergence of Ulster as its wealthiest and most populous province.

Efforts by landowners to establish linen operations elsewhere in the country proved less successful, but other initiatives continued. Indeed, at both local and national levels the ruling élite assiduously sought to remould both the rural and urban landscapes in the anglican image they held dear. Some of their schemes, like the proliferation of palladian and neo-classical residences and carefully landscaped demesnes, were primarily self-serving, but they did facilitate the dissemination of new techniques in construction and internal design and employed craftsmen from a multiplicity of trades. Other improvements such as the creation of a road network, widely regarded in the late 18th century as one of the best in Europe, the enhancement of internal navigation through the construction of canals and the drainage of rivers, and the creation of a network of estate villages were less personally motivated, though they well fitted the vision of a tidy landscape. Urban development on a substantial scale was fostered in cities like Dublin, Limerick, Cork and Waterford. In Dublin the crowded warrens of medieval streets were swept away by the Wide Streets Commissioners, and a lattice of straight, broad thoroughfares linking the elegant Georgian streets and squares on the north and south sides of the River Liffey was put in their place. Combined with fine new public buildings including a new parliament, customs house, city exchange and courts, they transformed the city into one of the most attractive of the period, and a crowning symbol of the vision and achievement of the Protestant interest in Ireland.

Below: Medieval buildings were swept aside to make room for Georgian ideas of elegance in buildings and landscapes. Here the home of the Duke of Abercorn sits in its well-groomed 'landscape'.

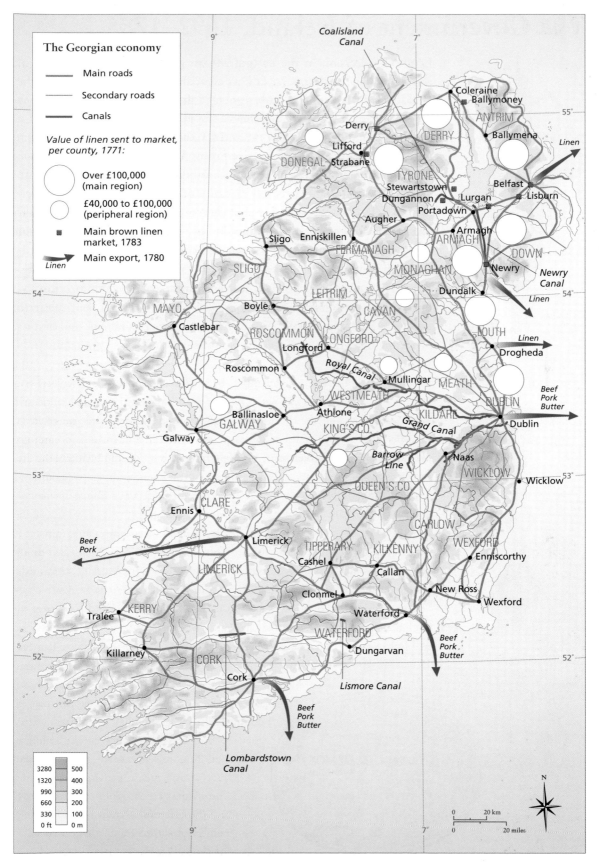

The Government of Ireland, 1692–1785

LONDON'S decision in the early 1690s to entrust the responsibility of raising revenue and making law to an Irish parliament determined the character of 18th-century government. Like its British counterpart, the Irish parliament had two chambers. The House of Lords consisted of a fluctuating number of temporal and a fixed number of religious peers, while the House of Commons comprised 300 representatives chosen from 150 constituencies of varying antiquity and franchise. It was an exclusively Protestant assembly because of the Irish parliament's decision to follow the Westminster precedent requiring all members to swear an oath of adjuration. The parliament sat for approximately six months every two years between 1692 and 1784, and annually thereafter, affording Irish Protestants a central role in the administration of their kingdom. The parliament's powers, however, were severely circumscribed by Poynings' Law and the Declaratory Act, and by the fact that the Irish executive at Dublin Castle was not responsible to parliament and that its head, the Lord Lieutenant, was a nominee of the British government.

Despite these constraints, the members of the Irish parliament, particularly the Commons, sought to play an active part in the administration of the kingdom. Because of this, and the disinclination of successive lords lieutenant to keep tight personal control of the levers of power by residing in Ireland throughout the terms of their appointment, the day-to-day duties of administration were shared between English-born officeholders and able Irish politicians (commonly termed undertakers) who agreed, in return for preferment and influence, to manage the parliament on the Lord Lieutenant's behalf.

This arrangement worked satisfactorily from its inception in 1695 until the 1750s, when a disruptive power struggle between Henry Boyle and John Ponsonby prompted a reassessment, and it was decided, eventually, that lords lieutenant should reside in Ireland for the duration of their appointment.

The decision of Lord Townshend to become a residential lord lieutenant in the late 1760s contributed to the emergence of the 'Patriots', whose object was to dilute the legal constraints on the legislative authority of the Irish parliament and to secure the right to free trade. Detachments of Volunteers —loosely organized associations of armed men whose primary purpose was to support the regular army— became politicized, and their extra-parliamentary lobbying was decisive in securing both free trade (1780) and legislative independence (1782). However, their attempts to secure direct admission to the political process by reforming the electoral system were thwarted by the small and unrepresentative élite that controlled most of the parliamentary constituencies.

Above: Silver-gilt mace, the symbol of authority of the old Irish House of Lords. This elegant silver work was made in Dublin around 1760.

Left: This medallion was presented to the 1st Ulster Regiment of Irish Volunteers and would be worn by the best shot in the regiment 'so long as he shall maintain his superior skill at the target'.

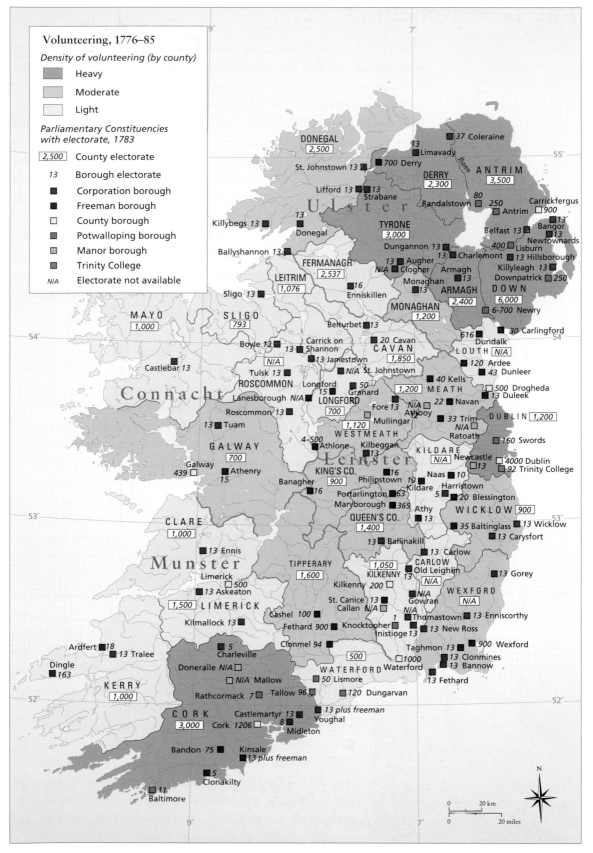

Volunteering, 1776–85

Density of volunteering (by county)

- Heavy
- Moderate
- Light

Parliamentary Constituencies with electorate, 1783

2,500	County electorate
13	Borough electorate
■	Corporation borough
■	Freeman borough
□	County borough
■	Potwalloping borough
■	Manor borough
■	Trinity College
N/A	Electorate not available

DONEGAL
2,500

37 Coleraine

13 Limavady

St. Johnston 13   700 Derry

DERRY
2,300

ANTRIM
3,500

Lifford 13 13
Strabane

Randalstown 80 250
Antrim 900

Killybegs 13   13
Donegal

TYRONE
3,000

Carrickfergus

Dungannon 13   13
Belfast 13 Bangor
Newtownards

Ballyshannon 13

FERMANAGH
2,537

13 Augher 13 Charlemont 400 Lisburn 13 Hillsborough
N/A Clogher   Armagh 13   Killyleagh 13

LEITRIM
1,076

Monaghan 13   Downpatrick 250

Sligo 13   16
Enniskillen

ARMAGH
2,400

DOWN
6,000

MONAGHAN
1,200

6-700 Newry

Belturbet 13   30 Carlingford

MAYO
1,000

SLIGO
793

20 Cavan   616   Dundalk
LOUTH N/A

Boyle 13   Carrick on   CAVAN
Shannon   13   *1,850*

120 Ardee   43 Dunleer

Castlebar 13

13 Jamestown   St. Johnstown   40 Kells
Tulsk 13   N/A   MEATH

500 Drogheda
13 Duleek

Longford   50   *1,200*
15 Granard   22 Navan

ROSCOMMON
Lanesborough N/A   LONGFORD
700

Fore 13   N/A   33 Trim
Athboy   N/A

DUBLIN *1,200*

Roscommon 13   Mullingar   Ratoath

13 Tuam   WESTMEATH
1,120

160 Swords

Connacht

4-500   Kilbeggan   KILDARE
Athlone   13   N/A   Newcastle

4000 Dublin
13   92 Trinity College

GALWAY
700

Leinster

KING'S CO.
900   Philipstown   Naas 10
16   19   Kildare   Harristown
Banagher   5   20 Blessington

Galway
439   Athenry
15

16   Portarlington 63   Athy   WICKLOW *900*
Maryborough   365   13

CLARE
1,000

QUEEN'S CO.
1,400

35 Baltinglass   13 Wicklow

13 Ballinakill   13 Carysfort

13 Ennis

TIPPERARY
1,600

13 Carlow

CARLOW
1,050   Old Leighlin
Kilkenny 200   13

13 Gorey

Munster

Limerick
500   Kilkenny 200   13

WEXFORD
N/A

13 Askeaton   St. Canice 13   Gowran
Callan N/A   N/A

13 Enniscorthy

1,500 LIMERICK   Cashel 100   N/A
Fethard 900   Knocktopher   1   Thomastown   13 New Ross
Inistioge 13

Kilmallock 13   Clonmel 94

Taghmon 13   900 Wexford

Ardfert 18   5   1000   13 Clonmines
13 Tralee   Charleville   500 Waterford   13 Bannow
Doneraile N/A

Dingle   N/A Mallow   50 Lismore   13 Fethard
163   Rathcormack 7   Tallow 96   120 Dungarvan

KERRY
1,000

WATERFORD
500

CORK   Castlemartyr 13   13 plus freeman
3,000   8   Youghal
Cork 1206   Midleton

Bandon 75   Kinsale
13 plus freeman

5
Clonakilty

11
Baltimore

N

0   20 km

0   20 miles

The 1798 Rebellion

THOUGH THE impression is often given, it is not true to say that 18th-century Ireland was peaceful until its last decade. The readiness of rural protesters to swathe themselves in Jacobite white suggests that they were already politicized, and that ancient sectarian loyalties remained strong. This conclusion is reinforced by the emergence in County Armagh in the 1780s of the Catholic Defenders to resist disarming raids by Protestant Peep O'Day Boys. At the same time, elements within the Protestant and Presbyterian middle classes offered an alternative non-sectarian vision and they were encouraged by the outbreak of the French Revolution in 1789 to launch a campaign to reform the representative system to satisfy their wishes. The organization they established in 1791 to spearhead their campaign took the name United Irishmen from Wolfe Tone's inspirational claim that it would only be possible to overcome the country's problems if Catholic, Protestant and Dissenter came together and Ireland broke the connection with England.

To begin with, the United Irishmen devoted their energies to the cause of reforming the representative system. Catholics were indeed conceded the franchise in 1793, but the fact that it was implemented on the insistence of London indicates how unimportant were the United Irishmen's efforts. The conservative dominated parliament embarked at the same time on a strategy to weaken its radical critics by replacing the Volunteers with a Castle-controlled militia. However, instead of destroying the movement, this strategy allowed revolutionary separatists within the organization to capitalize on the growing discontent throughout the country with the government's uncompromising policies and the premature recall, in 1795, of the liberal Lord Lieutenant, Earl Fitzwilliam. The United Irishmen then formed an alliance with the Catholic Defenders, and the movement was reconstituted along revolutionary lines. They were remarkably successful in recruiting members and in disseminating their message and, encouraged by the success of Wolfe Tone's diplomatic efforts to enlist the support of the French, were hopeful that a successful rebellion could be orchestrated.

Below: Members of the Society of United Irishmen take an oath to rise against English rule.

A large-scale invasion force attempted to land off Bantry Bay in 1796; if the fleet had not been disrupted by bad weather, the United Irishmen might have had a chance. Instead, the authorities were given time to embark on a ruthless campaign of disarmament. The damage inflicted on the organization ensured that when rebellion broke out in May 1798 it was fragmented and localized, being confined for the most part to east Ulster and, especially, County Wexford. Some French support was dispatched, but it came too late to alter the outcome, and the Crown forces won the day. The political initiative remained firmly in the hands of the establishment and the 1790s concluded, not with the declaration of the republic sought by the radicals, but with a legislative union.

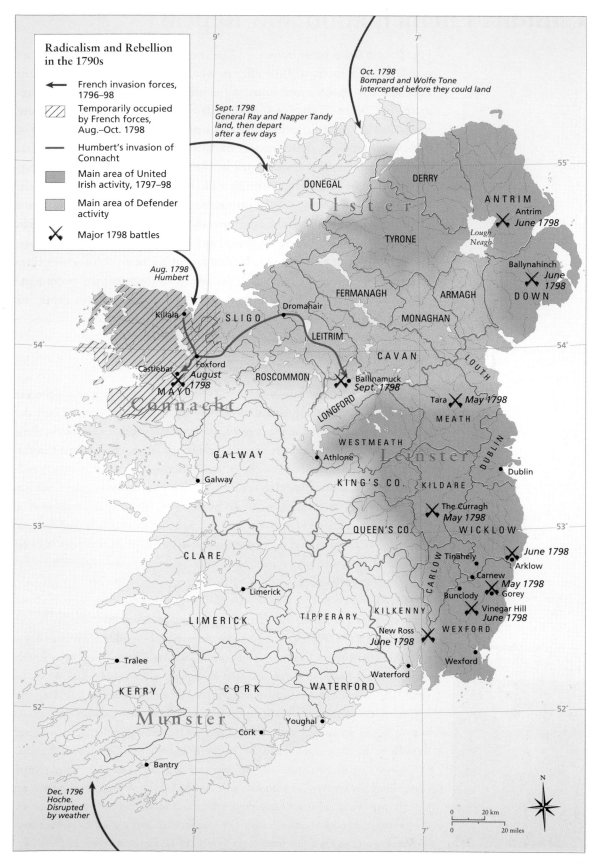

Radicalism and Rebellion
in the 1790s

⟵ French invasion forces,
1796–98

▨ Temporarily occupied
by French forces,
Aug.–Oct. 1798

— Humbert's invasion of
Connacht

▨ Main area of United
Irish activity, 1797–98

▨ Main area of Defender
activity

✕ Major 1798 battles

Oct. 1798
Bompard and Wolfe Tone
intercepted before they could land

Sept. 1798
General Ray and Napper Tandy
land, then depart
after a few days

Aug. 1798
Humbert

DONEGAL

DERRY

U l s t e r

ANTRIM
Antrim
June 1798

TYRONE

Lough
Neagh

Ballynahinch
June
1798

FERMANAGH

ARMAGH

D O W N

MONAGHAN

Killala
SLIGO

Dromahair

LEITRIM

CAVAN

LOUTH

Castlebar
Foxford
August
1798
MAYO
C o n n a c h t

ROSCOMMON

Ballinamuck
Sept. 1798
LONGFORD

Tara ✕ *May 1798*

MEATH

WESTMEATH

Athlone

L e i n s t e r

DUBLIN

Dublin

GALWAY

KING'S CO.

KILDARE

Galway

QUEEN'S CO.

The Curragh
May 1798

WICKLOW

CLARE

Tinahely

June 1798
Arklow

Carnew
May 1798
Gorey

Bunclody

Vinegar Hill
June 1798

Limerick

TIPPERARY

KILKENNY

CARLOW

WEXFORD

LIMERICK

New Ross
June 1798

Wexford

Tralee

KERRY

CORK

WATERFORD

Waterford

M u n s t e r

Youghal

Cork

Bantry

Dec. 1796
Hoche.
Disrupted
by weather

N

0   20 km

0   20 miles

Catholic Emancipation and Repeal

FOLLOWING the repeal between 1778 and 1792 of the bulk of the laws restricting the liberty of Catholics to worship, to own and lease land, to educate their children and to enter the professions, and the enfranchisement in 1793 of Catholic 40-shilling freeholders, the major remaining infraction of Catholic civil rights was the prohibition on their sitting in parliament. Hopes were raised in 1794–95 and in 1799–1800 that Catholic emancipation would not be long delayed, but Protestant conservatives in both kingdoms remained firmly opposed. In 1801, William Pitt failed to overcome royal opposition and was unable to honour an assurance he had given Catholics during the union negotiations. Together Catholics and Whig sympathizers like Henry Grattan tried to overcome Protestant resistance by proposing a Crown 'veto' over ecclesiastical appointments, but this only helped to fragment the pro-emancipation lobby. For many Catholics, including the bishops, the proposed veto powers went too far, and Daniel O'Connell emerged as the leader of those Catholics who chose to endure exclusion rather than to accept conditional emancipation.

By the early 1820s, O'Connell had concluded that a new strategy was necessary and, following the foundation of the Catholic Association in 1823, he oversaw its transformation into one of the most remarkable agencies of popular politicization yet seen in Ireland or Europe. As a consequence, in the landmark general election of 1826, Catholics throughout the country cast off the bonds of deference and returned MPs sympathetic to their cause. Catholic confidence was further boosted two years later when O'Connell won a remarkable by-election victory in County Clare, and fearful that the resultant rise in sectarian animosity could precipitate serious civil discord, the duke of Wellington persuaded the reluctant George IV to concede to Catholics the right to sit in parliament.

Emboldened by this, in 1830 O'Connell launched a campaign to repeal the Act of Union. The campaign did not register the decisive impression he hoped for, but it provided him with an issue around which he could organize an Irish party at Westminster. On the back of some striking electoral successes in the early and mid-1830s, O'Connell forged a working alliance with the Whigs to secure a number of adminstrative and political reforms. However, following the return of the Tories to power in 1841, he devoted his energies to repeal. Supported by an energetic group of intellectual nationalists called the Young Irelanders, by the Church and by his own formidable Repeal Association, O'Connell organized a series of 'monster meetings' in 1843 with the object of compelling the government to concede Ireland 'full and prompt justice or repeal'. Ministers, however, were unyielding, and following the proscription of the meeting scheduled for Clontarf in October and O'Connell's subsequent imprisonment, he spent his final years vainly trying to retrieve lost ground.

Below: Daniel O'Connell, known as 'The Liberator', was one of the most charismatic leaders of his generation and enjoyed a reputation as a libertarian that extended far beyond Ireland's shores.

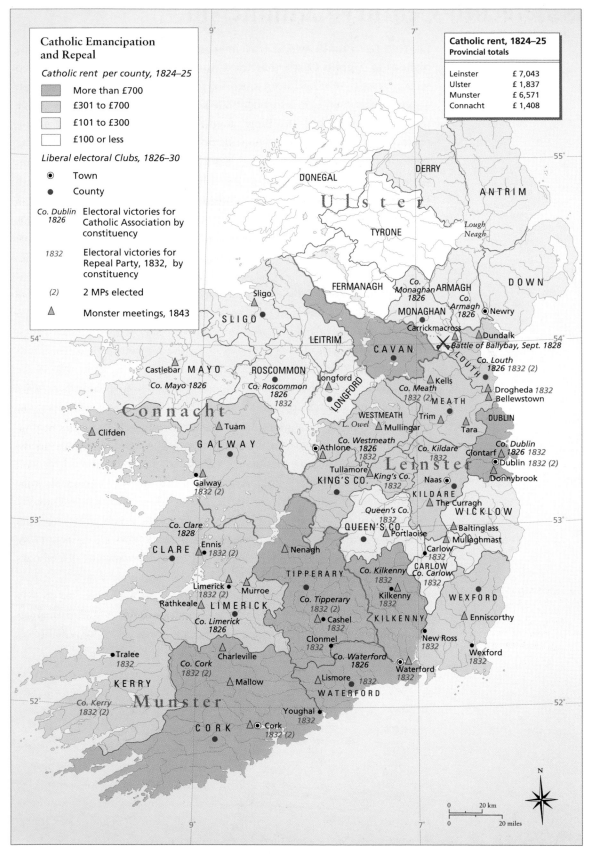

Catholic Emancipation and Repeal

Catholic rent per county, 1824–25

- More than £700
- £301 to £700
- £101 to £300
- £100 or less

Liberal electoral Clubs, 1826–30

- ◉ Town
- ● County

Co. Dublin 1826 — Electoral victories for Catholic Association by constituency

1832 — Electoral victories for Repeal Party, 1832, by constituency

(2) — 2 MPs elected

△ — Monster meetings, 1843

Catholic rent, 1824–25 Provincial totals	
Leinster	£ 7,043
Ulster	£ 1,837
Munster	£ 6,571
Connacht	£ 1,408

U l s t e r

DONEGAL

DERRY

ANTRIM

TYRONE

D O W N

FERMANAGH

Co. Monaghan 1826

ARMAGH

Co. Armagh 1826

MONAGHAN

● Newry

Carrickmacross

✕ *Battle of Ballybay, Sept. 1828*

△ Dundalk

Co. Louth 1826 1832 (2)

Sligo ●

S L I G O

LEITRIM

CAVAN

L O U T H

△ Kells

Co. Meath 1832 (2)

△ Drogheda *1832*

△ Bellewstown

△ Castlebar

M A Y O

Co. Mayo 1826

ROSCOMMON

Co. Roscommon 1826 1832

Longford △

LONGFORD

● Trim

M E A T H

DUBLIN

C o n n a c h t

△ Tuam

WESTMEATH

L. Owel

△ Mullingar

Co. Westmeath 1826 1832

Tara △

G A L W A Y

△ Clifden

◉ Athlone

Co. Kildare 1832

Co. Dublin 1826 1832

△ Clontarf

◉ Dublin *1832 (2)*

Tullamore ●

KING'S CO.

L e i n s t e r

King's Co. 1832

Naas ◉

Donnybrook ●

Galway △

1832 (2)

KILDARE

The Curragh

W I C K L O W

Queen's Co. 1832

△ Baltinglass

Ennis ●

1832 (2)

Co. Clare 1828

C L A R E

△ Nenagh

QUEEN'S CO.

△ Portlaoise

△ Mullaghmast

Carlow △ *1832*

CARLOW

Co. Carlow 1832

W E X F O R D

Limerick ◉

1832 (2)

● Murroe

Rathkeale △

L I M E R I C K

Co. Limerick 1826

T I P P E R A R Y

Co. Tipperary 1832 (2)

Co. Kilkenny 1832

Kilkenny △ *1832*

K I L K E N N Y

△ Enniscorthy

Cashel ● △ *1832*

New Ross ● *1832*

● Tralee

1832

Charleville ●

Co. Cork 1832 (2)

△ Mallow

Clonmel ● *1832*

Co. Waterford 1826

Waterford ◉ *1832*

Wexford ● *1832*

K E R R Y

Co. Kerry 1832 (2)

M u n s t e r

C O R K

△ Lismore *1832*

W A T E R F O R D

Youghal ● *1832*

◉ Cork *1832 (2)*

N

0   20 km

0   20 miles

Nineteenth-Century Catholicism

DESPITE THE Penal Laws, it is clear from the returns made by Catholic bishops to Dublin Castle that the Church in 1800 was better provided with priests than it had been a century earlier. It was also embarked on a campaign of church refurbishment and construction that was to see the humble thatched dwellings identified with the Penal era being replaced by the ornate, prominent stone edifices of the 19th century. The pace of this development varied from diocese to diocese, and within each diocese from parish to parish, depending on its leadership and resources. Widespread improvements commenced in the second half of the 18th century and accelerated in the early 19th, with the wealthier dioceses of Dublin and Cashel progressing more rapidly than those of Tuam and Armagh.

One important index of the growing strength of the Catholic Church is provided by the swelling ranks of its priests and nuns. In the first half of the 19th century their numbers were insufficient to permit the Church to administer equally to all its members: in 1840 there was one priest per 3,000 people. This problem was most acute in Connacht, and it is not surprising that in 1834 the Commissioners of Public Instruction found the church attendance here lower than elsewhere. In Connacht also there was the strongest adherence to popular religious practices associated with wakes, patterns and holy wells. These practices were a primary target for the burgeoning ranks of the Maynooth-trained secular clergy who oversaw the gradual countrywide extension of the Tridentine orthodoxies laid down by Reformist bishops like Murray of Dublin and Doyle of Kildare and Leighlin. Also, the Great Famine dealt its heaviest blows in the sectors of Irish society in which such practices were most deeply entrenched, and reduced the priest-people ratio in 1870 to 1:1,250. This alleviated endemic problems of clerical indiscipline and paved the way for the provision to all Catholics of a comprehensive religious service from birth to death. Indeed, priests became their communities' moral policemen, and as the Church continued to grow in wealth, numbers and influence, it assumed responsibility for an increasing network of social functions — schools, orphanages, hospitals, asylums and so on — through which it conveyed its message.

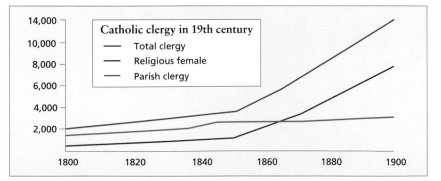

14,000
10,000
8,000
6,000
4,000
2,000

Catholic clergy in 19th century
—— Total clergy
—— Religious female
—— Parish clergy

1800   1820   1840   1860   1880   1900

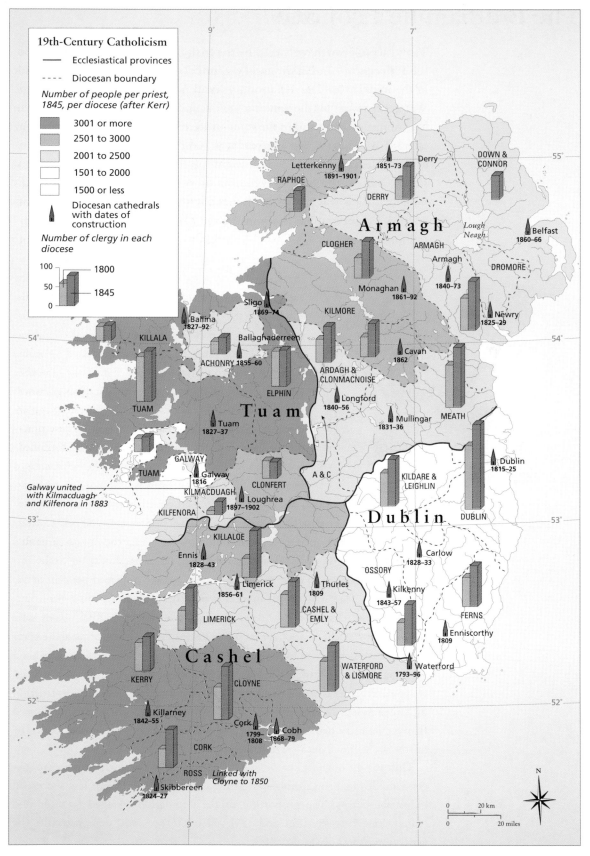

19th-Century Catholicism

— Ecclesiastical provinces

- - - Diocesan boundary

Number of people per priest, 1845, per diocese (after Kerr)

- 3001 or more
- 2501 to 3000
- 2001 to 2500
- 1501 to 2000
- 1500 or less

Diocesan cathedrals with dates of construction

Number of clergy in each diocese

100
50
0
1800
1845

Letterkenny 1891–1901
RAPHOE
Derry 1851–73
DOWN & CONNOR
DERRY
Armagh
Lough Neagh
Belfast 1860–66
CLOGHER
ARMAGH
Armagh 1840–73
DROMORE
Monaghan 1861–92
KILMORE
Newry 1825–29
Sligo 1869–74
Ballina 1827–92
KILLALA
Ballaghaderreen
ACHONRY 1855–60
Cavan 1862
ARDAGH & CLONMACNOISE
ELPHIN
Longford 1840–56
MEATH
Mullingar 1831–36
TUAM
Tuam
Tuam 1827–37
GALWAY
Dublin 1815–25
TUAM
Galway 1816
KILMACDUAGH
CLONFERT
A & C
KILDARE & LEIGHLIN
Loughrea 1897–1902
KILFENORA
DUBLIN
Galway united with Kilmacduagh and Kilfenora in 1883
KILLALOE
Carlow 1828–33
Ennis 1828–43
OSSORY
Limerick 1856–61
Thurles 1809
Kilkenny 1843–57
FERNS
LIMERICK
CASHEL & EMLY
Enniscorthy 1809
Cashel
WATERFORD & LISMORE
Waterford 1793–96
KERRY
CLOYNE
Killarney 1842–55
Cork 1799–1808
Cobh 1868–79
CORK
ROSS
Linked with Cloyne to 1850
Skibbereen 1824–27

N

0   20 km
0   20 miles

87

The Pre-Famine Economy

THE STRONG growth registered by the Irish economy in the second half of the 18th century and in the early years of the 19th came to an abrupt halt in the mid-1810s. The deflationary fiscal policy of the post-Napoleonic War government hit the banking sector especially hard, but the decline in the volume of linen and in the value of agricultural goods exported in the late 1810s indicates that the problem went deeper. The crisis was most acute in the countryside, which was affected not only by the agricultural slump, but by the general economic downturn, for much of Ireland's manufacturing was domestically based. It was compounded too by the country's demographic position: by 1820 its rising population neared 7 million.

Above: *Weighing potatoes, the staple of the agrarian community. Reliance on this single crop, together with the relative unsophistication of the Irish economy, left country people, particularly in the West, vulnerable to sudden change.*

In the late 18th century this had been accommodated by expanding employment in linen and tillage, and by the subdivision of holdings by landowners and middlemen. So long as domestic and international conditions were favourable, and the landless and landed labourers (cottiers) who constituted 56 per cent of the labour in 1841 could rely on the potato, this rising population was not a cause of concern. However, as rent arrears climbed sharply in the early 19th century, it quickly became apparent that substantial holdings were more economically viable than small tenancies. Evictions increased, but the sheer number of tenants on most estates and their mutual solidarity prevented all but the most determined landlords from restructuring land occupancy along sound economic lines. Cottiers and labourers eked out a precarious existence, but while the potato remained free from disease they remained reasonably well nourished.

In 1841 farmers with more than 50 acres represented only four per cent of the labour force. They had a ready market in industrial Britain for their grain, cattle and butter. Ulster linen-workers also found a market in Britain, but were threatened by mechanization. From the 1820s the development of machine-spinning and particularly of wet spinning forced a dramatic contraction in hand spinning in north Leinster, north Connacht and south, west and central Ulster. It appeared briefly that linen might be displaced by cotton, but the construction of a linen mill in 1828 on the site of a burnt-out Belfast cotton works indicated that the industry had a brighter future, and the building of another 60 in the north-east within a decade confirmed this.

This was the only area of Ireland to industrialize. Elsewhere, there were successful individual enterprises such as the Guinness brewery, but few successful industrial sectors. The proportion of the population engaged in trade and manufacture between 1821 and 1841 fell by 15 per cent, demonstrating the general weakness of the economy.

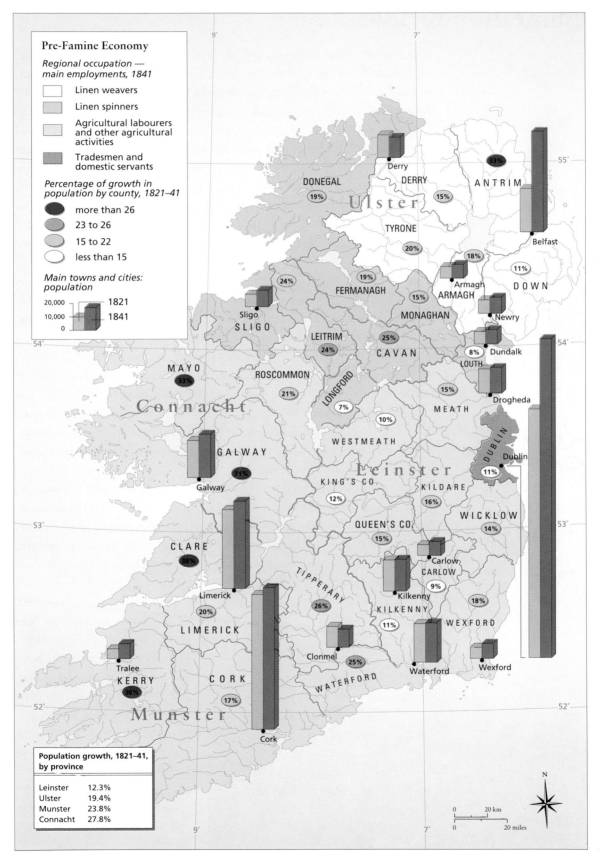

Pre-Famine Economy

Regional occupation — main employments, 1841

- Linen weavers
- Linen spinners
- Agricultural labourers and other agricultural activities
- Tradesmen and domestic servants

Percentage of growth in population by county, 1821–41

- more than 26
- 23 to 26
- 15 to 22
- less than 15

Main towns and cities: population

20,000
10,000
0

1821
1841

Population growth, 1821–41, by province	
Leinster	12.3%
Ulster	19.4%
Munster	23.8%
Connacht	27.8%

Ulster

DONEGAL 19%
DERRY 15%
ANTRIM 33%
Derry
TYRONE 20%
DOWN 11%
ARMAGH 18%
Armagh
MONAGHAN 15%
FERMANAGH 19%
Belfast
Newry
SLIGO 24%
Sligo
LEITRIM 24%
CAVAN 25%
LOUTH 15%
Dundalk 8%
Drogheda 15%

Connacht

MAYO 33%
ROSCOMMON 21%
LONGFORD 7%
MEATH 10%

WESTMEATH
DUBLIN 11%
Dublin
GALWAY 31%
Galway
KING'S CO. 12%
Leinster
KILDARE 16%

CLARE 38%
QUEEN'S CO. 15%
WICKLOW 14%

Limerick
TIPPERARY 26%
CARLOW 9%
Carlow

LIMERICK 20%
KILKENNY 11%
Kilkenny
WEXFORD 18%

Tralee
KERRY 36%
CORK 17%
Clonmel
WATERFORD 25%
Waterford
Wexford

Munster
Cork

N

| 0 | 20 km |
| 0 | 20 miles |

Emigration to 1845

THOUGH THE Irish are today widely perceived as an emigrant people, emigration from the island is in fact only a comparatively recent phenomenon. Prior to the 18th century, the country gained more people than it lost.

The best known of 18th-century Irish emigration was that of the Ulster Scots, who were tempted by the opportunities in the American colonies, and chose to settle there in small numbers from the late 1710s, rising to as many as 50,000 in the early 1770s. Much of this emigration, distinct from the seasonal migrations to Britain and Newfoundland, was by relatively affluent families, but the practice of indentured servitude provided a means by which the poor and restless could also leave.

The American War of Independence (1775–83) temporarily prevented access to what had become the main destination for Irish emigrants. By the early 1770s emigration to America was an established aspect of Irish life, though it was small enough to make little impression on the fast-growing population.

From 1827, the number of emigrants to North America exceeded 20,000 for the first time since the 1780s, and the trend was upwards. In 1831–32, it reached 65,000 for the first time, and average annual emigration to North America exceeded 65,000 between 1841 and 1845. In total, almost 1 million people left Ireland for North America between 1815 and 1845, and while a majority of these first set foot on Canadian soil, this was a reflection of the cost of their passage, not their choice of destination.

While to reach the United States was the ambition of most Irish emigrants, an increasing number were also drawn to industrial Britain. There were significant concentrations of Irish in several English cities by 1800, but these were dwarfed by the 500,000 or so emigrants that moved to Britain in the early 19th century. This trend may reflect the strong tradition of seasonal migration to Britain that had been established in the 18th century.

Below: People gather at the Government Inspector's Office determined to take a ship for America. Engraving from the Illustrated London News.

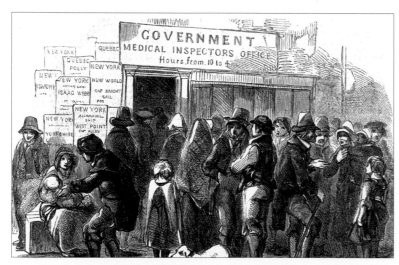

Irish convicts were transported to Australia from the late 1780s, when America's newly-won independence ruled it out as an option. Between the 1780s and 1845, Australia was the destination of between 50,000 and 65,000 Irish felons. A minority, among them some United Irishmen, were political prisoners, but most were common criminals exiled by a penal system that preferred expulsion to the cost of imprisonment.

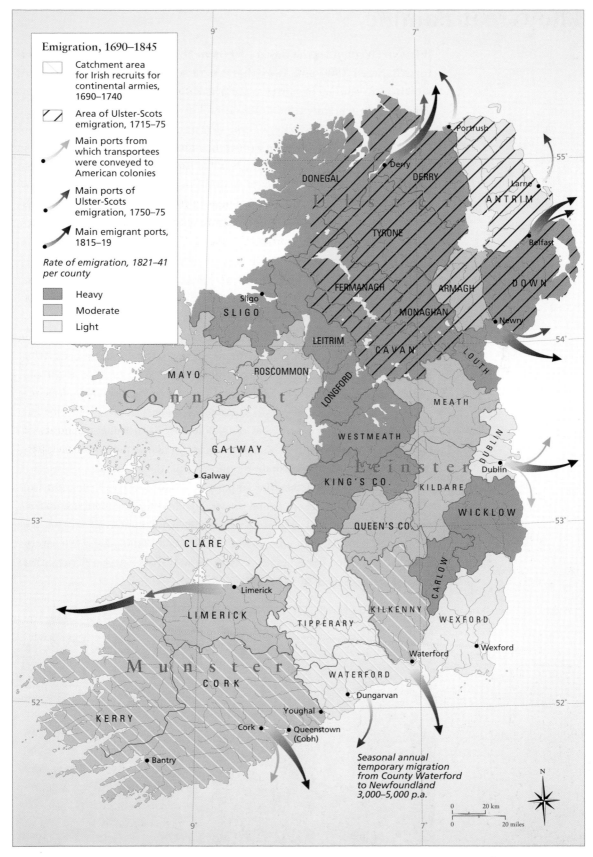

Emigration, 1690–1845

Catchment area for Irish recruits for continental armies, 1690–1740

Area of Ulster-Scots emigration, 1715–75

Main ports from which transportees were conveyed to American colonies

Main ports of Ulster-Scots emigration, 1750–75

Main emigrant ports, 1815–19

Rate of emigration, 1821–41 per county

Heavy

Moderate

Light

Seasonal annual temporary migration from County Waterford to Newfoundland 3,000–5,000 p.a.

ULSTER

DONEGAL

DERRY

Derry

Portrush

Larne

ANTRIM

Belfast

TYRONE

FERMANAGH

ARMAGH

DOWN

Newry

MONAGHAN

Sligo

SLIGO

LEITRIM

CAVAN

LOUTH

MAYO

ROSCOMMON

LONGFORD

Connacht

MEATH

WESTMEATH

GALWAY

Leinster

Dublin

Galway

KING'S CO.

KILDARE

WICKLOW

QUEEN'S CO.

CLARE

CARLOW

KILKENNY

WEXFORD

Limerick

LIMERICK

TIPPERARY

Wexford

Munster

Waterford

CORK

WATERFORD

Dungarvan

KERRY

Youghal

Cork

Queenstown (Cobh)

Bantry

N

0   20 km

0   20 miles

The Great Famine

IRELAND LIVED under the threat of famine throughout the early 19th century. Between 1800 and 1845 there were some 16 food crises most of which were caused by adverse weather conditions. Because the emergencies were generally overcome with relatively modest loss of life, there was no reason to anticipate an epic disaster, and the fact that the country annually produced enough food, not just to feed its own population but to export a healthy surplus gives the lie to those who maintain that the Great Famine was a disaster waiting to happen. Population growth had already declined appreciably from its 18th-century peak, and by the early 1840s increasing numbers were emigrating. The rural poor were nevertheless vulnerable to disaster, and in 1845 it came from Europe in the form of an incurable fungal disease, Phytophthera infestans, which decimated their staple food stuff, the potato crop.

The blight spread rapidly because of the wet harvest season, and 40 per cent of the crop was destroyed. This was enough to plunge the country into crisis, though imports of Indian meal at first kept mortality within bounds. If the blight had not recurred, the setback of 1845 would not have been much more consequential than any of the previous regional crises. Unfortunately, in three of the following four years the potato blight again took a heavy toll, with the result that when relief from private and official sources proved inadequate, tens of thousands died annually from malnutrition and epidemic disease. According to recent calculations approximately 1 million people died, of which an estimated 40 per cent came from Connacht, 30 per cent from Munster, 21 per cent from Ulster and 9 per cent from Leinster. Inevitably the crisis was most severe in the poorest areas: death and emigration reduced the population to 6.5 million, with the proportion of landholdings of less than five acres falling from 35 to 20 per cent, and those of 15 or more acres rising from 31 to 48 per cent between 1841 and 1851. Post-Famine rural Ireland was to be quite different as a consequence.

Right: The poor and destitute gather outside the gates of a workhouse hoping for shelter and food. By 1847 the local systems of relief were utterly overwhelmed by the magnitude of the crisis.

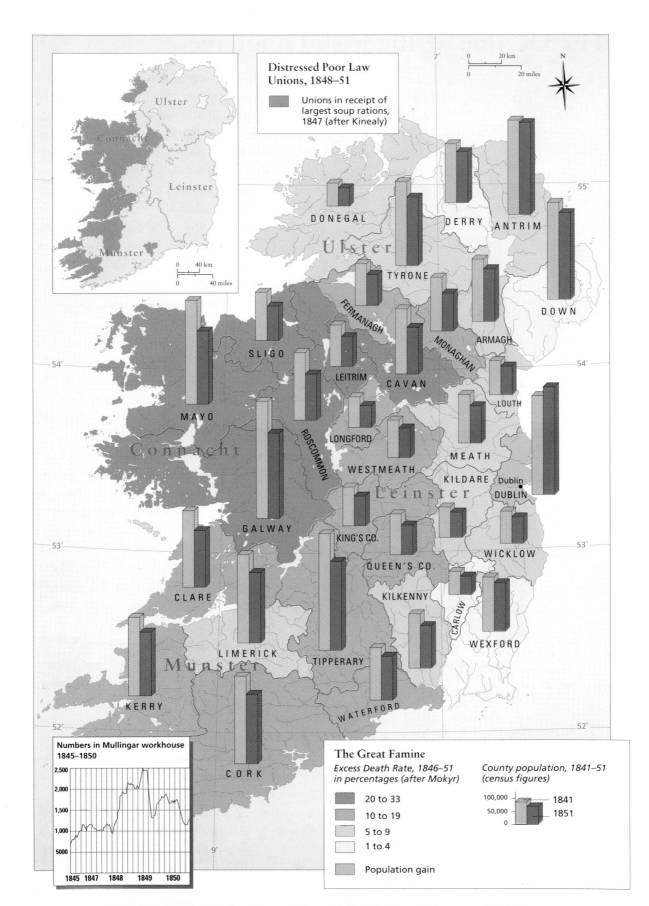

Distressed Poor Law Unions, 1848–51

Unions in receipt of largest soup rations, 1847 (after Kinealy)

Ulster
Connacht
Leinster
Munster

0   40 km
0   40 miles

0   20 km
0   20 miles

N

DONEGAL

DERRY   ANTRIM

Ulster

55°

TYRONE

FERMANAGH

DOWN

SLIGO

LEITRIM   CAVAN   MONAGHAN   ARMAGH

54°

MAYO

ROSCOMMON

LOUTH

Connacht

LONGFORD

MEATH

WESTMEATH

KILDARE   Dublin
DUBLIN

Leinster

GALWAY

KING'S CO.

WICKLOW

53°

QUEEN'S CO.

CLARE

KILKENNY

CARLOW

LIMERICK   TIPPERARY

WEXFORD

Munster

KERRY

WATERFORD

52°

CORK

7°

9°

Numbers in Mullingar workhouse
1845–1850

2,500

2,000

1,500

1,000

5000

1845 1847 1848 1849 1850

The Great Famine

Excess Death Rate, 1846–51
in percentages (after Mokyr)

20 to 33

10 to 19

5 to 9

1 to 4

Population gain

County population, 1841–51
(census figures)

100,000

50,000

0

1841
1851

The Decline of the Irish Language

The Irish language, of which Scottish Gaelic and Manx are dialects, is of Celtic and ultimately Indo-European origin, and has been spoken in Ireland for perhaps 2,500 years. Although it began to exhibit some minor Norse influences in the aftermath of the Viking invasions, its position as the language of Ireland only underwent serious challenge with the introduction of substantial communities of English speakers in the aftermath of the English invasion in the late 12th century.

Nevertheless, Irish retained its dominance, and, indeed, by the 14th century was spoken by an increasing number of settlers, Gaelic culture undergoing a considerable resurgence, in spite of attempts by the Dublin government to legislate against it. English language and influence were never eradicated, however, especially from the towns, and the Tudor reconquest put Irish very much on the defensive. By the early 17th century, the native aristocracy, the principal patrons of Gaelic culture, had been overthrown, and the language lost its ascendancy. Plantation of new English-speaking settlers, and a comprehensive redistribution of landownership following the Cromwellian and Williamite wars, meant that the new proprietorial, professional and mercantile classes were English-speaking virtually without exception.

Although Gaelic literature survived, and its merits increasingly gained an antiquarian appreciation, it was now predominantly the expression of an underclass, and for those anxious to gain social or economic advancement a knowledge of English was essential. Ironically, as the population began to rise rapidly, by the early 19th century there were probably more Irish-speakers than at any time previously (4 million or more), but they were the poorest sections of society, and an accelerating abandonment of Irish had begun well before the Great Famine struck in the mid-1840s. Death and massive emigration had the effect of decimating the language, aided by a hostile education system and a largely unsympathetic Church, so that by the end of the century its future seemed bleak.

At this point, however, a vibrant language revival movement emerged in the form of the Gaelic League (*Conradh na Gaeilge*), interest growing in tandem with the demand for political independence. The establishment of the Irish Free State in 1922 had the not entirely healthy effect of institutionalizing the language movement (except in the six counties which became Northern Ireland) and government efforts to promote Irish, especially by maintaining the viability of the Gaeltacht, the remaining Irish-speaking areas, and insisting on compulsory instruction in schools, have thus far attained only limited success. Perhaps the best hope for the language's future lies in the enthusiasm which individual groups of parents are showing for the provision of all-Irish primary education for their children in the form of *Gaelscoileanna*.

Below: *Early premises of Conradh na Gaeilge (the Gaelic League) in Sackville Street, around the turn of the century.*

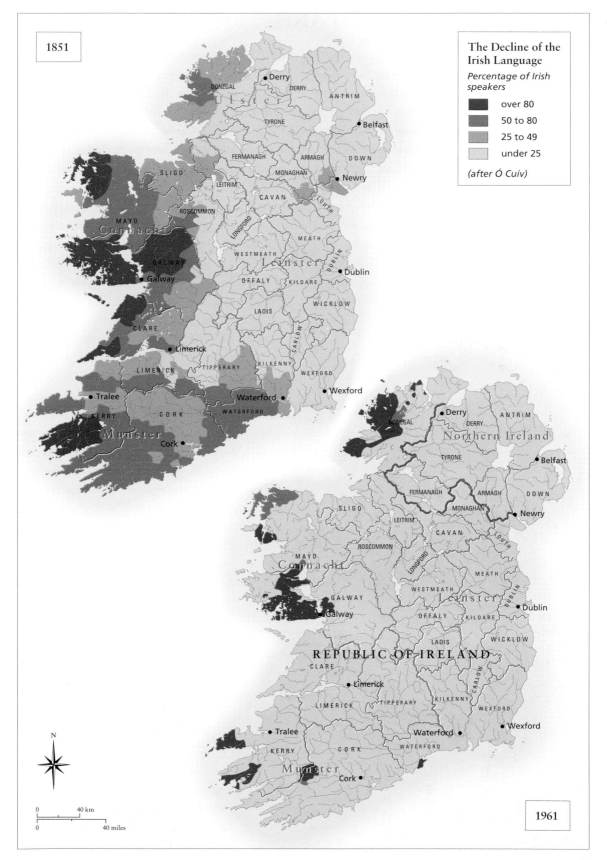

1851

The Decline of the
Irish Language

*Percentage of Irish
speakers*

over 80
50 to 80
25 to 49
under 25

(after Ó Cuív)

1961

PART V: MODERN IRELAND

Gabriel Doherty

AT FIRST SIGHT the history of Ireland over the course of the last 150 years manifests many similarities with the process of political, economic and social modernization evident in the evolution of its western European neighbours during the same period. A market-oriented economy characterized by a commercialized agricultural sector and substantially augmented manufacturing and service sectors; a literate population, increasingly urbanized, who live longer, marry less and have smaller families compared to their forebears; a sophisticated social welfare system designed to cater for the multifarious needs of its citizens; and a social culture which has become daily more variegated and influenced by international trends — in all these respects and more Ireland has changed since the Famine and changed quite dramatically, but only, it appears, to become less distinctively national and more routinely cosmopolitan.

Below: Charles Stewart Parnell entered parliament in 1875 and was active in the 'obstructionist' faction of the Home Rule Party. Their intention was to obstruct the day-to-day business of parliament in order to highlight Irish issues.

Other important changes should also be noted, most notably the dramatic decline in the island's population since the Famine (which stands in stark contrast to the unprecedented rate of expansion in the pre-Famine era, and also to the expansion evident elsewhere in Europe since the middle of the last century) and the formal partition of the island in 1920 into two distinct political entities. This latter development in particular, although in some respects only the formal political confirmation of a pattern of regional social and economic differentiation evident for over a century, nonetheless marked a significant point of departure for the subsequent history of the island, albeit not a very propitious one.

Such changes notwithstanding, however, there are characteristics of Irish life which have withstood the passage of time and which continue to set off Irish politics and society from those obtaining in other countries. The issues of ownership, dis-

Below: *Presidents John F. Kennedy and Eamon de Valera together during JFK's triumphant visit to Ireland in June 1963. He was seen as the supreme symbol of Irish-American success and was received like a conquering hero. But he had barely four month to live.*

Below: Dr Noel Browne, seen here being chased by police following a protest outside the American embassy in Dublin in the 1960s, had been Minister for Health from 1948 to 1951. A passionate socialist and radical, he had spearheaded the campaign which effectively eradicated tuberculosis as an epidemic disease in Ireland. In doing so, he removed one of the country's greatest scourges.

tribution and utilization of land have proved to be as contentious in this era as they were in the more distant past. The 'quiet revolution', by which ownership of land was transferred in the late 19th and early 20th centuries from landlord to tenant, was effected with less difficulty than many expected bearing in mind its uniquely controversial history, but changes in formal patterns of tenure were less significant than the contemporaneous and accelerated shift from arable to pastoral usage. While similar developments were taking place elsewhere, the social consequences of such a reorientation were perhaps more problematic for Ireland than for any other western European country, given the complex political context within which it took place, although one should note that the political disturbances of the period between 1915 and 1923 were not, in the main, economically determined.

Concern with land, however, has not been the only issue which has served to highlight the continuities between the pre- and post-Famine eras. The enduring cultural achievements of the Irish people, exemplified in the international acclaim accorded to such outstanding literary figures as Oscar Wilde, George Bernard Shaw, W.B. Yeats, James Joyce, Samuel Beckett and, more recently, Seamus Heaney, have also been widely attested to. Less straightforward has been the intellectual legacy of modern Irish nationalism which has provided the inspiration for some of the most dramatic developments of the period, most obviously the achievement of political independence for the greater part of the island under the terms of the 1921 Anglo-Irish Treaty, but which, in common with the equally problematic phenomenon of unionism, has left a complex and frequently divisive mark on the political and social landscape of the north-eastern part of the island in particular.

The form of Ireland's relationship with Britain has thus been one of the constant, defining features of the modern Irish experience, north and south, but the fluctuating fortunes of that relationship should not obscure the more nuanced but equally interesting links which have been forged between

Ireland and the wider world over the course of the last century and a half. The most tangible of those bonds have come in the shape of its people, the hundreds of thousands of emigrants who, for a variety of reasons, left their homeland to seek a new life elsewhere. Many of these, particularly during the middle of the 20th century, settled in the neighbouring isle but for the earlier period and again more recently other, more distant destinations have figured prominently — most obviously in America but also in Canada, Australia, New Zealand and elsewhere. Not that their departure meant that

Below: Charles Haughey, the most charismatic and controversial Irish Taoiseach of modern times.

they or their offspring lost interest in matters affecting the 'mother country'; on the contrary, these communities sustained a vibrant sense of Irish nationality in their adopted homes, albeit one attenuated by the conditions of the host society.

In addition to the legacy of the Irish abroad, numerous bonds have also served to incorporate the Irish experience into that of mainland Europe during these eventful years, a mutual interaction given institutional recognition in 1973 with the entry of both the Republic of Ireland and Northern Ireland (as part of the United Kingdom) into the European Economic Community (subsequently the European Union). It is the economic impact of this association which has, perhaps not surprisingly, received the lion's share of attention over the last quarter of a century but this should not blind one to its powerful social and political undercurrents — undercurrents which may, in the fullness of time, come to be regarded as its most enduring legacy.

It is, however, the story of what happened, and those who remained, in Ireland with which we are most concerned here. In this respect the transfer of political power from London to administrations in both Dublin and (to a lesser extent) Belfast in the early 1920s provided an opportunity for these governments to formulate policies designed to promote the specific interests of the Irish people. The development of two distinctive socio-political regimes north and south of the border — the former self-consciously British and Protestant, the latter explicitly Gaelic and Catholic in its cultural for-mation — bore testimony to the deep divisions within the country which pre-dated even the Famine, but even here the enduring ties of history between the two political areas should not be ignored. It is one of the enduring ironies of modern Irish history that the regional differences within the island — east/west as well as north/south — are in many respects less manifest now than in the middle of the 19th century, but are widely known and more

Above and right: *During the late 1980s and 1990s Ireland has enjoyed outstanding economic success, growing consistently around 6/7%. The high standard of education has attracted inward investment from the global economy, backed by infrastructural investment from the EU. The establishment of new activities, such as computers and financial services, has led to an increasing sophistication and diversification of opportunity, alongside Ireland's traditional and well established industries.*

keenly felt, and it is in this context that the debate on national identify, the nature of the Irish quintessence, which has proliferated over the last century, must be studied.

In short, while the island of Ireland has undoubtedly experienced massive and at times painful social and political change since 1851, evidence of the pervasive influence of its historical inheritance is as much in evidence on its contemporary intellectual landscape as it is on its physical one.

Post-Famine Emigration

THE FAMINE was a milestone in modern Irish history, not merely because of the sheer horror of the human suffering it carried in its wake (awful though this was) but also because it gave an added impetus to the development of profound social changes which had become evident during the years immediately prior to 1845.

Of these changes it was perhaps the scale of emigration which was the most important. So huge was this emigration that Ireland, which had experienced substantial population expansion over the course of the previous 100 years, now entered a period of population decline which had no contemporary comparison in Europe and which was to continue almost unchecked for well over a century. This phenomenon affected all creeds and classes and touched all parts of the country, although the poorer elements of the Catholic agricultural population of the south and west manifested the greatest relative decline, with Munster experiencing the largest absolute losses. The scale of female emigration was particularly noticeable, with the number of female emigrants at times outnumbering their male counterparts (contrary to the experience of most other countries).

While some emigrants settled in the growing industrial towns across the Irish Sea, most found themselves embarked on the hazardous sea journey towards a new life in North America, and in particular the United States. Initially finding themselves the subject of suspicion and distrust in their adopted homeland they nonetheless quickly adjusted and made an enormous contribution to the subsequent development of the country. Notwithstanding the fact that they had in the main come from an agricultural background, most of these emigrants settled in large cities on the east coast of America, and while the numbers returning to Ireland remained small in comparison to other nationalities, yet they retained an interest in Irish affairs which has persisted to the present day.

Back in Ireland other important demographic trends were becoming noticeable. In particular the marriage rate, which had been quite high prior to the Famine, now slowly declined (although as can be seen from the map this process did not proceed at the same pace throughout the island). This was due to the increase in the number of individuals who never married, together with an increase in the average age at the time. Notwithstanding this significant development the birth rate remained well above the European average, although this was also subject to significant geographic variation.

Below: 'Steerage emigrants', a wood engraving by Arthur Boyd Houghton, published in the Graphic, March 1869, shows poor emigrants sailing the cheap steerage passage to North America.

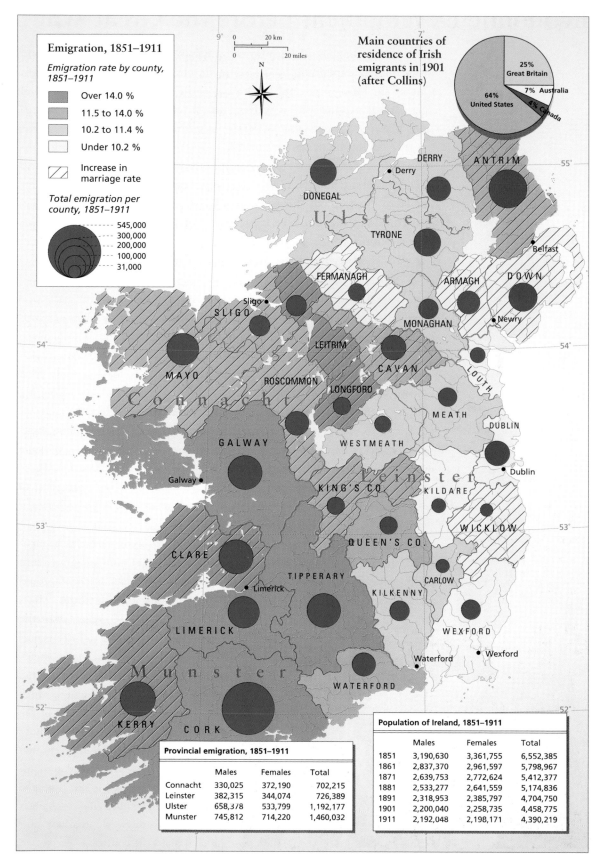

Emigration, 1851–1911

Emigration rate by county, 1851–1911

- Over 14.0 %
- 11.5 to 14.0 %
- 10.2 to 11.4 %
- Under 10.2 %
- Increase in marriage rate

Total emigration per county, 1851–1911

- 545,000
- 300,000
- 200,000
- 100,000
- 31,000

Main countries of residence of Irish emigrants in 1901 (after Collins)

- 64% United States
- 25% Great Britain
- 7% Australia
- 4% Canada

Provincial emigration, 1851–1911

	Males	Females	Total
Connacht	330,025	372,190	702,215
Leinster	382,315	344,074	726,389
Ulster	658,378	533,799	1,192,177
Munster	745,812	714,220	1,460,032

Population of Ireland, 1851–1911

	Males	Females	Total
1851	3,190,630	3,361,755	6,552,385
1861	2,837,370	2,961,597	5,798,967
1871	2,639,753	2,772,624	5,412,377
1881	2,533,277	2,641,559	5,174,836
1891	2,318,953	2,385,797	4,704,750
1901	2,200,040	2,258,735	4,458,775
1911	2,192,048	2,198,171	4,390,219

Economic Development before the Great War

THE HUMAN changes which followed the Famine were accompanied (and indeed partly explained) by dramatic changes in the national economy. One of the most important of these was the acceleration of the shift in agricultural production away from small-scale intensive tillage operations towards a more extensive dairy system. There were many reasons for this development, which involved the frequently controversial consolidation of large numbers of small holdings into more substantial and efficient units. Undoubtedly the Irish climate played a part, being conducive to grazing, but the government also exercised a direct influence, particularly by means of the legislation which it passed in the aftermath of the Famine which simplified the rather cumbersome existing procedures for the transfer of the ownership of land.

Such chances, together with the now near-universal tendency for land to be inherited en bloc rather than be divided up among competing offspring, produced large numbers of individuals and families who could find no role in the new economic dispensation and who formed the bulk of the emigrants discussed earlier. In the north, however, the second major development in the Irish economy during the second part of the century — the growth of manufacturing industry in the area (particularly in Belfast and Derry) — provided for many an alternative to the emigrant ship. Large numbers of agricultural workers, both Catholic and Protestant, now settled in these cities, hoping to find work in the new ship-building yards or linen mills which were opening at that time. These workers frequently had to endure appalling working and living conditions, to which were added the tensions which had long characterized relations between the two major religious blocs in the area.

A number of other developments in the national economy must also be mentioned. In particular the Irish economy was becoming ever more integrated into the British economic sphere of influence, a development aided by the improved road, rail and port facilities which developed in the 60 years after the Famine. Irish economic activity generally became more commercially-oriented and moved decisively away from the subsistence-type of production which had characterized certain areas in the earlier decades of the century. Partly as a consequence of this development, living standards across the island gradually improved, although it did leave the economy rather vulnerable to changes in European and world markets over which it had little control.

Below: Shipyard workers leaving the Harland and Wolff yard in Belfast at the end of a working day. Belfast and its environs were the centre of Ireland's industrial revolution, thus marking the north off even more from the agricultural south and west.

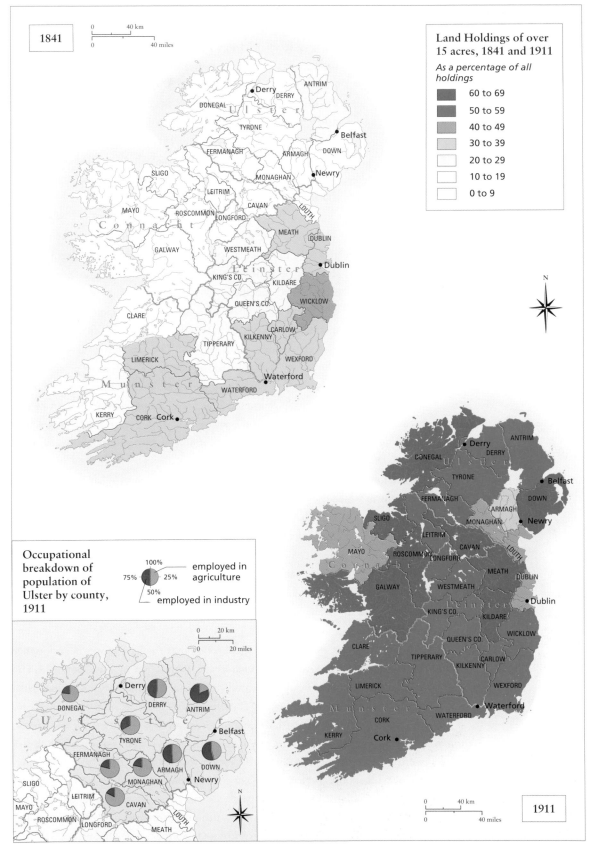

1841

0 ____ 40 km
0 ____ 40 miles

Land Holdings of over 15 acres, 1841 and 1911

As a percentage of all holdings

60 to 69
50 to 59
40 to 49
30 to 39
20 to 29
10 to 19
0 to 9

Occupational breakdown of population of Ulster by county, 1911

100%
75%   25%
50%

employed in agriculture

employed in industry

0 ____ 20 km
0 ____ 20 miles

1911

0 ____ 40 km
0 ____ 40 miles

The Growth of Irish Nationalism

Above: *Thomas Davis, editor of* The Nation, *was a popular idealist and the chief ideologue of the Young Ireland movement.*

THE TRAUMA of the Famine and the consequent readjustments provided an important impetus to the growth of political and cultural nationalism in the country. Building on the foundations laid by the United Irishmen and Daniel O'Connell, a series of individuals and groups during the latter part of the 19th century sought to cultivate a nationalist consciousness which would be the precursor to new and distinctively Irish political and social arrangements.

The first of these bodies — the Young Ireland movement of the 1840s — provided a coherent if not necessarily programmatic doctrine of nationality which was to inspire later generations. After failed rebellions in 1848 and 1867, it was only in the 1870s and 1880s that demands for the recognition of Ireland's distinctive inheritance found practical political expression through the activities at Westminster of the Irish Parliamentary Party, under the leadership initially of Isaac Butt and subsequently (and most impressively) of Charles Stewart Parnell. That both these men were Protestants bestowed upon the movement a deceptively ecumenical façade — in practice Irish nationalism became increasingly defined with the majority Catholic community (a development mirrored by the growth in support amongst Protestants for the maintenance of the Union of 1800).

A number of gains were made by the Irish Party, particularly in the area of land reform which the government undertook in the hope that it would forestall the growth of separatist sentiment, but on the key issue of political reform no progress was made and the controversial downfall of Parnell following his involvement in a divorce case seemed to stymie such hopes for the foreseeable future. Some felt that such a development was the inevitable consequence of constitutional action, and a revolutionary wing to the nationalist movement, the Irish Republican Brotherhood (the 'Fenians') was developed, albeit with little overt popular support.

It was, however, not just in political terms that the new sense of nationality manifested itself. Developments such as the foundation of the Gaelic Athletic Association (1884), a body dedicated to the maintenance of traditional Irish sports, and of the Gaelic League (1893), which sought to stem the apparently inexorable decline of the Irish language, bore testimony to a dynamic perception of nationality independent of political arrangements, a perception which found enduring cultural expression in the varied works of the Irish 'literary renaissance' evident during these years. The foundation in 1905 of Sinn Féin, a broadly-based nationalist organisation with a distinctive economic agenda, was but the latest in a long line of such bodies, although it was arguably to become the most influential in the renewed drive towards political independence.

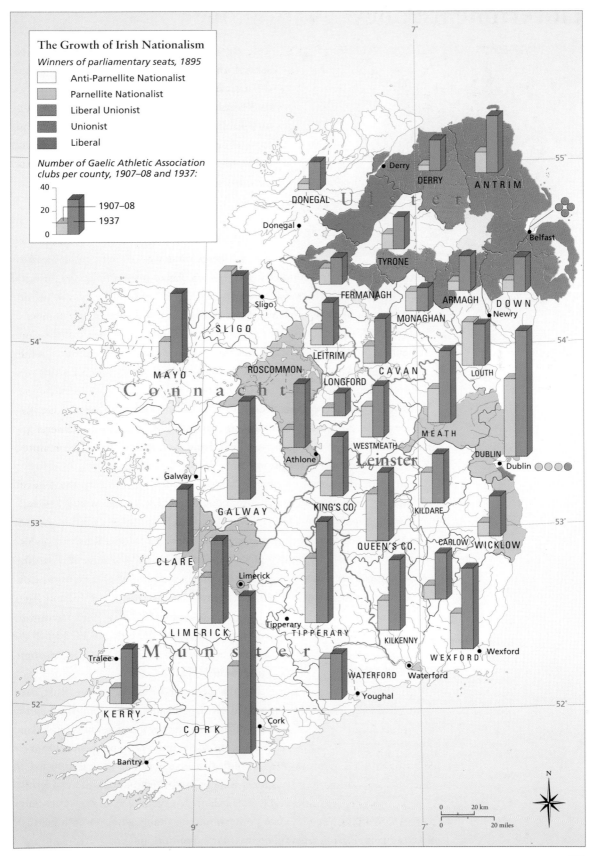

The Growth of Irish Nationalism

Winners of parliamentary seats, 1895

- Anti-Parnellite Nationalist
- Parnellite Nationalist
- Liberal Unionist
- Unionist
- Liberal

Number of Gaelic Athletic Association clubs per county, 1907–08 and 1937:

40 20 0
1907–08
1937

Government Policy

Above: This well-known staged photograph features a means rarely used in case of eviction for non-payment of rent: the battering ram.

THE GROWTH of nationalist sentiment presented the British government with severe difficulties. On the one hand the refusal to make concessions to the burgeoning nationalist lobby ran the risk of alienating the moderate majority; on the other, to give in to such demands raised the possibility of further, perhaps unpalatable demands.

The government's response had two elements. On the one hand it enacted wide-ranging social reforms where these were deemed to be compatible with existing constitutional arrangements. These reforms included the Land Acts (which essentially transferred ownership from landlord to tenant), the disestablishment of the Church of Ireland (1869), the establishment of a number of state agencies to assist with the task of developing the poorest areas of the country, and so on. In its latter stages this policy was accurately described as 'killing Home Rule by kindness', that is, the removal of the social grievances which were felt to underpin the demand for political separation.

However the government proved itself willing to employ coercive methods whenever the political situation became unacceptably tense. This strategy was particularly evident during the so-called 'Land War' of 1879-82, when a number of individuals and organizations, notably the 'Land League' led by Michael Davitt, were the object of official harassment, and also during the 'Plan of Campaign' from 1886-92, which also focused on the key issue of land reform.

Two attempts were made to find a solution to the political question. In 1885 Gladstone, the Liberal Prime Minister, introduced a 'Home Rule' Bill, which sought to bestow very limited powers on an all-Ireland Parliament. Even this was too much for Conservatives and Unionists, who launched a vigorous campaign of opposition to the Bill, which was defeated when the Liberal Party split on the issue in 1886. A second attempt by Gladstone to pass the Bill failed in 1893 when the measure was vetoed by the Conservative-dominated House of Lords.

For the next 20 years the Home Rule issue dropped off a political agenda dominated by the ruling Conservative Party, and attention in Ireland switched to social and economic issues. However the political and emotional capital invested in Home Rule by both Irish nationalists and British Liberals meant that the return of that latter party to power would inevitably witness a resurgence of interest in the question.

Land Legislation, 1870–1903

1870	*Made customary tenant right enforceable at law and provided compensation for disturbance.*
1881	*Concession of the 'Three Fs': right of free sale; judicial power to fix rents; conversion of ordinary tenancies to fixed tenancies.*
1885	
	Allowed land commission to lend to tenants to purchase holdings from landlords.
1903	
	Wyndham's Act. Provided for long-term low-interest government loans to buy out landlords' interests. This crucial piece of legislation effectively ended the land question and created the typical 20th-century pattern of independent family farms.

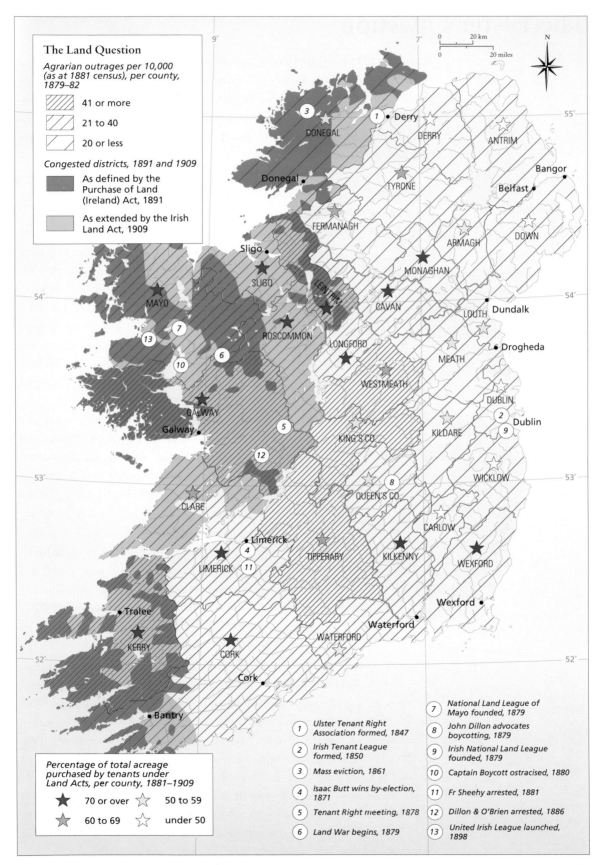

The Land Question

Agrarian outrages per 10,000 (as at 1881 census), per county, 1879–82

- 41 or more
- 21 to 40
- 20 or less

Congested districts, 1891 and 1909

- As defined by the Purchase of Land (Ireland) Act, 1891
- As extended by the Irish Land Act, 1909

0   20 km
0   20 miles

N

9°   7°

55°

54°

53°

52°

DONEGAL
Derry
DERRY
ANTRIM
Donegal
Bangor
Belfast
TYRONE
FERMANAGH
ARMAGH
DOWN
Sligo
SLIGO
LEITRIM
MONAGHAN
CAVAN
LOUTH
Dundalk
MAYO
13
7
ROSCOMMON
LONGFORD
MEATH
Drogheda
10
6
5
WESTMEATH
DUBLIN
12
KING'S CO.
KILDARE
2
9
Dublin
Galway
GALWAY
WICKLOW
CLARE
8
QUEEN'S CO.
CARLOW
Limerick
4
TIPPERARY
KILKENNY
WEXFORD
11
LIMERICK
Tralee
Wexford
KERRY
CORK
WATERFORD
Waterford
Cork
Bantry

Percentage of total acreage purchased by tenants under Land Acts, per county, 1881–1909

- ★ 70 or over
- ☆ 60 to 69
- ★ 50 to 59
- ☆ under 50

1. Ulster Tenant Right Association formed, 1847
2. Irish Tenant League formed, 1850
3. Mass eviction, 1861
4. Isaac Butt wins by-election, 1871
5. Tenant Right meeting, 1878
6. Land War begins, 1879
7. National Land League of Mayo founded, 1879
8. John Dillon advocates boycotting, 1879
9. Irish National Land League founded, 1879
10. Captain Boycott ostracised, 1880
11. Fr Sheehy arrested, 1881
12. Dillon & O'Brien arrested, 1886
13. United Irish League launched, 1898

The Ulster Question

IT WAS IN 1912 that the British government, once more led by a Liberal prime minister and supported by the votes of the Irish Parliamentary Party, returned to the issue of Home Rule. The terms of the Bill introduced in April of that year were similar to earlier proposals, but provoked an even more hostile response from its opponents, particularly in Ulster.

There were several reasons why the campaign of opposition to Home Rule during 1912–14 was markedly more bitter than those of the previous generation. The Liberal Party had been shorn of its unionist wing and so a repetition of the internal divisions of 1886 was not to be expected; the veto of the House of Lords had been removed some years earlier, so a repeat of the disappointment of 1893 was impossible; and unionist support had become more concentrated in Ulster, the area of Ireland with the highest concentration of Protestants, than theretofore, when the opposition had been characterized by an all-Ireland dimension.

Led by such men as Edward Carson and James Craig, the campaign became increasingly bellicose in tone. Actions during 1912–14 such as the signing of the Solemn League and Covenant, the formation of the Ulster Volunteer Force and the Larne gun-running signalled a determination at all costs to maintain the Union intact; and when allied with other developments such as the Curragh 'mutiny' and the formation of the opposing National Volunteers, the situation in Ulster seemed to threaten the possibility of civil war.

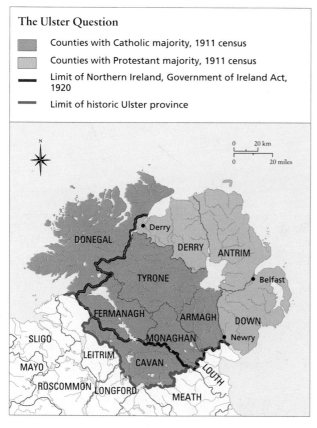

The Ulster Question

- Counties with Catholic majority, 1911 census
- Counties with Protestant majority, 1911 census
- Limit of Northern Ireland, Government of Ireland Act, 1920
- Limit of historic Ulster province

The crisis was temporarily 'solved' by the outbreak of war in Europe in August 1914, with the Bill being passed by parliament but being suspended for the duration of hostilities. Perhaps more importantly provision was also made for the possibility of special treatment for Ulster as compared to the rest of the country. The exclusion of some or all of the nine counties of Ulster from the terms of the Bill had been bitterly opposed by nationalists, although John Redmond, leader of the Irish Parliamentary Party, had been willing to concede the principle of temporary exclusion of certain counties in order to secure the passage of the Bill as a whole. The failure adequately to resolve the objections of Ulster unionists, however, was to have fatal consequences when the question was re-examined, in even more unfavourable conditions, after the end of the war in Europe.

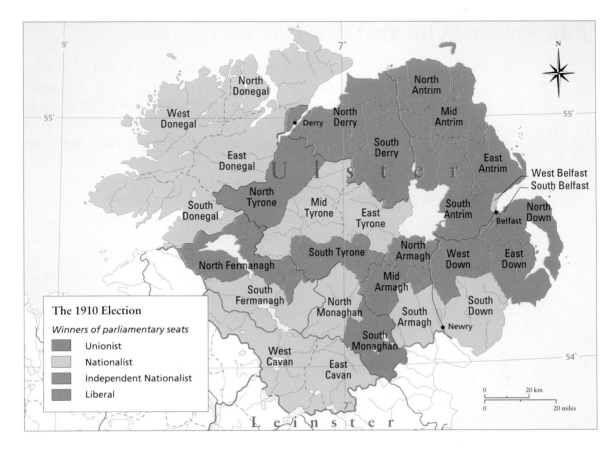

The 1910 Election

Winners of parliamentary seats

- Unionist
- Nationalist
- Independent Nationalist
- Liberal

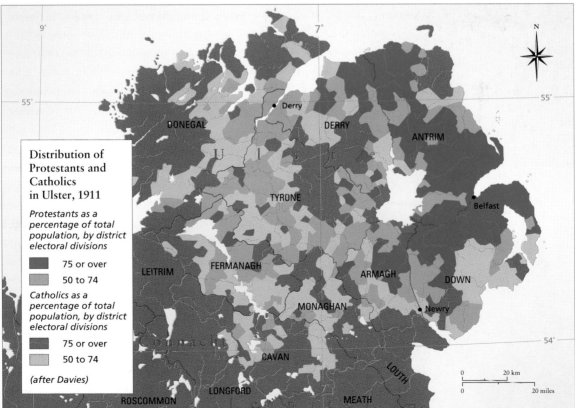

Distribution of Protestants and Catholics in Ulster, 1911

Protestants as a percentage of total population, by district electoral divisions

- 75 or over
- 50 to 74

Catholics as a percentage of total population, by district electoral divisions

- 75 or over
- 50 to 74

(after Davies)

The Great War and the Easter Rising

Above: *Éamon de Valera, commander of the rebel garrison in Boland's Mills, under arrest and escorted by British troops, Dublin, 1916.*

IN COMMON with the rest of Europe the 'Great War' of 1914–18 had far-reaching consequences for Ireland. The human dimension of Ireland's contribution to the war effort was enormous, with over 270,000 men (40per cent of the adult male population) serving in the British armed forces, and many thousands more working in the new munitions factories. The front line soldiers were to endure the same horrifying conditions as the other combatants, and casualties also reached the same appalling levels — barely a village escaped those years without the death of at least one local young man, with particularly savage losses being inflicted at the battle of the Somme in July 1916.

These human sufferings had a political as well as a military dimension. Many of the large numbers of nationalists who enlisted did so because they felt that their actions would serve to guarantee Home Rule for Ireland; conversely members of the Ulster Volunteer Force who volunteered felt that their sacrifices would be sufficient to ensure the defeat of the same measure. The apparent preference shown by the British government to the claims of the latter group added to the sense of discontent within the ranks of radical nationalist opinion, a discontent which was to become manifest with the events of the Easter Rising of April 1916.

This insurrection, which lasted less than a week, was fatally hindered by poor planning, inappropriate tactics and sheer bad luck. As a consequence of divisions within the leadership of the movement the Rising, which was originally intended to encompass the entire country, was concentrated almost entirely in the centre of Dublin. In spite of the personal bravery shown by many of the insurgents, the outcome of the drama was never really in doubt and on Saturday 29 April an unconditional surrender was signed by the leaders of the Volunteers, after a mere six days of fighting.

Below: *After the battle, citizens of Dublin walk through the rubble-strewn streets, the painful aftermath of the 1916 Easter Rising.*

In military terms the Rising was an unmitigated disaster for the Volunteers — casualties were high, with all those not killed or injured being interned by the British, and all of the munitions so painstakingly stockpiled being lost in a few short days. What the Rising did signal, however, through the actions and rhetoric of figures as diverse as Pádraig Pearse and James Connolly, was a militancy which could not be accommodated within the old Home Rule framework, and which was to become a determining factor in the Irish political scene over the next seven years.

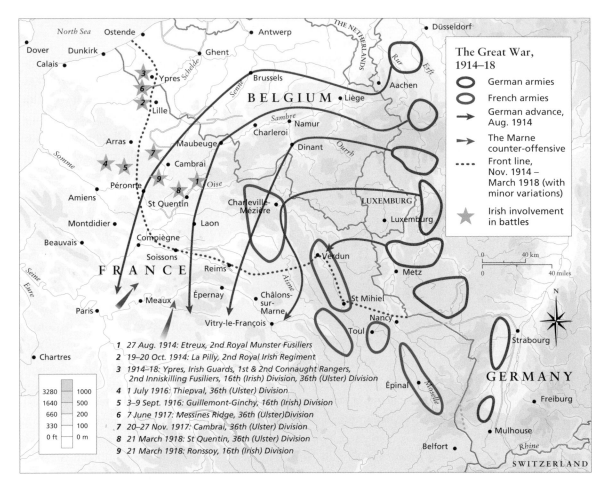

The Great War,
1914–18

⬭ German armies

⬭ French armies

→ German advance,
Aug. 1914

➡ The Marne
counter-offensive

⋯ Front line,
Nov. 1914 –
March 1918 (with
minor variations)

★ Irish involvement
in battles

1 27 Aug. 1914: Etreux, 2nd Royal Munster Fusiliers
2 19–20 Oct. 1914: La Pilly, 2nd Royal Irish Regiment
3 1914–18: Ypres, Irish Guards, 1st & 2nd Connaught Rangers,
   2nd Inniskilling Fusiliers, 16th (Irish) Division, 36th (Ulster) Division
4 1 July 1916: Thiepval, 36th (Ulster) Division
5 3–9 Sept. 1916: Guillemont-Ginchy, 16th (Irish) Division
6 7 June 1917: Messines Ridge, 36th (Ulster) Division
7 20–27 Nov. 1917: Cambrai, 36th (Ulster) Division
8 21 March 1918: St Quentin, 36th (Ulster) Division
9 21 March 1918: Ronssoy, 16th (Irish) Division

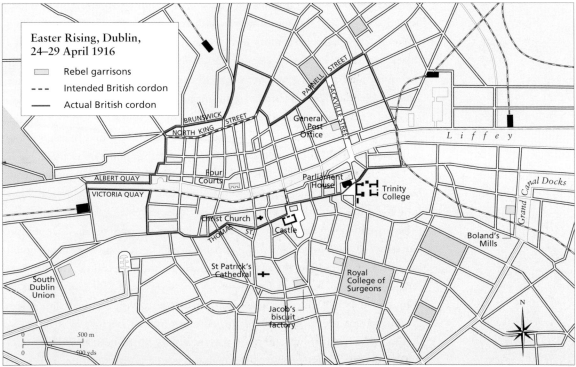

Easter Rising, Dublin,
24–29 April 1916

▢ Rebel garrisons

-- Intended British cordon

— Actual British cordon

Separation 1916–23

Above: *King George V opening the first parliament of the new Northern Ireland on 21 June 1921.*

NATIONALIST MILITANCY was compounded by serious government errors in the aftermath of the Rising, such as the execution of the leaders of the Rising and an ill-judged proposal to introduce conscription. It gained further momentum during 1917–18, with reorganizations both of the Volunteer movement (now known as Irish Republican Army) and of Sinn Féin, which now became the main vehicle for the expression of radical nationalist sentiment. The party's sweeping victory in the 1918 General Election, where it dominated the vote outside much of Ulster, gave added momentum to the separatist effort.

This momentum was consolidated by the foundation of Dáil Eireann, a republican assembly, in January 1919 and by the commencement in the same month of a vigorous guerrilla war undertaken by the IRA. Over the course of the next two years a number of violent incidents occurred, including 'Bloody Sunday' (marked by the deaths of 23 soldiers and civilians), the burning of Cork City and the destruction of the Custom House in Dublin. In an effort to stem the activities of the IRA the government introduced a number of specially-recruited and ruthlessly aggressive units into Ireland, most notoriously the so-called 'Black and Tans', but the excesses of these units only served to diminish further the moral authority of the government in the face of world opinion. A truce between the two sides was brokered during July 1921, following the formal partition of the country and the establishment of Northern Ireland under the Government of Ireland Act, and some months later a republican negotiating team was dispatched to London, led by Arthur Griffith and Michael Collins.

The 'Treaty' signed by this delegation with the British government in December 1921 was unacceptable to many republicans, who felt that it did not fully recognize Ireland's legitimate claim for independence. Prominent amongst these dissenters was Éamon de Valera, who had led the underground republican Government during the War of Independence. These disagreements erupted into Civil War in June 1922, with an attack by the Provisional Government established by the terms of the Treaty on the republican-held Four Courts in Dublin. The next 12 months saw widespread unrest, with the deaths of many leading figures on both sides, but in truth government victory was rarely in doubt. What was in doubt, however, was the ability of the new 'Irish Free State' to overcome the severe problems facing it as a young European state.

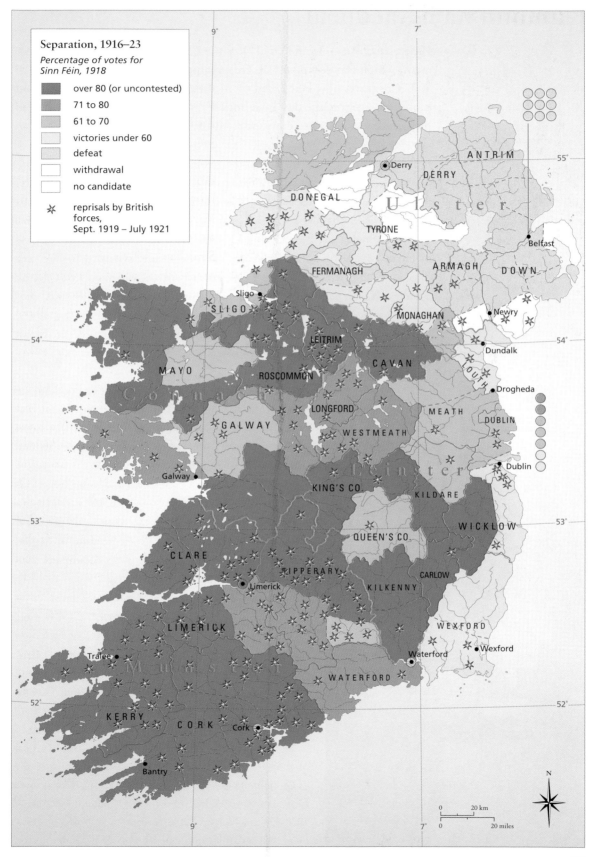

Separation, 1916–23

*Percentage of votes for
Sinn Féin, 1918*

- over 80 (or uncontested)
- 71 to 80
- 61 to 70
- victories under 60
- defeat
- withdrawal
- no candidate

✴ reprisals by British
forces,
Sept. 1919 – July 1921

Cumann na nGaedheal

HAVING PREVAILED in the Civil War the Cumann na nGaedheal government, which was composed of Treaty supporters under the leadership of W.T. Cosgrave, now embarked on a comprehensive political, social and economic programme designed both to promote stability and growth in the country and also to consolidate its own electoral position.

In the main the government's programme was characterized by cautious continuity rather than daring innovation. In terms of the structure of the civil service, legal system, police force, army, and the education system it was content to follow the broad principles laid down by the British administration. In economic affairs continuity was also the hallmark. The government completed the process of buying out the landlords but in most other respects refused to intervene directly in the economy, although its support for the Shannon hydroelectric scheme for example demonstrated a willingness to undertake substantial projects where necessary. Ireland remained, however, a predominantly agricultural country, with most exports destined for Britain from whom she in return imported most of her manufactured goods. Taxation remained low but poverty was rife.

The government also pursued a cautious line in its foreign policy, building up a small diplomatic corps in Europe and America but concentrating on the crucial relationship with Great Britain. The issue of Northern Ireland was a persistent problem, with the border between north and south being only finally ratified in 1925, when the Boundary Commission established under the Treaty collapsed in chaos. While the government was keen to maintain good relations with the British government it also sought to consolidate its own freedom of action, and it played an important role in the Commonwealth Conferences during these years.

Internal security remained a problem, however. A potential mutiny in the Army was averted in 1924, while the defeat of the IRA in the Civil War had not removed the threat of republican sedition. De Valera was frustrated by the rather sterile abstentionist policies of Sinn Féin and founded his own party, Fianna Fáil, in 1926. In the following year he led his followers into the Free State Dáil when it appeared that the government was trying to exclude them permanently following the assassination of Kevin O'Higgins, a leading government minister.

Cumann na nGaedheal managed to hang on to power for five more years, but following the General Election of 1932 Fianna Fáil was able to form a minority government and set about implementing its radical manifesto.

Below: William Thomas Cosgrave, President of the Irish Free State, making a speech in 1922. The new government had a dual task of rebuilding the country after the struggle for freedom and providing politically for the nation's desire for independence with unity.

The Anti-Treaty Vote in the General Election, 1923

- - - proposed change of border

Percentage of first-preference votes for Sinn Féin (anti-Treaty)

31 or over

21 to 30

14 to 20

20 km

20 miles

N

9°   7°

55°

ANTRIM

Coleraine

DERRY

Derry

Larne

Northern Ireland

DONEGAL

Belfast

Donegal

TYRONE

D O W N

Downpatrick

FERMANAGH

ARMAGH

Enniskillen

MONAGHAN

Newry

SLIGO

Sligo

LEITRIM

Dundalk   54°

Connacht

CAVAN

LOUTH

MAYO

ROSCOMMON

LONGFORD

Drogheda

Roscommon

WESTMEATH

MEATH

DUBLIN

GALWAY

Athlone

7

Leinster

Dublin   2

Galway

OFFALY

9

4

KILDARE

5

IRISH FREE STATE

6

R. Shannon

WICKLOW

7   53°

53°

LAOIS

CLARE

TIPPERARY

CARLOW

Arklow

8

3

Limerick

KILKENNY

1

LIMERICK

Tipperary

WEXFORD

Munster

WATERFORD

Wexford

Tralee

Waterford

Youghal   52°

52°

KERRY

CORK

Cork

Cobh

5   July 1927: assassination of
     Kevin O'Higgins

Bantry

1   January 1923: establishment
     of Garda training camp

6   August 1927: entry of Fianna Fáil
     into Dáil

2   March 1924: army 'mutiny'

7   Establishment of state
     broadcasting system: 1926 Dublin,
     1927 Cork, 1932 Athlone

3   1926: establishment of state
     power company

8   July 1929: opening of Shannon
     hydroelectric scheme

4   May 1926: public launch of
     Fianna Fáil

9   1931: IRA Wolfe Tone commemoration
     prohibited

9°   7°

Fianna Fáil

ON COMING to power in 1932 de Valera immediately set about the task of realizing his distinctive view of national development. One of his first actions was to suspend the payment of land annuities by Irish farmers to the British overnment, which led through a series of retaliatory measures into a full-scale 'Economic War', characterised on both sides by severe protectionist measures. De Valera seized on this opportunity to develop small domestic industries, although the damage to the agricultural sector, particularly to the small farmer group which formed the backbone of the party's rural vote, led to the gradual decline of the policy in the late 1930s.

In other areas too de Valera sought to influence Irish social development, particularly in the areas of education policy, Church-State relations and Anglo-Irish affairs. This latter issue was especially problematic, but by degrees the Cabinet succeeded in removing the most objectionable elements of the 1921 Treaty (particularly the Oath of Alliegance and the Office of Governor-General) and in 1937 de Valera successfully introduced a new Constitution.

The democratic tone of this Constitution was noteworthy at a time when fascism was at its height in Europe. Following an agreement with Great Britain in 1938, which ended the 'Economic War' and returned to Irish control several ports hitherto the responsibility of the Royal Navy, de Valera adopted a policy of military neutrality during the Second World War (or 'Emergency' as it was called in Ireland). The maintenance of this policy in spite of pressures both from the Allies (particularly after the entry of America into the War) and from Nazi Germany was a major diplomatic undertaking, one which required the government to take severe action against their former republican comrades in arms (de Valera had, in fact, immediately on coming to power, suppressed the quite distinct and quasi-fascist 'Blueshirt' movement in the country). In practice his policies favoured the Allies, but his formal adherence to neutrality gained the country few friends abroad.

The government found itself increasingly unpopular after the end of the War, when a combination of continued economic hardship, the emergence of new rival political parties and a series of scandals combined to present the image of a party too long in power. Its defeat in the 1948 election, however, only served to draw attention to the momentous changes witnessed during the previous 16 years.

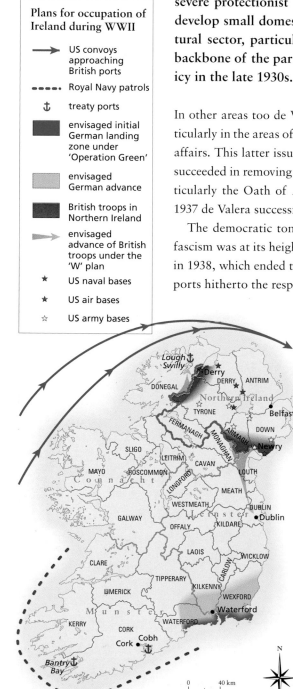

Plans for occupation of Ireland during WWII

→ US convoys approaching British ports

--- Royal Navy patrols

⚓ treaty ports

■ envisaged initial German landing zone under 'Operation Green'

■ envisaged German advance

■ British troops in Northern Ireland

➤ envisaged advance of British troops under the 'W' plan

★ US naval bases

★ US air bases

☆ US army bases

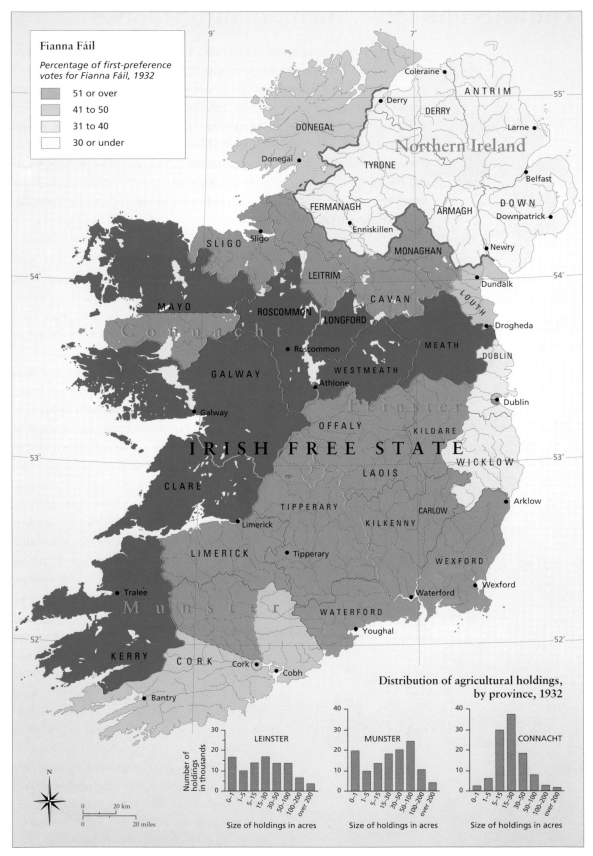

Fianna Fáil

Percentage of first-preference votes for Fianna Fáil, 1932

- 51 or over
- 41 to 50
- 31 to 40
- 30 or under

Northern Ireland

IRISH FREE STATE

Distribution of agricultural holdings, by province, 1932

LEINSTER

Number of holdings in thousands

Size of holdings in acres

MUNSTER

Size of holdings in acres

CONNACHT

Size of holdings in acres

The '40s and '50s: Turmoil and Malaise

THE 1950s in Ireland were characterized above all by severe economic difficulties, difficulties which were exacerbated by the political instability of the period. Having only experienced two, single-party governments during the first 25 years of the state's existence, three short lived governments (two 'inter-party' coalitions and one Fianna Fáil minority administration) now followed each other in quick succession. None of these cabinets was able to get to grips with the enormous problems facing the country during the period, although in 1949 the first inter-party government did take the dramatic step of formally declaring a Republic. The political scene during these years was dominated by a number of crises, most famously the 'Mother and Child' debacle of 1951, when a proposal to reform the health care provided to expectant mothers and young children collapsed amidst political indecision and pressure from the Catholic Church and the medical profession.

Such a political situation provided a decidedly unhelpful context in which to address the enormous economic problems facing the country. Foremost amongst these was a resurgence in emigration, which reached levels not witnessed since the 1880s and which came to symbolize the failure of the Irish state to provide a basic standard of living for its citizens, contrary to the hopes and expectations of those who had campaigned so hard for its independence. This increase in emigrants was due to a combination of factors, most notably the increasing use of machinery in rural areas which reduced the demand for farm labour, the lack of indigenous industrial development in urban centres and the enormous demand for labour in the major industrial centres in Britain. All these factors conspired to siphon off enormous numbers of young Irish men and women, with the poverty-stricken areas of the western seaboard being particularly badly affected.

While some efforts were made to arrest this loss of population, which was accentuated by a decline in the marriage rate, there was little scope for innovative policy given the restrictions imposed by the prevailing economic orthodoxies. It was only with the election in 1959 of Seán Lemass as Taoiseach and leader of Fianna Fáil in succession to de Valera (who was subsequently elected to two terms as President of Ireland) that the almost hermetically-sealed nature of the Irish economy and society was finally opened up to external influences.

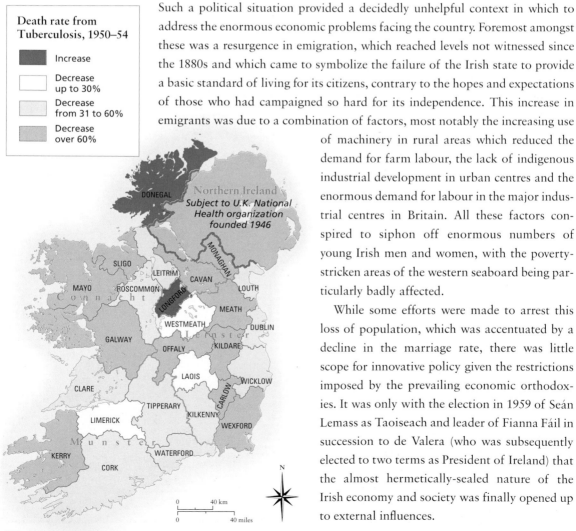

Death rate from Tuberculosis, 1950–54

- Increase
- Decrease up to 30%
- Decrease from 31 to 60%
- Decrease over 60%

Northern Ireland
Subject to U.K. National Health organization founded 1946

DONEGAL

SLIGO
LEITRIM
CAVAN
MONAGHAN
MAYO
ROSCOMMON
LONGFORD
LOUTH
Connacht
MEATH
WESTMEATH
GALWAY
OFFALY
DUBLIN
KILDARE
Leinster
LAOIS
WICKLOW
CLARE
CARLOW
TIPPERARY
KILKENNY
LIMERICK
WEXFORD
Munster
KERRY
WATERFORD
CORK

0   40 km
0   40 miles

N

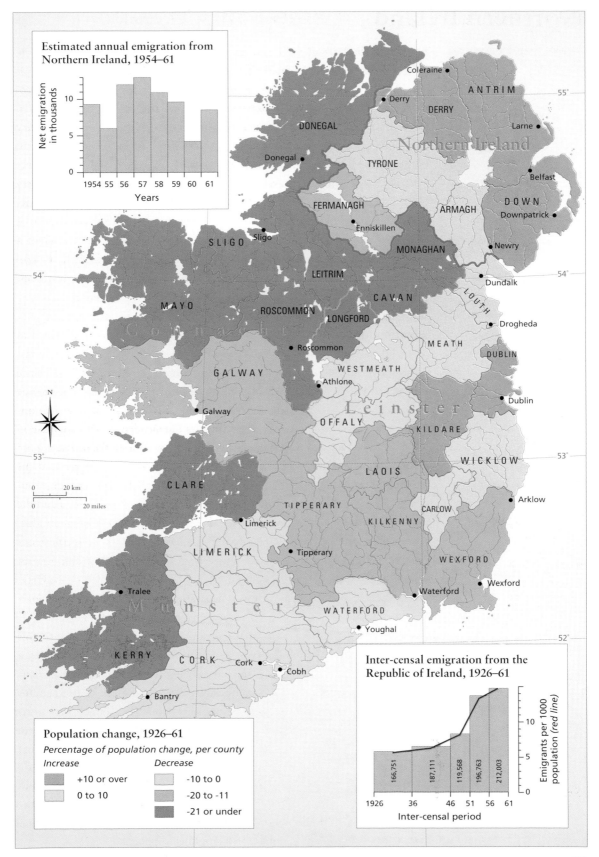

Estimated annual emigration from Northern Ireland, 1954–61

Net emigration in thousands

Years

Inter-censal emigration from the Republic of Ireland, 1926–61

Emigrants per 1000 population (*red line*)

166,751	187,111	119,568	196,763	212,003

1926 · 36 · 46 · 51 · 56 · 61

Inter-censal period

Population change, 1926–61

Percentage of population change, per county

Increase

+10 or over

0 to 10

Decrease

-10 to 0

-20 to -11

-21 or under

0 20 km

0 20 miles

N

Northern Ireland

Above: James Craig, Lord Craigavon, the first Prime Minister of Northern Ireland.

BY THE LATE 1950s the six county 'statelet' of Northern Ireland, established under the 1920 Government of Ireland Act, had also performed very badly in terms of social and economic development. One of the reasons for this stagnation was the nature of the original political settlement. Born out of Unionist opposition both to Home Rule and republican separatism, the territory encompassed by the state was a compromise between the historic nine county province of Ulster and the four counties where Protestants enjoyed numerical superiority over the Catholic community. The presence of substantial Catholic communities in border areas presented the new government (led by Sir James Craig) with severe difficulties, particularly during the years 1922–23 which were marked by severe communal violence. The confirmation of the border in 1925, by means of a tripartite agreement with the Free State and British cabinets (in return for which Dublin received financial concessions) meant that the Unionist government in Belfast was free to turn its attention to the consolidation of state and party interests.

Almost immediately complaints began to emerge regarding the abuse of the rights of the Catholic/nationalist minority. These complaints were concentrated in particular on electoral arrangements, which, it was suggested, were manipulated in the interests of the Unionist Party; on public and private employment, which Catholics alleged was characterized by severe religious discrimination; on security arrangements, which seemed at times geared more towards the suppression of political dissent rather than criminal activity; and on education, where, for a number of reasons Catholic schools received less financial assistance than their state-sponsored Protestant counterparts. While some of these grievances may have been exaggerated it seems clear that the political aspirations of the general Catholic community were regarded with hostility at the highest levels of the Northern state.

The decision of the Stormont government to participate in the Second World War drove a further wedge between it and neutral Éire. The experience of wartime industrial and military mobilization, and the tragedy of the Belfast Blitz, inevitably placed an emotional distance between north and south, a distance confirmed by the 1949 Ireland Act, which guaranteed the maintenance of the state so long as it enjoyed majority support. Notwithstanding the poor economic performance of the 1950s there seemed little danger that the government, now headed by Sir Basil Brooke, was in any danger of losing such support.

Below: Inter-communal violence has a long and depressing history in Northern Ireland. This newspaper headline dates from 1935, at which time the tradition of civil unrest was already almost a century old.

Religious denomination per county, 1926 and 1971

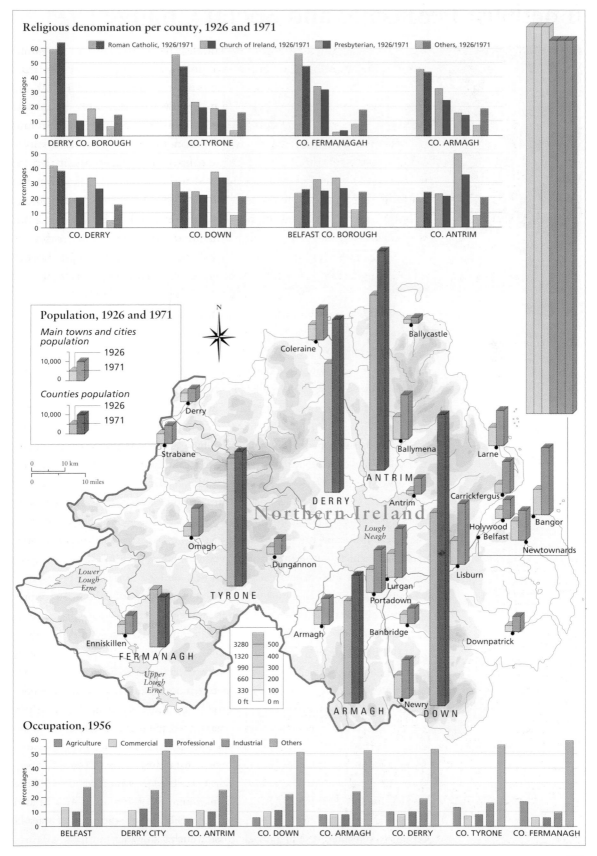

Roman Catholic, 1926/1971 · Church of Ireland, 1926/1971 · Presbyterian, 1926/1971 · Others, 1926/1971

DERRY CO. BOROUGH · CO.TYRONE · CO. FERMANAGAH · CO. ARMAGH

CO. DERRY · CO. DOWN · BELFAST CO. BOROUGH · CO. ANTRIM

Population, 1926 and 1971

Main towns and cities population

10,000 — 1926 / 1971

Counties population

10,000 — 1926 / 1971

0 10 km
0 10 miles

Northern Ireland

Coleraine · Ballycastle · Derry · Strabane · Ballymena · Larne · ANTRIM · Omagh · Antrim · Carrickfergus · Holywood · Belfast · Bangor · Dungannon · Lough Neagh · Lisburn · Newtownards · TYRONE · Lurgan · Portadown · Enniskillen · FERMANAGH · Lower Lough Erne · Upper Lough Erne · Armagh · Banbridge · Downpatrick · ARMAGH · Newry · DOWN

3280 500 / 1320 400 / 990 300 / 660 200 / 330 100 / 0 ft 0 m

Occupation, 1956

Agriculture · Commercial · Professional · Industrial · Others

BELFAST · DERRY CITY · CO. ANTRIM · CO. DOWN · CO. ARMAGH · CO. DERRY · CO. TYRONE · CO. FERMANAGH

The '60s: Economic and Social Change

A MAJOR DEPARTURE in economic policy in the Republic occurred with the publication in 1958 of the Programme for Economic Expansion. This report (which was followed by two more ambitious programmes) advocated the abandonment of self-sufficiency in favour of an economic policy based on free trade, with the emphasis now on increased exports and the attraction of foreign investment into Ireland.

Above: Jack Lynch (Taoiseach 1966–73, 1977–79) signing the treaty of accession to the European Economic Community on behalf of the Republic of Ireland in 1973.

In economic terms the new policy proved very successful, with output and employment reaching levels never before recorded in the history of the state, although both small farmers and those employed in the old 'protected' industries did not share equally in the new prosperity. Emigration fell and a substantial number of those who had left in the 1950s now returned to the country. People started to marry at an earlier age than theretofore, and the birth rate began to fall.

Not surprisingly these economic and demographic changes heralded new patterns of social development. Perhaps the most important was the establishment in 1961 of a national television station, Radio Telefís Éireann, which provided a forum for social and political debate hitherto rather lacking. Evidence of new thinking was also evident in religious practice building on the deliberations of the Second Vatican Council; in educational policy, with the introduction of free secondary education; in the area of gender relations, with new opportunities opening up for Irish women; in the field of popular culture, with exposure to new styles of music, literature and art, frequently imported from Britain and America and less subject to stultifying censorship; and in the party political field, with a new emphasis upon technocratic management at the expense of old-style nationalist rhetoric.

Not everything had changed, however, and not all change was progressive: the new materialist ethos inevitably meant that those on the margins of Irish society could not fully share in the new-found wealth. Many of the 'gains' of the period proved rather ephemeral, particularly when the international economic climate turned sour in the 1970s. That said, the 1960s were characterized by a social dynamic, which, while not revolutionary, was certainly a welcome change from the atrophied atmosphere of the 1950s. The decision to enter the EEC, overwhelmingly endorsed by popular referendum in 1973, seemed to symbolize this new era although such support was undoubtedly more the result of rational economic self-interest than any new-found interest in wider European affairs.

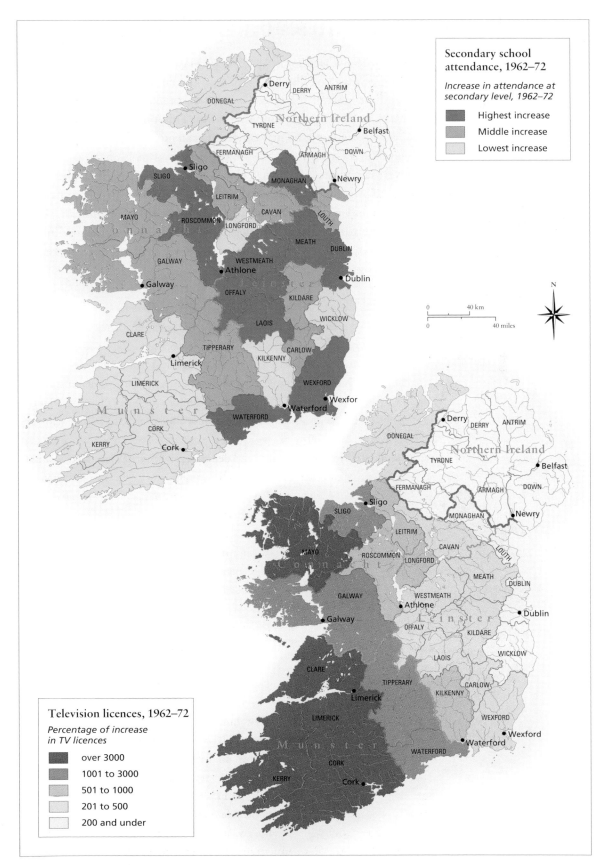

Secondary school
attendance, 1962–72

*Increase in attendance at
secondary level, 1962–72*

Highest increase
Middle increase
Lowest increase

Television licences, 1962–72

*Percentage of increase
in TV licences*

over 3000
1001 to 3000
501 to 1000
201 to 500
200 and under

The '70s and '80s: Political and Social Instability

The expansionist economic policy heralded by the First Economic Programme was dependent on a benign international trading environment, and for most of the next 15 years such was indeed the case. When this basis was destroyed by the 'stagflation' (high inflation accompanied by increasing unemployment) which afflicted most developed economies following the oil price rise of 1973, the country was plunged once more into severe economic difficulties. Over the next 15 years, through a combination of a series of international depressions, massive government borrowing, and a decline in the financial assistance forthcoming from the European Community (which affected rural areas particularly badly) the country experienced economic turmoil which threatened to undermine the progress made in the 1960s.

Such instability was evident in the political as well as the economic field. Having experienced 15 years of uninterrupted Fianna Fáil government between 1958 and 1973 the country now experienced a series of coalitions and short-term minority administrations (with the exception of the landslide Fianna Fáil victory of 1977, which was to be tarnished within two years by a series of internal disputes), with seven General Elections being held between 1973 and 1989.

The 1980s also witnessed a new style of political debate in the country, focused in particular on the provisions of the 1937 Constitution and which saw bitterly-contested referenda in 1983 (on the issue of abortion) and 1986 (on the issue of divorce). A host of new political issues also came to the fore, particularly with regard to the quality of the environment and the provision of local services. Few administrations devised satisfactory long-term solutions to these thorny problems, and a resurgence in emigration in the late 1980s bore eloquent testimony to the sense of crisis within the Irish body politic.

It was not all doom and gloom, however, and a number of developments in the sporting and cultural fields highlighted the latent potential beneath the political stalemate. The international acclaim earned by a series of Irish authors, playwrights and musicians was mirrored by a number of sporting successes, perhaps most notably the achievements of the national football team in reaching the finals of the European Championships in Germany in 1988 and the World Cup in Italy in 1990, events which gave rise to massive, spontaneous outpourings of national pride.

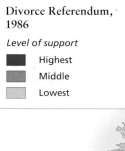

Divorce Referendum, 1986

Level of support

- Highest
- Middle
- Lowest

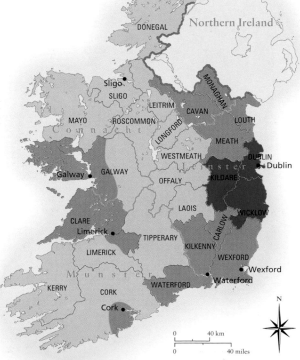

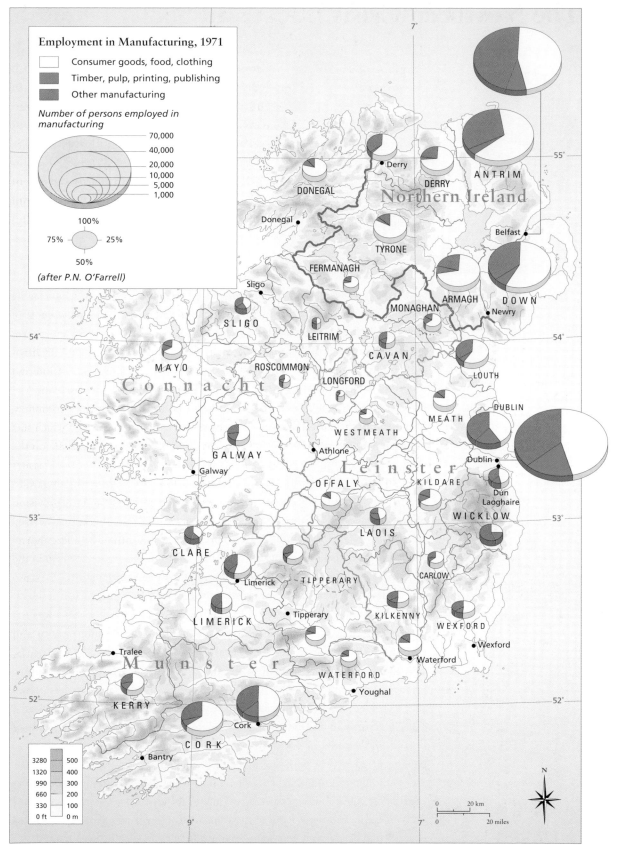

Employment in Manufacturing, 1971

Consumer goods, food, clothing
Timber, pulp, printing, publishing
Other manufacturing

Number of persons employed in manufacturing

70,000
40,000
20,000
10,000
5,000
1,000

100%
75%   25%
50%

(after P.N. O'Farrell)

Derry

DONEGAL

DERRY   ANTRIM

Northern Ireland

Donegal

Belfast

TYRONE

FERMANAGH

Sligo

MONAGHAN   ARMAGH   D O W N

SLIGO   LEITRIM   Newry

C o n n a c h t   CAVAN

MAYO   ROSCOMMON   LOUTH

LONGFORD

MEATH   DUBLIN

WESTMEATH

GALWAY   L e i n s t e r   Dublin

Galway   Athlone   Dún
Laoghaire

OFFALY   KILDARE

WICKLOW

CLARE   LAOIS

Limerick   T I P P E R A R Y   CARLOW

LIMERICK   Tipperary   KILKENNY

WEXFORD

M u n s t e r   Waterford   Wexford

Tralee   WATERFORD

Youghal

KERRY

Cork

C O R K

Bantry

3280   500
1320   400
990   300
660   200
330   100
0 ft   0 m

N

0   20 km

0   20 miles

127

The Northern Crisis

Above: Margaret Thatcher and Garret FitzGerald, whose governments negotiated the Anglo-Irish Agreement of 1985 which gave Dublin an input into the affairs of Northern Ireland, much to the fury of unionists.

THE 1960s were a decade of frustrated hope for Northern Ireland. Beginning with the promise of a new era based on improved economic performance and greater harmony between the Catholic and Protestant communities, these policies, associated with Captain Terence O'Neill, who was appointed Prime Minister in 1963, foundered on the rocks of social and political intransigence.

The frequent confrontations between Catholic Civil Rights demonstrators and Protestant opponents produced an increasingly tense atmosphere which erupted into open communal violence in 1969, in which year the British Army was deployed in Northern Ireland in an effort to restore calm.

Unfortunately, as a consequence of such mis-judged policies as the Falls Road curfew and internment without trial, the opposite occurred and the six counties experienced a spiral of violence which culminated in 1972 with an orgy of shootings and bombings unparalleled since the violence of 1922–23. Particularly prominent in these disturbances was a number of paramilitary groupings, most notably the Provisional IRA (an extreme republican organization) and the Ulster Defence Association (an equally ruthless loyalist force).

In an effort to deal with the deteriorating situation the British government prorogued Stormont and commenced 'direct rule' from Westminster. A series of initiatives followed — the Sunningdale Agreement (1973), the Power Sharing Executive (1974), the 'Rolling Devolution' plan of the early 1980s — each of which acknowledged the complexity of the situation but none of which could command cross-community support. The Anglo-Irish Agreement of 1985 institutionalized the recognition accorded by the British government to the legitimate interest of the Irish government in Northern Ireland, but notwithstanding such intermittent progress the violence associated with the unrest continued, with deaths from 'the Troubles' eventually exceeding 3,000.

A glimmer of light emerged in the late 1980s when provisional talks were arranged between the major parties as part of the 'three-strand' process, which acknowledged the three principal elements of the problem — the internal divisions in Northern Ireland, the relationship between the north and south of Ireland, and the issue of British/Irish relations. A major breakthrough appeared to have occurred in 1994, with the calling of cease-fires by both republican and loyalist paramilitary groups, but the opportunity was lost as a consequence of time-consuming political disagreements, and the IRA bomb attack on Canary Wharf in London in February 1996 seemed unfortunately to signal that the 'peace process' had been yet another false dawn for the people of Northern Ireland.

The Northern Crisis

1. *October 1968: Civil Rights march conflicts with police*
2. *January 1969: march attacked*
3. *August 1969: British troops deployed*
4. *July 1970: Falls Road curfew*
5. *August 1971: Internment swoop*
6. *January 1972: 'Bloody Sunday'*
7. *July 1972: 'Bloody Friday'*
8. *May 1974: Car bomb*
9. *January 1976: 10 workmen shot dead*
10. *August 1976: Peace People movement starts*
11. *1978: 'Dirty protest' by prisoners*
12. *August 1979: 18 paratroopers killed in explosion*
13. *August 1979: Lord Mountbatten assassinated*
14. *1980–81: hunger strikes*
15. *1982: 17 people killed in bombing*
16. *November 1985: Anglo-Irish Agreement signed*
17. *May 1987: 8 IRA members shot*
18. *November 1987: 11 killed at War Memorial bombing*
19. *January 1992: 8 killed in IRA bombing*
20. *October 1993: Shankill Road bombing*
21. *October 1993: Grey Steel shootings by Loyalists*
22. *1995–98: Orangemen march on Drumcree*

Seats Won at the General Election, 1997

- United Kingdom Unionist
- Ulster Unionist Party
- Social Democratic and Labour Party
- Democratic Unionist Party
- Sinn Féin

Ireland in the New Millennium

It is fair to say that Ireland emerged at the turn of the third Millennium as a more complex and rapidly changing society that at any time in its modern history. The Age of the Celtic Tiger had truly arrived. The population is now one of the most youthful in Europe, emigration has been reversed, new industries are daily established, old forms of religious faith and practice are coming under sustained pressure. Such social and economic change is also evident at the political level, with the emergence of a new cross-party economic consensus and a general blurring of traditional party lines derived from the Civil War period. Perhaps no other event highlighted this process of change more than the election in 1990 of Mary Robinson as President of Ireland. Female, an avowed liberal, youthful – she personified the challenge to the inherited patterns of power and authority in the country, and though many felt that the end of her seven-year term might herald a return to an earlier style of presidency, instead the challenge posed by President Robinson was maintained by her equally vibrant successor Mary McAleese.

Below: Mary Robinson's surprise success in the 1990 presidential elections broke the mould. A champion of women's rights, a left-of-centre social progressive, her victory shook the conservative, male-dominated, religious and Republican hold on Irish politics.

But while evidence of change is to be seen in abundance even amidst such contemporary dynamism powerful echoes of the national past remained. Perhaps the most abiding come from Northern Ireland, where the long-running failure to successfully implement the Good Friday Agreement of 1998 illustrated the difficulty of moving from entrenched positions. But there are other, more subtle and engaging expressions of continuity – the influential position occupied by agriculture in the national economy, the vibrancy of traditional forms of sport and culture, the impulse towards a satisfactory definition of nationality – in these and myriad other forms historic Ireland continues to exercise a degree of influence over the direction in which modern Irish society is moving. It seems reasonable to suggest that this tension between continuity and change, between fidelity to tradition and the accommodation of innovation, will continue to be a hallmark of the Irish experience of future generations as it has been of the past.

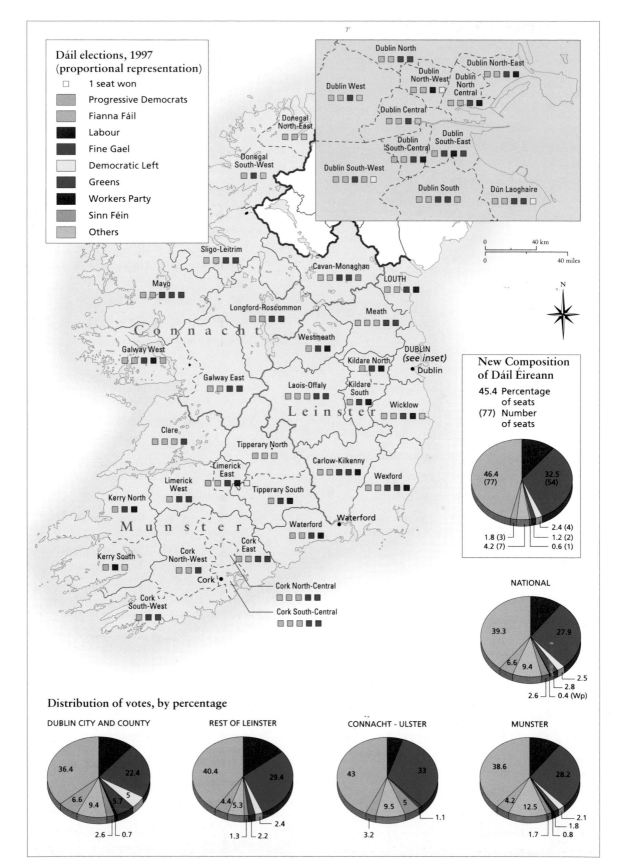

Dáil elections, 1997
(proportional representation)

- □ 1 seat won
- Progressive Democrats
- Fianna Fáil
- Labour
- Fine Gael
- Democratic Left
- Greens
- Workers Party
- Sinn Féin
- Others

New Composition
of Dáil Éireann

45.4 Percentage
of seats
(77) Number
of seats

46.4 (77) 32.5 (54)
2.4 (4)
1.8 (3) 1.2 (2)
4.2 (7) 0.6 (1)

NATIONAL

39.3   27.9
6.6
9.4
2.5
2.8
2.6 0.4 (Wp)

Distribution of votes, by percentage

DUBLIN CITY AND COUNTY

36.4   22.4
5
6.6
9.4   5.7
2.6 0.7

REST OF LEINSTER

40.4   29.4
4.4 5.3
2.4
1.3 2.2

CONNACHT - ULSTER

43   33
9.5 5
1.1
3.2

MUNSTER

38.6   28.2
4.2
12.5
2.1
1.8
1.7 0.8

Chronology

8,000 BC	First people arrive in Ireland, perhaps across the land bridge from Scotland.
3,000 BC	Arrival of New Stone Age people who built Newgrange.
c. 200 BC	Arrival of speakers of what develops into Gaelic.
AD 78–84	Roman Governor of Britain, Agricola, considers the invasion and conquest of Ireland.
c. 130–80	Ptolemy's account of Ireland.
367	Major offensive on Britain by the Irish, Picts and Saxons.
431	Pope sends Palladius as bishop to Irish Christians.
432	St Patrick arrives to help convert pagan Gaelic kings to Christianity (traditional date).
c. 550–650	The growth of monasticism in Ireland.
563	Foundation of Iona by Columba.
575	Convention of Druim Ceat.
7th and 8th centuries	Ireland's Golden Age, *Book of Durrow, Book of Kells,* Ardagh Chalice.
c. 670–700	Tírechán and Muirchú produce hagiographical works on St. Patrick.
697	Synod of Birr and the proclamation of the 'Law of the Innocents'.
c. 700	The Eóganacht become dominant in Munster.
721–42	Cathal mac Finguine King of Munster.
c. 725	Uí Briúm dynasty gain dominance in Connacht.
734	Abduction of Flaithbertach mac Loingsig. Cenél Conaill now excluded from Uí Néill overkingship.
743	Clann Cholmáin first take the overkingship of Uí Néill.
795	First Viking raid on Iona, Rathlin, Inishmurray and Inishbofin.
806	Vikings murder 68 members of Iona community.
820–47	Feidlimid MacCrimthainn King of Munster.
836	Viking raids penetrate deep inland.
837–42	Large Vikings fleets appear and overwinter on the Boyne, the Liffey, Lough Neagh and in Dublin.
842	First reported Viking-Irish alliance.
845	Abbot of Armagh captured by Vikings.
846–62	The reign of Máel Sechnaill I, powerful Overking of Uí Néill.
914	The Second wave of Viking raids.
980	Máel Sechnaill II becomes Overking of Uí Néill.
975–1014	Brian Boru King of Munster.
997	Brian Boru and Máel Sechnaill II divide Ireland.
999	Brian Boru defeats the Leinstermen and the Ostmen at Glenn Máma. Sitric Silkenbeard, King of Dublin, surrenders.
1002–14	Brian Boru King of Ireland.
1014	Death of Brian Boru at the Battle of Clontarf.
1142	Foundation of the first Cistercian house in Ireland.
1169	Arrival of English military leaders, FitzStephen, FitzGerald and others.
1170–71	Arrival of 'Strongbow' in person. Strongbow becomes King of Leinster. Arrival of Henry II. Submission of most Irish bishops and Irish Kings.
1175	Treaty of Windsor between Henry II and Rory O'Connor High King of Ireland, who submits to rule unoccupied regions as a vassal.
1176	Death of Strongbow.
1177	Prince John made Lord of Ireland — first visit 1185.
c. 1200	Start of Classical Irish period in literature, lasting until 1600.
1210	King John's second visit. Confiscation of the Earldom of Ulster and Honor of Limerick — submission of some Irish kings.
1260	Battle of Down, death of Brian O'Neill.
1261	Battle of Callan.
1315	Invasion of Ireland by Edward Bruce. Proclaimed by Irish allies as King of Ireland.
1316	Rebellious Irish Chiefs defeated at Athenry.
1318	Battle of Dysert O'Dea. Battle of Faughart, Edward Bruce killed.
1333	Murder of Earl of Ulster, William de Burgh. Crown looses control of Anglo-Norman Connacht and the Irish Chiefs in Ulster.
1366	Statutes of Kilkenny to try and prevent English settlers adopting the Irish language 1394–95 King Richard II's first expedition to Ireland.
1414–47	Continual feud between political groupings of James Butler, fourth Earl of Ormond and John Talbot Earl of Shrewsbury, for control of Royal government of Ireland.
1494	In the wake of Anglo-Irish support for Perkin Warbeck, Henry VII dismisses Kildare in 1492. Lord Deputy, Sir Edward Poynings, establishes 'Poynings Law' making all English parliamentary legislation applicable to Ireland.
1496	Kildare reappointed.
1504	Battle of Knockaoe. Kildare victorious.
1509	Accession of Henry VIII.
1515	Anarchy sweeps Ireland.

1534	The Kildare Rebellion leads to Kildare's arrest and death. Lord Offaly takes leadership of revolt.
1536	Fall of Maynooth Castle — arrest of Lord Offaly and five uncles (all brought to England).
1536–37	Meeting of the Irish Reformation Parliament.
1540	Sir Anthony St Leger becomes Governor of Ireland.
1541	A Parliamentary meeting declares Henry VIII King of Ireland. The establishing of the 'Surrender and Re-grant' programme.
1558	Accession of Elizabeth I following the death of Mary I. The strong state support Reformation unpopular in Ireland.
1565–71	Sir Henry Sidney governor of Ireland.
1569–71	Parliament declares the Lordship of Tyrone under the power of the Crown. Thus leading to revolts in Munster, Leinster and Connacht against the policy.
1571–75	Sir William FitzWilliam Governor of Ireland.
1573	Private Colonisation ventures continue in Ulster.
1576	Reappointed Sidney launches conciliatory policy halting any further private colonization.
1579–80	Rebellion in Munster. Exacerbated by a second revolt in Leinster led by James Eustace, Viscount Baltinglas and Feagh Mac Hugh O'Byrne. Support from discontented Palesmen. Arthur Lord Grey de Wilton is given the position of Governor to deal with the 'dual revolt'. Defeated at Glenmalure in Wicklow but success at Smerwick.
1582–83	The suppression of both revolts at Munster and Leinster culminates in the killing of Earl of Desmond.
1595	Rebellion of Hugh O'Neill, Earl of Tyrone.
1598	O'Neill victorious at Yellow Ford, Ulster.
1601	O'Donnell, O'Neill and Spaniards defeated by Mountjoy at the Battle of Kinsale.
1603	The assession of James I leads to the enforcement of English Law in Ireland, especially Ulster. Hugh O'Neill and Earl of Tyrone surrender.
1607	The 'Flight of the Earls', O'Neill, Earl of Tyrone, O'Donnell, Earl of Tyrconnell.
1608	Plantation of Derry (City of London). Six other confiscated counties planned.
1641	Great Catholic-Gaelic rebellion for return of lands. Ireland thrown into chaos.
1642	Irish suppression hoped for by English Parliament with the 'Adventurers Act'. Robert Munro and army land in Ulster in April. Civil War in England. Catholic Confederation assembles at Kilkenny.
1649	Execution of Charles I. Cromwell's arrival in Ireland leads to capture of Drogheda, Wexford, New Ross. There follows a Cromwellian conquest and subsequent implementation of plantations.
1658	Death of Cromwell.
1660	Restoration period — accession of Charles II. Uphold Cromwellian conquest but restore property to 'innocent papists'.
1665	'Act of Explanation' obliges grantees of Cromwell to surrender one third of their lands to 'innocents'.
1685	Accession of James II.
1686–87	The newly appointed Earl of Tyrconnell, Richard Talbot, replaces Protestant officials with Catholics.
1688	Deposition of James II in England. Gates of Derry closed to James' troops.
1695	Fourteen per cent of Irish land held by Catholics. Rights of Catholics restricted in education, arms-bearing, horse owning and the Catholic clergy banished.
1699	Acts restricting Irish woollen exports.
1704	Catholics' presence restricted in landholding and public offices.
1713	Jonathan Swift becomes Dean of St Patrick's.
1728	Act removing franchise from Catholics.
1741	First performance of Handel's *Messiah* in Fishamble Street Music Hall.
1775	Henry Grattan leader of Patriot Party.
1782	Irish Parliament successful in gaining 'legislative independence' from British.
1791	Wolfe Tone's *Argument on behalf of the Catholics of Ireland*. Leads to foundation of Society of United Irishmen.
1792	Relief Act allows Catholics to practice law.
1796–98	United Irishmen plotting rebellion. Rebellion in Wexford in May. Humbert lands in Killala in August. Tone arrested and dies in November.
1800	Act of Union — Ireland governed henceforth by Westminster.
1803	Robert Emmet's rising, trial and execution.
1822	Irish Constabulary Act (establishing county police forces and a salaried magistracy).
1823	Catholic Association founded, led by Daniel O'Connell.
1828	O'Connell elected for County Clare.
1829	Catholic Emancipation passed.
1837	Accession of Queen Victoria.

1840   O'Connell's Repeal Association founded.

1842   *The Nation* newspaper founded by Thomas Davis.

1843   O'Connell's 'Monster Meetings' for Repeal of the Union.

1845   Blight in the potato harvest. Beginning of Great Famine (1845–49).

1846   Repeal of Corn Laws. August sees Public Works started but stopped due to expectation of new harvest. Total failure of potato harvest. Public Works restarted. October sees first deaths from starvation.

1847   Foundation of Irish Confederation. Free rations first handed out from Government soup kitchens. Thus leading to distress thrown on localities.

1848–49 Worst years of Great Famine. Rebellion by Young Ireland movement. Battle of the Widow MacCormack's Cabbage Garden at Ballingarry.

1858   After James Stephens returns from France he establishes the Irish Republican Brotherhood. Fenian Brotherhood founded in the U.S.A.

1861   Beginning of American Civil War.

1866   Archbishop Paul Cullen becomes the first Irish Cardinal.

1867   Attempted Fenian rising.

1869   Disestablishment of the Church of Ireland by W.E. Gladstone.

1870   Gladstone's first Land Act recognizing tenant's right (August) and the foundation of Home Government Association by Isaac Butt (September).

1875   Charles Stewart Parnell elected MP for County Meath.

1879   Threat of famine in Ireland. Irish National Land League founded, instigated by Michael Davitt, widespread evictions.

1879–82 Land War.

1881   Gladstone's second Land Act.

1891   Parnell marries Katharine O'Shea (June), dies at Brighton (October).

1893   Second Home Rule Bill. Gaelic League founded.

1898   United Irish League founded.

1900   John Redmond elected chairman of Irish Parliamentary Party and United Irish League.

1907   Dockers' strike and riots in Belfast.

1914   Illegal importation of arms by Ulster Volunteers and Irish Volunteers. Buckingham Palace conference collapses just before outbreak of World War I.

1915   Reorganization of the Irish Republican Brotherhood and formation of military council formation (December).

1916   Irish Republic proclaimed in Dublin (24 April). There follows martial law, rebel surrender, imprisonments and 15 executions. The Ulster Division also loses significant numbers in the Battle of the Somme.

1917   The Irish Convention ineffectual and Sinn Féin and Irish Volunteers reorganize.

1918   The General Election sees Republican success and the formation of Dáil Éireann in following January.

1920   The Government of Ireland Act introduces partition between two Home Rule states. Dublin's 'Bloody Sunday'.

1921   IRA setback. King opens Northern Ireland Parliament in Belfast. Sir James Craig Prime Minister in Northern Ireland. A truce is called. December witnesses Anglo-Irish Treaty.

1922   Convention of Anti-Treaty IRA. 'Special' powers given to Northern Ireland police. National Army given emergency powers after murder of Collins. Irish Free State established, Northern Ireland excluded.

1923   End of Civil War — IRA 'dump arms'. Free State admitted to League of Nations.

1924   National Army re-organization, cutbacks and mutiny.

1925   Partition confirmed by tripartite agreement.

1926   De Valera founds Fianna Fáil. General election in Free State.

1929   Proportional representation abolished in Northern Ireland.

1930   Irish Labour Party and TU Congress separate.

1931   Banning of the IRA in Free State.

1932   In the general election Fianna Fáil prove successful.

1933   National Guard (Blueshirts) formed. United Ireland Party (Fine Gael) formed under O'Duffy (Blueshirts leader).

1934   Cosgrave reinstated as O'Duffy resigns.

1935   Importation and sale of contraceptives banned in Free State.

1936   Free State Senate abolished.

1937   Constitution of Éire replaces Free State.

1938   UK agree to subsidise Northern Ireland Social Welfare payments to UK standards.

1939   IRA bombing campaign on Great Britain in World War II. Éire neutral.

1940	Death of IRA hunger strikers in Éire. Anglo-Irish military consultations. Economic sanctions imposed on Éire.
1941	The most destructive German air raids on Belfast and Dublin. Death of James Joyce.
1945	Congress of Irish Unions formed after split in Trade Union Congress. Churchill's and de Valera's radio speeches post-World War II.
1946	Northern Ireland National Insurance in align with Great Britain.
1948	NHS introduced in Northern Ireland — Irish Republic enacted after Costello's repeal of External Relations Act. Fianna Fáil lose election, de Valera out of office after 16 years.
1949	Ireland Act, agreement that partition will be perpetuated.
1954	IRA attacks in Armagh.
1955	Republic admitted to UNO.
1956–62	Border campaign initiated by IRA.
1958	First programme for economic growth in the Republic.
1961	Republic unsuccessful in joining EEC.
1964	Lemass-O'Neill talks held on reconciliation.
1966	Anglo-Irish Free Trade Agreement.
1967	NI Civil Rights Association founded.
1968	First Civil Rights march. Clash in Derry between CRA and police. O'Neill's programme for the removal of discrimination of Catholics in local government, housing and franchise.
1969	People's Democracy march from Belfast to Derry in January. There follows a series of explosions. Chichester Clark becomes Prime Minister. British troops sent in.
1970	Dublin Arms Trial. Splits in Sinn Féin and IRA lead to provisional factions setting up.
1971	Paisley's Democratic Unionist Party founded. Re-introduction of internment. First British soldier killed by IRA in Belfast.
1972	Following Derry's Bloody Sunday in January, Direct Rule is imposed.
1973	Republic, UK and NI join EEC. Proportional representation restored in NI (December). Sunningdale Agreement.
1974	Multiple deaths in Dublin bombing. Guildford and Birmingham pub bombings in Nov. and Dec.
1975	NI internment suspended.
1976	British ambassador in Dublin killed. Republic's Emergency Powers Bill referred to Supreme Court by President.
1978	Twelve killed by Provisionals' fire bombs in a County Down restaurant.
1979	Earl Mountbatten and relations killed in County Sligo. Eighteen soldiers killed at Warrenpoint, County Down. Relaxation of Republic's ban on contraceptives.
1979	Visit of Pope John Paul II.
1981	Following the death of Republican hunger-strikers, the Provisionals' strategy of 'H-block' protests collapses.
1982	Mass killings of soldiers at Knightsbridge (July) and Ballykelly, County Derry, (December).
1983	Referendum bans abortion in Republic.
1985	Bitter Protestant disagreement over Anglo-Irish Agreement at Hillsborough.
1986	Confirmation of Republic's ban on divorce.
1987	Eleven killed before Enniskillen service on Remembrance Sunday.
1989	Fianna Fáil form coalition government for the first time in their history following general election. Their partners are the Progressive Democrats. Charles Haughey remains Taoiseach.
1990	Republic of Ireland reach quarter-finals of the soccer world cup in Italy under the management of Jack Charlton.
1990	Mary Robinson elected seventh President of Ireland, the first woman to hold the office.
1992	Dr Eamon Casey, bishop of Galway, flees country after it was revealed that he had fathered a child in the course of an affair nearly 20 years previously. The first of a succession of sexual scandals that eroded the authority of the Catholic Church in the course of the decade
1994	IRA and Loyalist paramilitary groups announce ceasefire.
1996	In the Republic of Ireland, a constitutional referendum to permit civil divorce and re-marriage is carried narrowly.
1996	End of IRA ceasefire.
1997	Following Labour victory in British general election, Dr Marjorie (Mo) Mowland appointed first woman Secretary of State for Northern Ireland.
1997	Fianna Fáil-PD coalition under Bertie Ahern replaces Rainbow coalition (Fine Gael, Labour, Democratic Left) following general election in the Republic.
1997	IRA declare a resumption of the 1994 ceasefire (July).

Further Reading

Aalen, F. H. A., Kevin Whelan & Matthew Stout (eds), *Atlas of the Irish Rural Landscape,* Cork University Press, 1997.

Andrews, J. H., *Ireland in Maps,* Dolmen Press, 1961.

Bagwell, Richard, *Ireland Under the Tudors,* Longman, 1885–90. *Ireland Under the Suarts,* Longman, 1909–16.

Bardon, Jonathan, *A History of Ulster,* Blackstaff, 1992.

Barnard, T. C., *Cromwellian Ireland: English Government and Reform in Ireland, 1649–60,* Clarendon Press, 1975.

Bradshaw, Brendan, *The Irish Constitutional Revolution of the Sixteenth Century,* Cambridge University Press, 1979.

Brown, Terence, *Ireland: a Social and Cultural History, 1922–79,* Fontana, 1981.

Buckland, Patrick, *A History of Northern Ireland,* Gill and Macmillan, 1981.

Byrne, F. J., *Irish Kings and High-Kings,* Batsford, 1973.

Canny, Nicholas P., *The Elizabethan Conquest of Ireland: A Pattern Established, 1565–76,* Harvester Press, 1976.

Curtis, Edmund, *A History of Medieval Ireland,* Barnes and Noble, 1983.

de Paor, Máire and Liam, *Early Christian Ireland,* Thames & Hudson, 1978.

Duffy, Seán, *Ireland in the Middle Ages,* Gill and Macmillan, 1997.

Ellis, Steven G., *Tudor Ireland: Crown, Community and the Conflict of Cultures, 1470–1603,* Longman, 1985.

Foster, R. F. , *Modern Ireland, 1600–1972,* Penguin, 1988. (ed) *The Oxford Illustrated History of Ireland,* Oxford University Press, 1989.

Gillespie, Raymond, *Colonial Ulster: The Settlement of East Ulster, 1600–1641,* Cork University Press, 1985.

Harbison, Peter, *Pre Christian Ireland*, Thames &
Hudson, 1988. (ed) *The Shell Guide to Ireland*,
Macmillan, 1989.

Kelly, James, *Prelude to Union: Anglo-Irish Politics in the
1780s*, Cork University Press, 1992.

Kinealy, Christine, *This Great Calamity, The Irish
Famine, 1845-52*, Gill & Macmillan, 1994.

Lee, Joseph, *Ireland, 1912–85*, Cork University Press, 1989.

Lennon, Colm, *Sixteenth-Century Ireland*, Gill and
Macmillan, 1994.

Lydon, James, *The Lordship of Ireland in the Middle
Ages*, Gill and Macmillan, 1972.

Lyons, F. S. L. (ed), *Ireland since the Famine*, Fontana, 1973.

Meeham, Bernard, *The Book of Kells*, Thames &
Hudson, 1994.

Mitchell, Frank, *The Shell Guide to Reading the Irish
Landscape*, Country House, 1986.

Moody, T. W., F. X. Martin and J. F. Byrne (eds), *A New
History of Ireland*, 9 vols, Clarendon Press, 1976–.

Ó Corráin, Donncha, *Ireland before the Normans*, Gill
and Macmillan, 1972.

O'Kelly, M. J., *Early Ireland*, Cambridge University
Press, 1989.

Orpen, G. H., *Ireland under the Normans*, 4 vols,
Oxford University Press, 1912–20.

O'Ríordáin, S. P., *Antiquities of the Irish Countryside*,
Methuen, 1979.

Otway-Ruthven, A. J., *A History of Medieval Ireland*,
Ernest Benn, 1968, 1980.

Stalley, Roger, *The Cistercian Monasteries of Ireland*,
Yale University Press, 1987.

Woodham-Smith, Cecil, *The Great Hunger*, Hamish
Hamilton, 1987.

Index

References in this index in **bold** face are for maps or pictures

A

Agricultural holding (1841 and 1911), **105**
distribution, by province (1932), **119**
Airgialla, 18
Anglo-Irish Agreement (1985), 128
Anglo-Irish Treaty (1921), 98
Anglo-Norman, invasion, 12
lordship, 50
Anglo-Saxons, 22
Anglo-Scottish Union (1707), 72
Annegray, 22
Antrim, 14
Ardagh chalice, 20
Armagh, 16
ecclesiastical province, 28
Arrival of Christianity, **17**
Augustinians, **32**
Auxilius, 16

B

Bagenal, Henry, 60
Bann, 18
Barrow, 18
Battles
Athenry (1316), **42**
Baggot Rath, (Rathmines), 66
Boyne, **68**
Clontarf, 26
Down, **41**
Somme, 112
Yellow Ford (1598), **60**
Beckett, Samuel, **98**
Bede, 22
Belfast
blitz on, 122
Falls Road, 128
linen mill constructed, 88
Unionist government in, 122
'Black and Tans', 114
Black death, 44, **45**
Blueshirts, 118
Bobbio, 22
Boyle, Henry, 80
Breifne, kingdom of, 36, 40
Brendan, St, 20
Brian Boru (Brian Boruma), 12, 30, 48
'emperor of the Irish', 26
campaigns of, **27**
Bríon, 18
British Army, deployed in Northern Ireland, 128
Bronze Age, 10
Brooke, Sir Basil, 122
Bruce, Edward, 42
defeated at Dundalk (1318), 42
Bruce invasions, **43**
Burntcourt, Co. Tipperary, plantation mansion, 66
Butler family, 35, 44, 46
Butt, Isaac, 106

C

Caledon House, Co. Tyrone, 73
Cambrensis, Giraldus, 32
Canary Wharf, London bomb
attack on, 128
Carew, Sir Peter, 58
Carrickfergus castle, Co. Antrim, **33**
Carson, Sir Edward H., 110
Cashel, 11, 18, 28
Catholic Association, 74, 84
Catholic emancipation and repeal, **85**
Catholicism, 19th-century, **87**
Celtic peoples, appearance in Ireland, 11, 14
language, P-Celtic, Q-Celtic, Gaelic, 14
Cennerig mac Lorcain, King of Thomond, 26
Charlemagne, 22
Charles I, King of England, executed (1649), 66
Charles II, King of England, 66
Charles the Bald, 22
Christianity, introduction of, 11, **17**, 18
spread of, 22
first encounter, 16
Church of Ireland (Anglican), 108
Church reform, the Gregorian movement, 28
Ciaran, St, 20
Cistercians, 32
Civil War, 114
Clare. *see* de Clare
Clare, County, 84
Clarendon, Lord Deputy, 68
Clonard, motte, **38**
Clontarf, battle of (1014), 12, 26, 48
Cnobesburh, 22
Collins, Michael, 114
Columba, *see* Colum Cille, 22
Columbanus, St, 22

Colum Cille, St, 20, 22
Connacht, 14, 18, 56, 86, 88
Connolly, James, 112
Cork city, 114
Cornwall, 11
Cosgrave, William T., **116**
Council of Trent (1545), 54
Countess of Ormond,
    carving, **38**
Craig, James, Lord
    Craigavon, **108**, 110, 122
Crannóg, lake-dwelling, 11
Cromwell, Henry, 66
Cromwell, Oliver, 53, **66**, **67**
Cumann na nGaedheal, 116,
    119
Curragh, mutiny, 110
Custom House, destruction
    of, 114

D

Dáil Éireann, 114, 116
    composition of (1997), **131**
    distribution of votes by per
    cent (1997), **131**
    election (1997), **131**
Dal Cais (dynasty), 26
Dal Riata, of Antrim, later of
    Argyll, 14, 16
    colony in Scotland, 16
    Scottish Kingdom, 22
Danes, 24
Dark Age, 11
Davitt, Michael, Land League
    leader, 108
Death rate, from tuberculosis,
    120
de Burgh, 42, 44
de Cantwell, Thomas, effigy
    of, **34**

Declaratory Act (1719), 71, 80
de Clare, Richard FitzGilbert,
    (Strongbow), 34, 12
    seal of, **36**
de Courcy, John, 33
Déisi, 16
Derry, name changed to
    Londonderry (1613), 62
    siege of, 68
Derrynaflan chalice, 20
Desmond, Earl of, 58
Devenish, round tower, 24
de Valera, Éamon, president,
    97, **112**, 114, 116, 118, 120
Dicuil, scholar, 22
Divorce referendum, 126
Down, 14
    battle of (1260), **41**
Downpatrick, 18
Drogheda, parliament held at,
    46, 64, 66
Dublin
    American Embassy, protest
    at, **98**
    Áth Cliath, ford of the
    hurdles', 48
    'Bloody Sunday', 114
    capital of country, 12, 48
    Castle, English
    headquarters, 48, 76, 86
    Charles II, proclamation as
    King, 66
    citizens' homage to Lord
    Deputy, 56
    Clontarf, Battle of (1014),
    12, 26, 48
    Custom House, destruction
    of, 114
    de Valera, Eamon, arrest of
    (1916), 122
    Duibhlinn, 'black pool', 48
    Easter Rising (1916), 112,
    112

empire, second city of, 48
Elizabethan
    administration, reform of,
    56
English, capture of (1170),
    36,48
English power, centre of, 50
Fingal (Fine Gall, 'the
    territory of the
    foreigners'), 48
Fishamble Street
    excavation, 30
Four Courts, attack on
    (1922), 114
Gaelic League premises in,
    94
growth of, 49
Henry II, King of England,
    in, 36
Irish political
    adminstration in, 99
kingship of, 30
military attacks on, 40, 42,
    66
Murray, Catholic bishop
    of, 86
new public buildings (18th
    century), 78
Ostmen revolt, 26
Pale, part of, 46
port expansion, 26
state ball, **70**
University of (Trinity
    College), 54, 66
Viking activity in, 12, 24
Volunteers in College
    Green, **71**
Wide Streets
    Commissioners, 78
Wood Quay excavation, **30**

E

Early Peoples and Politics, **19**
Easter Rising (1916), 112, **113**
Economic Expansion,
    programme for, 124
Economy,
    Pre-famine, (1821–41), **89**
    Georgian, 78, **79**
Edward III, 46
Elizabeth I, Queen of
    England, **52**, 54
Emergency, the, (World War
    II), 118
Emain Macha, 11, 14, 16, 18
Emigration, 90, **91**, 99, **103**,
    121
England, Normans conquer,
    32
English invasion, (1169), **37**
Eóganachta, 12, 18
Érainn, 14, 18
Ériu, 14
Eriugena, Johannes Scottus,
    22
Essex, earl of, 58, 60
European Economic
    Community, later
    European Union, 99, 124

F

Famine, 92, **93**
Fiachra, 18
Fianna Fáil, 116, 120, 126
Fiatach, Dál, 14
Finian of Clonard, 20
FitzGerald, Garret, **128**
FitzGerald, settler family, 35,
    42, 44, 46

Fleetwood, Charles,
    parliamentary
    commissioner, later Lord
    Deputy, 66
Flood, Henry, 78
Free Trade, 124

G

Gaelic
    culture, 44, 52
    church, hereditary clerical
    families, 54
    landholders, 58
    lordships, 50
    territories become shires,
    56
Gaelic Athletic Association,
    106, **107**
Gaelic League (Conradh na
    Gaeilge), 94, 106
Galloglass (gall-óglach,
    'foreign warrior'), 40
Galway, County, 14, 16,
Gaul, 16
General Election (1923), **117**
George IV, King, 84
George V, King, **114**
Gladstone, William E., 108
Golden Age, the, **21**
Government of Ireland Act,
    (1920), 114
Grandison, Lord, **75**
Grattan, Henry, **84**
Great War, (1914–18), 112,
    113
Gregorian, reform movement,
    12
Griffith, Arthur, 114

H

Harland and Wolff, shipyard,
    104
Haughey, Charles, **99**
Heaney, Seamus, 98
Henry II, King of England
    (1133–89), 12, 34,
    lands at Waterford, 1171,
    36
Henry VII, King of England,
    35, 46
Henry VIII, King of England,
    35, **50**, 54
Hiberno Scandinavian rulers,
    48
High king, of all Ireland, 11
    king of Tara, 18
Home Rule, 108, 110, 112,
    122
Households, percentage
    Catholic (1732), 76
House of Lords, British, 110

I

Ierne, 14
Inis Mór, 20
Iona, 22
Ireland, plans for the invasion
    of, WW II, **118**
Ireland Act (1949), 122
Ireton, Henry, 66
Irish (Brehon) law, 28
Irish Church, 12, 16, 20
    churchmen and scholars in
    Europe, **23**
    Viking plundering, 14
Irish colonies, 11
Irish Free State, 114, 116

Irish language, 44, 94, **95**

Irish Nationalism, growth of, **107**

Irish Parliamentary Party, in British parliament, 110

Irish Republican Army, 114, 128
guerrilla war, (*c.* 1919), 114

Irish Republican Brotherhood, 106

Iron Age, 14

Island of saints, 11

Iverni, 14

J

James I, King of England, 62

James II, King of England, 68

John, Lord of Ireland, later King of England, 34

Joyce, James, **98**

K

Kells, Book of, 18

Kells–Mellifont, Synod of (1152), 28

Kennedy, John F., **97**

Kilashee (Cill Usailli), 16

Kildare, 18, 20

Kilkenny, Statutes of, 35
federation of, 64

Kinsale, Spanish landing (1601), 60

L

Laigin, *see* Leinster

Land Acts, 108

Land annuities, 118

Land holdings (1841) and (1911), **105**

Land League, 108

Land Legislation (1870–1903), **108**

Land question, **109**

Laon, 22

La Tène style, 11, 14

Latin language, 18

Leighlinbridge, Co. Carlow, **46**

Leinster, 88
colony, 16
King of, 12
over kingdom, 18
Vikings in, 24

Lemass, Seán, 120

Liberal Party, British, 108, 110

Limerick, Treaty of, 68, 76

Lindisfarne, 22

Lionel of Clarence, 46

Lombardy, 22

Lough Neagh ship camp, 24

Luxeuil, 22

Lynch, Jack, 124

M

Mac Lochlainn, Muirchertach, 30

MacMail na mBo, Diarmait, King of Leinster, 30, **32**

Mac Murchada, Caomtranach Art, (Art McMurrough Kavanagh) King of

Leinster, 35

Mac Murchada, Diarmait, Leinster king, 12, 30, 36

MacMurrough, dynasty, Wicklow Mountains, 42

Máedoc, of Ferns, 20

Máel Sechnaill mac Domnaill, high king of Ireland, 26, 30

Maguire, Hugh, 60

Manufacturing, employment in (1971), **127**

Mayo, English colonies established, 42

Megalithic monuments, 10

Mellifont, Treaty of (1603), 60

Mesolithic period, 10

Molyneux, William, 72

Monasteries, 22

Monasticism, 20, 22

Mountjoy, Lord, 60

Mourne Mountains, 18

Muiredach's Cross, 20

Mullingar workhouse, numbers in (1845–50), **93**

Munster, 26, 28, 50, 56
and Vikings, 12, 24
famine in, 92
plantation, 58

N

Naas, royal site, 16

New English, community, **53**

Newfoundland, emigration to, **90**

Newgrange, passage tomb, Co. Meath, **10**

Niall Noígiallach, **18**

Neolithic peoples, 10

Neutrality, policy of, 118 *see*

also Emergency
Normans, 32, **34**
Norsemen, 24
Northern Ireland, 110, 112,
    114, 116, 122
    border ratified (1925), 116
    troubles, 128
    emigration from (1954–61),
    121
    general election (1997), **129**
Northumbria, 22

O

O' Connell, Daniel, **84**, 106
O' Connor, Aed, 40
O'Connor, Rory, high-king,
    12, 36, 40
O'Donnell, Hugh Roe, 60
Ogham script, 16
O'Higgins, Kevin, 116
Old English, community, 53,
    54, 56, 58, 60
O'Neill, Brian, 40
O'Neill, Captain Terence, 128
O'Neill, Hugh, Earl of
    Tyrone, **60, 61**
O'Neill, Sir Phelim, **64**
Ormond, peace of (1646), 64
O'Rourke, Tigernán, King of
    Breifne, slain, 40
Ostmen, 26

P

Pale, English, 46, 50, 54
Palladius, deacon of Auxerre,
    16
Parliament, colonial, 1297, 42

Irish, abolished (1650s), 66
Parliamentary army, English,
    lands in Ireland (1647), 64
Parnell, Charles Stewart, **96,**
    106
Partition, 96
Pearse, Pádraig, 112
'Peep O'Day Boys', 82
Penal laws, 76, **77**, 86
Péronne, Picardy, 22
Picts, 22
Pitt, William, 84
Plantations, 58, **59**, 62, **63**
Ponsonby, John, **80**
Poor Law Unions (1848–51),
    93
Pope Urban II, 32
Population, 88
    change, (1926–61), **121**
    females outnumber males,
    102
    growth by province
    (1821–41), **89**
    male–female (1851–1911),
    103
    1926–71, **123**
Potatoes, 92
Power sharing executive
    (1974), 128
Poynings' law, 71, 80
Poynings, Sir Edward, 46
Promontory forts, 11
Protestant Reformation, 54, **55**
Ptolemy, 14, 18

R

Radio Telefís Éireann, 124
Raths, 11
Redmond, John, E., 110
Reformation, Protestant, 54, **55**

Repeal Association, 84
Republic, declaration of, 120
Richard II, King of England,
    34, **35**, 46
Ring fort, 11
Rinuccini, Giovanni, Papal
    Nuncio, 64
Robert I, King of Scotland, 42
Robinson, Mary, President,
    130
Roman Empire, 11, 16
Rosserk, Co. Mayo,
    Franciscan Friary, 44

S

St Aidan, 22
St Augustine, 28
St Benedict, 22
St Brigid, 20
St Columbanus, 22
St Enda, 20
St Firsa, 22
St Gall, 22
St Malachy Ua Morgair,
    Bishop, 28
St Ninian, 20
St Patrick, 11, 16
St Patrick's Cathedral, **48**
Scandinavia, influence, 24
Sceilg Mhicil (monastery), 20,
    24
Scotland, Normans in, 34
Secondary School attendance,
    (1962–72), **125**
Secundinus, 16
Sedulius Scottus, scholar, 22
Separation, (1916–23), **115**
Shannon hydro-electric
    scheme, 116
Shaw, George Bernard, 98

Simms, J. G., 71
Simnel, Lambert, 46
Sinn Féin, founded (1905), 106, 114, 116
Smith, Sir Thomas, 58
Society of United Irishmen, 82
Solemn League and Covenant, 110
Statutes of Kilkenny, 35, 44
Stephen, King , 36
Stormont, 122, 128
Strongbow, *see* de Clare, Richard
Stuart dynasty, 53
Sunningdale Agreement (1973), 128

T

Tara, 14, 18, 30
Television licenses, (1962–72), **125**
Thatcher, Margaret, **128**
Tone, Theobald Wolfe, 82
Topographia Hiberniae, **32**
Trinity College (University of Dublin), 54, 66
Tuam, archbishopric (1152), 28
Tudor dynasty, 50
    conquest of Ireland, 53
Turoe Stone, 14
Tyrconnell, earl of, Lord Deputy, 68

U

Ua Briain, Tairdclbach, Brian Boru's grandson, 30

Uí Briúlin, 18
Ua Conchobhair, Ruaidri, 12
Ua Conchobhair, Tairdelbach, 30
Uí Chennselaig, 18
Uí Dúnlainge, 18
Uí Fiachrach, 18
Uí Liatháin, 16
Uí Néill, leading dynasty, 11, 34
    high kingship, 12
    origins, 18
    Northern, 26, 30
    Southern, 26
Ulaid, 14, 18
Ulster, 14, 56, 62, 68, 78, 82
    concentration of Protestants in, 110
    distribution of Protestants and Catholics (1911), **111**
    gun running, 110
    invaded (1315), 42
    linen workers, 88
    Ulster Volunteer Force, 110, 112
    Ulster Defence Association, (UDA), 128
Union, act of (1800), 74, 75, 84, 106
United Irishmen, 72, 82, 106

V

Vikings, 12
    attacks, 24, **25**, 26
    Danes compete with Norse, 24
    raiders, 32
    settlement, 24
    warship, 24
Volunteering, 80, **81**

W

Wales, 11, 12, 36
Waterford, 24, 36, 66
Western Scotland, 11
Westminster, (British Parliament), direct rule from, 128
Wetenhall, Edward, bishop of Limerick, 76
Wexford, 16, 82
Wide Streets Commissioners, 78
Wilde, Oscar, **99**
'Wild Geese', **68**
Williamite Revolution, **69**
William of Orange, later King William III of England, **53**, 68
World Cup, soccer, 126
World War I. *see* Great War
World War II. *see* Emergency

Y

Yeats, W. B., 99
York, 24
Young Ireland movement, 106

Acknowledgements

THE PUBLISHERS would like to thank to following for the photographs and illustrations produced in this atlas:

Peter Newark's Historical Pictures, Bath, England: 14, 24, 26, 28, 35, 50, 52, 53, 56, 60, 62, 64, 66, 68, 71, 73, 78, 82, 90, 92, 94, 96, 102.
Other photographs and illustrations:
Con Brogan
Industrial Development Agency of Ireland
National Gallery of Ireland
National Library of Ireland
National Museum of Ireland
Private Collections
Trinity College, Dublin

For Arcadia Editions Limited:

Design and Cartography: Peter Gamble
                        Elsa Gibert
                        Isabelle Lewis
                        Jeanne Radford
                        Malcolm Swanston
                        Jonathan Young

Editorial: Shirley Ellis
           Andrew Lavender
           Elizabeth Wyse

Illustration: Peter Massey
              Peter Smith

Typesetting: Jeanne Radford

Dance Umbrella
The First Twenty-One Years

Bonnie Rowell

Photographs by
Hugo Glendinning
Chris Harris
Chris Nash

DANCE BOOKS
Cecil Court London

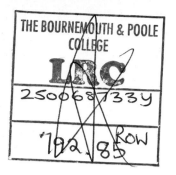
Published in 2000 by
Dance Books Ltd
15 Cecil Court
London WC2N 4EZ

ISBN 1 85273 077 3

A CIP catalogue record for this book
is available from the British Library

Editing: Rod Cuff
Design: Sanjoy Roy

SUPPORTED BY
THE NATIONAL LOTTERY
THROUGH
THE ARTS COUNCIL
OF ENGLAND

Printed in Great Britain by
H. Charlesworth & Co. Ltd, Huddersfield

Contents

Foreword and Acknowledgements   viii

Introduction   1

1   Foundations and Diversifications   13

2   The Early Years: 1978–1984   29

3   The Europeans Make their Mark: 1985–1989   63

4   An International Festival: 1990–1994   95

5   A New Role for Dance Umbrella: 1995–1999   127

Appendix 1: Listings by Year   165

Appendix 2: Digest of Events, Innovations and Themes   239

Appendix 3: Dance Umbrella Personnel   242

Appendix 4: Dance Umbrella Board of Management   246

Appendix 5: Dance Artists in Education Conference, 1979   249

Notes to the Chapters   250

Select Bibliography   255

Index   256

Illustrations

Five Car Pile Up, devised by artist-in-residence Yoshiko Chuma, 1984.   x

Eiko (of Eiko and Komo) in *Fur Seal*, 1981.   12

Paper presented by Val Bourne to the Dance Theatre Subcommittee, 1977.   15

Steve Paxton at Riverside Studios, 1980.   19

First-night party, 1981.   21

Advertisement included in the 1980 Umbrella Festival souvenir programme.   22

Michael Clark in *New Puritans*, 1984.   28

Flyer for Second Stride's first US tour, 1982.   34

Douglas Dunn in his solo show *Gestures in Red*, 1978.   37

Musician David Moss with Steve Paxton, 1980.   41

Steve Paxton and Lisa Nelson, 1980.   41

Charles Moulton and Dancers in *Through Movement Motor*, 1981.   43

Karole Armitage, with Joseph Lennon, 1981.   44

Molissa Fenley in her solo programme *Between Heartbeats*, 1981.   45

Eiko and Koma in *Fur Seal*, 1981.   46

Maedée Duprès in her solo programme *Time Within Time*, 1981.   46

Jeremy Nelson and Ian Spink of the Ian Spink Group, in Spink's *De Gas*, 1981.   48

Sally Banes and Deborah Jowitt at the Dance Writing and Criticism course, 1981.   49

Tim Miller and Company in *Postwar*, 1982.   51

Rosalind Newman and Dancers, 1982.   52

Mary Fulkerson and Dancers, 1982.   53

Bill T. Jones, Arnie Zane and Company, 1983.   56

Second Stride in Ian Spink's *Further and Further Into Night*.   59

Mark Morris and Company, *Not Goodbye*, 1984.   59

Shiro Daimon in *Kabuki-Woogie*, 1984.   60

Miranda Tufnell in *Huge Veil*, 1984.   61

Compagnie Charles Cré-Ange, *Noir Salle*, 1989.   62

Laurie Booth and Nick Pile in *Terminus Terminux*, 1989.   67

Greg Nash.   68

Pauline Daniëls and Harry de Wit in *13*, 1984.   73

David Gordon rehearsing members of the Pick Up Company, 1985.   76

Miranda Tufnell, Dennis Greenwood and David Ward's *Urban Weather*, 1985.   77

Ashley Page and Gaby Agis in *Refurbished Behaviour*, 1985. 78
Jonathan Burrows in *Hymns*, 1986. 82
Lea Anderson of The Cholmondeleys in *Marina*, 1987. 85
Extemporary Dance Theatre, 1988. 86
Adventures in Motion Pictures, *Spitfire*, 1988. 89
Groupe Emile Dubois in Jean-Claude Gallotta's *Mammame*, 1989. 91
The Cholmondeleys, *Flesh and Blood*, 1989. 92
Shobana Jeyasingh Dance Company, 1992. 94
Doug Elkins, solo, 1993. 100
A member of the Newcastle Cloggies. 102
Yolande Snaith's Dance Quorum in *Court by the Tail*, 1990. 107
Stephen Petronio, *Middlesex Gorge*, 1990. 108
Shobana Jeyasingh Dance Company, 1991. 111
Laurie Booth, 1991. 112
Members of the Trisha Brown Company at Canary Wharf, 1991. 114
Paul Douglas and Gill Clarke in Siobhan Davies's *White Bird Featherless*, 1992. 116
Sue MacLennan Dance Company in rehearsal at Chisenhale, 1992. 117
Nigel Charnock and Liz Brailsford in *Original Sin*, 1993. 118
Vtol dance company, *32 feet per second per second*, 1993. 120
Javier De Frutos, *The Palace Does Not Forgive*, 1994. 122
Ricochet Dance Company, 1994. 123
Ellen van Schylenburch, solo, 1994. 124
Russell Maliphant in *Paradigm*, 1995. 126
Twyla Tharp's *One Hundreds* project at the Barbican Centre, 1998. 131
Vivian Wood in Tom Sapsford's *Where Her Voice?* 1995. 137
Say a Little Prayer, installation by Chris Nash and René Eyre, 1996. 139
Tobias Tak, studio shot. 141
Mark Baldwin Company, studio shot, 1995. 143
Cathy Quinn in Siobhan Davies's *Wild Translations*, 1995 144
Stephan Koplowitz's *Genesis Canyon* at the Natural History Museum, 1996 147
Javier De Frutos, *Transatlantic*, 1996. 149
Rosemary Butcher's *Fractured Landscapes, Fragmented Narratives*, 1997. 151
Wendy Houston in *Haunted, Daunted, Flaunted*, 1997. 153
Ricochet Dance Company, 1998. 156
Michael Clark and Susan Stenger in *current/SEE*, 1998. 158
Darshan Singh Bhuller, in Richard Alston's *Orpheo*. 162
The Featherstonehaughs, *24-Hour Featherstonehaughs*, 1994. 164
Steve Paxton at Riverside Studios, 1982. 178
Bill T. Jones and Arnie Zane Company, 1983. 182
Pauline Daniëls in her solo programme, *Profile*, 1984. 185
Katie Duck and Group O, 1985. 189
Maedée Duprès, Riverside Studios, 1986. 192
Michael Clark in *Heterospective*, at the Anthony d'Offay Gallery, 1989. 202
Douglas Wright and Company at Canary Wharf, 1991. 210
Nigel Charnock Company, 1997. 232
Mark Baldwin Dance Company rehearsing *Song of the Nightingale*, 1998. 236

Foreword and Acknowledgements

This book is intended as an overview of the work of Dance Umbrella over its first twenty-one years, documenting the events and developments initiated by this very important organisation. It also attempts to trace the changing face and attitudes of British dance over that time, by giving a flavour of each year's festival and by putting them into a context of longer-term trends and influences. Certain themes emerging from the material are concerned with artistic influence and identity, and I have organised the discussion accordingly by dividing the years into major sections. This sectioning is inevitably somewhat arbitrary, since there is considerable overlap between spheres of influence.

The book may be read in many different ways: for instance, as a straight-forward documentation of Dance Umbrella's activities since its inception, or as a discussion of Dance Umbrella's role in the development of dance in the UK since the 1970s. It could also be used as a reference book covering particular years: annual overviews are therefore led by information, rather than by strong opinion. Appendix 1 fleshes these out to provide a further informative layer, while the introductory chapter could be used as a digest for students on the context of the festivals. The charts do, I hope, provide enough detailed information of events, participants and background to enable students at all levels to gain an impression of the festivals and changes to their function and make-up through the years, as well as providing a first point of departure for researchers.

The introduction draws largely upon secondary sources, in particular two seminal overviews of modern dance in the UK: Stephanie Jordan's *Striding Out* and Judith Mackrell's *Out of Line.* The remainder draws upon festival reports, annual overviews for the Arts Council, various project reports, journal and newspaper reviews and articles, and interviews with Val Bourne. Jan Murray's *Dance Umbrella* and Stephanie Jordan's and Chris de Marigny's special edition of *Dance Theatre Journal* provided invaluable overviews of the first six and ten years respectively.

Thanks are due to my researcher, Kate Etheridge, for archive work and for her painstaking cataloguing of material in the early stages of writing the book. I would also like to thank Ann Nugent for the generous loan of some of her programmes and other resources. I am especially grateful to Stephanie Jordan, for her patience in reading the text and for her many fundamental and detailed suggestions. Lastly, Val Bourne has provided fascinating and invaluable material in interviews, has allowed me free access to Dance Umbrella documents and has read the full text, making detailed corrections and suggestions. Many thanks to her for all these things, as well as to the members of her team who dug out material and who put up with my intrusions at busy times with good humour and grace.

The documentation is as accurate as I can make it, but as in all these things, variations in spelling and information abound in the first-source material, and those last-minute changes of personnel that have come to light only serve to make me aware of the many I have missed. I have attempted to cross-check all information from at least two sources.

Val Bourne is adamant that everything that has happened, has happened as the result of a team effort, and has been quick to correct me whenever I use Dance Umbrella and her name synonymously. If this tendency persists within the text, however, it is only because of the enormous respect in which I hold her.

Bonnie Rowell

Five Car Pile Up, devised by festival artist-in-residence Yoshiko Chuma, 1984. PHOTO: CHRIS HARRIS

Introduction

Dance Umbrella burst on to the scene in 1978 with four American guest soloists and a handful of British-based dance companies and dance artists. The performances, particularly those of the Americans, provoked and astonished – it was clear that the festival organisers had hit upon a winner. Here finally was an event that met the needs of the embryonic dance community in this country for a platform on which to show and share work. It could appeal to a wider audience and draw them in, *and* be financially viable.

But this first festival was significant in other ways too. It reflected a wider scenario, and contributed to a process already under way within the arts in general. Radicalism had been rife within the other arts in the UK since the 1950s, and yet most people involved in dance seemed more intent on consolidating its hard-won position than on experimentation, most probably because the risk-taking involved in the latter raised the possibility of making mistakes and losing ground. Dance Umbrella played a crucial role in reversing this situation, but its precise contribution must be seen within the context of the complex set of circumstances presiding over dance in this country in the second half of the twentieth century.

In 1954 Martha Graham brought her modern dance company to London. With a few notable exceptions, nobody noticed. Yet by 1963 when she returned, British audiences were showing they were ready for an American-style modern dance culture. The Graham company was followed by those of Cunningham, Taylor and Ailey – José Limón and Company had visited in 1957. Robin Howard, who was among the few to have originally championed Graham,[1] was inspired to set up the London School of Contemporary Dance (LSCD) and London Contemporary Dance Theatre (LCDT) in successive

1

years. Norman Morrice, another who was moved by the Graham spirit, was able to save the fortunes of our oldest classical ballet company, Ballet Rambert, by changing to a modern dance repertoire. Scarcely had our dancers and dance students absorbed Graham-style modern technique than they showed themselves keen to explore beyond its confines. They wanted to experiment with Cunningham-style chance procedures, to absorb influences from the visual arts and from performance art, and in some cases to harness the new social consciousness and make dances with a hard-edged political message.

What had happened in those few intervening years so to change the climate within Britain that modern dance was now not only acceptable, but to many a preferred alternative to ballet? In the following decade, the 1970s, a new generation of dancers and dance-makers emerged who were keen, in Richard Alston's words, to 'align dance with the other arts'[2] – that is, to catch up with the radicalism apparent within the arts in post-war Britain and to accord to dance a similar status. The reasons for this rapid genesis are of course complex, involving an adolescence for dance that was very swift indeed. Audiences could not always keep up with the fast development of this sometimes recalcitrant youth and neither for that matter could arts providers and funding bodies. It was at this point in the late 1970s that Dance Umbrella started to play its part. It has continued up to the present day – guiding, protecting, supporting, educating – and changing roles as and when necessary. A brief survey of the years leading up to the first festival will help to locate the Dance Umbrella organisation within the emergence of what amounted to a 'modern period' in dance in the UK as well as to explain and underline its importance.

Teachers and Visitors

Exposure to forms of dance other than ballet had begun as a trickle during the first half of the century, increasing to a small but steady stream during the 1960s and 1970s thanks largely to Robin Howard. In between there were several significant developments. There had been an interest in 'barefoot' dancing (one might even say a vogue for it) from around the 1920s, with classes and performances either inspired by Isadora Duncan or more directly influenced by her through her brother Raymond. Strong and influential women inspired by Duncan, such as Madge Atkinson, her pupil Anita Hayworth, Ruby Ginner and Margaret Morris, set up schools of what we now identify as 'early modern' dance and promoted styles such as 'Natural Movement'. Their influence extended between the wars and was primarily within education, therapy and recreation rather than theatre, although all these women were performers.

There had also been an infiltration of ideas from both American and European modern dance traditions, from teachers such as Margaret Barr and Dorothy Madden, who taught respectively Graham- and Humphrey-style techniques during the 1930s.[3] Kurt Jooss and his company had been based at Dartington from 1933; his strength had been in the synthesis of classical and modern dance. The Hungarian teacher and choreographer Rudolf von Laban came to England in 1938, initially to continue working with his collaborator Jooss. He founded his Art of Movement Studio in Manchester in 1946, then later in Addlestone, Surrey, from which his methods were continued by a second generation of important educators, Lisa Ullmann and Marian North. However, it was in the area of modern educational dance that Laban was to have the most influence in this country, and not as a choreographer. On the other hand, Jooss's 1932 ballet *The Green Table* was enormously influential, not least on Ninette de Valois, director of the Vic–Wells Ballet as it was then known. Nevertheless, ballet *classicism* remained the most influential form at this time and it seemed that all the dance world's energies were committed to the promotion of a traditional form with classical values. Some would argue that this was an understandable ploy, when our classical companies had such a short history.

Post-war Regeneration

After World War II things changed rapidly. The economy was booming, encouraging full employment to such an extent that a larger work force was needed. People were encouraged to immigrate to Britain during the 1950s, mainly from the West Indies and from South Asia at this stage, and this infiltration was to have an enormous influence on British culture in later years. Arts spending increased and experimental projects were supported and encouraged. All this added up to a confident and forward-looking climate in the arts, under which musicians, visual artists, writers and theatre directors all explored new subject matter and questioned existing forms – for a short time, at least.

Critiques of society appeared in film as well, with the Boulting brothers' *I'm All Right Jack* in 1959 and the film version of *Room at the Top* with its daring treatment of sex and class. Jerome Robbins's *West Side Story* to music by Leonard Bernstein and lyrics by Steven Sondheim opened in London in 1958, with the film version following in 1961. This musical combined balletic virtuosity with jazz energy in a way previously unseen in this country. The imagination of young British audiences responded to the vibrancy of its dancing, and to the storyline that heralded a new social realism on the musical stage quite distinct from the escapist musicals of the war years.

The economic expansion continued into the 1960s, but along with it came a population expansion. The 'baby boom' of the immediate post-war era led to a generation of teenagers numerically far larger than before in relation to the population as a whole, and consequently with real economic power for the first time. The result was a huge expansion in interest in popular culture – in pop music and fashion. Andy Warhol provided album covers for the Velvet Underground and the Rolling Stones, while the Beatles turned to our own Peter Blake for the cover of their *Sergeant Pepper* album. Thus popular music and pop art joined forces, and not for the last time. There was also a new political awareness with the student demonstrations of 1968 and renewed interest in feminism, sparked in this country by Germaine Greer's *The Female Eunuch* (1970).

Meanwhile in dance, Stephanie Jordan[4] recalls that Graham's film *A Dancer's World* (1957) was available and being promoted in Britain during the 1960s, thus enabling a generation of enlightened teachers to show children alternative and exciting ways of expressing themselves in movement. But the major developments of this period lay in the establishment of two modern-dance companies together with the activities of a new generation of dance students.

Companies, Schools, Collectives and More Visitors

After the 1964 influx of American companies came many that were based on a post-Cunningham aesthetic. Yvonne Rainer appeared at the Commonwealth Institute in 1965; Twyla Tharp, Sarah Rudner and Margaret

Jenkins all appeared at the Royal College of Art in 1967. In the 1970s Yvonne Rainer, Lucinda Childs and Trisha Brown all visited. These choreographers displayed what was becoming known as post-modern dance to a British audience that had scarcely had time to absorb modernism. Some of our own emergent choreographers, however, were more than willing to take these new ideas and run with them. This was thanks largely to a new supportive modern dance culture, with structures either instigated by an enlightened outsider such as Howard,[5] or resulting from like-minded individuals banding together for mutual benefit, as in the case of X6.

London Contemporary Dance Theatre

London-based entrepreneur and dance enthusiast Robin Howard established the LSCD in 1966. Originally he had promoted a series of moveable classes, which found a permanent address first in Berner's Place off Oxford Street, then at its present home, The Place, in Duke's Road near Euston. The LCDT was established the following year under the Graham Company dancer and choreographer Robert Cohan. Both company and school had originally a strong Graham commitment, but the early intake of students to the school included some with a background in the visual or other arts who were eager to explore beyond its confines from the very beginning. For instance, Richard Alston and Siobhan Davies had both attended art school prior to their dance training, and Sally Potter had a keen interest in film-making. Howard also encouraged experimentation and cross-fertilisation with the other arts, so the early years at The Place saw enormous experimental fervour.[6] Many of the early students went on to found small independent companies such as Strider and Extemporary Dance Theatre, or they became associated with the New Dance movement, with the festivals of the late 1970s and ultimately with Dance Umbrella itself.

A variety of styles were taught in these early years.[7] Teachers at Berner's Place included Merce Cunningham, Viola Farber and Margaret Jenkins for brief periods. Teachers at The Place in Euston included Rosalind Newman, while Alwin Nikolais and Murray Louis gave lecture demonstrations. Regular classes included those in Cunningham, Limón and Nikolais techniques and there were workshops for dancers, musicians, designers, actors and theatre directors, some of them open to the public. Howard brought Twyla Tharp to the School in 1967, where she held open rehearsals. Meredith Monk came in 1972 and mounted a huge performance piece (*Juice* from 1969), which Richard Alston recalls included 'hundreds of students [it was actually about thirty] doing things all round the building . . . you kind of found them as you went around'.[8]

Thus there emerged from this environment a number of choreographers and dancers who were to become significant in their own right during the 1970s as well as important contributors to the Dance Umbrella festivals. Alston, Davies and Potter have already been mentioned, but we may add to these Lloyd Newson (who was to found DV8 Physical Theatre), Emilyn Claid, Fergus Early and Maedée Duprès (who were all founding members of the X6 collective). Claid went on to become artistic director of Extemporary Dance Theatre and later an important independent artist. Early went on to found the community dance company Green Candle.

Ballet Rambert

Ballet Rambert gained the distinction in 1966 of becoming Britain's first major modern dance company. Choreographer and artistic director to the company, Norman Morrice, talked Marie Rambert into changing the repertoire of the ailing ballet company to a modern one. Morrice had been influenced also by Graham, this time as a result of having studied in the United States. The company always retained its ballet links, however. It preserved many dances from its older repertoire, for example Antony Tudor's *Dark Elegies* (1937), programming them alongside choreography by the American Glen Tetley. From the early years, too, it forged a strong and important link with design artists and musicians. In 1967 Morrice instituted the first *Collaborations* in which young choreographers were given the opportunity to show work they had made with students from the Central School of Art and Design. Rambert dancers and choreographers were to provide programmes for early Dance Umbrella festivals as well as feature in some of the choreographic platforms of new work.

Dartington College

Dartington Hall in Devon had provided a base for both Rudolf Laban and Kurt Jooss and company. In 1963 it established a course for teachers of modern dance based on the Graham technique and taught by Flora Cushman. American dancer and choreographer Mary Fulkerson was appointed the main movement tutor for the Theatre Department in 1973. She radically altered the style and structure of the course in favour of release-based movement – a technique evolved from a more relaxed way of moving that avoids unnecessary tensions or forced posture and is often based upon imaging, to help the dancer become more aware of the body's physical structure.

Fulkerson attracted a succession of American colleagues to teach alongside her at the college. One was Steve Paxton, who was regularly giving classes in contact improvisation. This was a way of moving developed by Paxton himself only a few years earlier, strongly related to release work in terms of its aesthetic but based upon partnering. Paxton became a full-time teacher at the college between 1978 and 1980. Richard Alston was closely associated with the course during the late 1970s, and contact improvisation greatly affected his attitude to movement and to the dancing body within his choreography at that time. Other choreographers who were to become stalwarts of the experimental dance stage in general and of Dance Umbrella in particular either trained at Dartington or had some connection with it. Rosemary Butcher, for example, trained under Cushman in the pre-Fulkerson days, while Sue MacLennan, Laurie Booth, Miranda Tufnell and Yolande Snaith were all Dartington–Fulkerson students. There was another radical movement afoot, however, this time started largely and perhaps surprisingly by ballet-trained dancers.

Balletmakers Ltd, X6 and New Dance

As early as 1963 Teresa Early founded a group, Balletmakers Ltd, that ran weekly composition classes and workshops for student and professional choreographers, independent of the larger ballet-based companies.[9] Those it attracted were mainly from the Royal Ballet and the Ballet Rambert, dancers and choreographers whose opportunities for making work at that time were limited. By the mid-1960s, however, this group had become more and more interested in modern dance techniques. Dancers felt liberated to create new, ambitious and experimental work, and in some ways this group served as a forerunner for the New Dance movement in the UK.

The X6 collective[10] derived its name from the X6 dance space in the London Docklands where members used to meet, exchange ideas and hold classes and workshops up until 1980 when it moved to Chisenhale. Its founding members were Claid, Duprès, Fergus Early (brother of Teresa), Jacky Lansley and Mary Prestidge. Many, such as Claid, Early and Lansley, had become disenchanted with the opportunities open to them within their earlier ballet careers and had gone on to train or to teach at The Place alongside Duprès. Prestidge, a gymnast and member of the Ballet Rambert, met this group later. From the very beginning they were committed to radicalism and polemical subject matters, and feminist themes often featured. They offered classes and workshops in alternative forms, and dances were dedicated to democratic, non-hierarchical structures performed in small, intimate dance spaces where the audience was very often integrated into the performance. This movement became known as New Dance, after the magazine of that name edited by the group from 1977 to September 1988 in which issues concerning the nature and function of dance were hotly disputed. New Dance deliberately distanced itself from American post-modern dance and sought a distinctly British character.

Judith Mackrell makes the important point that X6 was run as a collective, in keeping with their radical politics.[11] This extended from the ways in which organisational decisions were made to the ways in which dances very often were made, developing out of input and ideas from a number of people and credited to all of them.

*   *   *

All this activity resulted in a number of independent dancers wanting to show their work to a wider audience, and also in a proliferation of small companies. Some originated from the new LSCD graduates, but there were other new companies that were regionally based and regionally funded: for example, Cycles, EMMA and Ludus Dance Company in Education. For financial reasons, the Arts Council was encouraging the more established companies such as Rambert and LCDT to tour as much as possible, and heavy touring schedules were having a demoralising effect on the dancers because of inadequate facilities at many of the venues and high injury rates as a consequence.[12]

So although there was a great deal of creative activity in dance at this time, its supporting structures were inadequate. To make matters worse there were cuts in government expenditure all round, but particularly for the arts, which the government of the day regarded as a luxury. America was seen as the economic model; over there, modern and experimental dance seemed to be flourishing under the banner of free enterprise. In answer to this invidious situation a number of festivals were instigated on the American Dance Festival model.

Festivals

ADMA Festival

Even though money for the arts was generally being cut, there was a proportionate increase in money available for project grants in 1977. The Association of Dance and Mime Artists was founded in September 1976, as a 'kind of trade union' for dancers. It acted as an information-sharing body and as a pressure group for funding, modelled on similar organisations that had been successful in promoting and advancing fringe theatre groups. Jordan notes that the organisation was started as a support structure for independent and new dancers and to counteract what was perceived as the Arts Council's hostility towards new and experimental work in the mid-1970s.[13]

The organisation ran only two festivals, both of which received Arts Council grants and took place at the Drill Hall in Action Space off Tottenham Court Road, London. There was no selection process, the only provisos being that performers and teachers had to be members of ADMA. The festivals included classes and workshops that were diverse and varied, offering ballet, release-based work, improvisation, contemporary techniques, folk dance and acrobatics. Performances were understandably varied in terms of quality, though their strength lay in the celebration of the range and diversity of new work. The first festival ran for two weeks in May–June 1977.

The second Festival in 1978 was more ambitious and ran for three weeks, but it encountered difficulties over last-minute cancellations and, it was noted, a general air of disorganisation. In addition, the Arts Council deemed the venue inadequate for professional performances and noted that some of the participants were non-professional in any case. At that time, Arts Council policy was to fund only professional work and so a further grant was not forthcoming.

Dartington

The first festival in Dartington took place in June 1978 as a weekend event with Steve Paxton, Richard Alston and Dancers, Janet Smith and Dancers plus classes and workshops. The festivals developed into annual intensive and distinctively comradely events, generally stretching over a five-day programme of classes, workshops and performances, and attracting students from other institutions. Participants camped in the picturesque Dartington Hall grounds or stayed nearby. Work shown tended to be based on release or contact improvisation, or was more overtly political, such as the performance work of Jacky Lansley. Contributors were unpaid, with only expenses, food and accommodation being covered.[14]

Jordan notes a cosmopolitan flavour at Dartington,[15] interestingly in light of the development of Dance Umbrella festivals, and by 1979 there were participants from eight countries. In the early years choreographers and teachers tended to be drawn from the ranks of guest teachers at the college or were former colleagues at the American universities where Fulkerson had taught previously. (However, little Graham-based work was apparent.) The festivals were all directed and organised by Fulkerson herself with assistants, but did not survive Fulkerson's departure as head of department, the last festival being held in 1987.

* * *

Noel Goodwin, in a review of the first Dance Umbrella festival of 1978,[16] noted the change in Britain's dance scene, highlighted by the fact that no home group showing work in the festival had existed five years previously. His comments say much about the rapid expansion of dance during that decade. The only problem was that the public remained largely unaware of it, and it was to addressing this situation that Val Bourne and her team at Dance Umbrella were to dedicate themselves over the next twenty years and more.

10

Bourne is swift to point out that the enterprise depended on some absolutely key people. Two in particular were Fiona Dick, Dance Umbrella administrator until 1990, and Mary Caws, who held a similar position (under various titles) for a further eight years. They were, states Bourne, particularly crucial to the operation, given that for much of the time there *were* only two members of staff![17] Others including Julia Carruthers, Clare Cooper, Greg Nash and currently Betsy Gregory have also made considerable contributions. (See Appendix 3 for a full list of Dance Umbrella personnel.) Bourne recalls too that individual members of the Dance Umbrella board of management, in particular in its early days, were very much 'hands on', and their contributions are discussed in Chapter 1.

That the forum for this expansion was the festival platform is no accident either, but reflects the favoured arena of the times both within the UK and in continental Europe, where similar political changes were occurring. David Edgar eloquently argues that the 1960s and 1970s heralded a challenge by the new Left to the post-war years' patrician model of arts establishment, a challenge that 'sought to encourage autonomous activity by the grassroots (sometimes for festive, more often with subversive purposes in mind).' He continues: 'the generic art form of the short-lived provocative hegemony in the great cities of Europe was the carnival'.[18]

Eiko (of Eiko and Komo) in *Fur Seal*, at Riverside Studios, 1981. PHOTO: CHRIS HARRIS

1

Foundations and Diversifications

Events and Developments 1977–1981

Dance Umbrella folklore now has it that the festivals started by chance, when in 1977, at a meeting of the dance subcommittee of the Arts Council of Great Britain (ACGB), Noël Goodwin suggested – quite off the cuff – that what London needed was a dance festival. This would be a showcase, featuring the exciting new dancers and choreographers graduating from the schools and mainstream modern dance companies, by now well established in the wake of the dance boom. The idea appealed and Jane Nicholas, ACGB's Dance Officer, asked Val Bourne and Nicholas Hooton (then administrator at Riverside Studios) to work together on a proposal for a two-week London-based festival. Bourne had trained at the Royal Ballet, later working at Ballet Rambert as press and publicity representative before becoming assistant to Nicholas at ACGB.

Normally, any idea as unpremeditated as this would never have survived twenty years, let alone survive them well, as Umbrella has done. 'I'd never presented anything, let alone a festival – we had to learn on the job!', says Bourne,[1] who doubts very much whether anyone as inexperienced would get funding now. Even Bourne, who has been the guiding light behind the Umbrella's ventures, could not have foreseen the extent to which Umbrella would be instrumental in establishing the buoyant dance culture that now exists throughout the country. It is well documented (see Jordan, 1992 and Mackrell, 1992) that considerable pressure had been building to recognise dance as an art form as equally deserving of representation as any other, and therefore equally deserving funding and encouragement for experimental projects. The ADMA and Dartington festivals, too, had important roles to play. Bourne proved to be a champion with the insider knowledge and expertise needed to capitalise on the progress made thus far. These attributes she harnessed to an advanced intuitive sense and seemingly inexhaustible energy.

The paper presented to the Dance Theatre Subcommittee in November 1977 proposed a festival to be run along the same lines as New York's Umbrella festivals. Underpinning the latter was the idea that groups and soloists who might otherwise lack resources could come together for a series of performances, and be sheltered financially and administratively under a single management. It is apparent that, even then, the issue of the twin roles of management service and administration for independent companies and artists was a prominent consideration. In her short paper, Bourne also discussed the viability of the ADMA festivals as an ongoing concern, about which she had reservations. Firstly, she argued that the policy of non-selection advocated by ADMA, while praiseworthy on democratic grounds, would not work for a larger showcase event. Secondly, the festival would need venues suitable for professional theatrical companies. These perhaps were unpalatable truths to some at the time; nevertheless, had this line not been taken, it is very doubtful that the festival movement would have survived in the robust form that it has.

Money was finally approved for the festival,[2] a steering committee was set up to establish artistic policy shortly afterwards and the name of Dance Umbrella was adopted. 'Later we wanted to change it to Dance Exchange', recalls Bourne, 'but the Arts Council would not accept the name, because it implied international exchange, and at that time the Arts Council did not fund international companies.'[3] Whatever the reasons for its adoption, the name Dance Umbrella can now be seen as the more appropriate, reflecting a longer-term and wider-ranging enterprise. The aims of the first festival were:

- to give British artists an opportunity to present their work to its best advantage in established arts centres with proper technical facilities and staff;
- to focus public attention on an area of work thought to be important and worthy of support;
- to prove that there was an interested public for these artists when

'Umbrella' Festival

At previous meetings allusions have been made to 'umbrella' festivals held in New York and suggestions have been put forward that perhaps something on the same lines could be operated here. It seemed worthwhile to investigate a little further both as to the need for such festivals in this country and the possible costs.

An exact parallel to the American situation does not exist here, as we have nothing comparable to the Managements in the States, specialising in dance administration and publicity, each of which represents several of the small dance companies. It is they who, on behalf of their several clients, apply to funding bodies, such as the New York State Arts Council, for funds to present a two or three week festival of dance at a central venue.

Our nearest equivalent to an umbrella festival would be the Festival of Dance and Mime, presented by the Association of Dance and Mime Artists in May/June last. The Arts Council gave ADMA £1,350 towards their administrative costs and it is understood that ADMA will be applying for financial help with a similar festival next year. More than 20 groups were given opportunities to perform in central London during this year's Festival and classes and workshops were also offered and well attended. However ADMA steadfastly refuses to make qualitative judgements as to the groups taking part and operate on a first come, first served basis. This is obviously a very democratic approach, befitting a political organisation such as ADMA, but it does make for a very uneven level of performance. Also the venue - Action Space - though perfectly suitable for workshops, classes and the more experimental of the artists concerned, is less than ideal for the more theatrically orientated of the groups and its audience capacity and, therefore, box office income is minimal.

In addition, experimental and emergent groups are quite well-catered for already with the minimal budget Dance-Ins, established on a monthly basis at Battersea Arts Centre and soon to start at the ICA and possibly Jackson's Lane Community Centre. Oval House offers another alternative venue.

Mime groups have their own Festival at the Cockpit. The Arts Council gave £700 towards the cost of the 1977 one and has already recommended £1,880 towards the next.

However, it does seem that a strong case could be made for umbrella festival which would feature the more established of the smaller groups, such as Basic Space Dance Theatre, the Rosemary Butcher Dance Company, Cycles Dance Company, EMMA Dance Company, Extemporary Dance Group, the Janet Smith Dance Group, Junction Dance Company and Moving Visions Dance Theatre. If Riverside Studios, the Jeannetta Cochrane Theatre or The Place Theatre (when completed) were chosen as the Festival venue, this would give these groups the chance to be seen in a decent theatre, offering the possibility of attracting 200 - 400 people per performance, depending on which venue were chosen. In addition to actual performances, workshops and master classes would be included in the programme, making the fortnight not only a showcase for talent but a really exciting and rewarding dance event.

Costings are being investigated and will vary enormously according to the venue chosen. Richard Jarman has had informal preliminary discussions with Riverside Studios and will be able to give an idea of probable costs of a Festival there.

Paper presented by Val Bourne to the Dance Theatre Subcommittee, 9 November 1977.

presented as part of a festival, with the kind of attendant publicity, promotion and press coverage that they could not command independently.
(*Dance Umbrella Festivals: a paper for discussion*, 7 June 1982)

After the steering group had been convened, its members found out about a one-week festival of American dance that the Institute of Contemporary Arts (ICA) was planning in conjunction with the London magazine *Time Out* in November 1978. Jan Murray revealed the plan at the very first steering group meeting. Murray, who at the time combined the roles of dance consultant for the ICA and dance editor for *Time Out*, had been commissioned to visit New York to look for suitable American dance artists.

The members of the steering group were later to form themselves into Dance Umbrella's first board of management (see Appendix 4), and were all actively involved with the first festival. In addition to Murray there were David Gothard, Nicholas Hooton, John Ashford and Jeremy Rees, all of whom did a huge amount of work. 'So with Ruth [Glick] obviously, it was very much a collaborative thing and this collaboration only really changed in 1980 when we went "part time" into new premises,' Bourne recollects. 'But the thing that really made it all possible in the first place was that Riverside Studios was directed at that time by Peter Gill and Peter brought in Rosemary Butcher to work with his actors, because Rosemary at that time was the only dancer wearing sneakers, and Riverside had a concrete floor'.[4] Gill's interest in dance was a critical factor for the first festival, as was that of David Gothard,[5] who became involved as Gill's assistant at Riverside Studios. 'The culture at Riverside with Peter and David was immensely important; they kept the impetus going with all-year-round activities – you were able to see everything at Riverside then.'[6] John Ashford, then at the ICA, was mainly interested in theatre, but nevertheless gave his full support to the dance project, as well as allowing the ICA premises to be used.[7]

Concerning the independently mooted Dance Umbrella and ICA festivals, Bourne recalls, 'we made a virtue out of necessity and fused the two'.[8] It transpired that four soloists were all that could be afforded – these formed the overseas representatives for the first festival. In addition, and as part of Bourne's original plan, several small companies from the UK (some with an educational bias) were scheduled to appear – basically, all those funded by the Arts Council.

The first Dance Umbrella was held from 7 to 25 November 1978. It had one paid festival co-ordinator, Ruth Glick, appointed for a total of eight weeks – a period later described in the festival report as 'grossly insufficient'. Murray and Bourne put in a number of voluntary hours, and *Time Out* and GLAA both donated resources. All the artists had to be put up in the team's flats or with friends or relatives, who also provided all the transport. Two venues were used: the ICA and the newly reopened Riverside Studios. The festival was a great success, and only then was the idea of a second Festival mooted.[9]

Dance Umbrella had been set up originally as a one-off project. 'The panel had thought "Give them enough rope and they'll hang themselves" (the panel was heavily ballet-orientated at the time),' remembers Bourne.[10] But it rapidly became apparent that an organisational void existed where foreign and local dance presentation was concerned. Members of the newly formed Dance Umbrella board of management campaigned to fund the Dance Umbrella as a 'permanent catalyst, research, co-ordination and presentation body for contemporary dance'.[11] It was envisaged that at first the organisation would handle the presentation of foreign companies, run the annual festival and provide a management service with an information service running alongside. Once these services were established, it was hoped that others would follow, such as the promotion of regional activity and fundraising.

A highly influential conference, Dance Artists in Education, was held at the end of 1979 with Dance Umbrella involvement. Another important seminar to arise out of Dance Umbrella activity took place during the 1980 festival to debate the possibility of a National Lobby for Dance and Mime. Although it is not common knowledge, we can see that even at the outset Umbrella activity was not confined to the showcase events, but concerned itself with establishing and promoting an infrastructure that would ensure the nourishment of those events over a longer term. These activities, though less 'sexy' than the festivals, provide the key to the continued success of the whole venture.

In January 1980 the second Umbrella festival was held over six weeks in five London venues: to the original two were added the newly renovated Place Theatre, the Whitechapel Art Gallery and the Shaw Theatre. At one time the line-up was to have included Pina Bausch and her company, funded by the Goethe Institute. It would have been their first London appearance, presenting *Café Müller,* but the idea had to be dropped at the very last minute because of an outbreak of conjunctivitis in the company,[12] and Springplank came instead. It would be interesting to consider the effect on the American/

European balance of the festivals (which was to become a key issue) had Bausch appeared in London at that time.

The First Two Programmes

The importance of an educational dimension is apparent from the very first festival, with Ludus dance-in-education company and East Anglian Dance Theatre presenting programmes aimed at school children. The focus on these types of groups ceased to be a central issue fairly early on, but the role of education has continued in a different guise, with related events such as films, seminars, platforms and classes forming an integral part of Umbrella activity. In this way the audience is encouraged to participate both physically and critically and thus become an active part of the festival. Seminars and fora tackled issues of the moment that were often provocative. As a direct consequence of these debates, organisations were set up to develop the discussion and to continue to lobby on matters of importance to dance.

The first festival had a multi-cultural flavour, with performances and workshops given by Maas Movers, the UK's first professional black dance company. Ludus presented *No. 5 Empire Street,* whose subject was racial prejudice. The American choreographer and teacher, John Jones, who had danced in Katherine Dunham's pioneering ensemble and Jerome Robbins' Ballets USA, taught some brilliant workshops for Maas Movers as well as making a piece for the company, *Party Blues.*

The flavour of the opening programmes set the tone for future festivals, with American innovations drawn largely from the post-Cunningham stable. The American performers were real eye-openers because of their stylistic diversity and individual experience: choreographers generally had had several years with other mainstream or well established avant-garde companies before embarking on their own careers. UK companies on the other hand were newly established, and in some cases their dancers lacked professional experience. (One of the few exceptions was Richard Alston, with his experience of experimentation and performance.) In short, avant-garde, experimental dance had a much longer history in the US than in the UK: a history, it was apparent, from which our artists could learn. Even so, there was some resistance to the notion of importing ideas, rather than showcasing British talent alone.

Steve Paxton at Riverside
Studios, 8 February 1980.
PHOTO: CHRIS HARRIS

British performances showed diversity in their own ways, too, their choreographic concerns running from political statement (for example, Tamara McLorg) to pure dance experiment (Rosemary Butcher). There was also the Extemporary Dance Company (later, Extemporary Dance Theatre), a repertory company keen to try more theatrically based work. The practice of commissioning work from influential visitors to the festivals was another trend that started early on, and some long-term relationships were fostered during this period. This was to be most important for the development of the British companies' repertoire. In 1980 choreographers from the dance-ranks of some of our major companies were added, thereby contributing to the development of some important innovators from the more mainstream dance culture – Ashley Page being one example.

Even in 1978, British representation was marked by the presence of regional groups: for example, Cycles, EMMA and Ludus. But associated regional events really became established with the third festival in 1981.[13]

19

Regional Activity

The 1980 Umbrella festival had several offshoots: for instance, the Arnolfini and Bristol Arts Centre presented a joint season of dance. Bristol's involvement came about through Jeremy Rees, a founder member of the Dance Umbrella board and also director of the Arnolfini Gallery. The season took place between Thursday 1 May and Saturday 10 May, and included Moving Earth, the New-York-based company of the innovative Japanese choreographer Kei Takei; a 'Dance International' programme over two days with local groups representing different national roots; classes in Graham, Cunningham and contact improvisation; and the EMMA Dance Company in residence from 7 to 10 May. Events were also programmed that year at the Arts Centre in Plymouth and at the Sherman Theatre in Cardiff.

By autumn 1981 and the advent of the third festival, a measure of regional interest had developed, with a total of ten associated events throughout the UK. This area of activity was to form another crucial and far-reaching strand of Umbrella influence. Associated festivals in the regions blossomed, with Danceabout North West in the Manchester area starting up in 1983 and festivals in Leicester and Nottingham gaining independence in the late 1980s and early 1990s – all with Dance Umbrella's guidance. To these were added the Woking festivals, begun in 1995, which Dance Umbrella continues to manage. Dance Umbrella was an important initiator of the regionalisation of dance throughout the 1980s and was instrumental in establishing funding systems that persist to this day. We shall consider these developments later, within the context of each year's activities.

The Management Service

We have seen how the role of management and the need for effective administration were recognised as immediate concerns for the home artists, and with this in mind a feasibility study for a management service was put together by Gale Law, who was to have administered the scheme. Law pulled out of the project in the summer, and his role was taken over by Fiona Dick.

The management service and the festival, although entirely separate ventures, were closely related from the outset. Funding to encourage and support new talent was of course vitally important to the whole enterprise of

First-night party, Dance Umbrella 1981. Centre: Charles Moulton and Val Bourne. PHOTO: CHRIS HARRIS

showcasing new groups. With the 1978 festival it became even more apparent that British groups and artists needed professional support in order to develop. Dick states that the management service was 'based on the demands expressed at an open forum during the 1978 festival.'[14] Its organisation followed the model of an American enterprise called Arts Services, which represented Douglas Dunn and Sara Rudner at the time. Bourne says of the American organisation: 'It was marvellous just to be able to ring them up and they got you the information'.[15] With funding of £7,000 from the Calouste Gulbenkian Foundation, the Dance Umbrella Management Service was piloted under Dick's administration. An original eleven-month trial period was stretched to two years, from April 1980 to March 1982. Dick and Bourne shared the workload for that period, with Ruth Glick coming in to administer the festivals.

The aims of the Management Service were:

- to provide a shared administrative service for small London-based dance companies and solo artists;
- to organise conferences and seminars concerned with dance;

- to develop a central information service for such groups and for those wishing to promote dance events.[16]

The original intention was not only to have four 'quality' London-based companies or solo artists, but also to provide a free information service to anyone who needed it, on topics such as dance venues, addresses of promoters or advice on publicity. An advertisement in the 1980 Umbrella festival souvenir programme invited applications from companies and dancers who wished to be considered. By the end of the year, Dance Umbrella had acted on behalf of Janet Smith and Dancers, the Ian Spink Group, Maedée Duprès, Tara Rajkumar, Siobhan Davies and Dancers and Ingegerd Lonnroth. Soon afterwards, it took on Mantis and Rosemary Butcher as well, making a total of six companies and two soloists.

The office attracted many visitors, including theatre and festival directors from Europe, Canada and the United States as well as dancers and choreographers, so that the Service became a hands-on affair as well as the originally

Advertisement included in the 1980 Umbrella Festival souvenir programme.

intended communications network. Perhaps this is another clue to Umbrella's success: its ability to respond immediately and informally to situations and areas of need and to keep bureaucracy down to an absolute minimum.

The Information Service was launched with the December 1980 *Dance and Mime Newsheet*. This journal was sent to its subscribers every two months, giving information on the work of the Service. It covered proposed visits to the UK by overseas companies (for promoters), forthcoming special events, the availability of British dancers and choreographers, and information about new dance publications. In 1982 the Service contacted Ian Spink and Siobhan (Sue) Davies to suggest that their companies merge and that they join forces with Richard Alston. These choreographers already shared many of their dancers, and Dance Umbrella's original idea was that they amalgamate into a new company, Second Stride, to be represented by Dance Umbrella. The management organised annual tours, the company's first US tour being such a success that Second Stride became 'a standard bearer for the best in new dance'. (See *Second Stride's First US Tour, 1982,* in Chapter 2.)

The Management Service also helped to make good-quality promotional videos featuring Umbrella artists. 1984 videos featured both Laurie Booth and Second Stride. This was a direct consequence of the 1983 festival's Dance and Camera workshops, which had created videos featuring Mantis, Janet Smith, Extemporary Dance Theatre, Ludus, Indian classical dance and the Moving Picture Mime Show. These videos gave overseas promoters far more immediate access to UK companies and artists, and thus began another important dimension of the Service's work.

The Service had always intended to enable artists to develop to the point at which they could acquire their own paid administration, and this is indeed what happened. The success of the Management Service in promoting its companies meant that several of them required full-time management, a job larger than the original remit. In 1984 Jenny Mann joined the team (leaving her position of education officer at Ballet Rambert), originally with a press and marketing brief. The Service also acquired publicity trainee Melanie Gilbert on an Arts Council training scheme. However, by this time some companies, such as Janet Smith's, had become so well established that they could afford to have their own full-time administration, run from an independent company office. In April 1985, Mantis became a revenue client of the Arts Council, and so Mann took over both the company and its director Micha Bergese as full-time clients – Bergese by that time was forging a successful career on his own in films. Shortly afterwards Mann found new premises separate from the Umbrella office.

By 1987, Dick recalls, the work load had increased 'as demands from artists and presenters grew apace', and 'trying to provide a full support service for artists working at the "difficult" end of the spectrum and competing with more entertaining, accessible work, took so much time and effort that the Festival was beginning to suffer.'[17] She comments that the 1987 Arts Council appraisal 'concluded that the service was fulfilling no one's expectations and was draining resources from the Festival, and that the Umbrella could better serve the dance community through high-profile, concentrated events spanning a whole range of work.' Possibly the main factor in the decision to stop the Management Service was that Dance Umbrella had been asked to run several regional festivals. This too was an effective way of making sure groups had an airing outside London, at well-publicised events in well-appointed venues. The Service's role in raising funds for new works was replaced in the short term by galas, such as the DecaDance gala in January 1988. Some of the proceeds from this event enabled Siobhan Davies to make *White Man Sleeps* and *Wyoming,* performed late that year in the festival for the relaunch of her independent company. This commissioning of work by Dance Umbrella (rather than by an individual or company) had begun in a small way as early as 1980 and was clearly an effective way of funding projects. Bourne says now of the Management Service, 'I miss it, because you never are as close to artists again, but then again, there were the sleepless nights . . .'[18]

The National Lobby for Dance and Mime

A meeting was held at Riverside Studios during the 1980 Dance Umbrella festival with the express intention of debating the poor status of dance, its consequent underfunding compared to the other arts and the possibility of forming a National Lobby for Dance and Mime. Those taking part included directors, administrators and board members of many of the major companies; representatives from most of the smaller ones; representatives from education at all levels; as well as dancers, choreographers, critics, television producers and dance enthusiasts – in other words, a very good cross section of all interested parties. Speakers included Norman Morrice (director of the

Royal Ballet), Robert Cohan (director of London Contemporary Dance Theatre), Andrew Welch (director of the Warwick Arts Centre), Jan Murray (dance editor of *Time Out* magazine) and Joan White (senior lecturer in dance at Roehampton Institute). The meeting was chaired by John Drummond, then director of the Edinburgh Festival.

The problem of relative underfunding, it was felt, was caused primarily by dance's lack of public voice. Val Bourne wrote at the time:

> We believe that the case for Dance is a very strong one indeed and we should be able to justify its claim for a bigger slice of the financial cake, by drawing attention to the large audiences for the major companies throughout the country, to the emergence of so many small groups and soloists presenting exciting new work and to the success of the Umbrella and other Dance Festivals.[19]

The discussion also ranged over venues and dance spaces, training grants for dance students and media coverage of dance events. In 1982, arising directly from the seminar, a steering group was formed entitled the Dance and Mime Action Group (DAMAG), changing its name to the National Organisation of Dance and Mime (NODAM) in 1983. The aims of this group included:

- the provision of a major Dance House in London;
- the provision of non-commercial performance and rehearsal space for small dance and mime groups;
- the establishment of mandatory rather than discretionary grants for the vocational training of dancers;
- the extension of dance coverage by the media.[20]

Understandably enough, the implicit criticism of inadequate coverage was not well received by the press.

Dance Artists in Education Conference

Over the weekend of 30 November to 2 December 1979, Ruth Glick organised a seminar at the Midlands Arts Centre in Birmingham, with the focus on dance in education. The seminar was originally an Arts Council initiative, but Dance Umbrella became involved because Glick was also working as Dance Umbrella festival co-ordinator. The weekend included performances, film, lecture demonstrations and discussion groups. Its aims were to examine and evaluate the current practice of professional dance companies working within the context of formal education in the UK, and to make proposals for future developments in this area. There was an impressive line-up of important contributors to the field (see Appendix 5), and participants included dancers, administrators, teachers, lecturers and choreographers.

Bourne recalls that it was very much 'a "night of the long knives" – it was the first time the dancer practitioners and the teachers of dance in education had faced each other'.[21] Two dance-in-education companies met their demise shortly afterwards as a result: Educational Dance-Drama Theatre and Ballet for All. A follow-up report on the seminar listed key issues that needed urgent attention. Important considerations included:

- the role of the professional dance artist in education (with a recommendation that vocational training schools should reflect opportunities for this sort of work within their curricula);
- a recommendation for a scheme to encourage professional choreographers to create material for companies working in education;
- the proper assessment of dance programmes for schools;
- recommendations that more effective training was needed for specialist dance teachers in schools, and that dance should have its own Inspectorate at the Department of Education and Science;
- a call for greater co-operation between the professional and educational sectors.

Other Special Projects

A number of other projects arose as a result of early festival activity. This was to set the tone of events over the next few years, when Bourne and her team found themselves increasingly taking on the roles of consultants and advocates to similar or related projects. These included a British Dance Fortnight at the Centre George Pompidou in Paris in 1983 on behalf of the British Council. Dance Umbrella undertook the overall management of this two-week season and presented four British groups: Janet Smith and Dancers; Mantis; the improvisational duo Julyen Hamilton and Kirstie Simson; and Maedée Duprès and Friends. This Fortnight came about as a direct result of an earlier initiative in which Dance Umbrella had presented a showcase of British dancers at the Riverside Studios for the benefit of Jannine Charrat and Marcel Bonnard from the Pompidou Centre. Dance Umbrella also handled the fundraising for the visit of Merce Cunningham and Company in May/June 1980, jointly with the British American Arts Association.

Related activities formed – and continue to form – an important adjunct to the festivals, which after 1980 were to become annual events. We now move on to discuss the artistic flavour of these festivals, their development and their unique contribution to the dance scene in this country.

Michael Clark in *New Puritans*, 1984.
PHOTO: CHRIS NASH

2

The Early Years: 1978–1984

Trends and Activities

Artistic Trends

It is generally agreed that American visitors artistically dominated the early years of the Dance Umbrella festival, but there are three important qualifications to make. Firstly, the Americans did not exemplify a single style: indeed, what was striking was their stylistic diversity, perhaps one that was endemic to the art of contemporary dance in the US. Certainly their very different choreographic concerns provided a broad palette from which our own choreographers could draw inspiration, and, more pragmatically, from which our own companies could commission new work. A few years later the integrity of some younger-generation American post-modern choreographers appears to have become somewhat compromised, with perhaps a trend towards high-energy slickness to the detriment of content. However, this did not seriously detract from the overall quality of the American work, nor from the challenge it posed to our own choreographers.

The second qualification is to do with European contributions, which, although less dominant, gained influence throughout the period. These date back to as early as the second festival, but on the whole the work of European avant-garde artists was less well known and their reputations less established than those of the Americans – though Pina Bausch, seen at the Edinburgh Festival in 1978 and in London in 1982,[1] was fast building hers. Some artists attracted attention in their own right: in 1982 Anne Teresa de Keersmaeker

made a huge impression with a minimalist duet for herself and Michele Anne de Mey, quite unlike anything seen from America, or anything seen thus far from Béjart's Mudra School, from which both dancers came. The difference was even more startling because she contrasted with the more traditionally expressionist German choreographer Susanne Linke,[2] the other European artist to perform that year. Suddenly we became aware that very different styles were available across the Channel, different from our own and from American dance. So a fresh challenge was posed as we began to question our cultural roots and question our artistic allegiances.

The third qualification concerns our own growing strengths. British companies were able to commission work from these visitors, strengthen their own repertories and show their dancers to advantage. A good example is Extemporary Dance Theatre, long hailed as having particularly strong, technical dancers, who came into their own in the work of David Gordon and Karole Armitage. But British choreography itself acquired a much broader perspective during this period, with collaborative projects involving the visual arts, video, music and text. Contrasting points of departure were also becoming noticeable, employing different movements as a base – Cunningham-derived, or based on release or contact improvisation. These forms were being personalised and made more sophisticated.

The Made in Britain series set out to showcase experimental work by young choreographers, and sometimes by more established choreographers who simply wanted to push their ideas further than would be possible elsewhere. Out of this experience emerged Matthew Hawkins, Ashley Page and Yolande Snaith, among others. Alongside these were experimental artists, such as Rosemary Butcher, Laurie Booth, Sue MacLennan and Julyen Hamilton, whose single-mindedness would perhaps have led them to pursue their own more esoteric ideas come what may, but for whom the Umbrella provided a predictable platform and therefore some stability. Then of course there was Michael Clark, whose performance charisma seems to have guaranteed him a cult status, even before he started to show his own work. The success of Second Stride in America, discussed later in this chapter, is testament to the success of the Umbrella management.

In support of this activity were courses such as those in dance and video and in dance and criticism, seminal courses whose role we should not underestimate. They not only extended the artists' own ideas and perspectives, but also enriched dance's peripheral culture – supporting its academic study, for example, educating a new audience or simply encouraging artists from different disciplines to collaborate.

Administrative Trends

Given an increasing array of venues, various schemes were tested to encourage audiences both through economic incentives and by simplifying booking procedures. These should be seen in the context of general economic trends. Insecure almost throughout its history, Umbrella's funding from its various sources diminished, partly because of the recession of the eighties, but also because of government policy promoting business sponsorship to replace public spending. An audience survey questionnaire carried out in 1980 revealed that 80% of the festival audience were in the age range 18–35.[3] This perhaps accounts for the diminishing box-office returns from 1981–83, with a predominantly young audience being the first group to be affected by the recession.

Among the ticket-purchasing strategies employed was a season ticket scheme in 1983, whereby books of tickets for five or nine performances could be bought in advance, giving discounts on single-ticket prices. The saving of up to 35% was found to be over-generous, but the principle of concessions for advance sales proved itself a sound economic measure. This scheme was replaced the following year by one in which vouchers were offered for sale in books of six or ten, each voucher being worth more than its face value. These could be used to offset the purchase of single tickets. A mobile central box-office was tested in 1981 (funded by the Gulbenkian Foundation) with the aim of allowing advance ticket sales without the problem of visiting several different sites. The scheme proved unhelpful, as in reality 'it didn't help sell any more tickets – rather it provided a sort of information service to callers who would ring to ask advice on what to go and see!'[4] The plan to run a central box-office from the Criterion Theatre the following year was abandoned as a consequence. (However, voucher schemes persisted in various guises until 1988.)

There were some small forays into business sponsorship, with Marks and Spencer giving small grants towards the overall costs of the Festival from 1980 and a contribution towards the Made in Britain series in 1984, and Sotheby's making a small contribution in 1982. The encouragement of regional activity can be seen to some extent as a financial ploy as well, enabling visiting artists to extend their stay in this country and so allowing costs to be spread more widely.

However, 1983's financial crisis, when two expected sources of funds either did not materialise or were at a significantly lower level than requested, meant that the festival only narrowly avoided cancellation that year.[5] Fortunes improved markedly for Dance Umbrella 84 owing to a number of factors, not least of which was a collaboration with Sadler's Wells Theatre.

Video and TV

Dance on film was a feature of the Umbrella festivals from the very beginning. The 1978 festival featured seven films at Riverside Studios, the majority of which were receiving their London premieres. Riverside also featured a Film Forum, and the ICA held a special film evening featuring Channel 4's *Dance in America* TV series. The absence of Fred Astaire films provoked comment, but the balance was amply redressed by a special 'musicals of the thirties and forties' theme during the 1980 festival. The ambitious film and video season projected for 1981 had to be abandoned, owing to lack of funds. In its place the ICA held a week-long lunchtime series which featured American and British films and which opened with a lecture by John Mueller. This was followed in 1982 by a fortnight's season of dance films and videos previously unseen in this country.

It was during the 1983 festival, however, that hands-on experience became a feature, and in which 'Dance and the Camera' became a major secondary theme, a decision that was partly artistic, partly pragmatic. It had become apparent that good-quality videos of companies and artists were crucial if the Management Service was to provide much-needed exposure for its clients. In 1982 two separate video/television projects had involved Management Service clients Second Stride, Laurie Booth and Janet Smith and Dancers. For the following year's festival, a three-week Dance Video Project at the Riverside Studios was proposed, including workshops and recording sessions. The first part of the project was given over to a week-long workshop led by three experienced directors from very different backgrounds: Colin Nears, Susan Dowling and Charles Atlas. Nears had won the Prix Italia prize for his film of Christopher Bruce and Lindsay Kemp's *Cruel Garden* in 1982 for the BBC.

Dowling, a producer with WGBH TV in Boston, had made films featuring Trisha Brown, Douglas Dunn and Meredith Monk, among others. Atlas had for many years been film-maker-in-residence for the Merce Cunningham Company. From the many applicants, eight film makers were chosen to take part, alongside eight dance artists, Mantis (as the 'resource' company), Michael Clark and Matthew Hawkins (currently involved in making work for Mantis), plus Mantis's director and choreographer Micha Bergese. The 'graduates' from these workshops then went on to make films for a number of selected companies during the following three weeks.[6]

As a result of the project, six educational or promotional dance films were made (see Appendix 1, *1983 Festival: Related Events*, for details.) Of equal importance with their promotional role was the excitement generated by the project among dance artists; the ensuing years are marked by choreographic and video collaborations and by the incorporation of film, for example, either into the choreographic process or as source material.

Second Stride's First US Tour, 1982

Second Stride was formed as a temporary touring project. Throughout 1981 it became apparent that Siobhan Davies and Dancers and the Ian Spink Group, both of whom were under Dance Umbrella's management, were competing in many instances for the same dancers. They decided to combine forces, at Dance Umbrella's suggestion, forming a company considerably larger than the usual independent dance groups and consequently able to tackle larger-scale work. The company comprised twelve dancers with a repertoire of nine pieces. Three of these were new commissions, and four were dances that had been in the repertoires of Spink's and Davies's companies. The remaining two were revivals contributed by Richard Alston: *Doublework* (1978) and *Field of Mustard* (1980). Many of the dancers, such as Davies, Duprès, Smith and Spink, had previously performed for Richard Alston and Dancers during Dance Umbrella 1978, and Duprès and Davies had appeared in his first company, Strider (1972–1975). Strider had been Britain's very first independent dance company; it was in homage to this that the group was named, although Alston's connection with the group was short-lived due to his commitments to Ballet Rambert.

Because the group was formed for this single project, it disbanded shortly

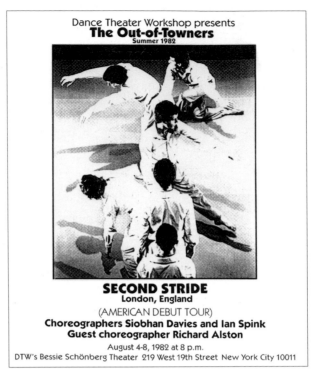

Flyer for Second Stride's first US tour, 1982.

afterwards, only to be reformed just as quickly for a second tour in 1983. The first tour met with particular success, not least in the United States, giving heart to the British independent dance fraternity, which had suffered somewhat from unfavourable comparisons with their American counterparts in the early Umbrella days. British independent dance, it seemed, had found its voice, and American as well as British critics acknowledged a newly developed ability to deal with the American modern dance legacy in a distinctively British way. In a much vaunted article for the *Village Voice,* reprinted in *Dance and Dancers* in January 1983, the New York critic Deborah Jowitt proclaimed: 'What I've seen . . . convinces me that youngish contemporary British choreographers are finally developing their own style – or styles – of "modern dance" analogous to the British Ballet style that Ashton, Tudor and others created when their sensibilities began to work creatively on the imported Russian tradition.'

She goes on to describe the style as 'overwhelmingly gentle, pastoral almost; the dancers seem to be musing with their bodies – lyrically or in mild despair.' This qualitative difference is confirmed by Val Bourne, who adds that perhaps British modern dance is less concerned with a message, with making a point, but is more interested in dance for its own sake.[7] This observation is astute, even though the differences in choreographic concerns within Second Stride were soon to become apparent. These differences were to provide mutual inspiration for Davies and Spink throughout the following years, but inevitably would result in their parting, Davies to hone and refine her more abstracted style and Spink to develop the theatrical side of his, continuing the group with Antony McDonald after Davies' departure in 1985.

Danceabout North West

Danceabout North West was really the forerunner of the later independent regional festivals. It was started in 1981, almost by accident, when the North West Arts Dance Panel decided that their budget was so small that year that the only way forward was to spend it all on one big event. This led to the largest regional season in the Dance Umbrella calendar (although Bristol's Arnolfini can claim to have had the longest association, having taken part from the very first festival up to 1994). A very able administrator was found in Lorna Hempstead, although several performances and activities had already been arranged before she took over. Also, the initiative deliberately coincided with the London festival in order to take advantage of overseas groups that could tour the regions. Hempstead comments in her festival report of December 1981 that there was little dance activity in the Manchester region at that time. It seems a major coup, therefore, that this ambitious project got under way and progressed so successfully. In 1981 the festival ran for some eight and a half weeks in twenty-one venues spread throughout the region. Its success was due partly to an astute mix of prestigious and well-known companies such as London Festival Ballet, Ballet Rambert, Northern Ballet Theatre and Sadler's Wells Royal Ballet, and less well-known visitors, such as Tim Miller, Jim Self, Nina Wiener and Dancers, Rosalind Newman in 1982, Bill T. Jones and Arnie Zane and La La La (Lock Danseurs) in 1983, Katie Duck and Group O in 1984, alongside classes, workshops, films and exhibitions.

The festival's fortunes increased in 1982 and 1983, though using the same strategy as in London of spreading events more thinly. By 1984, the festival took in thirty-five different centres in the Manchester area, but sadly was no longer sustainable after 1986. Danceabout, however, had brought a major increase of funding for dance to the North West over these years.

Year Overviews, 1978–1984

1978

The very first performance of the very first Dance Umbrella festival was by the American Douglas Dunn. Dunn's solo *Gestures in Red* very nearly caused a riot akin to the first night of Nijinsky's *The Rite of Spring*. 'A load of rubbish', 'an insult to my intelligence' were some of the responses, with some members of the audience noisily walking out. Val Bourne recalls that she was almost physically assaulted for having spent public money in such a way.[8] Others happily hailed it as a masterpiece, recognising the Californian dancer's remarkable technique and choreographic rigour. It later transpired that Dunn was on the verge of cancelling his second scheduled performance, so fearful was he for his own safety after the outcry provoked by the first.

Dunn was just part of the varied programme offered by the American visitors; three (Remy Charlip, Sara Rudner and Dunn) had been part of the Judson Dance Theater experimental venture of the 1960s. That Dunn's work was challenging is undeniable: his solo performance lasted fifty minutes and was performed in silence, with the exception of breath sounds and foot beats. In four sections, the second (the one that seems to have provoked most outcry) was performed on the spot.

Dunn's 'pure dance' explorations of time and space showed his Cunningham background. Sara Rudner's solo shared some similar concerns as well as again displaying brilliant technique. Her performance in general, though also described as 'pure dance', had a more accessible, emotional content with greater light and shade, containing images that were more easily connected to the external world. For example, her sections, though again predominantly in silence, were punctuated by changes of costume or simply 'taking time out', sitting on a chair at the side of the stage. A sound score provided intermittent music, at one point suggesting images of the sea, which in turn provoked swimming motions from the dancer.

Brooke Myers' dramatic *Once Again to Zelda* drew upon her theatrical experience, incorporating script and movement to explore and reassess the

Douglas Dunn in his solo show *Gestures in Red* at Riverside Studios, Dance Umbrella 1978.
PHOTO: CHRIS HARRIS

life of Zelda Fitzgerald, through her unhappy marriage and subsequent mental breakdown. Lastly, Charlip included in his *Solo Dances* programme a series of disparate sketches, drawing upon his experience in different media. *Painting Flying,* we are told, included an assistant who had to trace the dancer's image on paper in various positions, while *Imaginary Dances* included Britain's Richard Alston, who read text on stage.

Of our own representatives, most were repertory-based companies with the exception of three soloists and the companies of Alston and Butcher. (I am not counting the 'pick-up' companies of Smith and North, Warren and Owen.) Maedée Duprès scored successes both in her own solo show *Dance and Slide,* and also for Richard Alston in *Home Ground,* a solo made by him for

Duprès to Purcell's music. Another success was Alston's jazzy solo for himself, *Unknown Banker Buys Atlantic,* to music by Cole Porter. Richard Alston and Dancers played to the largest audience in the first week.[9]

But, with the exception of the performers already mentioned, an unevenness in the technical accomplishment of the British dance groups was frequently noted. Extemporary Dance Company members were singled out for praise in terms of their dance skills, but less so for their repertoire, deemed by many to be insufficiently challenging. Maas Movers gained the distinction of attracting the largest single audience of the entire festival, playing to near capacity in Riverside's Studio 1, while Extemporary played to a full house in the smaller Studio 2.

There were a number of commissioned scores, and evidence of a courageous collaboration in Tamara McLorg's *Solo,* which combined text, music and dance and was described by the choreographer as a 'one-woman show'. This epithet, though, perhaps referred to its feminist subject matter rather than to its personnel, as McLorg collaborated with composer Michael Simmonds and director Alan Lyddiard and included taped voices of Gillian Kerr and Diana Kyle.

Another success for the festival as a whole was Riverside's front-of-house displays and its exhibition of Mark Lancaster designs for the Merce Cunningham Dance Company plus Remy Charlip's drawings; these set up a very helpful festival ambience. Classes and workshops were so well attended that the possibility of residences was mooted. They ranged from exhausting master classes given by Rudner, Jones and Dunn, through Charlip's 'creativity' sessions for adults and children, to voice and movement exercises from Myers. All told, Umbrella 78 was a runaway success, which brilliantly fulfilled its remit of introducing the best of overseas work and of providing a much-needed showcase for our own. It also served to highlight the need for shared management under just such an umbrella scheme, so much so that a follow-up festival was immediately projected, and won an increased budget.

1980

Innovations during the 1980 Dance Umbrella festival included the introduction of groups from Europe (Pauline de Groot's company and Springplank) and a company from Canada, that of Danny Grossman. The idea of a longer-term relationship with the visiting artists was fostered through the first Dance Umbrella commission (though John Jones had made a piece for Maas Movers the previous year). This was *By Appointment Only* made for Extemporary Dance Theatre by Kathryn Posin. This work marked the beginning of an important development for Umbrella, the cross-fertilisation of ideas from visiting choreographers for our comparatively less established companies.

Another innovation was that choreographers from our larger mainstream companies – Ballet Rambert, LCDT and the Royal Ballet – were invited to show work in shared programmes. This contrasted with noticeably fewer dance-in-education companies than in 1978, possibly in answer to criticisms concerning poor technique the previous year, though due also to the Dance in Education Conference held late in 1979 under Umbrella auspices. Whatever the reason, it is clear that the precise festival 'concept' was still up for grabs to some extent. The 1980 report mentions that the idea of an exclusively 'post-modern' festival had been considered and rejected in favour of a more flexible format. Jan Murray's programme notes make this clear: 'The focus is firmly on new and sometimes experimental work, on providing a showcase for the current generation of young British choreographers and recent entries to the ranks of professional dance, on stimulating both participants and spectators with influential forces from overseas.'

It would seem that the decision to cast the net more widely was subsequently validated by the number of exciting, innovative (and undeniably 'post-modern') choreographers who emerged from the Royal Ballet in subsequent years, and who used the festival for experimentation in a way that was denied them in their companies. Jonathan Burrows and Matthew Hawkins both showed work that year and were to become stalwarts of future festivals, joined by the likes of Ashley Page in subsequent years. (Page performed in 1980, but did not show choreography.)

Among the performances, two tacit themes emerged. The first concerned technical training; many of the American visitors had Cunningham somewhere in their past, as did our own Richard Alston and Siobhan Davies. However, the diversity of post-Cunningham explorations in the US was apparent too. Steve Paxton, the dancer responsible for developing the form of contact improvisation and currently teaching at Dartington College in Devon, opened the festival and attracted almost as much critical reaction as had Douglas Dunn the previous year. However, audience and critics had had over twelve months in which to get to grips with post-Cunningham, post-Judson experimentation, and most were bowled over by the intensity of his performances. Paxton shared both his programmes: the first with percussionist David Moss in a mutually inspired and by all accounts wholly engrossing improvisation; the second with fellow contact-improviser Lisa Nelson. Jan Murray for *Time Out* drew upon a recent review of Paxton by Yvonne Rainer to describe the impact of his style:

> In any given set or segment of activity, his movement flow and the shapes through which his body passes may glance off memories of Graham, Cunningham, beefcake, Paul Taylor, Rainer, St. Denis, Duncan, Nijinsky, classic and pre-classic reliefs and murals, gymnastics, you name it. Delsarte gesture. Eastern Martial arts. Trisha Brown. He is a dancing encyclopaedia.[10]

With David Gordon and Valda Setterfield, the audience got a retrospective glimpse of Judson Theater performance in the 1960s. Gordon was forced to abandon his regular Pick-Up Company, and appeared in solos and duets with his wife and partner, Setterfield. The performances were at the cutting edge of performance art, employing photographic projections, tape, props and text. For example, Gordon's solo for himself, *An Audience with the Pope*, had a back projection of dance writer David Vaughan dressed as the Pope in different attitudes, with his taped voice reciting various pun-filled definitions of 'Popery'. However, this backdrop, according to John Percival, acted merely as 'camouflage to a perfectly serious, beautifully modulated and impeccably danced solo'.[11] In other words, at the core of Gordon's dances, however outlandish they might at first appear, there is always an exploration into the nature of dance.

The other theme was collaboration, and the addition of the Whitechapel Gallery meant that two exciting multimedia events could take place. In a work specifically designed for the Upper Gallery at Whitechapel, Miranda Tufnell, Dennis Greenwood and sculptor Tim Head, helped by dancers Sue McLennan and Hugh Davies, collaborated on a series of short dances that made use of projections of light and film, live and taped sounds and various

Opposite above: Musician David Moss with Steve Paxton at the ICA, 21 January 1980.
Opposite below: Steve Paxton and Lisa Nelson at Riverside Studios, 8 February 1980.
PHOTOS: CHRIS HARRIS

props. The space was a long and narrow room in which the audience was invited to sit on benches or cushions against the long walls so that the central space plus the two end walls were used for performance. Critics noted and welcomed an audience in which art students predominated; this was to be a growing trend for Umbrella performances.

Another husband and wife team, dancer Simone Forti and her musician husband Peter van Riper, also performed in the gallery, such being their preferred type of venue in their native New York. Forti displayed an astute understanding of the importance of performance space; and the experience of Pauline de Groot's company of dancers and musicians showed that performances do not always transfer well from one type of venue to another. De Groot's company, originally seen at the Dartington Festival, met with poor reviews when they performed in Riverside Studios. Some writers noted that perhaps the performance would have been better suited to the Whitechapel or Arnolfini, venues that could provide the required intimacy.

Our own artists were praised more as dancers demonstrating a level of technical accomplishment this year (in contrast with the last) than for choreographic inventiveness, and LCDT dancers seemed to be everywhere – in their own choreographic platform and in Ingegerd Lonnroth's company, while LCDS students appeared in Richard Alston's *Dumka*. Maedée Duprès's performance qualities again came in for particular praise, especially in Alston's solo for her, *Schubert Dances,* in which Duprès danced, dressed and made up as the composer.

Dance Umbrella 80 ran for six weeks (seven, counting the week of the Camden Arts Festival for which Umbrella was invited to provide the dance programme) and in four London and three regional venues. The success of these regional outcrops was noted and put forward as an area for possible expansion in following years. This was to prove crucial in helping to make available more funds for visitors to extend their stay. The two series of dance films on show at Riverside and at the ICA represented a vast increase from those of previous years and helped put dance on film at the very forefront of the Umbrella agenda. LWT's *South Bank Show* managed to televise The Merce Cunningham *Travelogue* on 2 March, the final day of the festival proper. Perhaps the enduring theme of the event was the spectre of Cunningham that lurked behind so many of the performances. Steve Paxton gives a powerful analogy, neatly capturing Cunningham's cerebral qualities as well as his illusory ones:

In a period when other art-dance choreographers tended to paint Greek or antique or modern pictures, Cunningham introduced us to the mirror. He produced clean mirrors, mirrors in fragments and whole, darkened mirrors and distorting mirrors. From some viewpoints they were empty, and from others they were full of reflections, images of the watcher's mind . . .[12]

1981

1981's festival ran a deficit for the first time, with ticket sales, healthy in the first four weeks, diminishing in the final week. This, it was thought, might be due to the long and densely packed programme leading to 'festival fatigue'. Artistically, however, it was agreed to have been the best to date by far, an irony that often blights arts planning. Dance Umbrella 81 was also the most cosmopolitan to date, with groups from the US, Japan, Canada, Sweden, Holland and France. It was still the Americans who generated most excite-

Charles Moulton and Dancers in *Through Movement Motor*, Dance Umbrella 1981. PHOTO: CHRIS HARRIS

Left and below: Karole Armitage, with
Joseph Lennon, 1981.
Opposite: Molissa Fenley in her solo
programme *Between Heartbeats*, 1981.
PHOTOS: CHRIS HARRIS

ment and controversy, though Caroline Marcade and Dominique Petit – theatre-trained and from Carolyn Carlson's experimental group at the Paris Opera – also made an impression with a sort of theatrical intensity different from that of the Americans and different from anything seen here before.

The sheer diversity of the American contingent once again amazed and provoked and was again dominated by ex-Cunningham dancers in their very different ways. Charles Moulton's Company was not to everyone's taste, but Jordan remarks on their deceptive accessibility.[13] They opened the Riverside festival in a style that combined relaxed, improvisational, pedestrian movement with tight structuring – hence their deceptiveness. The final piece, *Nine Person Precision Ball Passing,* used nine volunteers in three layers of three, passing coloured tennis balls between them, providing complex patterning, likened by more than one reviewer to a crazed Busby Berkeley routine and by Ann Nugent to a danced version of the Rubik's Cube.[14] The company also performed this piece in Manchester, and some of the audience volunteers from Manchester were matched with a team from London to perform the

Above: Eiko and Koma in *Fur Seal*, 1981.
Below: Maedée Duprès in her solo programme *Time Within Time*, Riverside Studios, 1981.
PHOTOS: CHRIS HARRIS

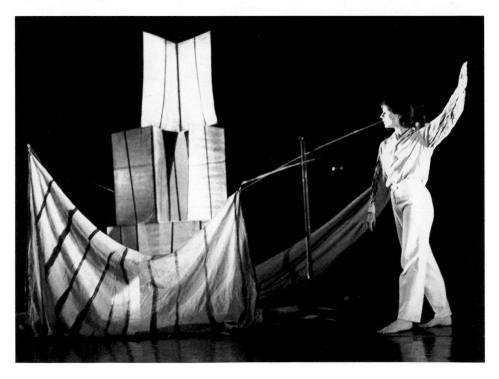

piece at a gala event. Bourne recalls that during rehearsal it was discovered that many of the parts were duplicated, with the Manchester team having learned the same parts as had the London team. 'Oh, it was a nightmare!'[15]

The remarkable athleticism and energy of Karole Armitage and of Molissa Fenley provided a new influence. For Armitage, audience members were offered cotton wool at the door for their ears, and the performance certainly had the sound and the look of punk. But Mary Clarke noted that they had an altogether more serious intent, in their challenge to our ideas about dance and music, albeit with the same anarchic approach.[16] The key was once again tight structure, with Armitage and musician/composer Rhys Chatham both showing their inherent classicism. Molissa Fenley's solo programme had the audience gasping at her athleticism and stamina, and at her ability to cover the stage space leaving intricate afterimages, and seemingly without drawing breath. Again the nuances of her movement, particularly of the arms and hands against the backdrop of pace, were picked up only by a few reviewers.

Different again was the solo programme of Dana Reitz, who appeared at the more intimate and newly reopened Almeida Theatre – a new venue for the Umbrella. Sensitive to the fact that her T'ai-chi-influenced improvisations might not be readily accessible to all, she invited questions from the audience. It happened that the audience included on this occasion a most unlikely group of schoolboys who nevertheless asked the most interesting questions,[17] and her clear explanations plus their lack of pretentiousness proved a huge success. This practice was formally incorporated into the Umbrella format the following year and ever since, with 'meet the choreographer' sessions. The idea was prompted also by a scheme started in New York, in which dancers were sent to locations where dance had never been seen before (a Shaker community was one example) and where the performers had to explain their work verbally in order to make it accessible.

In less need of explanation were Bill T. Jones and Arnie Zane, who made their UK debut in 1981 and would return to the festival for many years to come. They had been collaborating for some ten years and here introduced us to their autobiographical dances about their relationship and about their lives. Their good-natured, joint, largely improvised choreography exploited to the full the differences in their sizes. Perhaps the most unusual and arguably the most affecting performance came from the Japanese-Americans Eiko and Koma with their allegorical *Fur Seal:* 'a view of the human condition seen through the eyes of the post-Hiroshima generation of Japan'.[18] In it, the

Jeremy Nelson and Ian Spink of the Ian Spink Group, in Spink's *De Gas*, ICA, 1981. PHOTO: CHRIS HARRIS

husband and wife team depicted the harsh and lighter sides of both animal and human life in an intense and deeply moving performance.

If American work was marked by its sophistication and professionalism, the British contingent's was marked by the integrity of its intentions. There were important commissions, collaborations and cross-fertilisations, many of which took full advantage of the festival's subsidiary theme of dance and design. Rosemary Butcher and company performed two collaborative works: *Spaces 4* was her latest piece with the sculptor Heinz-Dieter Pietsch, and *Shell: Forcefields and Spaces* was made with visual artist Jon Groom. This had a wailing trombone solo by Jim Fulkerson, and movement suggested by the spirals and circles of the title. Reviews suggest greater understanding and

Sally Banes and Deborah Jowitt in conversation during the Dance Writing and Criticism course at the ICA, 1981. PHOTO: CHRIS HARRIS

sympathy for Butcher's highly eclectic style this year, perhaps in recognition of its integrity and originality.

Maedée Duprès also featured design and commissioned music in her solo programme. Duprès's own *Splitter* had an electronic score from Stephen Montague and design by Craig Givens – a red silk kinetic sculpture. Givens also designed for two of the other works on Duprès's programme, with Maria Liljfors supplying designs for Fulkerson's *Song from the Country*. Fulkerson's choreography also featured in her own slot: of particular note was a duet *The Raft is not the Shore* for Michael Clark (appearing this year as a dancer only) and Beverley Sandwith, to music again by Jim Fulkerson. Clark's skills as a dancer were also noted in his appearances for Ian Spink's company. Dancework included work by Judith Moss (seen the previous year with Rosalind Newman's Company) and Ruth Barnes, a solo performer in this year's festival. One of Rosemary Butcher's dancers, Sue MacLennan, 'graduated' to her own Umbrella slot, and this trend of the creative performer showing her or his own work would be seen again.

Perhaps the most unusual of the British offerings was artist Lizzie Cox's *A Year in the Life of a Field at Nettlecombe, Somerset*, which was a piece about seasonal change. Action was set in an eight-foot cube with one side open to the audience. Dancer Kirstie Simson interacted with the set, revealing different layers of printed fabric, to Stuart Gordon's specially written music (played, unfortunately according to some, on a tape recorder).

The Dance Writing and Criticism course deserves mention for its innovatory nature, being the first course in a Dance Umbrella festival, and for its excellent tutors: Sally Banes, Deborah Jowitt and John Mueller. It also demanded an approach that some regarded as unusual, as it included practical workshops integrated with analysis and lectures. For once the master class series was not a huge success. This seems to have been due to something of a mismatch between artists, venues and clientele, involving prejudice on all sides. The classes were held at the Pineapple Centre, a venue deemed inappropriate by some dance students ('flashy' and 'commercial' were epithets frequently overheard), while the usual Pineapple clientele had never heard of the guest teachers. However, Gina Levete's workshops for people with disabilities were a success and were repeated the following year.

1982

In 1982, performance art and dance theatre were strongly emphasised, with Tim Miller and Kei Takei's Moving Earth the leaders of the genre. The Tate Gallery was added to the list of venues, which emphasised the idea of a strong link with the visual arts – a carry-over from the previous year's theme. The official sub-theme was dance and music, with many commissioned scores, collaborations and courageous choices of accompaniment as well as the first live music concert of the festival series, led by Jim Fulkerson. Something of an autobiographical flavour pervaded the festival as well, with a return by popular demand of Jones and Zane (whose work inevitably contained elements of their own lives), Dan Wagoner's film *George's House* shown during the ICA series (in which Wagoner evokes childhood memories), and Tim Miller's *Postwar.*

Another of this year's innovations was the series of meet-the-choreographer sessions, sparked off by Dana Reitz at the Almeida Theatre the previous year. Val Bourne has said that one idea she had in mind was that of residences in London and the regions along the lines of the French *stages*, or courses, in which influential visitors can interact with local artists. This proved over-ambitious, and instead the festival included informal sessions during which the audience could question the artists about their work. In the same broadly educative vein, the Judson Dance Theater Exhibition was the first major exhibition that the Umbrella had hosted. It was accompanied by Sally Banes, who gave contextual lectures on American contemporary dance as well as on the Judson Dance Theater years. The organisers noted the 'festival fatigue' brought about by simultaneous performances in 1981, and so activity was now more spaced out between venues. Classes and workshops continued, this time at various venues in and around London, including The Place, ICA, Goldsmith's College, Pineapple West Dance Centre and Froebel College, Roehampton.

British representation could have been stronger across the board, but there were some important exceptions. Extemporary Dance Theatre drew much attention, as did Michael Clark, and Laurie Booth for his idiosyncratic performance. An important precedent was set with the 'British Independents' spot, giving young choreographers a platform to try out experimental work. This was to lead to important developments in later years, but this year Matthew Hawkins made a particular impression with his solo *Advent II* and

Tim Miller and Company in *Postwar*, ICA, 1982. PHOTO: CHRIS HARRIS

trio *Current Response.* These pieces were Cunningham-inspired in both their movement vocabulary and their process.

The repertory-based Extemporary Dance Theatre benefited from commissions from former Umbrella alumni that showcased the dancers to best advantage. Karole Armitage's *It Happened at Club Bombay Cinema* highlighted the tension ever present in her work between classical control and postmodern anarchy, while David Gordon's *Counter Revolution* was at once a series of puns, an exposé of a dancer's mental processes and a spoof of 1960s task-based choreography from the Judson era.

Clark presented a much revised version of his own *of a feather, flock*, the Alston solo *Dutiful Ducks*, and a five-minute piece entitled *Rush*. The programme notes for *Rush* gave all manner of dictionary definitions for the title word. In fact, the piece consisted of material hitherto shown, recycled at speed with a 'fast forward' version of *Dutiful Ducks* played on a video screen and with Clark stopping and starting it on occasions to repeat steps. Booth presented a solo *Crazy Daisy and the Northern Lights* with a puppet 'partner' attached to his body. The dance depicted the journey through life of 'eighties

Rosalind Newman and Dancers at Riverside Studios, 1982. PHOTO: CHRIS HARRIS

Mary Fulkerson and Dancers, 1982. PHOTO: CHRIS HARRIS

girl' Daisy, with Booth as her puppeteer/manipulator, her lover or an extension of the puppet character herself. Clark charmed and Booth fascinated.

But yet again it was the Americans who provoked the most controversy. Tim Miller presented a theatrical event in his full-length *Postwar,* which included the cooking of a hamburger on stage, multiple recordings of a telephone voice, photocopies of his birth certificate thrown into the auditorium, blown-up family snapshots, a dancer with a carnival-style President Reagan mask, acting, dancing and mime in an altogether hysterically toned production. All this, while contrasting the American Dream with Cold War American reality and within the context of Miller's youthful autobiography.

Different again was Kei Takei's Moving Earth. Based in New York but born in Tokyo, Takei presented excerpts from her life's work, *Light,* with a chamber group of two male performers. This piece was begun in 1969 and has gradually evolved ever since, as a cross-fertilisation of ideas from Japanese and American theatre cultures. The sections, we are told, are based on parables from the Buddhist and Christian traditions, so that each is a small morality play, making use of props, chanting and theatrically charged movement. In 1982 the full dance lasted over four hours and consisted of seventeen sections, each with a single theme, of which four that were suitable for duets and solos were selected for the Umbrella. Stephanie Jordan and Howard Friend felt that the reduced version did less than full justice to the piece: 'There is accumulated effect in the larger context of the structures; like a series of selected woodcuts, each with a single theme, there is greater richness in greater display.'[19]

Of the Europeans, Anne Teresa de Keersmaeker undoubtedly made the most impact when appearing with Michele Anne de Mey in *Fase, four movements on the music of Steve Reich*, a seventy-minute work that was only her second composition. In its form, *Fase* follows Steve Reich's earliest compositions in their development of a small amount of material with repetition and imperceptibly shifting variations, producing mesmerising effects. Yet again, the sheer diversity of the work shown – from de Keersmaeker to Tim Miller, not forgetting the crucial educative value of Banes's exhibition and lectures – further opened the audience's eyes to the possibilities for dance.

1983

This year, the festival came close to being cancelled altogether, as funds from two expected sources were lost just a couple of months before the festival was due to begin. In the event it had to be cut by a week, losing David Gordon and his Pick-Up Company, and there were fewer regional events. Innovations this year included the Made in Britain series and the voucher scheme.

Dance and film was the festival's secondary theme. This was seen in the ground-breaking video project at Riverside Studios, but was also apparent within many of the dances: Tony Thatcher's collaboration with film-maker David Robinson for Dancework's *Grey Window*; Michael Clark's *Parts I–IV* collaboration with video artist Cerith Wyn Evans; Robert Rauschenberg's black-and-white film projections for Trisha Brown's *Set and Reset*; and Laurie Booth's, Giovanna Rogante's and Nicolas Cincone's *From Ordinary Lives,* which had videos made by Pete Anderson and Steve Littman.

Brown played to capacity audiences on every night of her five-day residence at Riverside, which was her second visit to London.[20] She opened the final week of the festival with the visually stunning *Set and Reset*, with designs by Rauschenberg of semi-transparent wings and black-and-white news clips projected onto hanging three-dimensional frames, and with music by

Laurie Anderson. (Anderson seemed to provide another sub-theme, her music being used by Sally Sykes for the Made in Britain series, by Basic Space Dance Theatre and by Jane Dudley in her piece for Extemporary Dance Theatre.) *Son of Gone Fishin'* has a commissioned score by Robert Ashley that changes with every performance: the dancers can choose from a range of sound tapes. The programme managed to combine the effects of seemingly uncontrived groupings and regroupings of dancers, like so many iron filings, with unexpected entrances and exits and abrupt catches, to provide mind-bending conundrums in terms of structure.

Lisa Kraus's full-evening solo piece *Going Solo,* marking her departure from the Trisha Brown Company after five years, combined spoken commentary with dance in an essentially autobiographical work. Counteracting the suspicion from the previous year that some American artists were tending a little too much towards slick shows of virtuosity, Kraus's performance was marked by its understatement. Richness in diversity was again apparent, with the soloists Kraus and Dana Reitz, together with Robert Kovich and company, offering essentially formalist explorations. At the other end of the scale, Jones and Zane were back with a small company extended by three female dancers, offering a more populist entertainment that spoke of street culture, graffiti and pop. The Canadian group La La La offered a different sort of post-modernism, with rock music and forty-five cut-out Scottie dogs (one of which 'spoke') plus bravura performances of risk-taking and aggressive physicality, during which the extraordinary and charismatic performer Louise Lecavalier was introduced to the London audience.

Diversity was apparent within the British camp too. Extemporary Dance Theatre again had their repertory boosted by commissions, including one by Clark. Then there were the risk-takers: Booth, Julyen Hamilton and Kirstie Simson, Rosemary Butcher with her 'cool and quasi-mystic brand of minimalism',[21] Sue MacLennan and Tamara McLorg. MacLennan used dancers and non-dancers as two separate groups in her *New Moves.* Following on from Tim Miller's hamburger the previous year and not to be outdone, Micha Bergese cooked a whole Italian meal on stage.

Second Stride presented pieces from its three choreographers, all stretching the powerful techniques of its freelance performers in different ways. *Minor Characters*, a text-based piece by Siobhan Davies, explored the relationship between speech and movement in its evocation of character, using a 'Greek chorus' of Sally Owen and Betsy Gregory. Alston's light-hearted *Java,*

Bill T. Jones, Arnie
Zane and Company,
1983.
PHOTO: CHRIS HARRIS

danced to Inkspots recordings, contrasted with his newest work, the more formal *The Brilliant and the Dark* to a Benjamin Britten score. Spink's *Some Fugues* had four of its five dances tightly structured in fugue form according to the music, the middle dance departing into improvisation.

Once again Booth provided much to provoke and inspire. This year he was seen in collaboration with Italian performers Rogante and Cincone, designer Kate Owen and video-makers Anderson and Lipman. *From Ordinary Lives* traced the lives of various characters in movement, speech, music and video. For *Musk: Red*, Hamilton collaborated with Matthieu Keijser and British dancer Simson, with props including giant windchimes, one mobile of gongs and percussion instruments and another of saucepans. This was a development of the previous year's duet for Hamilton and Keijser, and contained inter-action between improvising dancers and a musician keen to play anything, set and dancers alike.

As if to draw a comparison between French post-modern dance and the rest, a French 'New Wave' Festival was held at Riverside during the Umbrella dates. The anarchically humorous Daniel Larrieu appeared in both, with a temporary company called Chelsea Quick Pick-Up in the New Wave Festival and with dancers Pascale Henrot and Pascale Houbin from his group Astrakan for Dance Umbrella. For the latter, Larrieu presented *Chiquenaude,* which relied heavily on minute distinctions of gesture, plus the surreal *Volte-Face,* which made use of dramatic classical scores.

1984

Dance Umbrella 84 was something of a turning point: there was no company with status on a par with that of Trisha Brown, but there were several compensatory factors, not least a growing recognition of the quality of some of our own performers. The festival also marked the first collaboration with Sadler's Wells Theatre, an event described by Bourne as a 'quantum leap' in terms of the festival's growing status.[22] Second Stride was seen in two pieces full of suppressed passion, shown in very different ways. Ian Spink's *Further and Further into Night* was the choreographer's response to Alfred Hitchcock's 1946 film *Notorious.* Scenes from the film were literally deconstructed to reveal their basic components and then rearranged, repeated in tape-loop sequences and explored as variations *ad infinitum.* Siobhan Davies's *Silent Partners* was an exploration of different couple-relationships, developing to an intense emotional climax.

The Made in Britain series also reached a turning point. Although it was proving immensely popular with choreographers, many of whom had a devoted following (the second programme was a sell-out and several others were close to selling out), it was widely believed that the format was not yet quite right. Made in Britain's five programmes for Dance Umbrella 84 presented work by twenty-two choreographers, many showing more than one piece. The result of keeping an open policy was that evenings were extremely long and of variable quality, sometimes stretching the audience's patience to the limit. However, there were some powerful pieces, and some young choreographers – Gaby Agis, Ashley Page and Yolande Snaith among them – made an impact. Other contributors were perennial Umbrella performers who were showing new work. Singled out for praise were Laurie Booth's *Beyond Zero,*

Richard Alston's duet *Coursing* for Bruce Sansom and Page, Agis's and Page's *Between Public Places* (a highly acclaimed and unusual duet in which release-based movement met ballet training) and Sue MacLennan's and Matthew Hauxwell's *Seven Desperate Years*. Clearly the series was performing a most important function within the remit of the Umbrella. Policy needed to maintain some flexibility to embrace this need, while rendering the events more easily digestible.

Extemporary Dance Theatre had three new commissioned pieces in its repertoire this year, as well as a recent work by Michael Clark. Clark also made a piece for English Dance Theatre, the witty and intricate *Morag's Wedding* in which Scottish dancing, ballet and pop are all explored. For Clark's own company, *New Puritans* had outrageous cut-away costumes; but, for all that, both pieces contained a density of challenging movement material that endeared him to audiences and critics alike.

For the Americans, newcomer Mark Morris presented a perhaps atypical repertoire at the festival, as he was reduced to only three dancers. However, the dance and music sub-theme was certainly evident within his work and Morris was to play an important role in later Umbrellas. Yushiko Chuma, festival artist-in-residence, led a community dance project that she rehearsed and organised over a period of one month. (The residency and the community dance project were both festival 'firsts'.) The sheer scale of the epic *Five Car Pile-Up* was interesting enough, with some one hundred people performing ritualised unison movements. The participants included her own company as well as some of our dancers – Agis, MacLennan, Simson and Anna Furse among them. There were no cars, but there were chairs, umbrellas, newspapers, toothbrushes and other assorted props, a huge weather balloon that hovered throughout the proceedings at the back of the hall, and music sampling by Christian Marclay. A very good time was had by all who experienced it.

Alongside the theme of dancer/musician collaboration, there seemed to be a general broadening of the scope of choreographic parameters to include more multimedia events, and there were some very interesting theatrical collaborations. We had become used to a meeting of different cultures in previous festivals with Japanese-Americans Eiko and Koma and Kei Takei's Moving Earth. This year, American Jazz musician Steve Lacy performed with Noh and kabuki artist Shiro Daimon. Lacy provided accompaniment and commentary while Daimon acted out three scenes. Regardless of what the

Above: Second Stride in Ian Spink's *Further and Further Into Night*. PHOTO: CHRIS HARRIS
Below: Mark Morris and Company, *Not Goodbye*, 1984. PHOTO: CHRIS NASH

title *Kabuki-Woogie* might imply, the performance was slow, atmospheric and contemplative. Macaulay wrote: 'Both are performers of deep absorption. Daimon's rapid-shuffle, tortoise-advance, diagonal in the scene of wizened, bent-double *vieillesse*, his raw and tender fall to the floor and to life in the scene of birth: these were the most haunting images in Umbrella's first three weeks'.[23]

Visual artist David Ward, with dancers Miranda Tufnell and Dennis Greenwood, presented *Huge Veil*, based on lighting effects on the human body. Tufnell and Greenwood were clothed in white silk costumes designed by Katherine Hamnett, and performed against a billowing white sail stretched across the performance space so that only a few feet remained in front, with patterns of light playing on all the surfaces. The performance gave rise to some stunning photographs by Chris Harris, which were displayed at Riverside. MacLennan, Ian Mitchell and Steven Montague turned the idea of collaboration on its head with dancer MacLennan making music and musician Mitchell dancing. Mitchell later interpreted Stockhausen's *The Little Harlequin* in which he played clarinet while following notated foot rhythms. Katy Duck had been resident since 1979 in Florence, from whence hailed her Group O, but was relatively well known to British audiences through her

Shiro Daimon in
Kabuki-Woogie, 1984.
PHOTO: CHRIS NASH

Miranda Tufnell, Dennis Greenwood and David Ward's installation, *Huge Veil,* 1984. PHOTO: CHRIS HARRIS

teaching at Dartington College. *Rutles* combined dance, conversation, games and song to explore two very different sources, the film *The Deerhunter* and Beatles songs, in a surreal juxtaposition that sparked off the dancers' own associative fantasies.

* * *

During this whole period, from 1978 to 1984, it became apparent that British artists were broadening their ideas, had taken counsel from the US and from Europe but had emerged with their own distinctive style. The development of British choreographers under the Umbrella is dealt with in greater detail in Chapter 4, but it is clear that by 1984 Britain had artists and companies that were developing fast, with some showing work that was now on a par with that of the visitors. One critic, Alastair Macaulay, compared the two new works in Second Stride's repertory with those shown by Trisha Brown the previous year, in their ability to 'light up the Umbrella'.[24] Here was praise indeed.

Compagnie Charles Cré-Ange, *Noir Salle*, 1989.
PHOTO: CHRIS NASH

3

The Europeans Make their Mark: 1985–1989

Trends and Developments

European and American Influences: Questions of Identity

Although the Americans had dominated the earlier period, this one was marked by the increasing prominence of European work. The previous six years had seen a trickle of European groups, but their numbers had been far outweighed by their American contemporaries. However, Pina Bausch had made an enormous impression on British audiences, and her influence on other European companies was also clear from Umbrella performances. In 1984, the 'Rates of Exchange' seminar debated the problems of funding in this country, when it became apparent that other European countries enjoyed more favourable levels of state aid than those found in the UK and USA. For whatever reason, European dance became an issue, which seemed to fuel an obsession with questions of national identity and stylistic influence.

In 1985, an exchange of performers with France and Holland was high on the agenda, and Dance Umbrella 85 was the first festival in which European companies outnumbered the Americans. Although this situation did not continue every year, some European companies, for example those of Daniel Larrieu, Charles Cré-Ange and Angelin Preljocaj, successfully insinuated themselves into the consciousness of the Dance Umbrella audience over the period leading up to the bicentenary celebrations of 1989. Larrieu had first appeared in Dance Umbrella 83 with his company Astrakan, and then again in 1985, having been commissioned in the interim to make a new work (*Ombres Eléctriques*, 1984) for Extemporary Dance Theatre. Compagnie Cré-

Ange, one of the most successful French companies of Dance Umbrella 89, had established themselves through visits in 1986 and 1988. However, perhaps the most influential of the Europeans was Rosas, the company led by Belgian choreographer Anne Teresa de Keersmaeker, whose work stressed a formalism that often appeared to be neglected by many of the French companies.

Some critics were less than ecstatic about French dance in general, and hinted that the main reason for its inclusion in the festivals was financial. In her editorial for the Dance Umbrella 85 programme, Val Bourne had warned darkly that the imminent demise of the GLC, along with the Government's insistence on commercial sponsorship as the only solution to funding problems, would inevitably mean a different kind of festival. Priority would have to be given to larger, more prestigious overseas companies, rather than to the independent and new British artists that it had previously promoted. From this period onwards, we saw European companies being showcased more prominently. This was particularly true of the French, who enjoyed large state subsidies in their own country, and the press was understandably sceptical. The truth is, however, that support from AFAA (L'Association Française d'Action Artistique) was always very modest. Val Bourne points out that 'Revolutionary Tactics' was dependent mostly on British money and on a successful collaboration with John Ashford at The Place, and that 'we've very rarely been influenced by money!'[1]

Nevertheless, the funding situation prompted a useful contextual discussion in the press, comparing funding patterns and artistic influence in France and the UK. Two critics, Andrew Lucre of the *Sunday Times* and Jann Parry of the *Observer*, offered interesting information and analysis. Certainly France enjoyed a flourishing dance culture, which owed a great deal to government grants that were huge by our standards: in 1988 the budget for dance was FF 100M (about £10M).[2] Parry argued that this situation stemmed from a tradition cultivated by Louis XIV, when dance and the arts were perceived as symbols of power and prestige. Nowadays, instead of the spectacular court of the Sun King, the French government 'proudly subsidises companies to travel abroad as cultural ambassadors, and Paris and the regions set up dance festivals to attract business and tourism'.[3] Lucre added that the French government's recent recognition of contemporary dance stemmed from the early 1970s, when young choreographers were first making an impact on the dance scene and were influenced by two extreme and different sources: Merce Cunningham and Pina Bausch. Today's choreography from France still

sometimes shows discernible influence from both sources: emotional intensity from Bausch, rigorous crafting from Cunningham and an eccentric,
unorthodox and iconoclastic approach to movement from both choreographers. To these, Bourne would add the influence of Carolyn Carlson and
Alwin Nikolais.[4]

These discussions form a fascinating backdrop to the activities of the
festivals throughout this period, and references to identity and stylistic precedent are made again and again within the longer reviews. The best of the
French companies, such as those mentioned above, were very interesting
indeed and certainly served as an alternative model to the American guests.
During Dance Umbrella 87, Fiona Burnside identified a distinctly Bausch-
influenced expressionism within the work of some of our own companies –
DV8 Physical Theatre, for example – and in Ashley Page's work at the time.[5]
These experiences, together with American influence over the years,
strengthened British work to such an extent that Alastair Macaulay could
claim that the 1990 festival showed the British now presenting the strongest
work by comparison.[6]

The period began, however, with a celebration of American dance, with
the Merce Cunningham Dance Company at Sadler's Wells Theatre in August
1985 (just before the Umbrella festival) and a Bite of the Big Apple season at
the Bloomsbury Theatre around this time. American issues were also apparent within the Umbrella-organised Parallels in Black season of 1987 (discussed below), which celebrated the diversity of new American black dance.
We also saw some powerful American visitors returning: for example, David
Gordon (1980 and 1985) and Trisha Brown (1983 and 1987). The Cunningham
Company made its Dance Umbrella debut in 1989. These choreographers
consolidated their influence, but in addition there were new flavours, choreographers such as Mark Morris and Karole Armitage who constituted a second
generation of post-Cunningham dance makers. These choreographers
Macaulay identified as displaying a new interest in tradition, in forms taken
from earlier dance history and in dance's past narratives.[7] In Sally Banes's
terms, they were 'post-modernist': forming an apparent contradistinction
with the earlier 'analytic' phase of post-modernism in dance, while aligning
themselves more overtly with the post-modernism of other art forms.[8]

Macaulay made another important point on this topic.[9] He first acknowledged our seduction by the French, commenting that their sexiness and
worldly-wise qualities contrasted with our puritan new dance world. How-

ever, he claimed that British dance, in common with American, retained its allegiance to formal concerns, over and above those of theatrical and dramatic effect and in marked contrast to the general ethos of European companies. What all this adds up to is that British independent dance was all the while taking sustenance from exposure to both American and European dance, and yet was developing apace its own distinctive styles. For example, the dance programmes of Siobhan Davies's new company and of DV8 were proclaimed the major successes of Dance Umbrella 88. If there was a common thread to these two groups, it was that both Davies and Newson had been influenced by contact improvisation, an influence that could be traced directly or indirectly to Steve Paxton; but they had developed these ideas in ways that produced more highly polished and theatrical performances. The new finesse apparent in British work might have stemmed from a European influence, with the tight presentation of groups such as Rosas and Cré-Ange having been noted in previous years in comparison with our own companies. By 1998 Jann Parry was drawing our attention to the fact that the Umbrella was now largely empty of a generation of performers such as Julyen Hamilton and Kirstie Simson, who were also influenced by Paxton-style improvisations but whose work tended to favour a 'loosely structured, work-in-progress' style of presentation.[10]

British Independents – From Platform to Graduation

Chapter 2 showed how the independent dance platforms developed and flourished during the preceding period. This development continued, despite the financial constraints of which Val Bourne had warned. In 1985 there was an explosion of 'new works' programmes, with four Triple Bills and five Late Extras (shows starting after the main performances at The Place Theatre). But critics complained of over-programming, were suffering from dance indigestion, or simply voted with their feet and did not turn up.

1986, then, saw a cutback in independent dance activity. There were no designated new-work platforms, but to some extent the Flying Starts programmes took over the role of showcasing young British talent, introducing The Cholmondeleys amongst others. Dance Umbrellas 87 and 88 each provided a relatively modest two programmes dedicated to new work. Dance Umbrella 89 had a different emphasis again, owing to its French theme, and contained four platform performances entitled 'British Independents for Bagnolet'. These enabled British choreographers to show works for consideration for entry into the prestigious Bagnolet International Choreographic Competition. As a result, Liz Aggiss and Lea Anderson were invited to participate in the 1990 competition.

Underpinning this shift in emphasis was the graduation by some of our artists either to their own slot or to an enhanced programme. Ashley Page, for example, showed work with Gaby Agis during the 1984 and 1985 Made in Britain series. He then expanded to a double bill with Jonathan Burrows in 1986, for which he received a Dance Umbrella commission; then to his own programme in 1987 with one of the major commissions of that year, *The Angel of Death is in My Bed Tonight* – a full evening's work. A second example

Laurie Booth and
Nick Pile in *Terminus
Terminux*, The Place
Theatre, 1989.
PHOTO: HUGO GLENDINNING

Greg Nash.
PHOTO: CHRIS NASH

is Laurie Booth, who, from solo performances in Dance Umbrellas 81 and 82, went on to ever more complex and ambitious collaborations. He joined with musician Harry de Wit in 1985 and 1987, and in 1989 collaborated with audiovisual artist Lol Sargent, composer Philip Jeck and a small company, to produce *Terminus Terminux*, the second part of his ambitious trilogy, *Danse Noire*.

The commissioning of work increased considerably during this period, with money now going almost entirely to home-grown choreographers. Thus the emphasis changed from commissioning works from visitors in order to extend our companies' repertoires, to enabling choreographers such as Davies and Page to finance a whole evening's performance. Dance Umbrella was demonstrating its confidence that a new generation of young choreographers was now ready and able to show work alongside the best from other nations.

British choreographers were also taking over some of the roles previously created by and around prestigious foreign guests. Dance Umbrella persisted in occasional community projects, though now on a grander scale, perhaps here too showing a changed attitude to such work, one that no longer associated community-based work necessarily with the second rate. Yoshiko Chuma, the first festival artist-in-residence, had set the ball rolling with the huge project of Dance Umbrella 84, *Five Car Pile-Up*. Greg Nash followed up in 1986 with *Momentum Rush*, a youth project involving over a hundred participants and divided between four city centres. In 1990 Lloyd Newson was appointed the first British artist-in-residence at the festival, itself an accolade, and DV8 did not perform during that year's festival, Newson preferring to devote his energies to teaching.

Two important questions were posed for Dance Umbrella's tenth anniversary in 1988. Firstly, how had British independent dance developed? Secondly, given that other venues (Riverside, ICA and The Place) all now ran strong dance programmes emphasising the cutting edge of dance, what then was the role of Dance Umbrella? Our account so far bears testimony to the very strong development and diversity of British dance. It appeared that Dance Umbrella, after a great deal of trial and error, had by the end of the decade largely redefined its identity. It was now presenting more ambitious work by artists who had reached a level of maturity. This left Chisenhale Dance Space, among others, to showcase the rawer works-in-progress, while Dance Umbrella's experimental platform could exercise a tighter control than in previous years.

Themes and Linked Projects

The London-based festivals during these years tended at first to continue an emphasis on particular aspects of dance culture, alternately focusing on 'dance and film' and 'dance and music' and occasionally on both. However, as the period progressed, the thematic idea changed direction and began to serve dance in a different way, possibly as a result of themes becoming driven less by artistic concerns and more by marketing needs. Around this time too, Dance Umbrella started to diversify its operations. It presented short seasons outside the autumn London Umbrella event, promoted British choreographers abroad and encouraged and helped kindred festivals to develop in the regions. A notable instance was the first Leicester International Dance Festival in 1989, with a similar festival in Newcastle already in the pipeline.

Within London, 1988 provided the opportunity to celebrate the Umbrella's tenth anniversary with a gala programme, DecaDance, at Sadler's Wells. This featured artists from our independent sector as well as from mainstream companies, and included guests from France and the USA. The following year saw a similar enterprise, Legs Eleven, this time emphasising the French connection in honour of the bicentenary. The main purpose of each enterprise was to raise funds for the commissioning of work for the Umbrella festival proper.

Some of the theme-based seasons are dealt with in greater depth later in this chapter. They continued the work of Umbrella in exposing British audiences to dance experiences drawn from beyond our shores. The 'Parallels' season also raised important issues and advanced their debate.

1987 saw 'The British are Coming' (10 April – 10 May), a season of new British dance in Copenhagen featuring Rosemary Butcher, Yolande Snaith, Laurie Booth and DV8, as well as musicians Michael Nyman, Loose Tubes and Courtney Pine, the Penguin Café Orchestra, Bow Gamelan and theatre groups Théatre de Complicité, Cheek by Jowl and Royal Court Theatre. This was not, however, the first event of its kind, for Umbrella had promoted a visit by dance artists to the Munich New Dance Festival in March 1985. The local press generally acclaimed the 'English' [sic] evening as the major success of the festival.[11] It opened with Laurie Booth and musician Philip Jeck in *Beyond Zero*, and continued with two more duos, Ashley Page and Gaby Agis who presented *Between Public Places,* and Sue MacLennan and Matthew Hauxwell in *Seven Desperate Years*.

Parallels in Black: New Black American Dance

These performances (23–24 and 28–29 February 1987, Place Theatre) were presented jointly by Dance Umbrella and The Place Theatre as part of The Place's 'Spring Loaded' season. Parallels in Black came about in response to criticism that British black and Asian artists had been under-represented in recent Dance Umbrella festivals. In fact the situation flagged up an anomaly within dance funding: Dance Umbrella was committed to innovative and experimental dance, but few African, Afro-Caribbean or Asian artists were choosing to work specifically within this area. This was because Greater London Arts, while prioritising what was then called Black Arts, excluded all those artists 'whose work lies within the Western European tradition and who are in effect artists who just happen to be black'.[12] In an attempt to draw attention to this Catch-22 situation and perhaps prompt a change in funding criteria, young American choreographers were invited to show work, to provoke debate and to raise the issue of what young British choreographers are to do if their interests lie within their present cultural situation, rather than exclusively within their cultural heritage. The 'parallels' referred to the idea that all six artists lived parallel lives: as black Americans and as avant-garde artists whose value systems, as Elizabeth Zimmer pointed out, 'often appear to conflict with the strong community-oriented feeling in much black American dance'.[13] The original Parallels series was curated by Ishmael Houston-Jones and included work by five of the six artists visiting Britain, with Jawole Willa Jo Zollar being the relative newcomer.

The season featured Bebe Miller, Ralph Lemon, Zollar (who later and highly successfully brought her troupe, the Urban Bush Women, to the autumn Umbrella festival), Blondell Cummings, Fred Holland and Houston-Jones. As well as performances, there were opportunities to exchange ideas and to interact with our own choreographers. Jayshree Naidoo, on behalf of the Black Dance Forum, hosted a party at the October Gallery to start the season, and there were workshops with London-based dance groups. Cummings worked with Irie Dance Theatre and IDJ; Zollar taught Adzido; and Miller and Houston-Jones each worked separately with Union Dance Company. Islington Arts Factory hosted a series of three workshops and Independent Dance arranged a further four. Cummings stayed on an extra few days to teach two sessions for West Sussex Institute of Higher Education in Chichester. As a follow-up, the BBC's *Saturday Review* featured a special programme on black dance in Britain on 6 March.

The point to be made was that these artists all worked in totally diverse ways, though all tended to emphasise autobiographical material and collaboration and to make use of multimedia, with Zollar's work drawing perhaps more than the others specifically upon traditional historical sources. She observed at the time, 'There's something really strong happening in the black performing arts right now, a strong creative energy. The cultural explosion of the Sixties and Seventies is being reshaped from a much less reactionary point of view'.[14] The artists preceded their London performances with dates in Europe, and, far from being the racial gimmick that some had feared, the tour fulfilled its commitment to widening the debate. Ralph Lemon wrote from New York, 'By the final performance and discussion in London, I was convinced that this tour, with all its complications, was extremely important not only to my artistic needs but also to a personally felt social obligation. Granted this tour did not answer all my "life" questions, but it did create a clearer picture of my relationship to the dance world as a Black artist.'[15] In this instance then, it seems that Umbrella exposure helped an overseas artist to clarify his own situation. Certainly the season seemed to provide a useful injection for future British developments along the lines of Shobana Jeyasingh, who draws upon elements from more than one cultural tradition, bearing in mind that the first performances of her company took place the following year.

Going Dutch

Going Dutch (4–12 March 1989) took place at The Place Theatre, at Phoenix Arts in Leicester and at Chapter Arts Centre, Cardiff, and was advertised as a spotlight on new dance from Holland. The season featured performances by leading dance artists Beppie Blankert and Angelika Oei as well as an exhibition of photography by Hans van Manen at The Place Theatre, film and video screenings and a seminar, plus the ubiquitous 'meet the artists' sessions. Holland provided yet another example of a country in which dance had flourished since the war, owing in more recent years to generous state support. Its dance culture gave priority to new works for all the companies, both major and independent, and this too provided an important cue for our own companies.

Organised by Dance Umbrella, ostensibly to celebrate the William and Mary tercentenary and with the expressed intention of expanding the British dance public's knowledge of Dutch dance, Going Dutch built upon our experience of performers who had appeared in Dance Umbrella festivals in previous years. As early as the second festival in 1980, Springplank had made their British debut, followed by Werkcentrum Dans in 1981, Pauline Daniëls in 1984 and Dansproduktie in 1985, not forgetting early frequent contributors to the festivals, Julyen Hamilton and Kirstie Simson, who had made Holland their home. However, of Holland's three major companies, only the Dutch National Ballet had been seen in London relatively recently. The remaining two, Nederlands Dans Theater and Scapino Ballet, had not

Pauline Daniëls and Harry de Wit in *13*, 1985. PHOTO: CHRIS NASH

been seen for well over a decade. Few people, for example, knew of van Manen's reputation in photography, as a highly professional adjunct to his choreography for, and direction of, the Dutch National Ballet and Nederlands Dans Theater. Going Dutch was supported by the Netherlands Theatre Institute as well as by our own Arts Council's International Initiatives Fund.

Revolutionary Tactics

Revolutionary Tactics was a joint initiative by Dance Umbrella and John Ashford of The Place Theatre. It aimed to introduce British audiences to a broad spectrum of French dance throughout 1989 and to provide what was in effect a year-long celebration of French dance. To kick off the theme, 'April in Paris' (17–29 April 1989, at The Place Theatre) featured Claude Brumachon, Brigitte Farges, Kelemenis, Jean François Duroure, Joseph Nadj and Mark Tompkins, and Odile Duboc. Curated by John Ashford, this mini-season was really a separate venture and formed part of a series of 'April in Paris' seasons. However, Dance Umbrella was able to capitalise on the name and use it as part of the festivities.

Dance Umbrella was solely responsible for 'Brolly Breaks', including an excursion to the Montpellier Festival in the summer, for which Umbrella organised travel, accommodation and tickets.[16] There were related events at the Queen Elizabeth Hall and the French Institute, a planned fortnight of dance at the Pompidou Centre in May, contributions to the programmes of the newly established Epinal Dance Festival and a culmination in Dance Umbrella 89 with its bicentenary theme.

Leicester International Dance Festival

The first Leicester International Dance Festival ran for a modest two-and-a-half weeks, from Thursday 2 March to Sunday 19 March 1989. Val Bourne was contacted initially by Peter Lichtenfels and David Gothard of the Haymarket Theatre, Leicester, to organise and run the festival from London with Fiona Dick (with the Haymarket Theatre providing contracts for the Cunningham Company). Linda Ludwin from Leicester Polytechnic (now De Montfort University) acted as administrator, whilst students from her arts administration degree course were active in all aspects of the festival.[17] Gregory Nash provides a useful context for the first regional festivals: dance provision in the regions had been a hit and miss affair, with larger companies such as Rambert and LCDT making regular visits to the major centres, while smaller-scale companies tended to visit arts centres and universities. But there was no regularity to these visits, and, with little dance experience or continuity in the type of dance they might view, audiences often found it difficult to relate to what were, in essence, isolated performances. The festival format was intended to provide a sustained contemporary dance experience, with an overview of new developments in dance.[18]

The festival opened with a British premiere from the Compagnie Cré-Ange and included the Merce Cunningham Dance Company in four different *Events*, specially created for the Haymarket Theatre. Other performers included the Rambert Dance Company (with its first performance of Trisha Brown's *Opal Loop*), the Mayurbhanj Chau Dancers from India, The Cholmondeleys, The Featherstonehaughs, Occasional Dance Company, Peter Badejo, Jonathan Burrows, Yolande Snaith and Glasshouses. The festival ended with a special commission, *Bhangra Variations*, led by Gurcharan Mall and Apna Sangeet, which acknowledged the fast-developing Bhangra culture within the city's flourishing Asian community. There were also workshops, video screenings and an open forum.

The importance of this first festival lies in the model created by Dance Umbrella – one that inspired others to follow, and proved that a dance festival outside London not only could provide an important asset to the community, but also could make sound economic sense. These features contributed to the setting up of the National Dance Agencies and to the continued regionalisation of dance throughout the 1990s. The success of the first festival gave rise to a second in 1991 with Donna McDonald employed as administrator after Fiona Dick had left, and to a third in 1993. The 1993 festival formed a part of the Year of Dance, being run by that organisation, for which Val Bourne acted as artistic director.

Year Overviews, 1985–1989

1985

The demise of the Greater London Council (GLC) cast a shadow over the proceedings this year, with future funding becoming even more insecure. The forecast for Dance Umbrella looked particularly bleak, as the GLC funded Umbrella directly as well as nearly all its London venues. Nevertheless, an exciting and geographically far-reaching programme was planned and enacted. This year marked the start of a gradually increasing European connection that was to reach a climax in Dance Umbrella 89. There were some hints of a change in focus, in that winners and past winners of the Bagnolet Choreographic prize were mentioned for the first time in the programme notes: L'Esquisse, we were told, won first prize in 1981. Also, the film series Dance in Focus included presentations by Patrick Bensard (France) and Stefaan Decostere (Belgium), both leading figures in the film world of their native countries, plus video programmes of current French and Belgian dance. With representatives from France, Holland and Italy, European groups for once outnumbered those from the US, and the idea of European influence can be extended, if stretched, by Laurie Booth's collaboration with Dutch musician Harry de Wit. However, the press concentrated on David Gordon, Karole Armitage and Mark Morris, all returning from previous years, and gave fewer in-depth reviews of the less familiar European groups.

David Gordon rehearsing members of the Pick Up Company, 1985. PHOTO: CHRIS HARRIS

The available reviews paint a picture of strong and highly individual performance styles. Jann Parry described L'Esquisse as being akin to the expressionist theatre of Beckett or Peter Brook.[19] Dansproduktie's *I Etcetera* was based on a story by Susan Sontag and successfully combined words on tape and words spoken by soloist Beppie Blankert with some powerful dancing. Laurie Booth's excursions into spoken text were less highly praised, except for an occasion when technical difficulties brought forth a riveting impromptu commentary from Booth that saved the situation.

It is true that 1985 saw the return of two of the most eye-catching American guests, Gordon and Armitage, after five and four years respectively, and of another who had made an impact the previous year, Morris. Gordon baffled many with his sophisticated brand of post-modern irony wrapped up in a deceptively casual look, in what he calls his constructions. References abounded – to his choreographic past in *Nine Lives* (one of his 'chair' pieces, but a chair piece to end all chair pieces), and to his ethnic past in *My Folks*, which used traditional Jewish Klezmer music and reams of cloth to help weave choreographic patterns. Gordon's comments in his programme notes –

'I support changes in context, the freedom to re-examine, to alter, to abandon materials or to re-use them for a good laugh at myself and my world' – amply demonstrate his utter lack of pretentiousness, as well as a reflexive recycling of material.

Thanks partly to a cover feature in *Time Out,* both Riverside performances of Armitage's *Watteau Duet* were sold out. Here she shared the stage with dance partner Joseph Lennon, composer/musician David Linton and musician Conrad Kinnard. Armitage continued her exploration of issues posed by classical ballet, primarily those surrounding the representation of male and female, their relationship and its relevance today.

Morris's ensemble had increased to five from the previous year's three, and revealed more facets of his choreographic style, including a rather darker side in *Lovey,* which takes child sex abuse as its theme, with music from the Violent Femmes as its uncomfortable accompaniment. *Jealousy* showed him in high-camp, early-modern-dance mode, while *Minuet in G* to Beethoven

Miranda Tufnell in Tufnell, Dennis Greenwood and David Ward's *Urban Weather,* 1985.
PHOTO: CHRIS HARRIS

demonstrated both his respect for and his iconoclasm with regards to music, as well as his lack of fear in debunking some of its pretensions (even Beethoven's). Critics were divided over whether they found his mock-naivety irritating or were knocked out by the utter commitment he demonstrated to his themes.

Gordon, Armitage and Morris can all be said to have theatricality in their performance make-up one way or another, whereas our own artist, Rosemary Butcher, tends towards the opposite end of the artistic spectrum, drawing inspiration from the visual arts rather than from the stage. Butcher's *Flying Lines* was very well received, and hailed as fast-paced by her standards, at least in the final section – full of dancers criss-crossing the stage space at speed, with some near (and some actual) collisions. In its conception it

Ashley Page and Gaby Agis in *Refurbished Behaviour*, The Place Theatre, 1985. PHOTO: CHRIS HARRIS

brought to mind some of Trisha Brown's work, in particular *Set and Reset*, seen at the festival two years earlier. Miranda Tufnell and Dennis Greenwood continued to explore the interaction of light, movement and sound in *Silver*, in which a black 'sound ball' by designer Bob Bielechi housed Annea Lockwood's sound tape, playing all manner of games with the audience's perceptions, as did the effects of lighting on the movement.

Extemporary Dance Theatre was seen in a double bill that demonstrated a two-way divide between their former identity – that of dance *company*, with Richard Alston's *Cutter* providing the dance – and their post-1982 alter ego of dance *theatre*. For the latter, festival artist-in-residence Katie Duck collaborated with the company and composer Tristran Honsiger for *On the Breadline*, a theatre piece radical in its abrupt switches of focus and tone. Meanwhile, Ashley Page was still busy exploring various styles, from the marriage of contact improvisation with ballet for *Refurbished Behaviour*, to *This is What You Get!!*, for a quartet of Royal Ballet ballerinas, a classical critique that was more Armitage- or Clark-inspired. So perhaps a covert theme to this festival emerged, one concerned with contrasts between theatricality and pure dance exploration, and with the differences between European and American dance.

1986

The official theme for this year's festival was 'contemporary music', with commissions from contemporary composers and a proliferation of jazz scores. John-Marc Gowans worked with Maedée Duprès (both artists improvising on stage) and with Ashley Page for his *'Accident' Ballroom*. Perhaps one of the most significant trends in the use of music was the juxtaposition of new and classical scores, a device displayed by both of the French companies as well as by the American, Tim Miller.

But perhaps this festival had a second, covert theme, concerned with the creation or exploration of new forms that integrated movement, theatre, sound and film without giving precedence to any one of them, and which left many a critic bemused about the performer's inclusion in a *dance* festival. One performer who seems obsessed by exploring new forms and who provided the most significant contribution to Dance Umbrella 86 was Meredith Monk, who had stopped performing in dance festivals by that time, having provoked too much controversy in the past.[20] Monk's *Turtle Dreams: Cabaret* was, she said, 'abstract cabaret', though in the past she has described her works as 'opera-epic', 'live movie', even 'theatre cantata'.[21] Monk states, 'My work lies in the cracks between what people think this or that is: it gives some audiences a lot of trouble because they like to see what they already know.'[22]

Turtle Dreams provided a sequence of music, movement and film scenarios. On the one hand it evoked the informality of a cabaret setting with sequined and satin costumes; on the other it hinted at darker and more intense rituals with an underlying theme of the nuclear threat, apparent from the opening number 'Engine Steps'. Thus, in a film projection a turtle named Proton lumbers across a map of the world and Godzilla-like through a model urban landscape – the sole survivor of a holocaust. The cabaret started outside the auditorium, with two films in the foyer to set the scene, and ended with a lullaby, a solo for Monk as a sort of hymn to Gaia. In between there had been precision routines, humour, show-biz razzmatazz and poignancy. Yet Monk's dances do not contain a 'message' – or rather, not one that can easily translate into a medium other than that in which it communicates. She says, 'I think there is a layer of political consciousness but it's not the main thrust of my work. I always feel that any artist is trying to be in a way connected to something that is the undercurrent of the unconscious, or what's going on in our culture; a bit like an antenna so that you're picking up essences of what is going on'.[23]

Fellow American Miller also confused the audience, this time over issues of art or life. His autobiographical *Buddy Systems* was highly explicit and personal, and included his real-life partner, non-dancer Douglas Sadownick. Reviewers were divided over whether it was more important for Miller's act to be authentic or to be artistically coherent.

Comparisons were still being drawn between British, American and European dance, showing a fascination that was fast growing into an obsession with issues of national identity. This year, the argument tended to focus on their respective degrees of theatricality and professionalism, with the French companies displaying more chic in their presentation style and the Americans courting more extremes in theirs. Judith Mackrell stated:

> There are American choreographers whose style is almost identical on paper to that of British New Dance. But where British New Dance seems soft and even introverted, the Americans have taken the style to

its fastest and hardest extremes. Replacing slow deliberation with break-neck speed, their idea of relaxing into the body's weight means either nose-diving recklessly to the floor or hurling each other around with pugnacious relish.[24]

This was an apt description of the companies of Stephen Petronio and Susan Marshall. At his 'meet-the-choreographer' session, Petronio stated, 'I'm always looking for a surprise in the body. I like ridiculous physical moments.' This seemed to be so in his programme, which displayed a style at once more violent and more angular than that of his mentor, Trisha Brown. In his solo *#3* he kept his feet firmly rooted to the spot throughout almost the entire dance, performing complex twists and turns of the torso and gestures of the arms and hands. He made up for this lack of momentum within the group dance *The Sixth Heaven,* which involved bodies hurtling through the air, flung at each other or simply at the floor.

Dana Reitz, on the other hand, this festival's artist-in-residence, exploited neither American 'over-the-top', nor the official festival theme of contemporary music. Her improvisational performances, without accompaniment, used naturally occurring sounds, such as that of a plane flying overhead, to suggest a mood that governed the movement. The result was unusually concentrated.

Of French chic there were two exponents. The company of Angelin Preljocaj displayed both Cunningham and punk influences and made much use of facial expression and detailed movements of the head, with sharply structured movement phrasing. Compagnie Charles Cré-Ange presented *Euridice Disparue*, which had taken a year to make and incorporated ballet, mime, slapstick and acrobatics. Sophie Constanti likened it to Paul Taylor's *Cloven Kingdom*, transposed to the Kingdom of the Dead.[25]

Compared with the confidence and wider range of both American and French work, British dance did not fare so well. This may have been partly because two of our leading choreographers, Siobhan Davies and Ian Spink, did not appear in live performance, participating instead in the Channel Four *Dance Lines* project, the results of which were later broadcast. Also, one potentially exciting project, with Fergus Early, Sue MacLennan and Pablo Ventura all choosing electronic scores from the EMAS (Electro-Acoustic Music Association) library, suffered from lack of sufficient production time. However, there were British successes in the double bill of Jonathan Burrows and Ashley Page. Page presented an ambitious work, *'Accident' Ballroom,*

Jonathan Burrows in *Hymns*, 1986. PHOTO: CHRIS NASH

which strongly displayed his interest in the other arts. With its slightly sinister design by Spyros Coscinas of a 1920s setting, and a powerful, commissioned score from John-Marc Gowans, it combined classical and contemporary styles with social dancing. Burrows's highly individual and humorous *Hymns* and the intensity of his trio *Squash* also made an impact.

Elsewhere, 'cabaret' once again prevailed in the Flying Starts programmes, which were really parties at the ICA, held to kick off the Umbrella. These contained some gifted and hilarious compèring from Ralf Ralf, circus tricks from Ra Ra Zoo, The Cholmondeleys, the Jiving Lindy Hoppers, Royal Ballet student William Tuckett and Petronio. But it takes a Meredith Monk to integrate the elements into one meaningful and powerful statement and make it entertaining too.

1987

Dance Umbrella 87 boasted an extremely strong line-up from Britain as well as from Europe and America, with emotion-based works more prevalent than before. The formalist components of the programme, however, were by no means marginalised and were ideally championed by Trisha Brown.

Brown appeared to packed houses at Sadler's Wells, showing two of the pieces performed during her previous visit in 1983: *Set and Reset* (1983), which again showed her dancers' exuberance and pleasure in performance, and *Opal Loop* (1980). The recently made *Newark* seemed to demonstrate a new departure, however, coming from a different movement base that was more positional, more angular with an emphasis on line. Donald Judd's set, using coloured backdrops, moved in and out, determining the dancing space. At one point the dancers dived beneath the backdrops before they quite reached the ground, giving the impression that the dance continued behind them (just as *Set and Reset* gave the impression of continuing in the wings). Audiences could draw comparisons directly between Brown and alumnus Stephen Petronio. Petronio delights in movement for its own sake, faster and more aggressive than Brown's, full of horizontal dives and catches as in *Simulacrum Reels*, which also has elements of classical ballet.

Jawole Willa Jo Zollar, director of the Urban Bush Women, had scored a hit when she had appeared solo at the Umbrella-organised *Parallels in Black* season earlier in the spring. For Umbrella, her company fostered an almost party-like atmosphere (even though their subject matter was very serious), as they romped through a programme based on their shared experience as feminist, African-American women, dancing and chanting while depicting various images of women as sexual stereotypes. For these reasons, perhaps it should not have come as quite such a surprise as it did to some, when the final number, the solo *Life Dance II,* took a serious, almost violent turn as Zollar cracked an egg on her bare chest, rubbing the contents down her arms and across her body.

Another act that seemed to defy categorisation was that of Eiko and Koma, returning after their acclaimed performance for Dance Umbrella 81. Their concentrated and introverted performance of *Grain* was about primitive rituals. Their almost overwhelming sense of commitment perhaps showed up the lack of a similar sense in the performance of Marc Vanrunxt and Hyena from Belgium. On the face of it, Vanrunxt displayed artistic concerns similar to those of his compatriot, Anne Teresa de Keersmaeker, with repeated movements and the subversion of images of *fin de siècle* decadence, all with a highly polished and professional veneer. Vanrunxt, however, lacked de Keersmaeker's choreographic rigour and succeeded only in displaying a more violent and more mannered performance.

De Keersmaeker had first appeared in Dance Umbrella 82 with Michèle Anne de Mey in *Fase*, to music by Steve Reich. This time she brought her company, Rosas, and gave us *Bartók/Aantekeningen*, performed by four women with the same unison, repetition and rhythmic precision. This was less successful than *Fase*. Mackrell noted that, whereas in the earlier work a sort of drama unfolded without the help of narrative, in *Bartok/Aantekeningen* 'de Keersmaeker is more interested in studying the stylistic clash between minimalism and expressionism than in exploring the situation of the four women on stage'.[26] The piece also displayed a somewhat suspect and ambiguous eroticism in the schoolgirl-uniform nature of the women's costumes. Be that as it may, many a student performance in this country followed, dressed in short black slips and Doc Martens. *Bartók* took as its theme Peter Weiss's *Marat/Sade* and interspersed text and Bartók's *Fourth String Quartet*, supplied by a tape-deck on stage that was operated by one of the dancers – a device, like the stuffed deer in one corner, reminiscent of Bausch.

There were three Dance Umbrella commissions: for Ashley Page, Images Dance Company and DV8 Physical Theatre. DV8 proved such a resounding success that there had to be two extra performances to accommodate demand. *My Body, Your Body* was an unnerving performance that explored alienation in human relationships, and was based on Robin Norwood's book *Women Who Love Too Much*. Thus began that group's highly productive choreographic process of performers tapping into their own individual emotional states, given a situation or stimulus.

Page had been a regular participant since 1983, but here he was given his first chance at an Umbrella programme devoted solely to a single work. In *The Angel of Death is in My Bed Tonight*, dancers were cast as angels and messengers in erotic power encounters, the piece dealing with decadence and degeneracy. Page continued his project of rewriting classical vocabulary, in this piece contrasting two movement styles and using one contemporary dancer (Catherine White) with four Royal Ballet dancers, of whom Page was one. He provided some delicious movement phrases that were 'tirelessly ingenious' with '*jetés* dropping into skidding slides, *ronds de jambes* skewed

Lea Anderson of The
Cholmondeleys in *Marina*,
1987.
PHOTO: CHRIS NASH

off-course by a kink of the hip and balances thrown out of kilter by a jutting
pelvis.'[27]

This year 'Flying Starts' again featured mixed bills of young British artists,
but greater attention was paid this time to orchestrating the evening as a
whole, with a designer brought in to transform The Place Theatre into a
cabaret venue. The Cholmondeleys featured prominently, and Lea Anderson's distinctive style – witty with a strong performance presence – made its
mark in *The Big Dance Number*, *Marina* and *No Joy*, amongst other pieces.

1988

This year was marked by the first of the gala fundraising evenings,
with DecaDance at Sadler's Wells Theatre in January. The programme ostensibly celebrated Dance Umbrella's tenth year, but also aimed to raise funds

Extemporary Dance Theatre, *Suddenly Out of the Blue*, 1988. PHOTO: CHRIS NASH

in order to commission work for the autumn festival. In this way Dance Umbrella was able to make the biggest commission of its career, providing funds for the whole of Siobhan Davies's programme to launch her new company, as well as part-funding Image's programme. The gala evening itself showed acts as diverse as Michael Clark and Company, 'Popular Song' from Ashton's *Façade* and morris dancers from the Royal Ballet. Choreographers from the very beginning of Umbrella's history were invited back, such as Richard Alston (with an excerpt from his recent work for Rambert, *Strong Language)*, Second Stride, Ingegerd Lonnroth and Steve Paxton. The evening also included popular acts from recent festivals, such as Compagnie Charles Cré-Ange.

The 1988 autumn festival programme notes remind us of 'how much contemporary dance in the UK has developed since that first Umbrella season in 1978', and as if to vindicate its judgement, Davies and DV8 provided two of the most exciting and successful programmes of the event, even though the two performances could scarcely be more dissimilar in kind. In the context of 1988, it was perhaps Siobhan Davies's emphasis on the primacy of movement that swam against the tide of fashion, as other British Umbrella contributions seemed to be taking inspiration from recent European dance/theatre. Following her Fulbright-funded stay in the United States, Davies created *Wyoming*, to a commissioned score by John-Marc Gowans, and *White Man Sleeps,* which took its inspiration from an existing score – that of Kevin Volans's *String Quartet*, played live by the Degas Quartet. (A related work, *Embarque,* was made for the Rambert Dance Company in the same year.) Davies's style seemed to have developed in two ways. First of all there was an increased awareness and acknowledgment of space and location. Judith Mackrell identified the choreography's 'old clarity of line, but [with] an even greater fluidity.'[28] To this can be added an increased weightiness, a quality that can perhaps be attributed to the influence of some of her new dancers, in particular the American Scott Clark with his background in Feldenkrais technique. These works marked the beginning of Davies's mature choreographic style with its delicious fluidity and barely hinted characterisation and narrative. The entire programme was filmed by Channel Four and televised the following spring, justifiably so.

At the other end of the dance theatre scale, DV8, the company headed by former Extemporary Dance Theatre member Lloyd Newson, had in previous years struck a sympathetic chord with its risk-taking explorations of sexual politics and gender stereotypes, but earlier works, though undoubtedly inventive, were stronger on issues than on choreographic cohesion. In the company's new full-length work, *Dead Dreams of Monochrome Men* – by far their most ambitious to date – these issues were communicated on dance's own terms, theatrically and physically, to intense and disturbing effect. *Dead Dreams* was performed on the intimate, and in this case claustrophobic, ICA stage and lasted for one hour and twenty minutes without interval, during which no latecomers were allowed access. These strictures were fully justified by the painful intensity of the four-man performance, which evoked Brian Masters's book *Killing for Company*, the story of the serial killer Dennis Nilsen. Within the dance, the four protagonists explored different aspects of Nilsen's psychosis as well as portraying his victims. The result was an uncomfortable exploration of loneliness and isolation taken to extremes. The work's power and its ability to move stemmed from its tight choreographic structure: the 'club scene' in particular was an admirable example of a device attempted by some other groups who lacked DV8's formal nous, and who consequently made far less impact.

Of the other British contributions, Second Stride's *Dancing and Shouting* offered an ambitious and courageous exploration of dance, text and music in a sort of *Brave New World* vision. The piece had much unrealised potential, and was strong on theatrical ideas, in particular a set consisting of office blocks upon which the cast could climb. The platform performances (a feature that took over from British Independents and Made in Britain platforms for new choreographers), featured work by a relatively unknown choreographer, Matthew Bourne, for Adventures in Motion Pictures. His *Spitfire* was memorable in its comic send-up of *Pas de Quatre,* danced by four men in variations of male underwear, and full of male-model posturings. This relatively light piece displayed a confident touch in its manipulation of various movement styles to comic effect, but had a serious undercurrent. Another brave performance/art collaboration took place at the Whitechapel Art Gallery, involving sculptor Bruce McLean and photographic artist David Ward. McLean danced *In the Shadow of the Hat* in a huge white sombrero whose shadow moved with the dancer within a larger, static circle of light on stage, and all this to the extraordinary voice of Yma Sumac.

Compagnie Charles Cré-Ange presented a taut and economical version of dance theatre, all the more so for having to prepare a piece at the very last moment, owing to copyright problems with their scheduled show. The resulting 'structured improvisation', *Blackmail,* was clever and witty in conveying its characters' anxieties and obsessive game playing, and gave a good indication of how well the company would have tackled Pinter, had they been allowed to do so. It confirmed their status as one of the foremost French groups. They shared a bill with choreographer Jean Gaudin, whose duet with dancer Sophie Lesard, *L'Ascète de San Clemente at la Vierge Marie* also displayed elements of European theatrical tradition, combining the surreal and the absurd. The piece was also very well received.

Groups from outside Europe for once failed to dominate. The Canadians La La La had much to live up to after the hype that had preceded their show, owing partly to an appearance with David Bowie at the Dominion Theatre the previous June. Performer Louise Lecavalier once again stole the show with her androgynous stage persona and her heart-stopping horizontal spins

Adventures in Motion Pictures, *Spitfire*, 1988. PHOTO: CHRIS NASH

in the air. From America, Molissa Fenley had proved in the past that she was one of the few solo performers able to sustain an entire evening. In the event, her version of *Rite of Spring* to the full orchestral score could not be denied its ambition. More successful was the Philip Glass piece in which the musical structures allowed her to develop and vary her athletic movements against Glass's rhythms, without fear of the choreography being swamped.

Potentially the most interesting project was that of Liz Lerman with her two companies that spanned the age divide. While the workshops were well attended, the performances were less so, and neither were they very well received. Despite the development in the 1990s of groups using older dancers, for example DV8 and Matthew Hawkins's company, perhaps London audiences were not yet ready for such innovations; or there again, perhaps our choreographers were among the few to take note of Lerman's work.

1989

British contributions to the French bicentenary celebrations culminated in Dance Umbrella 89 with five visiting French companies. Audiences enthusiastically received most programmes, showing that Dance Umbrella was once again fulfilling its brief to make home audiences more aware of what was happening elsewhere. The festival received a mixed response from the press, with some critics revelling in the novelty and sheer difference of French contemporary dance, while others bemoaned the lack of any real substance in some contributions, seeing instead an overriding emphasis on fashionable posing. This made it sound as if all the French companies produced similar work, which could not have been further from the truth.

Amongst the pick of the bunch was the company of Jean-Claude Gallotta, whose jokey and idiosyncratic choreography (even the company has an enigmatic title, Group Emile Dubois) offered us a bleak but affectionate view of humanity. Dancers came in all shapes, sizes and ages, which once again offended some; and in *Mammame* they were apparently playing children. Compagnie Angelin Preljocaj gave us overtly erotic dance-theatre with *Liqueurs de Chair*, whose English translation, *Carnal Cocktails*, did not convey the French title's ambiguity. Programme notes referred to 'la sueur, le sperme, les larmes et le sang' – other possible meanings of *liqueurs* – and the dance made reference to all of these, coming complete with a huge sculpture at the back of the performance space, full of steaming pistons and glistening parts.

Compagnie Charles Cré-Ange presented *Noir Salle,* which took as its source Molière's *Le Misanthrope,* and used fragments of its text. Five dancers enacted a series of social and sexual encounters, using a mixture of dance, mime, slapstick comedy and acrobatics: 'I would like to find my own language where each emotion has its gesture,' said the choreographer.

Merce Cunningham's and his company were the only American visitors this year, offering a complete contrast to the Europeans. In a two-week season at Sadler's Wells, the company provided four different programmes. Jann Parry rightly made the point that Cunningham's work, far from dehumanising the dancers as some of his critics contended, actually celebrated their individuality as people and as dancers.[29] This was amply demonstrated by the diversity of the programmes. They included *Rainforest* from 1968, which comes close to narrative content; a new work, *Carousel*, with its sexual encounters; *Fabrications,* with its sense of dance community; and *Points in Space,* made first for BBC television in 1986.

Karas Company, like previous Japanese visitors, showed choreography that was meticulous in its crafting, with utmost attention to detail and intense effect. The traditional and the modern came together in Teshigawara's *Ishi No Hana* which drew upon Noh theatre and Kabuki, as well as breakdance, bicycle riding, classical ballet, mime and martial arts. The performance was hypnotic, enigmatic, surreal and visually arresting in its decor and costumes, with blue stones on the stage and a pile of green glass.

Against this backdrop, British dance showed that it could hold its own while demonstrating influences from both the United States and Europe. Lea Anderson and her Cholmondeleys concluded the festival at Riverside Studios with *Flesh and Blood*, for which she won a Digital Award. Described by Sophie Constanti as 'probably the darkest exit this annual festival has ever known',[30] *Flesh and Blood* offered the same sort of obsessive and ritualised movement that we had come to expect from previous Anderson dances. This, though having the same ironic tone, was altogether more sombre, deriving more from European expressionism in its contortions and writhings. Laurie Booth

Groupe Emile Dubois in Jean-Claude Gallotta's *Mammame*, 1989. PHOTO: CHRIS NASH

offered another dark and obsessive piece with *Terminus Terminux*. This was inspired by J.G. Ballard's *The Atrocity Exhibition*, and marked a confident departure for Booth in that it was a group choreography. Reviewers noted that, whereas in the past the dancers looked as if they had been given Booth's movements to perform, here they looked at ease with the material and had made it entirely their own.

Siobhan Davies Dance Company, on the other hand, offered a more formal, less emotionally intense dance style and impressed with the warmth of their performances as well as with sure-footed choreography whose development continued in its range and confidence. Second Stride once again

The Cholmondeleys, *Flesh and Blood*, 1989. PHOTO: CHRIS NASH

attempted a daring and difficult integration of speech, song, dance and portentous narrative with *Heaven Ablaze in His Breast*. This was a collaboration with the composer Judith Weir and director Antony McDonald, based upon the Hoffmann tales, *Girl with the Enamel Eyes* and *The Sandman,* that had provided inspiration for the Romantic ballet *Coppélia.* It provided a sophisticated reappraisal of the narrative, and well deserved its television screening.

Last but by no means least, Michael Clark appeared with Stephen Petronio in *Heterospectives*, a related event at the Anthony d'Offay Art Gallery. The programme was thoroughly outrageous, contained much nudity, and as part of its decor had a row of plastic penises mounted on the wall.

*   *   *

The diversity and continuing development of British dance notwithstanding, at this time funding and marketing seemed to be uppermost on the Umbrella's agenda for reasons of sheer survival. The idea of a French theme had been successful in marketing terms, and artistically the festival had been more diverse than ever, yet two financial constraints dominated the year's report. The first was to do with visiting artists' increased fees, as well as with their increased demands in terms of standards of accommodation, demands that were fully justified but not easy to meet. The second was to do with budget cuts. The Visiting Arts Planning Grant was in its final year, and with the introduction of the poll tax, things were, as usual, worrying. Dance Umbrella 89 had its budget inflated by a grant from the Arts Council's International Initiatives Fund for Revolutionary Tactics, which enabled not only the French companies but also Karas and the Cunningham Company to perform. So the decade was able to come to a close with a resounding confirmation of Umbrella's role in bringing developments in dance to the attention of a wider audience. That it looked forward to a changing role was also to become apparent.

Shobana Jeyasingh Dance Company, 1992.
PHOTO: HUGO GLENDINNING

4

An International Festival: 1990–1994

Overview

Losses, Gains and Reorganisation

The opening of this period was far from auspicious, given the fate of some important companies that had been Dance Umbrella stalwarts. The demise of Extemporary Dance Theatre, following in the wake of Janet Smith and Dancers, Mantis and English Dance Theatre among other casualties, had severely reduced the number of small- to middle-scale companies providing artistic alternatives to the mainstream companies. Their loss was mourned, and yet perhaps taken overall as a necessary sacrifice to the march of progress. But the dance community could scarcely take in the reality that the mainstream contemporary companies, London Contemporary Dance Theatre and Rambert Dance Company, were also on the verge of disbanding by 1992/93. Ironically the fates of these two companies, which had provided a healthy competition for each other throughout most of the 1970s and 1980s, followed very contrasting paths from this point. LCDT disbanded as a repertory company, and from 1994 was replaced in residence at The Place by a smaller choreographer-led company, Richard Alston Dance Company. Rambert, on the other hand, survived by increasing its company and by enhancing its already eclectic repertoire from international sources, taking Nederlands Dans Theater 1 as its model.

One important topic of debate at this time, then, was the basis of a company's work: whether to be repertory- or choreographer-led. Judith Mackrell[1] identified reasons for the current vogue for single-choreographer companies as being to do with the unwillingness of choreographers at the cutting edge to make work for companies other than their own, because their idiosyncratic style requires dancers well versed in that specific mode of expression.[2] She identified the problems of LCDT and Rambert as stemming from their having followed the repertory model of the Royal Ballet and of our theatre companies, unlike dance companies in the US and Europe, which tended towards the choreographer-led model. Bourne observes that the loss of LCDT is still felt, as there is no longer any bridge between the smaller contemporary companies and the major ballet companies. 'Rambert is all that remains, and I would classify it now as neo-classical.'[3] (Interestingly, from the later 1990s there has been a move back towards repertory- and dancer-led companies such as Ricochet and Diversions; and Shobana Jeyasingh's commissions for her company support this idea too.)

There were signs, however, that some British dance makers who had matured with the Umbrella were flourishing, and these provided the Umbrella festivals throughout this period with a highly respectable and respected home-grown dance presence. The companies of Siobhan Davies, Shobana Jeyasingh and DV8 Physical Theatre in particular can be seen to have established themselves at the forefront of British contemporary dance in their very different ways. Laurie Booth and Lea Anderson also increased their following, and there were notable contributions from Yolande Snaith and Second Stride.

The defining qualities of British dance were once again debated within the dance press, with technical strength and an emphasis on the expressive potential of movement *per se* identified as important characteristics, though not exclusively so. In her overview of the 1990 festival, and recalling Deborah Jowitt's comments about Second Stride in 1982, American critic Marilyn Hunt identified a British style that displayed 'a creamy control, an easy, light fluidity'.[4] Hunt went on to comment, 'I find in English dancing a riveting, satisfying movement logic when the flow is given light and shade by a variety of dynamics', and these qualities were extended to Laurie Booth's *Spatial Decay II*, which evoked 'a meditative ritual, based on self-mastery and mystery'. Fiona Burnside noticed similarities between the styles of Davies and Jeyasingh: 'A strong technical base is common to both, the exploration of technique and the intrinsic, expressive capacity of movement is another common aim'.[5] But then the whole debate about national characteristics is thrown into question by the transculturalism of Jeyasingh's work. Perhaps it is Jeyasingh who lays to rest this 'national identity' introspection, replacing it with a focus upon movement as the primary means of expression in dance, with the ability to draw upon many cultural references.

Anyway, the distinction between 'national' and 'international' was becoming increasingly difficult to define. It grew ever more problematic to ascribe national identities to festival artists; moreover, DV8, for example, drew upon the international dance community for its performers, while a great many British dancers were currently appearing in European companies. Furthermore, 'the Americans think that Richard [Alston] and Sue [Davies] are sub-American, and the French think that too'.[6] 'Internationalism', then, was raised in relation to a variety of issues, but most importantly in terms of status on the world stage, with comments in reports and reviews ascribing inter-national status to companies, festivals and venues. As a final testimony to its worth, the Davies Company performed at Sadler's Wells in 1990 – the first British single-choreographer company to appear there. The title of Chris de Marigny's editorial for the Dance Umbrella 91 programme, 'London, A Cultural Capital?', underlined what was at stake. The Dance Umbrella festivals were seen alongside other international festivals and judged to be on a par – if not always in terms of budget size,[7] then certainly in terms of quality and, importantly, in terms of concept. Dance was no longer being viewed against the narrow confines of national characteristics, but more against a world stage.

New Platforms, Changing Roles

With the Umbrella's 'international' status came a change of role. We have already noted that one of the main strengths of Dance Umbrella is its flexibility, its ability to identify the needs of the dance community and the opportunities by which to meet them. By 1990, Dance Umbrella's role had already changed. In the previous chapter we saw how the experimental and less polished works of fledgeling choreographers, championed in the early Festivals, were almost entirely absent from festivals by the late 1980s. We suggested that other venues had stepped in to provide platforms for the rawer experimental work. The festival had gained in prestige, and while maintaining its educative role, as we shall see, Dance Umbrella increasingly needed to ensure very high standards of artistry and performance from all participants. It is a further mark of Dance Umbrella's success that people from outside the Umbrella organisation were starting other platforms, and these too were taking on some of the earlier roles of the festival.

One such platform was begun by a former member of Dance Umbrella's board of management, John Ashford. Ashford was ambitious for The Place Theatre, having taken over its management in 1986, and wanted to enhance its role as a dance venue. We have seen that his original interest lay in theatre, and that his interest in dance developed after seeing Anne Teresa de Keersmaeker's *Fase* in 1982. 'John was a late convert to dance,' says Bourne, 'and they always make the best evangelists'.[8] Mackrell noted that Ashford became aware of a significant group of determined young students and recent graduates from the relatively newly established dance degree programmes 'with confident, privately invented movement languages to show the world. They needed a venue which would turn their disparate activities into a visible London scene.'[9] The Spring Loaded seasons were begun in 1987 at The Place Theatre and have expanded to include the Royal Festival Hall as a venue. These seasons showcased work from established young companies and artists, by invitation only, and by now stretch over two-and-a-half months.

Then in 1990 Ashford opened 'Resolution!' as a new platform, providing some six or so weeks of triple bills changing nightly. 'Resolution!' had an evolutionary ethos and comprised three 'stages'. 'First Footing' was an open platform for choreographers just starting in their careers and who had not previously shown work in 'Resolution!'. 'Evolution' selected work from those who had shown previously. 'Aerwaves' provided an opportunity to show the work of European companies visiting London for the first time, and for our young companies to show work in Amsterdam in exchange.[10] Mackrell continued: 'Before Ashford's reign at The Place, these choreographers could scrabble for two or three nights at one of the half-dozen available fringe venues, or they could hope for a date in the prestigious Dance Umbrella festival . . . but Umbrella only lasted for a few weeks a year, was partly geared to presenting international work, and was also moving up market to show larger scale work.'[11] 'Resolution!' then, may be regarded as having taken over and extended the role of the Made in Britain platforms of earlier Umbrellas, releasing Umbrella to develop in other directions.

Ashford also started the Turning World seasons in 1990, in which companies from all over the world were featured, giving a further opportunity for selected 'Aerwaves' graduates to present work. Repertory-led companies were significantly absent. This series soon encompassed other venues – the South Bank Centre and Sadler's Wells. As the seasons were scheduled for May/June, there was never a clash with the autumn Dance Umbrella festival. They were rather an extension of another aspect of Umbrella's role, that of showcasing international choreographer-led companies.

Touring

Another set of changes to Umbrella's role concerned its touring policies. In the early years, the pattern had been for overseas companies to perform in the London festival, then to undertake regional dates to help cover the initial costs of travel to the UK. By the mid-1980s, Umbrella realised that touring was actually costing it money, rather than making a profit or even covering costs. This was because visiting companies were getting bigger: whereas previously artists had been prepared to come with a scaled-down version of their companies (for example, Mark Morris in 1984), they were now appearing with extended companies. Umbrella was also attracting more high-profile artists at greater expense; by the mid-1980s it was apparent that regional venues could no longer pay their fees and that Dance Umbrella was being forced to step in to subsidise them.[12] The sporadic regional touring of earlier Umbrellas seemed to have all but petered out by the early 1990s in favour of larger-scale tours by one or two overseas companies. This was partly due to the Umbrella-managed regional festivals – in particular Newcastle Dance 90 and Newcastle Dance 92, which bore the thrust of regional touring for those years – but due also to changes in policy and funding patterns.

From 1989 onwards, in partnership with the Arts Council, Dance Umbrella undertook a series of pilot projects, part of which was the 'Revolutionary Tactics' initiative, responsible for the Compagnie Cré-Ange tour. In 1990, with the support of Arts Council Touring (ACT), Dance Umbrella was able to tour Stephen Petronio and Company. In 1991, again with ACT support, it toured several artists, but sought a more ambitious, longer-term solution. Dance Umbrella initially proposed setting up a Tours Unit with a core staff of three and sufficient funding to manage and promote tours by overseas dance

Doug Elkins, solo, 1993. PHOTO: HUGO GLENDINNING

companies throughout the UK. This was not to be; but in 1992 it implemented a greatly scaled-down version of the proposal. Under its own auspices, Dance Umbrella created the full-time post of tours manager with the touring of overseas companies as its sole remit, appointing Belinda Regio to the post. In this first year two tours were undertaken from the London festival base: by Blok and Steel (from the Netherlands) and by Urban Bush Women (USA); with Groupe Emile Dubois (France), Transatlantic Tap and the Margaret Jenkins Dance Company (USA) also taking part in the Newcastle festival. From the Newcastle festival base, Wim Vandekeybus and his company Ultima Vez (Belgium) toured the regions without visiting London.

Policy changed in 1993, to tour only those overseas companies whose work was markedly better than or substantially different from that of our own companies, thus paving the way for the nation-wide tours, independent of the festivals, that were set up later in the decade. A short tour for Doug Elkins and Company was organised for 1993 and the Stephen Petronio Company and Urban Bush Women were toured in 1994. But ACT suffered a massive 30% funding cut, which it passed on to Dance Umbrella Touring with the direct consequence that Regio's contract had to be terminated in 1995.

Regional Festivals

The stimulation of regional activity, however, continued on a different track well into this period, with the establishment of a biennial festival in Newcastle, the continuation of the Leicester festivals and a proposed festival for Woking. These festivals followed the same format, with Dance Umbrella providing artistic direction in the early stages (as well as management for Newcastle and Woking) and with events geared to the specific community in order to provide a foothold for the enterprise. However, there were differences in terms of overall responsibility: the Newcastle festivals were totally run from London by Dance Umbrella, who employed Catherine Nunes, based in Newcastle, to co-ordinate them in 1990 and 1992. Because of the financial risks involved in this arrangement, the organisation for the Woking festivals was to be different again (see Chapter 5).

Newcastle Dance Festival

Nash again suggests various factors contributing to the decision to hold an international festival in Newcastle. Newcastle already possessed a building specially converted for dance activity in its Dance City, which in 1989 became a pilot National Dance Agency (NDA).[13] A dance culture had been established within the region from the early 1980s through the residency of English Dance Theatre in this building, through their programme of public classes and performances and through visits by other touring companies. Suzanne Burns, then dance officer for Newcastle Arts, invited Dance Umbrella to set up a festival. The first of these, Newcastle Dance 90, ran for five weeks from 3 November to 8 December and involved ten companies in four of the city's venues: the Theatre Royal, Newcastle Playhouse, the Gulbenkian Studio Theatre and Newcastle Arts Centre. Before the festival officially opened, a series of events collectively known as the Citywide Project was staged on the city's renowned Swing Bridge and at other well-known sites around town.

This ambitious and eye-catching project was directed by American artist Elise Bernhardt (director of 'Dancing in the Streets', New York), choreographer Yoshiko Chuma and London-based choreographer Rosemary Lee. All three had worked previously on large-scale projects for non-traditional

A member of the
Newcastle Cloggies.
PHOTO: HUGO GLENDINNING

venues. The idea here was to involve a much wider audience by increasing the scale and level of participation, but also by providing a familiar 'home' context for events. In this spirit also, the project drew upon many local dance groups, dance artists and musicians, including Fast Forward, a musician based in New York but originally hailing from Newcastle. The project also drew attention to the splendour of some of the local buildings, now seen in a new light.

Events began on the floodlit Swing Bridge, which completed three revolutions for the very first time in its history, animated by dancers and accompanied by music specially composed for the event by Fast Forward, and played (also on the bridge) by five local musicians on drum-kits, oil drums and sirens. The event, preceded by the city's Guy Fawkes display, had an audience estimated at 50,000. Other venues included the Greenmarket in Eldon Square Shopping Centre, Grey's Monument, All Saints Church and the Central Arcade of Central Station. This last venue played host to Stomp, who had been in a residency for two weeks, working with young people from Newcastle West End; this was just before Stomp became hugely successful following their first New York appearance. Site-specific choreography was provided by those artists already mentioned, with choreography provided by regionally based artists for the All Saints Church project, as well as entertainment from local dance schools.

In line with the London festivals, there was a gala evening as the 'official' opening, for local dignitaries and sponsors both actual and potential. This included artists from English National Ballet, Rambert Dance Company,[14] LCDT and Phoenix Dance Company sharing the stage with local talent Bamboozle, Clan na Gael, the Highspen Diamond Rapper Sword Dancers and clog dancer Shona Harper (who was to steal the show at the London 'Baker's Dozen' gala in 1991). Other artists appearing throughout the festival included The Featherstonehaughs, Laurie Booth and Russell Maliphant, Mallika Sarabhai and Yolande Snaith's Dance Quorum, Margaret Jenkins Dance Company and Siobhan Davies Dance Company. On offer too were the Chris Nash Dance Photography Exhibition, a film and video programme and a seminar with a regional focus, hosted by NODM.

A second Newcastle festival ran from 25 October to 5 December 1992. Following the success of the first, it again instigated a themed project, this time 'Percussive Feet'. It took as its starting point Northumberland clog dancing, and included flamenco, tap, Kathak and African dance. As before, the festival's timing meant that international artists appearing at the London festival could also visit. These included Blok and Steel (from Holland), Groupe Emile Dubois (France) and Transatlantic Tap (USA). Another theme was 'European Overtures', to link in with festivals in Norway, Holland and Belgium. Of significance also, the Belgian choreographer Wim Vandekeybus and his company Ultima Vez toured the regions from the base of the Newcastle festival without appearing in the London festival this year, something that was significant in promoting the independence of the festivals. This second festival was highly successful, more so even than the first.

By 1991, Dance City had become a full NDA, and so, after two years of Dance Umbrella management, the festival was handed over to Dance City. The 1994 festival followed the model created by Dance Umbrella. Dance

City's director, Janet Archer, is clear that deviation from this model, in the form of less community participation and more high-profile international work, was responsible for the less successful 1996 festival, and that 'the planned festival in 1999 should return to the proven formula'.[15]

The Second Leicester International Dance Festival, 1991

The second festival ran for six weeks from 15 March to 28 April 1991. It retained Dance Umbrella as artistic consultants, but was managed by Phoenix Arts on behalf of the Leicester Arts Consortium, which included the Leicester Haymarket Theatre, Phoenix Arts Centre and Phoenix's owners, Leicester Polytechnic (now De Montfort University). Drawing upon the experiences of the first festival, the idea was to include as many local groups as possible and to increase community involvement, with more workshops and participatory projects. Lea Anderson's *Opéra Sportif,* a site-specific work for the Granby Halls, included a cast of 500 local gymnasts, footballers, cyclists and bowlers. A number of groups and events acknowledged the local Asian community, including the first-ever forum to address Asian dance education in the UK, plus a display centred upon classical and folk traditions in Asian dance. The display featured costumes, photographs and jewellery and was organised by dancer Indra Thiagarajah. The festival programme promised an eclectic mix of dance events, ranging from internationally known artists such as Petronio, through the Czechoslovak State Song and Dance Ensemble, local groups and student groups, and on to workshops, video showings and seminars.

While it is clear that these enterprises were invaluable in flaming the spark of dance interest in their areas, it is also clear that Dance Umbrella had much to learn from their experiences. A major factor contributing to the successes in both Newcastle and Leicester was the level of community involvement, and this it had clearly got right. But Nash identifies a number of problems to do with inadequate local authority funding and the need for a more formal and financially realistic basis for the role played by Dance Umbrella (more specifically, by Val Bourne). Nash states, 'It was also clear to Dance Umbrella's board that in Bourne it had a major asset and her services were being provided to outside organisations at little cost but at great expense to the organisation itself.[16] These problems were both addressed for the Woking Dance Umbrella of 1995 (see Chapter 5).

Courses, Conferences and Residencies

Meanwhile, although the longer-established London festivals continued to be less community orientated in comparison with the regional festivals, they retained an educational agenda. Dance Umbrella's professed intention had always included an informative role – both in terms of bringing to London audiences what was new and innovative on the world dance stage, and in terms of exposing dance practitioners themselves to other influences. Bourne explained, 'I'm interested in underpinning the festival with, for example, Digital Dance or particular workshops like those in criticism or lighting. So every year we do something during the festival to make it more homogeneous, so that it's more than just a series of performances.'[17] This period included study days devoted to exploring the work of influential and long-standing choreographers from overseas (Trisha Brown in 1991, Merce Cunningham in 1992), as well as some lively and important dance residencies, such as Siobhan Davies's in 1992. The Doug Elkins residency in 1993 was based upon club dancing, for young people with no formal dance training. In the influential 'Necessary Weather' residency held by Jennifer Tipton and Dana Reitz, choreographers and lighting designers, amongst others, together explored collaborative possibilities, with all participants being required to choreograph.

The 1994 Dance Criticism course was aimed at would-be dance writers, fresh from the (by now) newly proliferated dance degree courses. Led by Alastair Macaulay, participants contributed to a Dance Umbrella news-sheet (edited by David Hughes), which was then freely distributed at venues. The course culminated in an open seminar in which festival participants, course participants and members of the audience were able to discuss the events, their reviews and articles.

Dance Technology: Trick or Treat was a two-day conference held in 1994 at the South Bank Centre, addressing the uses of interactive technology both within an educational context and for its potential for choreographers. For the former, Jacqueline Smith-Autard and Jim Schofield introduced their pioneering work in technology for Bedford Interactive, and presented their pilot interactive video disc, based upon Siobhan Davies's *White Bird Featherless*, to demonstrate ways in which interactive video can assist the critical and analytic appreciation of dances. Alternatively on offer was a project led by Illuminations Interactive, a company set up to produce interactive software for the arts. In this, eight choreographers were coupled with eight computer artists to create work, using Apple Macintosh computer software, including the Lifeforms program, and with each having their own Power Mac to work on. Participating choreographers included Ashley Page, Laurie Booth and Siobhan Davies. Some teams became so inspired that they were taken in directions quite away from dance, into fantastical works of visual art that were extraordinary, within the space of only two days.

The conference broadened possibilities both for those involved within the profession and for those within dance education. The choreographers acknowledged that the potential for collaboration was enormous, but felt the working process was painstakingly slow. Ashley Page's verdict was that the program, though unlikely to transform his work style, 'could be useful as a notebook, and maybe as a teaching tool'.[18] As a result, another workshop course was held in 1995 at Sadler's Wells, again directed by Terry Braun and expanded by request to one week (see Chapter 5).

Year Overviews, 1990–1994

1990

British artists tended to dominate the festival this year. Lloyd Newson was appointed the first British artist-in-residence at the festival; the best of young choreographers (Lea Anderson, Yolande Snaith and, at the gala event, Michael Clark) acquitted themselves well, as did more mature Dance Umbrella 'graduates' (Siobhan Davies and Laurie Booth); and Shobana Jeyasingh made a notable Umbrella debut. There were fewer events than in previous years; but to make up for it and impress sponsors, a glitzy gala incorporated the presentation of the Dance Umbrella/*Time Out* Dance Awards.

The Siobhan Davies Dance Company made its Sadler's Wells debut with one new work, *Different Trains,* and with *White Man Sleeps* from 1988. Macaulay called *Different Trains* 'the finest piece she has yet made for her company'.[19] The dance very much represented Davies's response to Steve Reich's score or 'documentary music theatre', as Reich called it. Davies's economical style of barely suggested narrative took Reich's sound-taped 'personal stories' as her base from which to weave abstracted gesture and layered interaction.

In many ways, Davies and Jeyasingh work along parallel lines: both raise issues within their choreography to do with our perception and understanding of dance movement. *Correspondences* was created by Jeyasingh and the composer Kevin Volans, whose score was played by the Smith Quartet, with narrative sung by Llewellyn Rayappen. It also included a taped voice, reading extracts from the writings of the Indian mathematician Srinivasa Ramanujan, on whose life and premature death the piece was based. Mathematics retains its mystic significance within Indian culture, a feature that has been largely lost from ours, but Jeyasingh provided an 'interesting and courageous attempt to reconcile two cultures',[20] though many critics found challenging and difficult the unpredictable rhythms of the music set against the complex rhythms of Bharata Natyam.

Booth found a worthy partner in Russell Maliphant for *Spatial Decay II*, a duet that had been developed from an improvised quartet presented at the Spring Loaded season earlier in the year. A dark and sinister atmosphere was set by Hans Peter Kuhn's 'environmental sound score', with sound emanating from different parts of the darkened auditorium, and by Michael Hulls's lighting design. Booth's general eccentricity and occasional moments

Yolande Snaith's Dance Quorum in *Court by the Tail*, 1990. PHOTO: HUGO GLENDINNING

107

of black humour led Sophie Constanti to liken the performance to David Lynch's *Eraserhead*[21] – a convincing analogy.

The other undoubted hit of the festival, and a Dance Umbrella graduate, was Snaith. Her new company, Dance Quorum, made a fine debut with *Court by the Tail,* which contained Snaith's trademark surrealist choreography, in which the protagonists occupied different time zones. Visually impressive, Peter Carlton's film was screened intermittently throughout, a sand ridge bordered all four sides of the stage space and Anthony Bowne supplied imaginative lighting. The only problem found by reviewers seemed to be

Stephen Petronio, *MiddleSex Gorge*, 1990. PHOTO: CHRIS NASH

making sense of the piece as a whole, though there were various starting points for the choreography, including an essay on *Time* by William Hazlitt, with Sophie Constanti also invoking Hermann Hesse's *The Glass Bead Game* together with Joseph Knecht's *Search For Reflection*.[22]

Stephen Petronio led the American visitors, preceded by advertisements that included provocative photographs of him by Chris Nash. Mention of Petronio's pink whale-boned corset even made it into the satirical magazine *Private Eye*. The company had Clark as a guest artist, to whom Petronio's new work *MiddleSex Gorge* was dedicated. There was something of a change in direction in Petronio's new work with its sexual-politics thrust, though pieces still had no direct message, instead emphasising movements that explored sensuality and sexuality. The company, too, still bore the same trademarks of speed and attack. 'Our aim is to find out how fast and how far off-balance you can be, especially if five other people are involved in propelling or inhibiting your movement'.[23]

The other two American companies were for once less successful than American visitors usually tended to be, but since this was in comparison with the success of our own companies, nobody much minded. Margaret Jenkins Dance Company presented strong and dramatic choreography in *Shelf Life*, in which the dancers were dressed as books with text written on their costumes. The company appeared in collaboration with performance artist Rinke Eckert, who sung/narrated the score and was individually something of a hit. However, although the performances included a post-modern *mélange* of text, video and narration, David Hughes and others pointed out that the work did not question very much, or allow the different media to pose questions about each other. Snaith's work, arguably along the same mixed-media lines, was more favourably reviewed in comparison.[24]

The sole representative from Europe after the previous year's extravaganza, Groupe Emile Dubois, was again extremely successful with audiences, but critics were divided on its worth. *Les Mystères de Subal* was set on an imaginary island where fantasies come true. Choreographer Jean-Claude Gallotta's mix of theatre and Bauschian anarchy was full of his own and his dancers' idiosyncrasies. Some reviewers found the work to be too loosely structured, but all acknowledged the commitment of the dancers.

It is true that our performers had less competition from overseas for this year, because of financial constraints on the festival budget; but still, there were welcome signs that our own choreographers could bear favourable comparison with the guests. This, then, mitigated to some extent the demise of Extemporary Dance Theatre, a company once at the forefront of innovative dance and this year making its final appearance.

1991

In spite of the previous year's fears, Dance Umbrella 91 was a greatly expanded festival, seeing an increase from thirty-four London performances to fifty-one. There were plenty of points of comparison within the programme to prompt commentary: between diverse styles, between dance styles from different cultures, between text and movement, and between the experimental and the mainstream and how one evolves into, or transposes to, the other. There could even be comparisons between international festivals: Montreal's International Festival of New Dance ended immediately prior to the Dance Umbrella, and the Japan Festival taking place on London's South Bank concurrently was providing funding for the Japanese companies appearing in the Umbrella. All of this gave rise to discussion, which also focused on the changing role of the Dance Umbrella festivals themselves.

In terms of diverse styles, the opening gala event's thirteen items ('A Baker's Dozen') contained contemporary dance, ballet, contact improvisation, tap and clog dance. This undifferentiated mixture provoked controversy but also debate. Judith Mackrell took the opportunity to overview the role of the festivals to date: finding that, in addition to educating audiences in contemporary dance, the Umbrella also provides 'a focus for the dance world to talk to itself',[25] and this, she pointed out, promotes development amongst our choreographers.

Dance Umbrella 91 offered two groups overtly concerned with cross-culturalism. Shobana Jeyasingh's programme entitled *New Cities, Ancient Lands* comprised three separate pieces, two by Jeyasingh and one by Madras-based choreographer Chandralekha. All three employed the language of Bharata Natyam within the framework of Jeyasingh's continued exploration of Western forms. By contrast, Valli Subbiah and Company offered less of a cultural fusion and more of a cultural comparison. Two leading Bharata Natyam dancers, Subbiah herself and Shantala Shivalingappa, danced alongside ballet-trained Koen Onzia in a programme that was also to have included a choreographic collaboration between Savitri Nair and Maurice Béjart.

Shobana Jeyasingh Dance Company, studio shot, 1991. PHOTO: HUGO GLENDINNING

Both Laurie Booth and Julyen Hamilton offered improvisational, text-based works this year in their separate programmes, but to very different effect. Booth's *New Text/New Kingdom* reminded audiences of how much improvisational dance can mature in terms of the richness of its movement palette, the sophistication of its structuring and working processes and the dramatic potential it unleashes in conjunction with other dancers. Booth's mesmeric and meditative style contrasted with Hamilton's quick-witted inventiveness. Mackrell likened his performance of *Of Solution and Answer and Understanding,* to that of a witty raconteur, in his physical response to Elizabeth Pike's text (read on stage by actress Jill Freud), which, the reviewer maintained, called upon the audience's ability to 'free float between text and movement'.[26]

The appearance of Trisha Brown's company, celebrating twenty-one years of the choreographer's work, also prompted overviews of her choreography as well as comparisons between experimental work, mainstream work and the possibility of moving between one and the other. On Brown's dance

Laurie Booth, 1991.
PHOTO: HUGO GLENDINNING

background (Graham, Horst, Limón, Cunningham), Mackrell reported her as commenting: 'You can say I've had a traditional modern dance training and it didn't take'.[27] She attributed this to the influence of Halprin, Rainer and Forti: 'What they sought, and in Brown's case found, was pure movement in which gestures were emptied of their content and dance was freed from its burden of narrative and symbolic weight'.[28] This year, in two programmes, Brown gave us her most up-to-date work, in contrast to previous years where her 'classics' had been revived – another mark of Umbrella's work having been well done. She showed two new collaborations with Robert Rauschenberg. The first, *For MG: The Movie,* had received its world premiere in France only the previous week, which explains its dedication to the organiser of the French festival, Michel Guy, who had recently died. The other, *Astral Convertible,* had banks of lights activated by the dancers' movements. The programme included two solos for Brown herself, in *Foray Forêt,* and *For MG.*

112

Changes that were charted over the years in her work included: move-ment content that was increasingly sensuous and complex; proscenium-arch rather than site-specific presentation; 'designed' costumes instead of practice gear; and greater emotional intensity. One element that seemed to persist was the carefully structured development of her dances, so that they ap-peared to have arrived organically – giving a sense of both order and chaos, but obeying material laws too complex for the comprehension of mere mortals. These ideas go part of the way towards explaining the seamless shift of Brown's work spanning twenty-one years, from cutting-edge experiment to mainstream stage. This shift is unusual in its accomplishment, as Laurie Booth noted at the time: 'Particularly in this country, there are not many success stories from the experimental wing'.[29] Alastair Macaulay made the point that in the audience's acceptance of Trisha Brown lay perhaps the Dance Umbrella's greatest achievement to date.[30]

Eiko and Koma were more polemical than in previous years, and appeared with two other performers, which was also a new departure for them. *Land* involved a collaboration with Native American Indian musicians Robert Mirabel and Ben Sandoval and with visual artist Sandra Lerner. As ever, their work was concentrated and slowly evolving; although, as Alastair Macaulay notes, 'in terms of meaning . . . Eiko and Koma proceed very rapidly indeed'.[31]

This was the second year with only one European company, but L'Esquisse from France gave London audiences the chance to see its seminal influence on fellow French choreographers such as Claude Brumachon, whose work had been seen more recently in London. This fact was missed by many who thought the reverse was the case and that it was Brumachon who had influ-enced the choreography of Joelle Bouvier and Regis Obadia.

1992

Dance Umbrella received the 1992 Prudential Award for the Arts – at £100,000 the largest single arts sponsorship in Britain at that time – and this provided further impetus for writers to take stock of the current situation. Audiences had grown from 4,000 in 1978 to 20,000 in 1991, ranking Dance Umbrella as one of the largest international festivals of contemporary dance, alongside the Festival International de Nouvelle Danse (FIND), Lyon and Montpellier. In an interview with Debra Craine, Val Bourne noted that Um-

Members of the Trisha Brown Company at Canary Wharf in a lunch-time special event, 1991.
PHOTO: HUGO GLENDINNING

brella audiences were more experienced than they had been fifteen years before, something which also made them more demanding.[32] The festival had expanded to Leicester and Newcastle and regional touring was now on a more financially viable basis, with the creation in 1992 of the full-time post of tours manager (which was, however, to be short-lived).

American versus European influence was still a hot topic, and Craine referred to 'the general schizophrenia in British contemporary dance' with regards to this 'contest',[33] adding that this ambivalence was echoed in the stated themes of this year's festival: the Transatlantic Tie-up idea and the European Arts Festival link. Boston Umbrella was involved in promoting and curating some events, notably Transatlantic Tap and Paula Josa Jones. There was to have been a further Anglo-American collaboration in a specially commissioned piece by Michael Clark and Stephen Petronio. This had been planned as the artistic centrepiece for the 1992 festival, and was also to be performed at the Dance Umbrella in Boston; but the respective companies found they were unable to work together. Alongside, there was a link-up with the European Arts Festival, which provided a crucial £168,000 to bring companies over from France, Belgium, Spain and Holland.

To these twin cultural influences, Bourne added a further dimension: 'I think you will see the pendulum go further; you might be looking at Japan or Australia. It's no longer a single focus'.[34] The Japanese representation had been strongly in evidence the previous year, but 1992 showed less of an international focus outside the USA and Europe. It should also be noted that some of the European companies let themselves down badly with below-par productions and last-minute changes from the programmes originally booked. By comparison the Americans were strongly led by the companies of Merce Cunningham and Petronio, with some powerful competition from Anne Teresa de Keersmaeker's company, Rosas.

The strongest programmes, then, were those from groups seen previously, with many choreographers, such as de Keersmaeker, showing revised work. *Rosas Danst Rosas* was the company's signature piece from 1983; with a running time of one hour and forty-five minutes with no interval, it displayed in equal measure the maturity, choreographic rigour and utter lack of compromise typical of de Keersmaeker, as well as the dancers' stamina. The piece was especially important this year because it showed European work at its best, as well as highlighting the number of derivatives that were currently on the market.

As far as the UK was concerned, too, 1992 tended to showcase established though still developing companies such as those of Siobhan Davies and Shobana Jeyasingh, although the Jonathan Burrows group attracted attention too. Burrows was appearing independently of the Royal Ballet for the first time, and showed an intriguing piece, *Very*, for four performers: Burrows, fellow Royal Ballet dancers Lynne Bristow and Deborah Jones plus the composer Matteo Fargion, who played, sang and participated in the action. Laurie Booth also deserves mention for once again leading the 'cutting edge'. This year he elected to improvise with violinist Alex Balanescu and poet Aaron Williamson, who is profoundly deaf, plus dance partner of some three consecutive years, Russell Maliphant.

Davies's programme had been preceded by an extremely successful week-long residency of classes and workshops led by the company, in which Val Bourne noted the utter delight at having Riverside filled with dance and dancers for a whole week.[35] This remark prophesied the 'Operation Riverside' project the following year, financed by the Prudential Award money. Davies presented two contrasting pieces, *Make-Make* and *White Bird Featherless*, the former dark and less formally structured, the latter light in atmosphere and

Paul Douglas and Gill Clarke in *White Bird Featherless*, Siobhan Davies Dance Company, 1992.
PHOTO: HUGO GLENDINNING

suggesting rule-based games. For both, however, Davies once again created a dance community specific to the individual piece, in which various aspects of what it is to be human are tested.

Jeyasingh too gave a double bill of works: this time a reworking of her 1988 piece, *Configurations,* and a new piece, *Making of Maps.* In Nyman's music for the former, Jeyasingh found an appropriate Western counterbalance to the rhythms of Bharata Natyam and showed an increased maturity in her deconstructions of Indian classical dance, such that she exploited the 'collective emotional and visceral power of her five dancers', transforming them into 'unmistakably . . . citizens of the 20th century'.[36] In *Making of Maps* Jeyasingh directly confronted the making of cultural identity. In possibly the most courageous of her works at that time, she pushed the movement further than ever from its origins.

As for the Americans, the Transatlantic Tap programme was the first time tap had been included in the festival proper (other than on gala occasions), and very popular it proved to be, encouraging a new audience to the Umbrella. The Petronio company gave a typical bravura performance with Petronio's predictable unpredictability. *Half Wrong plus Laytext* was his response to Stravinsky's *Rite of Spring* (the score for two pianos, here played by two performers on one instrument) and harked back to a joint venture for himself and Michael Clark. That venture had resulted in Clark's *Mmm . . .* seen previously for his company, and in Petronio's *Wrong Wrong*, incorporated in the current performance (hence the *Half Wrong*). Against custom, the dancers lay on the floor motionless for the Chosen Maiden section, putting the focus on the pianists Christopher Swithinbank and Gruffydd Owen. Urban Bush Women scored another resounding success with a series of short excerpts, including in their performance live music, text and *a cappella* vocalisations based on field hollers, chants and shape-note singing.

The Cunningham performances at the Queen Elizabeth Hall were described as a celebration of the life of John Cage, who had died earlier in the year. These were the London audience's first experience of Cunningham's *Events*[37] – programmes tailored to a specific performance space and incorporating excerpts from work seen previously and from work new to London. Cunningham, then aged seventy-three, danced two solos that demonstrated

Sue MacLennan Dance Company in rehearsal at Chisenhale, 1992. PHOTO: HUGO GLENDINNING

Nigel Charnock and Liz Brailsford in *Original Sin*, 1993. PHOTO: HUGO GLENDINNING

as much as anything his compelling stage personality. Mackrell noted: 'The *Event* not only celebrated Cunningham the sorcerer-choreographer, but also Cunningham the performer – enigma, seer and total showman'.[38]

So once again it was Cunningham who provided a clear perspective for what was then happening in contemporary dance: drawing comparisons between his own style and that based on European dance-theatre, and with companies on whom he had exerted so much influence, albeit indirect and by now indistinct. As if that were not enough, his programme also drew attention to new technologically-based choreographies, which appeared alongside older works from his 'canon'.

1993

The centrepiece for Dance Umbrella 93 was a project financed by the 1992 Prudential Award for the Arts – 'Operation Riverside', in which every inch of Riverside Studios was given over to dance and dance-related activity for close to three weeks. This 'celebration', together with an altogether darker introspection brought about by speculation on the future of the UK's two oldest contemporary dance companies, LCDT and Rambert, provided the context for the flavour of Dance Umbrella 93.

'Operation Riverside' opened with 'Necessary Weather'. This performance project involved Sara Rudner, who had performed in the very first festival, and Dana Reitz, who in Dance Umbrella 81 had been seminal in introducing 'meet the choreographer' sessions. The third member of 'Necessary Weather', and similarly billed as co-choreographer, was lighting designer Jennifer Tipton. This was by no means a fanciful billing, for it was Tipton who actively created the dance space by dividing the stage into pools or by creating columns of light, and who provided the ambience from which the other 'dancer/choreographers' could project movement ideas. With no set or accompaniment, lighting was seen as an equal choreographic determinant and Mackrell noted the lighting's 'alchemic reaction with the movement'.[39] The performances were rapturously received.

Other events recalling the strengths of previous years included two collaborations between artists from the UK. Dancer/choreographer Miranda Tufnell was working once again with artist David Ward, a collaboration that had resulted in memorable work in 1984 (*Huge Veil*) and 1985 (*Urban Weather*). Together with composer/musician Sylvia Hallett, with whom Tufnell had been working since 1988, they presented *In the Grain of the Body.* Prompted by capacity audiences for 'Necessary Weather', this lighting-emphasised collaboration also received very positive reviews, though its treatment was very different, focusing on 'texture, symbolism, sensuality and mystery'.[40] Hallett also appeared with Emilyn Claid in *Sweet Side Show* – a piece that emerged from an 'Operation Riverside' commission in Riverside Studio's Gallery and was based on a short story by Angela Carter – in which 'they successfully inhabited every area of the space, transforming it into a mysterious and atmospheric environment'.[41]

Doug Elkins's witty and vibrant dance style also showed to good effect in a residency for 'Operation Riverside'. His company's performances similarly found considerable favour with their fast and furious style, a natural audience-pleaser not lacking in reflexive wit: 'I'm a post-modern representative of junk culture, but that word post-modern seems to validate it somehow'.[42]

But Mackrell noted the prevalence of dramatic dance this year.[43] David Rousseve's style of 'confessional theatre' explored sexual and racial oppression in America, Victoria Marks responded to the Gulf War in *Dick* and Nigel Charnock dealt with sex and violence in his *Original Sin*, which claimed to be 'more slap than tickle, more S than M'. The Catalan troupe Mal Pelo were also representative of a more dramatic expression in their performance of *Sur Perros del Sur* (Southern Dogs), which included text and dialogue and had its roots in *commedia dell'arte*.

Matthew Hawkins and his new company marked the centenary of the death of Tchaikovsky with *Fresh Dances for the Late Tchaikovsky*. The opulence of the Hackney Empire was well suited to the outrageous baroque over-the-top costumes designed by Pearl and the dance's absurd comedic situations. To these qualities Hawkins added his own Cecchetti-style classical purity, and combined young, inexperienced dancers with more seasoned performers: actress Fenella Fielding and performance artist Rose English.

V-Tol dance company, *32 feet per second per second*, 1993. PHOTO: CHRIS NASH

Second Stride described themselves as 'physical music theatre with a dance focus'. The performance included more dance than in recent years, perhaps for financial reasons, since the company had recently found themselves in the invidious position of falling between funding categories for the Arts Council. *Escape at Sea* was no less challenging than previous performances, with texts that were spoken in English, French and Russian and a narrative that required intimate knowledge of *Sleeping Beauty* as well as of Chekhov's *The Seagull*.

But Siobhan Davies's choreography once again provided a contrast, and this year she confronted the issue that is really at the heart of all her work, directly in *Wanting to tell Stories,* by exploring just what dance can express and how it communicates at its most basic level. Working within a similar remit was Shobana Jeyasingh who this year commissioned a piece from Richard Alston, *Delicious Arbour,* to music by Purcell. 'It was as though Alston had gone abroad to learn a new language and submitted poetry as a first composition,' wrote Anne Sacks in admiration.[44]

1994

In 1994 the festival again came close to being cancelled. With no Prudential Award to buoy up its finances this year, it was back to (inadequate) core funding and had to withdraw its invitation to Merce Cunningham, as late in the year as May. The Cunningham Company was fortunately secured for the 1994 Edinburgh Festival instead. The 'Coast to Coast' initiative provided funding for most of the visiting European companies, and the result was a reduced festival over three weeks instead of the usual four or five (excluding The Featherstonehaughs' extravagant finale, scheduled for the weekend after the last performances). But the festival was able to provide a star attraction, with Lucinda Childs presenting her company for its very first London appearance, plus two important short courses, in dance and technology and in dance criticism. Neither was there any shortage of resonant themes to choose from, with many choreographers (visitors and our own artists included) airing issues of sexuality. Age-related issues were similarly to the fore, with many companies sporting more 'mature' dancers. The Childs's repertoire brought to a head the long-fermenting debate over pure dance versus dance theatre. Then there was classical ballet's resurgence, long heralded but particularly apparent this year in terms of both subject matter and technique. There were no less than two versions of *Rite of Spring,* plus versions of *Le Spectre de la rose* and *Les Noces.* Moreover, choreographers such as Childs, Mark Baldwin, Matthew Hawkins, Russell Maliphant, Angelin Preljocaj and Philippe Tréhet drew directly from the classical ballet vocabulary.

Compagnie Preljocaj, making its third Umbrella appearance, was one of four companies to be celebrating their tenth anniversary (the others were those of Stephen Petronio, Lea Anderson and Urban Bush Women) and proved to be the most successful of the European companies. The programme, with an overall title *Hommage aux Ballets Russes,* included Preljocaj's

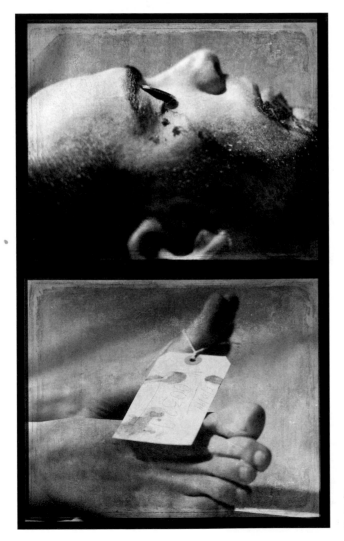

Javier De Frutos, *The Palace Does Not Forgive*, 1994.
PHOTO: CHRIS NASH

Ricochet Dance Company,
1994.
PHOTO: HUGO GLENDINNING

overtly erotically-charged versions of *Le Spectre de la rose* and *Les Noces.* Two other European companies, those of José Besprosvany and Philippe Tréhet, presented text-based work. They fared less well, partly through the inaccessibility of their French texts, partly because of the relatively lesser weight given to movement content and partly because of what was perceived as a somewhat naive and outdated portrayal of gender relationships. The tide seemed to have turned in terms of press, if not public, taste for dance that privileged movement for its expression.

The Spanish-born, Venezuelan-raised, British-based choreographer Javier De Frutos had been gaining notoriety elsewhere – he had been choreographer in residence at Chisenhale Dance Space this year. He made his Umbrella debut with a typical flourish, in a solo version of Stravinsky's *Rite of Spring,* an enterprise appropriately identified by Ann Nugent as 'either mad or inspired'.[45] The enigmatically titled *The Palace Does Not Forgive,* saw De Frutos (by now, familiarly) naked, save for a gold lurex tunic, which he used to 'flash' at the audience: 'the victim awaiting sacrifice, playing with traits of national-

123

Ellen van Schuylenburch,
solo, 1994.
PHOTO: HUGO GLENDINNING

ity, religion and sexuality'.[46] De Frutos's literal and metaphorical nakedness made an impact and ensured his return visits for many years to come.

The Lucinda Childs Dance Company presented what must have appeared the polar opposite to European narrative-based dance theatre with her minimalist, analytic strand of dance. Ironically, in light of the apparent European preference for dance-theatre at the time, she had been scoring enormous success in France (as had Trisha Brown) for the previous twenty or so years. 1991 had seen her creation of *Four Elements*, at the invitation of Richard Alston for Rambert Dance Company, and she had also been seen two months previously at the Edinburgh Festival; but, incredibly, the company was celebrating its twenty-first year and yet this was its first visit to London. For the Umbrella, audiences were fittingly able to compare past and previous works. Childs presented *Available Light* (1983), originally conceived for the opening of the Museum of Contemporary Art in Los Angeles. This was only the third time it had been seen with the double-level staging by architect

Frank Gehry. The other piece, *Concerto* (1993), to Górecki's *Concerto pour clavecin et cordes*, served as an example of her newer work. But many reviewers found her 1979 collaboration with composer Philip Glass and visual artist Sol Le Witt, *Dance*, which was shown only at the Edinburgh Festival, to be more richly textured and rewarding.

It was Siobhan Davies's *The Glass Blew In* that was designated a masterpiece by some quarters of the dance press. Tellingly, Davies had premiered the work earlier in the year and this seemed to set the precedent, with our established artists showing in the festival only material that had previously been tried and tested. This was in marked contrast to the practice of earlier years.

Childs (at the age of fifty-four, we were constantly reminded), had performed in her own work alongside the more youthful members of her company. Baldwin chose to separate his casts in a programme that made a very promising Umbrella debut for his new company, in choreography that allowed all performers to dance at strength. *A Collection of Moving Parts* was for a mature cast of four that included Lynn Seymour, Lucy Burge, Christopher Bannerman and Dale Thompson. The programme also included a younger cast of freelancers in *Excursions*. Mixed-age casting was however on the agenda for Matthew Hawkins's Fresh Dances Group. *Matthew and Diana on Manoeuvres* sent up the assumptions and preconceptions of both classical and contemporary dance, and included a *pas de deux* for Hawkins and sixty-nine-year-old Diana Payne Myers to Tchaikovsky's *Capriccio Italien*.

Inclusiveness was also on the bill for the two community-based projects, a feature of this Umbrella that returned us to the ethos of its history. In collaboration with playwright Goran Stefanovski, Fergus Early's Green Candle Company presented an ambitious piece, *Old Man Dragging Stones,* based loosely upon current events in Eastern Europe and incorporating students from City and Islington Colleges. Wheel of Fortune's *The Dancing Room* was the other community-based project at Riverside Studios, in which the 'room' was also situated somewhere in Eastern Europe and served as a site for community high spirits. Devised by Kate Flatt and designer Sally Jacobs, the performances included professional and ex-professional dancers alongside some forty workshop participants who had been involved with the project through the company's outreach programme.

Russell Maliphant in *Paradigm*, 1995.
PHOTO: HUGO GLENDINNING

5

A New Role for Dance Umbrella: 1995–1999

Major Developments

Dance Umbrella 94 reached a nadir, according to Bourne. With her renowned ingenuity she had just about got away with it, but with no prize money and no foreign arts festival upon which to 'piggyback', the festival had had to reduce its programme substantially, and Bourne did not want to relive the experience. More to the point, she knew that another such festival might mean the end of Dance Umbrella altogether, and so it was that she threatened to shut it down herself unless more secure funding was forthcoming from the Arts Council of England (ACE). Bourne eventually won her case, and Dance Umbrella 95 was a triumph that in some ways marked the end of this bleak period, but in turn heralded new uncertainties. For 1996/97, after eighteen years, Dance Umbrella was finally elevated to the status of regularly funded client of ACE. Status and security rose, therefore, even though the grant remained the same as for the previous year.

But in addition to funding, the other perennial problem that had so far dogged all dance programming in the capital was its lack of a decently sized performance space. For promoters this had meant either touring large companies (including many of the major overseas ones) away from the capital, or negotiating with the prohibitively expensive Coliseum. This situation was also to change, and we saw the prospects for dance turn around in the space of just a few years.

Dance Umbrella had been seminal in building up audiences for dance. As a result, organisations such as The Place, the South Bank and ICA have all independently increased their dance programming in the past few years.

These venues are now competitors for funding as well as for audiences; even though there are few simultaneous events, Bourne is well aware that tickets are expensive and that audiences' pockets are not limitless. Competition has stepped up, which means that Dance Umbrella cannot sit back and rest on its laurels even if it wanted to.

Needing to maintain its name at the forefront of dance programming, Dance Umbrella undertakes consultancies as well as collaborations with other large organisations, as we have seen, and these activities have increased. Dance Umbrella's co-production (with English National Opera) of the Mark Morris Dance Group's *L'Allegro, Il Ponseroso ed Il Moderato* at the Coliseum in June 1997 was just such an opportunity, allowing Dance Umbrella to 're-position itself within the arts world and to be seen as a potential player in the premier league.' The Dance Umbrella Annual Report for the Arts Council, 1995/96, continues: 'For the same reason, Dance Umbrella has undertaken Consultancies and Management for certain projects which it has thought strategically important, for reasons of scale, location etc.' Examples include the programming at the Barbican after its stage refurbishment, for which Val Bourne acted as consultant for a couple of years, and Dance Umbrella's continued management of Woking Dance Umbrella, alongside the large-scale tours of major international artists that have also become a feature of Dance Umbrella's work.

But it would be a mistake to think that success amounts to cool calculation and strategic planning. Dance Umbrella's initial premise was that the UK needed a dance festival to provide a platform for new choreography from the UK and to showcase the best from abroad (initially from the US, then from Europe as well, then internationally). As we have seen, since its inception things have changed: new choreography has other platforms; Dance Umbrella now organises major tours for overseas artists in their own right and separate from the London festival; and there are now several dance festivals in the regions. But at the heart of the enterprise there remain the needs of the profession and the continued education and augmentation of the audience for dance. This chapter examines Dance Umbrella's current roles, and speculates on what its future roles might be.

Touring

The pattern established during the previous period was one of touring fewer foreign companies and then only with work markedly different from that of our own groups or distinguished in some other way. From 1995, Dance Umbrella increased its touring of high-profile companies outside the autumn Dance Umbrella season. The Mark Morris company was toured in March and April 1995, the Trisha Brown company during May and June 1996. These tours were in addition to the festival spin-off tours of Elizabeth Streb/ Ringside (1995), Stephen Petronio (1997) and Michael Clark and Company (1998), all of whom took in the London Dance Umbrella festival as part of a nationwide tour. In the latter two cases the tour was extended over eight and ten different venues (including London) spread over three and six weeks respectively. All of these tours were undertaken in conjunction with Arts Council Touring, and in some cases attached to other events, for example regional festivals. The Morris Company appeared as part of the first Woking Dance Umbrella – a venue close enough to London to attract its audience. Trisha Brown's performances were also typical of the cross-fertilisation style of funding for such activities, in that the Brighton performances were pro- moted by the Brighton Festival as part of its venture, those at the Queen Elizabeth Hall were included in the Turning World Festival and the Newcastle performances were included in the Northern Electric Festival. This pattern decentralised dance in much the same way as the regional festivals had done in the 1980s, and acted in tandem with the concentrated events of the large regional festivals in Woking, Leicester, Newcastle and latterly Nottingham, independently of Dance Umbrella.

Both the Morris tour of 1995 and the Brown tour the following year were the first in Britain by these companies. In both cases, programming was most carefully undertaken, giving samples of the choreographers' work that spanned their careers and gave some indication of their choreographic range. Although Morris had been seen regularly in recent years at the Edinburgh Festivals, he had not been seen in London since 1985 and then with a company of only five. Within the UK, Trisha Brown's company had only ever appeared in London and Glasgow, and her last London appearance had been in 1991. Even given these factors, however, and that the companies had capacity or near-capacity audiences in many venues, the tours stretched Dance Umbrella's resources to the limit. The Brown tour in particular had to be underwritten by Dance Umbrella, and even though box office targets were met and the money was released back into the budget, programming of the London festival had been seriously affected. The 1996/97 report proposed accordingly that future tours of international companies be tied to the London or Woking festivals. Even with these constraints and with the drain on resources inevitably attending large-scale projects such as the collaboration with English National Opera at the Coliseum in 1997, Bourne still sees touring and company residencies as central and crucial components of Dance Umbrella's activities.

Management Consultancies

Consultancies increased dramatically during this period, which gives a good indication of Dance Umbrella's increased sphere of influence, as well as its increased international standing. One of the varied initiatives under this heading was to advise the Barbican Theatre on dance programming. The Royal Shakespeare Company vacates its London base for six months each year, during which time the Barbican becomes available to other companies. Programme director Graham Sheffield offered a six-month consultancy to Dance Umbrella to advise on an American-themed dance programme for 1998, to fit in with the Barbican's 'Inventing America' year. In the first season, BITE 98 (the Barbican's International Theatre Event), featured Trisha Brown's *Orfeo,* the Twyla Tharp company in repertory (plus Tharp's *One Hundreds* project), the Siobhan Davies company (whose double bill of dances that year featured American composers) and the Merce Cunningham Dance Company. Both Davies and Cunningham appeared under the twin auspices of Dance Umbrella and BITE, their performances simultaneously opening the former festival and marking the finale of the latter. The Barbican now offers one of the best and largest stages in London for contemporary dance for six months of the year.

The co-production, with English National Opera, of *L'Allegro, Il Ponseroso ed Il Moderato* at the Coliseum in June 1997 was the first time Mark Morris's full company of twenty-four dancers had been seen in London. The company had featured regularly at the Edinburgh Festivals since 1992 (they performed *L'Allegro* there in 1994) and Dance Umbrella had toured the company in repertory in 1995, but with no London venue in the itinerary. Bourne recalls,

Twyla Tharp's *One Hundreds* project at the Barbican Centre, July 1998. PHOTO: HUGO GLENDINNING

'We made a Faustian deal with Mark – no London date in 1995, but we would bring *L'Allegro* to London within the next two years'.[1] At that time, however, finding an available London venue large enough for the production was a problem – a situation which was to change considerably – and the Coliseum alone was found to be suitable. The performances were a huge success, with critic Jenny Gilbert suggesting that in an ideal world we would have the resources to enable regular visits from the company, with tickets available on the National Health, such was the feel-good factor promoted by this piece.[2] All performances were sold out, with queues for returns.

Woking Dance Umbrella Festivals 1995, 1997 and 1999

Woking Borough Council (WBC) wanted to celebrate its centenary in 1995 with a dance festival sited within its Peacocks Centre, a huge shopping and leisure complex which had opened in 1992 and included the New Victoria Theatre and the Rhoda McGaw Theatre. Ruth Glick (co-ordinator and administrator for the first three London festivals) had been brought in by WBC to advise, and she brought in Dance Umbrella in a consultative role on the study. Surprisingly, since the study proposed a more ambitious and expansive festival than WBC had originally envisaged, the Council accepted it and Dance Umbrella was engaged to run Woking Dance Umbrella 95. At the insistence of Dance Umbrella's accountant, who had been appalled at the financial risk involved in Dance Umbrella running the Newcastle festivals, a different arrangement was found for Woking. Dance Umbrella was employed to programme and manage the festivals only, and a separate Woking Dance Umbrella board was created to bear the financial brunt.[3] The board included representatives from the New Victoria Theatre and WBC.[4] Drawing on experiences learned during the Leicester and Newcastle festivals, Bourne selected a judicious mix of British and international companies, with an emphasis on community-based projects and showcases for local schools and companies, but also including a ballet company and a musical – events with a far more overtly commercial bent than was the current norm in London.

The first Woking Dance Umbrella caused mirth in the dance press, partly because of the town's dull commuter-belt reputation and partly for its venue, which led to billings such as 'dance in the shopping mall'. All the festivals to date have indeed sited dance within the shopping centre itself. The first festival included performances by the French 'vertical' dance group, Roc in Lichen, in the 20-metre-high glass atrium, their aerial manoeuvres providing a contrast with the escalators and glass lifts of the centre. Other companies, however, appeared in the more traditional settings of the centre's two theatres, the 1300-seat New Victoria and the more intimate Rhoda McGaw.

The first festival boasted eighteen days (16 March to 2 April 1995) of dance performances, classes, films and seminars, plus a charity gala. Programming aimed to animate the local dance scene on a long-term basis, but also had a canny eye on immediate marketing issues, with the Mark Morris company opening the festival. The Morris programme was perfect, as it offered a range of his work from Brahms's *New Love Song Waltzes,* through Gershwin and a solo for himself in *Three Preludes*, the ostensibly jokey *Going Away Party* (containing, however, darker undercurrents) and finishing with the overtly dark and primitive *Grand Duo* to Lou Harrison's monumental score. Dance Umbrella could not have picked a more appropriate dance group for the task. The Morris company had built a following amongst seasoned dance-goers and was now embarking on its first-ever British tour; Woking was the closest to the capital that it was to come, thus guaranteeing a London audience and providing full houses for the festival opening. For local audiences less accustomed to modern dance, Morris's company and choreography were extraordinarily accessible, showing that dancers are in fact normal people – with a talent for extraordinarily hard work maybe, but not out of this world.

With an eye on further encompassing all tastes, Scottish Ballet showed their new version of *Swan Lake* with designs by Jasper Conran, and the tap musical *Hot Shoe Shuffle* appeared fresh from its West End success. In the smaller venue appeared Candoco, Kathak dancer Nahid Saddiqui, V-Tol, Laurie Booth and Company, the Gandini Juggling Project and the Jiving Lindy Hoppers. All these events were interspersed with master classes, residencies and projects, plus showcases of local work – some in association with Brighton Dance Agency, thanks to Theresa Beatty. The first festival was such a success that WBC agreed to support further festivals on a biennial basis. As a follow-on, WBC created the post of community dance co-ordinator to maintain interest in between the two-yearly festivals as well as to intensify involvement during them. Dance Umbrella was ever aware of the need to keep interest bubbling away during the intervening years. An effective strategy for doing this was by occasional programming of varied dance events at the Rhoda McGaw Theatre, some traditional, some less so, such as the Spring into Dance festivals in 1996 and 1998.

The second festival ran from 25 February to 22 March 1997. In contrast with the first, it opened with Scottish Ballet and their much-acclaimed production of *La Sylphide*, mounted by Sorella Englund from the Royal Danish Ballet. But with the need to show a major international company that had not previously been seen in London, a prestigious modern dance company, Philippe Decouflé's Compagnie DCA, appeared the following week with his surreal 'circus-theatre' *Decodex*, giving the last-ever performances of this work on the final leg of their two-year European tour. The lavish musical *A Chorus Line* then completed the final two weeks of the festival in the large theatre. There were also ODC from San Francisco and David Dorfman from New York, Brighton-based artists Divas and Steve Parry, Wimbledon-based Kathak and contemporary dancer Akram Khan, a Youth Dance Showcase and classes for all abilities in styles that ranged from line dancing to flamenco. Basically, then, the formula that had proved so successful two years previously was little changed. However, the level of community participation was increased and was more ambitious for the 1997 festival. This included a project for a cast of 150 drawn from local schools and community groups and led by Chicken Shed Theatre Company, which culminated in a performance in The

H. G. Wells Suite at The Planets. The StopGap Project involved ten disabled and able-bodied dancers in a piece choreographed by Kuldip Singh Barmi – a result of nine months' work – while High Spin Dance Company, which comprised nine dancers with and without learning difficulties, worked on a performance devised in collaboration with Fiona Edwards and Jamie Watton.

The third Woking Dance Umbrella festival (7–27 March 1999) opened with a gala featuring highlights from the fare to come. The festival itself increased the number of overseas companies, with Cas Public from Montreal, Inbal Pinto and Company from Israel and Doug Varone and Dancers from New York appearing in 'shopping malls, schools and unexpected places around town'. Also from the US were Sara Pearson and Patrik Widrig, who adapted their dance theatre piece *Ordinary Festivals* for nine local performers. The more mainstream events on offer were Royal Ballet Dance Bites, *Cruel Garden* from Rambert Dance Company and a mixed bill from English National Ballet. This year also featured a site-specific work: a commission from Lea Anderson for the Peacocks Shopping Centre, *Bubblehead,* which included fifty local dancers. Participants from the 1997 event also featured, with Fiona Edwards and Jamie Watton's company, Physical Recall, Akram Khan and The StopGap Project. There was also a two-week residency for Varone, funded by the Arts Council's Arts for Everyone (A4E) initiative, a trend that Dance Umbrella is keen to reproduce and extend in future festivals both in London and in Woking.[5] The Woking Dance Showcase once again featured local talent, and included the Chance to Dance Weekend, which had also become something of a tradition, plus a 'Historic Dance Project' for children.

Programming of international companies then took on a different accent, featuring performers who had made their mark relatively recently under the auspices of the London Dance Umbrella festivals, rather than huge international names. For example, Varone had featured in Dance Umbrella 96, and Cas Public and Pearson and Widrig in Dance Umbrella 97. Another innovation was that the musical (*Grease*) was scheduled after the festival rather than being included as part of it.

At the time of the second festival, the press made something of the relationship between the festivals and the existing arts scene. The Rhoda McGaw Theatre was a 1970s building, purpose-built to encourage Woking's popular amateur dramatics groups; when the new complex was planned, this building alone was thought important enough historically to preserve and to incorporate within the site. Michael Wright for the *Daily Telegraph* contends that Woking Dance Umbrella was able to draw upon and reflect community arts in which 'the amateur and the professional coexist happily side-by-side'.[6] However, Bourne doubts that this relationship existed in the past to any significant degree, and is proud of the fact that Dance Umbrella forged new links with the community, with over one thousand local participants by 1999.[7]

Nash argues that the community links, alongside programming that had learned its lessons from Dance Umbrella's experience of the Leicester and Newcastle dance festivals, ensured that Woking's festival has become a model for partnerships between the commercial sector, local authorities and arts organisations.[8] Of equal importance were the adequate levels of funding available for the festivals from Woking Borough Council, ACE, South East Arts and other corporate sponsors.

The Jerwood Choreography Awards

The Jerwood Choreography Awards are managed by Dance Umbrella as a joint initiative between the Jerwood Charitable Foundation and ACE. Presently open to UK-based choreographers aged thirty-five or under, their distinctive quality is that they actively encourage experimental works. This may have something to do with the unusualness of the Trust itself, set up by the late John Jerwood in 1977 and managed by Alan Grieve. Grieve describes the organisation and its benefactor thus: 'John's life was colourful. That's why, in a way, the Jerwood Foundation isn't riddled with bureaucracy and committees . . . I think we have a freer spirit than most funding bodies.'[9] The brief of the organisation as a whole is similarly broad: to fund anything from painting and fashion to medicine, education and social welfare, with the choreography awards having become one of its enterprises in the early 1990s.

Dance Umbrella's association with the Awards began in 1994 with a project over three years that was undertaken in association with the Royal Ballet companies and the Arts Council. The first recipients in 1995 were Jillian Mackrill of the Birmingham Royal Ballet and Tom Sapsford of the Royal Ballet. Sapsford's piece, *Where Her Voice,* for four dancers, was so successful that it was included in Dance Umbrella 95. 1996 winners were William Tuckett and Matthew Hart. By 1996/97, the Jerwood Awards had been opened up to all young choreographers, not just those from the Royal Ballet companies. Dance Umbrella tendered for management of the new awards and was successful in its bid.

In 1997 there were two recipients of the awards, Yael Flexer and Henri Oguike, both receiving £17,000. In 1998 there were three: Charles Linehan received £17,000 and Ted Stoffer and Stephen Hughes each received £8,500. For 1997, choreographers had to be aged thirty or under, but the criteria changed for 1998, with the age limit raised so that the main prize was open to those aged thirty-five or under, with two smaller prizes with an age limit of thirty years. By 1999 all these awards were on offer to anyone aged thirty-five or under.

The project, now managed by Betsy Gregory of Dance Umbrella, is one which, according to Bourne, has become almost like an extension of the Management Service of the early years because of its closeness to people making work, and it therefore has become very dear to those involved.

Courses, Themes and Initiatives

The days of 'themed' festivals had long since passed, but one initiative dominated this period – that of dance and the new computer technology in all its varied guises. Other themes that emerge, such as the Percussive Feet festival and the commissioning of site-specific works, are to do with the perennial drive towards attracting new audiences. The relationship between dance makers and digital artists was one that was fostered in conjunction with Terry Braun of Illuminations Interactive and greatly enhanced by Dance Umbrella from 1994 onwards, but the feeling is now that it is time for others to take over the reins for this area of dance making.

Dance and Technology

The history of Dance Umbrella's involvement in the new technologies and their possibilities can be traced back to 1983 and the Dance Video Project, which included workshops for film and TV directors. Participants included Terry Braun, who, together with his company Illuminations Interactive, was to oversee all the dance and technology initiatives within the festival's related events up to 1998. The 1994 two-day conference, Dance and

136

Vivian Wood in
Tom Sapsford's
Where Her Voice? 1995.
PHOTO: HUGO GLENDINNING

Technology: Trick or Treat?, was led by Braun, Julian Blom and Anna Cutler. During it they discussed the application of new computer technologies in dance. The main focus was Lifeforms, the modelling program developed at Simon Fraser University in Canada and most famously used by Merce Cunningham, but which was then relatively new to most people.

The enthusiasm amongst participants in 1994 meant that for the following year Dance Umbrella hosted 'Techno Dance Bytes', a six-day course to explore the use of interactive technology. A specially constructed Cyberstudio set up in the Lilian Baylis Theatre at Sadler's Wells hosted five teams of choreographers and computer artists. This year, the interest in dance and technology was in any case much more apparent within the Festival programming itself, with the Merce Cunningham Company's repertory programmes of dances made with the aid of Lifeforms. Mark Baldwin too presented a programme entitled *Dances from Cyberspace* that made use of material created with Lifeforms software, while Chris Nash's photography exhibition at Riverside Studios also reflected the influence of the latest technology in producing images of dance. Wayne McGregor's *Cyborg* solo contrasted significantly with that of Steve Paxton with whom he shared a double bill, and who from the very early days had been an exponent of dance's re-invention at Judson's Yard, so the point was made there too.

1996 saw a widening of the area with 'Dance on Screen' – a whole week of events and screenings organised by The Place Dance Services, again in conjunction with Illuminations Interactive and Dance Umbrella. It included a showcase for the latest developments to come out of the previous year's 'Techno Dance Bytes'. Mark Baldwin, for example, had worked with French-born multimedia artist Carole Murcia in 1995, and had produced a prototypical multimedia performance piece called *Mirrors*, a narrative-based 'murder mystery' that was made available later on CD-ROM. René Eyre's and Chris Nash's interactive installation at the Union Chapel in Islington, in which the audience roamed over two floors of a former Sunday School room, triggering sound, lighting and video effects by their movements, provided an instance of the inclusion of digital wizardry within the main programme of the festival. Their film was also included in the Digital Dancing showcases.

It was in 1997, however, that the varied range of possibilities for this area of working really became apparent. Braun and Illuminations Interactive won a grant from A4E that funded a further two highly productive years in association with Dance Umbrella. Digital Dancing 97 consequently ran five separate and very different initiatives over a two-week period in Riverside Studio 2. These included Susan Kozel's *Ghosts and Astronauts*, in collaboration with digital artist Grechen Schiller. This was a live tele-presence performance, designed for Halloween, in which dancers at The Place Theatre and at Riverside Studios were linked through video-conferencing technology based on Macintosh computers and CU-See Me software. Former Graham dancer Jane Dudley worked with animator Gillian Lacey and digital artist Timo Arnall to produce *Dancing Inside*, which was later televised. The power of Dudley's performance in Green Candle's relatively recent *The Citadel* had impressed Lacey (head of animation at the National Film and Television School) and inspired her to make the piece. Sarah Rubidge and digital artist Simon Biggs produced *Halo,* an interactive installation that played in the Riverside foyer.

Part two of the A4E-funded initiative saw Digital Dancing 98 and six teams of choreographers working together with digital artists. Among the outcomes of these three weeks of workshops at the Jerwood Space in Union Street was Richard Lord's collaboration with digital effect animators Christian Hogue and Alex Rutterford (*Lost in Space* digital effects designers), which produced *Cyberkinesis* in which real dancers and computer animations were linked in an installation based on motion capture. Another project had Wayne McGregor beamed up live (by a process known as telematics) from the Jerwood Space into Company in Space's *Trial by Video* performance in Melbourne, enabling McGregor to 'materialise' and move among the Australian dancers, and vice versa. Sarah Rubidge, digital artists Garry Hill and Tim Diggins and composer Nye Parry produced *Passing Phases*, an interactive installation shown in the foyer of the Queen Elizabeth Hall and originally developed during Digital Dancing 96 at The Place Theatre.

At the end of this period, however, A4E funding ceased and, bearing in mind the huge cost of these projects, so too did the association with Dance Umbrella. Practitioners within the profession and dance audiences had both had their knowledge of the possibilities for the new technologies within dance greatly extended over the previous five years. Public response to the

Say a Little Prayer, installation by Chris Nash and René Eyre, 1996. PHOTO: CHRIS NASH

139

seminars and screenings was often overwhelming and there was never any shortage of professional applicants for places on the courses and workshops.

Dance and technology is still an exciting and important area, as it is 'yet another gateway for dance',[10] and choreographers such as Wayne McGregor are making huge creative strides. However, the interest and expertise that Digital Dancing 97 and 98 encouraged under its two-year funding now have to be fostered elsewhere. Bourne feels that this sort of work is probably best continued in a university environment, because of the skills and equipment needed and the considerable financial burden that they bring with them.[11] For example, Leeds Metropolitan University is experimenting with artists on-line, and Chichester Institute of Higher Education has held performance and technology laboratories in 1996 and 1998.

Percussive Feet

The idea for this festival developed from a percussive-feet theme for Newcastle Dance 92, which drew together acts seemingly as diverse as North-umberland clog dancers and Transatlantic Tap, a specially curated perform-ance of tap artists from the US who also appeared in the London festival.

Then in 1996 a festival was held at the Cochrane Theatre (see Appendix 2, 1996: Additional Events) with principal guest artists Ira Bernstein from the US and Dutch-born, New-York-trained but London-based Tobias Tak (who had also participated in the Transatlantic Tap performances). Bernstein acted as master of ceremonies for the festival, introducing the programmes and per-forming on the first and last nights, while both he and Tak conducted work-shops which culminated in performances by student participants. The idea was to present artists and companies who represented the international diversity of percussive dance forms, and to that end the programmes drew upon a diverse range of styles, from Kathak, flamenco, clog, Irish and African dance forms. In addition to the performances and residencies there were film screenings, a debate and a piece commissioned from Sue MacLennan that incorporated Irish step, Appalachian clog and contemporary movement.

The festival was yet another way of attracting a new audience for dance and, for Dance Umbrella, one that unashamedly exploited the current inter-est in percussive styles, with *Riverdance*, the Australian company Tap Dogs and Stomp all enjoying enormous popularity. But the programme also reflected the current interest in hybrid cultural forms, as a way of creatively experimenting as well as of breaking down barriers between ethnic forms, gender distinctions, class interests and generic forms within dance itself. We have seen how the dances of Jeyasingh reflect an interest in looking forward rather than in preserving the past; in the same vein, the festival included Akram Khan, who performed a much-acclaimed solo that melded Kathak with contemporary dance. His success was repeated in his appearances during the 1997 and 1999 Woking Dance Umbrella festivals, for which venue he counts as part of the local talent, being based in Wimbledon but teaching in Woking.

Tobias Tak, studio shot.
PHOTO: HUGO GLENDINNING

The Outside Eye Initiative

This was a two-week, A4E-funded course that took place during September 1998. The facilitators were David Gordon and his son Ain, whose services were procured by Dance Umbrella to guide seven established British-based choreographers (Gaby Agis, Laurie Booth, Mark Bruce, Emma Diamond, Paul Douglas, Matthew Hawkins and Fin Walker) and five dancers in a 'creative laboratory'. It was also, in Booth's words, 'an opportunity to spend extended quality time with colleagues.'[12] The Gordons drew upon a method developed by Liz Lerman (see listings for Dance Umbrella 88) of 'non-opinionated observations and de-biased queries', designed to 'sharpen the perceptual process and hone critical faculties without harming sensitive egos'.[13]

Year Overviews, 1995–1998

1995

The festival moved from the previous year's near-cancellation to this year's comparative riches: Dance Umbrella 95 boasted the largest budget ever, owing to increased funding from ACE and from the Foundation for Sports and the Arts together with the 1994 Prudential Award of £25,000. This last went towards commissioning work from Siobhan Davies and Lloyd Newson, as well as part-funding the visit by the Merce Cunningham Company. A showcase for 'Singular Soloists' put the spotlight on eleven diverse solo programmes, highlighting that most difficult of dance forms, while Techno Dance Bytes continued the previous year's education of choreographers in computer-aided dance generation.

The festival opened unusually, with two soloists, Dana Reitz and Russell Maliphant. This pairing presaged some interestingly contrasting qualities in the double bills, some by design, some governed by accident of availability. For example, the authority of Reitz whose 'twenty years of performing have honed her movements down to such luminous essentials'[14] was seen next to the extreme physicality of Russell Maliphant in his much-praised *film noir* solo, *Paradigm,* from the previous year. As another example, the seasoned improvisation of Steve Paxton was paired with the new and idiosyncratic

Mark Baldwin Dance Company, 1995. PHOTO: HUGO GLENDINNING

choreographic voice of Wayne McGregor, 'cool, remote and decidedly weird' in 'dance that owed nothing to postmodernism and everything to the new perspectives of space-age technology.'[15]

Certainly technology provided something of a sub-plot for this year's festival, with Cunningham and Mark Baldwin both presenting dances that used material generated by the Lifeforms computer program. To this were contrasted Reitz and Paxton, dance-makers who had been part of the re-invention of dance in the 1960s. Mackrell made the interesting observation that there is a tradition directly linking McGregor to Paxton, however un-likely that may seem. 'In [McGregor] you see the same blips and eddies of movement ricocheting around, see beauty in the body's oddest corners, even while the extremity of McGregor's appearance (delicate shaved head poised

143

Cathy Quinn of the Siobhan Davies Dance Company in *Wild Translations*. PHOTO: HUGO GLENDINNING

on incredibly long etiolated body) makes his style a unique thing of long boneless ripples, sharp angles and classic sweep'.[16]

Another extremely Singular Soloist was Javier De Frutos, making a return visit after the considerable acclaim of last year. Audiences were becoming acclimatised to the naked De Frutos and his eclectic body articulations, though *Meeting J* also gave us a 'scene stealing moment provided by a 100-mph bottom wobble that defies gravity and sends the eyes into a blur'.[17] Elizabeth Streb was also taking dance to extremities with Ringside, her company of athletes/gymnasts who presented what they termed 'pop action' movement, generated by a trampoline to bounce off, scaffolding to swing from and dive off and a wall of plexiglass to splat onto. The whole ensemble wore contact microphones so that the only audible sounds were made by the dancers themselves. Streb exploited and exposed the current vogue for extreme physicality, her stated aim being to break formal dance rules, 'exposing the guts of the genre with violent, percussive persistence'.[18]

If technology was appealing to a younger generation of dance makers, then one of its earliest exponents was still at it. Cunningham's influence has been discussed at some length previously, but this year audiences had a chance to compare two different sorts of programmes – the first time British audiences had had the chance to watch the company in both repertory and *Events* in a single season.[19] The repertory programme included three works new to the UK, all made within the previous four years and totally distinct from each other. *Beach Birds* was originally commissioned for the 1991 James Joyce/John Cage Festival in Zurich and was suggested by the opening passage from *Finnegan's Wake*. The other pieces were *Ground Level Overlay* (1995) and *CRWDSPCR* from 1993.

Richard Alston appeared to be in tribute mode, with a revival for his new company of *Rainbow Bandit*, the piece he had choreographed on his return from studying with Cunningham in the US in 1977. The dance was set to a text accompaniment by Charles Amirkhanian, but had a section in silence that was here greatly extended from the original.[20] Completing the bill was Alston's new work, set to various recordings and sharing the title of Hoagie Carmichael's classic, *Stardust*.

Baldwin had recently been appointed choreographer-in-residence at Scottish Ballet and appeared with a small group of dancers in a programme derived from experimentation with the software program Lifeforms (as did Cunningham). Baldwin's musicality was once again praised in a programme full of ideas, including a series of solos that had the choreographer in a send-up of himself (to silence) and (showing his new status with Scottish Ballet) a *pointe* solo for Antonia Franceschi.

Siobhan Davies again showed a double bill of works, *Wild Translations*, which had premiered in the spring, and the new *The Art of Touch*, a Dance Umbrella commission that contrasted with the serenity of the former work in its fast and furious pace. *The Art of Touch* juxtaposed Scarlatti's formal structures with contemporary harpsichord music by Matteo Fargion, for which David Jays observed, 'Davies reinvents Scarlatti as a grouchy old punk, spilling notes like a yob knocking over a line of dustbins'.[21] The day Davies opened for the Umbrella was also the day she went to Buckingham Palace to collect her MBE. Also part-commissioned by the Prudential Award was DV8's *Enter Achilles*, which examined male sexuality and male behaviour in general.

The piece was as impeccably researched as ever, and, with the action situated in a pub setting, contained a potent mixture of humour and more sinister message. The dance was performed somewhat against type, at the Queen Elizabeth Hall.

An unusual Anglo-French collaboration, inadvertently involving audience participation, was that between choreographer Hervé Robbe and British sculptor Richard Deacon in Riverside's Studio 1, with the seating removed. *Factory* was the product of a three-month residency in 1993 at La Ferne du Buisson Arts Centre in Marne-la-Vallée on the outskirts of Paris, and was part homage to Andy Warhol's Factory. The audience was encouraged to move around the space, which contained Deacon's metal tracks, grids and overhead machinery, as well as curved wooden shapes with which the dancers interacted. However, some members of the audience also tried interacting with the installation and this, together with overcrowding, made it difficult for the dancers to move through the throng, let alone for everyone to see the dancing. The audience was deliberately kept smaller for the second night and *Factory*, it was noted, could have run for a week.

Returning after their previous visit in 1993, the two performer/directors of Mal Pelo, Pep Ramis and Maria Muñoz, together with cellist/composer Tristan Honsinger, represented Spanish New Dance. The very strong performance skills of all three were seen to advantage in *Zarco*, which involved song and speech in Italian and Spanish plus role swapping between Honsinger and Ramis, who played cello while Honsinger participated in the action.

Ariadone's *Le Langage du Sphinx* was the first appearance of Carlotta Ikeda's all-woman company at the Umbrella, though Ikeda herself had performed in *Ai Amour* with her partner Ko Murobushi for Dance Umbrella 93. *Le Langage* was for many the highlight of the festival for its powerful and emotive performances and its extraordinary staging and lighting by Eric Loustau-Carrère.

1996

It was clear that this year the budget would be tighter after the previous year's riches, and so an altogether different emphasis had to be sought. It was provided by the first-ever site-specific work of the London festival, choreographed by the American Stephan Koplowitz. This event, together

Stephan Koplowitz's *Genesis Canyon* at the Natural History Museum. PHOTO: CHRIS NASH

with a backbone of very strong British company support and some outstanding soloists – Javier De Frutos, Matthew Hawkins, Wendy Houstoun, Julyen Hamilton and the Canadian José Navas – were the highlights of this year's Dance Umbrella.

The festival opened with *Genesis Canyon*, a piece for thirty-eight dancers and three itinerant vocalists, set within the main hall of the Natural History Museum. The piece followed a precedent set by the 'Swing Bridge' event for Newcastle Dance 90, Lea Anderson's *Opéra Sportif* event for the Leicester Festival in 1991 and Roc in Lichen's *Pigeons à la Tombée d'Echalotes* from Woking Dance Umbrella 95. Action took place in the galleries and on the stairs off the hall, with the audience placed in the downstairs area alongside the dinosaur fossils. *Genesis Canyon* took its inspiration from the cathedral-like architecture as well as from the Museum's function. During the performance the singers Jonathan and Barnaby Stone (a.k.a. Ralf Ralf) and Sarah-Jane Morris passed among the dancers, dressed as Victorians and eyeing the

147

'exhibits', muttering to each other in nonsense Latinate sounds. The performances were very well attended, the event proving an invaluable exercise in raising dance's profile and in bringing in a new audience. Val Bourne stated 'In a way, site-specific work is evangelical because it offers the possibility of erasing that pernicious idea that dance is for a select few who have been educated to understand it'.[22]

Another ambitiously conceived work was René Eyre's and Chris Nash's *Say a Little Prayer*, a collaborative dance and installation piece at the Union Chapel in Islington in which audience movement triggered sound, lighting and video effects within a stunning installation. Of our more theatrical companies, Yolande Snaith's Theatredance presented *Gorgeous Creatures*. Set in the Elizabethan court and with sumptuous costumes by Suzanne Slack and Kei Ho, the piece combined text and mime with dance movement to produce what many described as the strongest piece to date from one of the UK's most inventive choreographers. Meanwhile, the 'alarmingly amplified emotion'[23] of the Nigel Charnock Company's *Heroine* took as its subject the extremes of feeling and experience expressed within the songs of Billie Holiday and, though understandably somewhat overpowered by them, produced a moving performance.

At the other end of the dance-focus scale, Jonathan Burrows's *The Stop Quartet* received resounding acclaim. The choreography was noted for its challenge both to the dancers and to the audience, and was highly praised for its tantalising intricacy. The Richard Alston Dance Company had sold out in May as part of the Secret Theatres Festival, and here the dancers showed themselves to be a company much evolved in its understanding of the Alston style, in a world premiere, *Okho,* which had a score by Iannis Xenakis for djembes, played live on stage. Siobhan Davies again showed a pair of companion pieces in *Trespass* and *Affections.* These shared some material, albeit transposed and transmuted in its passage between the two, as well as sharing certain elements of design and lighting. They shared too the musicianship of Gerald Barry, who wrote for the former and arranged Handel for the latter. It had been a good couple of years for Davies – this year the company received the £50,000 Prudential Award for Dance, to add to the previous year's Olivier Award and MBE for Davies.

Shobana Jeyasingh gave us *Palimpsest,* which 'conjures up a world that is intimate, profound, mysterious, alluringly private, utterly self-contained and totally feminine'.[24] The title also provided a metaphor for Jeyasingh's experiments in dance: a palimpsest is a manuscript that has been erased and overwritten with a new text, but with traces of the original persisting.

Dance Umbrella 96 continued its Singular Soloists showcase with some outstanding performances. As ever, De Frutos gave an autobiographical show, this time based upon his experiences in New York, and set to the original cast recording of Styne and Sondheim's *Gypsy*, about the stripper Gypsy Rose. De Frutos was naked from the beginning, which gave added resonance to the show-stopping number 'You gotta have a gimmick'. Montreal-based Venezuelan José Navas was described as an astonishing performer (he has worked with Lucinda Childs, Stephen Petronio and Michael Clark). Matthew Hawkins gave his first full-length solo, a collaborative collage of dance, score and slide projections made while rehearsing publicly in the atrium of the Chelsea and Westminster Hospital. Hawkins danced in *pointe* shoes and high heels as well as bare feet.

Javier De Frutos, *Transatlantic*, 1996. PHOTO: CHRIS NASH

So although visiting companies were strong competition, there was no sense of their overshadowing our own artists this year. Tumbuka from Zimbabwe were praised for their enthusiasm and commitment. La La La had not been seen in the UK since 1990 and as a consequence they were sold out every night. The performance was as intense as ever, but its demonstration of extreme physicality, though breathtaking, was formulaic to some. Doug Varone from New York was another sure-fire audience pleaser with exuberant and technically accomplished performances, but his *Rise* to John Adams's score evoked unfavourable comparisons with *Fearful Symmetries*, Ashley Page's treatment of the same score for the Royal Ballet.

Mal Pelo brought an extended company of five to provide *La Calle del Imaginero*, a series of fragmented episodes that swept the audience along with its wit and invention. Deborah Weiss gave some indication of its kaleidoscopic and schizophrenic vision with her description of successive events: 'Jordi Casanovas performing his daily ablutions by excreting singularly blooming daisies from the top of the building gives new meaning to the phrase "toilet humour", a carefully choreographed dance with a dead chicken, a desperate need for water that involves various curious antics, a pirouetting religious icon[25] and a *pas de deux* for chins'.[26]

The Dance Umbrella 1995/96 annual report contained a plea to the Arts Council, either for Lottery funds or to become a regularly funded organisation. This plea had become a paean, but this year it was made all the more poignant by the closing words: 'We appreciate that such an elevation does not give any further security of tenure than we have at present but, nevertheless, the change of status would reflect the Arts Council's confidence in Dance Umbrella's ability to deliver what it promises. After all, the Arts Council has been regularly funding the organisation for nigh on 20 years.'

1997

This, the nineteenth Dance Umbrella festival, was a smaller affair than had been usual, encompassing only twenty-five London performances by fourteen companies over just less than four weeks. This was because of the £50,000 commitment to the Mark Morris Dance Group's performances of Morris's epic *L'Allegro, Il Ponseroso ed Il Moderato* at the Coliseum in June with English National Opera, which inevitably had repercussions on the autumn

Rosemary Butcher's *Fractured Landscapes, Fragmented Narratives*, 1997. PHOTO: CHRIS NASH

festival. Nevertheless the festival was able yet again to present a long overdue 'first', in Compagnie Maguy Marin's UK debut. Then there were the relative newcomers Compagnie Tandem from Belgium, Compañia Vicente Sáez from Spain and Montreal-based Cas Public with some inspirational choreography. Of previous festival favourites, many reviewers noted and welcomed the return to form of Stephen Petronio and his company. As a related event, Riverside Studios continued to host the Digital Dancing initiative, with more pioneering work in dance and technology.

The festival opened, as it had several times before, with Petronio, in his seventh Umbrella season with his own company. Petronio's *ReBourne* was fittingly dedicated to Val Bourne and her support of him over the years. Many noticed the renewed influence of his mentor Trisha Brown in this piece. Petronio had certainly abandoned the issues with which he had briefly flirted in previous years, albeit in a greatly abstracted way, and the choreography was less lightning-speed and more measured, consequently having a greater ability to show the multi-layering of images that was at its core.

Cas Public from Montreal provided a strongly theatrical performance with *Les Suites Furieuses*, which nevertheless developed from a distinctive movement base and involved costume and score, to push the movement to a more physical extreme. The cast of six was decreased from the piece's original staging for eight (seen earlier in Glasgow), but this did not seem to detract from its effect, and performances were generally deemed to be excellent.

Of the European visitors, Compagnie Maguy Marin was undoubtedly the star attraction. The company's work had never been seen here live, but even so their reputation had extended to this country, building upon the considerable following they had established in France and on the international circuit. *Waterzooi* ran at ninety minutes without interval and provided highly accomplished yet confidently experimental dance-theatre. The title translates as a type of Belgian stew, and the piece presented a hotchpotch in which the 'ingredients' were 'passions of the soul'. Marin trained with Béjart and claims influence from Bausch, the latter being manifest in the sheer intensity and completeness of the theatrical experience. But the all-pervading sensation was one of humour in all its manifestations – slapstick, irony, verbal humour and a sense of the absurd, as when all thirteen dancers donned cow masks near the end of the performance.

Compañia Vicente Sáez from Spain and Compagnie Tandem from Belgium provided powerful and moving performances. Sáez, together with Rafael Linares and Cinzia Scordia, provided a trio, *Atman,* to the music of Purcell in which solos, duets and trios evoked the music's period. The company was last seen with *Regina Mater* as part of the Turning World season in 1996, and *Atman* proved a very different experience with an altogether simpler structure. Tandem presented choreographer Michèle Noiret's *Les Plis de la Nuit*, inspired by the engravings of Maurice Pasternak and including projected film images. This company too had been seen earlier in the year at Glasgow's New Moves festival.

As if to maintain a balance of styles with the Europeans, the UK provided performances by Rosemary Butcher, Siobhan Davies and Mark Baldwin, all of whom favour movement referring to emotion more distanced from that of the everyday than that illustrated by their European counterparts. Butcher continued her retrospective at the Riverside Studios, with two duets spanning some twenty-one years of dance making. *Landings* from 1976 and *Fractured Landscape, Fragmented Narratives* from 1997 were beautifully performed by Fin Walker and Henry Montes, and a third show had to be scheduled to satisfy public demand.

Davies also presented something of a retrospective, with a considerably reworked version of *White Man Sleeps* from 1988 (to Kevin Volans's original instrumentation of viola da gamba, harpsichord and drums), a revival of *The Art of Touch* from 1995 and the London premiere of *Bank* with music played live by its composer, Matteo Fargion. The general impression was that of a company at the very peak of its form. Baldwin also had live music for all three of his pieces and drew inspiration from it for his chorcography, though what he hears in the music, as Judith Mackrell points out, is not at all predictable.[27] Thus *Tuireadh*, commissioned by the South Bank for its festival

Wendy Houston in *Haunted, Daunted, Flaunted*, 1997. PHOTO: CHRIS NASH

of James MacMillan's music, and a tribute by the composer to the Piper Alpha disaster, prefers to 'nail the tragedy through form', rather than to attempt the drama of naturalistic emotion. 'He gives each dancer a brief, beautiful solo that takes them off stage, creating a sense of complex individual lives being glimpsed, then lost.'[28]

Javier De Frutos's performances were all sold out weeks ahead, such was the reputation he had built over the previous few years. *Grass* was a harrowing trio to excerpts from Maria Callas's recording of Puccini's *Madam Butterfly,* in which De Frutos paid homage to the obsessive passion of the musical narrative. Two extraordinary soloists also deserve mention: Wendy Houstoun provided a *tour de force* in her solo trilogy *Haunted, Daunted* and *Flaunted,* and Eva Karczag, a former member of Richard Alston's Strider company and a long-term dancer with Trisha Brown, also proved herself to be a compelling solo performer.

The 1997 festival may have been economical in terms of dates and numbers, but it was anything but economical in terms of the quality of its artists. One component that had been developing steadily over the previous four years was Digital Dancing 97, once again presented in conjunction with Illuminations Interactive under the direction of Terry Braun. This event has been given separate consideration, but it is worth noting here that it ran for two weeks and demonstrated yet again Dance Umbrella's commitment to important innovations within the art form.

1998

This was a year of celebrations and landmarks: Dance Umbrella's twentieth festival, Richard Alston's fiftieth birthday, Shobana Jeyasingh's tenth year of dance-making for her company and the first appearance of Ballett Frankfurt in London. The festival was the most ambitious to date, running for a little over eight weeks – something of a record in itself – during which time it presented seventeen companies and three soloists in six different venues, plus a site-specific event at the British Library. To the fore, understandably, were artists with long-standing Dance Umbrella connections: Siobhan Davies, Eiko and Koma, Stephen Petronio, Merce Cunningham and Michael Clark, plus more recent festival attractions Javier De Frutos and Mark Baldwin. The exciting 'newcomer' to the festival was William Forsythe with his company of fourteen years, Ballett Frankfurt, making its UK debut, though with a formidable reputation borne out by Forsythe's work for the Royal Ballet and Nederlands Dans Theater, plus recently televised dance programmes and documentaries.

Alston was marking thirty years of choreography and four years of his new company, as well as a birthday. The birthday tribute was a onc-off occasion featuring *Sophisticated Curiosities*, an Alston 'Event' that included work spanning his career from 1970 to 1990, danced by his current company. Jenny Gilbert wondered why critics (herself included) had sometimes doubted the strength of his work, when these extracts looked so fresh in retrospect: 'It could be that Alston's very English qualities have simply weathered the short-lived fads that have sometimes looked more exciting . . . Whatever, it was wonderful'.[29] There was also a solo, an '*a cappella* dance poem' for Eva Karczag, just as impressive here as in her solo show for Umbrella the previous year, plus a new trio for Davies, Darshan Singh Bhuller and Alston himself, entitled *Dances of the Wayward Ancients*. Lastly, there was a Dance Umbrella commission, *Waltzes in Disorder*, to Brahms's *Liebeslieder Walzer* – a 'birthday present' from Umbrella, who provided funds for the music to be played live. It was Alston after all, who had opened the very first Dance Umbrella performance in 1978, on a double bill following Douglas Dunn, whose work that night had caused such a sensation.

Davies opened the festival at the Barbican and was billed under the Barbican's Inventing America season of American performing arts, as both pieces on her programme had accompaniment by American composers. Her most recent work, *Eighty Eight*, was set to Conlan Nancarrow's studies for player piano, played by Rex Lawson. 'This is piano music beyond the reach of mortals in terms of speed and contrapuntal craziness. Out of the music's arrhythmic mayhem, the choreographer creates a kind of serene visual logic, with its own inversions and surprises'.[30] Her 1992 piece for Rambert, *Winnsboro Cotton Mill Blues*, was to music by Frederic Rzewski, extended by Davies with taped sounds of a Lancashire cotton mill. The choreography evoked both the mill machinery and the social conditions of its workers. So Davies once again gave us two halves of the same coin in a single programme: setting the more abstracted *Eighty Eight* against *Winnsboro*, which is more evocative of time and place. Critics were full of superlatives: displaying admiration for Davies's crafting skills, but no less admiration for 'the choreography's portrayal of feeling, of social and emotional states.'[31]

Ricochet Dance
Company, 1998.
PHOTO: HUGO GLENDINNING

The Merce Cunningham Dance Company, fifteen strong, also appeared at the Barbican, and showed four works new to London and two *Events* in two different programmes. These retrospectives spanned three decades of dance making, including sections from *Suite for Five* from 1956 and from his 1964 piece, *Winterbranch*. The choreographer had a standing ovation when he appeared every night, sadly no longer during the action but after it. Alastair Macaulay wrote: 'These programmes of dances old and new add up into a single spiritual image: Merce Cunningham Dance Theatre, which is still like nothing else in the whole world. Or rather it is like everything else in the whole world: a poetic kaleidoscope of life itself in all its diversity.'[32]

Petronio presented his first full-length piece for his company, *Not Garden* – 'a sweeping millennial rant, apparently inspired by Dante's Inferno, that could be described as the choreographer's own vision of a contemporary hell'. Debra Craine thought it banal,[33] while David Jays saw it as 'the most finished, ambitious piece' of the festival.[34] Petronio had also created *Fetch Boy and Fox* for London-based Ricochet Dance Company, who were making their Festival

156

debut. Ricochet's other commission – just as challenging in its own way – was *5IVE part one* from Nigel Charnock.

Doug Elkins had always proved very popular with audiences, but this year critics found a new depth to his choreography in addition to his pleasing lack of pretentiousness. The former breakdancer with his roots in the street describes himself as a sampler of movement, similar to the way in which club DJs sample music, putting reference alongside abstracted versions of movement styles. He had not appeared for Umbrella since 1993, but in the meantime had made for Union Dance a piece, *A Knot Annulled*, of which *Narcoleptic Lovers* (in the current repertory of Elkins's own company) was a reworking.

Jonathan Burrows's idiosyncrasies continued to intrigue, with his minimalist *Hands* solo – a five-minute piece for himself seated on a chair – and *All Together,* a trio for Burrows, Dana Fouras and Ragnhild Olsen, using only their arms. In the second half, *Things I Don't Know* comprised a solo for Burrows and a duet for the women to music by Kevin Volans, in which the choreography gradually broke free from its earlier restrictions.

De Frutos's *The Hypochondriac Bird* was a Dance Umbrella commission and the choreographer's version of *Swan Lake*. He appeared this year at the Queen Elizabeth Hall, but, as John Percival pointed out, his dance is based upon minute gesture, for which the intimate space of The Place Theatre is better suited.[35] Eiko's and Koma's theatre, however, could sustain performances on the South Bank and this year's offering, *Wind*, which included their ten-year-old son Shin Otake, was 'bleak, but intensely moving'.[36] The other Butoh performer appearing in this year's festival, Carlotta Ikeda, presented a solo at The Place Theatre described simply as 'riveting'.

Enthusiastic audiences welcomed Michael Clark back to the dance stage after an absence of four years. *Current/SEE,* a Dance Umbrella commission, began with Clark being 're-animated' by bassist Susan Stenger, who summoned increasing volume to get the dancer on his feet both literally and metaphorically. With Clark were three dancers, including Kate Coyne, whose performance qualities were likened by Debra Craine to those of Clark himself, 'sharing his super definition in the lower body'.[37] There was nothing that was rude or outrageous – other people had taken over that particular mantle in the intervening years since Clark's last performance – and the show reportedly evolved greatly over its tour.

Dance Umbrella continued its run of site-specific works by commissioning a new piece from Stephan Koplowitz. The British Library had been

Koplowitz's first choice of venue for the 1996 commission. With the November 1997 opening of the Library building to the public, the project was once again possible and *Babel Index* was conceived. The piece had fifty-four dancers, twelve singers and slide projections, all put together by the same creative team as for *Genesis Canyon*. Like the latter, it aimed to evoke something of the function, ambience and architecture of the environment. The performance began outside, with dancers on plinths 'reading' from volumes that were literally 'illuminated', and the audience (an estimated 500 per night) was conducted in groups on a promenade around the building by tour guides, with each group seeing the movement from a different perspective. The final section was watched by everyone from the entrance hall, with the dancers on three balconies unfurling like a scroll from the spiral staircase.

The American choreographer Forsythe had built a huge reputation in

Michael Clark and Susan Stenger in *current/SEE*, 1998. PHOTO: HUGO GLENDINNING

Europe, and had created *Tight Roaring Circle* (an installation piece commissioned by Artangel) in London's Roundhouse in 1997, but this was the first appearance of his company in Britain. It had originally planned to show *Eidos: Telos*, but even Sadler's Wells' newly constructed stage proved inadequate for that work, and so Ballett Frankfurt presented a triple bill that ably demonstrated both the dancers' extraordinary capabilities and the range of Forsythe's choreography. The Forsythe programme brought the festival to an end, and Val Bourne concluded her festival report by saying: 'The fact that we could successfully sustain such a long festival proves that not only Dance Umbrella but contemporary dance in Britain has truly come of age.'

Future Roles – 1999 and Beyond

The 1999 Dance Umbrella featured a new work by Siobhan Davies, *Wild Air*, her first ever full-length piece, to a commissioned score by Kevin Volans. It also included a cabaret for five Cholmondeleys and five Featherstonehaughs by Lea Anderson involving long-term collaborators Sandy Powell and Steve Blake. Representing the 'home' team were programmes from Mark Baldwin, Aletta Collins and Russell Maliphant, and an installation performance from Nigel Charnock and Company.

There was a chance to see some European companies for the very first time in a Dance Umbrella festival. The Ljubljana-based choreographer Iztoc Kovac brought his company En-Knap (they had previously presented work at Chisenhale and The Place). The company formerly known as Werkcentrum Dans, now De Rotterdamse Dansgroep, had last been seen eighteen years previously at the festival, and this year returned with repertoire including a piece by Javier De Frutos, *Fortune Biscuit*. There was a return visit too for Compagnie Maguy Marin after their acclaimed UK debut in Dance Umbrella 97, this time with Marin's signature piece *May B*, inspired by the writings of Samuel Beckett. Compagnie Montalvo-Hervieu from France visited for the first time, and Tanzcompagnie Rubato, a Berlin-based duo, made their British debut.

American imports included a repertoire programme from Mark Morris (his first in London since 1985). *Martha@DanceUmbrella*, Richard Move's very much personalised interpretation of the work of Martha Graham, was derived from a show that achieved cult status in New York and was here performed at the Brick Lane Music Hall. Doug Varone also appeared, following the company's residence as part of the 1999 Woking Dance Umbrella festival, with a programme of UK premieres and a residency in Sunderland. American choreographer Meg Stuart's company Damaged Goods, now based in Belgium, collaborated with installation artist Ann Hamilton.

Also appearing was Johannesburg-based dancer and choreographer Vincent Mantsoe, whose solo performance was preceded by a screening of Gerald Fox's documentary film featuring Mantsoe and two other South African artists.

The site-specific work this year was supplied by Lea Anderson with *Sportorama* at Crystal Palace National Sports Centre, with 150 dance and sports people, plus members of her two companies. Its blueprint was *Opéra Sportif*, made for the Leicester International Dance Festival 91. The Mark Morris Company visited five other centres in the UK over a period of two weeks, following on from their Sadler's Wells shows.

*   *   *

If we compare current programming policies with those from the early years, we can see that, although there have been subtle changes, the thrust of the festival remains the same. The aims of the very first festival were to show British dance to advantage and to introduce to the UK the best and most innovative work from overseas. We have noted too that the early festivals had an educational aspect, as well as showcasing regional dance groups.

Taking these points one by one, what we see now within the festivals are British companies that have achieved international status, with even relative newcomers such as De Frutos having attracted considerable international attention prior to being offered an Umbrella platform. This points firstly to the general strengthening of British work over the years, both in terms of its quality and in terms of its professionalism. Secondly, it demonstrates greater overall 'quality assurance' on the programmes – a necessary step in order to have continued to attract funding for this length of time – but this does not mean that Bourne no longer takes risks. Rather it means that Dance Umbrella can now afford to pick the most interesting of experimental work from both the UK and overseas.

A more nebulous change has occurred within the realm of education: the commitment is still and always has been to increase the audience for dance.

If anything, Dance Umbrella has come up with ever more ingenious ways of exposing audiences and those within the profession to new ideas, new technological innovations and new ways of seeing dance, as well as attracting new and different audiences. Given top priority are tours by major artists with residencies attached. This idea actually dates back to when Bourne first conceived the 'meet the artists' sessions, for want of longer residencies along the lines of the French *stages* in which guest artists work alongside home artists in a free exchange of ideas.

Another idea is that of workshops for professionals, following the 'Necessary Weather' residency by Dana Reitz and Jennifer Tipton during Dance Umbrella 93. The idea of site-specific works will continue, with the British Museum Great Court or the British Library (again) mooted at the moment as two possibilities. Or there are what Bourne refers to as 'generic site-specific' works such as Anderson's *Sportorama*, where a large-scale piece is made for a sports centre and includes sports people as well as dancers. These have both been enormously successful in the past in attracting new and different audiences for dance.

When we come to the showcasing of dance groups from the regions during the London festivals, we see that a reverse process has in fact occurred. The regions now have their own major festivals where local companies and artists both amateur and professional can perform alongside international artists. It is not an overstatement to claim that Dance Umbrella has played a major role in the decentralisation of dance within the last two decades.

Postscript

A quality that has contributed to the festival's endurance is Bourne's apparent lack of fear of failure (though she claims she is always terrified). Another is her sense of responsibility towards her artists, many of whom clearly rank her amongst their closest friends. She says:

> If you're being adventurous, if you're trying new things, well, not all of it is going to succeed. When it does go wrong it is my responsibility to let the artist know that it is not the end of the world: 'We employed you to come here and do this. If it didn't work, it is as much our fault as it is yours.' And I do believe that.[38]

161

Darshan Singh
Bhuller, in Richard
Alston's *Orpheo*.
PHOTO: CHRIS NASH

Richard Alston has said that Bourne does what nobody else in this country does – she presents a cross-view. The Dance Umbrella may reflect the tastes of a single person, as inevitably all such programmes do; but in Bourne's case the range of her tastes is quite extraordinary, so that the diversity of works shown is also extraordinary. Neither does she see earlier generations of choreographers as old-fashioned or not contemporary – 'the breadth of her interests is unique.'[39] Bourne recognises the changes that have occurred over the last two decades, changes that are largely due to her enterprise, but to which, with characteristic modesty, she does not lay claim:

We have very good work here now, and, let's be honest, that was not true twenty years ago. Today, British dance is 100 per cent better than it was when Umbrella started. But, no, I do not think that was my doing. But I've been so very lucky. You see, I was part of something, an art form that was growing in so many different ways, and I was one of the things that was growing with it. I don't think it was me; I think it was us.[40]

Yet Bourne is adamant that it is far from a period of consolidation for Dance Umbrella, but instead a period of increasingly fast change. 'We live in interesting times', as she says, when predictions and 'reading the runes' become ever more of a haphazard business as far as audiences, funding and even artistic fashion are concerned. Still, Bourne has proved herself to be an prophet of uncommon accomplishment. As she sees it, the factors at play are:

- the changing complexion of government funding: trying to play the 'new audiences' funding initiative, with the present government's policy of making money available for attracting new audiences to any cultural event, and its wide interpretation of the concept of 'culture' (anything from sport, through the arts to heritage);
- the huge amount of dance currently on offer in the capital (particularly from ballet companies) and the very high prices that are being charged (particularly at Sadler's Wells but also at the Peacock Theatre and the Barbican), which leaves a question mark not so much over whether London audiences will have had a surfeit by the autumn, but over whether they will be able to afford more;
- an increase in the number of suitable theatres currently available: for example, the newly reopened Sadler's Wells, the Peacock Theatre which housed Sadler's Wells events during its closure and continues to be available for dance events, and the Barbican with its newly refurbished stage;
- theatre festivals such as LIFT (the biennial London International Festival of Theatre, which brings avant-garde overseas performers to London) that now include dance within their remit, as well as running seasons specifically for dance (such as Turning World), which deal with the same sorts of international companies as does Umbrella.

Because of these things, programming is far more speculative than it used to be, and because of funding patterns there is a need to keep coming up with new projects, some of which will happen, some of which will not. So applica-

The Featherstonehaughs, *24-Hour Featherstonehaughs*, 1994. PHOTO: CHRIS NASH

tions for funding have to include a certain amount of 'blanket bombing', with much-cherished – and nurtured – projects falling by the wayside, but some more opportunistic projects succeeding. 'The dance ecology has been thrown out,' as Bourne puts it, 'but temporarily, let's hope'.[41]

What the Dance Umbrella organisation has certainly overseen and led, as it enters its fourth decade, is an unparalleled explosion of dance since the first festival in 1978. This includes a vastly increased exposure of the European scene, overlapping generations of dancers and of dance-makers, a pluralism of styles and a reflection of social and cultural issues that is now on a par with that in the other arts, if indeed not leading them. Mark Baldwin sums it up: 'There's a certain climate in the contemporary dance world in London. Umbrella is like a weather forecast that way'.[42]

Appendix 1

Listings by Year

Information relating to the annual (from 1980) London Dance Umbrella festivals and their associated events, including related regional activity, separate gala performances and other special events organised by, or in association with Dance Umbrella.

1978

Tuesday 7 – Saturday 25 November (39 London performances)

Venues
London: ICA; Riverside Studios

Artists

UK
Richard Alston and Dancers[1]
Basic Space Dance Theatre[2]
Rosemary Butcher Dance Company[3]
Cycles Dance Company [4]
Maedée Duprès[5]
Fergus Early[6]
EMMA Dance Group[7]
Extemporary Dance Company[8]
Junction Dance Company[9]
Maas Movers[10]
Tamara McLorg[11]
Janet Smith and Robert North[12]
Leigh Warren and Sally Owen [13]

For Schools
East Anglian Dance Theatre[14]
Ludus[15]

USA
Remy Charlip[16]
Douglas Dunn[17]
Brooke Myers[18]
Sara Rudner[19]
John Jones[20] (guest teacher and choreographer)

Notes
Many evenings consisted of two or three separate performances.

[1] Presented *Single Dances*, a programme of solos including *Home Ground* to music by Purcell for Maedée Duprès (repeated from earlier in the year), the London premiere of *Connecting Passages* for Julyen Hamilton, a solo for Alston himself, *Unknown Banker Buys Atlantic* to music by Cole Porter, and *Distant Rebound* for Duprès, Julyen Hamilton, Michele Smith and Ian Spink.

[2] In a programme of new works by Don Asker and director Shelley Lee: *The Visit* (Asker), *Vienna Dream* and *Blackbird* (Lee).

165

3 Company-in-residence at Riverside Studios, in two different programmes for six female dancers including *Catch 5, Catch 6* and *First Step* (Butcher), plus a trio choreographed by company member Sue MacLennan.

4 Based in the West Midlands and run as a co-operative. Integral to the company's policy was the provision of contemporary dance-based performances and workshops for regional audiences. The programme included *Pon-toon* by company member Duncan Holt.

5 Presented *Dance and Slide*.

6 Presenting two solos: *Sergeant Early's Dream* and *Gymnopédies*.

7 Founded in 1976 by East Midlands Arts, the company presented Christopher Bruce's *Responses* (with designs by Nadine Baylis); Lenny Westerdijk's *In this Solitude* (with accompaniment, *Im Abendrot*, one of the *Four Last Songs* of Richard Strauss); Jaap Flier's *Dolly Mixtures* (with music by Biber, designs by Baylis); Janet Smith's *Return to Go* (to specially commissioned score by Christopher Benstead); and director Gideon Avrahami's *Negev* (also to a new score by Pip Greasley.) All these pieces were London premieres.

8 In Robert North's *Sometimes* (with a commissioned score by Christopher Benstead), and Domy Reiter Soffer's *Nightspells* (with music by Jacob Gilboa), both London premieres, plus a revival of Ingegerd Lonnroth's *Dreams* (commissioned score by Barrington Pheloung) and Alston's solo *Blueprint*.

9 Including new works by Ingegerd Lonnroth (*Fugue* and *Life Drawings*) and Kristin Donovan (*Dance for Three* and *The Marias*).

10 Founded in 1977 with the encouragement of MAAS (Minorities Arts Advisory Service), the company presented *Peace be Still* by their former artistic adviser William Louther, *Outreach* by Mikloth Bond and a new work, *Party Blues,* by guest choreographer John Jones.

11 In a new work *Solo*: 'not a Dance, nor a Play, but a marriage of words, movement and music' (programme notes) that was a collaboration with composer Michael Simmonds and director Alan Lyddiard.

12 In a new programme *Domestic Dances*. Robert North was on leave from LCDT.

13 Joined by Lucy Burge and Yair Vardi, all performers were on leave from Rambert, in a programme of new work, including Warren's *Escape from an Image* for Burge and Warren and Vardi's *Day Voices/Night Voices* for Owen and Vardi.

14 London debut of Dance in Education Company based in Ipswich and funded by Eastern Arts Association, here presenting programmes for 8- to 11-year-olds and 15- to 18-year-olds.

15 London debut of this North West dance-in-education company based in Lancaster, here presenting *The Adventures of Mr Lear and his cat, Foss* for ESN schools, and *No 5 Empire Street* for secondary schools. Both programmes focused on social themes.

16 Author, artist, dancer, choreographer, actor, designer and director, Charlip has performed with Merce Cunningham and Charles Weidman, designed for Cunningham, Dan Wagoner and James Waring and written and illustrated twenty-four books. The programme, entitled *Solo Dances,* included *Painting Flying, Imaginary Dances* (with text read by Richard Alston), *Travel Sketches* and *Glow Worm.*

17 Formerly a member of Yvonne Rainer, Merce Cunningham and Grand Union companies, presented *Gestures in Red.*

18 Actress and dancer, former member of the Firehouse Theatre Company, presented *Once Again to Zelda.*

19 Former leading dancer with Twyla Tharp's company, who has also appeared with Pilobolus Dance Theatre and Joffrey Ballet Company, presented *As Is As Solo.*

20 Former member of Katharine Dunham Dance Company and of Jerome Robbins's Ballets USA, combines ballet, jazz, martial arts and Afro-Caribbean techniques in his workshops, and is 'sharply conscious of his responsibility to other black dancers, in particular young people with whom he has been working as teacher and choreographer in Philadelphia'. Jones created *Party Blues* for Maas Movers while in the UK.

1978: Related Events

Films[1]

Late night screenings at Riverside. Hetty King Performer and *Gold Diggers of 1933* (Busby Berkeley), *Pas de deux* (Norman McLaren), *Summer Interlude* (Ingmar Bergman), *The Queen* and *Lola* (Jacques Demy), *Isadora* (Karel Reisz)

Film forum at Riverside. *A Dancer's World*, featuring Martha Graham; *Sue's Leg,* featuring Twyla Tharp; *Rhythmatron*, featuring the Dance Theatre of Harlem; followed by discussion.

Dance film evening (ICA). Screenings of films from the *Dance in America* television series, not previously shown in this country.

Seminars
Dance and Education (Riverside, Thursday 9 November)
Administration of Dance Groups (ICA, Sunday 19 November)
ICA Dance Platform (ICA, Sunday 19 November)

Classes and Workshops

Professional classes. Richard Alston; Douglas Dunn; John Jones; Sara Rudner.

Open workshops. Remy Charlip (cross-arts workshops, for adults and children); Brooke Myers' voice and movement workshop.

Schools workshops. Two schools workshops aimed at primary and secondary school children and given by John Jones[2] and Maas Movers

Exhibitions

Riverside exhibited Mark Lancaster's designs for the Merce Cunningham Dance Company and Remy Charlip's drawings.

Notes
[1] The majority of films received their London premieres. The absence of Astaire films was noted and rectified the following year.
[2] Also involved in two youth projects in Lambeth and Tower Hamlets as well as giving classes ancillary to the Festival in and around London.

1980

Saturday 19 January – Sunday 2 March (54 London performances), plus one extra week at the Shaw Theatre as part of the Camden Festival: Monday 17 – Saturday 22 March (6 performances)

Venues
London: ICA, The Place Theatre, Riverside Studios, The Shaw Theatre, Whitechapel Gallery. Bristol: Arnolfini Gallery (25 January – 23 February). Cardiff: Sherman Theatre (19 January – 9 February). Plymouth: Plymouth Arts Centre (25–26 January, 22–23 February)

Artists

Continental Europe
Pauline De Groot and Company[1]
   (Holland)
Springplank[2] (Holland)

UK
Richard Alston and Dancers[3]
Ballet Rambert choreographers[4]
Rosemary Butcher Dance Company[5]
Cycles Dance Company[6]
Dancework[7]
Maedée Duprès[8]
Fergus Early and Jacky Landsley[9]
EMMA Dance Company[10]
Extemporary Dance Company[11]
LCDT choreographers[12]
Ingegerd Lonnroth and Dancers[13]
Maas Movers[14]
Royal Ballet choreographers[15]

Janet Smith [16]
Janet Smith, Robert North and Dancers[17]
Miranda Tufnell, Dennis Greenwood and Tim Head[18]

International
Danny Grossman Dance Company[19]
   (Canada)

US
Simone Forti and Peter van Riper [20]
David Gordon and Valda Setterfield[21]
Elisa Monte and David Brown[22]
Rosalind Newman and Dancers[23]
Steve Paxton with David Moss or Lisa
   Nelson[24]
Kathryn Posin and Michael Kane[25]
Naomi Sorkin[26]

Notes

Some evening programmes consisted of two separate performances.

[1] The company comprised dancers and musicians, and presented *Stepping Stones*.

[2] Apprentice group of Nederlands Dans Theater in works by Nils Christie, Jirí Kylián, Christopher Bruce and Robert North. This was their British debut.

[3] In Alston's *Schubert Dances*, *The Field of Mustard* and *Dumka* (for students of LSCD), all to live music, plus *Recall*, a solo choreographed and danced by Siobhan Davies.

[4] Presented collaborative programmes by choreographers Ann Dickie, Nelson Fernández and Sally Owen, with dancer Tom Yang.

[5] Dancers Butcher, Julyen Hamilton, Sue MacLennan and Janet Smith performed Butcher's *Five Sided Figure* and MacLennan's solo *Uneven Time*.

[6] Presented *AWOL* (Another Way Of Living),

a collaborative venture by the company, directed by Fergus Early.

[7] Christine Juffs and Tony Thacker in a programme that included Stuart Hopps's *The Check Up*.

[8] Presented Ian Spink's *Standing Swing*, Jackie Lansley's *Jeanne*, and Duprès's *Footfalls* (with a commissioned score by composer Stephen Montague). The design for the programme was by Craig Givens.

[9] Presented *Fifty Million Robins*, developed from a dance first performed in September 1979.

[10] Presented (among other works) Australian choreographer Jacqui Carroll's *Play Back*, Royston Maldoom's *Doina*, Shelley Lee's *In Passing*, Tamara McLorg's *Ladylove* and Lenny Westerdijk's *Atolen*.

[11] In a programme that included new work by Kathryn Posin (the first work to be commis-

sioned by Dance Umbrella), Jonathan Burrows, Tom Jobe and Micha Bergese, plus company members Corrine Bougaard, Robb Fleming and Steven Giles.

[12] The programme comprised Christopher Bannerman's *Treading* and a new untitled work, Anca Frankenhauser's *Meeting Ground* and Patrick Harding-Irmer's *Picnic*.

[13] The programme included work by Jane Dudley, *Six Little Piano Pieces,* to Schoenberg.

[14] Presented a mixed programme including the premiere of a work by jazz choreographer Ivor Meggido.

[15] Michael Batchelor, Jonathan Burrows, Michael Corder, Nicholas Dixon, Matthew Hawkins, Jennifer Jackson and Richard Slaughter.

[16] In a solo programme *Studies in Solitude.*

[17] In choreography by Smith and North.

[18] Dancers Tufnell and Greenwood in collaboration with sculptor Tim Head were joined by dancers Sue MacLennan and Hugh Davies, in the Upper Gallery of the Whitechapel Gallery and presented 'a series of separate dance pieces in which the dancers work with a specific light and/or sound situation in the particular spatial context'.

[19] Presented *Curious Schools of Theatrical Dancing* (mus. Couperin), *Couples Suite* (mus. Terri Riley and Mbiri music of Zimbabwe), *Triptych* (mus. Milhaud), *National Spirit* and *Higher* (mus. Ray Charles), all choreographed by Grossman. This appearance formed part of a four-week tour of six cities, sponsored by the Department of External Affairs of Canada, and was the company's London debut.

[20] A collaboration between dancer Simone Forti and musician Peter van Riper, presenting the partly improvisational *Wood Fish*. Forti began her career with Anna Halprin.

[21] Gordon, founder member of Judson Dance Theater and the Grand Union, and Setterfield, former Cunningham dancer, presented four pieces by Gordon dating from 1972–79.

[22] Presented a programme: *Singles and Doubles,* which included Cliff Keuter's *Wood Blocks*, Monte's *Pell-Mell*, Molissa Fenley's *Boca Raton*, Marcus Schulkind's *Gentleman's Night at Home*, all specially created for Dance Umbrella 80, plus *Job* and *Ladies Night Out* (Schulkind) and *Treading* (Monte). Both dancers were former members of the Martha Graham Dance Company.

[23] Dancers Ellen Bogart, Judith Moss and Newman in Newman's *Necessary Adventures* (premiere)

[24] The collaborations involved dancer Paxton with percussionist David Moss, and Paxton with dancer Lisa Nelson.

[25] Kathryn Posin did not perform owing to illness, but was commissioned to create a piece for Extemporary Dance Company. The company stepped in on 19 March to perform Posin's *By Appointment Only* plus three other works from their repertory, and Michael Kane performed two solos in between. The second scheduled performance was cancelled.

[26] Presented a solo programme of works by Anna Sokolow, Rachel Lampert and Phylis Lamhut. This was the dancer's British debut.

1980: Related Events

Films[1]

Astaire retrospective (ICA). Shall We Dance[2] (Mark Sandrich,1937), *Swing Time*[3] (George Stevens, 1936), *Top Hat*[4] (Mark Sandrich, 1935), *Follow the Fleet*[5] (Mark Sandrich, 1936), *The Band Wagon*[6] (Vincente Minelli, 1953), *Funny Face*[7] (Stanley Donen, 1956)

Film season at Riverside. Let's Dance[8], *Footlight Parade*[9] (Busby Berkeley, 1933), *No Maps on my Taps*[10] (George T. Neirenberg, 1979), *Le Ballet Mechanique* (Fernand Leger, 1924), *Little Miss Broadway* (1934), *Taking Tiger Mountain by Strategy*[11] (1970), *Nine Variations on a Dance Theatre*[12], *For Me and My Gal*[13] (Busby Berkeley, 1942), *A Song is Born* (Howard Hawks, 1948), *Forty-Second Street*[14] (chor. Busby Berkeley, dir. Lloyd Bacon, 1933), *On The Town*[15] (Gene Kelly and Stanley Donen, 1949), *What Maisie Knew*[16] (Babette Mangolte,1976), *Invitation to the Dance*[17] (Gene Kelly, 1956), *Hooray for Love*[18] (1935), *Jitterbug,*[19] *Hellzapoppin*[20] (1942)

Film forum (Riverside). Under the Dance Umbrella[21]

Seminars
Foreign Touring and Exchanges[22] (2 February at ICA)
A National Dance Lobby[23] (9 February at Riverside)

Classes and Workshops
Master class: David Gordon. Workshops: Valda Setterfield, Patricia Bardi, David Gordon

Notes
[1] The film theme for 1980 was tap/jazz musicals of the 1930s and 1940s.

[2] With Fred Astaire and Ginger Rogers.

[3] With Fred Astaire and Ginger Rogers.

[4] With Fred Astaire and Ginger Rogers.

[5] With Fred Astaire and Ginger Rogers.

[6] With Fred Astaire and Cyd Charisse.

[7] With Fred Astaire and Leslie Caron.

[8] This was not the Astaire musical, but Burns and Allen in a film about dance halls.

[9] With Ruby Keeler, Joan Blondell and James Cagney.

[10] Veteran tappers Sandman Sims, Bunny Briggs and Chuck Green warm up for the onstage 'challenge' at Harlem's Small's Paradise and share reminiscences, accompanied by Lionel Hampton and his big band. First London showing.

[11] A collective ballet work by the Peking Opera Troupe of Shanghai.

[12] 'Hilary Harris's choreographic camera follows the movements of a ballerina rehearsing.'

[13] With Gene Kelly and Judy Garland.

[14] With Ginger Rogers and Ruby Keeler.

[15] With Ann Miller, Vera Ellen, Frank Sinatra, Jules Munshin and Kelly, music by Bernstein.

[16] With Yvonne Rainer.

[17] With Kelly, Tamara Toumanova, Igor Youskevitch and Claire Sombert.

[18] With Bill 'Mr Bojangles' Robinson.

[19] With Buster West and Jon Patriocilla.

[20] Described as a 'pop-surrealist' film with a dance number from the Lindy Hoppers.

[21] A programme of five films presented free of charge to members of Riverside's film club (membership 5p), comprising: *Modern Ballet* (1960) – a discussion with Antony Tudor; *Night Journey* (Graham, 1961); *Rainforest* (Cunningham, 1968); *Three Dances* (performed by Judith Dunn, Alex Hay, Steve Paxton and Robert Rauschenberg, 1963); *Trance and Dance in Bali* (by the anthropologist Margaret Mead).

[22] The invited panel included David White (director of Dance Theatre Workshop in New York and a member of the US National Endowment for the Arts, dance panel); Max Wagener (then director of the Netherlands Theatre Institute); Denise Luccioni (dance promoter in France and Holland); Gale Law and Val Bourne.

[23] This resulted in the establishment in 1982 of the National Organisation of Dance and Mime (NODM).

1981

Thursday 8 October – Sunday 15 November (73 London performances)

Venues
London: Almeida Theatre, ICA, The Place, Riverside
Brighton: Gardner Centre for the Arts (19–31 October)
Bristol: The Arnolfini (8 October – 12 November)
Cardiff: Chapter Arts Centre (2–15 November)
Coventry: Arts Centre, University of Warwick (2–7 November)
Glasgow: Third Eye Centre (9–17 October)
Leicester: Phoenix Theatre (2–6 November)
Liverpool: Everyman Theatre (19–25 October)
Danceabout North West: 21 venues in Manchester and region (26 September – 28 November)
Norwich: The Premises and Village Theatre (3–25 October)
Peterborough and Oundle (19-24 October)

Artists

Continental Europe
Caroline Marcadé and Dominique Petit[1] (France)
Werkcentrum Dans[2] (Holland)
Wind Witches[3] (Sweden)

UK
Laurie Booth[4]
Rosemary Butcher Dance Company[5]
Lizzie Cox with Kirstie Simson[6]
Cycles Dance Company[7]
Dance Theatre London[8]
Dancework[9]
Jane Dudley Dancers[10]
Maedée Duprès[11]
EMMA Dance Company[12]
Mary Fulkerson[13]
Inge Lonnroth and Dancers[14]
Sue MacLennan[15]
Tamara McLorg[16]
Mantis[17]
New Choreographers Award Winners[18]

Nin Dance Company[19]
Rambert Choreographers[20]
Janet Smith and Dancers[21]
Ian Spink Group[22]
Anthony van Laast[23]
Miranda Tufnell and Dennis Greenwood[24]

International
Le Groupe de la Place Royale[25] (Canada)
Junko Kikuchi[26] (Japan)

USA
Karole Armitage and Company[27]
Ruth Barnes[28]
Eiko and Koma[29]
Molissa Fenley[30]
Tom Jobe[31]
Bill T. Jones and Arnie Zane[32]
Charles Moulton and Dancers[33]
Dana Reitz[34]

Notes

[1] Former members of the Groupe de Recherches Théâtrales de l'Opéra de Paris (an experimental dance unit attached to the Paris Opera and directed by Carolyn Carlson). The programme included Marcadé's duet *Pierre Robert*, solo *These Arms of Mine* and Petit's solo *Variations*.

[2] The company's UK debut, in choreography by David Gordon, Bill T. Jones, Ian Spink, Hans Tuerlings, Toer van Schayk and company director Kathy Gosschalk. The latter incorporated film by Dutch painter Pieter Peereboom.

[3] Presented two pieces by company director Eva Lunqvist: *Three Women Dance Part 1* and *When the Water Turns*, both performed in silence.

[4] In a solo programme *Manipulatin' Motion (Pictures)*

5 The company premiered *Spaces Four,* Butcher's latest collaboration with Heinz-Dieter Pietsch and *Shell: Forcefields and Spaces* with installation by Jon Groom, sound score by Jim Fulkerson.

6 A performance arts piece in which printmaker Lizzie Cox presented a performance and exhibition *A Year in the Life of a Field at Nettlecombe, Somerset* with dancer Kirstie Simson to a commissioned score by composer Stuart Gordon (played on a tape recorder).

7 Presented *Marital Arts*, directed by Sara and Jerry Pearson, *Being British*, directed by Ian Spink.

8 The company was established in March 1981, co-directed by dancers/choreographers Stewart Arnold and Gary Hurst and financed itself by working on the London club and cabaret circuit.

9 Presented *New York Connexions*, including premieres by visiting American choreographers Judith Moss and Ruth Barnes, plus Tony Thatcher's *Answerphonedance*, Christine Juff's *Sixteen*, to a new score by Gavin Bryars, and Sally Gardner's solo, *Suds.*

10 Presented a full programme of Dudley's work: *Retrospectives 1938–1981* including *The Lonely Ones* (1946), *Harmonica Breakdown* (1938), *Several Brahms Waltzes* (1978), *Five Character Studies and a Conclusion* (1978) and *Dance Suite* (1981).

11 Presenting her fourth solo evening, *Time Within Time*, which included Fergus Early's *Three Sarabandes*, Mary Fulkerson's *Song from the Country* (commissioned score by Gordon Jones, design by Maria Liljfors), Duprès's *Splitter* (commissioned electronic score, *Scythia* by Stephen Montague, design by Craig Givens) plus an improvisation.

12 In a programme including work by new artistic director Nicholas Carroll, commissioned work by Janet Smith and American guest choreographers Sara and Jerry Pearson, plus Royston Maldoom's *Adagietto No. 5.*

13 Fulkerson presented a mixed programme, including two solos: her own *Testament to One Thought* and Richard Alston's *Swedish Dances*; Fulkerson's duet for Michael Clark and Beverley Sandwith, *The Raft is not the Shore* (score by Jim Fulkerson); and a collaboration with Chris Crickmay, *Field*, incorporating a film project.

14 Presented Lonnroth's *Helix*; *Ten Haikus on Bridges and Butterflies*, a premiere with commissioned score by Gary Carpenter; plus a new

work by Hannele Jansson. Many works were accompanied by the clarinettist and close associate of the company, Catherine Lewis.

15 Presented a full-length work, *Interruptions*, to a commissioned text-sound score by Jane Wells and Cris Cheek, with dancers Gaby Agis, Craig Givens and Kirstie Simson.

16 In *Profile: Solo Dances*, consisting of commissioned solos from Anthony Ellis, Stuart Hopps, Neil Murray and Lenny Westerdijk, plus an improvisation with live accompaniment by percussionist Simon Limbrick.

17 The all-male company founded by Micha Bergese with a commitment to educational work, in a programme, *Tripping the Light Fantastic,* that included *Dolly Sods* by Dan Wagoner; Bergese's *Some Dance and Some Duet, Encore* (music by Steve Reich) and *Social Life* (music by Laurie Anderson) plus a new work with a commissioned score by Dominic Muldowney and design by Liz da Costa.

18 A new scheme launched at the Laban Centre. The programme comprised works by the finalists: Paul Douglas, Beyhan Fowkes, Steven Goff, Rosemary Lee, Rosemary Lehan, Maggie Morris, Liana Nyquist, Ilana Snyder and Annelies Stoffel.

19 Founded in 1980 by Trinidadian Greta Mendez and American Michael Quaintance, the company presented Mendez's *Only a Memory* (commissioned score by Jon Keliehor), plus Quaintance's *Deception, Racks* and *Negatives,* with a jazz score by Charles Mingus.

20 Nelson Fernández, Michael Ho, Ikky Maas, Quinny Sacks and Yair Vardi all presented new work in a programme that also included Richard Alston's solo for Michael Clark, *Soda Lake.*

21 In a programme of Smith's works including *Square Leg, Until the Tide Turns* and *Should I?*

22 Presented *Canta 2* (accompanied by a score of tape loops and phased sound by David Cunningham), *Tap Dance*, with live music by Jane Wells, *De Gas*, with oboist Christopher Redgate, and *Some Fugues.* Spink also made a piece for Werkcentrum Dans.

23 Presented works by van Laast, Garey Hurst, Janet Smith plus a film collaboration with Antony Penrose.

24 Performed with Laurie Booth, Cris Cheek and Sue MacLennan in three improvised works devised by Tufnell.

25 Formed in Montreal in 1966 as a multi-arts company: the members were responsible

for choreography, music, vocal accompaniment, design, lighting design and text. They presented Jean-Pierre Perrault's *Dernière Paille*, the group's *Miniatures*, plus founder Peter Boneham's *The Collector of Cold Weather* or *What Happened*.

[26] A resident of New York since 1976, performed works by Carmen Beuchat, Carla Blank, Miyako Kato, Minako Manita and Mel Wong.

[27] In the full-length work *Drastic Classicism* for four dancers (Armitage, Chris Komar, Joseph Lennon and Nathalie Richard) and four musicians (Rhys Chatham, David Linton, Joe Dizney and Michael Brown). The music was composed by Chatham, and the piece was designed by Charles Atlas. Armitage and Lennon performed a duet programme, *The Decibel Diary* and *Vertige* with Chatham for Danceabout North West.

[28] Presented a solo programme: *A Very Short Umbrella Dance*; *Yeah, but can you make a flag out of it?* and *Another Time, Another Place*.

[29] In *Fur Seal* (1977), inspired by a poem of the same title by M. Kaneko. Eiko and Koma studied Buto with Kazuo Ohno and Tatsumi Hijikata in their native Japan and German Expressionist dance with Manja Ohmiel (a disciple of Mary Wigman) in Germany, before moving to the US.

[30] In a solo programme *Between Heartbeats*, to a commissioned score by Mark Freedman.

[31] Jobe with Linda Gibbs and Linda Brewer performed Jobe's *City* for the late shows (9.45 pm) at The Place.

[32] Performed *Blauvelt Mountain Act I, A Fiction* and *Valley Cottage* in the company's UK debut.

[33] Three dancers (Moulton, Barbara Allen and Beatrice Bogorard) plus musician A. Leroy in *Expanded Ball Passing, Thought Movement Motor, Motor Fantasy* and *Nine Person Precision Ball Passing*, which included local volunteers trained for this performance. UK debut.

[34] In *Steps, Changing Score* and *Steps 2*. At the end of her work, Reitz instigated a question and answer session with the audience, thereby beginning the 'meet the choreographer' slots that were to become a regular Dance Umbrella feature.

1981: Related Events

Films[1]

Lunchtime screenings (ICA). Paul Taylor,[2] Merce Cunningham,[3] *Making Dances*,[4] British Programme,[5] tap dance films.[6]

Dance in Education Week screenings (Riverside Studios). The Red Shoes, Bugsy Malone

Lecture

'The Art of Fred Astaire', illustrated lecture by John Mueller[7] which opened the ICA dance film week.

Seminars and Courses

Dance Writing and Criticism Course. An intensive five-day course taught by American guests Sally Banes, Deborah Jowitt and John Mueller, plus an open, concluding seminar[8] (ICA, 26–30 October)

Design for Dance[9] – open forum (Riverside, 24 October); *Children's Theatre*[10] – open forum (Riverside, 12 October); *Dance and Young People – A Fair Exchange*[11] – open forum (Riverside, 14 November)

Classes and Workshops

Master classes (Pineapple Studios). Bill T. Jones, Arnie Zane, Charles Moulton, Molissa Fenley

Workshops (Pineapple Studios and ICA). Gina Levete led movement workshops for professional dancers in combination with people with disabilities, organised by SHAPE.

Exhibitions

Photographs of postmodern or 'new' dance in New York and the UK. Nathaniel Tileston (US) (ICA, 6–25 October), Paula Court (US) (Riverside Studios, 27 October[12] – 5 November), Chris Harris[13] (UK) (Riverside Studios, 13 October – 8 November)

Associated Events

Dance in Education Week[14] (Riverside Studios, 10–15 October)
Artists: Dance Experience for Children, Tara Rajkumar, Ludus Dance in Education Company, Lynx Dance Group, London Festival Ballet, Mantis, Students from the Royal Ballet School, Jonathan Burrows, Nicolas Dixon, Matthew Hawkins[15]

Notes

[1] Originally an ambitious film and video season was planned, but was later abandoned through lack of funds.

[2] Merrill Brockway's television documentary on Paul Taylor and his company.

[3] Programme included *Locale*, co-directed by Cunningham and Charles Atlas.

[4] Michael Blackwood's TV film, featuring Trisha Brown, Lucinda Childs, Douglas Dunn, David Gordon, Kenneth King, Meredith Monk and Sara Rudner.

[5] The programme included *Dancers,* which focuses on members of the Ballet Rambert; *Other Rooms*, a film with Miranda Tufnell and Dennis Greenwood, co-directed by Nick Gonzalez and Chris Schwarz; and Bob Lockyer's *To Be A Choreographer* about the Gulbenkian International Dance Course for Choreographers and Composers.

[6] The programme included an Arts Council short, directed by John Tchalenko and featuring clog dancer Sam Sherry; *Tapdancin'* by Christian Blackwood featuring American tap artists The Hoofers, the Copasetics, John Bubbles, Honi Coles and Cholly Atkins; plus vintage clips of 'Bojangles' and the Nicholas Brothers.

[7] Author of *Films on Ballet and Modern Dance* and *Dance Film Directory*, founder and director of the dance Film Archive at the University of Rochester in New York, film producer.

[8] There were sixteen participants, some of whom were sponsored by Sotheby's and the Arts Council's Training Department. Support groups in Leeds and London were subsequently set up to continue the exchange of information.

[9] Chaired by Peter Williams, with panellists Nadine Baylis, Fergus Early, Antony McDonald and Peter Mumford.

[10] Arranged by GLAA drama panel as part of Dance in Education Week.

[11] Part of Dance in Education Week.

[12] Originally to have opened 14 October, but materials were delayed in transit.

[13] Harris was house photographer at Riverside Studios. The exhibition was also held at the Arnolfini Gallery in Bristol from 29 September – 10 October.

[14] Part of Allsorts Young People's Festival, hosted by Riverside and the London Borough of Hammersmith and Fulham. The week included performing and/or teaching units in performances, workshops and lecture demonstrations for children and teachers highlighting the use of dance as an educational resource. There were also two open fora and two film screenings (see above).

[15] Presented *JumbleDance* – an open choreographic workshop for people of all ages, with or without dance experience.

1982

Sunday 3 October – Sunday 14 November (75 London performances)

Venues
London: Almeida Theatre, ICA, The Place, Riverside Studios, Tate Gallery[1]
Aberdeen: Cowdray Hall, SchoolHill (16 October)
Bristol: The Arnolfini (22 October – 11 November)
Canterbury: Gulbenkian Theatre (7–9 October)
Cardiff: Chapter Arts Centre (22–26 October)
Coventry: Arts Centre, University of Warwick (19 October – 6 November)
Glasgow: Third Eye Centre (8–16 October)
Leicester: Phoenix Arts Centre (3-6 November)
Danceabout North West: venues in Manchester and region (11 October – 29 November)
Peterborough and Oundle (20–30 October)

Artists

Continental Europe
Anne Teresa de Keersmaeker[2] (Belgium)
Susanne Linke[3] (Germany)

UK
Stewart Arnold and Paul Henry[4]
Basic Space Dance Theatre[5]
Laurie Booth[6]
British Independents[7]
Rosemary Butcher Dance Company[8]
Michael Clark and Dancers[9]
Dancework[10]
Libby Dempster[11]
Extemporary Dance Theatre[12]
Mary Fulkerson[13]
Julyen Hamilton and Matthieu Keijser[14]
Ingegerd Lonnroth/Richard Sikes[15]
Sue MacLennan and Kirstie Simson[16]
Tamara McLorg[17]
Mantis Dance Company[18]

Midlands Dance Company[19]
Nin Dance Company[20]
Janet Smith and Dancers[21]
Ilana Snyder[22]
Spiral Dance Company[23]

International
Dancemakers[24] (Canada)

USA
Laura Glenn and Gary Lund[25]
Bill T. Jones and Arnie Zane[26]
Kei Takei's Moving Earth[27]
Ellen Kogan[28]
Tim Miller[29]
Charles Moulton and A. Leroy[30]
Rosalind Newman and Dancers[31]
Steve Paxton[32]
Jim Self and Dancers[33]
Nina Wiener and Dancers[34]

Notes
[1] Selected as the venue for special perform-ances by Jim Self's American Trio, near the Jackson Pollock collection.

[2] Presented *Fase, four movements on the mu-sic of Steve Reich* with fellow Mudra School graduate Michele Anne de Mey. UK debut for both artists.

[3] Trained in Mary Wigman School in Berlin, Essen Folkwang Hochschule, and also danced in Folkwang Tanz-Studio, directed at that time by Pina Bausch. Linke directs her own com-pany Folkwang-Tanz-Studio of Essen-Werden, but here presented a solo programme, *Im Bade Wannen* (1980, music by Satie).

[4] Former members of Maas Movers and Dance Theatre London. Presented their own solos and duets, plus works commissioned from Charles Augins, Gary Hurst and Anthony van Laast.

[5] Presented *Cocktails* with choreography by Jane Dudley, Howard Cooper, Patricia Mac-kenzie and Shelley Lee. The company also ap-peared in the Allsorts Festival.

[6] In his solo programme *Crazy Daisy and the Northern Lights*.

[7] Included work by Matthew Hawkins, Quinny Sacks and Tom Yang.

[8] With dancers Dennis Greenwood, Miranda

Tufnell and Gaby Agis in new collaboration with visual artist Heinz Dieter-Pietsch, and a revival of *Spaces 4.*

9 Presented *of a feather, flock* including film with a score by Eric Clermontet; a duo by and for himself and Owen Smith *A Wish Sandwich*, also using film and a Clermontet score; Alston's solo *Dutiful Ducks* and Clark's own *Rush.*

10 Presented *Objects that don't need names – A Composite of Dances* including a commissioned score by Gavin Bryars, recordings of insects and a 1929 tape of James Joyce reading from *Finnegan's Wake.*

11 Appeared with fellow performer and designer Simon Lloyd in late-night bill *One Man, Two Man.* (The item did not appear in the festival broadsheet, but came into the programme at the last minute, championed by Richard Alston.)

12 Presented a work commissioned from Karole Armitage, *It Happened at Club Bombay Cinema,* David Gordon's *Counter Revolution,* Jacky Lansley's *Speaking Part* and Fergus Early's *Naples.*

13 Included a duet *Put Your Foot Down,* a solo *The Same Story*, a trio *Tangle of Dreams* and *Undergrowth*, all to James Fulkerson's music.

14 Dancer Hamilton, currently based in Holland, collaborated with percussionist Keijser from Holland in *Musk.*

15 A double bill in which students from LSCD performed work by Lonnroth and dancers from the Genée Ballet performed some of Sikes's work.

16 Presented a programme of recent solos and duets.

17 Presented a solo programme *Sketches,* which was a collaboration with theatre director Alan Lyddiard, designer Neil Murray, composer Charles Barber and lighting designer Tim Haunton, with contributions from composer Chris Reason and photographer Jonathon Crick.

18 Presented Jones's and Zane's *Rotary Action,* expanded for the company; a duet *Encore,* plus Dan Wagoner's *Dolly Sods.*

19 Formerly EMMA Dance Company and now with joint funding from East Midlands and West Midlands Arts. The programme included Mitchell Rose's *Tales from Sherwood,* Lenny Westerdijk's *Atolen* and Sally Owens's *Muscaritas.*

20 Presented Greta Mendez's *Different Spot Along the Same Line* and Michael Quaintance's

Like Houses, Sonny's Letter, Scruffs and *Shine.*

21 The programme included *Holiday Sketches* and *Electra,* commissioned respectively from Christopher Bruce and Robert North; plus Smith's *Last of the Cotton Pickers.*

22 Presented a programme that included a reconstruction of Doris Humphrey's *Water Study,* plus her own choreography.

23 The London debut for this Merseyside-based company, in a programme *New Dances,* that included a new work by Jonathan Burrows, *Cloisters,* and Jacky Lansley's *Impersonations.*

24 Toronto-based company in a programme that included commissioned work from Robert Cohan, a revival of Doris Humphrey's *Two Ecstatic Themes: Circular Descent and Pointed Ascent* (1931) (with solos performed by Zella Wolofsky).

25 In Glenn's *After the Appointment Near Kerb* and Lund's *Trout Duet.* Glenn danced with the Limón Company for eleven years.

26 Jones and Zane also had their own season at Riverside Studios in September and appeared at the Edinburgh Festival the same year. Here they performed *Continuous Replay,* Jones's solo *Three Dances* and Zane's *Rumble in the Jungle.* They also extended *Rotary Action* (seen the previous year) for Mantis.

27 Takei was joined by two colleagues to perform sections of her epic *Light,* begun in 1969. (Nederlands Dans Theater have performed sections of *Light.*)

28 Currently a guest teacher at the Laban Centre, Kogan performed a solo programme with works by Cliff Keuter, Rachel Lampert, Igal Perry, Manuel Alum, Annabelle Gamson, James Waring and Jim Self.

29 Presented a performance art piece, *Postwar.*

30 Presented a new duo programme.

31 First appeared as a trio (including herself) for Dance Umbrella 80. Newman returned with her full company of eight and a programme that included *Juanita* (mus. Laurie Anderson), *Four Stories* and *Ropeworks* (music by Meredith Monk).

32 Appeared with Lisa Nelson in *PART* (score by Robert Ashley) and with Nelson and Laurie Booth in *Bound* (1981).

33 Former Merce Cunningham Dance Company member Self, with Rob Besserer and Ellen Van Schuylenburch presented a programme that included a solo, *Scraping Bottoms,* a duet, *Domestic Interlude,* a trio *Marking Time*

and excerpts from *The Phoenix City Story*.

[34] Wiener danced in Twyla Tharp's company, before forming her own. This programme included Wiener's *Condor Material*, *Lullabies for Elizabeth*, and *Kemo Sabe* plus company member Tim Buckley's *Irish Jumping Songs*.

1982: Related Events

Films and Video

Fortnight season at ICA Cinematheque.[1] *Dancing on the Edge*,[2] Remy Charlip's *Dances*[3] (dir. David Atwood), *George's House*,[4] *Dance Journeys*,[5] *You Little Wild Heart*,[6] *Rites of Passing* (chor. and co-dir. Nancy Schreiber), plus dance programmes to be shown on C4 during 1983, including *The Rake's Progress*[7] (chor. de Valois), a Canadian film featuring Pilobolus, *Troy Game* (Robert North, performed by LCDT), *Ellis Island* (chor. and dir. Meredith Monk), *Daphnis and Chloe* (chor. Graeme Murphy for Sydney Dance Theatre)

Seminars

Open fora. Dance and Mime Action Group (DAMAG) Second General Meeting (Riverside Studios, 3 October). *Dance and Music*[8] (The Place, 30 October), *Dance: As Art or Excercise?*[9] (Riverside, 7 November)

Lectures. Judson dance Theater[10] by Sally Banes in London (24 October, Riverside) and regions. *American Contemporary Dance* by Sally Banes (26 October, ICA)

Classes and Workshops
The Place, ICA, Goldsmith's College and Froebel College, Roehampton: Nina Wiener, Rosalind Newman,[11] Tim Miller, Jim Self, Kei Takei.
Movement workshops for people with disabilities organised by SHAPE

Exhibitions
Judson Dance Theatre 1962–66 Exhibition[12] (Riverside Gallery, previewed 3 October)
Dance Photographs by Dee Conway at The Place, Chris Harris at Riverside Studios, Irene Hall at the Almeida
Drawings of Indian classical dancers Uday Shankar and his Company 1939–1944 by Eilean Pearcey at the Place

Concerts
James Fulkerson and Musicians[13]

Meet the Choreographer[14]
The Almeida, ICA and Riverside: Steve Paxton and Lisa Nelson, Matthew Hawkins, Quinny Sacks, Mary Fulkerson, Rosalind Newman, Julyen Hamilton, Tim Miller, Ann Dickie

Associated Events
Dance and Education Week as part of Allsorts (see 1981).

Notes
[1] A series of early evening showings of videotapes from New York, previously unseen in this country and courtesy of the Kitchen Center for Video and Dance Theater Workshop/Video D plus commissioned dance programmes from WGBH New Television Workshop in Boston. The programmes were introduced by Susan Dowling, dance co-ordinator for WGBH. The selection was also shown at Bristol's Arnolfini and Edinburgh's Traverse

Theatre.

2. Featuring choreography by Trisha Brown, including *Watermotor*.

3. Five short pieces for a variety of dancers, including the choreographer Charlip.

[4] Created by Dan Wagoner and set in and around a log cabin.

[5] Including choreography by Meredith Monk, Ruth Wheeler, Dawn Kramer and Sam Costs.

[6] Marta Renzi's video-dance about young New York street dancers.

[7] Dame Ninette de Valois rehearsing her work with members of Sadler's Wells Royal Ballet, followed by a performance.

[8] Noel Goodwin, Barrington Pheloung and Gary Carpenter led the debate.

[9] A discussion chaired by Jan Murray, preceded by an open workshop in two contrasting exercise styles.

[10] Toured twelve different centres including London and regions.

[11] Newman also taught a week of classes at the Pineapple West Dance Centre.

[12] Included videos, interviews, posters, photographs and programmes.

[13] In the first live concert to be held by Dance Umbrella, the group presented the London premiere of *Forcefields and Spaces,* excerpts from which were choreographed by Rosemary Butcher.

[14] This marked the first series of informal sessions between choreographer and public that continues to the present day.

Steve Paxton at Riverside Studios, 1982.
PHOTO: CHRIS HARRIS

1983

Monday 3 October – Sunday 13 November (49 London performances, including the festival finale)

Venues
London: ICA; The Place; Riverside Studios
Aberdeen: The Art Gallery
Bristol: Arnolfini (22 September – 12 November)
Coventry: Warwick Arts Centre (17 October – 19 November)
Dundee: Bonar Hall, University of Dundee (22 October – 3 December)
Edinburgh: Traverse Theatre Club; Belford Church (25 October – 4 November)
Glasgow: Third Eye Centre (10 – 19 November)
Leicester: Phoenix Theatre (1 – 5 November)
Danceabout North West Festival: Manchester and region (3 October – 2 Dec)
Nottingham: Midland Group Arts Centre (14 October – 12 November)
Peterborough and Oundle (15 October – 10 December)
Swindon: Thamesdown Community Dance Studio (22 October & 5 November)

Artists

Continental Europe
Astrakan[1] (France)
Hamilton, Keijser and Kirstie Simson[2] (Holland)
Robert Kovich and Dancers[3] (France)

UK
Basic Space Dance Theatre[4]
Micha Bergese[5]
Booth, Rogante and Cincone[6]
Rosemary Butcher Dance Company[7]
Michael Clark[8]
Dancework[9]
Extemporary Dance Theatre[10]
Mary Fulkerson's Dance Alliance[11]

Ludus Dance Company[12]
Sue MacLennan[13]
Tamara McLorg[14]
Second Stride[15]
'Made in Britain' series[16]
Festival Finale[17]

International
La La La/Lock Danseurs[18] (Canada)

US
Trisha Brown Company[19]
Bill T. Jones, Arnie Zane and Company[20]
Lisa Kraus[21]
Dana Reitz[22]

Notes

[1] Founded by French choreographer Daniel Larrieu in 1982, the company presented Larrieu's recent *Trois Pièces, Cuisine* comprising *Chiquenaudes, Volte Face* and *Un Sucre ou Deux?*

[2] Hamilton and Simson, originally from the UK, with Dutch percussionist Matthieu Keijser in a development of last year's performance piece, *Musk:Red*.

[3] Originally from California (a graduate of Bennington College, soloist with the Merce Cunningham Company), Kovich moved to Paris in 1981. Here, he performed a solo, *Decoy*, and with Ségolène Colin duo works including *Pin-Up* and *Tarantula (with tarantella)*.

[4] Presented a full length work *Flying Blind* including music by Laurie Anderson, Mahler's

Songs and Edith Piaf's singing, plus a commissioned score by Robert Handleigh and John Sampson and design by David Bates.

[5] In a solo show *Crickets* (formerly *Spaghetti Junction),* with music by Glenn Branca and David Cunningham and design by Rebecca Neil.

[6] Laurie Booth with Giovanna Rogante and Nicholas Cincone in the collaboration *From Ordinary Lives,* with design by Kate Owen and with videos made by Pete Anderson and Steve Littman.

[7] In a new programme comprising *The Site* and *Imprints* created with Dieter Pietsch, with a taped score commissioned from Malcolm Clark; with dancers Gaby Agis, Butcher,

Dennis Greenwood and Helen Rowsell.

8 Choreographer-in-residence at Riverside Studios. Here performed with Catherine Tucker, Gaby Agis and Angus Cook in excerpts from *Parts I–IV,* in collaboration with video artist Cerith Wyn Evans, and with the Neo-Naturist Cabaret in *Sexist Crabs.*

9 The programme included choreography by Lisa Kraus, also *Grey Window* by Thatcher with film by David Robinson and a Gavin Bryars score.

10 The programme included Michael Clark's *1 2 X U* to a score by Wire, Dan Wagoner's *Spiked Sonata* (1981), Jane Dudley's *Dark is the Night, Cold was the Ground,* Sally Owen's *Giraffes and Jellyfish and Things* plus Emilyn Claid's solo for Annelies Stoffel, *Solo.*

11 Fulkerson collaborated with Eva Lundquist, director of Wind Witches on *Track Follows,* which also contained Wind Witches dancers, plus Fulkerson's *Julie and the Henchman* and *Fine Romance,* all to music by Jim Fulkerson.

12 Presented *Cut to Ribbons* choreographed by director Chris Thomson and guest Beyhan Fowkes, with a score by Tim Souster and design by Helen Turner.

13 Presented *New Moves* with music by John King and design by Johanna Agis.

14 In a solo programme *Moving,* comprising short works by Jonathan Burrows, David Glass, Ingegerd Lonnroth, Royston Maldoom, Sally Owen and Peter Purdie, with designs by Janet Newton.

15 Presented the London premiere of Siobhan Davies's *Minor Characters* (designed by Antony McDonald), Ian Spink's *Some Fugues* and Richard Alston's *Java, Doublework* and *The Brilliant and the Dark.*

16 Devised as a platform for young choreographers, the programmes included works by: Gaby Agis, Paul Clayden, Anne Dickie, Nelson Fernandez, Stephen Goff, Phillip Grosser, Luis Gonzalez (seen last year with Kei Takei's Moving Earth), Matthew Hawkins, Stephanie Jordan, Gregory Nash, Jeremy Nelson and Michael Popper.

17 Held at Riverside Studios on 13 November, the event was used as a showcase by the Association of British Sponsorship of the Arts (ABSA) to introduce potential sponsors to modern dance, and included artists from the Royal Ballet, LCDT and smaller dance companies appearing at the festival.

18 The Montréal-based company in Edouard Lock's *Businessman in the process of becoming an angel,* described as a *'danse musicale postmoderne',* with music by Michel Lemieux.

19 The programme included *Set and Reset* with designs by Robert Rauschenberg, music commissioned from Laurie Anderson, *Glacial Decoy,* decor and costumes by Rauschenberg, *Line-Up, Son of Gone Fishin'* to a Robert Ashley score and *Opal Loop.*

20 The company of five presented Jones's *Five Brahms Dances,* Zane's *Continuous Replay,* a duet *Shared Distance* (1982), a collaboration *Secret Pastures,* and a duet version of *Intuitive Momentum.*

21 Presented a full-evening solo, *Going Solo,* that marked Kraus's departure from Trisha Brown's company with which she had performed for the previous five years.

22 In a solo programme that included *Steps, Changing Score* and an extract from *Field Papers.*

1983: Related Events

Film and Video
Film screenings[1] (The Place, Riverside Studios)
Dance on Film (The Place), lecture by John Mueller
Dance Video Project[2] (Riverside Studios), workshops and recording sessions

Seminars
Dance and the Camera[3] (Riverside Studios), open forum

Classes and Workshops

Master classes and workshops. Robert Kovich, Bill T. Jones, Arnie Zane, members of the La La La and Trisha Brown Companies, Dana Reitz

Daily technique classes (Pineapple Dance Centre), June Anderson[4]

Exhibitions
Photographic retrospective (Riverside Studios, 25 October for four weeks): photographs by Chris Harris of Dance Umbrella 1978–83
Photographs by Dee Conway (The Place)

Meet the Choreographer
Trisha Brown, Bill T. Jones and Arnie Zane, Edouard Lock

Meet the Composers
Two 'in conversation' sessions featuring Morton Feldman and Philip Glass, (Riverside Studios)

Associated Events
Dance-in-Education Week[5] (Riverside, 31 October – 5 November)
Hammersmith and Fulham's third Allsorts Festival for Young People
Festival of French New Wave[6] (Riverside Studios, 4–9 October)
Studio Night[7] (Riverside, 10 October), Patricia Bardi
Performing Clothes[8] (ICA, 11–16 October)
Third International Symposium on the Orthopaedic and Medical Aspects of Dance (Pineapple West Dance Studios, 8–9 October)
The Place of Indian Dance in British Culture, Conference (Commonwealth Institute, 13–16 October)
A World of Dance in Britain[9] (Commonwealth Institute, 14–16 October)
Three programmes showing Western, Indian and Afro-Caribbean folk and theatre dance side by side.
Indian Classical Dance Series (Place Theatre, 18–29 October). Performances[10], classes, workshops and an open forum.

Notes

[1] These comprised dance films made for television, and were primarily British, but included films by independent US film-maker David Robinson, who showed a selection of his low-budget 16-mm and 8-mm pieces. Also screened were Geoff Dunlop's *De Gas* and *Canta* (made for C4) and his *Merce Cunningham Travelogue* made for LWT; Colin Nears's *Cruel Garden*; Tony Cash's profile of Richard Alston, made for LWT; and a selection of Bob Lockyer's dance films for the BBC.

[2] These workshop and recording sessions were led by Colin Nears, Charles Atlas and Susan Dowling. They resulted in six video programmes that featured: Mantis; Janet Smith and Dancers; Moving Picture Mime Show; Ludus; Extemporary Dance Theatre and Indian classical dancers Chitra Sundaram, Alpana Sengupta and Ranjala Gohar.

[3] Chaired by Michael Kustow, the panel comprised Colin Nears and Bob Lockyer (BBC), Susan Dowling (WGBH Boston), Geoff Dunlop, Kenneth MacMillan and Jan Murray.

[4] This New York choreographer also presented an informal concert at Pineapple West Dance Studio.

[5] Participating artists included members of: Direct Dance, Mexicolore, Ludus Dance Company, Education Units of the Royal Ballet and London Festival Ballet, London Youth Dance/Harehills Youth dance (shared performance) and Maedée Duprès. There was also a conference, *What is Youth Dance and Where is it Going?*

[6] Described as a plethora of fashion, rock, dance, video and film, to celebrate the current explosion of French creativity. The programme included Daniel Larrieu plus others appearing as the Chelsea Quick Pick-Up, Philippe Decouflé and Mogly Spex.

[7] Part of a regular series at the venue, in which choreographers tried out their work in front of an audience in an exploratory and informal setting.

[8] Choreographers (Micha Bergese, Stewart Arnold and Claude Paul Henry) dancers and fashion designers (Robin Archer, Michele Clapton, Sue Clowes, Richard Ostell, Elaine Oxford,

Bill T. Jones and Arnie Zane Company, 1983. PHOTO: CHRIS HARRIS

Willy Brown and Zwei) collaborated during London Fashion Week in a setting designed by Andrew McAlpine.

[9] Artist included: Laurie Booth, Royal Scottish Country Dance Society, Nahid Siddiqui, United Artists Dance Company No. 7, Greta Indian Dancers, Headington Morris Men, Tara Rajkumar, Chandrasekharan, London City Ballet, Chitra Sundaram, Priwa Pawar, Shobana Jeyasingh, Rajalaksmi Kanthan and students of the Academy of Indian Dance.

[10] Artists included: Tara Rajkumar, Chandrasekharan (Kathakali dancer), Madavi and Mugdal Odissi, Chitra Sundaram (Bharata Natyam) and Nahid Siddiqui (Kathak).

1984

Wednesday 3 October – Sunday 18 November (45 London performances, plus the last-night party)

Venues
London: Bloomsbury Theatre; Place Theatre; Riverside Studios; Sadlers Wells Theatre*
Bristol: Arnolfini Gallery (13 October – 7 Nov)
Danceabout North West: 35 different centres in the Manchester area (4 October – 18 November)
Glasgow: Third Eye Gallery (7–16 November)
Leicester: Scraptoft Campus and Phoenix Arts (25 October, 9–10 November)
Norwood: Nettleford Hall (17 & 24 November, 7 & 15 December)
Nottingham: various venues (5, 6, 8 & 26 October, 2 & 16 November, 7 December)
Peterborough: various venues (1–3 & 12 October, 10 & 16 November)

Artists

Continental Europe
Pauline Daniëls[1] (Holland)
Katie Duck/Group O[2] (Italy)
Steve Lacey and Shiro Daimon[3] (France)
Michele Anne de Mey and Roxane Huilmand[4] (Belgium)

UK
Michael Clark and Company[5]
English Dance Theatre[6]
Extemporary Dance Theatre[7]
Sue MacLennan, Ian Mitchell, Steven Montague[8]
Second Stride[9]
Miranda Tufnell, Dennis Greenwood and David Ward[10]

'Made in Britain' series[11]
Last-night party[12]

International
Russell Dumas' Dance Exchange[13] (Australia)

USA
Timothy Buckley and The Troublemakers with 'Blue' Gene Tyranny[14]
Yoshiko Chuma/The School of Hard Knocks[15]
Bill T. Jones, Arnie Zane and Company[16]
Lar Lubovitch Dance Company[17]
Mark Morris and Dancers[18]

Notes
* The first time this venue had been used.

[1] A member of the experimental collective in Amsterdam, Danspoduktie, here presented a solo programme *Profile* that included a film of herself in Helga Langen's *Gotspe*, a collaboration with musician Harry de Wit in *13*, and Hans van Manen's *Portrait*.

[2] American-born Duck formed Group O in Florence in 1979. Here they presented *Rutles*, including songs by the Beatles.

[3] American saxophonist Lacy and Japanese Noh and Kabuki artist Daimon, both resident in Paris, in the collaborative *Kabuki-Woogie*.

[4] Cancelled because of illness. Tim Buckley *et al.* consequently extended their season to one week with 'Blue' Gene Tyranny taking over the first half of the programme on the two nights de Mey and Huilmand were scheduled to appear.

[5] With a new ensemble comprising Clark, Matthew Hawkins, Julie Hood and Ellen van Schuylenburch. The group presented *Do You Me? I Did* plus *New Puritans*.

[6] The programme included Ethel Winter's solo *En Dolor*, director Yair Vardi's *Solare* and *Full Half Crescent*, company member Nicholas Burge's *Is a Rose . . . Is a Rose*, David Glass's *Golden Geiger Days*, Peter Darrell's *Murder Story*, and *Morag's Wedding* by Michael Clark.

[7] The programme included *Field Study* by David Gordon, Daniel Larrieu's *Ombres Electrique*, Lloyd Newson's *Beauty, Art and the Kitchen Sink* (all London premieres), and *1 2 X U* by Clark, all with an emphasis on new music.

[8] In a collaborative programme presented by Intermedia, an organisation run by composer Jane Wells. The programme included

dancer MacLennan's solo choreography *Uneven Time*; a solo for electro-acoustic musician Montague, *The Eyes of Music*; a Stockhausen clarinet solo performed by Mitchell followed by the collaborative *Gravity is Proving Most Difficult*.

[9] Presented Ian Spink's *Further and Further into Night* (to a commissioned score by Orlando Gough, design by Antony McDonald) and Siobhan Davies's *Silent Partners* (in silence until the final section to clarinet music by Orlando Gough, design by David Buckland)

[10] A collaboration between dancer/choreographers Tufnell and Greenwood and visual artist Ward, *Huge Veil*, was developed out of a shared concern with the use and manipulation of light in relation to the human body. Costumes were by Katherine Hamnett.

[11] Five programmes of work by: (1) Paul Clayden, Lucy Fawcett, Tony Thatcher, Yolande Snaith, Julyen Hamilton; (2) Peri Mackintosh, Luis Gonzalez, Philip Grosser, Beyhan Fowkes, Lesley Bryant, Darlene Stevens; (3) Mary Fulkerson, Gaby Agis, Sue MacLennan and Matthew Hauxwell, Gregory Nash; (4) Richard Alston, Laurie Booth, Rosemary Butcher, Henrietta Van Reesma, Russell Dumas; (5) Gaby Agis and Ashley Page, Richard Alston, Nelson Fernández.

[12] This involved a performance of *A Night at the Millionaire's Club* devised by Yoshiko Chuma, followed by a party.

[13] Dumas has performed with Ballet Rambert and Strider, and with the Twyla Tharp and Trisha Brown Companies. Here the company of three performed Dumas's *Circular Quay*.

[14] Buckley was first seen in this country during Dance Umbrella 82 in Nina Wiener's company, for which he choreographed *Irish Jumping Songs*. The company here comprised four dancers and performed Buckley's *Barn Fever* and *How To Swing a Dog*, to live music by Tyranny.

[15] The first Dance Umbrella artist-in-residence, Chuma recreated her project *Five Car Pile-Up* on a British cast of nearly one hundred, including a core group of six professional dancers, her own company The School of Hard Knocks and non-dancers. They gave the first public performance in Covent Garden Piazza.

[16] The fourth consecutive visit to Dance Umbrella by the company. They presented *Freedom of Information*, to music by British composer David Cunningham (of Flying Lizards) and design by.Gretchen Bender (later recreated for LCDT), prefaced by Jones's *Coffee*.

[17] Founded in 1969, the company of twelve dancers performed Lubovitch works including *North Star* (with music by Philip Glass), *Cavalcade* and *Tabernacle* (both with scores by Steve Reich) and *Big Shoulders*.

[18] Morris and two members of his company, Guillermo Resto and Penny Hutchinson, presented *Love, You have Won*, *Songs That Tell a Story*, *Not Goodbye*, *Slugfest*, *The Vacant Chair* and *Bijoux*.

1984: Related Events

Seminars

Music and Dance: Collaboration or Co-existence?[1] (Riverside Studios)
Dance International: Rates of Exchange[2] (Riverside Studios)

Classes and Workshops

Classes. Mark Morris, Timothy Buckley, Bill T. Jones and Arnie Zane, Lar Lubovitch, Katie Duck, Russell Dumas

Workshops. Two-day dance and music workshops at The Place led by composers Stephen Montague and Jane Wells.[3] Improvisatory sessions at The Place led by saxophonist Steve Lacey and Noh performer Shiro Daimon. Yoshiko Chuma in preparation for the performance *Five Car Pile-Up*.

Concerts and Collaborations
Orlando Gough,[4] Steve Lacey and Shiro Daimon, 'Blue' Gene Tyranny – solo show

Meet the Choreographer
Mark Morris, Bill T. Jones and Arnie Zane, Lar Lubovitch, Timothy Buckley

Associated Events
Performing Clothes II[5] (ICA, 10–20 October)

Notes
[1] The seminar was led by Richard Crossland, then GLAA Music Officer.

[2] A seminar funded by the British Council, to discuss problems of funding for visiting artists from overseas, touring abroad by home artists and the funding of dance in Britain and overseas (following on from the 1980 festival seminar, held at the Riverside Studios on a similar theme). Theatre directors and entrepreneurs from six different countries were invited to participate, chaired by Stephen Remington, director of Sadler's Wells. The panel also included Dieter Lange of the Theatre am Turm in Frankfurt, Ann Valois of the Montréal Festival, David White of the Dance Theatre Workshop in New York and Robert Sykes of the British Council.

[3] Montague worked with fellow composer James Fulkerson and dancer Sue MacLennan; Wells with composer and musician Christopher Benstead, voice teacher Elise Lorraine and dance artist Claire Hayes.

[4] Gough's commissioned score accompanied Ian Spink's new work for Second Stride and the concert followed Second Stride's performance.

[5] Ten new fashion designers, including Leigh Bowery, showed their work, using a team of professional dancers instead of models, with choreography by Micha Bergese. The set was designed by architect Piers Gough and the show directed by ICA's Michael Morris.

Pauline Daniëls in her solo programme, *Profile*, 1984. PHOTO: CHRIS HARRIS

1985

Wednesday 9 October – Sunday 1 December (63 London performances)

Venues
London: Almeida; ICA; Place Theatre; Riverside Studios; Sadler's Wells
Alsager: Crewe and Alsager College
Brighton: Pavilion Theatre
Bristol: Arnolfini
Bury: Derby Hall
Danceabout North West: throughout the Manchester region
Glasgow: Third Eye Centre
Leicester: Leicester Polytechnic
Nottingham: Midland Group Arts Centre
Oxford: St Paul's Arts Centre
Peterborough: Walton School
Portsmouth: The Drama Studio, Portsmouth Polytechnic
Swindon: Thamesdown Community Dance Centre
Wakefield: Bretton Hall College

Artists

Continental Europe
Dansproduktie[1] (Holland)
Katie Duck and Group O[2] (Italy)
L'Esquisse[3] (France)
Julyen Hamilton and Kirstie Simson[4]
   (Holland)
Daniel Larrieu[5] (France)

UK
Laurie Booth and Harry de Wit[6]
Rosemary Butcher and Dancers[7]
Extemporary Dance Theatre[8]
The Kosh[9]
Sue MacLennan, Jane Wells and Peter
   Anderson[10]
National Youth Dance Theatre[11]

Phoenix Dance Theatre[12]
Second Stride[13]
Miranda Tufnell and Denis Greenwood[14]
Triple Bills +[15]
Late Extras[16]
Regional Day[17]
Final Fling[18]

International
Marie Chouinard[19] (Canada)

US
Karole Armitage and Joseph Lennon[20]
David Gordon and the Pick-Up Company[21]
Risa Jaraslow and Dancers[22]
Mark Morris and Dancers[23]

Notes
[1] An experimental collective, formed in 1977, based in Amsterdam and represented last year by Pauline Daniëls. The company policy was to have commissioned music, performed live wherever possible. For Dance Umbrella 85 they presented Beppie Blankert's *En Suite* (accompaniment, Harry de Wit), Bianca van Dillen's *Gift* (music, George Antheil) and Tom Lutgerink's *I Etcetera* (music, Glenn Branca).
[2] This year's artist-in-residence, and involved in four different projects: *On the Breadline*, created by Duck and musician Tristan Honsinger for Extemporary Dance Theatre; *Reckless*, a collaboration with four dancers and four musicians, and commissioned by Dance Umbrella 85; classes and workshops taught by members of the *Reckless* cast throughout the rehearsal period; and Group O's latest work *The Orange Man*, performed at the ICA, as well as touring the UK.
[3] Formed in 1980, this was the company's UK debut. Presented *Les Noces d'Argile* and a trio *Terre Battue* with actor Jean-Marc Poiriez.
[4] These two improvisation artists also participated in Katie Duck's *Reckless*.
[5] With his company Astrakan Recherches Chorégraphiques in a Late Extra programme. Presented *Romance en Stuc*.
[6] Booth in collaboration with musician de

Wit presented *An Axe to Grind*, originally commissioned by the Klapstuk Festival in Belgium. Booth also orchestrated the Festival's Final Fling.

[7] Butcher again in collaboration with visual artist Heinz Dieter Pietsch, and newly collaborating with composer Michael Nyman for *Flying Lines*.

[8] This was the company's tenth anniversary year and they celebrated with two new commissions: Katie Duck's *On the Breadline* (music, Tristan Honsinger, design, Craig Givens) and Richard Alston's *Cutter* (music, a commissioned score by John-Marc Gowans).

[9] Presented company member Siân Williams' *Marked Cards*. To celebrate International Youth Year, the company included a special programme of dance events for youth clubs.

[10] MacLennan was accompanied by video artist Peter Anderson, composer/saxophonist Jane Wells and saxophonist Edward Pillinger in *The Scattering Matrix*, a mixed-media project for Intermedia. The collaboration involved professional workshops during the week prior to performances.

[11] The London debut of the company whose repertory included David Gordon's *Counter Revolution* and new commissions: Graham Lustig's *Across the Sky*, Emilyn Claid's *Gathering* and company member Dwight Powell's solo, *Freedom*.

[12] The official festival debut for the all-male group that originated from Harehills Middle School, Leeds, although they appeared unofficially in Dance Umbrella 83's Final Fling Programme Finale. Here they presented Jane Dudley's *Running* (with music by Joe Farrell, Herbie Hancock, Metal Health); Leo David Hamilton's *Story of the Phoenix*; and Donald Edward's *Blessed Are They That Mourn, For They Shall Be Comforted*.

[13] Presented two works by Siobhan Davies: a revival of *Silent Partners* and a new work, *School for Lovers Danced* to excerpts from Mozart's *Cosi Fan Tutte*.

[14] In a new programme that included *Silver* (with designs by Bob Bielechi and music by Annea Lockwood) and with dancers Claire Bushe, Merry Dufton and Helen Rowsell in *Urban Weather* (sound by performance artist

Stuart Brisley, lighting design by David Ward).

[15] Four separate programmes that featured: (1) Gregory Nash/Sally Sykes/Rosemary Lee; (2) Patricia Bardi/Sue MacLennan/Ashley Page and Gaby Agis/Quinny Sacks; (3) Michael Popper/Lloyd Newson/Scott Clark/Anna Furse; (4) Gwylan Dance Company/Belinda Neave and Jessica Cohen.

[16] All programmes started after the main programmes at 9.45pm at The Place and featured: (1) Belinda Neave; (2) Matthew Hawkins; (3) Yolande Snaith; (4) Danielle Hogan/Cathy Jefferson; (5) Anne Seagrove.

[17] Three programmes of dance from the regions were presented at Riverside Studios and featured: Gwylen Dance Company/Jessica Cohen/Belinda Neave (Wales); English Dance Theatre (Newcastle); Howard and Eberle/The Morganisation (Wales).

[18] The Festival Finale was organised by Laurie Booth and Philip Jeck, and included a performance of part of their collaboration *Yip Yip Mix*; plus the Moving Picture Mime Show with a scene from *The Compleat Berk*; Richard Lindsay; The Ethiopian Music Group and The Royal Ballet's Morris Men.

[19] Performance artist Chouinard had created films, videos, drawings, installations and texts, as well as dances. For her UK debut she presented the premiere of *Earthquake in the Heartchakra*.

[20] Presented Armitage's *Watteau Duet* with musicians David Linton and Conrad Kinnard, design and lighting by Charles Atlas.

[21] In Gordon's constructions: *My Folks* (music, nineteenth-century East European Jewish klezmer, design, Power Boothe); *Offenbach Suite* (music Offenbach, lighting Beverley Emmons) and *Nine Lives* (lighting Robert Cedar).

[22] Presented both the film and the staged versions of *Rites of Passing* (in collaboration with film-maker Nancy Schreiber), and *Fine Line* (in collaboration with visual artist Deborah Freeman and composer Elliott Randall).

[23] Morris's ensemble of five dancers performed *Lovey* (music, the Violent Femmes); *I Love You Dearly*; *Deck of Cards*; *Retreat from Madrid, Jealousy* and *Minuet and Allegro in G* (music, Beethoven). All were UK premieres.

187

1985: Related Events

Films

Dance in Focus (ICA). A series of screenings of varied programmes with presentations by three leading filmmakers:

Patrick Bensard[1] presented a variety of dance films from the library of the Cinémathèque Française

Régine Chopinot, Philippe Decouflé, Daniel Larrieu, L'Esquisse, Hideyuki Yano[2]

Daphnis et Chloe (Groupe Emile Dubois, chor. Jean-Claude Gallotta) plus the work of François Verret and Maguy Marin

David Gordon and the Pick Up Company including *Limited Partnership* (dir. Kathryn Ascher), *Changing Horses* (dir. Edward Steinberg) and *Ten Minute TV* (dir. Gordon and Steinberg)

Videos produced by Susan Dowling of WGBH in Boston including *The Secret of the Waterfall* (dir. Charles Atlas, chor. Douglas Dunn), *Summer Dances, Bill and Arnie – An Affectionate Portrait* (dir. Geoff Dunlop)

Charles Atlas[3] presented a selection of his video works, including *Parafango*

Stefaan Decostere[4] presented his film *Dance & Camera*

Seminars

Independent Dancers: An Endangered Species[5] – open forum (ICA)

Dance in the Regions: A Tale of Two Cities[6] – open forum (Riverside Studios)

Classes and Workshops

Open classes and workshops.[7] Julyen Hamilton, Maedée Duprès, Michele Smith, Mark Morris, Betsy Gregory, Cathy Burge, Viola Farber, Daniel Larrieu, Tony Thatcher, Yaakov Slivkin, Sue MacLennan, Carolyn Choa, Risa Jaraslow

Dance improvisation workshop. Led by Kirstie Simson and Julyen Hamilton

Intermedia Project. Three workshops in dance, music and video, led by Sue MacLennan, Jane Wells and Peter Anderson

Meet the Choreographer

David Gordon, Mark Morris, Risa Jaroslow, Karole Armitage, Katie Duck

Associated Events

Allsorts Festival[8] (Sadler's Wells)
Spiral Dance Company[9]
National Youth Dance Theatre[10]
Suraya Hilal: *A major new initiative in Egyptian Dance*[11]
Alston study day[12] (The Place, Oct 20)
La La La Human Steps[13] (ICA, Nov 26 - 30)

Notes

[1] Head of the dance section of the Cinémathèque Française in Paris.

[2] Videos of the works of these five contemporary French choreographers, commissioned by the French Ministry of Culture.

[3] Filmmaker-in-residence for Merce Cunningham Dance Company, also designer and filmmaker for Karole Armitage and Michael Clark.

[4] Belgian filmmaker, director of Arts Services for Belgische Radio en Televisie since 1979.

[5] An informal meeting called by NODM to discuss the crisis in funding for independent dancers, chaired by Dr Mollie Davies, Head of Movement Studies at Roehampton Institute.

Katie Duck and Group 0, 1985. PHOTO: CHRIS NASH

6 The session focused on recent developments in dance in two cities, Cardiff and Newcastle, and formed part of Dance Umbrella's Regional Day. Chaired by Graeme Kay.

7 A series of classes and workshops taught daily by festival guests, in conjunction with the Independent Dance Programme.

8 The festival for young people presented daily dance performances and workshops for schools, plus a public performance of *UBU* with Fergus Early and Patricia Bardi, and a performance by Hammersmith Dance Theatre.

9 With a show made specially for International Youth Year, to introduce dance to young inner-city audiences. Ideas for the work arose from work done in the recent past by Spiral with Chinese, Asian and Black communities in Liverpool.

10 The company led a variety of classes during the day and gave a public performance in the evening.

11 Four evenings of dance and music from Egypt, plus Arabian food and refreshments.

12 An all-day session exploring the work of choreographer Richard Alston, including practical workshop, illustrated lecture and video session

13 In Edouard Lock's latest production *Human Sex*.

1986

Monday 6 October – Saturday 8 November (52 London performances)

Venues
London: French Institute's Artaud Theatre; Bloomsbury Theatre; Chisenhale Dance Space;
  Donmar Warehouse; ICA; Place Theatre; Riverside Studios; Whitechapel Art Gallery
Bristol: Arnolfini
Danceabout North West: various venues throughout the Manchester region
Dursley, Gloucestershire: Prema Project
Nottingham: Midland Group
Oxford: St Paul's Arts Centre
Plymouth: Drum Theatre, Theatre Royal

Artists

Continental Europe
Compagnie Cré-Ange[1] (France)
Katie Duck and Allesandro Certini[2] (Italy)
Compagnie Preljocaj[3] (France)

UK
Adzido[4]
Gaby Agis and Kate Blacker[5]
Arc Dance Company[6]
Jonathan Burrows and Ashley Page[7]
Paul Clayden and Dancers[8]
Direct Current[9]
Maedée Duprès[10]
Fergus Early/Sue MacLennan/Pablo
  Ventura and Dancers[11]

Extemporary Dance Theatre[12]
Gregory Nash[13]
Josyulu Venkatachalapathi[14]
Flying Starts[15]
Final Flourish[16]

USA
Tim Miller and Douglas Sadownick[17]
Susan Marshall and Company[18]
Meredith Monk and Vocal Ensemble[19]
Stephen Petronio and Dancers[20]
Dana Reitz[21]
Steve Lacy and Jazz Ensemble/Douglas
  Dunn and Elsa Wolliaston[22]

Notes
[1] Presented *Eurydice Disparue* with a commissioned score by François Kokelaere, augmented by extracts from Glück and Verdi.

[2] Duck had been based in Italy, but was currently a member of staff at Dartington College. *Wild Card* for Dance Umbrella 86 involved live piano music, text and narration, all supplied by Alex Maguire.

[3] The company formed in December 1984 by Angelin Preljocaj in *Larmes Blanches* (music Bach, Balastre and Purcell), *Marche Noir* (score by Marc Kahnne augmented by Verdi) and *Peurs Bleues* (music Beethoven).

[4] The Adzido Community Project gave a performance followed by a workshop for children.

[5] Presented a collaborative project, *Trail*, that involved dancer/choreographer Agis and sculptor Blacker. Agis was choreographer-in-residence at Riverside and appeared with Charlotte Zerbey.

[6] Umbrella debut for the company formed in 1985 by Danish-born Kim Brandstrup and fellow LCDS graduates. Presented Brandstrup's *Chamber Play* and *The Soldier's Tale*.

[7] Music for Burrows's programme, which included *Hymns* and *Squash,* was composed and played live by Nicholas Wilson. Page collaborated with John-Marc Gowans for a new work *'Accident' Ballroom* (with designs by Spyros Coscinas), a Dance Umbrella commission, and also performed his duet *Refurbished Behaviour,* with Sue Hawkesley.

[8] Presented *Adverse Camber,* choreography and sound score by Clayden.

[9] The group was formed in 1984 by Michael Popper, a member of Second Stride. Here they presented Popper's *Mary Mary*, with a commissioned score by David Owen.

[10] In two new programmes, the first a double-bill of work by Arianna Economou, *I Owe*

You the Earth, and Kate Flatt's *La Divina* (design by Craig Givens). Duprès's second programme was a collaboration with composer John-Marc Gowans, and both provided live improvisations.

[11] The Electro-Acoustic Music Association installed a sophisticated sound system in Riverside's Studio II for two weeks and the choreographers were invited by Dance Umbrella to create new works to tapes selected from the EMAS library. MacLennan collaborated with visual artist David Ward on *Against Interpretation* (music William Schottstaedt).

[12] Presented a double-bill of Laurie Booth's *Elbow Room* and Steve Paxton's *Audible Scenery* with live music ranging from 'whistling to keyboards to percussion'.

[13] Co-ordinated and choreographed (with four group leaders who worked in Merseyside, Glasgow, Oxford and Leeds) the youth project *Momentum Rush* for a cast of 100 young people. *Momentum Rush* was directed by Ian Brown, had a commissioned score by James Beirne and included film by Bradford Independent Film Group, which was projected onto large screens as part of the performance environment.

[14] Joined by members of the Academy of Indian Dance in a programme that featured popular Indian tales for children.

[15] Umbrella 86 began with Flying Starts – two 'cabaret' evenings at the ICA, which featured entertainment by Stephen Petronio, The Cholmondeleys, Jiving Lindy Hoppers, William Tuckett and Ra Ra Zoo and was hosted by Ralf Ralf.

[16] The final-night party was held at Chisenhale Dance Space and featured music and cabaret entertainment by members of the Chisenhale collective and guests Michael Popper, dancers from the Maguire O'Shea Academy of Irish Dancing and members of the Trinidad Tent Theatre Company.

[17] Presented *Buddy Systems*, which included music, text and visual design, all by Miller.

[18] This was Marshall's UK debut. The company presented *Opening Gambits*, *Arena*, *Ward* (music by Linda Fisher) and *Arms*. Guillermo Resto of the Mark Morris Company was one of the dancers.

[19] Monk performed with seven members of her company, The House, in *Turtle Dreams: Cabaret*, a production that included film, dance and live music. C4 screened Monk's *Ellis Island* on 16 October to coincide with the Riverside performances.

[20] This was Petronio's UK choreographic debut (previously he had performed with Trisha Brown's Company and with her in Dance Umbrella 83). Presented *#3* (to music by Lenny Pickett, *Dance Music for Borneo Horns, No. 5*), *The Sixth Heaven* (to Pat Irwin's jazz score of the same name) and *Walk-In* with a score by David Linton, *Dias de Fugeo y Muerte*. (Linton was last seen at the Festival with Karole Armitage in Dance Umbrella 85.)

[21] Dance Umbrella 86 artist-in-residence. Presented *Solo in Silence*, as well as teaching classes and choreographic workshops.

[22] Presented a dance-theatre piece. *Futurities*, a collaboration between jazz saxophonist Lacy, American writer Robert Creeley (whose poetry Lacy set to music), painter Kenneth Noland, choreographer/dancer Douglas Dunn and African-born dancer Elsa Wolliaston.

1986: Related Events

Film and Video
'Dance Lines' Video Poject[1] (Riverside Studio I)

Seminars
Making Television Dance: New Initiatives[2] (ICA), open forum
Dance Videos: The Promotional Tool of the Future?[3] (ICA), open forum

Classes and Workshops

Music and dance workshops. Meredith Monk and company members, for professional dancers and musicians; John-Marc Gowans and Maedée Duprès, open workshop; Stephen Montague and Sue MacLennan, open workshop; Douglas Dunn and Steve Lacy.

Maedée Duprès,
Riverside Studios, 1986.
PHOTO: CHRIS HARRIS

Independent Dance Programme (in collaboration with Dance Umbrella). Classes and workshops held by Stephen Petronio; Dana Reitz; Tim Miller; Mestre Panca (Capoeira); Gaby Agis

Meet the Choreographer
Dana Reitz, Stephen Petronio, Meredith Monk

Associated Events
Education: DaCi Evening[4] (Logan Hall, Oct 11); the Adzido Community Project (see main events); Josyulu Venkatachalapathi (see main events)

Notes

[1] A four-week project, the initiative of video-maker Terry Braun and designer Peter Mumford in conjunction with Limehouse Productions and Channel 4. The project involved twelve dancers, plus choreographers Siobhan Davies and Ian Spink who created experimental dance performances for and with TV. During the final week the public had access to recording sessions, and a library of tapes was available in the 'video lounge' for viewing by appointment.

[2] The four key artists from the 'Dance Lines' project, Mumford, Braun, Davies and Spink, were joined by video/film makers and producers from Europe in a discussion led by the BBC's Bob Lockyer.

[3] A debate chaired by Jodi Myers, Assistant Controller of Touring at the Arts Council.

[4] National launch of Dance and the Child International, with a gala performance by young people between 7 and 18 years of age from all over the UK.

1987

Wednesday 14 October – Saturday 14 November (54 London performances)

Venues

London: Almeida Theatre; ICA; Place Theatre; Riverside Studios; Sadler's Wells
Brighton: Gardner Arts Centre, University of Sussex
Bristol: Arnolfini
Cardiff: Chapter Arts
Dursley: Prema Project
Leicester: Leicester Polytechnic
Manchester: Royal Northern College of Music; The Green Room
Plymouth: Drum Theatre

Artists

Continental Europe
Rosas[1] (Belgium)
Sosta Palmizi[2] (Italy)
Studio DM[3] (France)
Marc Vanrunxt and Hyena[4] (Belgium)

UK
Laurie Booth and Harry de Wit[5]
The Cholmondeleys[6]
Direct Current[7]
DV8 Physical Theatre[8]
Extemporary Dance Theatre[9]
Images Dance Company[10]

National Youth Dance Company[11]
Ashley Page and Dancers[12]
New Works Platforms[13]
Flying Starts[14]

International
Eiko and Koma[15] (Japan/USA)

USA
Trisha Brown and Company[16]
Victoria Marks Performance Company[17]
Stephen Petronio Company[18]
Urban Bush Women[19]

Notes

[1] Formed in 1983 by Anne Teresa De Keersmaeker, who made her UK debut in Dance Umbrella 82, with Michele Anne de Mey. Presented *Bartok/Aantekeningen* (1986) to Bartók's *Fourth String Quartet*. The piece also included Charlotte Corday's monologue from Peter Weiss's play, *Marat/Sade* and text from George Buchner's *Lenz*, spoken by the dancers. Rosas also appeared at the ICA in December.

[2] Performed in Manchester and Cardiff only.

[3] Catherine Divèrres and Bernado Montet trained at the Mudra School and then studied Butoh in Japan with Kazuo Ohno. Presented *Instance* (1983).

[4] Presented *A Dieu* to a soundtrack by Thierry Genicot and Marie-Jeanne Wijckmans, that included excerpts from Offenbach's *Gaité Parisienne*.

[5] Presented *A Bone to Pick*.

[6] Appeared as leading performers in both 'Flying Starts' programmes, presenting *The Big Dance Number* and *Marina* among other dances.

[7] Presented *The Superhero Project* or *What are You Doing Eugene?*, with script by Marcia Kahan and a live score by David Owen.

[8] Formed in the Summer of 1986, here presented a new work commissioned by Dance Umbrella, *My Body, Your Body*. Performances were sold out and an extra performance was added.

[9] Presented *Grace and Glitter*, made and performed by an all-woman team, co-directors, Emilyn Claid and Maggie Semple, live music by Sylvia Hallett and Lucy Wilson, designs by Jacqueline Dunn and script by Tasha Fairbanks.

[10] Formed in 1986 and winners of Concours Chorégraphique International de Bagnolet, here presented *Left of Centre*, *Filligree* and *Penumbra*, commissioned by Dance Umbrella. These were all collaborations between choreographer Earl Hepburn, composer Walter Fabeck, designer Joanna Parker and lighting specialist Tina McHugh.

[11] Presented new work by Lucy Bethune,

Susan Crow, Viola Farber and Janet Smith, plus a solo by Namron, Sharon Wray's *it be glory* and the finale from Tony Lardge's *Blood Dance.*

[12] Presented a Dance Umbrella commission: *The Angel of Death is in My Bed Tonight* to an electronic score by 'this heat', with costumes and set by Isobel Work (a hanging metal mobile) and lighting by Anthony Bowne.

[13] In two programmes: (1) Jayne Lee/Ingegerd Lonnroth/Jonathan Lunn; (2) Suzie Ater and Scott Clark/Lucy Fawcett/Gregory Nash/Catherine Tucker.

[14] Flying Starts once again opened the festival, this time with four performances, two nights each of two programmes in cabaret format. Both featured Rose English as MC and the shows included The Cholmondeleys (in both programmes), the B-Shops Saxaphone Quartet, Rosemary Lee, a ballet by William Tuckett, Adventures in Motion Pictures, Pushkala Gopal and Unnikrishnan, Pyramid, Edgar Newman, 4D, Laurie MacLeod and Dwight Powell.

[15] Performed *Grain* which incorporated video, and for which they received a Bessie Award in New York in 1984.

[16] Presented *Set and Reset* and *Opal Loop*, both shown in Dance Umbrella 83, plus *Newark* (1987) to a score by American composer Peter Zummo and designs by Donald Judd.

[17] Presented five short works made between 1985 and 1987: *Solo* (design by Swanger, film by Phillip Jones and Marks), *What Holds You* (in collaboration with visual artists Lorie Novack and Janet Zweig, using slide projections), *Armed Response* (with music by Rhys Chatam), *Java Jumping* (with slides by Lorie Novack), and *A Last Place* (with music by the Bulgarian Women's Choir). Marks began a seven-month residency at The Place Theatre with these performances, culminating in a performance for Spring Loaded in 1988.

[18] Presented two works to percussive scores by David Linton, *Walk-In* (seen the previous year), new work *Simulacrum Reels* (set by Justin Terzi, costumes by Yonson Pak), which received its UK premiere, and *# 3*, a solo seen the previous year.

[19] Directed by Jawole Willa Jo Zollar, who appeared in London in February during the season 'Parallels in Black'. Presented *Girlfriends, Anarchy, Wild Women and Dinah, The Aretha Chronicles* and *New Moon Fantasies.* The performances involved jazz and folk musicians, and the seven dancer-actresses also sang and chanted. Jawole also made a piece for Union Dance Company.

1987: Related Events

Film and Video

Video screenings at the ICA
1. *Alive from off centre: Geography and Metabolism*[1]
   Airdance and *Landings* (chor. Elizabeth Streb, dir. Michael Schwartz)
   Two pieces by Michael Clark and Charles Atlas, music by The Fall)
   Daytime Moon (chor. Min Tanaka, dir. Sandy Smolan)
   Women of the Calabash (dir. Skip Blumberg)
   Sticks on the Move (chor. Pooh Kaye and Elizabeth Ross)
   Aquamirabilis (chor. Dee MacCandless and Gene Menger)

2. *Spiegels*[2] (1983, chor. Bart Stuyf)
   Trio[3] (chor. Krisztina de Chatel, dir. Luk Blancquaert)

3. *Charon*[4] (chor. Mirjam Berns, Shusaku Takeuchi, Ed Wubbe and Julyen Hamilton, dir. Franz Zwartjes)
   Muurwerk[5] (chor. Roxane Huilmand[6])

Seminars
Perspectives: Dance Videos in Education,[7] open forum
Dance and the Media: as others see us[8]

Classes and Workshops

Technique classes: Stephen Petronio, Jeremy Nelson, Irene Hultman[9] (member of the Trisha Brown Company)

Workshops: Jawole Willa Jo Zollar, Victoria Marks, Lloyd Newson.

Delicious Movement: a weekend held by Eiko and Koma.

International Dance Course for Young People,[10] for young people aged 14–25

Meet the Choreographer

Extemporary Dance Theatre, Victoria Marks, Urban Bush Women, Ashley Page, Images, Lloyd Newson, Marc Vanrunxt, Stephen Petronio.

Associated Events

Chisenhale Dance Space held a collaborative project with the Camerawork gallery that focused on the relationships between photography and dance. Both venues featured programmes and exhibitions throughout November.

Notes

[1] A collaboration between Molissa Fenley and video artists John Sandborn and Mary Perillo.

[2] With music by Philip Glass, Johanna d'Almagnac, Samuel Barber, Chick Corea and Taj Mahal.

[3] With music by Warner van Es.

[4] Conceived by Ruth Meyer and with music by Harry de Wit.

[5] With music by Walter Hus.

[6] Huilmand performed with Rosas in Dance Umbrella 87.

[7] Organised jointly with the Arts Council's Dance Department.

[8] Representatives from the various media met with members of the dance profession to discuss dance's standing and status and how to improve it. Chaired by Chris Cook.

[9] Gave a technique/repertory workshop.

[10] Dance Umbrella, in conjunction with the London Borough of Hammersmith and Fulham gave an intensive one-week course in a variety of dance techniques. Morning classes were taught by festival performers including Victoria Marks, Rosemary Lee, members of the Urban Bush Women and Images Dance Company Afternoon creative workshops were taken by Joanna Blake, the Hammersmith dance fellow, with a showing at the end of the week.

1988

Sunday 16 October – Sunday 20 November (65 London performances)

Venues
London: ICA; Place Theatre; Riverside Studios and Gallery; Sadler's Wells; Whitechapel
  Art Gallery; Theatre Museum (Awards evening)
Brighton: Gardner Arts Centre, University of Sussex
Bristol: Arnolfini
Cardiff: Chapter
Dursley, Gloucestershire: Prema Project
Leeds: Northern School of Contemporary Dance
Leicester: Phoenix Arts
Liverpool: The Blackie
Manchester: The Green Room
Norwich: St Andrew's Hall
Plymouth: Drum Studio, Theatre Royal

Artists

Continental Europe
Compagnie Cré-Ange[1] (France)/Jean
  Gaudin[2] (France) (double bill)

UK
Gaby Agis and Bill Culbert[3]
Amici Integrated Dance Theatre
  Company[4]*
  /Hammersmith Dance Theatre[5] *
  /Islington Arts Factory-Young People's
  Dance Theatre[6]*
Siobhan Davies Dance Company[7]
Jane Dudley[8]
DV8 Physical Theatre[9]
Extemporary Dance Theatre[10]
Images Dance Company[11]
Ludus[12]*
Bruce McLean and David Ward[13]

National Youth Dance Company[14]
No-Go A-Go-Go[15]
Phoenix Dance Company[16]
Second Stride[17]
Yolande Snaith[18]/Company Blú[19]
Platform Performances[20]

International
Danceworks[21] (Australia)
La La La Human Steps[22] (Canada)

USA
Molissa Fenley [23]
Liz Lerman – Dance Exchange/Dancers of
  the Third Age[24]*
Urban Bush Women[25]
Randy Warshaw Dance Company[26]

London Dance and Performance Awards
The first Awards event was presented at the Theatre Museum on 16 October to launch the
10th Anniversary season of Dance Umbrella and was held in conjunction with *Time Out's*
20th anniversary. Awards were presented for:
Choreography: Rosemary Butcher, Lloyd Newson, Lea Anderson
Performers: Kirstie Simson, Philippe Giraudeau, Lucy Burge, Shobana Jeyasingh
Performance Art: Bow Gamelan, Rose English, Julian Maynard Smith, Alistair MacLennan
Exceptional Contributions: John Ashford, Fergus Early, George Dzikunu
Music: Orlando Gough, Stephen Montague
Design: Antony McDonald, Peter Mumford
Special Citation: Arts Admin

Notes

* Performers took part in the education week at Riverside Studios.

[1] Following his first appearance in Dance Umbrella 86, Charles Cré-Ange created a piece for Transitions at the Laban Centre. The company intended to show *L'Encontre* (which was to have incorporated a flashback sequence by David Buckland), but was prevented from doing so because of an injunction from the agent of Harold Pinter, upon whose play, *The Dumb Waiter,* the performance was based. The company performed *Blackmail* instead – a 'structured improvisation'.

[2] In a *pas de deux* by Gaudin for himself and Sophie Lessard, *L'Ascete de San Clemente et la Vierge Marie.*

[3] A collaboration between dancer Agis and installation artist Cullberg. Music included scores by Gavin Bryars, Michael Nyman and Père Ubu and a commissioned score by David Sylvian. The programme was commissioned by Dance Umbrella.

[4] The company was founded by Wolfgang Stange in 1976 and integrates people with and without disabilities. They showed a work in progress created by company members.

[5] Based at Riverside Studios and funded by the London Borough of Hammersmith and Fulham, the company presented a new work *Two Minute Grab*, directed by Joanna Blake.

[6] In a piece *Just Under*, choreographed by Images member Isabel Mortimer.

[7] The launch of Davies's new company with a programme of her own choreography commissioned to celebrate Dance Umbrella's 10th anniversary, *White Man Sleeps,* to music by Kevin Volans, performed live by the Degas String Quartet, and *Wyoming* with a commissioned score by John-Marc Gowans. The programme was subsequently filmed for C4.

[8] *Then and Now* was a programme of new and old dances by Dudley, created over a period of 50 years, and included: *Harmonica Breakdown* (1938), *The Lonely Ones* (1946), *Five Characters and Conclusion* (1978), *Paying My Dues* (1982), *Bird as Prophet* (1983), *Daybreak* (1986), *Spindrift* (1988) to music by Schumann and *Island; I see my City Again* (to Bartók's 4th Quartet), which was choreographed for this celebration.

[9] Lloyd Newson's company won a second Digital Dance Award for the creation of *Dead Dreams of Monochrome Men*, which was commissioned by the Third Eye Centre, Glasgow.

[10] Presented the London premiere of *Suddenly Out of The Blue*, which consisted of three out of four possible sections. Section one, *Where the Moon Rises*, was choreographed by leading aerialist Sue Broadway and performed on trapezes above the stage; section two, *Dead Steps,* was by Liz Aggiss; section three, *Pheasant China*, was a fusion of text by Tashe Fairbanks and movement by Emilyn Claid; section four, *Can Monsters Get Inside You Mrs Berry?*, was choreographed by Jacob Marley. Live music was commissioned from Billy Cowie, Sylvia Hallett, Stephanie Nunn and Jeremy Peyton Jones.

[11] Presented *Tectonics,* a collaboration with designer Inga Rogers and composer/musician Barry Ganberg. The work was part-commissioned by Dance Umbrella.

[12] Presented *The Whale in Your Back Yard*, a new dance theatre programme for children of primary school age and featuring live music.

[13] New collaborative works by sculptor McLean and photographic artist Ward, with dancers Catherine Tucker and Dennis Greenwood, in a programme entitled *A Ball is not a Dancing School.* This included *Partition* ('an architectural ballet in parts'), *In the Shadow of the Hat* and *Lullaby*, a collaboration between Ward and Greenwood. Performances were commissioned by Dance Umbrella.

[14] Presented Janet Smith's *Save the Last Dance* (score by Christopher Benstead), Kim Brandstrup's *Thracian Steps*, Aletta Collins's *Truce*, Tony Lardge's *Blood Dance*, Dwight Powell's *The Lady Sings the Blues* and Sheron Wray's *The Eye Fell on the Dance.*

[15] 'A cabaret of professional dancers', coordinated by Edgar Newman.

[16] The programme included the London premiere of *Revelations*, and *The Path* by Donald Edwards; Villmore James's *Leave Him Be* and Neville Campbell's *Misfits.*

[17] Presented *Dancing and Shouting*, with choreography by Ian Spink, design by Antony McDonald, music by Evelyn Ficarra, played live by Gemini. The programme was supported by a 1988 Digital Dance Award and an Arts Council Composers for Dance Award.

[18] Snaith was to have presented a work-in-progress, *Lessons in Social Skills*, but was prevented through illness. Instead, she reworked her solo *Can Baby Jane Can Can?* for the festival.

[19] Presented *Verso la Madre del Turco*, a col-

laboration between Alessandro Certini (known here through his work with Group O), Julyen Hamilton, Sacha Waltz (who replaced Charlotte Zerby who was injured in a road accident) and musician Steve Noble.

[20] Two mixed programmes of new work by: Adventures in Motion Pictures; Caroline Pope and Darlene Stevens; Ingegerd Lonnroth; The Chaos Sisters; Jeanne Ayling and Kate Dalton (Saturday performance only).

[21] Danceworks' artistic director, Nanette Hassall worked with the first British independent dance group, Strider. One of the dancers was injured in Norwich prior to the London performances, and so only two of the three works were performed with the remaining seven dancers: *As the Crow Flies* and *Gond-Wana-Dance* which included live music by Gondwanaland, a group that mixes indigenous Australian instruments with electronic sound.

[22] Presented Edouard Lock's 1987 work *New Demons,* to live electronic music by the West India Company.

[23] In a solo performance of *State of Darkness*

to Stravinsky's *Rite of Spring, Forgotten Memories* (an excerpt from the full-length *Esperanto*) to wind chimes and percussion by Ryuchi Sakamoto, and a new solo, *Provenance Unknown*, to a score by Philip Glass.

[24] Lerman's two companies Dance Exchange, consisting of young performers and Dancers of the Third Age (performers in their fifties and sixties), presented performances, workshops and lectures. This was the UK debut for both companies.

[25] A return appearance of the dance/theatre company rooted in the folklore and religious traditions of African American Women. Edwina Lee Tyler, composer, choreographer, percussionist, vocalist and dancer, appeared as a guest.

[26] Warshaw danced with the Trisha Brown Company before setting up his own group in 1986. The company performed *Sanctus* with a commissioned score from John Cale, and *Fragile Anchor* with designs by Yugoslav artist Miran Mohar.

1988: Related Events

Film and Video

Video screenings (ICA)
  Vigil,[1] plus a selection from the 'Alive from Off-Center'[2] season: *Commitment, 2 Portraits*;[3] *Dancing Hands*;[4] *Number 3*;[5] *Endance*[6]
  Premier Danceur (dir. Andreas Missler-Morrell); *Passages* (chor. Michael Pink, dir. Chris Bowman); *Opus 123*[7]

Film season (The Cinema,[8] Riverside Studios)
  Carlos Saura and Antonio Gades triple bill: *Blood Wedding* (1981), *Carmen* (1983), *A Love Bewitched* (1986)
  West Side Story (1961, chor. Jerome Robbins, dir. Robert Wise)
  The Red Shoes (1948, Michael Powell/Emeric Pressburger)
  Black Orpheus (1958, Marcel Camus)

Seminars
Study Day organised by the Society for Dance Research in collaboration with Dance Umbrella to celebrate the tenth birthday.[9]
Dangerous Liaisons?: Towards an International Performance Network[10] – open forum
Coming of Age: An Investigation into Growing Older[11] – open forum

Classes and Workshops
Creative workshops. Lloyd Newson (Connecting Meaning to Movement: all-day workshops); Ludus (for 7–11 age range); Ian Spink; Dance Exchange/Dancers of the Third Age

Technique classes. Nanette Hassall, Molissa Fenley, Scott Clark

Meet the Artists
Second Stride, Danceworks, Urban Bush Women, DV8, Jean Gaudin, Molissa Fenley, Randy Warshaw, Siobhan Davies, Extemporary Dance Theatre

Associated Events
Education week at Riverside Studios (15–19 November). Participants included Amici Integrated Dance Theatre Company, Hammersmith Dance Theatre, Islington Arts Factory – Young People's Dance Theatre, Ludus, Liz Lerman's Dance Exchange/Dancers of the Third Age. See main event.

Deca
Dance: Gala Programme to celebrate Ten Years of Dance Umbrella
Sadler's Wells Theatre – 31 January 1988
Compèred by Tom Jobe, the gala included performances by:

Adventures in Motion Pictures
Gaby Agis
Bow Street Rappers (Royal Ballet morris dancers)
Michael Clark and Company
Scott Clark
Michael Corder
Compagnie Charles Cré-Ange
4D
David Glass

Philippe Giraudeau and Lizie Saunderson
Pushkala Gopal and Unnikrishnan
Gary Lambert
Ashley Page and Ian Spink in 'Popular Song' from Ashton's *Façade*
David Parsons
Steve Paxton
Ralf Ralf
Rambert Dance Company
Second Stride
Kenneth Tharp
Randy Warshaw

Notes

[1] A collaboration between choreographer Suzanne Watson and video artists Nicola Baldwin and Richard Hodson.

[2] From Twin Cities Public Television: KTCA/TV in Minneapolis.

[3] A treatment of two pieces choreographed and performed by Blondell Cummings and directed by Bernard Herbert.

[4] A collage of dance images directed by Skip Blumberg.

[5] Solo by Stephen Petronio, directed by Jean-Louis le Tacon.

[6] Collaboration between choreographer Tim Buckley and video maker John Sanborn with music by Blue 'Gene' Tyranny.

[7] An abstract treatment of dance images by Chris Bowman.

[8] Newly opened.

[9] The day included a contextual and historical overview of Umbrella's development, interviews with Val Bourne and Fiona Dick, plus an illustrated lecture on Second Stride by Stephanie Jordan.

[10] In which was discussed the possibility of setting up a network along the lines of the national Performance Network in America, set up to support and encourage emerging experimental, minority and non-mainstream performing artists.

[11] Liz Lerman, artistic director of Dance Exchange/Dancers of the Third Age in open discussion with others on the topic of ageism in dance and age-related issues.

199

1989

Monday 9 October – Saturday 18 November (57 London performances)

Venues[1]
London: ICA; Place Theatre; Riverside Studios; Sadler's Wells; South Bank Centre, Queen Elizabeth Hall*
Basildon: Towngate Theatre
Brighton: Gardner (Arts) Centre, University of Sussex
Bristol: Arnolfini Live
Bury St Edmunds: Theatre Royal
Colchester: University of Essex Theatre
Coventry: Arts Centre, University of Warwick
Leicester: Phoenix Arts
Manchester: Green Room
Norfolk: City College[2]

Artists

Continental Europe
Compagnie Cré-Ange[3] (France)
Groupe Emile Dubois[4] (France)
Compagnie Angelin Preljocaj[5] (France)
Roc in Lichen[6] (France)
Studio DM[7] (France)

UK
Laurie Booth and Company[8]
The Cholmondeleys[9]
Extemporary Dance Theatre[10]
Siobhan Davies Company[11]
National Youth Dance Company[12]

Yolande Snaith[13]
Second Stride[14]
Young Choreographers of the Royal Ballet companies and school[15]
Platform Performances (British Independents for Bagnolet)[16]

International
Karas Company[17] (Japan)

USA
Merce Cunningham Dance Company[18]

Notes
* The first time this venue had been used.
The 1989 London Dance and Performance Awards took place at the Royal Festival Hall immediately prior to the first Festival performance, which featured Groupe Emile Dubois in the Queen Elizabeth Hall.
[1] This year, in addition to the London Festival, regional touring concentrated on one company, Cré-Ange, which visited seven centres. The Siobhan Davies Dance Company appeared in Coventry and The Chomondeleys in Bristol.
[2] Part of the Norfolk and Norwich French Festival.
[3] Presented *Noir Salle*, based upon Molière's *Le Misanthrope* for the Umbrella. The company also opened the Leicester International Dance Festival in March.
[4] Choreographer Jean-Claude Gallotta and his company presented *Mammame* with a jazz/rock score by Henri Torge and Serge Houppin.
[5] Presented *Liqueurs de Chair*, with a sound

collage by Laurent Petitgand.
[6] UK debut for the company, which performed *Grenadier Weaver* on three vertical walls. During the interval a video of the company's first performance *Le Creux Poplite* was shown: a piece in which the set had been transported to the sheer face of a gorge in Verdon and the performance filmed by helicopters. *Grenadier Weaver* featured contemporary music by Glenn Branca and Sonic Youth.
[7] Return of French duo Catherine Divèrres and Bernado Montet after two years' absence, with other company members in *Fragment,* premiered at the festival after the choreographers' month-long residence at the Laban Centre. The piece had a sound score by Eijo Nakasawa and lighting by Pierre-Yves Lohier, Studio DM's regular collaborators.
[8] Presented *Terminus Terminux* in association with the Third Eye Centre, Glasgow, by whom it was originally commissioned as part

of its New Move season in January 1989. The work formed the second part of the trilogy *Danse Noire,* made in collaboration with audiovisual artist Lol Sargent and composer Philip Jeck. Booth was joined by dancers Sally Doughty, Helen Stanley, Nick Pile and Fin Walker.

[9] Premiere of Lea Anderson's *Flesh and Blood*, with a specially commissioned chamber-systems/jazz score by Steve Blake, performed live. The work was awarded a Digital Dance Award 1989 during the Riverside Studios performances.

[10] Presented *Up To Something*, a show in three parts including *101 Scenes from the Revolution* by Michael Popper; *Private Heart* by Karen Greenhough and *The Peculiar Grin* by Kevin Finnan and Louise Richards. The show featured live music by Stephanie Nunn, Paul Bartholomew and Andrew Dodge.

[11] Presented two new works, *Cover Him With Grass* to music by Kevin Volans, and *Drawn Breath* to specially commissioned live music by Andrew Poppy.

[12] Performed works by Peter Curtis, Earl Lloyd Hepburn, Shobana Jeyasingh, Jacob Marley, Euan Forbes and Evan Williams. The company's evening performance included a special appearance by the Hammersmith Youth Dance Group.

[13] Snaith and partner Kathy Crick presented *Germs: Advanced Lessons in Social Skills,* which included film.

[14] Ian Spink's new work for the company, *Heavan Ablaze in His Breast,* was premiered at the festival. Spink collaborated with director Antony McDonald, who also designed the piece, and with Vocem Electric Voice Theatre. Two pianists performed a specially commissioned score by Judith Weir.

[15] The Royal Ballet Choreographic Group under Norman Morrice, in collaboration with Dance Umbrella, presented a revival of Ashley Page's *This is what you get* (1985), two new works by company members Simon Rice and William Tuckett, and three new works by students at the School (Matthew Hart, Francesca Trippa and Evan Williams).

[16] The programme comprised four platform performances for British choreographers to showcase works for consideration by the Bagnolet International Choreographic Competition director Lorrina Niclas, for entrance in the 1990 Independent Choreographers section. Liz Aggiss and Lea Anderson were invited to take part in the 1990 competition as a result.

[17] UK debut for Saburo Teshigawara and the Karas Company, who presented *Ishi No Hana* (The Stone Garden). Teshigawara studied sculpture before becoming involved in classical ballet and mime

[18] The company's first performance for Dance Umbrella included five British premieres: *Inventions* (1989), *Field and Figures* (1989), *Carousal* (1986), *Cargo X* (1989) and *Eleven* (1988); plus *Rainforest* (1968), *Pictures* (1984) (which won a Laurence Olivier Award in 1985), *Points in Space* (1987), *Fabrications* (1987) and a revival of *Native Green* (1985). The opening night of Programme Two was the first time that the company had ever performed without Cunningham himself dancing. See also 'Related events'.

1989: Related Events

Film and Video
Video screenings:[1] (ICA Theatre)
Film season[2] (The Cinema, Riverside Studios)

Seminars
Revolutionary Tactics: French Lessons in Political Skills[3]
Get It In Writing: NODM meeting[4] (Riverside Studios, 12 November)
Montpellier conference: Panorama of Dance in Northern Europe[5]
Anglo-French Colloque[6] (French Institute)

Classes and Workshops

Classes. Cunningham (2)

Workshops. Compagnie Cré-Ange, Laurie Booth, Scott Clark, Second Stride (whole day), Studio DM

Michael Clark in *Heterospective,* at the Anthony d'Offay Gallery, 1989. PHOTO: CHRIS NASH

Cunningham Study Day[7] (Sadler's Wells, November 4)

Meet the Artists[8]
With participants from: Groupe Emile Dubois; Compagnie Cré-Ange; Roc in Lichen; Compagnie Angelin Preljocaj.

Exhibitions
Cocteau et la Danse[9] (French Institute), accompanied by two films: *Le Jeune Homme et la Mort* and *Phèdre* (Dominique Delouche)
Dancers on a Plane[10] (Anthony d'Offay Gallery, 31 October – 2 December) John Cage, Merce Cunningham, Jasper Johns
Andy Warhol Retrospective[11] (Hayward Gallery)

Associated Performances
Heterospective[12] - Michael Clark (Anthony d'Offay Gallery, 14–24 October)

Legs Eleven: Dance Umbrella Gala
5 February, Sadler's Wells Theatre. A gala to celebrate the second decade of Dance Umbrella. Since it coincided with the bicentenary, it seemed appropriate to have a French flavour. Compèred by Christopher Gable.

Artists

Continental Europe
Compagnie Cré-Ange[13] (France)
Michel Kelemenis[14] (France)
Vicente Saez[15] (Spain)

UK
Peter Adegboyega Badejo[16]
Adventures in Motion Pictures[17]
Laurie Booth and Philip Jeck[18]
Central School of Ballet[19]

Cholmondeleys and Featherstonehaughs[20]
Graham Fletcher[21]
London Festival Ballet[22]
Matthew Hart[23]
Michael Popper/Gateway to Freedom[24]
Transitions[25]
William Tuckett and Dancers[26]

USA
Charles Moulton and Company[27]

Notes
[1] The ICA ran programmes of specially selected French dance videos.
[2] Presented in consultation with the Cinemathèque de la Danse in Paris.
[3] A debate about the public and political profile of dance in the UK in comparison with France, and what and how we can learn from the French experience. Speakers included: Brigitte Lefèvre (dance delegate of the French Ministry of Culture) and choreographers Dominique Bagouet and Karine Saporta.
[4] Open meeting for choreographers and administrators to launch the *Choreographers' Handbook*.
[5] As part of the 'Revolutionary Tactics' initiative, Dance Umbrella organised a package tour to Montpellier from 3 to 9 July, to coincide with the Montpellier Dance Festival and with this conference. The conference focused on Belgium, Britain and The Netherlands, and British representatives included David Prateley, Richard Alston, Lloyd Newson, Peter Kyle and John Ashford.
[6] Dance Umbrella invited eighteen leading personalities in French dance, led by Brigitte Lefèvre, to meet their opposite numbers from this country for a one-day conference.
[7] Included talks by the choreographer, contributions from David Tudor and David Vaughan and opportunities to view two of the works (Programme Two) in rehearsal.
[8] Sessions presented by Oonagh Duckworth, Dance Umbrella's French consultant.
[9] To mark the centenary of Cocteau's birth, the show included models, designs, photographs, costumes, drawings and documents relating to his association with dance.
[10] An exhibition of works by Merce Cunningham, John Cage and Jasper Johns to coincide with the Sadler's Wells season.
[11] Included Warhol's silver inflatables for *Rainforest*.
[12] Performed in the upper rooms of the gallery, with part of the action taking place in two adjoining rooms so that the audience had to peer through doorways.
[13] Presented an extract from *Noir Salle*.
[14] Presented a piece by Kelemenis and Priscilla Danton, *Faune Fomitch*.
[15] In *Ens*, 1987.
[16] In *Ijo Ayo*, with musicians Boladji Adeola, Ayam Amoo, Bode Lawal and Rufus Orishayomi.
[17] Presented *Kalenda Maia*, a work specially created for the company by French choreographer Brigitte Farges.
[18] In a specially devised improvisation.
[19] Presented a short demonstration of contemporary classwork.
[20] In an extract from *Flag*, 'Five Finalists'.
[21] In *First Time Live*.
[22] In Christopher Bruce's *Swansong*.
[23] In his own solo choreography *And I*.
[24] Presented Popper's *O Speako Tico*.
[25] Presented *Naufragés*, a work specially created for the company by French choreographer Claude Brumachon.
[26] In Tuckett's *You May May You Find*.
[27] In Moulton's *Nine Person Precision Ball Passing*.

1990

Saturday 6 October – Saturday 10 November (35 London performances, including the gala evening)

Venues
London: Place Theatre; Riverside Studios; Sadler's Wells; Queen Elizabeth Hall, South Bank Centre
Bracknell: Wilde Theatre, South Hill Park Arts Centre
Bristol: Arnolfini
Newcastle:[1] Theatre Royal, Playhouse, Gulbenkian Studio Theatre, Newcastle Arts Centre
Northampton: Derngate

Artists

Continental Europe
Groupe Emile Dubois[2] (France)

UK
Laurie Booth[3]
The Cholmondeleys[4]
Siobhan Davies Dance Company[5]
Diversions Dance Company[6]
Extemporary Dance Theatre[7]

Shobana Jeyasingh Dance Company[8]
National Youth Dance Theatre[9]
Yolande Snaith's Dance Quorum[10]
Jonathan Stone (Ralf Ralf)[11]

USA
Margaret Jenkins Dance Company[qw]
Susan Marshall and Company[13]
Stephen Petronio Company[14]

Awards Gala
Sadler's Wells Theatre, 7 October (during which the London Dance and Performance Awards were presented, a joint Dance Umbrella/*Time Out* venture).

Gala artists: featuring a number of past award winners or their representative companies, including *. Presented by participants Rose English, John Ashford and Nigel Charnock.

UK
Adzido* [15]
Jonathan Burrows and Dancers[16]
Michael Clark[17]
Siobhan Davies Company* [18]
The Featherstonehaughs* [19]
Suraya Hilal*[20]

Shobana Jeyasingh*[21]
Phoenix Dance Company[22]
Artists from Rambert Dance Company [23]

USA
Stephen Petronio and Jeremy Nelson[24]

Notes
[1] This formed part of Newcastle Dance 90 (November 3 – December 8). See 'Regional Festivals'.

[2] Jean-Claude Gallotta's company presented *Les Mystères de Subal* (1990), with music by Henry Torgue and designs by Jean-Yves Langlais.

[3] Presented *Spatial Decay II* in collaboration with sound artist Hans Peter Kuhn and performed with Russell Maliphant. The performance was developed as a Dance Umbrella 90 commission from a quartet first presented at the 1990 Spring Loaded season.

[4] The company premiered *Cold Sweat*, with two specially commissioned scores by Steve Blake and Drostan Madden, performed live, and with costumes by Sandy Powell.

[5] The company presented *Different Trains* (a Dance Umbrella 90 commission) to music by Steve Reich played live by the Smith Quartet, and including train sounds and spoken text; and *White Man Sleeps* (1988).

6 Umbrella debut for the company, with works choreographed by Quinny Sacks (*Over the Edge*), David Dorfman (*Oakfield Ridge*) and Roy Campbell-Moore (*Caprice*). The company won a 1990 Digital Dance Award for the production of a work by Bill T. Jones.

7 Presented the London premiere of Sean Walsh's *A Flaming Desire,* with music by Trevor Jones and Stephanie Nunn, design by Tim Hatley.

8 Presented the premiere of *Correspondences*, a full-length dance-opera in collaboration with composer Kevin Volans and theatre director Steve Shill. The music was performed live by The Smith Quartet and actor-singer Llewellyn Rayappen. The company was awarded its second Digital Dance Award in 1990.

9 With recreated work by Janet Smith (*Con Spirito*), Shobana Jeyasingh (*Janpath*) and Mark Bruce; and new work by Matthew Hart and NYDC dancers Craig James, Mark Mitchell, Peter Anderson and Jonathan Mitchell. A new work by Chick Eldridge included a specially commissioned score by Matteo Fargion.

10 This was the launch of Snaith's new company with *Court by the Tale,* produced in collaboration with film maker Peter Carlton, with film sections screened intermittently throughout the piece, and lighting by Anthony Bowne.

11 Stone's first major project, *Dinner,* for Ralf Ralf, was a British–American co-production with set design by Rae Smith. The company featured an international cast.

12 The company's debut Umbrella appearance included *Shelf Life* (1987), with text narrated by collaborator Rinde Eckert and score performed live by the Paul Dresher Ensemble; *Miss Jacobi Weeps* (1989), also with live music

composed by Miguel Frasconi, performed by Frasconi and Gene Reffkin; and *Woman Window Square* (1990) with text and score by Rinde Eckert.

13 Presented *Family Quartet & Duet* (1988, music, Luis Resto); *Kiss* (1987, music by Arvo Pärt); and the world premiere of *Contenders* (with a commissioned score by Pauline Oliveros), a specially commissioned work by Brooklyn Academy of Music's Next Wave Festival. All dances were billed as the products of a choreographic process involving movement and idea contributions from the dancers.

14 Petronio presented a solo, *#3* (1986, music, Lenny Pickett); and a duet with Jeremy Nelson, *Surrender II* (1989, music, David Linton). The company also performed the British premiere of *MiddleSex Gorge* (music, Wire) and the London premiere of *AnAmnesia* (music, Peter Gordon).

15 In an extract from *Under African Skies*, choreography by George Dzikunu.

16 In an extract from *Stoics*.

17 Performed solo.

18 In an extract from *White Man Sleeps*.

19 Performed *Strangers*.

20 In *Drum Improvisation*.

21 In an exclusive performance of a stage version of *Late* (a work specially commissioned by the BBC Late Show) in collaboration with composer Orlando Gough.

22 Winners at the 1990 Bagnolet International Choreographic Competition, with an extract from *Human Scandals*.

23 Mark Baldwin and Amanda Britton in an extract from Richard Alston's *New York Counterpoint*.

24 Performed the duet *Surrender II*.

1990: Related Events

Film and Video
Dance film and video season: (The Cinema, Riverside Studios)
1. *Twyla Tharp: Making TV Dance* (USA, 1990) + supporting programme
2.[1] *Memories of Jazz*[2] + an extract from *The Spirit Moves*[3] (1950, director Mura Dehn)
3. Taped: Dance and Videos in Education[4]
   Flesh and Blood: The Cholmondeleys (1990, dir. Margaret Williams)[5]
   Jazz Dance: The Jiving Lindy Hoppers (1990, dir. Yossi Bal)
   Egg Dances: Rosemary Lee (1990, dir. Peter Anderson)

Seminars
Devolution to Greater London Arts: Cause for Concern or Celebration?[6]

Dance Umbrella: The First Twenty-One Years

Classes and Workshops

Classes (Place Theatre). Lloyd Newson;[7] Margaret Jenkins; Scott Clark (Feldenkrais)

Workshops: (Place Theatre). Stephen Petronio; Laurie Booth; Shobana Jeyasingh; Lloyd Newson.

Meet the Artists
Stephen Petronio; Groupe Emile Dubois;[8] Siobhan Davies; Shobana Jeyasingh; Diversions Dance Company; Margaret Jenkins; Laurie Booth; Susan Marshall; Yolande Snaith; The Cholmondeleys

Exhibitions
Beyond Dance (Portfolio Gallery), photography by Chris Nash[9]

Notes
[1] Programme 2 was screened in association with the Cinémathèque de la Danse, Paris.

[2] From the collection of Jo Milgram. Performers include Sammy Davis Jnr, Betty Boop, Fats Waller, Louis Armstrong, Duke Ellington and Slim and Slam.

[3] A record of the Saturday night lindy-hop dance competitions at the Savoy Ballroom, Harlem.

[4] Premieres of the 1990 winners of the Arts Council/British Council scheme to encourage high-quality dance videos for use in education. In association with the Arts Council.

[5] Lea Anderson was present at the screening for discussion.

[6] To consider the prospects of the sixty London-based dance companies and independent artists funded at the time by the Arts Council, and now coming under the funding remit of the GLA. Hosted by the NODM and chaired by David Pratley (chair of the National Campaign for the Arts).

[7] The first British artist-in-residence at Dance Umbrella, Newson had been awarded a Digital Premier Award in 1989. DV8 did not perform during the 1990 festival, but instead Newson led the 'meet the artists' sessions and held weekend workshops and classes for professional dancers.

[8] Chris de Marigny led the discussion with Jean-Claude Gallotta.

[9] The exhibition featured a selection of recent commissions and collaborations, such as those with Lauren Potter, Siobhan Davies, Jonathan Lunn and Viviana Durante.

1991

Sunday 6 October – Saturday 16 November (51 London performances, including the gala)

Venues
London: Cabot Hall, Canary Wharf;* Chisenhale Gallery; ICA; Place Theatre; Riverside
    Studios Royalty Theatre;* Sadler's Wells; Purcell Room,* South Bank Centre
Cambridge: Arts Theatre
Leicester: Phoenix Arts
Manchester: Green Room; Royal Northern College of Music
Newcastle upon Tyne: Newcastle Playhouse
Nottingham: The Playhouse

Artists

Continental Europe
L'Esquisse[1] (France)

UK
Gaby Agis[2]
Laurie Booth and Company[3]
Jonathan Burrows/Julyen Hamilton[4]
Rosemary Butcher[5]
Shobana Jeyasingh Dance Company[6]
Rambert Dance Company[7]
Valli Subbiah and Company[8]
Yolande Snaith's Dance Quorum[9]

International
Eiko and Koma[10] (Japan/US)
Pappa Tarahumara[11] (Japan)
Saburo Teshigawara and Karas[12] (Japan)
Douglas Wright[13] (New Zealand)

USA
Trisha Brown Company[14]
Doug Elkins Dance Company[15]
Muscle Voice[16]

A Baker's Dozen Gala
The thirteenth Dance Umbrella festival opened with a charity gala to raise money for
Dance Umbrella's Commissioning Fund. Hosted by Wayne Sleep and Tom Jobe, the gala
was directed by Stephen Jefferies and featured 13 items.

Artists

UK
Laurie Booth and Russell Maliphant[17]
Shona Harper[18]
London Contemporary Dance Theatre[19]
Ashley Page and Ann de Vos[20]
Rambert Dance Company[21]
Scottish Ballet[22]

Tobias Tak [23]
Clair Thomas, Euan Forbes, Anna Tetlow
    and Andrew Stone[24]

USA
Bill T. Jones and Arthur Aviles[25]
Tim Miller[26]

London Dance Performance Awards (Dance Umbrella and *Time Out*) winners
Keith Khan, Wim Vandekeybus, Anne Teresa de Keersmaeker, Krystina Page, Germaine
Acogny and Arona N'Diaye, Caroline Broadhead and Rosemary Lee, Pushkala Gopal, Lea
Anderson, Dance Lines, Theresa Beattie, Anne Bean, Scott Clark, Russell Maliphant,
Second Stride, Yolande Snaith, Bobby Baker.

Notes
* New venues for the festival.
[1] The company founded by choreographers
Joelle Bouvier and Regis Obadia, presented the
'avant première' of *Une Femme Chaque Nuit Voy-*

age En Grand Secret, prior to its proper premiere in the Holland Dance Festival, and with
score commissioned from composer Guedalia
Tazartes. Films by the choreographers and a

photographic exhibition by collaborator Guy Delahaye appeared at the French Institute: see 'Related Events'.

2 Presented *A Cold Dark Matter* in collaboration with visual artist Cornelia Parker, performed in the Chisenhale Gallery, with music by Gavin Bryars, John Lever and Henry Threadgill.

3 Presented the London premiere of *New Text, New Kingdom,* a work produced in collaboration with Deborah Levy (text from *The Egyptian Book of the Dead,* spoken on tape by Booth), Graham Snow (design), Philip Jeck (sound) and Jeanne Spaziani (costumes).

4 In a shared programme: Burrows presented *Stoics* (1990), performed by fellow members of the Royal Ballet; Hamilton presented the London premiere of improvisational work *Of Solution and Answer and Understanding,* in collaboration with actress and director Jill Freud, with text by Elizabeth Pike.

5 Presented *Of Shadows and Walls,* produced in collaboration with video-maker Nicola Baldwin and composer Jim Fulkerson. On the opening night, Michael Popper and Lizie Saunderson performed with one fewer dancer because of injury.

6 In a programme, entitled *New Cities, Ancient Lands,* the company presented *Speaking of Sakti* with choreography commissioned from Chandralekha to music by V.V. Subrahanyam, recorded in Madras; and two dances choreographed by Jeyasingh, *Late* (1990, music, Orlando Gough) and *Byzantium* (music, Christos Hatzis).

7 Presented two programmes, which included: *Four Elements* (1990) by Lucinda Childs (designs by Jennifer Bartlett); Laurie Booth's *Completely Birdland* (1991), his first work for the company, and in collaboration with Graham Snow (set design), Jeanne Spaziani (costumes) and composer Hans Peter Kuhn; Alston's *Roughcut* (1990, design, Tim Hatley) to specially commissioned score by Gavin Bryars, performed live; *Signature* (1990) by Siobhan Davies (commissioned score by Kevin Volans, performed live; designs by Kate Whiteford); and Davies's 1981 *Plainsong* to music by Satie.

8 One of Britain's leading Bharata Natyam dancers, Subbiah collaborated with dancer/ choreographer Savitry Nair in *Trikonam,* a contemporary treatment of an Indian myth, performed by Bharata Natyam dancers Valli Subbiah, Shantala Shivalingappa and former English National Ballet dancer Koen Onzia.

9 Presented the London premiere of *No Respite,* devised, choreographed and performed by Snaith, Barnaby Stone and Jamie Walton, which included film, soundscape, objects and text.

10 Presented the British premiere of *Land* – a first collaboration with native American musician and composer Robert Mirabal and New York painter Sandra Lerner.

11 British debut for the company, presenting performance artist Hiroshi Koike's *Parade* (1989): 'neither pure drama nor pure dance but both'. This also formed part of the 1991 Japan Festival on the South Bank.

12 Presented Teshigawara's most recent production *Dah-Dah-Sko-Dah-Dah,* part of the 1991 Japan Festival.

13 UK debut of the company, founded in 1988. Wright danced with the Paul Taylor Company for five years and with DV8 in *Dead Dreams of Monochrome Men.* The company here performed Wright's choreography: *Hey Paris* (1987), *A Far Cry* (1989, music Bartók's *Sonata No. 2* for violin and piano) and *Gloria* (1991, music, Vivaldi).

14 Presented British premieres of *Foray Forêt* (1990) made in collaboration with Robert Rauschenberg; *For M.G. The Movie* (received world premiere in France the previous week and was renamed from *Lever Best* after the programmes were printed) with a score by Alvin Curran; *Astral Convertible* (1989), in collaboration with Rauschenberg and *Line Up* (1977). The company also performed free of charge at Canary Wharf in a lunchtime, mid-week special event as part of Olympia and York's Arts and Events programme.

15 In Elkins's choreography: *Testosterone Diversions* (1989, music, Telemann, David Byrne); *Danforth & Multiply (The Rituals of Democracy)* (1990) and *The Patrooka Variations* (1989, music Bizet, flamenco and James Brown).

16 Muscle Voice was a touring project of P.S.122, New York, a collaboration between choreographers David Rousseve, Sarah Skaggs and David Dorfman and composer/performance artist Dan Froot. Dorfman also performed with Froot on saxophones.

17 Performed an extract from *Spatial Decay II* (1990).

18 With a display of Northumberland and Durham clog dancing.

19 In an extract from Liat Dror and Nir Ben

Gal's *Rikud* (1991), music Shostakovich Piano Quintet.

[20] In Pages's new duet, *Dumb.*

[21] In an excerpt from Alston's *Roughcut* (1990).

[22] This was the company's first appearance in London for twelve years. They performed Jiří Kylián's *Forgotten Land* to Britten's *Sinfonia Da Requiem*, played by the Purcell Orchestra.

[23] Tap dancer Tak in an excerpt from *Tobias on Swing Street,* accompanied by pianist Mauric Horhut.

[24] Winners of the 1991 Cosmopolitan/C&A Dance Awards.

[25] In Jones' *Forsythia*, to music by Arnie Zane.

[26] Presented *Civil Disobedience Weekend.*

1991: Related Events

Film and Video

Film season:
Happy Feet: a BBC film written and directed by Mike Bradwell[1] (Riverside Studios)
Memories of Jazz[2] (French Institute)
Company L'Esquisse and recent choreography in France[3] (French Institute)
Dance Videos: Beyond Television[4] (Riverside Studios)

Parallel Lines:[5] film and dance discussion (and video screenings) (Riverside Studios)

Seminars

Discussions:
Shobana Jeyasingh with music collaborators, in a discussion about her latest work (The Place Theatre)
Dance UK and the National Arts Strategy[6] (Chelsfield Room, Royal Festival Hall)
Space Invaders[7] (Chisenhale Dance Space)

Study day (Sadler's Wells): *Trisha Brown: 21 Years of Choreography*[8]

Classes and Workshops
Repertoire class: Doug Elkins, with members of the company, led a repertoire class.
Technique class, with members of Trisha Brown Company
Workshops: Yolande Snaith; Julyen Hamilton; Laurie Booth

Meet the Artists
Laurie Booth; Rosemary Butcher; Doug Elkins; Eiko and Koma; Shobana Jeyasingh; Yolande Snaith; Valli Subbiah and Company; Pappa Tarahumara; Douglas Wright.

Exhibitions
Exhibition of photographs by Guy Delahaye, who has worked with L'Esquisse since the company's formation (French Institute).

Associated Events
Voiceover (ICA): Nigel Charnock in *Resurrection*, his first solo show.

Notes
[1] Advertised as 'a hysterical view of the Northern dance competition circuit'. Bradwell was present to answer questions after the screening.

[2] A compilation of short films, cartoons and 'soundies' from the 1930s and 1940s, featuring

Douglas Wright and Company at Canary Wharf, 1991. PHOTO: HUGO GLENDINNING

Sammy Davis Jnr, Betty Boop, Fats Waller, Louis Armstrong, Duke Ellington, Cab Calloway and the Nicholas Brothers.

[3] Films shown included *La Chambre* and *L'Etreinte* (both by Bouvier and Obadia of L'Esquisse), *La Noce,* awarded 'best choreography created for the camera' at the 1991 IMZ Dance Screen Competition, Frankfurt, and *La Lampe.* The films were supported by an exhibition of photographs by L'Esquisse collaborator Guy Delahaye.

[4] A panel discussion to consider why dance video festivals are so much a part of the European cultural calendar, but have yet to catch on in Britain. The panel included Pia Kalinka (IMZ Dance Screen), Anne Bedou (Centre George Pompidou), Geneviève Charras (APA Geneva), Peter Packer (Tyneside Cinema, Newcastle), Rodney Wilson (Arts Council) and a BFI representative. A selection of videos was also shown from the IMZ Dance Screen Competition for audiovisual dance productions, held each summer in Frankfurt.

[5] A panel of critics, choreographers and programme-makers examined the creative possibilities of dance, film and video. The event included a special showing of four new Arts Council education videos featuring the work of Mark Murphy and Sue Cox, Motion House, Carousel and Shobana Jeyasingh. To coincide with the seminar, the Arts Council and John Libbey published a critical anthology entitled *Parallel Lines: a History of Dance and the Media* (edited by Stephanie Jordan and Dave Allen).

[6] An opportunity for dance professionals to consider the key issues in the Arts Council's discussion document: 'Dance Strategies: the Turning Point', chaired by Peter Brinson. The meeting was preceded by the Annual General meeting of Dance UK, members of which also reported on the event.

[7] A discussion to consider the phenomenon of collaborative projects between contemporary choreographers and visual artists, and dancers' use of art gallery spaces, chaired by David Hughes. Contributors included Cornelia Parker, Gaby Agis and Jonathan Watkins, director of the Chisenhale Gallery.

[8] Organised by the Society for Dance Research to coincide with the final Dance Umbrella performance. The day included a lecture by Stephanie Jordan, a discussion with Trisha Brown, a slide and video presentation and the opportunity to watch company class and rehearsal prior to the evening performance.

1992

Wednesday 14 October – Wednesday 11 November (47 London performances)

Venues
London: ICA; Place Theatre; Purcell Room; Queen Elizabeth Hall; Riverside Studios;
   Royalty Theatre; (French Institute – associated event)
Brighton: Gardner Arts Centre, University of Sussex
Bristol: Arnolfini
Edinburgh: Dancebase, The Assembly Rooms
Guildford: Main Hall, University of Surrey
Leicester: Phoenix Arts Centre
Newcastle upon Tyne[1]: Newcastle Playhouse, Gulbenkian Studio Theatre
Northampton: Derngate Theatre
Nottingham: Nottingham Playhouse
Swindon: Town Hall Studios

Artists

Continental Europe
Compagnie Bagouet[2] * (France)
Blok and Steel[3] * (Holland)
Groupe Emile Dubois[4] * (France)
Lanonima Imperial[5] * (Spain)
Paola Rampone[6] (Italy)
Rosas[7] * (Belgium)
Santiago Sempere[8] * (France/Spain)

UK
Laurie Booth[9]
Jonathan Burrows Group[10]
The Cholmondeleys[11]
Aletta Collins/Victoria Marks[12]

Siobhan Davies Dance Company[13]
Julyen Hamilton[14]
Shobana Jeyasingh Dance Company[15]
MacLennan Dance and Company[16]
Royal Ballet Choreographic Group[17]
Second Stride[18]

USA
Merce Cunningham Dance Company[19]
Paula Josa-Jones[20]
Stephen Petronio Company[21]
Transatlantic Tap[22]
Urban Bush Women[23]

The London Dance and Performance Awards (Cochrane Theatre)
Winners included Candoco, DV8 Physical Theatre, 'No respite', Bode Lawal, Tim Etchells,
Fiona Wright, Joanne Barrett, Lea Anderson, Liz Ranken, Chandralekha, Yuva, Betty
Bourne, Platform and Steve Whitson. The presentations were preceded by entertainment
from Transatlantic Tap.

Notes
* These artists appeared in association with
the European Arts Festival, July–December 92.

[1] All Newcastle events were part of Dance
Umbrella's Newcastle Dance 92 Festival (25
October – 5 December)
[2] The company's UK debut, presenting *So
Schnell* by director Dominique Bagouet, to a
Bach Cantata, and *One Story as in Falling*,
choreography by Trisha Brown, commissioned
score by Alvin Curran. The latter piece came
about as a result of creative collaboration between the two companies during residences in

Montpellier and Chicago.
[3] Choreographers Suzy Blok and Christopher
Steel led a company of four in two separate
but thematically linked duets: *Still You/Belong*
and *(Breaking) The Back of Love*.
[4] UK premiere of *La Legende de Don Juan*
commissioned by Expo 92, Seville, to live music by Henry Torgue, Serge Houppin and LO-
CAL Groupe.
[5] Choreographer-director Juan Carlos Garcia's company made its UK debut with *Afanya't
A Poc A Poc* (More Haste, Less Speed).
[6] Presented a solo programme *Tap Stairs*

with choreography by Americans Tere O'Connor, Sarah Skaggs, Susan Rethorst for *Four Dead Women Live, Estatic Tap* and *Under The Stairs* respectively, plus *Steps* by Rampone herself. UK debut.

[7] The company presented their 'signature' piece, *Rosas Danst Rosas* (1983), to music by Thierry de Mey and Peter Vermeersch. The piece won two 'Bessie' Awards, for choreography and lighting.

[8] Choreographer Sempere was born in Spain but resident in France from the age of fourteen. The company presented *Don Quixote, Duels et Amours,* replacing the originally scheduled *Ribera* at the last minute, owing to production difficulties. UK debut for the company.

[9] *Improvisations with Dance/Music/Poetry* was a collaboration with violinist Alex Balanescu, poet Aaron Williamson who is profoundly deaf and dancer Russell Maliphant. Booth won a 1991 Digital Dance Award.

[10] The group performed *Very,* made with a Digital Dance Award, to songs composed and performed live by co-director Matteo Fargion, with costumes by fashion designer Joe Casely-Hayford and light installations from Peter Mumford. The piece was performed by Burrows and ex-Royal Ballet dancers Lynne Bristow and Deborah Jones, who also collaborated in the work.

[11] Presented *Walky Talky,* with choreography by Lea Anderson, in collaboration with writer/ performer Anne Rabbitt (dialogue), Drostan Madden (music) and Sandy Powell (costume design): a Contemporary Archives Commission for Now '92.

[12] An Anglo-American initiative: Collins creating a series of solos for Marks and dancers: *8 Parts Water* to Handel's *Water Music*; Marks creating a solo for Collins, *Present* (to Beethoven's *Moonlight Sonata*), a duet, *Dick,* for Paul Douglas and Sean Feldman plus a revival of *Dancing to Music* (1988, music Wim Mertens), a piece for four women that included Jane Dudley.

[13] Presented London premieres of *White Bird Featherless* (score by Gerald Barry for two pianos and counter-tenor, played live) and *Make-Make* (sound score by David Buckland and Russell Mills, mixed live during performance)

[14] Presented a solo, *Song In Two Sets,* in collaboration with saxophonist Becke Hinnerson, on a double bill with Paola Rampone.

[15] The performance comprised a re-worked version of *Configurations* (1988, with commissioned score by Michael Nyman, played by the Smith Quartet); the premiere of *Making of Maps* (with a commissioned score by electronic composer Alistair MacDonald, incorporating specially composed music by Christos Hatzis and Indian composer/singer R A Ramamani).

[16] Presented *Continental Drift* (1991), a work in two parts: *Wound in Slow Motion* and *Ignorance Toboggans Into Know,* to Simon Limbrick's score, performed live.

[17] The group paid tribute to its founder Leslie Edwards, and celebrated its twenty-fifth anniversary year. The performance included choreography by Matthew Hart, Ashley Page, Christopher Wheeldon, Stephen Wicks and Simon Rice

[18] The company presented *Why Things Happen (the things people do when they fall out of love)* directed by Ian Spink in collaboration with writer Marty Cruickshank, designer Antony McDonald; with music arranged and directed by Judith Weir.

[19] Presented a series of *Events* specially conceived for the Queen Elizabeth Hall and including works never seen before in London. Sound accompaniment was by four on-stage musicians including David Tudor. Cunningham performed.

[20] British debut for this performance art company, appearing care of the Boston Dance Umbrella. The company presented *Eine Kleine Nachtmusik* (1992) and *The Messenger* (1991).

[21] In a programme specially assembled for Umbrella 92, which included the British premiere of *Half Wrong plus Laytext* to Stravinsky's *Rite of Spring,* transposed for two pianos (played live on one by Christopher Swithinbank and Gruffydd Owen), plus *Previous* – a reconstruction of *Walk-In* (1986), score by David Linton.

[22] A performance specially curated by Jeremy Alliger, director of Dance Umbrella Boston and featuring tap artists from the US: Manhattan Tap Company, Buster Brown, Steps Ahead, Savion Glover and Tobias Tak from the UK.

[23] Presented a programme of short pieces and excerpts: 'Girlfriends' and 'Madness' (excerpts from *Anarchy, Wild Women and Dinah*); *Lifedance III … The Empress (Womb Wars)* (described as a work in progress); 'Lipstick … A Doo-Wop Dilemma' (an excerpt from *Heat*) and *I Don't know, but I've Been Told If you Keep on Dancin' You'll Never Grow Old.*

1992: Related Events

Film and Video

Film and video weekend (The Cinema, Riverside Studios)
1. IMZ Dance Screen[1]
   Dance Videos in Education – 1992[2]:
   Siye Goli[3] (Return to Johannesburg)
   Big Feature[4]
   Gift of Tradition[5]
   On Tap[6] + *The Bandwagon* (1953, dir. Vincente Minelli)

2. L'Esquisse/DV8 on film:
   The Fall[7]
   Never Again[8]
   La Noce + *L'Etreinte* + *La Chambre*[9]
   Montalvo et L'Enfant[10]

Seminars
Dance USA/Dance UK[11] (ICA)

Classes and Workshops (The Holborn Centre)
Sue MacLennan; Julyen Hamilton; Urban Bush Women
Writing dance; through the limitations of physical language: discussion and workshop led by
   Jonathan Burrows
Touchdown Dance Project:[12] residency at Riverside Studios
Classes: Siobhan Davies Dance Company Residency[13] (Riverside Studios)

Meet the Artists
Siobhan Davies; Shobana Jeyasingh; Urban Bush Women; Paula Josa-Jones; Blok and Steel; Stephen Petronio; Jonathan Burrows; Sue MacLennan; Lanonima Imperial; The Cholmondeleys (Lea Anderson); Laurie Booth

Education
Merce Cunningham study day[14]

Associated Events
The Meredith Monk Vocal Ensemble[15] (US, Queen Elizabeth Hall)
Astrakan in Daniel Larrieu's *Gravures*[16] (France, The French Institute)

Notes

[1] A screening of the winners and most notable entrants of the 1992 IMZ Dance Screen Competition, including *Rosa* (chor. Anne Teresa de Keersmaeker, dir. Peter Greenaway). The screenings were introduced by Stephanie Jordan, a member of the 1992 competition jury, and Pia Kalinka of IMZ.

[2] Showing three premieres of work produced under a scheme by the Dance and the Film and Video Broadcasting departments of the Arts Council.

[3] Featuring the Adzido Pan African Dance Ensemble, produced and directed by Terry Braun.

[4] Featuring The Featherstoneshaughs, choreographed by Lea Anderson, directed by Maxwell Bailey.

[5] Featuring the Sampad Dance Company, with choreography by Piali Ray, directed and produced by Maxwell Bailey.

[6] An illustrated talk by Sally Sommer to place the Transatlantic Tap performances in context.

[7] A celebration of the life of Celeste Dandeker; choreographed and directed by Darshan Singh Bhuller, 1991.

8 Featuring DV8 Physical Theatre; choreography, Lloyd Newson, directed by Bob Bentley, 1989.

9 Featuring L'Esquisse, choreographed and directed by Joelle Bouvier and Regis Obadia, 1988–91.

10 Choreographed by Jean-Claude Gallotta, directed by Claude Mourieras, 1989. London premiere. Gallotta was present at the screening as guest of honour.

11 The panel, chaired by Bonnie Brooks, director of Dance USA, included Susan Fait-Meyers, a member of the Trisha Brown Company.

12 A company of blind and sighted people, led by Steve Paxton and Anne Kilkoyne (a performance psychologist) in residence, offering two workshops (exploring contact improvisation, release technique, relaxation and massage) and informal open performances.

13 The residency included masterclasses for dancers, open rehearsals, lecture demonstrations and discussions.

14 The South Bank season included a Merce Cunningham Dance Company study day led by Stephanie Jordan, focusing upon the fusion of dance and technology in Cunningham's work. Hands-on experience with the Lifeforms computer program was available to participants. The day also included Elliot Caplan's Cage–Cunningham film.

15 A special concert version of Monk's opera Atlas, for her first British tour with the Vocal Ensemble, including the vocal piece Facing North. Followed by an after-show talk.

16 The performance was at the invitation of the French Institute. Gravures featured Larrieu's company Astrakan.

1993

Tuesday 12 October – Sunday 7 November (53 London performances)

Venues
London: French Institute; Hackney Empire;[1] ICA; Place Theatre; Queen Elizabeth Hall; Riverside Studios Riverside Gallery

The Doug Elkins Dance Company embarked on a short regional tour in a mixed programme of performance and workshops:
Newcastle: Playhouse
Manchester: Green Room; NIA Centre
Swindon: Thamesdown Centre; Wyvern Theatre

Operation Riverside[2] (4–24 October)
Over a period of nearly three weeks, every available space at Riverside Studios was given over to dance activities: performances, films, video, classes, debates and seminars. Marked with an *.

Artists

Continental Europe
Beppie Blankert[3] (Holland)
Angelika Oei[4] (Holland)
Mal Pelo[5] (Spain)
Annamirl van der Pluijm[6] (Holland)
Compagnie Philippe Tréhet[7] (France)

UK
Bedlam[8]
Laurie Booth[9]
Nigel Charnock[10]
*Emilyn Claid, Sylvia Hallett, Hermione Wiltshire[11]
Siobhan Davies Dance Company[12]
Matthew Hawkins and the Fresh Dances Group[13]
Shobana Jeyasingh Dance Company[14]

Michael Popper[15]
Second Stride[16]
*Miranda Tufnell, David Ward, Sylvia Hallett[17]
V-Tol Dance Company[18]

International
Ariodone[19] [Carlotta Ikeda and Ko Murobushi] (Japan)
Batsheva Dance Company[20] (Israel)
Saburo Teshigawara[21] (Japan)

US
*Doug Elkins Dance Company[22]
Victoria Marks Performance Company[23]
*Dana Reitz and Sara Rudner[24]
*David Rousseve Reality Dance Company[25]

Notes
[1] New venue.
[2] Financed by the 1992 Prudential Award for the Arts, awarded to Dance Umbrella.
[3] Presented *Charles* (1991) and *Ives* (1992) about the composer Charles Ives, for seven dancers. The performance also included text, music and song. Music was performed live by baritone Charles van Tassel, pianist Gerard Bouwhuis and violinist Josje ter Haar.
[4] Dutch choreographer Oei's company included Britain's Jamie Watton and Jordi Cortés Molina, who has appeared with DV8 Physical Theatre. They presented *Kepler's Kamer.*
[5] Dance Umbrella debut for the company,

which comprised performers Maria Muñoz, Pep Ramis (both directors) and Jordi Casanovas. Presented *Sur – Perros Del Sur*, to a commissioned sound score by Leo Lankhuyzen.
[6] Making her Dance Umbrella debut in a solo performance. *Solo 1* was performed at Leicester International Dance Festival earlier in the year.
[7] British debut for Tréhet's company of eight dancers, Le Galet Gris, who presented *Une Ville Peut Mourir.*
[8] Yael Flexer, the Place Theatre's recent choreographer-in-residence presented a short new work for founder member of Bedlam,

Rachel Krische, to music by composer/violinist Jonathan Podmore, played live on stage, in a free performance entitled *Dot..Dot..Dot.*

[9] Presented a solo extension of the material originally used in the Laurie Booth and Company performance *River Run*, entitled *River Run/A Lone* with sculptures by Anish Kapoor, and a specially constructed 'octophonic' sound by German sound artist Hans Peter Kuhn.

[10] Dancer/choreographer Charnock joined forces with actress/singer Liz Brailsford and musician Nicholas Skilbeck for *Original Sin.*

[11] *Sweet Side Show* was a live art collaboration between choreographer/performer Claid, composer/musician Hallett, lighting designer Jeremy Radford and visual artist Wiltshire, with guest performers Betsy Gregory and Odette Hughes.

[12] Davies was the winner of the 1993 Olivier Award for Outstanding Achievement in Dance. Presented two programmes included *Wanting to Tell Stories,* receiving its London premiere here with a commissioned score from Kevin Volans, made possible by a Digital Dance Award; *White Bird Featherless* and *Make-Make,* both from 1992.

[13] Hawkins' staging of *Fresh Dances for the Late Tchaikovsky* included actress Fenella Fielding and performance artist Rose English plus live music 'Souvenir de Florence' for string sextet, played by the Endymion Ensemble. Commissioned by Dance Umbrella, and a Digital Dance Award Winner.

[14] The company presented a new work commissioned from Richard Alston, *Delicious Arbour,* made possible by a Digital Dance Award, and Jeyasingh's *Romance With Footnotes* with a commissioned score from Glyn Perrin. Jeyasingh received the 1993 Prudential Award for Dance.

[15] In a solo performance choreographed by Popper: *The Moment.*

[16] Presented *Escape at Sea,* a .collaboration with choreography by Ian Spink, Ashley Page and Eyal Rubin; composer Orlando Gough and director/designer Antony McDonald plus Peter Mumford. Singers Amanda Dean and Jozik Koc performed on stage.

[17] The collaboration between choreographer/dancer Tufnell, artist Ward and musician Hallett, *In The Grain Of The Body* received its premiere in the 1992 Newcastle Dance Festival.

[18] Formed in 1991 by Mark Murphy, the company presented *32 feet per second per second,* which included film footage, cinema screens and a sound track by rock drummer Nic Murcott.

[19] The two performers were working together again after a break of seven years and presented the London premiere of *Ai Amour* (music, Osamu Goto.)

[20] The company presented *Mabul* (1992), with choreography by artistic director Ohad Naharin, music by Vivaldi (performed live by James Bowman and the Academy of Ancient Music), John Zorn, Arvo Pärt, Livingston and Evans Ray, and Carl Orff.

[21] This solo performance, *Bones In Pages,* was originally commissioned as a gallery installation and included a soundscape by Kunu Kunu.

[22] Billed as 'Breakdancing meets hip-hop as the New York based company slices through issues of gender, race and politics with a large dose of humour.' The company presented *More Wine For Polyphemus, Where Was Yvonne Rainer When I Had Saturday Night Fever?* and *The Stuff of Recoiling,* and held a major residency at Riverside Studios, involving local young people.

[23] The company included dancers from New York and London and performed *Present* (1993), made for and performed by Aletta Collins, *This Way* (1993), *Dick* (1991), and *Dancing To Music* (1988) performed by four women aged between 16 and 70 (including Jane Dudley for one performance).

[24] *Necessary Weather* was an ongoing collaborative venture between dancers Reitz and Rudner and lighting designer Jennifer Tipton. Performed in silence with no set, these performances were followed by a professional workshop at Riverside Studios.

[25] Formed by choreographer/writer/director Rousseve in 1988, Reality included gospel singer B. J. Crosby. *Coloured Children Flying By* combined text with movement, unaccompanied gospel singing and music by James Brown, Marvin Gaye and Tammy Terrell, Public Enemy and The Supremes amongst others, to 'unfold a tale of racism, sexual oppression and loss in the USA'.

216

1993: Related Events

Film and Video
* European Broadcasting and Dance[1] (Riverside Cinema)
* Launch of Dance Videos in Education – 1993[2] (Riverside Studios)
* Dance on Film Screening (Riverside Cinema) including:
  Little Titch and his Big Boots (1902)
  Tango (Poland, 1983)
  Rosa (1992, chor. Anne Teresa de Keersmaeker, dir. Peter Greenaway)
  46 Bis; Rue de Belleville; Topic 1 & 2 (chor. Sarah Denizot, dir. Pascale Baes)
  La Lampe (chor/dir. Joelle Bouvier and Regis Obadia)

Seminars
* Dance and Design[3]
* Dance and the Camera[4]
* European Broadcasting and Dance[5]
* Lighting for Dance: an open lecture demonstration led by Dana Reitz and Jennifer Tipton
* Classic and Contemporary?[6] open discussion

Dance Umbrella Debates:
* Whose Art is it anyway?[7]
* Arts Marketing: The Great Growth Industry.[8]

Classes and Workshops
Classes: *Richard Alston[9]
Workshops (Holborn Centre and Hackney Empire): Gill Clarke, Mark Murphy, Matthew Hawkins, Nigel Charnock

Exhibitions
Peggy Jarrell Kaplan: Portraits of Choreographers[10]

Meet the Artists
Batsheva Dance Company, Miranda Tufnell, Siobhan Davies Company, David Rousseve and Reality, Victoria Marks, Shobana Jeyasingh Dance Company, Doug Elkins Dance Company, Mal Pelo, Saburo Teshigawara, Nigel Charnock, Angelika Oei, V-Tol, Second Stride

Education
Residencies:
*Necessary Weather[11] (Riverside Studio 2)
*Doug Elkins Dance Company Residency[12] (Riverside Studios, 4–22 Oct)

Notes
[1] A one-day conference that explored the creative range of dance for TV, with a European perspective. Directors and choreographers introduced extracts from their work and short programmes, and answered questions from participants.

[2] Three premieres of work produced under a scheme by both the Dance and the Film and Video Broadcasting departments of the Arts Council: Rosemary Butcher (choreographer): *Body as Site*; Nomads: *No Means No*; Physical State International: *The Julyen Hamilton Project*, with members of the cast and crew present at the screenings.

[3] Chaired by Sarah Rubidge, with a panel that included Ashley Page, Mark Baldwin, Michael Craig Martin, Emilyn Claid and Hermione Wiltshire.

[4] Chaired by Chris de Marigny, the panel included Chris Nash, Catherine Ashmore and

Martha Oakes.

5 Chaired by Rodney Wilson, the panel included European producer George Brugmans, plus directors and choreographers who collaborated for the BBC/Arts Council Dance and Camera series: Bob Lockyer, Anne Beresford and Milfid Ellis.

6 A discussion addressing the question of when contemporary dance becomes classic, chaired by Sarah Rubidge, with a panel including Richard Alston, Shobana Jeyasingh, Alessandra Iyer and Alastair Macaulay.

7 A public debate about who really controls the art form in this country, chaired by John Drummond, who was joined by Robert Breckman, Dana Reitz, Lloyd Newson and Janet Archer.

8 A panel comprising marketing managers, promoters, graphic designers and artists debated the increasing amounts spent on arts marketing. Chaired by Maggie Sedwards, who was joined by Alec Jessel, Keith Cooper, Rebekah MacLeary and Val Bourne.

9 Richard Alston took daily technique classes for professionals and advanced level students during one week of Operation Riverside.

10 Featuring choreographers who had performed in Dance Umbrella Festivals over the previous fifteen years, including portraits of Merce Cunningham, Anne Teresa de Keersmaeker, Trisha Brown, Jean Claude Gallotta, Michael Clark, Lea Anderson, Shobana Jeyasingh, Jonathan Burrows, Mark Morris and Bill T. Jones.

11 Following on from the performances, an intensive week-long workshop led by Dana Reitz and Jennifer Tipton, open to professional choreographers, lighting designers and artists from other disciplines. Participants included Gaby Agis, Jonathan Burrows, Rosemary Butcher, Michael Clark, Ippy Donnellan, Cathy Kerr, Russell Maliphant, Caroline Pope, Ellen van Schuylenburch, Anthony Bowne, Ross Cameron, Larry Coke, Mark Galione, Paul Keogan, Simon Robertson, Mike Segnior, Francis Watson, Sophie Fiennes, Craig Givens, Hugo Glendinning and Jane Joyce. This was the first of its kind in this country.

12 Inspired by the club scene, the company worked with a group of young people aged 17–23 years with no formal dance training in a series of workshops culminating in a performance. The residency was supported by the London Borough of Hammersmith and Fulham plus the Community Education Department at Riverside Studios.

1994

Monday 17 October – Saturday 5 November, and Saturday 12 November (38 London performances)

Venues

London: Brixton Academy (new venue); Hackney Empire; ICA; Lilian Baylis Theatre; Place Theatre; Queen Elizabeth Hall; Riverside Studios; Sadler's Wells Theatre
Stephen Petronio Company tour:
    Brighton: Gardner Arts Centre, University of Sussex
    Leicester: Haymarket Theatre
    Newcastle upon Tyne: Playhouse
    Nottingham: Playhouse
Urban Bush Women tour:
    Bristol: Arnolfini
    Manchester: NIA Centre
    Nottingham: Playhouse
    Oxford: Playhouse

Artists

Continental Europe
José Besprosvany[1] (Belgium)
Michel Kelemenis*[2] (France)
Koffi Koko*[3] (France)
Compagnie Angelin Preljocaj*[4] (France)
Hervé Robbe*[5] (France)
Compagnie Philippe Tréhet*[6] (France)

UK
Mark Baldwin Dance Company[7]
Siobhan Davies Dance Company[8]
Featherstonehaughs[9]
Green Candle Dance Company[10]
Matthew Hawkins and the Fresh Dances Group[11]

Javier de Frutos[12]
Russell Maliphant/Ellen Van Schuylenburch[13]
Ricochet Dance Company[14]/Company Vertigo
Wheel of Fortune[15]

International
Company Vertigo[16] (Israel)

USA
Lucinda Childs Dance Company[17]
Stephen Petronio Company[18]
Urban Bush Women[19]

Notes

* Brought to Dance Umbrella by the Coast to Coast project: an ongoing Anglo-French initiative.

[1] Presented *Cuarteto*, with text from Marguerite Dumas's *La Maladie de la Mort*, read on stage by Micheline Hardy, and a commissioned score by cellist Johan Van Weerst, who played live on stage.
[2] Following appearances in the Legs Eleven gala event of 1989 and April in Paris (also in 1989), Kelemenis presented his latest work *Clins de Lune*, (a solo) in homage to the late French choreographer Dominique Bagouet; a duet, *Image;* and *Anthère.*

[3] Born in Benin, now resident in Paris, Koffi Koko presented a solo *D'une rive à l'autre* accompanied by three musicians and created for the Lyon Biennale Dance Festival.
[4] Celebrating its tenth anniversary, the company presented *Hommage aux Ballets Russes,* which comprised new versions of *Les Noces* and *Le Spectre de la Rose,* plus a duet, *Un Trait d'Union.*
[5] London debut for Robbe's company Le Marietta Secret in a programme of recently created works, including *Made Of* and *Flowing Along.*
[6] Tréhet's company, Le Galet Gris, comprising seven dancers, an actor and a singer pre-

sented *Le Couloir de Galilée* with text written by Tréhet.

[7] The company's Dance Umbrella debut with Lynn Seymour, Lucy Burge, Christopher Bannerman and Dale Thompson in *A Collection of Moving Parts*, to Chopin; plus a different cast for *Excursions*, to Samuel Barber's *Excursions 20*, and *More Poulenc*, to Poulenc's *Soirée de Nazelles*.

[8] The company presented *The Glass Blew In*, to a score for nine clarinets by Gavin Bryars, performed live and multi-tracked by Roger Heaton; plus *Wanting to Tell Stories* (1993).

[9] Choreographer Lea Anderson's all-male group presented a 24-hour extravaganza as the finale to the festival, *24-hour Featherstonehaughs*, including 'film, performance and clubbing'. Preceded by screenings of films including *Battleship Potempkin* and *Das Boot,* the performance included film projections and installations by Cash Aspeek.

[10] Artistic director Fergus Early in collaboration with playwright Goran Stefanovski presented *Old Man Dragging Stones*, during a festival residency at the Lilian Baylis Theatre. The performance involved students from Islington College.

[11] Hawkins, now choreographer-in-residence at the Hackney Empire, joined forces with Diana Payne Myers, 'London's busiest postmodern sexagenarian', to present *Matthew and Diana on Manoeuvres,* which included live accompaniment by guitarist Steve Smith.

[12] De Frutos's Umbrella debut with *The Palace Does Not Forgive* – a solo version of Stravinsky's *Rite of Spring.*

[13] Double bill that featured Schuylenburch's trio *Company* for herself, dancer Tamsin O'Donnell and bass guitarist Shrikanth Sriram; and Maliphant's solo for himself, *Paradigm*, made in collaboration with lighting designer Michael Hulls and composer Titch English.

[14] Ricochet Dance Company and the duo Company Vertigo from Israel together presented a programme that included *Symbiosis*, choreographed by Vertigo's Noa Wertheim.

[15] A project led by Kate Flatt and Sally Jacobs that provided opportunities for community involvement with professional and ex-professional dancers, co-ordinated by Riverside Studios' Education department. Performances of *The Dancing Room* included music performed by Hungarian string band Muzsikas.

[16] See Ricochet Dance Company.

[17] The company's London debut in a programme that included *Concerto* (1993), to Henryk Gorécki's *Concerto for Harpsichord and Strings*; and *Available Light* (1983) to music by John Adams and set by architect Frank Gehry.

[18] The company's tenth anniversary, in a programme that included the London premiere of *The King is Dead*, to live music by David Linton and a recording of Elvis Presley's *Love Me Tender* and design by Cindy Sherman, costumes by Manolo; the London premiere of *She Says*, to music by Yoko Ono; *Full Half Wrong* to a score that includes Stravinsky's *Rite of Spring.*

[19] In a programme that included *Nyabinghi Dreamtime* (1994), to a percussion score by Junior Wedderburn; *Girlfriends* and *Shelter.*

1994: Related Events

Film and Video
Dance on Video[1] (Riverside Studios Cinema):
The Spark (chor. Ludus Dance Company, dir. Maryn Hollingsworth)
Dark Hours and Finer Moments (chor. Gaby Agis, dir. Douglas Hart)
Not Just a Somersault[2]

Dance on Film[3] (Riverside Studios Cinema):
Achterland (chor. Anne Teresa de Keersmaeker, winner of the Dance Screen Award)
Le P'tit Bal (chor. Philippe Decouflé, joint winner of the Screen Choreography Award)
Outside In (Candoco Dance Company, chor. Victoria Marks, dir. Margaret Williams)
Love Sonnets (chor. Michele Anne de Mey)
Our/Film (chor. Jonathan Burrows, dir. Adam Roberts)

Seminars
London: First or Last?[4] (ICA, 18 Oct)

Classes and Workshops

Workshops (for professional/experienced dancers): Urban Bush Women; Mark Baldwin

Classes. Michel Kelemenis (pre-performance technique and repertory class for experienced dancers); Stephen Petronio (masterclass)

Exhibitions

Chris Nash[5] (Riverside Studios, 17 October – 5 November)

Meet the Artists

Urban Bush Women, Matthew Hawkins, Koffi Koko, Ellen van Schuylenburch, Lucinda Childs Dance Company, Stephen Petronio Company, Wheel of Fortune, Mark Baldwin Dance Company, José Besprosvany, Compagnie Philippe Tréhet, Hervé Robbe, Vertigo/Ricochet, Michel Kelemenis, Siobhan Davies Dance Company, Green Candle Dance Company

Education

Dance and Technology: Trick or Treat?[6] (Royal Festival Hall)
Dance Writing and Criticism course[7] (Riverside Studios)

Notes

[1] Three premieres of work produced under a scheme by the Dance and Film departments of the Arts Council.

[2] A study of Martha Graham's technique by two of her former pupils, Bonnie Bird and Thea Barnes.

[3] A selection from the recent IMZ Dance Screen 1994, followed by an informal discussion.

[4] A debate concerning London's position and status within European culture.

[5] New work that demonstrated the photographer's experimentation with the latest available technology, and a product of three days of workshops held at the Royal Festival Hall using a Kodak digital camera and computer retouching system.

[6] An artist-led two-day conference, which explored the application of new computer technologies in dance, led by Terry Braun, Julian Blom and Anna Cutler.

[7] Participants wrote and edited two newsletters, which included features, news items and reviews of Dance Umbrella events and which were distributed throughout the festival's venues. The course was led by Alastair Macaulay.

1995

Tuesday 10 October – Saturday 11 November (56 London performances)

Venues

London: Greenwich Borough Hall;[1] ICA; Place Theatre; Purcell Room; Queen Elizabeth
Hall Riverside Studios; Sadler's Wells
Elizabeth Streb/Ringside regional tour included:
Frome: Merlin
Manchester: Dancehouse
Nottingham: Playhouse
Oxford: Playhouse

Artists

Continental Europe
Ariadone[2] (France)
Compagnie D.I.T.[3] (France)
Koffi Koko (France)/Peter Badejo (UK)[4]
Mal Pelo[5] (Spain)
Hervé Robbe (France)/Richard
  Deacon (UK)[6]

UK
Richard Alston Dance Company[7]
Mark Baldwin Dance Company[8]
Christopher Bannerman and Candoco[9]
Emilyn Claid[10]/Laurie Booth[11]
Aletta Collins Dance Company[12]
Siobhan Davies Dance Company[13]

DV8 Physical Theatre[14]
Javier de Frutos[15]
Matthew Hawkins and the Fresh Dances
  Group[16]
Russell Maliphant[17]
Wayne McGregor[18]
Henry Montes[19]/Wendy Houston[20]
Phoenix Dance Company[21]
Tom Sapsford[22]

USA
Merce Cunningham Dance Company[23]
Steve Paxton[24]
Dana Reitz[25]
Elizabeth Streb and Ringside[26]

Notes

[1] The venue was new this year, and the first association with Greenwich Dance Agency.

[2] Carlotta Ikeda's all-female Butoh company, now based in France, presented *Le Langage du Sphinx*, comprising seven scenes following the different stages of women's existence, with lighting by Eric Loustau-Carrère.

[3] Choreographer and former member of Groupe Emile Dubois, Robert Seyfried's company made their UK debut in a duet, *No Comment*, and *Légèrement Deplacé*, a quartet to music by Gorécki, both with lighting by Manuel Bernard. The company shared a double bill with Tom Sapsford.

[4] Presented *Sisi Agbe Aye (Opening the Gourd of Life)* in which the choreographer/dancers drew upon their experiences as Africans working in Europe, as well as their Yoruba ancestry. Accompanied by African musicians, working in Britain and France.

[5] Presented *Dol,* a solo for Pep Ramis, and *Zarco,* a collaboration between Ramis, co-per-

former/director Maria Muñoz and composer and cellist Tristan Honsinger.

[6] An Anglo-French collaboration between choreographer Robbe and sculptor Deacon to produce *Factory,* a piece in which audience, dancers and sculpture moved around the performance space – Riverside's Studio 1, cleared of its seats.

[7] In a revival of Alston's *Rainbow Bandit* (1977) to Charles Amirkhanian's score and new work, *Sometimes I Wonder,* to different versions of the Hoagy Carmichael classic, *Stardust.*

[8] In a programme, *Dances from Cyberspace,* which included dances created using material made on the software program LifeForms. The programme included *Concerto Grosso,* to Handel; *Out of Doors* to Bartók's First Piano Suite, played live by Jeremy Sweeney; *Vespri* to Monteverdi's *Vespers;* and three solos: *Even More,* a pointe solo for NYCB's Antonia Franceschi, set to Poulenc's *Sonata for Four Hands;*

Julia, to a John Lennon song; and a solo in silence for Baldwin, *Factual Nonsense*.

9 Bannerman reworked his inaugural professorial lecture, including his performance of 'The Swan' solo from Siobhan Davies' *Carnival of the Animals*, and included performances by Candoco, by members of the Shobana Jeyasingh Company and by Dana Fouras, who danced an excerpt from Ashley Page's *Fearful Symmetries*.

10 Presented *Le Flesh*, a solo commissioned by Islington Dance Project, on a double bill with Laurie Booth.

11 In an improvised duet *Condition Red* with viola player Beverley Davidson. Shared double bill with Emilyn Claid.

12 Presented *This is the Picture*, in collaboration with opera and theatre director/designer Tom Cairns and writer Helen Cooper with music by Richard Strauss and Graham Fitkin. *Alistair Fish*, a short film by Collins and Cairns, was shown as part of the programme.

13 Presented new works *The Art of Touch* to music by Scarlatti and Matteo Fargion, played live by Carole Cerasi, costumes by Sasha Keir, and *Wild Translations*, to music by Kevin Volans, played live by the Duke Quartet, designs by David Buckland and Peter Mumford. The programme was part-commissioned from the Prudential Award given to Dance Umbrella 94.

14 Presented *Enter Achilles*, a Dance Umbrella commission made possible by the 1994 Prudential Award.

15 Presented two solos: *Sweetie J*, to one of Bartók's Romanian Folk Dances, and *Meeting J*, to Bartók's *Sonata for Two Pianos and Percussion*. The music for both pieces was performed live by Elena Riu and Peter Bridges with percussionists Daniella Ganeva and Lavon Parikian.

16 In a performance to mark Purcell's tercentenary, *Great Moments of Purcell – and Blow*, to music by Henry Purcell and John Blow. The performance included a choir on stage.

17 Maliphant presented a reworking of *Paradigm*, first shown in Umbrella 94, and shared a double bill with Dana Reitz.

18 Presented a solo, *Cyborg*, and shared a double bill with Steve Paxton.

19 Presented a solo *Dunk* in collaboration with visual artist Bruce Sharp who constructed the sound and light score. Shared a double bill with Wendy Houston.

20 Presented *Haunted* with new music by John Avery and shared a double bill with Henry Montes.

21 In a new work by company member Chantal Donaldson, *Never Still*, to music by Hughes le Bars; plus a revival of Philip Taylor's *Haunted Passages* (music, Benjamin Britten's *Lachrymae*) and *Movements in B*, a collaboration between jazz musician Orphy Robinson (with music performed live), choreographer Gary Lambert and company artistic director, Maggie Morris.

22 Sapsford is an artist with the Royal Ballet and recipient of a Jerwood Young Choreographers Award, which enabled him to create *Where Her Voice*, for four dancers (Tammy Arjona, Dana Fouras, Rachel Lopez and Vivian Wood), to a commissioned score from Hans Peter Kuhn and designs by Kitty Percy. Shared a double bill with Compagnie D.I.T.

23 Presented three evenings of *Events* with a backdrop by Robert Rauschenberg, plus a mixed bill of British premieres, comprising: *Beach Birds* (1991) to *Four* by John Cage, lighting and costume, Marsha Skinner; *Ground Level Overlay* (1995) to Stuart Dempster's *Underground Overlay* which used ten trombone players recorded in a giant watertank, decor by Leonardo Drew, costumes by Suzanne Gallo, lighting by Aaron Copp; and *CRWDSPDR* (1993) with a score by John King, design by Mark Lancaster.

24 Showed his latest work, *Some English Suites*, to Glenn Gould's recording of Bach's *English Suite*. Shared a double bill with Wayne McGregor.

25 Presented *Private Collection*, on a double bill with Russell Maliphant.

26 Founded in 1985, this was the UK debut for the company from New York, exponents of 'pop action'. The programme included *Action Occupation*, *Wall*, and a solo for Streb, *Little Ease*, all with the sole accompaniment of contact microphones to amplify the sound of the dancers. The company also toured and held workshops – see 'Related Events'.

1995: Related Events

Film and Video
Dance on Film (Riverside Studios Cinema), double bills:
Showboat[1]; *Cabin in the Sky*[2]
Take Me Out to the Ball Game[3]; *Seven Brides for Seven Brothers* [4]

Dance on Screen[5] (The Video Place):
Il Combattimento di Ettore e Achille[6]
Launch of new screenings from *Editions à Voir*[7]
Unknown Territory[8] by Union Dance, *Lounge*[9] and *Pure Visions*[10]
Video Dance in Europe;[11] launch of *Dance for the Camera*[12]
The Dance Films of Merce Cunningham and Elliot Caplan[13]

Seminars
Come Surfing[14] (Lilian Baylis Theatre)
Fit to Dance? Aspects of Fitness, Injury and Nutrition for Dancers[15] (Middlesex University)

Classes and Workshops
Workshop: Dana Reitz
Masterclasses: Elizabeth Streb and Ringside

Exhibitions
Pushing the Boundaries - Advancing the dance[16] (Lethaby Gallery, Central St Martins College of Art and Design)
Chris Harris Photographs[17]

Pre-performance Talk
Siobhan Davies Dance Company

Meet the Artists
Dana Reitz, Elizabeth Streb, Steve Paxton, Mal Pelo, Henry Montes, Siobhan Davies Dance Company, Matthew Hawkins, Mark Baldwin, Koffi Koko/Peter Badejo, Richard Alston, Aletta Collins, Javier De Frutos, Mallika Sarabhai and the Darpana Dance Company

Education
Techno Dance Bytes course[18] (Lilian Baylis Theatre)
Doris Humphrey: A Centenary Celebration[19] (The Place Theatre)
Elizabeth Streb/Ringside residency[20]

Associated Events
Badenheim 1939 with Second Stride[21] (Riverside Studios)
The Hour We Knew Nothing of Each Other with the National Youth Dance Company[22] (The Place Theatre)
Mallika Sarabhai and the Darpana Dance Company[23] (Bloomsbury Theatre)

Notes
[1] James Whale/USA, 1936
[2] Vincente Minelli/USA, 1943
[3] Busby Berkeley/USA, 1949
[4] Stanley Donen/USA, 1954, choreography by Michael Kidd.
[5] A collaboration between The Video Place and European Partners in Barcelona and Köln, presented by Anita Belli.
[6] A video opera for two screens, by Fabio Cirifino and Pablo Rosa.
[7] Included dance videos from Spain and Belgium and a documentary on the work of Anna

Teresa de Keersmaeker.

[8] Chor. Doug Elkins, dir. Jeff Baynes.

[9] Dir/chor. Miranda Pennell.

[10] Chor. Ted Stoffer, dir. Bob Bentley, Milfid Ellis, Ross MacGibbon.

[11] Screenings of Spanish and German dance films, including from Spain: *Aral* (chor. Pep Ramis); *Graons* (chor. Toni Mira); *Maria Muñoz* (chor. Maria Muñoz); *Subur, 305* (chor. Angel Margarit); *Escenari* (chor. Oscar Dasi/Carmelo Salazar); *Mundana* (chor. Pep Ramis and Maria Muñoz); *Peix* (Angel Margarit) and from Germany: *Impressing Uncle Bill* by Gerd Weigelt; *Effort Public* by Stefan Schneider; *Obfer Clip* by Gerd Weigelt; *Kontakt Triptychon* by Lutz Gregor. Followed by a debate *Dance on Screen across Europe*, chaired by Pia Kalinka.

[12] Including *Cover Up* (chor. Victoria Marks, dir. Margaret Williams); *T-Dance* (chor. Terry John Bates, dir. John Davies); *Horse Play* (chor./dir. Alison Murray); *boy* (chor. Rosemary Lee, dir. Peter Anderson); *Pace* (chor. Marisa Zanotti, dir. Katrina Mc Pherson); *Echo* (chor. Mark Baldwin, dir. Ross MacGibbon); *Man Act* (dir. Mike Stubbs with Roland Denning and Man Act); *Hands* (chor. Jonathan Burrows, dir. Adam Roberts); *The Storm* (chor. Aletta Collins, dir. Tom Cairns); *Never Say Die* (chor./dir. Nigel Charnock); *Dwell Time* (chor. Siobhan Davies, dir David Buckland).

[13] Including *Cage Cunningham; Deli Commedia; Changing Steps; Beach Birds for Camera*.

[14] Provided an opportunity to meet the participants of Techno Dance Bytes in the multimedia and networked Cyberstudio in Lilian Baylis Theatre and to explore the internet. Followed by a discussion chaired by David Hughes and with a panel of artists, multimedia experts and promoters to discuss the impact of technology on dance and the arts in general.

[15] A day-long conference that looked at the results of research initiated by Dr Peter Brinson as part of the Healthier Dancer Programme. Organised by Dance UK in association with the Society for Dance Research and Middlesex University.

[16] An exhibition exploring the role of design in the work of Robert Cohan, Peter Darrell, Kenneth MacMillan and Norman Morrice.

[17] A selection of the photographs of Harris, former resident photographer and graphic artist at Riverside Studios, who died in November 1994 in Perth.

[18] A six-day course to enable choreographers and digital artists to explore the use of interactive technology in dance, directed by Terry Braun. Five teams of choreographers, including Sue MacLennan, Yael Flexer, Mark Baldwin and Susan Crow, together with multimedia designers collaborated on making digital dance. Courtesy of the Illuminations Interactive website, the project was put on the Internet and linked to the South Bank, the ICA and selected overseas sites, remaining on-line until the New Year.

[19] A study day organised by the Society for Dance Research, featuring excerpts from Humphrey's early dances as well as a full performance of *Passacaglia in C*, with guest speakers and a panel discussion.

[20] A week-long residency in Greenwich, working with local schools.

[21] Directed and choreographed by Ian Spink, designed by Antony McDonald, with music by Orlando Gough, played live on stage. Second Stride was joined by ten local performers of varying ages.

[22] The first British production of Peter Handke's play with no words, co-directed by Ian Spink and Peter Brooks.

[23] The company from Ahmedabad in the only UK performance of a programme that formed part of Pan Projects' CHAKRA Cycle of Indian Dance Theatre. The programme included *Jazz Tillana*, with music by Trilok Gurtu, *Mean Streets on Earth* with music by the Karnataka College of Percussion, and *Ceremony One*.

1996

Saturday 28 September – Friday 8 November (50 London performances)

Venues

ICA, Natural History Museum, Peacock Theatre, Place Theatre, Purcell Room, Queen Elizabeth Hall, Riverside Studios, Union Chapel Islington[1]

Artists

Continental Europe

Compagnie Carmen Koko[2]
  (France/Spain/Benin)
Compagnie Cré-Ange[3] (France)
Julyen Hamilton[4] (Netherlands)
Mal Pelo[5] (Spain)

UK

Richard Alston Dance Company[6]
Mark Baldwin Dance Company[7]
Jonathan Burrows Group[8]
The Charnock Company[9]
Jordi Cortès[10] (Spain/UK)/Marisa Zanotti[11]
Siobhan Davies Dance Company[12]
Rene Eyre and Chris Nash[13]
Javier de Frutos[14]
Gateway to Freedom and The Strike
  the Man Band[15]

Green Candle Dance Company[16]
Matthew Hawkins[17]
Wendy Houstoun/François Testory[18]
Shobana Jeyasingh Dance Company[19]
Yolande Snaith Theatredance[20]
V-TOL Dance Company[21]

International

La La La Human Steps[22] (Canada)
José Navas[23] (Venezuala/Canada)
Tumbuka Dance Company[24] (Zimbabwe)

USA

Stephan Koplowitz[25]
Doug Varone and Dancers[26]

Notes

[1] New Dance Umbrella venue.

[2] Flamenco artist Mari Carmen Garcia from Spain and Paris-based Koffi Koko, born in Benin, joined forces to present *Scorched Earth*, with live music. The piece previewed during Dance Umbrella's Percussive Feet festival earlier in the year.

[3] The company made a return appearance after an absence of seven years, and presented a new piece, *Squares*, to 1960s music, including Jimi Hendrix, Otis Redding, Lou Reed and Duke Ellington with narrator, Citizen Smart a.k.a. Geoffrey Carey (US).

[4] Presented two programmes (numbers 25–27 and 28–30) from Hamilton's series of improvised solos, *40 Monologues*, with lighting by Svante Grogarn.

[5] The extended company of five performers presented *La Calle del Imaginero*, with designs by Jorda Ferrer, Laforja and Juan Gonzalez.

[6] Presented the world premiere of *Okho*, to Iannis Xenakis's score for djembes, played live on stage by Richard Benjafield, Simon Lim-brick and Andrew Martin; *Orpheus Singing and Dreaming*, to the Harrison Birtwistle score *Nenia*, with singer/narrator Nicole Tibbels; and *Beyond Measure* (expanded from *Bach Measures*) to Bach chorales and organ choral preludes.

[7] Presented the London premiere of *Confessions*, to James MacMillan's *The Confession of Isobel Gowdie, Mirrors*, to Ravel's *Miroirs*, played by John Sweeney, *Homage*, a quartet danced in silence and *Sister* to James MacMillan's *The Berserking* (first movement).

[8] Presented *The Stop Quartet* to piano music by Kevin Volans, played live by the composer, and recorded music by Matteo Fargion, with lighting design by Michael Hulls. Performers were Jonathan Burrows, Henry Montes, Ragnhild Olsen and Fin Walker.

[9] Presented *Heroine*, based on the life and work of Billie Holiday.

[10] In a solo, *Day Dreaming at Dusk*, inspired by the dark paintings of Goya, with music by Shostakovich and lighting by Michael Man-

nion. Shared a double bill with Marisa Zanotti.

[11] Glasgow-based Zanotti presented her solo, *Runner,* inspired by Brian Keenan's memoirs.

[12] In a programme featuring Davies's latest work, *Trespass* (music by Gerald Barry), and *Affections* to Handel arias, arranged by Barry, sung on stage by mezzo-soprano Buddug Verona James. Lighting was by Peter Mumford, design by David Buckland.

[13] A collaboration between dancer/choreographer Eyre and photographer Nash to produce an interactive multimedia installation, made in collaboration with digital interaction technician, Gerald Wells, plus two performances of *Say a Little Prayer,* performed by René Eyre and Bo Chapman.

[14] Presented *Transatlantic,* a personal memoir set to the original cast recording of Styne and Sondheim's *Gypsy,* with lighting by Michael Mannion. De Frutos appeared as part of the South Bank Centre's American Independents season.

[15] Independent artist Michael Popper's company, founded in 1986, presented *Also Available in White.*

[16] In *Tales from the Citadel,* in which all the dancers were over 45, and included Brian Bertscher, Jane Dudley, Fergus Early, Jacky Lansley and Tim Rubidge. Directed by Early, with designs by Craig Givens and featuring live music with a score commissioned from Sally Davies.

[17] In a full-length solo *Alone – in Your Company,* commissioned by Tanzprojekte Cologne, in collaboration with composer Fabienne Audéoud, photographer Chris Nash and sound and light technician Charles Balfour.

[18] A double bill, featuring Houstoun's solo *Daunted* with music by John Avery; Testory's duet *Spectre* had music by long-time collaborator Luca Mainardi and masks by Rea David.

[19] Presented a double bill, including *Romance ... with footnotes* (1993) and new work *Palimpsest* to a score by Graham Fitkin, designs by carnival artist Keith Khan. The performance was accompanied throughout by a chamber ensemble on stage.

[20] In a new production *Gorgeous Creatures,* with music by Graeme Miller, design by Barnaby Stone, costume design by Suzanne Slack and Kei Ho.

[21] In Mark Murphy's fusion of dance and film, *By Force of Fantasy.*

[22] Edouard Lock's company returned to London with *2* (1995), which featured action, punctuated by twin-screen film sequences, with commissioned music by Gavin Bryars, played on stage on two harpsichords by Denis Bonenfant and Kong Kie Njo.

[23] Born in Venezuela, Navas moved to Montreal in 1991. The programme of solos comprised *Sterile Fields, Luna Llena, Postdata* and *Celestiales.*

[24] The company was formed in 1992 in Harare by artistic director Neville Campbell and here made its British debut with a programme that included Campbell's *Quartet, Solo for a Street Child* and *And Rwande,* plus Robyn Orlin's *And At Midnight We Aired Our Soles.* Tumbuka dancers also enjoyed a week-long residency, taking classes and choreography workshops at the London School of Contemporary Dance.

[25] Koplowitz – a specialist in large-scale works – created the site-specific piece *Genesis Canyon* set in the main hall of the Natural History Museum for thirty-eight dancers. Design was by Craig Givens, lighting by Simon Corder and vocal score by Jonathan Stone in collaboration with Adam Peacock, with live accompaniment by Sarah-Jane Morris, Barnaby Stone and Jonathan Stone.

[26] British debut for the company founded ten years ago in New York. The programme included a duet, *In Thine Eyes,* to Michael Nyman's *Noises, Sounds and Sweet Airs; Aperture,* to Schubert's *Moments Musicaux, No. 2; Motet,* to Mozart's *Exsultate, Jubilate;* and *Rise,* to John Adams' *Fearful Symmetries.*

1996: Additional Events

Percussive Feet Festival
(Cochrane Theatre, 19–23 February 1996). Hosted by Ira Bernstein (US)

Artists

Ira Bernstein/John Kirk (musician)
Tobias Tak
High Spen Blue Diamond Rappers
The 25 Northumberland Cloggies
The Jiving Lindy Hoppers

Maricarmen Garcia
Koffi Koko
Sonia Kundi and Akram Khan
Irish Folk Ballet Company

Related Events
Debate, chaired by Val Bourne.
Film and video screenings: *Sam Sherry: Step Dancer;* two videos by Gerald and Michelle Fox of LWT.

Residencies:
Tobias Tak (UK) worked for two hours each week over nine weeks with young people aged 18-plus at the Weekend Arts College. Extra rehearsals were held closer to the festival, where they performed as part of Tak's programme.

During the festival week, Ira Bernstein and John Kirk worked every day with eleven 20- to 25-year-old women students on the BTEC dance course at Kingsway College. The students performed on the closing night of the festival as part of Bernstein's programme.

Commission:
Sue MacLennan was commissioned to create a 20-minute piece in collaboration with composer Jamie McCarthy for the opening night, including dancers Ben Craft and Andrea Buckley, and drew upon Irish step, Appalachian clog and contemporary movement.

1996: Related Events

Film and Video

Dance on Screen[1] (The Place Theatre):
Elliot Caplan Masterclass[2]
Screening of *CRWDSPCR*[3]
TAPED:[4] *Car on the Road;*[5] *Where Angels Fear to Tread;*[6] *Tenement – a multi-story*[7]
European Festivals, programmes 1 and 2[8]
Lloyd Newson programme[9]

Seminar/discussion: Dance Versus Camera – does video really serve dance, or is it a distraction?[10]

Open Forum[11] – for dance-film makers
Digital Dancing 96[12]

Seminars
So Many Islands: issues of meaning in the work of Shobana Jeyasingh[13] (Place Theatre)
Beyond the Tea Dance [14]

Classes and Workshops

Workshops for professional dancers: Julyen Hamilton, Doug Varone and Dancers

Meet the Artists

Julyen Hamilton, Mal Pelo, Matthew Hawkins, Javier De Frutos, Jonathan Burrows, Jordi Cortés Molina, Compagnie Cré-Ange, Charnock Dance Company, Wendy Houstoun, François Testory, Siobhan Davies, Yolande Snaith, Doug Varone, Green Candle, Shobana Jeyasingh

Notes

[1] A five-day event organised by The Place Dance Services in association with Illuminations Interactive and Dance Umbrella.

[2] Film-maker with the Merce Cunningham Dance Foundation, Caplan held a three-day masterclass on dance-film making for directors and choreographers, culminating in a public showing of work from the class.

[3] The London premiere of Caplan's film of Cunningham's choreography, which explores the making of the dance, with Cunningham using the Lifeforms program.

[4] Two screenings of the three dance videos commissioned by ACE, for use in education.

[5] Choreography by Lea Anderson, director, Ross McGibbon, featuring The Cholmondeleys.

[6] Directed and choreographed by Mark Murphy for V-Tol.

[7] A documentary based upon Edwards and Watton's latest show, directed by Mark Parry.

[8] A selection of the best short dance films shown in Europe this year, chosen by Bob Lockyer and Mark Baldwin.

[9] Newson presented excerpts from films of DV8's work, including *Enter Achilles*, and provided commentary and background information.

[10] The panellists were: John Ashford, Alison Murray, Robert Penman and Yolande Snaith, and the debate was chaired by arts consultant Jenny Waldman.

[11] This provided an opportunity for dance film and video makers to show and discuss their work with eight out of those films submitted being shown.

[12] An intensive follow-up to the 1995 Techno Dance Bytes held in four two-hour sessions over one and a half days, in which work was shown that had developed from the previous year's initiative, as well as keynote introductions from Terry Braun of Illuminations Interactive and reports and work from the alt.dance project at Yorkshire Dance Centre, the Split Screen Conference in Chichester, and Lantaren/Venster in Rotterdam. Works shown were: Simon Grosser, Sue MacLennan and Nye Parry's *Breathless*; Tim Diggins and Sarah Rubidge's *Passing Phases*; Chris Nash, René Eyre and Simon Grosser's *Say A Little Prayer*; Richard Lord's *Progressive 2* and *Brownian Motion*; Bruno Martelli and Ruth Gibson's *Igloo* and *Windows 96*; Mark Baldwin, Carol Murcia, Nye Parry, Richard Lord and Bruno Martelli's *Who Killed Me?*; Jonathan Jones-Morris, Tessa Elliot, Andrew Deacon and Rebecca Skelton's *Odyssey*; and Tim Diggins and Susan Crow's *Six*. There was also a discussion on future developments in dance and technology, led by Braun.

[13] A debate chaired by Christopher Cook, with Shobana Jeyasingh, Sarah Rubidge and Stephanie Jordan.

[14] A one-day conference for dance artists, companies, animateurs and others working to create dance with, by and for older people, organised by the Foundation for Community Dance, and based around the performances of Green Candle Dance Company at Riverside.

1997

Tuesday 21 October – Saturday 15 November (25 London performances)

Venues
Place Theatre, Queen Elizabeth Hall, Riverside Studios
The Stephen Petronio Company presented a national tour, following their London performances:
Basingstoke: The Anvil
Brighton: Dome
Cambridge: Arts Theatre
High Wycombe: Swan
Manchester: The Dancehouse
Sheffield: Lyceum Theatre
Warwick: Arts Centre

Artists

Continental Europe
Lanónima Imperial[1] (Spain)
Compagnie Maguy Marin[2] (France)
Compañia Vicente Sáez[3] (Spain)
Compagnie Tandem[4] (Belgium)
Raz/Hans Tuerlings[5] (Netherlands)

UK
Mark Baldwin Dance Company[6]
Rosemary Butcher[7]
Siobhan Davies Dance Company[8]

Javier De Frutos[9]
Wendy Houstoun[10]

International
Cas Public[11] (Canada)
Eva Karczag[12] (Australia)

USA
Sara Pearson/Patrik Widrig and Company[13]
Stephen Petronio Company[14]

Notes
[1] Presented the British premiere of artistic director Juan Carlos Garcia's *Moving Landscapes*, (1995) which included six dancers and four musicians.
[2] British debut for the company of thirteen dancer/actor/musicians in Marin's *Waterzooi* (1993), with score by Denis Mariotte for toy instruments.
[3] Presented Sáez's trio *Atman*, to Purcell's music, with lighting by Bruno Garny.
[4] Choreographer Michèle Noiret's ensemble presented *Les Plis de la Nuit*, inspired by the engravings of Maurice Pasternak, in the company's London debut.
[5] The four dancers who comprise Raz made their London debut with Tuerlings's *De Reis 2 sans peau et sans arêtes*, the third part of a four-part composition inspired by the work of French writer Céline. Music by Jeroen van Vliet.
[6] Presented *Tuireadh*, a piece commissioned by the Royal Festival Hall as part of the *Rising Sparks* festival, in celebration of James Mac-

Millan's music. MacMillan's *Requiem* for clarinet and string quartet was dedicated to those who lost their life in the Piper Alpha tragedy, and was played live for the performance by the Nash Ensemble of London. Also on the bill were *Intimate Letters* to Janácek's *String Quartet No. 2*, played by The Sorrel String Quartet and a re-staging of *Samples* to Ravel's *Introduction and Allegro* for solo harp, flute clarinet and string quartet, played by the Nash Ensemble.
[7] As part of an ongoing retrospective of Butcher's work, Fin Walker and Henry Montes performed two duets: *Landings* (1976) and *Fractured Landscapes, Fragmented Narratives* (1997), a collaboration between Butcher, visual artist Noel Bramley and composer Johnny Clark. 'Riverside Studio 2 was converted into a gallery space for the installation/performance, where images obtained with a video camera allowed the live performers to integrate with a collage of sound and with still and moving images.' (Brochure notes)
[8] To celebrate 25 years of dance making,

Davies presented a triple bill that included her latest work *Bank* to a percussive score *Donna Che Beve* performed live by composer Matteo Fargion, lighting design by Ian Beswick; *White Man Sleeps* (1988); and *The Art of Touch* (1995).

[9] Presented the London premiere of his trio *Grass*, set to Puccini's *Madam Butterfly*, danced by De Frutos, Jamie Watton and Pary Naderi, with set and costumes by Terry Warner and lighting by Michael Mannion. De Frutos was the winner of the 1996 Bagnolet Prix d'auteur.

[10] Soloist Houstoun performed her trilogy *Haunted, Daunted* and *Flaunted*.

[11] The Montreal-based group made its London debut with Hélène Blackburn's *Les Suites Furieuses,* to music by Stravinsky, Hindemith and Zoran Eric.

[12] Now based in the Netherlands, Karczag presented a solo performance that formed a double bill with Sara Pearson, Patrik Widrig and Company.

[13] Presented Pearson's solo, *Dr Pearson's Guide to Loss and Fear*; and a duet *Heimweh* (homesick). The performance formed a double bill with Karczag.

[14] Opened the festival with five UK premieres: *ReBourne* (1997) to the Beastie Boys and Sheila Chandra's *A BoneCroneDrone2; La-reigne* (1995) to the Stranglers's *No More Heroes* and an original score by David Linton; *Drawn That Way;* a new solo *I Kneel Down Before You,* and *#4* (1996).

1997: Related Events

Film and Video

Dance on Screen (The Place), Dance on Screen masterclass[1]

Insights - a series of discussions and film screenings with the focus on dance for television, including: *Whirlpool - a case study*[2]

Taped:[3] Bullies Ballerinas' *Bare Feet and Crazy Legs;*[4] JazzXchange's *Special Request;*[5] *Macbeth Taped*[6]

Choreographers Choice: 1 and 2[7]

Dance for the Camera, Retrospective[8]

Open Forum[9]

Digital Dancing 97[10] – 'Beyond the Screen' (Saturday 25 October – Sunday 9 November, Riverside Studios)

Classes and Workshops

Masterclass: Stephen Petronio and Kristen Borg (Greenwich Dance Agency)

Meet the Artists

Stephen Petronio, Lanónima Imperial, Cas Public, Siobhan Davies, Maguy Marin, Raz, Javier De Frutos, Tandem

Notes

[1] A four-day masterclass for choreographers to acquire the technical training to make work with film makers, including choreographer/film maker Alison Murray.

[2] A new film by Jayne Parker, commissioned by the London Production Fund for Carlton Television. Parker was also present for a discussion of the process, with Maggie Ellis from the London Production Fund.

[3] The launch of new dance videos for use in education, commissioned by the Arts Council of England.

[4] Chor. Pearl Jordan and Jeanefer Jean Charles, dir. Alison Murray.

[5] Chor. Sheron Wray, dir. Henry Letts.

[6] Chor. Jonathan Lunn and Phyllida Lloyd, dir. Margaret Williams.

[7] Two programmes of new dance films from around the world, selected by Javier De Frutos and Alison Murray.

[8] Rodney Wilson, director of the Film, Video and Broadcasting Unit of the Arts Council presented highlights from the BBC2 television series of films made collaboratively by choreog-

Nigel Charnock Company, 1997. PHOTO: HUGO GLENDINNING

raphers and directors.

⁹ A selection of new films or extracts for viewing and discussion.

¹⁰ Five teams worked simultaneously in Studio 2 on separate digital initiatives, involving, for example, different uses of motion capture, a surveillance project and a fusion of digital animation and live performance. The projects were run in conjunction with Illuminations Interactive, and directed by Terry Braun with a team that included Suzanne Kelly and Henry Johnson. A first venture for Digital Dancing was a live tele-presence performance on Halloween, *Ghosts and Astonauts*, devised by Suzan Kozel, that linked choreographers and dancers performing simultaneously at The Place Theatre and Riverside Studios via a videoconference link facilitated by Macintosh computers and CU-SeeMe software.

1998

Thursday 1 October – Saturday 28 November (53 London performances)

Venues
Barbican Centre,* British Library,* ICA Brandon Room, Place Theatre, Queen Elizabeth Hall, The Roundhouse,* Sadler's Wells
The Michael Clark Company presented a national tour, surrounding the London performances:
Bath: Theatre Royal
Birmingham: Repertory Theatre
Blackpool: Grand Theatre
Cambridge: Arts Theatre
Canterbury: The Marlowe Theatre
Epsom: Playhouse
High Wycombe: Swan
Oxford: Playhouse
Sheffield: Crucible Theatre

Artists

Continental Europe
Ariadone[1] (France)
Ballett Frankfurt[2] (Germany)
Dance Company Leine and Roebana[3] (Netherlands)
Provisional Danza[4] (Spain)

UK
Richard Alston Dance Company[5]
Mark Baldwin Dance Company[6]
Jonathan Burrows Group[7]
Michael Clark Company[8]
Aletta Collins[9]
Siobhan Davies Dance Company[10]

Javier De Frutos[11]
Shobana Jeyasingh Dance Company[12]
Russell Maliphant/David Hughes[13]
Ricochet Dance Company[14]

International
Eiko and Koma[15] (Japan)
Kinetic Theatre[16] (Russia)

USA
Merce Cunningham Dance Company[17]
Doug Elkins Dance Company[18]
Stephen Koplowitz[19]
Stephen Petronio Dance Company[20]

Notes
* New venues
[1] Presented *Waiting*, a new solo by Carlotta Ikeda, inspired by Marguerite Duras' account of childhood in Indochina, with lighting by Eric Loustau-Carrère.
[2] The company made its British debut with *Hypothetical Stream 2* (1997): music, Stuart Dempster's *Standing Waves* and Ingram Marshall's *Fog Tropes*; *Enemy in the Figure* (1989, integrated in 1990 into the full-length *Limb's Theorem*): music, Thom Willems; *Quintett* (1993) to Gavin Bryars's *Jesus' Blood Never Failed Me Yet*.
[3] Making their Dance Umbrella debut, the company presented choreographers Andrea Leine and Harijono Roebana's *Tales of Eversion*

and *If we could only even if we could*.
[4] The Madrid-based company made its London debut with Carmen Werner's *Coraje, escena 13 (Courage, scene 13)*, a work that incorporated characters drawn from Brecht's *Mother Courage*, with music by Mozart and Penderecky.
[5] A performance in celebration of Richard Alston's fiftieth birthday. Special guests Eva Karczag (former member of Strider), Darshan Singh Bhuller and Siobhan Davies performed alongside Alston himself. The programme comprised *Sophisticated Curiosities*: a collage drawn from pieces that spanned Alston's career, danced by his current company, and including excerpts from *Nowhere Slowly* (1970),

Combines (1972), *Blue Schubert Fragments* (1974), *Rainbow Ripples* (1980), *Apollo Distraught* (1982), *Strong Language* (1987), *Roughcut* (1990); *Dances of the Wayward Ancients* (a trio for Davies, Alston and Singh Bhuller to Bach); as well as a new Dance Umbrella commission *Waltzes in Disorder* to Brahms *Liebeslieder Walzer* for four voices and piano, performed live on stage.

[6] Presented a bill of new works to twentieth-century piano music, played by Martin Jones: *Song of the Nightingale* to Stravinsky's *Le Rossignol*, costumes Rifat Ozbek; *Pulcinella Disperato* to music by Hans Werner Henze, *Darkness Visible* to music by Thomas Ades, lighting by Stephen Munn; *M-Piece*, a solo for Bart De Block, performed *en pointe*, to a commissioned score by Roxanna Panufnik.

[7] Presented Burrow's solo for himself, *Hands* (1995), *All Together*, a trio for Burrows, Dana Fouras and Ragnhild Olsen, plus *Things I Don't Know*, with music by Kevin Volans.

[8] Clark presented his first full-length work in four years: *current/SEE*, to specially commissioned live music from Susan Stenger's bass guitar ensemble, Big Bottom plus drummer Andrew Tween, with lighting by Charles Atlas and costumes by Hussein Chalayan. Performing with Clark were dancers Kate Coyne, Lorena Randi and Dominik Schoetschel.

[9] In a solo show (her first) *My Half of the Painting*, inspired by the Poulenc/Cocteau opera *La Voix Humaine* for solo soprano.

[10] With a company enlarged to ten dancers, presented *Winnsboro Cotton Mill Blues* (1992) to Frederic Rzewski's piano blues; *Eighty Eight* (1998) to Conlan Nancarrow's studies for player piano, played by Rex Lawson.

[11] Presented his latest work commissioned by Dance Umbrella, *The Hypochondriac Bird*, a duet with Jamie Watton, sets by Terry Warner and lighting by Michael Mannion.

[12] The company celebrated its tenth year with a Dance Umbrella commission *Memory and Other Props*, which made references to works created over the last decade, and had a specially composed score by Alistair McDonald; plus a revival of *Intimacies of a Third Order*, to music by Michael Gordon.

[13] A double bill, in which Hughes performed two solos made specially for him: Robert Cohan's *Adagietto,* to Mahler's *Adagietto for Strings;*

Siobhan Davies' *L'Après-Midi d'un Faune* to Debussy's music. Maliphant performed his own choreography: *Shift* with lighting by Michael Hulls, and presented two solos commissioned by Dance Umbrella: *I* for himself and *II* for Dana Fouras.

[14] In a double bill of new commissions: Stephen Petronio's *Fetch Boy and Fox*, score by British composer Stuart Jones, costumes by H Petal; and Nigel Charnock's *5IVE part one*.

[15] The Japanese–American Butoh artists' return to London after eight years with a British premiere, *Wind*, with a score arranged by Joseph Jennings. The performance included their son Shin Otake.

[16] Sasha Pepelyaev founded the company in 1994 in order to establish a Russian contemporary dance style, and in their British debut they presented *The View of Russian Grave from Germany* and *Violators of Disorder,* which featured teachers and pupils from the Modern Art School in Ekaterinberg.

[17] Presented *Windows* (1995), music *Microcosmos*, by Emanuel Dimas de Melo Pimenta, backdrop by John Cage; *Scenario* (1997), score by Takehisa Kosugi, design by Rei Kawakubo of Comme des Garçons; *Rondo* (1996), score by John Cage *FOUR6*, costumes Suzanne Gallo and Merce Cunningham; *Pond Way* (1998), to Brian Eno's *New Ikebukuro* (for three CD-players), design by Roy Lichtenstein's *Landscape with Boat* (1986); plus two *Events: Barbican Event 1*, set design by Robert Rauschenberg: *Immerse* (1994); *Barbican Event 2*, set design by William Anastasi: *Points in Space* (1986).

[18] Elkins returned to Dance Umbrella after an absence of eight years with *Narcoleptic Lovers* (1995); *Bipolar NOS* (1998); and a solo *Roda* for Elkins himself.

[19] Choreographer/director Koplowitz returned to London to make a site-specific piece for the new British Library building at St Pancras, *Babel Index*, with collaborators: costume designer Craig Givens; lighting designer Simon Corder; composer Jonathan Stone and fifty-four dancers.

[20] Presented the British premiere of *Not Garden*, inspired by Dante's *Inferno*, with music by Gounod, Bach, David Linton and Sheila Chandra, set against a series of video projections and with costumes by Ghost.

1998: Related Events

Film and Video
Digital Dancing 98[1] (The Jerwood Space, over three weeks)
Dance on Screen[2] (The Place):
   Dance on Screen Masterclass[3]
   Insights[4]
   Canadian Insight[5]
   Masterclass Screening[6]
   Choreographers' Choice, Programmes 1 and 2[7]
   Breakdancing[8]
   Lecture/demonstration by Lea Anderson
   Open Forum[9]
   Informal screenings and discussions
Passing Phases[10] (Queen Elizabeth Hall foyer, 24–29 October)

Classes and Workshops
Masterclass: Stephen Petronio (Greenwich Dance Agency)
Delicious Movement Workshop: Eiko and Koma (Greenwich Dance Agency)
Workshop: Doug Elkins (Greenwich Dance Agency)

Meet the Artists
Siobhan Davies, Shobana Jeyasingh, Rusell Maliphant and David Hughes, Javier De Frutos, Stephen Petronio, Provisional Danza, Ricochet, Kinetic Theatre, Leine and Roebana, Eiko and Koma, Doug Elkins

Pre-performance Talk
Siobhan Davies

Notes

[1] Six teams of choreographers and digital artists produced: *Trial by Video* – a real-time/live collaboration between Wayne McGregor and Random Dance Company in London and Company in Space in Melbourne; *The Body Within* – choreographer Gill Clarke, digital artist Shelley Williams and dancer Kirsty Alexander; *Dancing Inside* – a collaboration between Jane Dudley, animator Gillian Lacey, digital artist Timo Arnall and dancer/choreographer Frank Bock; *Daylight Robbery* – choreographer Ruth Gibson, designers Bruno Martelli and Dan Ray, composers Tim Norman and Luke Boucher and dancers including Mark Bruce; *Cyberkinesis* – an interactive installation for public spaces created by Richard Lord with *Lost in Space* digital effects designers Christian Hogue and Alex Rutterford, designer Emma Fryer, composer Max Richter and dancer Enid Gill; *Untitled* – in which RCA researcher Jane Harris experimented with optical motion capture from Oxford Metric, together with choreographer Ruth Gibson. The project also included a debate, *The Future of Dance and New Technology in Higher Education.*

[2] A week of screenings, events and workshops, celebrating dance made for screens of every size, from computer to cinema, directed by Theresa Beattie, director of The Place Dance Services.

[3] An advanced masterclass for choreographers with some experience working with film or video, led by director Peter Anderson.

[4] A series of daily events designed to give an insight into the thoughts and ideas of the people who commission, create and fund dance for the screen. It included a talk by masterclass leader Peter Anderson; a discussion chaired by Terry Braun about collaborations between choreographers and digital artists; Australian Insight, presented by Peter Kaufmann, Exhibition Programme Manager at the Australian Film Institute and film-maker Alyson Bell; Dance for the Camera – Bob Lockyer and Rodney Wilson talked about the new format for the 1999 series of BBC's *Dance for the Camera.*

[5] Presented by film-maker Laura Taler and Kathleen Smith, director of *The Moving Pictures Festival of Dance on Film and Video in Toronto.*

[6] A screening of work produced by the par-

235

Mark Baldwin Dance Company rehearsing *Song of the Nightingale*, 1998. PHOTO: HUGO GLENDINNING

ticipants of this year's masterclass.

[7] A selection of new international dance films, chosen by Shobana Jeyasingh and Carol Brown.

[8] Short screenings of a selection of television advertisements, including Sony's *The Perfect Copy* and the Eurostar commercial choreographed by Wayne McGregor.

[9] Screening and discussion of eight short films by emerging dance film-makers and choreographers.

[10] An interactive multi-screen installation by Sarah Rubidge, Tim Diggins, Gary Hill and composer Nye Parry. The project was originally developed during Digital Dancing 96 at The Place.

1999

Wednesday 29 September – Sunday 14 November (43 London performances)

Venues
*Brick Lane Music Hall, *Crystal Palace National Sports Centre, Greenwich Dance Agency, Place Theatre, Queen Elizabeth Hall, Riverside Studios, Sadler's Wells Theatre

The Mark Morris Dance Group tour:
   Birmingham: Repertory Theatre
   Canterbury: The Marlowe Theatre
   High Wycombe
   Stoke on Trent: Regent Theatre
   Woking: New Victoria Theatre

Artists

Continental Europe
En-Knap Dance Company (Slovenia)
Compagnie Maguy Marin (France)
Compagnie Montalvo-Hervieu (France)
De Rotterdamse Dansgroep (Netherlands)
Tanzcompagnie Rubato (Germany)
Meg Stuart, Ann Hamilton and
   Damaged Goods (Belgium)

UK
Lea Anderson
Mark Baldwin Dance Company
The Cholmondeleys and The
   Featherstonehaughs

Nigel Charnock and Company
Aletta Collins Dance Company
Siobhan Davies Dance Company
Russell Maliphant Company

International
Vincent Mantsoe (South Africa)

USA
Bill T. Jones
Mark Morris Dance Group
Richard Move
Doug Varone and Dancers

Notes
*New venues for the festival.
[1] Part of the Canterbury Festival.
[2] Part of the Taking Risks Festival.
[3] The company of Iztok Kovac made its Umbrella debut with *Far From Sleeping Dogs*, that also included a filmed performance by avantgarde composer Vinko Globokar.
[4] Presented the company's signature piece *May B*, to music including Schubert's *Death and the Maiden* and Gavin Bryars' *Jesus's Blood Never Failed Me Yet.*
[5] Choreographer José Montalvo, dancer/collaborator Dominique Hervieu and their company of ten presented *Paradis.*
[6] The repertory-led company founded in 1975, formerly Werkcentrum Dans and led by Käthy Gosschalk, presented Gosschalk's *Zonder Tiel* (mus. Beethoven's String Quartet No. 12), Jacopo Gordani's *Mars in Aries* and Javier De Frutos's *The Fortune Biscuit.*
[7] Berlin-based Jutta Hell and Dieter Baumann (Rubato's artistic directors) presented a

duet for themselves, *This is Not a Love Song*, to Wolfgang Bley-Borkowski's contemporary arrangement of Beethoven's *Grosse Fugue* in B minor.
[8] Presented *appetite*, a collaboration between American choreographer Stuart, her Belgium-based company Damaged Goods and installation artist Hamilton. London debut for the company.
[9] Anderson collaborated with designer Simon Foxton and composer Steve Blake to present the latest Dance Umbrella commissioned site-specific work, *Sportorama*. The performance at Crystal Palace National Sports Centre included 100 athletes, 40 dance students, members of The Cholmondeleys and The Featherstonehaughs and the Dulwich Orchestral Society.
[10] Presented *Julius Tomb* (mus. Luke Stoneham, performed live by the Bournmouth Sinfonietta, des. Michael Howells) plus revivals of *Hommage* and *A Collection of Moving Parts*

(mus. Chopin).

[11] Presented Lea Anderson's latest show *The Victims of Death in Smithereens*, inspired by cabaret, to music by Steve Blake, lighting design by Simon Corder and costumes by Sandy Powell.

[12] Presented an installation performance, *The Room*, in which the audience was invited to view the action through windows, spy-holes or on a bank of monitors and large screens.

[13] Presented *Alice is Back in Wonderland* to Gershwin's *Rhapsody in Blue*.

[14] Presented the company's first full-length work, *Wild Air*, to music by Kevin Volans, set and lighting by David Buckland and Peter Mumford.

[15] Presented two solos: *One*, for Maliphant himself, and *Two* for Dana Fouras (Dance Umbrella commissions), plus company work *Liquid Reflex* with lighting design by Michael Hulls and music by Andy Cowton.

[16] Dance Umbrella debut for the Soweto-born dancer/choreographer, with an evening of solos performances: *Gulu*, *Mpheyane* and *Phokwane*. The performances were accompanied by a screening of the South Bank Show documentary film directed by Gerald Fox and featuring the work of Mantsoe and two fellow South Africans.

[17] Presented the UK premiere of his solo project *The Breathing Show*, that included a series of new dances to music by Schubert and the reworking of some earlier solos.

[18] Presented the London premiere of *Gloria* (mus. Vivaldi) and the UK premieres of *The Argument* (mus. Schumann's *Fünf Stücke in Volkston*) and *Rhymes With Silver*, to a specially commissioned score by Lou Harrison and a set by Howard Hodgkin.

[19] Presented *martha@danceumbrella*, a homage to Martha Graham, developed from performances first given in New York.

[20] Presented a programme of UK premieres including *Possession* (mus. Philip Glass) and *Sleeping with Giants* (mus. Michael Nyman).

1999: Related Events

Film and Video
Dance on Screen (The Place):
Dance Documentaries and The Place[1]
Insights[2]
International Screenings[3]
Pop Promos and Dance[4]
Kicking and Screening – What makes a good dance film?[5]
Open Forum[6]

Classes and Workshops
Masterclasses: Iztoc Kovac; Vincent Mantsoe[7]

Meet the Artists
En-Knap Dance Company, De Rotterdamse Dansgroep, The Cholmondeleys and The Featherstonehaughs, Compagnie Maguy Marin, Doug Varone, Aletta Collins, Meg Stuart, Ann Hamilton and Damaged Goods, Tanzcompagnie Rubato

Notes
[1] Including Bob Lockyer's recollections of working with Robert Cohan and London Contemporary Dance Theatre, plus extracts from *Cell, Forest, Class* and early BBC and LWT documentaries.

[2] A discussion with Miranda Pennell and David Hinton.

[3] Two programmes of new dance films, curated and presented by Rosemary Lee and Laura Taler, including Philippe Decouflé's *Abracadabra* and Thierry de Mey's *Musique de Table.*

[4] Screenings of music promos which use dance.

[5] Panel discussion hosted by Christopher Cook with Margaret Williams, Ross MacGibbon, Alison Murray and Rodney Wilson.

[6] Including the work of eight emerging dance film makers and the presentation of the Dance on Screen production Award.

[7] Mantsoe led a masterclass in Afrofusion technique – integrating elements of African dance and music with western contemporary dance.

Appendix 2

Digest of Events, Innovations and Themes

1978

Theme – dance and film

Performers – avant-garde American soloists

British groups were funded by Arts Councils

Emphasis on education

Emphasis on regional groups

Many programmes consisted of two and sometimes three separate performances

Venues – Riverside Studios, ICA

Riverside held film screenings and a film forum

1980

Theme – dance films

Management Service established

National Lobby for Dance and Mime established, 9 February

First international groups outside UK and US: two from Holland and one from Canada

First commissioned work (for Extemporary Dance Theatre)

Three regional venues take part

First business sponsorship (Marks & Spencer)

Many programmes consisted of two separate performances

Added venues – The Place Theatre, Whitechapel Gallery

1981

Theme – design for dance

Dance Writers' course with Sally Banes, Deborah Jowitt and John Mueller

Exhibition of dance photographs

Influential artists are asked to return and/ or have works commissioned

Music commissions

Dana Reitz explains her work and precipitates 'Meet the Choreographer' sessions

Development of regional activity: ten associated festivals

Danceabout North West begins

Central box-office scheme starts

Greater concentration of events

Added venue – Almeida Theatre

1982

Theme – dance and music

Performances run consecutively

Judson Dance Theater exhibition

'Meet the Choreographer' sessions begin officially

First live music concert – Jim Fulkerson

Second general meeting of DAMAG

Subscription scheme for tickets begins

Jim Self's performance at the Tate Gallery

1983

Theme – dance and the camera

Video dance workshops

British Independents performances (sponsored by Marks & Spencer)

Performing Clothes I – related event

Festival Finale – gala benefit

Season ticket scheme introduced

Michael Clark is choreographer in residence at Riverside Studios

Trisha Brown Company

Dance Umbrella: The First Twenty-One Years

1984

Theme – dance and music

Concerts by musician collaborators and a commitment to live music

Yoshiko Chuma is first festival artist-in-residence

Festival project – *Five Car Pile-Up*

Made in Britain expands to five programmes

Performing Clothes II at ICA

Added venue – Sadler's Wells

Slight cut back in regional activity

Festival voucher scheme introduced

First 'last-night party'

1985

Change of emphasis – to Europe

Dance in Focus series – continues video and dance film emphasis

Intermedia Project (MacLennan, Wells and Anderson)

Katie Duck is festival artist-in-residence (with Group O)

Festival project – *Reckless*

Independents now showcased in Triple Bills (four) and Late Extras (five)

Late Extras start at 9.45pm

Voucher scheme continues

Val Bourne awarded Bessie in New York

1986

Theme – dance and contemporary music

Dana Reitz is festival artist-in-residence

Festival Youth project – *Momentum Rush*

Dance Lines Video Project

Last Danceabout NorthWest

Flying Starts – cabaret opening

Final Flourish at Chisenhale

Voucher scheme continues

Meredith Monk and Vocal Ensemble

1987

Flying Starts

Umbrella commissions – DV8, Images and Page

New Works platforms

Parallels in Black season, February

Trisha Brown Company

1988

Theme – tenth birthday.

'DecaDance' Gala programme at Sadler's Wells

First London Dance and Performance Awards

Siobhan Davies Dance Company receives first full Dance Umbrella commission

Liz Lerman in residence at Riverside

Platform performances of new work

Voucher scheme continues

1989

Theme – contemporary French dance, in celebration of Bicentenary

Legs Eleven gala

First Leicester International Dance Festival

Added venues – South Bank Centre, Queen Elizabeth Hall

April in Paris season

Going Dutch season

Val Bourne wins Digital Premiere Award

Regional touring concentrates on Compagnie Cré-Ange

Second London Dance and Performance Awards

Merce Cunningham Dance Company

1990

Gala and third annual Dance Umbrella/ *Time Out* London Dance Awards;

Lloyd Newson is first British festival artist-in-residence

Siobhan Davies Dance Company is first British one-choreographer company to appear at Sadler's Wells

First Newcastle Dance Festival

1991

A Baker's Dozen gala opens festival

Bourne awarded OBE in 1991 Birthday Honours List

Twenty-first anniversary of Trisha Brown Company

Japan Festival funds Eiko and Koma, Pappa Tarahumara and Karas

Added venues – Canary Wharf, Royalty Theatre, Purcell Room

Second Leicester International Festival

1992

Tie-ups with other festivals:

Transatlantic Tie-up: Boston Dance Umbrella; European Arts Festival

Prudential Award for the Arts to Dance Umbrella

Siobhan Davies Dance Company residency

Full-time post of Tours Manager created

Second Newcastle Dance Festival

Appendix 2: Digest of Events, Innovations and Themes

1993

Operation Riverside
Necessary Weather workshop
Added venue – Hackney Empire
Regional activities concentrate on Doug
   Elkins Company tour
Third Leicester International Dance
   Festival

1994

Coast to Coast project
Lucinda Childs's Umbrella debut
Hawkins and Baldwin companies include
   'mature' dancers
Festival sponsored by Häagen-Dazs
Prudential Award (second time)
Two important education ventures: Dance
   and Technology, and Dance Writing
   and Criticism
Dance and Technology develops into
   Digital Dancing series
Newsletters started, a result of the Dance
   Writing and Criticism course
Added venue – Brixton Academy
Tours – Stephen Petronio Company and
   Urban Bush Women
Jerwood Choreographic Awards

1995

Theme – Singular Soloists
Association with Greenwich Dance
   Agency
Techno Dance Bytes
Tour – Elizabeth Streb/Ringside
First Woking Dance Umbrella
Mark Morris tour (excludes London)
Cunningham Company in *Events* and
   mixed bills of British premieres
Retrospective exhibition of Chris Harris
   photographs

1996

Singular Soloists
First site-specific piece at Natural History
   Museum – *Genesis Canyon*
Jerwood Foundation sponsorship (*Genesis
   Canyon*)
Digital Dancing 96
New venue – Union Chapel, Islington
Percussive Feet at the Cochrane Theatre
Trisha Brown Company tour
Val Bourne is awarded the Chevalier dans
   l'Ordre des Arts et des Lettres

1997

Compagnie Maguy Marin British debut
Digital Dancing 97
Second Woking Dance Umbrella
Mark Morris and ENO at Coliseum in
   L'Allegro, Il Ponseroso ed Il Moderato

1998

Site-specific work at British Library – *Babel
   Index*
Ballett Frankfurt British debut
Alston birthday tribute
Michael Clark commission and national
   tour
Public appeal launched to raise money for
   commissions
Digital Dancing 98
Dance Umbrella News 1 and 2
Added venues – Barbican Centre, British
   Library, Roundhouse
Outside Eye Initiative

1999

Anderson's *Sportorama* at Crystal Palace
   National Sports Centre
Dance On Screen at The Place
Added venue – Brick Lane Music Hall
Mark Morris Company tour
Third Woking Dance Umbrella

241

Appendix 3

Dance Umbrella Personnel

1978
Ruth Glick: Festival Co-ordinator (with the additional, unpaid services of
    Val Bourne and Jan Murray)

1980
Ruth Glick: Festival Administrator
Fiona Dick: Management Service Administrator
Jan Murray: Programme Editor (continues in this role until 1988)
Erica Bolton, Sandy Broughton: Festival Press Coverage

1981
Val Bourne: Director
Fiona Dick: Administrator
Ruth Glick: Festival Co-ordinator
Erica Bolton, Sandy Broughton: Festival Press Coverage

1982
Val Bourne: Director
Fiona Dick: Administrator
Ruth Glick: Festival Co-ordinator
Erica Bolton, Jane Quinn: Press and Publicity

1983
Val Bourne: Director
Fiona Dick: Administrator
Anne Valois: Festival Co-ordinator
Jenny Mann: Marketing Officer
Steve Whitson, Scott Windsor: Technical Co-ordinators
Erica Bolton, Jane Quinn: Press and Publicity
Libby Wilsea: Festival Assistant

1984
Val Bourne: Director
Fiona Dick: Administrator
Debbie Vielvoye: Assistant
Tamara Essex: Festival Co-ordinator
Steve Whitson: Technical Co-ordinator

Erica Bolton, Jane Quinn: Press and Publicity
Jenny Mann: Manager of Mantis

1985
Val Bourne: Director
Fiona Dick: Administrator
Tamara Essex: Festival Co-ordinator
Bridget Sutton: Festival assistant
Donald Auty, Cassie Doran: Technical Co-ordinators
Erica Bolton, Jane Quinn: Press and Publicity

1986
Val Bourne: Director
Fiona Dick: Administrator
Julia Carruthers: Festival Co-ordinator
Jo Wood: Festival Assistant
Fiona Williams: Technical Co-ordinator
Erica Bolton, Jane Quinn, Flicky Ridel, Caroline Roche: Press and Publicity

1987
Val Bourne: Director
Fiona Dick: Administrator
Julia Carruthers: Festival Co-ordinator
Simon Byford: Technical Co-ordinator
Faith Wilson, Sandy Broughton: Press Representatives
Bolton & Quinn Ltd: Sponsorship/Development Consultants

1988
Val Bourne: Artistic Director
Fiona Dick: Administrative Director
Clare Cooper: Festival/Projects Co-ordinator
Caroline Roche: Publicity/Marketing Officer
Simon Byford: Technical Co-ordinator for the Festival
Sarah Hill: Festival Assistant
Faith Wilson, Sandy Broughton: Press Representatives

1989
Val Bourne: Artistic Director
Fiona Dick: Administrative Director
Clare Cooper: Festival/Projects Co-ordinator (to 4/89)
Mary Caws: Festival and Projects Co-ordinator (from 4/89)
Simon Byford: Technical Co-ordinator for the Festival
Oonagh Duckworth: French Consultant
Christopher Winter: Festival Assistant
Faith Wilson: Press Representative

1990
Val Bourne: Artistic Director
Fiona Dick: Administrative Director (to summer 1990)
Ian Gugan: Administrative Director (from autumn 1990)
Mary Caws: Festival and Projects Co-ordinator
Ruth Glick: Gala Organiser
David Scholefield: Technical Co-ordinator
Catherine Nunes: Festival Co-ordinator, Newcastle Dance 90
Faith Wilson: Press Representative

Dance Umbrella: The First Twenty-One Years

1991
Val Bourne: Artistic Director
Ian Gugan: Administrative Director (to 4/91)
Mary Caws: Adminstrative Director (from 5/91)
Robert Jude: Gala Organiser
Julian Sleath: Technical Co-ordinator
Douglas Thackway: Marketing Assistant
Faith Wilson, Rosalyn Fry: Press Representatives

1992
Val Bourne: Artistic Director
Mary Caws: General Manager
Lucy Curry: Marketing/Development Officer (from 6/92)
Jenny Goss: PA (from 4/92)
Belinda Reggio: Tours Manager (from 7/92)
Julian Sleath: Technical Co-ordinator
Catherine Nunes: Festival Co-ordinator, Newcastle Dance 92
Faith Wilson, Claudia Stumpfl: Press Representatives

1993
Val Bourne: Artistic Director
Mary Caws: General Manager
Jenny Goss: PA
Catherine Nunes: Associate Director
Belinda Reggio: Tours Manager
Simon Byford: Technical Co-ordinator for the Festival
Lucy Curry: Marketing Manager (to 7/93)
Faith Wilson, Claudia Stumpfl: Press Representatives

1994
Val Bourne: Artistic Director
Mary Caws: General Manager
Jackie Friend: Marketing Manager
Deborah O'Brien: Freelance tour manager (Spring)
Claire Cooper: Fundraiser
Catherine Nunes: Associate Director (to 11/94)
Emma Gregory: Festival Organiser
Faith Wilson: Press Representative

1995
Val Bourne: Artistic Director
Mary Caws: Administrative Director
Candida Ronald: Marketing Manager (from 5/95)
Chantal Bougnas: Festival co-ordinator
Simon Byford: Technical Director
Gregory Nash: 'Percussive Feet' Festival Administrator
Simon Byford: Technical Co-ordinator
Theresa Beattie: Festival Director, Woking Dance Umbrella
Faith Wilson: Press Representative

1996
Val Bourne: Artistic Director
Mary Caws: Administrative Director
Candida Ronald: Marketing Manager
Gregory Nash: Festival Co-ordinator and Administrator (6/1996 – 6/1997)

244

Chantal Bougnas: Festival Assistant
Simon Byford: Technical Director for the Festival
Teresa Szczotka: Finance Officer (p/t)
Susan Davenport: Development Consultant (p/t)
Faith Wilson: Press Representative (to 11/96)

1997
Val Bourne: Artistic Director
Candida Ronald: Marketing Manager (Deputy Director from 8/1997)
Debbie O'Brien: Tour Manager for Petronio, and Administrator,
    May – September
Mary Caws: Administrative Director (to 4/97)
Toby Beazley: Administrator (from end of September)
Gregory Nash: Programme Manager
Betsy Gregory: Programme Manager (from 11/97)
Charlotte Semlyen: Festival Co-ordinator
Robin Baxter: Finance Officer (from the summer, p/t)
Susan Davenport: Sponsorship Consultant (p/t)
Tony Shepherd: Press Representative (from 11/97)

1998
Val Bourne: Artistic Director
Candida Ronald: Deputy Director/Marketing Manager
Toby Beazley: Administrator
Betsy Gregory: Programme Manager
Charlotte Semlyen: Festival Co-ordinator
Robin Baxter: Finance Officer (p/t)
Susan Davenport: Sponsorship Consultant
Tony Shepherd: Press Representative

1999
Val Bourne: Artistic Director
Toby Beazley: Administrator
Betsy Gregory: Programme Manager
David Pratt: Marketing Manager
Henrietta Esiri: A4E Project Manager
Vicky Thompson: Assistant to A4E Project Manager
Brian Horton: Finance Officer
Tony Shepherd: Press Representative

Appendix 4

Dance Umbrella Board of Management

1978
John Ashford
David Gothard
Nicholas Hooton (Chair)
Jan Murray
Jeremy Rees

1980
John Ashford
David Gothard
Nicholas Hooton (Chair)
Jan Murray
Jeremy Rees

1981
John Ashford
Richard Bayliss
Geoff Dunlop
David Gothard
Nicholas Hooton (Chair)
Jeremy Rees
Seona Reid

1982
John Ashford
Richard Bayliss
Geoff Dunlop
David Gothard
Nicholas Hooton (Chair)
Jeremy Rees
Seona Reid

1983
John Ashford
Richard Bayliss
Anthony Blackstock
Peter Brinson

Geoff Dunlop
David Gothard
Nicholas Hooton (Chair)
Jeremy Rees
Jennifer Williams

1984
John Ashford
Richard Bayliss
Peter Brinson
Geoff Dunlop
David Gothard
Nicholas Hooton (Chair)
Jeremy Rees
Jennifer Williams

1985
Mary Allen
John Ashford
Richard Bayliss
Lawrence Brandes
Mollie Davies
Geoff Dunlop
David Gothard
Nicholas Hooton (Chair)
Jeremy Rees
Andrew Welch

1986
Mary Allen
John Ashford
Richard Bayliss
Lawrence Brandes
Mollie Davies
David Gothard
Nicholas Hooton (Chair)
David Pratley

246

Appendix 4: Dance Umbrella Board of Management

Jeremy Rees
Andrew Welch

1987
John Ashford
Richard Bayliss
Lawrence Brandes
Mollie Davies
David Gothard
Nicholas Hooton (Chair)
David Pratley
Jeremy Rees
Andrew Welch

1988
Richard Bayliss
Lawrence Brandes
Mollie Davies
Steven Garrett
David Gothard
Colin Hicks
Nicholas Hooton (Chair)
David Pratley
Jeremy Rees
Andrew Welch

1989
Richard Bayliss
Jennifer Bird
Lawrence Brandes
Colin Hicks
Nicholas Hooton (Chair)
David Pratley
Jeremy Rees
Andrew Welch

1990
Chris Barlas
Mark Baxter
Lawrence Brandes
Colin Hicks
Nicholas Hooton (Chair, to 7/90)
David Pratley (Chair, from 7/90)
Nick Pride
Jeremy Rees (to 7/90)
Neil Wallace
Andrew Welch

1991
Chris Barlas
Mark Baxter
Lawrence Brandes
Colin Hicks
Nicholas Hooton
David Pratley (Chair)

Jenny Rogers
Maggie Sedwards
Neil Wallace
Andrew Welch

1992
Chris Barlas
Mark Baxter
Lawrence Brandes
Colin Hicks
Nicholas Hooton
David Pratley (Chair)
Jenny Rogers
Maggie Sedwards
Neil Wallace
Andrew Welch

1993
Chris Barlas
Mark Baxter
Lawrence Brandes
Angela Diakopoulou
Colin Hicks
Nicholas Hooton
Jack Phipps (Chair)
Jenny Rogers
Maggie Sedwards
Neil Wallace
Andrew Welch

1994
Chris Barlas
Mark Baxter
Anthony Blackstock
Lawrence Brandes
Angela Diakopoulou
Colin Hicks
Jack Phipps (Chair)
Jenny Rogers
Maggie Sedwards
Neil Wallace
Andrew Welch

1995
Chris Barlas
Mark Baxter
Anthony Blackstock
Angela Diakopoulou
Colin Hicks
Danny Melita
Jack Phipps (Chair)
Andrew Welch

1996
Chris Barlas

247

Dance Umbrella: The First Twenty-One Years

Mark Baxter
Keith Bayliss
Anthony Blackstock (Chair)
Angela Diakopoulou
Morag Macdonald
Danny Melita

1997
Peter Barker
Chris Barlas
Chris Barron
Mark Baxter
Keith Bayliss
Anthony Blackstock (Chair, to 9/97)
Sheila Colvin
Angela Diakopoulou
Richard Jarman (Chair, from 10/97)
Peter Kyle
Morag Macdonald
Danny Melita

1998
Peter Barker
Chris Barlas
Chris Barron

Mark Baxter
Keith Bayliss
Sheila Colvin
Angela Diakopoulou
Richard Jarman (Chair)
Peter Kyle
Morag Macdonald
Danny Melita
Judith Unwin (from 10/98)

1999
Peter Barker
Chris Barlas
Chris Barron
Mark Baxter
Keith Bayliss
Sheila Colvin
Angela Diakopoulou
Nicholas Elam
Richard Jarman (Chair)
Peter Kyle
Morag Macdonald
Danny Melita
Judith Unwin

Appendix 5

Dance Artists in Eudcation Conference

30 November – 2 December 1979

Sources: *Dance Artists in Education* – Follow-up Report on Birmingham Conference, undated; conference Report by John Allen, member of the dance panel for CNAA; Dance Umbrella 80 programme.

Performers included:
Ballet for All
Ludus Dance in Education Company
EMMA (demonstration of training methods, plus one piece of choreography)
Educational Dance-Drama Theatre (samples from its repertoire)
Tara Rajkumar
Scaramouche
Anthony van Laast (class to group of twelve-year-olds)
Nancy Stark Smith (contact improvisation demonstration with Laurie Booth)

Notes to the Chapters

Introduction

[1] Howard had been Graham's manager in New York City for three years, which was how he was able to persuade company members to visit the London school and teach. (Interview with Val Bourne, 7 September 1999.)

[2] Alston in discussion with Melvin Bragg on the ground-breaking *South Bank Show* dedicated to Alston's choreography, first broadcast 14 March 1982 for London Weekend Television.

[3] Jordan, Stephanie, 'American Dance Abroad. Influence of the United States Experience', *Proceedings of the Society of Dance History Scholars, Fifteenth Annual Conference,* Riverside: University of California, 1992, p. 264.

[4] *Ibid.*

[5] Howard chose to call the Graham style 'contemporary' in this country, rather than 'modern', because he did not want it to be confused with the style of the 'early moderns'. (Interview with Val Bourne, 7 September 1999.)

[6] See Jordan, 1992, p. 208. Appendix 1 gives information from a publicity leaflet from 1971 listing events in the years from 1969 to 1971, under the banner headline 'Barriers between the arts are disappearing; The Place is where they meet...'

[7] See Jordan, 1992, Chapter 1 for a full account of activities summarised here.

[8] Alston in Mackrell, 1992, p. 8.

[9] Mackrell, 1992, p. 4.

[10] Jordan, 1992, Chapter 3.

[11] Mackrell, 1992, p. 32.

[12] Deirdre McMahon, 'Dance Umbrella '80. After the Dance Explosion', *What's on in London,* 18 January 1980, pp. 38–39.

[13] Jordan, 1992, p. 60.

[14] Mary Fulkerson in *New Dance,* Summer 1978, pp. 14 and 32; Spring 1985, p. 17.

[15] Jordan, 1992, p. 93.

[16] Noel Goodwin, 'Dance Collective for London', *Dance and Dancers,* January 1979, p. 18.

[17] Interview with Val Bourne, 7 September 1999.

[18] David Edgar, *The State of Play,* Faber, 1999, p.12.

Chapter 1

[1] Interview with Val Bourne, 14 October 1997.

[2] The official date for the approval of funds was January 1978, although Bourne thinks the timescale was tighter than this: 'I seem to remember having only six or seven months to put the whole thing together'. This would mean that funds became available only in April or May 1978. Interview with Val Bourne, 7 September 1999.

[3] *Ibid.*

[4] *Ibid.*

[5] Later, Gothard went to Leicester Haymarket after leaving Riverside Studios. It

was he and Peter Lichtenfels who invited Dance Umbrella to organise the first Leicester festival.

[6] *Ibid.*

[7] 'The seminal point for John was when Anne Teresa [de Keersmaeker] did *Fase*, in 1982. He then went to The Place and made a huge difference there, resigning from the Dance Umbrella Board as he decided, quite rightly, that it might pose a conflict of interests.' *Ibid.*

[8] Val Bourne in Claudia Cooke, *Classical Music,* 20 November 1982.

[9] Riverside Studios ran a follow-up week for dance, 11–14 January 1979, with performances by Lucinda Childs, Kate Flatt and Elizabeth Walton.

[10] Bourne 1997, *ibid.*

[11] Ruth Glick, *Feasibility Study*, April 1979.

[12] The event came about through David Gothard's connections. Bourne, *ibid.*

[13] Douglas Dunn and Remy Charlip had visited Bristol and Cardiff as an extension of their 1978 Umbrella performances. Charlip caused havoc, Bourne remembers, because he refused to appear in a certain theatre until it had been repainted, after which Bourne received the bill. *Ibid.*

[14] Fiona Dick, 'Ten Years of Development and Change', *Dance Theatre Journal,* Vol. 6 No. 3, 1988, p. 30.

[15] There were two possible models: Arts Services and Pentacle. 'With Arts Services, the artist had a manager who did everything for them. With Pentacle, on the other hand, you bought into different parts of their service and you would, for example, deal with somebody over grant applications, someone else for accounts, so you would be working with three or four different people within the same organisation. At the Management Service we opted for the Arts Services type of model.' Bourne, *ibid.*

[16] Murray, 1985, p. 5.

[17] Fiona Dick, 1988, *ibid.*

[18] Bourne, *ibid.*

[19] Letter from the GLAA office to interested parties, dated 30 January 1980.

[20] *Dance Umbrella Festival Report,* 1980.

[21] Bourne, *ibid.*

Chapter 2

[1] Bausch's Wuppertal Dance Theatre had presented a programme *Das Frühlingsopfe* at the Edinburgh Festival in 1978, that included *The Rite of Spring.* In 1982 the company presented *Kontakthof* and *1980, a piece by Pina Bausch* at London's Sadler's Wells Theatre.

[2] Linke was from the Wigman and Essen Folkwang schools.

[3] The questionnaire was funded by the Calouste Gulbenkian Foundation and had practical assistance from the Arts Council's Research department.

[4] Interview with Val Bourne, 7 September 1999.

[5] £7,000 from the London Tourist Board was withdrawn; £5,200 was forthcoming from the GLC, as against the £14,000 that had been requested. Cancellation was averted when the GLC doubled the amount to £10,500. *Dance Umbrella Festival Report,* 1983, p. 5.

[6] Appendix, 'Dance Video Project' in *Dance Umbrella Festival Report,* 1983.

[7] Bourne in Eleanor Blau, 'British Dancers to Bow', *The New York Times,* Friday 6 August 1982.

[8] Bourne in Allen Robertson, 'Preview', *Time Out,* 27 September 27 – 3 October 1984, p. 12.

[9] *Dance Umbrella Festival Report,* 1978.

[10] Jan Murray, 'Dancing into the '80s', *Time Out,* 18 – 24 January 1980, p. 12.

[11] John Percival, 'Halfway Under the Umbrella', *Dance and Dancers,* February 1980, p. 26.

[12] Steve Paxton, in Jan Murray, *ibid,* p. 13.

[13] Stephanie Jordan, 'Dance Umbrella 1981, Part 1', *Dancing Times,* December 1981, p. 171.

[14] Anne Nugent, 'Rubik Cube of Dance', *Stage,* 22 October 1981.

[15] Val Bourne, 1999, *ibid.*

[16] Mary Clarke, 'Karole Armitage', *Guardian,* 21 October 1981.

[17] Bourne has an amusing and illuminating story to tell about the incident: 'The first piece was in silence. There was a group of boys from a Sixth-Form College and we were quite surprised to see them there. When it came to the second half (I had seen them all puffing away outside during the interval), I

said, "Listen guys, if you're not going to come back, could you clear off, because things are about to start?" and they said, "Oh no, we're going back in!" Dana came back, and said, "I realise that there are a lot of people who have never seen work like this before, so I'm going to talk to you about it, and you can ask me questions." So there were the usual sort of questions and then the boys started up, and they asked the most perceptive questions. One of them asked "Do you choreograph your hair?" (Reitz has a shiny bob that moves all-of-a-piece). She said, "Well, I guess I do, because my hair moves in a certain way." Another boy asked if she always danced alone, or did she 'clone' herself? Then she launched into the second piece and the audience was absolutely rapt.' Val Bourne, 1999, *ibid.*

[18] Stephen Goff, 'Reviews: Dance Umbrella', *Labanews*, Vol 2 No 1, February 1982, p. 8.

[19] Stephanie Jordan and Howard Friend, 'Dance Umbrella 1982: Part II', *Dancing Times*, January 1983, pp. 283–4

[20] For Brown's first visit in 1979, which was organised by David Gothard, Val Bourne remembers, 'Nobody came, no critics, nobody.' Bourne, 1999, *ibid.*

[21] Alastair Macaulay, 'Umbrelladom', *Dancing Times,* January 1984, p. 304.

[22] Val Bourne, 1999, *ibid.*

[23] Alastair Macaulay, 'Umbrellissima', *Dancing Times*, December 1984, p. 219.

[24] Alastair Macaulay, *ibid*, p. 220.

Chapter 3

[1] Interview with Val Bourne, 7 September 1999.

[2] Andrew Lucre, 'Child's Play with Adult Meanings', *Sunday Times,* 8 October 1989.

[3] Jann Parry, 'French Lessons in Polished Performances', *Observer*, 22 October 1989.

[4] Bourne, *ibid.*

[5] Fiona Burnside, 'Birds Do It, Bees Do It and Dancers Do It Again and Again and Again', *Dance Theatre Journal*, Vol. 5 No. 4, Spring 1988, pp. 32–5

[6] Alastair Macaulay, 'The Lack of the New', *Dancing Times,* January 1991, pp. 363–4.

[7] Macaulay, *ibid.*

[8] Sally Banes, 1987, Introduction to the Wesleyan Paperback edition.

[9] Alastair Macaulay, 'Dance Umbrella', *Financial Times*, 27 October 1989.

[10] Jann Parry, 'Unfurled Umbrella', *Observer*, 20 November 1988.

[11] E. Linenmeier, 'Mit Humor gegründelt', *tz*, Munich, 18 March 1985.

[12] Dance Umbrella press release, undated.

[13] Elizabeth Zimmer, 'Parallels in Black', *Dance Theatre Journal,* Vol. 5 No.1, Spring 1987, p. 5

[14] Zollar in Zimmer, *ibid*, p. 7.

[15] Ralph Lemon in Dance Umbrella press release, undated.

[16] A similar excursion to Rouen was planned but never happened.

[17] Bourne, *ibid.*

[18] Gregory Nash, *Dance Umbrella. The First Twenty Years, 1978–1997*, unpublished MA dissertation for the City University, December 1997.

[19] Jann Parry, 'Electrifying Laurie', *Observer,* 17 November 1985.

[20] Bourne, *ibid.*

[21] Judith Mackrell, 'A Dance with a Turtle Called Proton', *Independent*, 16 October 1986.

[22] Monk in Mackrell, *ibid.*

[23] Interview with Monk, Ramsay Burt and Valerie Briginshaw, *New Dance*, No. 39, New Year 1987, p. 12.

[24] Judith Mackrell, 'Dancing with a Flytrap', *Independent*, 18 October 1986.

[25] Sophie Constanti, 'American Glob, French Kisses, British Love Letters', *Dance Theatre Journal*, Vol. 5, No. 1, Spring 1987, p. 25.

[26] Judith Mackrell, 'Umbrella Dance and Dancers', *Dance Theatre Journal*, Vol. 5, No. 4, Spring 1988, p. 5.

[27] Judith Mackrell, 'Heavy Metal, Light Feet', *Independent*, 2 November 1987.

[28] Judith Mackrell, 'Flights without Fancy', *Independent*, 12 November 1988.

[29] Jann Parry, 'Revolution in the French Class', *Observer*, 5 November 1989.

[30] Sophie Constanti, 'First and Last', *Dancing Times*, January 1990, p. 363.

Chapter 4

[1] Judith Mackrell, 'Feet, Please Don't Fail Them Now', *Independent*, 19 October 1993.

[2] Bourne recalls that when Rosemary Butcher formed her company in 1976, it was thought immodest in the UK to use your own name. Interview, 7 September 1999.

[3] Bourne, *ibid.*

[4] Marilyn Hunt, 'British Undercurrent at Dance Umbrella', *Dance Theatre Journal*, Vol. 8 No. 4, Spring 1991, p. 13.

[5] Fiona Burnside, 'Can They Tell Stories?', *Dance Theatre Journal*, Vol. 11, No. 1, Winter 1993/94, p. 36.

[6] Interview with Val Bourne, 14 October 1997.

[7] Bourne states that Lyon, Montpellier and FIND (Festival International de Nouvelle Danse) are all larger festivals in terms of programming. 'Dance Umbrella can afford one, maybe two major companies, while Montpellier can afford six or seven each year'. Bourne, 1999, *ibid.*

[8] Bourne, 1997, *ibid.*

[9] Judith Mackrell, 'Best Foot Forward: Power and Influence in the Arts: Dance', *Independent*, 31 January 1994.

[10] Guidelines and application forms for the 1999 seasons, supplied by The Place Theatre.

[11] Mackrell, *ibid.*

[12] Dance Umbrella Touring Document: proposal, undated

[13] Gregory Nash, *Dance Umbrella. The First Twenty Years, 1978–1997*, Unpublished MA dissertation for the City University, December 1997.

[14] Rambert premiered Richard Alston's *Roughcut*, a piece dedicated to Val Bourne.

[15] Janet Archer, in Nash, *ibid,* p. 35.

[16] *Ibid,* p. 36.

[17] Bourne, 1997, *ibid.*

[18] Ashley Page, in Philip Blenkinsop, 'Network: Keyboard of the Dance', *Independent*, 31 October 1994.

[19] Alastair Macaulay, 'Siobhan Davies Dance Company', *Financial Times*, 8 November 1990.

[20] Val Bourne, *Dance Umbrella 90*: report, February 1991, p. 3 .

[21] Sophie Constanti, 'Improvising Steps through Space', *Guardian*, 18 October 1990.

[22] Sophie Constanti, 'Yolande Snaith', *Guardian*, 27 October 1990.

[23] Petronio, cited in Jann Parry, 'Power and the Body in Question', *Observer*, 10 October 1990, p. 57.

[24] David Hughes, 'The Poetics of Exhaustion', *Dance Theatre Journal*, Vol. 8 No. 4, Spring 1991, pp. 17–19.

[25] Judith Mackrell, 'Fully Baked Evening', *Independent*, 9 October 1991, p. 18.

[26] Judith Mackrell, 'Speaking with the Body', *Independent*, 5 November 1991.

[27] Trisha Brown, 1986, cited in Mackrell, 'Purity in Motion', *Independent*, 9 November 1991.

[28] *Ibid.*

[29] Laurie Booth, in Mackrell, 9 November 1991, *ibid.* One exception is Richard Alston, who at that time was director of Rambert.

[30] Alastair Macaulay, 'Dance Umbrella '91', *Dancing Times*, January 1992, p. 322.

[31] Macaulay, January 1992, *ibid* p. 322.

[32] Val Bourne, cited in Debra Craine, 'Spokesperson for an Umbrella', *The Times*, 13 October 1992.

[33] Craine, *ibid.*

[34] Bourne, cited in Craine, *ibid.*

[35] Val Bourne, *Dance Umbrella 1992 Festival Report*, p. 5.

[36] Judith Mackrell, 'Making of Maps', *Independent*, 20 October 1992.

[37] These were not new to Umbrella audiences, since he had presented two *Events* at the first Leicester Festival in 1989.

[38] Judith Mackrell, 'Selected Steps', *Independent*, 26 October 1992.

[39] Judith Mackrell, 'Narrative Force', *Independent*, 19 October 1993, Arts, p. 24.

[40] *Dance Umbrella 1993 Year Report*, 5 January 1994, p. 4.

[41] *Dance Umbrella 1993 Year Report*, 5 January 1994, p. 3.

[42] Elkins, in Clifford Bishop, 'Swing-Slap-Hop-Jump-Clap', *Sunday Times*, 10 October 1993.

[43] Judith Mackrell 'She Wants to Tell You a Story: Narrative Force or Empty Gesture?' *Independent*, 13 October 1993, Arts, p. 26.

[44] Anne Sacks, 'Mixed Marriage Made in Heaven', *Independent on Sunday*, 24 October 1993, The Critics, p. 27.

[45] Anne Nugent, 'Opening Out the Umbrella', *Dance Now*, Winter 1994, p. 25.

[46] Josephine Leask, 'The Sacred and the Profane', *Dance Umbrella News*, Issue No. 2, 3 November 1994, p. 1.

Chapter 5

[1] Interview with Val Bourne, 7 September 1999.

[2] Jenny Gilbert, 'Dance: Mark of Genius for Handel', *Independent on Sunday*, 8 June 1997.

[3] Bourne, September 1999, *ibid*.

[4] Bourne, *ibid*.

[5] Interview with Val Bourne, 25 July 1999.

[6] Michael Wright, 'Dullsville Rises from the Dead', *Daily Telegraph*, 28 March 1995.

[7] Bourne, September 1999, *ibid*.

[8] Gregory Nash, *Dance Umbrella. The First Twenty Years*, 1978–1997, Unpublished MA dissertation for the City University, December 1997, pp. 38–39.

[9] Grieve in Donald Hutera (ed.), *Dance Umbrella News*, Issue No. 3, Summer 1999.

[10] Interview with Val Bourne, 26 June 1999.

[11] Bourne, June 1999, *ibid*.

[12] Booth in Donald Hutera (ed.), *Dance Umbrella News*, Issue No. 2, Autumn 1998.

[13] Donald Hutera, *ibid*.

[14] Judith Mackrell, *Guardian*, 11 October 1995, Home Page 2.

[15] Debra Craine, 'Soloists in Space: Dance Umbrella', *The Times*, 18 October 1995, p. 38.

[16] Judith Mackrell, 'Ringside/Singular Soloists', *Guardian*, 17 October 1995, p. 11.

[17] Keith Watson, 'Dance Umbrella', *Dance Now*, Winter 1995, p. 21.

[18] Cheryl Smyth, *Guardian*, 7 October 1995, p. 30.

[19] *Events* were held at Riverside Studios, while the repertory programmes were shown at Sadler's Wells Theatre. This was not planned, but happened because Sadler's Wells had a double booking at the beginning of the week. Bourne, September 1999, *ibid*.

[20] Alston made a version of this dance for Strider in 1974 (see Angela Kane in Jordan, 1992, p. 221). These performances of *Rainbow Bandit* were based upon the 1977 version made for LCDT, which included Tom Jobe in its cast, to whom the current piece was dedicated.

[21] David Jays 'Review', *Dancing Times*, December 1995, p. 271.

[22] Val Bourne cited in Allen Robertson, 'Barefoot in Jurassic Park', *The Times*, 25 September 1996, p. 34.

[23] David Jays, *Dancing Times*, December 1996, p. 219.

[24] Allen Robertson, 'Shobana Jeyasingh', *Dance Europe*, December 1996/January 1997, p. 15.

[25] Val Bourne recollects that the head came off on the first night. Bourne, September 1999, *ibid*.

[26] Deborah Weiss, 'Mal Pelo', *Dance Europe*, December 1996/January 1997, p. 19.

[27] Judith Mackrell, 'Review', *Guardian*, 27 October 1997, Home, p. 2.

[28] Mackrell, *ibid*.

[29] Jenny Gilbert, *Independent on Sunday*, 8 November 1998.

[30] Gilbert, 'Among the Balletic Mills', *Independent on Sunday*, 4 October 1998.

[31] Clement Crisp, 'Dance Umbrella: Siobhan Davies', *Financial Times*, 6 October 1998.

[32] Alastair Macaulay, *Spectator*, cited in the festival report 1998/99.

[33] Debra Craine, 'Hell is the Twentieth Century', *The Times*, 28 October 1998, p. 34.

[34] David Jays, 'Dance Umbrella '98', *Dancing Times*, December 1998, p. 243.

[35] John Percival, 'De Frutos Forgets that Less Can Be More', *Independent*, 23 October 1998.

[36] *Dance Umbrella Festival report*, 1998/99.

[37] Debra Craine, 'He's Got Rhythm Again', *The Times*, 16 October 1998, p. 43.

[38] Bourne in Allen Robertson, 'There's a Riot Going On', *The Times*, 25 September 1998, p. 44.

[39] Alston cited in Donald Hutera (ed.), *Dance Umbrella News*, Issue No. 2, Autumn 1998.

[40] Val Bourne in Hutera, *ibid*.

[41] Bourne, June 1999, *ibid*.

[42] Mark Baldwin in Hutera, *ibid*.

Select Bibliography

Banes, Sally, *Democracy's Body: Judson Dance Theatre 1962–1964*, Ann Arbor, Michigan, UMI Research Press, 1983.

Banes, Sally, *Terpsichore in Sneakers*, Middletown, Connecticut, Wesleyan University Press, 1987.

Jordan, Stephanie, *Striding Out: Aspects of Contemporary and New Dance in Britain*, London, Dance Books, 1992.

Mackrell, Judith, *Out of Line: The Story of British New Dance*, London, Dance Books, 1992.

Murray, Jan, *Dance Now*, Harmondsworth, Middlesex, Penguin Books, 1979.

Murray, Jan, *Dance Umbrella*, London, Dance Umbrella, 1985.

Sources

Periodicals

Classical Music
Dance and Dancers
Dance Now
Dance Theatre Journal
Dancing Times
Dance Umbrella News
Labanews
New Dance
Spectator
Stage
Time Out

National Newspaper Reviews

Daily Telegraph
Financial Times
Guardian
Independent
Independent on Sunday
Observer
Sunday Times
Times

Index

Italics indicate references to titles and illustrations. Companies are listed under name of founder where appropriate, e.g. 'Companie Charles Cré-Ange' is listed under 'Cré-Ange, Charles', references under 'Cunningham, Merce' indicate both the individual and the company.

'Accident' Ballroom   81–2
Advent II   51
Adventures in Motion Pictures   88, 89
Affections   148
Agis, Gaby   58, 67, 70, 78
Ai Amour   146
All Together   157
Allegro, il ponseroso ed il moderato, L'   128, 130–31, 150
Alston, Richard   7, 10, 18, 23, 33, 37, 39, 52, 95, 145, 148, 155
American dance   1, 3, 4–5, 9, 16, 18, 29, 43–44, 63–66, 79, 80–81, 114–115, 155
Anderson, Lea   85, 96
Angel of Death is in my Bed Tonight, The   67, 84
April in Paris   73
Armitage, Karole   30, 44, 47, 52, 65, 76, 77, 78
Art of Movement Studio   3
Art of Touch, The   153
Arts Council   8, 9–10, 13, 14, 73, 93
Ascete de San Clemente et la Vierge Marie, L'   88
Asian dance   23, 74–5, 104, 107, 110, 116
Ashford, John   16, 64, 73, 98–9
Association of Dance and Mime Artists (ADMA)   9, 14
Astrakan   63
Astral Convertible   112
Atman   152

Audience with the Pope, An   40
Available Light   124

Babel Index   158
Bagnolet International Choreographic Competition   67
Baldwin, Mark   143, 145, 153–4, 236
Ballet Rambert   2, 6, 7, 8, 39
   see also Rambert Dance Company
Balletmakers Ltd   7–8
Banes, Sally   49, 50
Bank   153
Barnes, Ruth   49
Bartók/Aantekeningen   84
Bausch, Pina   29, 63, 64, 65
Béjart, Maurice   30, 152
Beach Birds   145
Between Heartbeats   45
Between Public Places   70
Beyond Zero   70
Bhuller, Darshan Singh   155, 162
Big Dance Number, The   85
Bite of the Big Apple   65
Black American dance   70–72, 83
Blackmail   88
Booth, Laurie   7, 30, 32, 51, 52–3, 67, 68, 70, 75, 76, 96, 103, 111, 112
Bourne, Matthew   88
Bourne, Val   13–14, 15, 21, 161–2
Brailsford, Liz   118
Brilliant and Dark, The   56

British are Coming, The 70
British dance 1–2, 7–9, 19, 26–7, 30, 34–5, 61, 66–9, 70, 80–81, 96–7, 160, 162–3
Brown, Trisha 5, 65, 83, 111–13, *114*
Bruce, Christopher 32
Bubblehead 134
Buddy Systems 80
Burrows, Jonathan 39, 67, *82*
Butcher, Rosemary 7, 16, 19, 22, 30, 48, 70, *151*
By Appointment Only 39

Calle del Imaginero, La 150
Carousel 90–91
Charlip, Remy 37
Charnock, Nigel *118*, 148, *232*
Chandralekha 110
Childs, Lucinda 5, 121, 124–5
Chiquenaude 57
Cholmondeleys, The 66, *92*
Chorus Line, A 133
Chuma, Yoshiko *x*, 69
Citadel, The 138
Claid, Emilyn 6
Clark, Michael *28*, 30, 49, 51, 52, 86, 93, *202*
Clark, Scott 87
Clarke, Gill *116*
Cloven Kingdom 81
Cohan, Robert 5, 25
Collaborations 6
Collection of Moving Parts, A 125
Concerto 125
Configurations 116
Correspondences 107
Counter Revolution 52
Court by the Tail *107*, 108
Coursing 58
Craizy Daisy and the Northern Lights 52–3
Cré-Ange, Charles *62*, 63–4, 66, 74, 81, 86, 88, 90
Cruel Garden 32, 134
CRWDSPCR 145
Cummings, Blondell 71
Cunningham, Merce 1, 5, 27, 42–3, 64–5, 74, 90, 117–18, 130, 145, 156
Current Response 52
Current/SEE 157 *158*
Cutter 79
Cyborg 138
Cycles 8, 19

Daimon, Shiro *60*
Damaged Goods 160

Dance and Slide 37
Dance and Mime Action Group (DAMAG) 25
Dance City 101, 103
Dance Lines 81
Dance Quorum *107*, 108
Dance Umbrella
   aims 14–16, *15*
   educational aspects 17, 18, 25–6, 39, 50, 105–6, 160–61
   financial aspects 14, 31–2, 43, 54, 63, 64, 75, 93, 99, 127–8, 129–30, 163–4
   international development 96–7, 110, 113, 130, 160
   Management services 20–24, *22*, 130–31
   role 93, 95–9, 110
   touring 99–100, 114, 129–130
Danceabout North West 35–6
Dancer's World, A (film) 4
Dances from Cyberspace 138
Dances of the Wayward Ancients 155
Dancing and Shouting 88
Dancing Inside 138
Dancing Room, The 125
Dancework 49
Daniëls, Pauline 72, *73*, *185*
Danse Noire 68
Dansproduktie 76
Dark Elegies 6
Dartington 7, 10, 14
Davies, Siobhan 22, 33, 35, 39, 66, 68, 81, 86, 87, 92, 96–7, 103, 106–7, 115–16, 121, 130, 145, 148, 155
De Gas 48
Dead Dreams of Monochrome Men 87
DecaDance 70, 85
Decodex 133
Deerhunter, The 61
Delicious Arbour 121
Dick 119
Different Trains 106
Doublework 33
Douglas, Paul *116*
Dubois, Emilie 90, *91*
Duck, Katie 35, 79, 60–61, *189*
Duncan, Isadora 2
Dumka 42
Dunn, Douglas 33, 36, *37*
Duprès, Maedée 22, 27, 33, 42, *46*, 49, 79, *192*
Dutch dance 72–3, 95
Dutiful Ducks 52
DV8 Physical Theatre 6, 65, 66, 69, 84, 87, 96

Early, Fergus 6, 8
Early, Teresa 7
East Anglia Dance Theatre 18
Eidos: Telos 159
Eighty Eight 155
Eiko *12, 46*, 47, 83
Elkins, Doug *100*
Embarque 87
EMMA 8, 19, 20
En-Knap 159
English Dance Theatre 95
English National Ballet 134
Enter Achilles 145–6
Eraserhead 108
Escape at Sea 121
Esquisse, L' 75, 76, 113
Euridice Disparue 81
European dance 29, 63–6, 75, 79,
   114–15
Events 117, 156
Excursions 125
Extemporary Dance Company 19
Extemporary Dance Theatre 5, 23, 30,
   38, 51, 52, 79, *86*, 95, 110
Eyre, René 138, *139*

Fabrications 91
Façade 86
Factory 146
Farber, Viola 5
Fase 54, 84
Fearful Symmetries 150
Featherstonehaughs, The 103, *164*
Fenley, Molissa *45*, 47, 89
Fetch Boy and Fox 156
Field of Mustard 33
Films and dance 4, 23, 32–3, 42, 50, 54,
   69, 75, 105, 108–9, 138, 160
Five Car Pile Up *x*, 58, 69
5IVE Part One 157
Flesh and Blood 91, *92*
Flying Lines 78
Flying Starts 82, 85
For MG: The Movie 112
Foray Forêt 112
Forsythe, William 154–5, 158–9
Forti, Simone 42
Fortune Biscuit 159
Four Elements 124
*Fractured Landscapes, Fragmented
   Narratives* 151
French dance 64–5, 67, 70, 73–4, 93, 113,
   146, 161
Fresh Dances for the Late Tchaikovsky 120

From Ordinary Lives 54
Frutos, Javier De *122*, 123–4, 144, *149*,
   154
Fulkerson, Mary 7, 10, *53*,
Fur Seal *12, 46*, 47
Furse, Anna 58
Further and Further into Night 57, *59*

Gallotta, Jean-Claude 90
Genesis Canyon *147*
George's House (film) 50
Gestures in Red 36
Ghosts and Astronauts 138
Gill, Peter 16
Glass Bead Game, The 109
Glass Blew In, The 125
Going Away Party 132
Gordon, David 30, 40, 65, 75, *76*, 78
Gorgeous Creatures 148
Graham, Martha 1, 4, 5, 7, 159
Grain 83
Grand Duo 132
Grass 154
Green Candle 6, 125, 138
Green Table, The 3
Greenwood, Dennis 60, 79
Grey Window 54
Groot, Pauline de 38, 42
Grossman, Danny 38
Ground Level Overlay 145
Group O 60, *189*

Half Wrong Plus Laytext 117
Halo 138
Hamilton, Julyen 27, 30, 56, 66, 72,
   111
Hands 157
#3 81
Haunted, Daunted, Flaunted *153*, 154
Hauxwell, Matthew 58, 70
Hawkins, Matthew 30, 39, 51, 120
Heaven Ablaze in his Breast 93
Heroine 148
Heterospectives 93, *202*
Holland, Fred 71
Home Ground 37
Hommage aux Ballets Russes 122
Hooten, Nicholas 13, 16
Hot Shoe Shuffle 133
Houstoun, Wendy *153*, 154
Huge Veil 60, 119
Hyena 83

Hymns 82
Hypochondriac Bird 157

I etcetera 76
Ikeda, Carlotta 146
Images Dance Company 84
Imaginary Dances 37
In the Grain of the Body 119
In the Shadow of the Hat 88
Institute of Contemporary Arts (ICA) 16,
42, 69, 87, 127
Ishi no hana 91
It Happened at Club Bombay Cinema 52

Java 55
Jealousy 77
Jeck, Philip 70
Jenkins, Margaret 4, 5, 103, 109
Jerwood choreography awards 135–6
Jeyasingh, Shobana *94*, 96–7, 107, *111*,
116, 121, 148–9
Jones, Bill T. 35, 47, *182*
Jones, John 18
Jooss, Kurt 3, 7
Jowett, Deborah 34, *49*, 50
Judson Dance Theater 36, 40, 51
Juice 6

Kabuki-Woogie 60
Karas 91
Keersmaeker, Anne Teresa de 29–30, 54,
84
Keijser, Matthieu 56
Kemp, Lindsay 32
Knot Annulled, A 157
Koma *46*, 47, 83
Koplowitz, Stephen *147*, 157
Kovac, Iztoc 159
Kovich, Robert 55
Kraus, Lisa 55

La La La 35, 55, 88, 150
Laban, Rudolf von 3, 7
Land 113
Landings 152
Langage du Sphinx, Le 146
Lansley, Jacky 8, 10
Larrieu, Daniel 63
Legs Eleven 70
Leicester festivals 69, 74–5, 101, 104, 160
Lemon, Ralph 71

Lennon, Joseph *44*
Lerman, Liz 89
Life Dance II 83
Light 53
Limón, José 1, 5
Linke, Susanne 30
Liqueurs de Chair (Carnal Cocktails) 90
Little Harlequin 60
London Contemporary Dance Theatre
(LCDT) 1, 5, 8, 39, 42, 74, 95–6
London School of Contemporary Dance
(LSCD) 1, 5, 42
Lonnroth, Ingegerd 22
Louis, Murray 5
Lovey 77
Ludus 8, 18, 19, 23

Maas Movers 18, 38
MacLennan, Sue 7, 30, 40, 49, 58, 60, 70,
117
Make-Make 115
Making of Maps 116
Maliphant, Russell *126*, 142
Mammame 90, *91*
Mantis 22, 23, 27, 33, 95
Mantsoe, Vincent 160
Marin, Maguy 151, 152, 159
Marina 85
Martha@DanceUmbrella 159
Marshall, Susan 81
Matthew and Diana on Manoeuvres 125
May B 159
McDonald, Antony 35
McLorg, Tamara 19, 38
Meeting J 144
Mey, Michèle Anne de 30, 54, 84
MiddleSex Gorge *108*, 109
Miller, Bebe 71
Miller, Tim 35, *51*, 53, 79, 80
Minor Characters 55
Minuet in G 77
Mmm.... 117
Momentum Rush 69
Monk, Meredith 6, 79–80
Morag's Wedding 58
Morrice, Norman 2, 6, 24
Morris, Mark *59*, 65, 75, 76, 77, 78,
132–3
Moss, David *41*
Moss, Judith 49
Moulton, Charles *21*, *43*, 45
Moving Earth 20, 50, 53
Moving Picture Mime Show 23
Moving Visions Dance Theatre 15

Mueller, John 50
Munich New Dance festival 70
Murobushi, Ko 146
Musk: Red 56
My Body, Your Body 84
My Folks 76
Myers, Brooke 36
Mystères de Subal, Les 109

Naidoo, Jayshree 71
Narcoleptic Lovers 157
Nash, Greg *68*, 69, 138, *139*
National Dance Agency (NDA) 101, 103
National Lobby for Dance and Mime 17, 24–5
National Organisation of Dance and Mime (NODM) 25
Necessary Weather 119
Nelson, Jeremy *48*
Nelson, Lisa *41*
New Cities, Ancient Lands 110
New Love Song Waltzes 132
New Moves 55
New Puritans *28*
New Text/New Kingdom 111
New York festivals 14
Newark 83
Newcastle Cloggies, member *102*
Newcastle festivals 99, 100, 101–4, 129, 140
Newman, Rosalind 5, 35, *52*
Newson, Lloyd 6, 66, 69, 87
Nikolais, Alwin 5, *65*
Nine Lives 76
Nine Person Precision Ball Passing 45
No. 5 Empire Street 18
No Joy 85
Noces, Les 122, 123
Noir salle *62*, 90
Not Garden 156
Not Goodbye 59

Of a feather, flock 52
Of Solution and Answer and Understanding 111
Okho 148
Old Man Dragging Stones 125
Ombres éléctriques 63
On the Breadline 79
Once again to Zelda 36
One Hundreds 130, *131*
Opal Loop 74, 83
Operation Riverside 115, 118–19

Opera sportif 147, 160
Ordinary Festivals 134
Original Sin *118*, 119
Orpheo 130, *162*

Page, Ashley 19, 30, 39, 65, 67, 70, *78*, 79, 81–2, 84–5
Painting Flying 37
Palace does not Forgive, The *122*, 123
Palimpsest 148–9
Paradigm *126*, 142
Parallels in Black 65, 70–72, 83
Parts I–IV 54
Party Blues 18
Paxton, Steve 7, 10, *19*, 39–40, *41*, 42–3, 66, *178*
Percussive Feet 103, 136, 140–42
Petronio, Stephen 83, 93, 100, *108*, 109, 151, 156
Pick-Up Company 40, 54, *76*
Pigeons à la Tombée d'Echalotes 147
Pile, Nick *67*
Place, The 5, 17, 69, 70, 72, 95, 98, 127
Plis de la nuit, Les 152
Points in Space 91
Postwar 50, *51*, 53
Preljocaj, Angelin 63, 81, 122
Prestidge, Mary 8
Profile *185*

Quinn, Cathy *144*

Raft is not the Shore, The 49
Rainbow Bandit 145
Rainforest 90
Rainer, Yvonne 4–5
Rajkumar, Tara 22
Rambert Dance Company 74, 95–6, 103, 134
    see also Ballet Rambert
Rambert, Marie 6
Rates of Exchange 63
ReBourne 151
Refurbished Behaviour *78*, 79
Regina Mater 152
regional festivals 20, 69, 101, 129
Reitz, Dana 47, 50, 55, 142
Resolution 98
Revolutionary Tactics 64, 73–4, 93, 99
Ricochet Dance Company *123*, *156*
Riper, Peter van 42
Rise 150
Rite of Spring 89, 122, 123

Riverdance 140
Riverside Studios 13, 17, 24, 32, 38, 45, 54, 66, 69, 77, 91, 115, 118, 125
Rogante, Giovanna 54
Rosas 66, 84, 115
Rosas Danst Rosas 115
Royal Ballet 7, 35, 39, 86, 115
Rudner, Sarah 4, 36
Rush 52
Ruttles 61

Sadler's Wells 65, 70
Sáez, Vicente 151
Say a Little Prayer 139, 148
Schubert Dances 42
Schuylenburch, Ellen van 124
Scottish Ballet 133
Search for Reflection 109
Second Stride 23, 32, 33–5, *34*, 59, 88, 92–3, 121
Set and Reset 54, 79, 83
Setterfield, Valda 40
Seven Desperate Years 70
Shelf Life 109
Shell: Forcefields and Spaces 48
Silver 79
Simson, Kirstie 27, 56, 66, 72
Simulacrum Reels 83
Singular Soloists 149
Sixth Heaven, The 81
Smith, Janet 10, 22, 23, 27, 32, 33, 95
Snaith, Yolande 7, 30, 70, 96, 108, 148
Solo 38
Solo Dances 37
Some Fugues 56
Son of Gone Fishin' 55
Song from the Country 49
Song of the Nightingale 236
Sophisticated Curiosities 155
Spaces 4 48
Spanish New Dance 146
Spatial Decay II 96, 107
Spectre de la rose, Le 122, 123
Spink, Ian 33, 35, *48*, 56, 81
Spitfire 88, *89*
Splitter 49
Sportorama 160, 161
Spring Loaded 70, 98
Springplank 17
Squash 82
Stardust 145
Stenger, Susan 157, *158*
Stomp 140
Stop Quartet, The 148

Streb, Elizabeth 144–5
Strider 5, 33
Strong Language 86
Stuart, Meg 160
Subbiah, Valli 110
Suddenly out of the Blue 86
Suite for Five 156
Suites furieuses, Les 151
Sur perros del sur (Southern Dogs) 120
Swan Lake 133, 157
Sweet Side Show 119
Sylphide, La 133

Tak, Tobias 140, *141*
Takei, Kei 20, 50, 53
Tandem 151
Tap Dogs 140, 151
Taylor, Paul 1, 81
technology and dance 105–6, 136–9, 143, 151, 154, 161
Terminus Terminux 67, 68, 92
Teshigawara, Saburo 91
Tetley, Glen 6
Tharp, Twyla 4, 5–6, 130, *131*
Things I Don't Know 157
13 73
32 feet per second per second 120
This is What You Get 79
Three Preludes 132
Through Movement Motor 43
Tight Roaring Cirle 159
Time 109
Time within Time 46
Tipton, Jennifer 119
Transatlantic 149
Transatlantic Tap 116–17, 140
Travelogue 42
Trespass 148
Tudor, Antony 6
Tufnell, Miranda 7, 40, 60, *61*, *77*, 79
Tuireadh 153–4
Turning World 98–9
Turtle Dreams: Cabaret 79–80
24-hour Featherstonehaughs 164

Unknown Banker buys Atlantic 38
Urban Bush Women 71, 83, 100, 122
Urban Weather 77,

V-Tol *120*
Valois, Ninette de 3
Vanrunxt, Marc 83–4

Very   115
video, *see* film
Volte-face   57

Waltzes in Disorder   155
Wanting to Tell Stories   121
Ward, David   60, 119
Waterzooi   152
Watteau duet   77
Where Her Voice?   137
White Bird Featherless   105, 115, *116*
White Man Sleeps   24, 87, 106, 153
Wild Air   159
Wild Translations   *144*
Wind   157
Winnsboro Cotton Mill Blues   155
Winterbranch   156
Wit, Harry de   *73, 75*

Woking festivals   101, 104, 129, 130,
   131–5, 141
Women who Love Too Much   84
Wood, Vivian   *137*
Wright, Douglas   *210*
Wrong Wrong   117
Wyoming   24, 87

X6   6, 8

*Year in the Life of a Field at Nettlecombe,
   Somerset, A*   49–50

Zane, Arnie   *56, 182*
Zarco   146
Zollar, Jawole Willa Jo   71–2, 83

Classic
Biscuits
& Family Favourites

JACQUELINE BELLEFONTAINE

JOHN BEAUFOY PUBLISHING

This edition first published in the United Kingdom in 2013 by
John Beaufoy Publishing, 11 Blenheim Court, 316 Woodstock Road,
Oxford OX2 7NS, England
www.johnbeaufoy.com

10 9 8 7 6 5 4 3 2 1

ISBN 978-1-909612-04-4

Project manager: Rosemary Wilkinson
Design: Glyn Bridgewater
Photography: St.John Asprey
Illustration: Stephen Dew

Printed and bound in Malaysia by Times Offset (M) Sdn. Bhd.

RECIPE NOTES

■ Where milk is used in a recipe, this can be full-fat, semi-skimmed or skimmed.

■ All eggs are medium unless otherwise stated.

■ All spoon measurements are level unless otherwise stated.

■ Metric and imperial measurements are not always exact equivalents, so only follow one set of measurements within each recipe.

■ Oven temperatures have been given for conventional electric and gas ovens. For fan ovens, use the following equivalents:

Electricity °C	Electricity (fan) °C
110	90
120	100
130	110
140	120
150	130
160	140
170	150
180	160
190	170
200	180
220	200

Contents

Introduction 6

1 Everyday treats 16

2 Fancy fun 36

3 The healthier cookie 54

4 World classics 72

Recipe index 96

A great place to start

If you are new to baking then making cookies is a great place to start. You only need a little equipment and there are many recipes here that are very simple to make but also a few more challenging recipes for the more experienced cook to try his or her hand. There are quick and easy drop cookies, ideal everyday treats; more involved, rolled, shaped and decorated cookies; lots of classic favourites from around the globe and even some slightly healthier cookies for those on special diets. There is something for everyone.

Is it a cookie or a biscuit? Americans tend to refer to them as cookies, the name of which comes from the Dutch word *koekje*, meaning 'little cake'. Whereas the British tend to use the word biscuit from the French *bis cuit*, which means 'twice baked'. Others choose to refer to them as cookies if they are soft, almost cake-like, and biscuits if they are crisp and brittle.

Methods of making cookies

You can divide most cookies into the following methods of making:

Drop cookies:

The quickest and easiest to make and perfect for beginners. Often made by the creaming method, the fat and sugar are beaten together, then the flour and any additional ingredients are added and beaten until evenly combined. The mixture is soft and can be spooned or 'dropped' onto the baking sheet. Allow room for the cookies to spread during baking: the softer the mixture, the more it will spread.

Sliced cookies:

Probably the next easiest method. The dough is firm and can be shaped into a log. The biscuits are then cut at the desired thickness. The uncooked biscuit dough can be stored in the fridge for several days and a few cookies cut and baked from the log as desired. The uncooked dough can also be frozen either pre-sliced or whole, in which case it should be left in the fridge overnight to defrost before slicing. Ideal for fresh baked biscuits everyday.

Rolled cookies:

The dough is rolled out and cut into shapes with a knife or a cookie cutter. If a dough is very soft, you may find it easier to roll out between two sheets of cling wrap. Chilling the dough

will also help. Do not add too much extra flour and try to avoid re-rolling too many times or the cookies may become tough.

Moulded cookies:

A soft dough is used and the cookies are shaped into logs, balls or crescents, with lightly floured hands. Take care not to add too much extra flour when rolling and shaping as this will

alter the careful balance of the ingredients and make the dough tough.

Piped biscuits:

Made from a dough which is soft enough to be piped from a plain or fluted nozzle to produce attractive biscuits. The consistency of the biscuit dough needs to be just right, so

very careful measuring is essential. Too stiff and the biscuits will be hard to pipe, too soft and the biscuits will lose their shape when baked.

Wafers: Probably the hardest to make as they cook very quickly so timing is critical. The mixture is very soft (a batter) and is spooned onto a baking sheet and spread out to form a circle. They are sometimes shaped  into rolls or curled. In this case you need to work fast only cooking a couple at a time, as they need to be shaped whilst warm.

Storage: Cookies should be stored in an airtight container and most will last for up to a week, many longer, unless otherwise stated in the recipe. Always store soft and crisp cookies separately or you will end up with all soft cookies. Undecorated cookies can be frozen for up to 2 months and some uncooked cookie dough can be stored for up to 1 month. Make sure cookies are completely cold before storing.

Tips for success

Oven temperature: Always preheat the oven. Cookies often cook best if cooked one sheet at a time, especially in conventional ovens with top and bottom heat. They are best cooked on the middle shelf. But if you do cook more than one sheet at a time, remember to swop the position halfway through the cooking time.

Fan ovens: These generally cook more evenly especially if cooking more than one sheet at a time, so are ideal for cookie baking but you will need to adjust the temperature according to the manufacturer's instructions, usually reducing by 10–20oC. See the chart on page 4.

Greasing baking sheets and tins: When using good quality baking sheets, you often do not need to grease them, unless otherwise stated. When required, grease lightly using a little cooking oil or butter. Over greasing may cause cookies to spread excessively and may cause the bottom of the cookies to burn.

Always use a cold baking sheet, or the cookies may spread excessively. If you need to reuse the baking sheet, allow to cool between batches.

Softened butter: Many recipes call for softened butter. If the butter is too hard it will not mix into the sugar properly. Soften butter by leaving at room temperature for 1 hour. If you forget you can soften for a few seconds in a microwave but take care: it is very easy to over soften and reduce the butter to liquid which again will not blend with the sugar properly and will make the cookies oily.

Children in the kitchen

Children often enjoy helping to make cookies and as they are relatively easy and fun, they make a good introduction to the joy of baking but do remember that a kitchen can be an unsafe environment especially for children, so NEVER leave them unsupervised.

When cooking with children, allow extra time and take extra care when putting things into and taking out of the oven, and also when using hot liquids, knives and electrical equipment.

Equipment to get you started

Scales: Accurate measuring is essential. Electronic or balance scales are more accurate than measuring cups which measure by volume and it is recommended that you invest in a set of scales if you intend to take up baking.

Measuring spoons: A set of measuring spoons is also a must for measuring ingredients. All spoon measures in books are always level unless otherwise stated.

Bowls: You will need a selection of bowls of various sizes.

Spoons: Wooden spoons are used to beat ingredients together. They can be used to beat fat and sugar together until pale and fluffy, although an electric whisk will make this job easier. For cookie making they can also be used to beat in dry ingredients, although when bringing the mixture together to form a dough, you will need to use your hands to complete the process.

Although measuring spoons must be used for measuring ingredients, a standard dessert or tablespoon can be used to spoon free-form cookies onto the baking sheets. The larger the spoon, the larger the cookie, which may take a minute or two longer to cook.

Spatula: Silicone or plastic spatulas are ideal for scraping out bowls with the minimum of waste.

Baking sheets: It is advisable to invest in a few good quality baking sheets. They will distribute heat more evenly, are less likely to twist or buckle in the oven

and the cookies are also less likely to stick or burn. Choose tins that feel relatively heavy and do not twist or bend easily.

Timer: Because cookies and biscuits cook quickly, you will need to keep a close eye on the baking. Times given in the recipes are a guide as ovens and the thickness and size of the cookies may vary. A timer with a loud ring is ideal to help make sure they do not overcook.

Wire racks: When cookies first come out of the oven they are often a little soft and need to be left for a minute or two to crisp up. They should then be moved to a wire rack to cool completely – the clean rack from a grill will do if you do not have a specific cooling rack. If the cookies are left to cool on the baking sheet they may stick or become soggy.

Some useful extras

Knives: A sharp knife is useful for cutting cleanly through a dough in some recipes. A rounded, flat blade palette knife is useful for transferring cookies to the cooling rack and also for spreading fillings or icings.

Electric whisks and mixers: A hand-held whisk is ideal to use in place of a wooden spoon to beat the fat and sugar together, as it is quicker and easier. Swap to a wooden spoon to beat in the dry ingredients. Also useful for whisking egg whites and batters for some cookie mixtures.

Food processor: Can be used to rub fat into flour quickly and efficiently. Also ideal for chopping or grinding nuts.

Rolling pin: You will need this when making cookies that are rolled out and cut into shapes before baking.

Cookie cutters: Use for cutting cookies into shapes before baking. They are available in many shapes and sizes and are

usually made from plastic or metal. Metal cutters often have a sharper edge and give a better 'cut'. When using cutters, press down firmly, then lift off without twisting. If dough is sticky, dip the cutters in a little flour first. If you do not have any cutters, use an upturned glass.

Pastry brush: For glazes and greasing baking sheets when using oil.

Piping bags and nozzles: Required for some cookie recipes and for piping icing. Reusable and disposable piping bags and plastic or metal nozzles are available from cook shops.

Ingredients

Many cookies are made from three basic ingredients, fat, sugar and flour with the addition of other ingredients, such as chocolate, fruit and nuts, for flavour and oats, semolina, etc., for texture. The best ingredients will give the best flavour.

Fats: Butter gives the best flavour. Using salted butter eliminates the need to add salt but some recipes require unsalted butter. Use butter that is at room temperature as beating cold butter is very difficult. Baking margarine can be used but the flavour is seriously compromised and the biscuits will have a less 'melt-in-the-mouth' texture. Spreads and reduced fat spreads are not suitable. Oil is used in a few recipes. In these cases the fat does not contribute to the overall flavour, so use a lightly flavoured oil, such as sunflower or corn oil.

Sugar: Most sugar is produced from two sources: sugar cane or sugar beet. Unrefined sugars are made from sugar cane and have a higher mineral, vitamin and trace element content than refined sugars and although not essential they improve the flavour of the cookie.

The most common types of sugar used are caster, icing and light muscovado sugar (unrefined light brown sugar). It is important that the correct type of sugar is used for the best result.

Flour: Most recipes use plain or self-raising flour. If you do not have self-raising flour you can make your own by adding 2 tsp baking powder to each 225 g/8 oz plain flour. Wholemeal flour, which is flour that has been milled from the whole of the wheat grain, is used in some recipes.

Eggs: The size of eggs in baking is important. All recipes use medium-sized eggs unless otherwise stated. Remove from the fridge to come up to room temperature if possible before using, as cold eggs do not combine well with other ingredients or trap as much air.

I

everyday
treats

Makes 18
Prep time: 10 mins
Cook time: 12–15 mins

175 g/6 oz self-raising flour
75 g/3 oz butter, cut into cubes
75 g/3 oz caster sugar
1 egg, lightly beaten
6 tbsp maple syrup
approx. 18 pecan halves

Maple pecan cookies

1 Preheat the oven to 180°C/350°F/Gas 4.

2 Place the flour into a mixing bowl and add the butter. Rub in the butter with your fingertips until the mixture resembles fine breadcrumbs. Stir in the sugar. Add the egg and 4 tbsp of the maple syrup and mix until well combined.

3 Place small spoonfuls of the mixture onto baking sheets, allowing space for the cookies to spread. Push a pecan half into the centre of each one.

4 Bake for 12–15 minutes until golden. Brush the cookies with the remaining maple syrup whilst still hot, then transfer to a wire rack to cool completely.

Makes about 20
Prep time: 20 mins plus chilling
Cook time: 10–12 mins

50 g/2 oz butter, softened
50 g/2 oz caster sugar

1 egg
175 g/6 oz plain flour
a little milk
40 g/1½ oz toasted hazelnuts, finely chopped
2–3 tbsp lemon curd

Lemon and hazelnut slices

1 Beat together the butter and sugar until pale and fluffy. Beat in the egg, then beat in the flour, finally using your hands to bring the mixture together to form a soft dough. Divide the dough into 2 pieces and roll into logs about 25 cm/10 in long. Brush each log with a little milk.

2 Spread the chopped hazelnuts on a sheet of non-stick baking parchment. Place the logs on the nuts and roll to press lightly into the nuts to coat.

3 Place the logs on a lightly greased baking sheet. Flatten each log slightly. Using the handle of a wooden spoon, press a channel down the centre of each log. Fill the hollows with lemon curd. Chill for 30 minutes.

4 Preheat the oven to 190°C/375°F/Gas 5. Bake for 10–12 minutes until pale golden brown. Leave on the baking sheet until the lemon curd has set but the dough is still warm. Cut diagonally into slices and transfer to a wire rack to cool completely.

Makes about 18
Prep time: 15 mins
Cook time: 12–15 mins plus setting

100 g/4 oz butter, softened
100 g/4 oz caster sugar

1 egg, lightly beaten
75 g/3 oz plain chocolate chips
175 g/6 oz self-raising flour
3 tbsp cocoa powder
1/2 tsp chilli powder
25 g/1 oz white chocolate (optional)

Chilli choc cookies

1 Preheat the oven to 180°C/350°F/Gas 4. Lightly grease 2 or 3 baking sheets.

2 Beat the butter and sugar together until pale and fluffy, then gradually beat in the egg. Stir in the chocolate chips. Sift the flour, cocoa and chilli powder into the bowl and beat together until combined to form a soft dough.

3 Place the dough on a large sheet of non-stick baking parchment and roll out to a 30 x 20 cm/12 x 8 in rectangle. If the dough is very soft, place another sheet of parchment on top to make rolling easier. Cut the dough into 18 rectangles and place on the prepared baking sheets.

4 Bake for 12–15 minutes. Allow to cool for 2–3 minutes before transferring to a wire rack to cool completely.

5 To decorate if desired, melt the white chocolate in the microwave or over a pan of hot water. Drizzle the white chocolate back and forth over the cookies. Allow to set.

Makes about 16
Prep time: 15 mins
Cook time: 15–20 mins

100 g/4 oz butter
100 g/4 oz caster sugar
2 tbsp orange juice

grated zest of 1 orange
100 g/4 oz self-raising flour, sifted
100 g/4 oz rolled oats
50 g/2 oz dried cranberries, roughly chopped
25 g/1 oz chopped candied orange peel

Orange and cranberry biscuits

1 Preheat the oven to 180°C/350°F/Gas 4. Lightly grease 2 baking sheets.

2 Place the butter and sugar in a saucepan and heat gently, stirring until the butter melts and the sugar dissolves. Stir in the orange juice and zest. Remove from the heat and beat in the remaining ingredients.

3 Place dessertspoonfuls of the mixture on the baking sheets allowing space for the mixture to spread a little.

4 Bake for 15–20 minutes. Allow to cool for a minute, then transfer to a wire rack to cool completely.

Makes about 24
Prep time: 20 mins
Cook time: 10–12 mins plus setting

150 g/5 oz butter, softened
175 g/6 oz caster sugar
3 tbsp lime juice
grated zest of ¹/₂ lime

50 g/2 oz desiccated coconut
225 g/8 oz self-raising flour

ICING
150 g/5 oz icing sugar
1–2 tablespoons lime juice
grated zest of ¹/₂ lime

Lime and coconut biscuits

1 Preheat the oven to 180°C/350°F/Gas 4. Lightly grease
2 baking sheets.

2 Beat together the butter and sugar until pale and fluffy.
Beat in the lime juice, zest and coconut. Add the flour and
beat into the coconut mixture.

3 Place rounded dessertspoonfuls of the mixture well spaced
on the baking sheet. Bake for 10–12 minutes or until golden.
Allow to cool on the baking sheet for 2–3 minutes, then
transfer to a wire rack to cool completely.

4 Sift the icing sugar into a bowl and stir in the lime juice and
zest to form a smooth icing. Spread over the biscuits. Allow to
dry for 1–2 hours or until the icing sets. Store in an airtight
container for up to 5 days.

VARIATION
If time is short omit the icing, the cookies are still delicious!

Makes 16
Prep time: 15 mins
Cook time: 15–20 mins

125 g/4½ oz granulated sugar
1 tbsp dried lavender flowers

225 g/8 oz butter
225 g/8 oz plain flour
125 g/4½ oz ground rice
or semolina
caster sugar, to sprinkle (optional)

Lavender shortbreads

1 Place the sugar and lavender in a food processor and whiz for about 10 seconds. Add the butter and process until pale and fluffy. Add the flour and ground rice or semolina and whiz briefly until the dough begins to come together.

2 Tip out onto a work surface and continue bringing the mixture together to form a soft dough with your hands. Divide the dough into two. Form each piece into a ball, then roll out to form an 18 cm/7 in circle. Transfer to a baking sheet.

3 Press a fork into the edge of the circles to make a crinkled border and prick all over the surface. Mark each into 8 wedges, then chill for 30 minutes.

4 Preheat the oven to 190°C/375°F/Gas 5. Bake for 15–20 minutes until pale golden. Sprinkle with caster sugar if desired, then transfer to a wire rack to cool completely.

TIP
If you cannot find dried lavender, substitute the same amount of fresh, chopped rosemary for a similar scented biscuit.

Makes about 15
Prep time: 15 mins plus chilling
Cook time: 15–18 mins

100 g/4 oz butter, softened
50 g/2 oz icing sugar
1/2 tsp vanilla essence
175 g/6 oz plain flour
a little milk, if needed
fruit jam of your choice

Thumbprint cookies

1 Beat the butter and sugar until pale and fluffy, then beat in the vanilla essence. Gradually beat in the flour, bringing the mixture together to form a soft dough with your hands as you add the last of the flour. Add a little milk or water if the mixture is too dry.

2 Lightly dust your hands with flour and roll the dough into small balls about the size of a small walnut. Arranged well spaced on a baking sheet. Flatten slightly, then, using your thumb, make a deep hole in the centre of each cookie. Chill for 30 minutes.

3 Preheat the oven to 180°C/350°F/Gas 4. Bake for 10 minutes, then fill each hole with a little jam and return to the oven for 5–8 minutes until pale golden. Allow to cool on the sheet for a few minutes before transferring to a wire rack to cool completely.

VARIATION

For a chocolate thumbprint cookie: bake the cookies for 15 minutes until golden. Meanwhile, melt 50g/2 oz plain chocolate with 25 g/1 oz butter in a microwave or in a bowl over a pan of hot water. Beat in 25 g/1 oz icing sugar. Once the cookies are baked, spoon or pipe the melted chocolate into the centre of the cookies and allow to set.

Makes about 20
Prep time: 20 mins
Cook time: 15–20 mins

100 g/4 oz chopped toasted hazelnuts
2 medium egg whites
225 g/8 oz caster sugar
1 tsp cornflour
about 20 whole hazelnuts, to decorate

Hazelnut macaroons

1 Preheat the oven to 170°C/325°F/Gas 3. Line 2 baking sheets with non-stick baking parchment.

2 Place the hazelnuts in a grinder and whiz until very finely chopped. Put the egg whites in a large mixing bowl and whisk until standing in soft peaks. Gradually add half the sugar and whisk until combined and stiff peaks are formed.

3 Carefully fold in the remaining sugar, ground hazelnuts and cornflour. Place spoonfuls of the mixture well spaced on the baking sheets and press a whole hazelnut into the centre of each.

4 Cook for about 15–20 minutes until the macaroons are pale golden and can be easily removed from the paper.

TIP
Dip the base of the macaroon into melted chocolate for a special treat.

Makes about 15 small cookies
Prep time: 15 mins
Cook time: 12 – 15 mins plus setting

grated zest of 1 orange
8 large basil leaves, chopped
175 g/6 oz plain flour

50 g/2 oz butter, softened
50 g/2 oz caster sugar
2 tbsp orange juice

ICING
50 g/2 oz icing sugar
2 tsp orange juice

Orange and basil cookies

1 Preheat the oven to 180°C/350°F/Gas 4.

2 Place the butter and sugar in a mixing bowl and beat until pale and fluffy. Beat in the orange juice, zest and basil. Add the flour and beat until combined using your hands to finish bringing the mixture together.

3 Roll walnut-sized pieces of the dough into balls using lightly floured hands. Place on baking sheets, flatten slightly and bake for 12–15 minutes until pale golden. Allow to cool for a couple of minutes before transferring to a wire rack to cool completely.

4 Sift the icing sugar into a bowl and stir in the orange juice to form a smooth icing. Spread over the biscuits. Allow to dry for 1–2 hours or until the icing sets.

VARIATION
Add 25 g/1 oz candied orange peel or mixed chopped peel.

2

fancy fun

Makes about 20–40 depending on size of cutters used
Prep time: 30 mins
Cook time: 10–12 mins plus setting

100 g/4 oz butter, softened
100 g/4 oz light muscovado sugar
225 g/8 oz plain flour
1 tbsp golden syrup

2 tbsp milk
2 tsp ground ginger (optional)

TO DECORATE
150 g/5 oz icing sugar
approx. 4 tsp tbsp water
food colouring and sprinkles (optional)

Iced Christmas cookies

1 Preheat the oven to 190°C/375°F/Gas 5. Grease 2 baking sheets.

2 Place the butter and sugar in a mixing bowl and beat until light and fluffy. Add the remaining ingredients and mix to form a soft dough.

3 Roll out the dough to 5 mm/$^1/_4$ in thick and cut out different shapes using cookie cutters. Place on the baking sheets and bake for 10–12 minutes until crisp and golden.

4 Allow to cool on the baking sheets for 2–3 minutes, then transfer to a wire rack to cool completely.

5 To decorate, sift the icing sugar into a bowl, stir in enough water and mix to form a smooth icing. Colour the icing, if desired, with a few drops of food colouring. Spread or pipe over the biscuits and add sprinkles if desired. Allow to dry for 1–2 hours or until the icing sets. Store in an airtight container for up to 2 weeks.

TIP
If you want to hang the cookies on the tree make a hole in each cookie with a skewer before baking. Tie onto the tree with ribbon threaded through the hole.

Makes about 20
Prep time: 20 mins
Cook time: 12 mins plus setting

100 g/4 oz butter, softened
100 g/4 oz caster sugar
2 tbsp instant coffee
4 tbsp boiling water
225 g/8 oz plain flour
50 g/2 oz ground rice

FILLING
50 g/2 oz unsalted butter
175 g/6 oz icing sugar
2 tsp milk
2 tsp vanilla essence

ICING
100 g/4 oz icing sugar
1/2 tsp instant coffee
drinking chocolate or cocoa powder, to dust

Cappuccino creams

1 Preheat the oven to 180°C/350°F/Gas 4.

2 Beat together the butter and sugar until light and fluffy. Dissolve the coffee in the boiling water, then beat in. Add the flour and ground rice and mix to form a firm dough.

3 Roll out the dough on a lightly floured surface to about 3 mm/1/8 in thick, then cut into 5 cm/2 in rounds with a cookie cutter. Place on baking sheets. Repeat until all the dough is used, re-rolling as necessary.

4 Bake for 12 minutes until golden. Allow to cool for a few minutes before transferring to a wire rack to cool completely.

5 To make the filling, beat the butter until fluffy, then gradually beat in the icing sugar, milk and vanilla. Use to sandwich the biscuits together in pairs.

6 To make the icing, sift the sugar into a bowl. Dissolve the coffee in 1 tablespoon of boiling water and stir into the icing sugar until smooth. Spread over the cookies and allow to set. Dust with a little drinking chocolate or cocoa powder.

Makes about 24
Prep time: 30 mins
Cook time: 15–20 mins plus setting

1 tbsp instant coffee
2 tbsp milk

175 g/6 oz butter, softened
50 g/2 oz caster sugar
1 egg yolk
175 g/6 oz plain flour
approx. 24 walnut halves
150 g/5 oz milk or plain chocolate

Walnut whirls

1 Preheat the oven to 170°C/325°F/Gas 3. Grease 2 baking sheets.

2 Place the coffee in a small pan with the milk and heat gently, stirring until the coffee dissolves. In a mixing bowl beat together the butter and sugar until light and fluffy. Beat in the egg yolk, then the coffee mixture. Stir in the flour to form a smooth thick paste.

3 Spoon into a piping bag fitted with a large star nozzle and pipe rosettes measuring about 5 cm/2 in across onto the baking sheets. Press a walnut half gently into the centre of each.

4 Bake for 15–20 minutes or until pale golden. Allow to cool on the baking sheets for 2–3 minutes, then transfer to a wire rack to cool completely.

5 Melt the chocolate in a bowl set over a pan of gently simmering hot water or in the microwave. Place the cookies on a sheet lined with baking parchment and drizzle the chocolate over them, then leave in a cool place until set.

VARIATION
Omit the coffee and replace with 2 tsp vanilla essence instead.

Makes about 36
Prep time: 20 mins plus chilling
Cook time: 10–12 mins

150 g/5 oz butter, softened
75 g/3 oz caster sugar

1 tsp vanilla essence
5 tbsp double cream
250 g/9 oz plain flour
4 tbsp demerara sugar
1 tbsp ground cinnamon

Cinnamon twirls

1 Place the butter and sugar in a mixing bowl and beat until pale and fluffy. Beat in the vanilla essence and 3 tbsp of the double cream. Add the flour and mix to a smooth soft dough.

2 Roll out the dough on a sheet of non-stick baking parchment to form a rectangle about 30 x 20 cm/12 x 8 in. Brush the remaining cream over the surface of the dough. Mix together the demerara sugar and cinnamon, then sprinkle over the cream. Roll up from the long side like a Swiss roll. Cover and chill for 30 minutes.

3 Preheat the oven to 180°C/350°F/Gas 4. Cut the dough into 5 mm/$^{1}/_{4}$ in slices and place well spaced on baking sheets.

4 Bake for 10–12 minutes until crisp. Cool for 2–3 minutes on the baking sheets, then transfer to a wire rack to cool completely.

Makes about 24
Prep time: 25 mins
Cook time: 12–15 mins

175 g/6 oz plain flour
100 g/4 oz butter, cut into cubes
50 g/2 oz ground almonds
50 g/2 oz caster sugar
3 tbsp apricot jam

TOPPING
75 g/3 oz plain flour
1/2 tsp ground cinnamon
50 g/2 oz butter, cut into cubes
40 g/1 1/2 oz demerara sugar
50 g/2 oz ready-to-eat dried apricots, finely chopped

Streusel-topped cookies

1 Preheat the oven to 180°C/350°F/Gas 4.

2 Place the flour in a mixing bowl and rub in the butter with your fingertips until the mixture resembles fine breadcrumbs. Stir in the almonds and sugar. Add the jam and work the mixture together to form a smooth dough.

3 Roll out on a lightly floured work surface and cut into 7 cm/2 1/2 in rounds with a cookie cutter. Place on baking sheets.

4 To make the topping, sift the flour and cinnamon into a bowl. Rub in the butter until the mixture resembles breadcrumbs. Stir in the demerara sugar and chopped apricots. Pile a little of the streusel mixture on top of each cookie. Bake for 12–15 minutes or until the topping is golden.

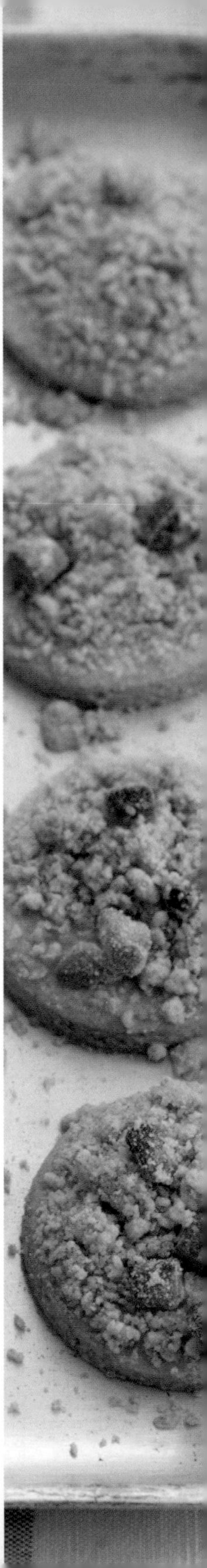

Makes about 24
Prep time: 30 mins plus chilling
Cook time: 10–12 mins

PLAIN CHOCOLATE LAYER
50 g/2 oz plain chocolate
50 g/2 oz butter, softened
50 g/2 oz caster sugar
150 g/5 oz plain flour
a little milk or water

WHITE CHOCOLATE LAYER
50 g/2 oz white chocolate
50 g/2 oz butter, softened
50 g/2 oz caster sugar
150 g/5 oz plain flour

MILK CHOCOLATE LAYER
50 g/2 oz milk chocolate
50 g/2 oz butter, softened
50 g/2 oz caster sugar
150 g/5 oz plain flour

Chocolate stacks

1 Break up the plain chocolate and place in a bowl over a pan of gently simmering water. Stir until melted. Allow to cool.

2 Place the butter and sugar in a mixing bowl and beat until pale and fluffy. Beat in the cooled chocolate. Add the flour and beat until combined using your hands to finish bringing the mixture together. Add a little milk or water if the mixture is too dry.

3 Repeat steps one and two twice but using first the white chocolate, then the milk.

4 Shape each of the doughs into a sausage, then flatten to form a rectangle about 5 x 25 cm/2 x 10 in long. Brush the tops of the plain and white chocolate dough with a little water to dampen. Make a stack of 3 layers, first the plain chocolate, then the white, then the milk. Chill for 20 minutes. Preheat the oven to 180°C/350°F/Gas 4.

5 Cut into about 24 slices and place on baking sheets with room for spreading. Bake for 10–12 minutes until firm. Cool for 3–4 minutes, then transfer to a wire rack to cool completely.

Makes about 20
Prep time: 15 mins
Cook time: 12–15 mins

100 g/4 oz butter, softened
50 g/2 oz caster sugar

2 tbsp milk
75 g/3 oz glacé cherries, chopped
50 g/2 oz almonds, chopped
175 g/6 oz self-raising flour
75 g/3 oz marzipan

Cherry marzipan bites

1 Preheat the oven to 180°C/350°F/Gas 4.

2 Place the butter and sugar in a mixing bowl and beat until pale and fluffy, then beat in the milk. Add the cherries, almonds and flour and mix together to form a soft dough.

3 With lightly floured hands, break off small walnut-sized pieces of the dough and roll into balls. Place on a baking sheet allowing space for the cookies to spread and flatten with a palette knife.

4 Grate the marzipan coarsely and sprinkle a little over each cookie.

5 Bake for about 12–15 minutes until pale golden. Transfer to a wire rack to cool completely.

Makes about 24
Prep time: 25 mins
Cook time: 8–10 mins

75 g/3 oz butter, softened
75 g/3 oz caster sugar
100 g/4 oz smooth peanut butter
3 tbsp golden syrup
175 g/6 oz self-raising flour
fruit jam of your choice

Peanut jelly dodgers

1 Preheat the oven to 180°C/350°F/Gas 4.

2 Beat the butter and sugar together until pale and fluffy. Add the peanut butter and golden syrup, beating until well combined. Add the flour and work into the mixture to form a soft dough. Knead lightly.

3 Roll out the dough 5 mm/¼ in thick and cut out cookies using a 5 cm/2 in round cutter. Cut out the centre of half the cookies using a small round cutter. Re-roll these centre cut-outs to make further cookies. Place on baking sheets, with a little space around each. Bake for 8–10 minutes, until pale golden. Allow to cool on the sheets for a few minutes before transferring to a wire rack to cool completely.

4 Spread a little jam over the whole circles and place the rings on top.

3

the healthier cookie

Makes 10
Prep time: 15 mins
Cook time: 20 mins

1 egg
50 g/2 oz light muscovado sugar
100 g/4 oz stoned dates, chopped
50 g/2 oz dried figs, chopped
75 g/3 oz walnuts, finely chopped
50 g/2 oz wholemeal flour
1 tsp mixed spice

Date and walnut fingers

1 Preheat the oven to 180°C/350°F/Gas 4. Grease and line an 18 cm/7 in shallow, square cake tin.

2 Place the egg and sugar in a bowl and whisk until frothy and the whisk leaves a short trail when lifted from the mixture. Stir in the dates, figs and walnuts. Sift the flour and spice over the mixture and carefully fold in.

3 Spread the mixture out in the cake tin and bake for 20 minutes until firm and golden.

4 Allow to cool in the tin for 5 minutes, then cut into fingers and transfer to a wire rack to cool completely.

TIP
These cookies are high in fibre and low in fat. To save preparation time, chop the fruit and nuts in a food processor.

Makes 24
Prep time: 20 mins
Cook time: 15 mins

75 g/3 oz butter, softened
50 g/2 oz light muscovado sugar
50 g/2 oz barley malt syrup or honey
50 g/2 oz sunflower seeds
75 g/3 oz self-raising flour
75 g/3 oz wholemeal flour

Seedy wedges

1 Preheat the oven to 180°C/350°F/Gas 4.

2 Place the butter and sugar in a bowl and beat together until pale and fluffy, then beat in the malt syrup or honey. Stir in the sunflower seeds. Mix in the flours to form a soft dough.

3 Divide the dough into 2 pieces and roll each piece into a circle about 18 cm/7 in in diameter. Place on baking sheets and cut each into 12 wedges.

4 Bake for 15 minutes until golden. Allow to cool slightly, then break into wedges and transfer to a wire rack to cool completely.

TIP
Seeds are a good source of trace elements and essential oils. Try using a mixture of seeds to increase the health value of these cookies.

Makes about 40
Prep time: 15 mins plus chilling
Cook time: 8–10 mins

175 g/6 oz butter, softened
75 g/3 oz light muscovado sugar

1 egg yolk
grated zest of 1/2 lemon
2 tbsp lemon juice
1 tbsp poppy seeds
225 g/8 oz plain flour

Lemon poppy seed cookies

1 Place the butter and sugar in a bowl and beat together until pale and fluffy. Beat in the egg yolk, lemon zest and juice. Mix the poppy seeds with the flour, then beat into the butter mixture to form a soft dough.

2 Shape into a long log about 5 cm/2 in thick. Wrap the log in a sheet of non-stick baking parchment and chill until required.

3 Preheat the oven to 190°C/375°F/Gas 5. Cut 5 mm/1/4 in thick slices from the log and place on baking sheets. Leave enough space for the cookies to spread.

4 Bake for 8–10 minutes until just firm. Allow to cool on the baking sheet for a few minutes before transferring to a wire rack to cool completely.

TIP
The uncooked biscuit log can be stored in the fridge for up to 1 week or place in a polythene bag and freeze for up to 2 months.

Makes about 20
Prep time: 15 mins
Cook time: 10–12 mins

225 g/8 oz plain flour
1 tsp baking powder
1 tsp allspice

1/2 tsp ground cinnamon
1/2 tsp ground nutmeg
125 ml/4 1/2 fl oz sunflower oil
1 egg
150 g/5 oz full-flavoured clear honey

Honey and spice cookies

1 Preheat the oven to 190°C/375°F/Gas 5. Lightly grease 2 baking sheets.

2 Place the flour, baking powder and spices in a mixing bowl and stir to combine. In another bowl, beat together the oil and the egg, then pour into the centre of the dry ingredients. Add the honey. Mix well.

3 Place spoonfuls of the mixture onto the baking sheets allowing a little space for them to spread.

4 Bake for 10–12 minutes until golden. Allow to cool for a few minutes on the baking sheets before transferring to a wire rack to cool completely.

TIP
Suitable for a dairy-free diet. You can replace the spices listed with 2 tsp of mixed spice.

Makes about 38
Prep time: 15 mins plus chilling
Cook time: 8–10 mins

175 g/6 oz butter, softened
100 g/4 oz light muscovado sugar
75 g/3 oz walnuts, very finely chopped

1 tsp dried rosemary or 2 tsp chopped fresh rosemary
175 g/6 oz plain flour
1 tsp baking powder
50 g/2 oz plain wholemeal flour

Walnut and rosemary cookies

1 Place the butter and sugar in a bowl and beat together until pale and fluffy. Add the walnuts and rosemary and mix to combine. Sift the plain flour and baking powder into the bowl, then add the wholemeal flour and mix to form a soft dough.

2 Shape into a long log about 5 cm/2 in thick. Wrap the log in a sheet of non-stick baking parchment and chill until required.

3 Preheat the oven to 190°C/375°F/Gas 5. Cut 5 mm/^{1}/$_{4}$ in thick slices from the log and place on baking sheets, leaving enough space between for the cookies to spread.

4 Bake for 8–10 minutes until just firm. Allow to cool on the baking sheets for a few minutes before transferring to a wire rack to cool completely.

TIP
Walnuts are a good source of Vitamin E and essential oils.

Makes about 24
Prep time: 15 mins
Cook time: 12 mins

150 g/5 oz rolled oats
50 g/2 oz self-raising flour
100 g/4 oz ready-to-eat dried
apricots (unsulphered if possible),
chopped

50 g/2 oz unblanched almonds,
roughly chopped
75 g/3 oz light muscovado sugar
1 tbsp barley malt syrup
150 ml/5 fl oz sunflower oil

Apricot and almond cookies

1 Preheat the oven to 190°C/375°F/Gas 5. Lightly grease 2 baking sheets.

2 Place the oats, flour, apricots, almonds and sugar in a mixing bowl and stir to combine. Add the malt syrup and oil and beat into dry ingredients, making sure the syrup is well blended into the mixture.

3 Place spoonfuls of the mixture on the baking sheets.

4 Bake for 12 minutes until golden. Allow to cool slightly for a few minutes on the baking sheet before transferring to a wire rack to cool completely.

TIP
Dried apricots are a
good source of iron.

Makes 16–20
Prep time: 15 mins
Cook time: 20–25 mins

225 g/8 oz butter
150 g/5 oz dark or light muscovado sugar

2 tbsp barley malt syrup or golden syrup
500 g/1lb 2 oz rolled oats
1 Granny Smith apple, peeled, cored and chopped
50 g/2 oz dried figs, chopped

Fruity flapjacks

1 Preheat the oven to 180°C/350°F/Gas 4. Lightly grease a 30 x 20 cm/12 x 8 in square, shallow cake tin.

2 Place the butter, sugar and syrup in a small saucepan and heat gently, stirring until combined. Place the oats in a mixing bowl and stir in the apple and figs. Make a well in the centre and pour in the butter and sugar mixture. Beat until well combined.

3 Pour into the cake tin and level the surface. Bake for 20–25 minutes. Allow to cool for 5 minutes in the tin, then cut into pieces whilst still warm and transfer to a wire rack to cool completely.

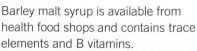

TIP
Barley malt syrup is available from health food shops and contains trace elements and B vitamins.

Makes about 18
Prep time: 15 mins
Cook time: 10–15 mins

100 g/4 oz light muscovado sugar
100 g/4 oz sunflower margarine
175 g/6 oz rolled oats

50 g/2 oz plain wholemeal flour
1 piece stem ginger in syrup, chopped plus
2 tbsp of the ginger syrup from the jar
1 egg

Ginger oat cookies

1 Preheat the oven to 180°C/350°F/Gas 4. Lightly grease 2 baking sheets.

2 Place the sugar and margarine in a saucepan and heat gently, stirring until combined. Place all the remaining ingredients, except the egg, in a large mixing bowl. Beat in the sugar mixture, then add the egg and beat until all the ingredients are well combined.

3 Place rounded tablespoonfuls of the mixture onto the baking sheets. Flatten slightly with the back of the spoon.

4 Bake for 10–15 minutes until golden. Allow to cool on the baking sheet for a few minutes before transferring to a wire rack to cool completely.

TIP
Suitable for a dairy-free diet. Oats and wholemeal flour are complex carbohydrates that release energy slowly helping you to feel fuller for longer.

4

world classics

Makes about 18 large cookies
Prep time: 15 mins
Cook time: 10–12 mins

50 g/2 oz plain chocolate
50 g/2 oz white chocolate

50 g/2 oz milk chocolate
150 g/5 oz butter, softened
150 g/5 oz caster sugar
1 egg
1 tsp vanilla extract
200 g/7 oz self-raising flour

Triple choc chip cookies

1 Preheat the oven to 190°C/375°F/Gas 5. Lightly grease
2 baking sheets.

2 Chop all the chocolate into small chunks. Beat the butter
and sugar together until pale and fluffy. Beat in the egg and
vanilla extract. Stir in the chocolate. Sift the flour and beat
into the mixture, until well combined.

3 Place round tablespoons of the mixture onto the
baking sheets leaving plenty of space around each one. Shape
each mound into a round and flatten slightly with the back
of a spoon.

4 Bake for 10–12 minutes until golden. Allow to cool on the
baking sheets for a few minutes before transferring to a wire
rack to cool completely.

TIP
The irregular
chunks of chocolate
make these biscuits
taste more
'homemade' but you
can use ready-made
chocolate chips if
you prefer.

Makes about 16
Prep time: 25 mins
Cook time: 8–10 mins

100 g/4 oz butter, softened
100 g/4 oz icing sugar
1 egg, lightly beaten
grated zest of $1/2$ orange
2 tbsp orange juice

150 g/5 oz plain flour
3 tbsp cocoa powder

FILLING
50 g/2 oz unsalted butter
grated zest of $1/2$ orange
100 g/4 oz icing sugar
1 tbsp orange juice

Chocolate orange creams

1 Preheat the oven to 200°C/400°F/Gas 6. Line 2 or 3 baking sheets with non-stick baking parchment.

2 Beat the butter and sugar together until light and fluffy, then gradually beat in the egg. Beat in the orange zest and juice. Sift in the flour and cocoa powder together and beat well.

3 Place the mixture in a piping bag fitted with a large star nozzle. Pipe spirals onto the baking sheets about 3 cm/$1^1/4$ in wide, allowing plenty of space for the cookies to spread.

4 Bake for 8–10 minutes. Allow to cool on the baking sheets for a few minutes before transferring to a wire rack to cool completely.

5 For the filling, beat the butter until soft, then beat in the orange zest and gradually beat in the icing sugar. Finally beat in the orange juice. Use to sandwich two biscuits together. Store in a cool place and eat within 2 days.

Makes about 30
Prep time: 20 mins
Cook time: 8–10 mins

175 g/6 oz butter, softened
225 g/8 oz caster sugar
1 large egg, lightly beaten
1 tsp vanilla essence

275 g/10 oz plain flour
1 tsp cream of tartar
1/2 tsp bicarbonate of soda

TO COMPLETE
1 tbsp caster sugar
2 tsp ground cinnamon

Snicker doodles

1 Preheat the oven to 200°C/400°F/Gas 6. Lightly grease 2 or 3 baking sheets.

2 Beat the butter and sugar together until pale and fluffy. Gradually beat in the egg and vanilla essence. Sieve the flour, cream of tartar and bicarbonate of soda together and beat into the butter and sugar mixture to form a soft dough.

3 Mix the sugar and cinnamon together and place in a shallow dish. With lightly floured hands, break off pieces of the dough about the size of a small walnut and roll into a ball. Roll each ball in the cinnamon mixture and place on the baking sheets allowing space for the cookies to spread.

4 Bake for about 8–10 minutes until pale golden. Transfer to a wire rack to cool completely.

TIP
Traditionally made with cream of tartar and bicarbonate of soda, you can replace these with 1 tsp baking powder.

Makes about 20
Prep time: 20 mins plus cooling and chilling
Cook time: 10 – 12 mins

120 g/4 1/2 oz unsalted butter
75 g/3 oz caster sugar
1 tsp vanilla essence
150 g/5 oz plain flour

Swedish butter cookies

1 Place the butter in a heavy-based saucepan and heat gently until it melts, then continue to cook until the butter turns a pale golden brown colour. Take care not to let it burn. Carefully pour the butter into a mixing bowl leaving behind the residue. Allow to cool and solidify.

2 Add the sugar to the cooled butter and beat until pale and fluffy. Beat in the vanilla, then beat in the flour and mix to form a firm dough. Form into a thick log and wrap in non-stick baking parchment. Chill for 30 minutes.

3 Preheat the oven to 190°C/375°F/Gas 5.

4 Cut the log into 3 mm/1/8 in thick slices and place on baking sheets. When you slice them, gently push the edges to form a round and they will re-form as they cook. Don't worry if the cookie cracks slightly. Bake for 10–12 minutes until pale golden. Allow to cool on the baking sheets for a few minutes before transferring to a wire rack to cool completely.

Makes about 24
Prep time: 15 mins
Cook time: 8–10 mins

100 g/4 oz self-raising flour
100 g/4 oz rolled oats

75 g/3 oz desiccated coconut
100 g/4 oz caster sugar
150 g/5 oz butter
1 tbsp golden syrup
1 tsp bicarbonate of soda
2 tbsp boiling water

Anzac biscuits

1 Preheat the oven to 180°C/350°F/Gas 4. Lightly grease 2 or 3 baking sheets.

2 Place the flour in a mixing bowl with the oats, coconut and sugar and stir to combine.

3 Melt the butter with the golden syrup in a small saucepan. Dissolve the bicarbonate of soda in the boiling water and add to the pan. Pour over the dry ingredients and mix well.

4 Place spoonfuls of the mixture onto the baking sheets, well spaced to allow the biscuits to spread.

5 Bake for 8–10 minutes until golden. Allow to cool for a few minutes on the baking sheets before transferring to a wire rack to cool completely.

Makes about 18
Prep time: 25 mins
Cook time: 15–20 mins

225 g/8 oz butter, softened
50 g/2 oz icing sugar
1 tsp vanilla essence
225 g/8 oz plain flour
25 g/1 oz cornflour

Viennese shells

1 Preheat the oven to 170°C/325°F/Gas 3.

2 Beat together the butter and sugar until pale and fluffy. Beat in the vanilla essence. Sift together the flour and cornflour and beat into the mixture. Place the mixture in a large piping bag fitted with a star nozzle.

3 Pipe small shells onto baking sheets.

4 Bake for 15–20 minutes or until pale golden. Allow to cool on the baking sheets for 2–3 minutes, then transfer to a wire rack to cool completely.

VARIATIONS
CHOCOLATE SHELLS: Melt about 150 g/5 oz milk or plain chocolate in the microwave or in a bowl over a pan of hot water. Half-dip each cooked shell in the melted chocolate. Place on sheets of non-stick baking parchment and allow to set.
CHERRY SHELLS: Decorate some or all of the shells by pressing a half glacé cherry into the cookie before baking.

Makes about 30
Prep time: 30 mins
Cook time: 20 mins

150 g/5 oz butter, softened
50 g/2 oz caster sugar

225 g/8 oz plain flour
100 g/4 oz chopped almonds, finely chopped
40 g/1^1/$_2$ oz granulated sugar
2 egg yolks, lightly beaten

Finnish shortbread

1 Preheat the oven to 180°C/350°F/Gas 4.

2 Beat the butter and caster sugar together until pale and fluffy. Beat in the flour and mix to a soft dough.

3 Divide the dough into 2 or 3 pieces and roll into long sausages about 1 cm/^{1}/$_2$ in thick. Cut into 5 cm/2 in lengths. Combine the nuts and granulated sugar. Dip each piece of dough into the egg yolks, then roll in the chopped nut mixture to coat. Place on baking sheets.

4 Bake for 20 minutes until golden. Cool on the baking sheets for a couple of minutes before transferring to a wire rack to cool completely.

TIP
You could use other nuts, such as chopped pecans, walnuts or hazelnuts instead of the almonds, if preferred.

Makes about 24
Prep time: 20 mins
Cook time: 10–12 mins plus setting

50 g/2 oz butter
75 g/3 oz caster sugar
2 tbsp double cream

1 tbsp plain flour
50 g/2 oz sultanas
50 g/2 oz glacé cherries, chopped
25 g/1 oz crystallized ginger, chopped
100 g/4 oz flaked almonds
100 g/4 oz milk or plain chocolate

Florentines

1 Preheat the oven to 180°C/350°F/Gas 4. Line 2 baking sheets with non-stick baking parchment.

2 Place the butter and sugar in a small pan and heat gently until the butter has melted and the sugar dissolved. Remove from the heat and stir in the cream. Stir in the flour, sultanas, cherries, ginger and almonds until well mixed.

3 Place dessertspoonfuls of the mixture onto the baking sheets allowing plenty of space for the biscuits to spread. Bake for 10–12 minutes until pale golden. While the cookies are still hot use a greased circular cookie cutter to pull the edges of the cookies in to form neat circles. Take care not to touch the mixture as it will be very hot. Allow to cool completely before removing from the sheet.

4 Place the chocolate in a bowl over a pan of hot water until melted. Allow to cool, then spread onto the backs of the Florentines. Use a fork to mark squiggles in the chocolate and allow to set.

Makes about 50
Prep time: 20 mins
Cook time: 40 mins

175 g/6 oz pistachio nuts
100 g/4 oz butter, softened
200 g/7 oz caster sugar
3 eggs

grated zest of 1 lemon
2 tbsp lemon juice
1 teaspoon aniseed (optional)
450 g/1 lb plain flour
100 g/4 oz coarse cornmeal or polenta
2 tsp baking powder

Cantucci

1 Preheat the oven to 180°C/350°F/Gas 4.

2 Roughly chop half the pistachios. Beat together the butter and sugar until pale and fluffy. Beat in the eggs one at a time. Beat in the lemon zest, juice and aniseed if using, then beat in the chopped and whole nuts.

3 Sift together the flour, cornmeal and baking powder and beat into the butter mixture, using your hands to finish bringing it together to form a soft dough. Divide the mixture into 4 pieces and roll each into a log shape about 30 cm/12 in long. Place on baking sheets and flatten slightly.

4 Bake for 30 minutes until risen and golden. Remove from the oven and allow to cool slightly. Reduce the oven temperature to 170°C/325°F/Gas 3.

5 When the logs are cool enough to handle, cut the biscuits diagonally into 1 cm/¹/₂ in slices. Place cut side down on the baking sheets and return to the oven for 10 minutes until crisp and golden.

Makes about 16
Prep time: 15 mins
Cook time: 20 mins

175 g/6 oz self-raising flour
100 g/4 oz butter
75 g/3 oz caster sugar

2 tsp ground cinnamon
1 egg, separated
2 tbsp milk
40 g/1½ oz flaked almonds
1 tbsp natural sugar crystals or granulated sugar

Dutch Jan Hagel cookies

1 Preheat the oven to 180°C/350°F/Gas 4. Grease a shallow baking tin about 25 x 20 cm/10 x 8 in.

2 Place the flour in a mixing bowl. Cut the butter into pieces and add to the bowl. Rub in with your fingertips until the mixture resembles fine breadcrumbs. Stir in the sugar and cinnamon. Add the egg yolk and enough milk to bring the mixture together to form a soft dough.

3 Roll out into a rectangle that almost fits the tin. Place in the tin and press out to fit with your fingers to fill the tin completely, pressing together any cracks in the dough.

4 Brush the top of the dough with beaten egg white and sprinkle the flaked almonds over the top. Sprinkle with sugar crystals or granulated sugar and bake for about 20 minutes until golden. Cut into pieces whilst still warm and transfer to a wire rack to cool completely.

Makes about 18
Prep time: 45 mins
Cook time: 5 mins

50 g/2 oz butter
50 g/2 oz caster sugar
1 egg, lightly beaten
4 tbsp double cream
50 g/2 oz self-raising flour

Tuiles

1 Preheat the oven to 220°C/425°F/Gas 7. Lightly grease 2 baking sheets.

2 Beat the butter and sugar together until pale and fluffy. Gradually beat in the egg and cream. Carefully fold in the flour.

3 Place about 6 dessertspoonfuls of the batter on the baking sheet and spread each into a 7.5 cm/3 in circle. Bake for 5 minutes until just golden around the edges.

4 Working quickly, remove the cookies from the baking sheet with a palette knife and drape over a rolling pin to make a curved shape. Allow to cool.

5 Repeat with the remaining batter until all the tuiles are made, alternating the baking sheets, so that they have time to cool between each batch.

VARIATION
Add some finely chopped pistachio nuts or flaked almonds to the mixture.

Recipe index

Anzac biscuits 82
Apricot and almond cookies 66
Cantucci 90
Cappuccino creams 40
Cherry marzipan bites   50
Cherry shells 84
Chilli choc cookies 22
Chocolate
    Chilli choc cookies 22
    Chocolate orange creams 76
    Chocolate shells 84
    Chocolate stacks 48
    Chocolate thumbprint cookies 31
    Triple choc chip cookies 74
Chocolate orange creams 76
Chocolate shells 84
Chocolate stacks 48
Chocolate thumbprint cookies 31
Cinnamon twirls 44
Date and walnut fingers 56
Dried fruit:
    Apricot and almond cookies 66
    Cherry shells 84
    Date and walnut fingers 56
    Florentines 88
    Fruity flapjacks 68
    Orange and cranberry biscuits 24
Dutch Jan Hagel cookies 92
Finnish shortbread 86
Florentines 88
Fruity flapjacks 68
Ginger oat cookies 70
Hazelnut macaroons 32
Honey and spice cookies 62
Iced Christmas cookies 38

Lavender shortbreads 28
Lemon and hazelnut slices 20
Lemon poppy seed cookies 60
Lime and coconut biscuits 26
Maple pecan cookies 18
Nuts
    Apricot and almond cookies 66
    Cantucci 90
    Date and walnut fingers 56
    Hazelnut macaroons 32
    Lemon and hazelnut slices 20
    Maple pecan cookies 18
    Peanut jelly dodgers 52
    Walnut and rosemary cookies 64
    Walnut whirls 42
Orange and basil cookies 34
Orange and cranberry biscuits 24
Peanut jelly dodgers 52
Seedy wedges 58
Snicker doodles 78
Spice
    Chilli choc cookies 22
    Cinnamon twirls 44
    Ginger oat cookies 70
    Honey and spice cookies 62
    Snicker doodles 78
Streusel-topped cookies 46
Swedish butter cookies 80
Thumbprint cookies 30
Triple choc chip cookies 74
Tuiles 94
Viennese shells 84
Walnut and rosemary cookies 64
Walnut whirls 42

Chocolate
Cakes, Biscuits,
Tarts & Puddings

WENDY VEALE

JOHN BEAUFOY PUBLISHING

This edition first published in the United Kingdom in 2013 by
John Beaufoy Publishing, 11 Blenheim Court, 316 Woodstock Road,
Oxford OX2 7NS, England
www.johnbeaufoy.com

10 9 8 7 6 5 4 3 2 1

ISBN 978-1-909612-02-0

Project manager: Rosemary Wilkinson
Design: Glyn Bridgewater
Photographs: Michael Prior (except p. 70, Ian Garlick)
Illustration: Stephen Dew

Printed and bound in Malaysia by Times Offset (M) Sdn. Bhd.

RECIPE NOTES

■ Where milk is used in a recipe, this can be full fat, semi-skimmed or skimmed.

■ All eggs are medium unless otherwise stated.

■ All spoon measurements are level unless otherwise stated.

■ Metric and imperial measurements are not always exact equivalents, so only follow one set of measurements within each recipe.

■ Oven temperatures have been given for conventional electric and gas ovens. For fan ovens, use the following equivalents:

Electricity °C	Electricity (fan) °C
110	90
120	100
130	110
140	120
150	130
160	140
170	150
180	160
190	170
200	180
220	200

Contents

Introduction 6

1 Cakes & tray bakes 14

2 Cookies, buns & bars 38

3 Desserts & indulgences 60

4 Tarts & pies 82

Recipe index &
acknowledgements 96

Cooking with chocolate

Chocolate has to be the best loved flavour, at least in the western hemisphere. Used as a flavouring ingredient, a drink and as a confectionary, it is hard to imagine a world without the cocoa bean. Unsurprisingly, the scientific name for the Cacao tree is *theobroma cacao* – 'theobroma' meaning 'the food of the gods'!

Did you know?

Chocolate is believed to boost serotonin and endorphin levels in the brain – a feel-good factor.

A 125 g/4^1/$_2$ oz bar of chocolate contains more caffeine than a cup of instant coffee. Other stimulants in chocolate include theobromine. Chocolate increases alertness and gives an instant lift but energy levels are low.

Choosing the perfect chocolate

Choosing the right chocolate for baking or eating could prove confusing: some are smoother than others, some more bitter, sweeter, harder, some are melt-in-the-mouth – the sign of quality chocolate with a

high percentage of cocoa butter which melts just below body temperature – hence it literally does melt in the warmth of the mouth!

More cocoa solids mean a more distinctive chocolate flavour and more cocoa butter gives a smooth, creamy richness to the chocolate.

Some chocolates include other vegetable fats to supplement a lower content of cocoa butter. This not only results in a less distinct flavour but also raises the temperature at which chocolate melts.

Dark or bittersweet chocolate: This is the darkest of all eating chocolates and has a high concentration of cocoa solids and little sugar. It must have a minimum of 35% cocoa solids. Premium brands have 50–55% cocoa solids. The higher the percentage, the more intense the chocolate flavour, but more sugar may be required in baking. There is a semisweet version which has a higher sugar content and is interchangeable with bittersweet chocolate. With good keeping, wrapped and kept in a cool place, it will last a year.

Continental style: This top quality chocolate has a high cocoa butter content of between 32% and 39%. The total cocoa butter and cocoa solids can then be from around 70% and the very bitter version is as high as 90%. With good keeping, wrapped and kept in a cool place, it will last a year.

Milk chocolate: Semi-sweet and with a high cocoa butter content, this chocolate also contains milk. It is difficult to use for baking as it cannot take any moderate heat without burning. It does not store well, so should be wrapped and kept in a cool place but not the fridge as this causes a cloudy 'bloom' on the chocolate.

White chocolate: An imposter really as white chocolate does not contain any cocoa solids but it does contain rich cocoa butter for that creamy taste. Ivory or cream in colour with added sugar and milk, it does not tolerate heat well, so requires gentle handling. It has a short shelf life, so is best stored in the freezer! Choose the continental style (i.e. Belgium) chocolate for best quality.

When the cocoa butter is replaced with other vegetable fats it is no longer white chocolate but a chocolate-flavoured coating.

Chocolate chips, drops or chunks: Often used as an ingredient in cookies, muffins, cupcakes and for decorations, plain, milk or white chocolate drops are available in small drums or packs and have a shelf life of about 1 year. Store in a cool place.

Chocolate coating or covering: Once called Cooking Chocolate, this chocolate 'flavour' compound reacts well to heating and does not burn easily as most of if not all the creamy cocoa butter has been replaced with soya bean, palm oil and emulsifiers.

Cocoa powder: When the cocoa butter is removed from the chocolate liquor, the 'cake' left is processed to cocoa powder. Unsweetened and simple to use, it can be added in place of a couple of tablespoons of flour to chocolate cakes and cookies. And if using a low cocoa solid chocolate in cooking, a couple of teaspoons blended to a paste will add richness.

Drinking chocolate: Unsweetened cocoa powder blended with milk powder and sugar to make a comforting chocolate drink. Not ideal in cooking. Many low-calorie/low-fat versions are available and also malted chocolate drinks.

Fair Trade label
You can choose to support farmers and their families by buying chocolate with the Fair Trade Certified label which guarantees farmers a minimum price for their cocoa and thus protects their livelihood.

Handling and melting

There are two rules to handling and melting chocolate: do not hurry and do not overheat. For all the care that has been taken from farm to factory to produce your bar of chocolate, simple mistakes at this final stage of sheer enjoyment are often irreversible.

Dark chocolate is much easier to handle, heat and melt than milk or white chocolate with their higher fat content and tendency to burn or 'seize' resulting in a stiff, tacky mess that has to be thrown away. But for all types:

■ Break the chocolate into a heatproof bowl and set over a pan of gently simmering water. Make sure the water is not touching the base of the bowl or that steam cannot escape and be in contact with the chocolate.
■ Take the pan off the heat and leave the chocolate for 5 minutes or so – it will still retain its shape until the last minute – then stir and use as required.
■ If required, cream should be melted with the chocolate, whilst butter should be added as soon as the chocolate has melted.
■ If making a sauce which contains ingredients with a high water content i.e. fruit juice, these should be added right at the beginning of the melting process.
■ To melt chocolate in a microwave always refer to the manufacturer's instructions as ovens vary considerably. However, as a rule of thumb, break 100 g/4 oz chocolate into a small bowl, then microwave on 'defrost' for 2 minutes depending on the thickness of the bar used. The pieces will appear to remain whole but will have softened all the way through. Stir only occasionally to produce a smooth glossy liquid.
■ A foolproof way of melting or softening chocolate is to place it in a bowl in the airing cupboard overnight!
■ When cooling melted chocolate to be used to cover a cake or for decorations, the chocolate should be left to set in a cool place and not in the fridge as rapid cooling may affect its appearance.

Decorating with chocolate

Use a small, double thickness greaseproof bag for piping chocolate. If the chocolate hardens, simply soften in the piping bag in the microwave or if the opening gets clogged up, just snip off the tip of the bag.

Have chocolate at room temperature, not too cold, when grating, chopping or making large curls.

■ To make chocolate curls (top), melt the chocolate in a small heatproof bowl set over simmering water, then cool for 10 minutes. Spread onto a cold work surface – a slab of marble is ideal. When cold, use a sharp knife almost parallel to the surface and push through the chocolate.

■ Chocolate shavings (middle), are easy to make: use a swivel vegetable peeler along the flat side of a large bar of chocolate, shaving it off in curls.

■ To make chocolate leaves (bottom), brush or coat the underside of clean, unblemished rose or bay leaves with melted chocolate, then leave to set. Peel the leaf away from the chocolate. Store the fragile leaves in an airtight container.

■ To make chocolate triangles (see page 73), melt chocolate in a small bowl set over simmering water, then cool for 10 minutes. Spread onto a piece of baking parchment and when cold, cut into triangles.

Baking tips

Baking tins: Invest in good quality bakeware that will last for years. Loose-bottomed and non-stick tins make for easier removal of fragile cakes and also only require base lining. Spring-form tins are ideal for delicate or fragile recipes – but do make sure they are released carefully once you have eased around the edge with a small palette knife.

Lining cake tins: Use greaseproof or baking parchment paper. Lightly grease the base and sides of the tins before lining, then do the same to the paper. Vegetable oil sprays often used for low-calorie cooking are ideal for this. Line the tins carefully and accurately. Paper creases can spoil the look of the cooked cake.

Cakes that have longer cooking times i.e. fruit cakes will require the base and sides of the tin lining for added protection.

Base-line tins by cutting out a circle of greaseproof paper to fit. If you make cakes on a regular basis, it's worth cutting a number of circles for your most often used tins. Or you can buy ready-cut standard circles.

Dropping consistency: This describes the ideal consistency of the cake mixture – just right to plop off a spoon if gently tapped. Hence if the cake mixture seems dry, add enough milk to form a soft, dropping consistency.

For a flat top: When making a creamed cake mixture make a slight hollow in the centre of the cake before baking. This will then rise in the oven to give a flat top for icing.

For a level top: Use a small flexible palette or butter knife to level off the top of creamed cakes. Do not bang the tin to level as this will knock air out of delicate mixtures.

What went wrong?

Scorching or burning through excessive heat will cause the chocolate to go gritty and it will have a burnt taste. It can easily happen when using the microwave oven to melt chocolate. This is irreversible, so only microwave for very short periods.

Thickening or 'seizing' of a solid mass may be due to uneven heating, the addition of high water content ingredients or steam/water from the saucepan. This is irreversible.

In the oven: Bake cakes on the middle shelf of the preheated oven unless the recipe states otherwise. All ovens are different, so cooking times and temperatures may vary slightly. Check the cake just before the end of cooking time.

To test if a cake is cooked: Insert a skewer or sharp-tipped knife into the centre of the cake – it should come out clean.

Cooling: Allow the cake to cool in the tin for at least 5 minutes before inverting it onto a wire cooling rack. Carefully peel away the paper, then turn the cake the right way up to cool. Ensure the cakes are cold before storing.

Storage: Store cakes in an airtight container. They will keep for a few days.

Freezing cakes: Elaborately decorated cakes should be open frozen until firm, then packed into a rigid container. Stand the cake on a strip of foil or greaseproof paper inside the container, so that it can be lifted out with ease. Label stating 'this way up' to prevent accidental damage. Undo the top of the container before thawing and lift out onto a plate whilst frozen if it will be more difficult to do when thawed.

Rich tea cakes, tea bread, tray bakes, etc can be sliced and separated with paper then reassembled and over-wrapped before freezing. This makes it easy to remove just the required number of slices – ideal for packed lunches.

Meringues are best frozen as undecorated shells. Once defrosted, fill with cream and decorate.

Cooked cheesecakes do not freeze as successfully as uncooked ones and may loose their freshly baked texture.

For best results always leave the cakes to defrost at room temperature. Allow 5–6 hours, or overnight.

A 'bloom' on the chocolate – whitish, mottled spots – can be due to a number of reasons, such as rapid cooling in the fridge, moisture from the steam when melting over a pan of water or the addition of ingredients which do not mix well with the chocolate. Whilst still edible, the appearance of the chocolate is spoilt.

I

cakes &
tray bakes

Makes 24
Prep time: 10 mins
Cook time: 25–30 mins

175 g/6 oz butter
175 g/6 oz caster sugar
3 eggs

175 g/6 oz self-raising flour
1 tsp baking powder
100 g/3½ oz ready-to-eat apricots, chopped
100 g/3½ oz good quality white chocolate, chopped
1 tbsp icing sugar, sieved

Apricot & white chocolate tray bake

1 Grease and line a 30 x 20 cm/12 x 8 in tray bake tin. Preheat the oven to 180°C/350°F/Gas 4.

2 In a mixing bowl, cream the butter and sugar together until light and fluffy. Beat in the eggs, flour and baking powder.

3 Mix in the apricots and white chocolate. Spread evenly into the tin and bake for 25–20 minutes or until firm to the touch and golden.

4 Cool in the tin for 5 minutes before turning out onto a wire rack to cool completely. Dust with icing sugar and cut into fingers.

TIP
Replace the apricots with dried apple and the white chocolate with dark chocolate.

Makes 8–10 slices
Prep time: 15 mins
Cook time: 50 mins–1 hour

225 g/8 oz butter
225 g/8 oz caster sugar

4 eggs, beaten
a few drops of vanilla extract
225 g/8 oz self-raising flour
1 tbsp cocoa powder
100 g/3^{1}/$_{2}$ oz plain chocolate

Chocolate marble slice

1 Grease and line a 900 g/2 lb loaf tin. Preheat the oven to
180°C/350°F/Gas 4.

2 In a mixing bowl, cream together the butter and sugar until
light and fluffy, then gradually beat in the eggs and vanilla.
Fold in the flour.

3 Transfer half the mixture to another bowl. Sift and fold the
cocoa powder into this portion.

4 Break the chocolate into a small heatproof bowl and set over
a pan of barely simmering water. Stir until the chocolate
melts. Leave to cool slightly, then fold into the chocolate
mixture.

5 Put alternative spoonfuls of the chocolate and plain
mixtures into the loaf tin. Use a knife to swirl together
creating a marbled effect.

6 Bake for 50 minutes–1 hour or until well risen and firm to
the touch. Turn out onto a wire rack to cool. Serve sliced.

VARIATION
Add the finely grated zest of 1 lemon or 1 orange or
chopped stem ginger to the plain sponge mix. For a spicy note
add ^{1}/$_{2}$ tsp ground cinnamon to the chocolate sponge mix.

Makes 14 slices
Prep time: 30 mins
Cook time: 1–1¼ hours

200 g/7 oz dark chocolate (min.
70–75% cocoa solids)
200 g/7 oz butter, cubed
1 tbsp instant coffee granules
85 g/3 oz self-raising flour
85 g/3 oz plain flour
¼ tsp bicarbonate of soda
400 g/14 oz light soft brown sugar

3 tbsp cocoa powder
3 eggs, beaten
5 tbsp buttermilk or soured cream

GANACHE
200 g/7 oz dark chocolate (min.
70–75% cocoa solids), chopped
50 g/1¾ oz butter
284 ml/10 fl oz carton double cream
2 tbsp caster sugar
white and dark chocolate curls (see
page 11), to decorate

The ultimate chocolate cake

1 Grease and line a 20 cm/7 in deep, round, loose-bottomed cake tin. Preheat the oven to 160°C/325°F/Gas 3.

2 Break the chocolate into a medium saucepan together with the butter and coffee. Add 125 ml/4 fl oz boiling water. Warm through over a low heat, stirring until melted and smooth.

3 Put all the dry ingredients into a large bowl. Make a well in the centre and add the eggs and milk or cream. Pour on the warm chocolate and mix to a smooth batter. Pour into the cake tin and bake for 1–1¼ hours or until a skewer inserted in the centre comes out clean. Leave to cool in the tin, then turn out onto a wire rack to cool completely. Cut into 3 horizontal layers.

4 To make the ganache, place the chocolate and butter in a mixing bowl. Heat the cream and sugar together in a saucepan and when just scalding, pour onto the chocolate. Cover and leave for a few minutes, then stir until smooth and glossy.

5 Sandwich the layers together with some of the ganache, then pour the rest over the cake. Decorate with chocolate curls.

Serves 8–10
Prep time: 25 mins
Cook time: 1 1/4 hours

225 g/8 oz self-raising flour
40 g/1 1/2 oz cocoa powder
1 level tbsp baking powder
1/2 tsp salt
2 large eggs
175 ml/6 fl oz semi-skimmed milk
75 g/2 3/4 oz caster sugar

100 g/3 1/2 oz butter, melted
250 g/9 oz firm dessert plums, stoned and finely chopped

TOPPING
25 g/1 oz butter
75 g/2 3/4 oz self-raising flour
75 g/2 3/4 oz demerara sugar
50 g/1 3/4 oz chopped toasted hazelnuts
25 g/1 oz good quality white or milk chocolate chips

Chocolate streusel cake

1 Grease and line a 20 cm/8 in spring-form cake tin. Preheat the oven to 190°C/375°F/Gas 5.

2 Place the flour, cocoa powder, baking powder and salt into a large bowl.

3 In another large bowl whisk together the eggs, milk and sugar, then whisk in the melted butter.

4 Sift the dry ingredients onto the egg mixture and swiftly fold in, together with the plums. Don't worry if the mixture looks lumpy; it must not be over-stirred. Spoon into the tin.

5 For the topping, rub the butter into the flour to resemble breadcrumbs, then stir in the sugar and hazelnuts with 1 tbsp cold water to form a rough crumble. Scatter over the cake.

6 Bake for 1 1/4 hours until risen and springy. (Cover the tin with foil if the cake darkens too quickly). As soon as it is ready, scatter on the chocolate chips. Leave to cool in the tin for 30 minutes before transferring to a wire rack to cool completely.

Serves 8
Prep time: 3–5 mins
Cook time: 25–35 mins

175 g/6 oz self-raising flour
25 g/1 oz cocoa powder
1 rounded tsp baking powder
125 g/4½ oz caster sugar
150 ml/5 fl oz groundnut oil

150 ml/5 fl oz semi-skimmed milk
2 eggs

BUTTER FILLING
25 g/1 oz cocoa powder
175 g/6 oz butter, softened
225 g/8 oz icing sugar + 1 tsp
a few drops vanilla extract

Five minute chocolate wonder

1 Grease and base-line 2 x 18 cm/7 in sandwich tins. Preheat the oven to 160°C/325°F/Gas 3.

2 Place all the ingredients for the cake in a food processor and blend together. When the mixture becomes smooth, dark and creamy, divide it between the 2 tins.

3 Bake for 25–35 minutes or until risen. Turn out onto wire racks to cool.

4 For the butter filling, mix the cocoa powder to a paste with a very little hot water. Leave to cool. Cream the butter in a bowl. Sift in the 225 g/8 oz icing sugar and a few drops of vanilla extract. Whisk really well until pale in colour and fluffy, then beat in the cocoa paste.

5 Sandwich the cooled cakes together with the butter filling. Sprinkle the top with a dusting of icing sugar.

Makes 9 squares
Prep time: 20 mins
Cook time: 1–1¹/₂ hours

250 g/9 oz plain flour
2 level tsp ground ginger
2 level tsp baking powder
1 level tsp bicarbonate of soda
50 g/1³/₄ oz cocoa powder

175 g/6 oz medium oatmeal
175 g/6 oz unsalted butter
175 g/6 oz dark soft brown sugar
300 g/10¹/₂ oz golden syrup
300 ml/10 fl oz semi-skimmed milk
1 egg, beaten
85 g/3 oz dark chocolate (min.
50–55% cocoa solids), chopped

Chocolate & ginger parkin

1 Grease and base-line a 23 cm/9 in square, deep cake tin.
Preheat oven to 180°C/350°F/Gas 4.

2 Sieve the first 5 dry ingredients together into a large
bowl. Stir in the oatmeal.

3 Meanwhile gently heat together the butter, sugar and
syrup in a saucepan until the sugar has dissolved. Whisk in
the milk and egg, then beat into the dry ingredients,
combining well to a smooth thick batter.

4 Fold in the chocolate. Pour into the tin and bake for
1–1¹/₂ hours or until firm to the touch but still slightly moist
in the middle when tested with the point of a knife. Leave
to cool in the tin before turning out onto a wire rack to
cool completely.

Makes 9 squares
Prep time: 20 mins
Cook time: 1¼ hours

225 g/8 oz butter, softened
175 g/6 oz soft light brown sugar
1 tsp vanilla extract
3 large eggs

425 ml/15 fl oz unsweetened chunky apple sauce
225 g/8 oz self-raising flour
50 g/1¾ oz ground almonds
100 g/3½ oz cocoa powder
1 tsp baking powder
1 tsp ground ginger or cinnamon
175 g/6 oz dark chocolate (min. 50%–55% cocoa solids), chopped

Spiced chocolate applesauce cake

1 Grease and line a 20 cm/8 in deep, square cake tin. Preheat the oven to 180°C/350°F/Gas 4.

2 Cream the butter and sugar together until light and fluffy, then beat in the vanilla and eggs. Fold in the apple sauce.

3 Sift the flour, ground almonds, cocoa powder, baking powder and spice onto the applesauce mix and carefully fold in, finally adding the chopped chocolate.

4 Spoon into the cake tin and bake for 1¼ hours or until a skewer inserted into the centre comes out clean. Leave to cool in the tin for 10 minutes before transferring to a wire rack to cool completely.

TIP
To make your own apple sauce, peel, core and dice 4 Bramley apples. Place in a pan with 1–2 tbsp caster sugar and 1–2 tbsp water. Cover and cook gently for 10 mins or until soft.

Serves 10–12
Prep time: 30 mins
Cook time: 40 mins

The alternative Christmas chocolate cake

100 g/3^1/$_2$ oz dark chocolate
(min. 70–75% cocoa solids)
150 ml/5 fl oz soured cream
175 g/6 oz unsalted butter
300 g/10^1/$_2$ oz soft brown sugar
zest of 2 oranges
3 eggs, beaten
300 g/10^1/$_2$ oz plain flour
2 tbsp cocoa powder
^{1}/$_2$ tsp baking powder
1^1/$_2$ tsp bicarbonate of soda

FILLING
300 g/10^1/$_2$ oz fresh cranberries
juice of 2 oranges
125 g/4^1/$_2$ oz caster sugar

FROSTING
2 egg whites
350 g/12 oz caster sugar
a good pinch of salt
juice of 1 lemon
^{1}/$_2$ tsp cream of tartar

DECORATION
foil-wrapped chocolate coins
whole physalis
cocoa powder, to dust

1 Grease and line a 23 cm/9 in spring-form cake tin. Preheat the oven to 180°C/350°F/Gas 4.

2 Heat the chocolate in a bowl set over a pan of gently simmering water. Remove from the pan and leave to cool a little. Stir in the soured cream.

continued next page

3 In a large bowl cream together the butter and brown sugar until pale and fluffy. Whisk in the orange zest, then the eggs, a little at a time, followed by the cooled chocolate and cream.

4 Sift on the remaining dry ingredients. Gently fold through to form a smooth batter. Pour into the tin and bake for 40 minutes or until risen and a skewer inserted into the centre comes out clean. Leave in the tin for 10 minutes before turning out onto a wire rack to cool.

5 Meanwhile make the filling: simmer the cranberries with the orange juice until the cranberries have softened and most of the fruit juice has evaporated. Stir in the sugar, leave to cool, then chill.

6 Now make the frosting: place all the ingredients in a large, grease-free bowl. Add 1 tablespoon of water. Set over a pan of gently simmering water and whisk with electric beaters for 10 minutes or until smooth and light. Remove from the pan and leave to cool, then cover with cling film until ready to use.

7 Split the chocolate cake in half horizontally and prick the lower half with a skewer. Spread the cranberries evenly over this and top with the other half.

8 Spread the frosting liberally over the top and sides of the cake. Leave to harden slightly, then decorate with coins and fruit and dust with cocoa powder.

Makes 8 slices
Prep time: 15 mins
Cook time: 40–45 mins

175 g/6 oz butter
175 g/6 oz caster sugar
zest and juice of 2 oranges
2 tbsp milk

3 eggs
175 g/6 oz self-raising flour
1 tsp baking powder
75 g/2¾ oz good quality white chocolate, roughly chopped
½ tsp ground cinnamon (optional)
3 tbsp granulated sugar

White chocolate & orange drizzle cake

1 Grease and line a 900 g/2 lb loaf tin. Preheat the oven to 180°C/350°F/Gas 4.

2 In a large bowl cream together the butter, sugar and orange zest until light and fluffy. Whisk in the milk, then gradually beat in the eggs, one at a time with a spoonful of flour.

3 Fold in the remaining flour, baking powder, chocolate pieces and cinnamon, if liked.

4 Spoon into the tin, levelling the surface and bake for 40–45 minutes until well risen, golden and a skewer inserted into the centre comes out clean.

5 Meanwhile make the syrup: place the orange juice in a small saucepan and bring to the boil until reduced to 3 tablespoons. Leave to cool. Gently stir in the granulated sugar until it is just starting to absorb the juice and dissolve.

6 As soon as the cake comes out of the oven, prick it with a skewer several times and drizzle over the orange syrup. Leave the cake in the tin to cool completely before turning out.

Serves 8–10
Prep time: 15 mins
Cook time: 30–40 mins

100 g/3½ oz butter, diced
125 g/4½ oz dark chocolate
(min. 70–75 % cocoa solids)

6 eggs, separated
a pinch of salt
6 tbsp caster sugar
150 g/5½ oz ground almonds
whole almonds, to decorate
cocoa powder or icing sugar, for
dusting

Sunken gluten-free chocolate cake

1 Grease and base-line a 23 cm/9 in spring-form cake tin. Preheat the oven to 160°C/325°F/Gas 3.

2 Melt the butter and chocolate together in a large, heatproof bowl set over a pan of gently simmering water. Remove from the pan and beat until smooth. Leave to cool for 5 minutes, then beat in the egg yolks.

3 In a large clean bowl whisk the egg whites with a pinch of salt until soft peaks form. Continue whisking, adding in the sugar 1 tablespoon at a time, until the whites become stiff. Stir 2 tablespoons of this into the chocolate mixture and stir in the ground almonds, then carefully fold in the remainder of the egg whites.

4 Dust the sides of the cake tin with a little cocoa powder to help prevent sticking, then spoon in the mixture. Bake for 30–40 minutes or until well risen and just firm to touch. Cool in the tin.

5 When ready to serve, decorate with whole almonds and dust liberally with cocoa powder or icing sugar.

2

cookies,
buns & bars

Makes 12
Prep time: 15 mins
Cook time: 20 mins plus chilling

200 g/7 oz self-raising flour
200 g/7 oz soft light brown sugar
6 tbsp cocoa powder, sieved
150 ml/5 fl oz sunflower or
groundnut oil

300 ml/10 fl oz carton soured cream
2 eggs
100 g/3½ oz dark chocolate (min.
50–55% cocoa solids), finely
chopped
200 g/7 oz good quality white or milk
chocolate, broken into pieces
3 tbsp caster sugar, to taste
milk chocolate shavings (see page
11), to decorate

Chocolate cupcakes

1 Line a 12-hole muffin tin with deep paper cases. Preheat
the oven to 180°C/350°F/Gas 4.

2 In a large bowl mix together the flour, sugar, cocoa powder,
sunflower or groundnut oil, 150 ml/5 fl oz of the soured
cream and the eggs together with 6 tablespoons cold water.
Whisk to combine all the ingredients to a smooth batter.

3 Stir in the dark chocolate. Carefully divide the mixture
between the paper cases and bake for 20 minutes or until
risen and firm to the touch. Transfer to a wire rack to cool.

4 Meanwhile make the icing: gently heat together the white or
milk chocolate, remaining soured cream and caster sugar in a
bowl over a pan of simmering water. Stir until smooth. Cool,
cover and chill the icing until firm enough to swirl on top of
the cupcakes, then decorate with the chocolate shavings.

TIP
Finely chop the dark
chocolate in a food
processor or use
chocolate chips for
ease.

Makes 16 squares
Prep time: 15 mins
Cook time: 30–40 mins

175 g/6 oz dark chocolate (min. 70–75% cocoa solids)
175 g/6 oz butter
3 eggs, beaten

200 g/7 oz caster sugar
a few drops natural vanilla extract
85 g/3 oz self-raising flour
25 g/1 oz cocoa powder + extra for dusting
75 g/2³/₄ oz whole walnuts or pecan nuts, coarsely chopped

Boston brownies

1 Lightly grease and line a 20 cm/8 in square baking tin, 5 cm/2 in deep, with parchment paper allowing a paper collar 2.5 cm/1 in above the tin. Preheat the oven to 160°C/325°F/Gas 3.

2 Melt the chocolate and butter together in a large heatproof bowl set over a pan of simmering water.

3 Remove the bowl from the heat and briskly stir in all the remaining ingredients until well blended. Pour into the tin, then bake for 30–40 minutes or until springy to the touch but slightly soft in the centre.

4 Leave to cool in the tin for 2 hours, then turn out onto a board. Cut into squares and dust with cocoa powder.

VARIATIONS
· Replace the nuts with chunks of white chocolate for a really decadent brownie.
· For a thoroughly adult brownie, soak 50 g/2 oz pitted prunes in brandy overnight, then fold in with chopped almonds instead of walnuts at stage 3.

Makes 16
Prep time: 15 mins
Cook time: 40 mins

175 g/6 oz dark chocolate
(min. 50–55% cocoa solids)
175 g/6 oz unsalted butter
225 g/8 oz light soft brown sugar

3 large eggs, beaten
85 g/3 oz plain flour
50 g/1¾ oz cocoa powder
½ tsp baking powder
200 g/7 oz full-fat cream cheese
a few drops of vanilla extract
1 tbsp icing sugar

Chocolate cheesecake swirls

1 Grease and base-line an 18 cm/7 in square baking tin,
5 cm/2 in deep. Preheat the oven to 180°C/350°F/Gas 4.

2 Gently melt together the chocolate, butter and brown sugar
in a large saucepan over a moderate heat. Stir until all
ingredients are smooth. Remove from the heat, leave to cool
slightly, then whisk in the eggs. Keep whisking until the
mixture is smooth.

3 Sift on the flour, cocoa powder and baking powder, folding
into the mixture. Pour into the tin.

4 Beat together the cream cheese, vanilla extract and icing
sugar. Dollop small spoonfuls over the chocolate mix then,
using a rounded knife, swirl the cream cheese through to
create a marbled effect.

5 Bake for 40 minutes or until just firm. Cool in the tin
before marking into squares.

Makes approx. 30
Prep time: 20 mins
Cook time: 8–12 mins

225 g/8 oz butter
125 g/4½ oz soft brown sugar
125 g/4½ oz caster sugar
2 eggs

a few drops vanilla extract
325 g/11½ oz plain flour
1 tsp bicarbonate of soda
½ tsp baking powder
200 g/7 oz dark chocolate (min. 50–55% cocoa solids), chopped or chocolate chips

Chocolate chip cookies

1 Lightly grease 2 baking sheets. Preheat the oven to 190°C/375°F/Gas 5.

2 In a large bowl, cream the butter and sugars together until light, pale and fluffy, then gradually beat in the eggs and vanilla extract.

3 Sift in the flour, bicarbonate of soda and baking powder, then add the chocolate. Using a rubber spatula, work all the ingredients together to a pliable dough.

4 To bake straightaway, shape the dough into 30 walnut-sized balls and place well-spaced on the baking sheets. Use a fork to gently press down each ball. Bake for 10 minutes or until the centres are just firm to the touch. Transfer to a wire rack to cool. Serve warm or cold.

5 To bake as required, split the dough in half, roll each out into a sausage shape approx. 5 cm/2 in in diameter, wrap in cling film and refrigerate until required. When required, simply slice into 2 cm/¾ in thick cookies, space out on a baking sheet and bake as above.

Makes 20
Prep time: 20 mins
Cook time: 50–60 mins

2 egg whites
50 g/1¾ oz caster sugar
50 g/1¾ oz icing sugar, sieved
2 level tbsp cocoa powder, sieved,
plus extra for dusting

FILLING
250 ml/9 fl oz whipping cream
1 tbsp icing sugar, sieved
75 g/2¾ oz dark or white chocolate,
finely grated

Chocolate kisses

1 Line 2 baking sheets with parchment. Preheat the oven to 140°C/275°F/Gas 1.

2 Whisk the egg whites in a clean bowl until they form soft peaks. Very gradually whisk in the caster sugar, icing sugar and cocoa powder until the meringue is really stiff and dry.

3 Spoon or pipe small whirls onto the baking sheets. Bake for 50–60 minutes or until dry and crisp. Turn the meringues over and leave in the turned-off oven to cool completely. Store in an airtight container until required.

4 When ready to serve, whisk the cream until just stiffening, then fold in the icing sugar and grated chocolate. Spoon a small dollop of the cream onto half of the meringues, then add the remaining halves and press lightly together. Dust lightly with cocoa powder.

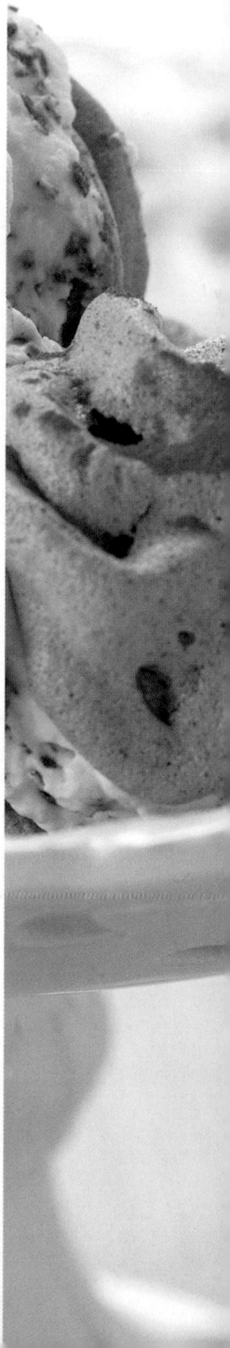

TIP
Do not sandwich
the meringues until
just ready to serve as
they will soften.

Makes 12
Prep time: 20 mins plus resting
Cook time: 12–15 mins

150 g/5¹/₂ oz icing sugar
3 rounded tbsp cocoa powder

150 g/5¹/₂ oz ground almonds or hazelnuts
3 egg whites
50 g/1³/₄ oz caster sugar
a few drops of vanilla extract

Chocolate macaroons

1 Line 2 large baking sheets with parchment. Preheat the oven to 160°C/325°F/Gas 3.

2 Make a stencil for the meringues by dipping the rim of a 4 cm/2 in pastry cutter in flour, then gently tapping onto the baking sheets. Mark out 12 circles, 2.5 cm/1 in apart.

3 Blend the icing sugar, cocoa powder and nuts in a food processor until very fine.

4 In a large clean bowl, whisk the egg whites until soft peaks form. Gradually add the caster sugar, whisking until the meringue is stiff and glossy. Fold in the ground nut mixture and the vanilla extract.

5 Gently spoon into a large disposable piping bag, snip off the bottom to make a 1 cm/³/₈ in hole, then pipe into rounds using the flour circles as a guide. Give the baking sheets a sharp rap to eliminate any air bubbles and leave to 'set' in a cool dry place for 30 minutes.

6 Bake one sheet at a time for 12–15 minutes or until they feel just firm, risen and glossy with a bubbled rim around the base. Cool on the sheets before carefully removing from the parchment paper.

Makes approx. 30
Prep time: 30 mins plus cooling
Suitable for freezing

250 g/9 oz dark chocolate (min. 70–75% cocoa solids)
150 ml/5 fl oz double cream

75 g/2¾ oz unsalted butter
2 tbsp rum or brandy
50 g/1¾ oz cocoa powder mixed with a little icing sugar, for dusting
30–36 white paper sweet cases (optional)

Rocky chocolate truffles

1 Gently melt the chocolate with the cream and butter in a heatproof bowl set over a pan of simmering water.

2 Remove from the heat and stir in the rum or brandy. Beat well until the mixture is shiny and smooth. Leave to cool completely, cover and refrigerate for 3–4 hours or until the mixture has firmed up enough to shape into truffles.

3 Have the paper cases ready on a tray or plate, if using. Sift the cocoa powder and icing sugar onto a plate. Scoop half a heaped teaspoon of truffle mix and toss into the cocoa powder mix, then spoon into a case.

4 Store in the fridge for up to 3 days. They also freeze well.

VARIATION
For smooth, round truffles, dust your hands with cocoa powder, then roll the mix into a small ball, roll it in the cocoa powder and icing sugar, then place in a case. Work as quickly as possible and do not over-roll the truffles.

Makes 12–16
Prep time: 10 mins
Cook time: 20–25 mins

225 g/8 oz butter
150 g/5½ oz light soft brown sugar
75 g/2¾ oz desiccated coconut
75 g/2¾ oz dried blueberries

50 g/1¾ oz cornflake cereal
2 tbsp cocoa powder
150 g/5½ oz self-raising flour
150 g/5½ oz white chocolate, broken into pieces
150 g/5½ oz dark chocolate (min. 50–55% cocoa solids), broken into pieces

Chocolate, coconut & blueberry cereal bars

1 Base-line a 15 x 25 x 2.5 cm/6 x 10 x 1 in baking tin. Preheat the oven to 180°C/350°F/Gas 4.

2 In a large saucepan, melt the butter over a low heat. Stir in the sugar, coconut, blueberries and cornflakes. Gradually sift in the cocoa powder and flour. Mix together well.

3 Turn into the tin and level with a knife. Bake for 20–25 minutes. Leave in the tin, then cut into bars whilst still warm.

4 Meanwhile, melt the white and dark chocolate separately in heatproof bowls set over pans of simmering water. Spoon the melted plain chocolate in thick lines over the top of the tray bake, then fill in the gaps with the melted white chocolate. Use a palette knife to swirl the chocolates together to create a marbled effect. When the chocolate has just set, cut again into bars. Allow to cool completely before transferring to an airtight container.

Makes 32 small cookies
Prep time: 20 mins
Cook time: 10–15 mins

225 g/8 oz unsalted butter, softened
150 g/5½ oz golden granulated sugar plus extra for topping
1 egg

300 g/10½ oz plain flour
1 tsp baking powder
1 tsp cream of tartar
100 g/3½ oz white chocolate, chopped (or chocolate chips)
100 g/3½ oz dried cranberries
100 g/3½ oz pistachio nuts, coarsely chopped

White chocolate, cranberry & pistachio cookies

1 Line 2 baking sheets with parchment paper. Preheat the oven to 190°C/375°F/Gas 5.

2 Cream the butter and sugar together in a large bowl until light, pale and fluffy, then beat in the egg.

3 Sift in the flour, baking powder and cream of tartar. Use a wooden spoon to combine well, then fold in the white chocolate, cranberries and nuts. If the dough seems sticky, sift in a little more flour.

4 Roughly shape the dough into small walnut-sized balls and space evenly apart on the baking sheets. Dip the prongs of a fork into cold water, then into granulated sugar and lightly press cookies into rounds.

5 Bake for 10–15 minutes or until tinged golden brown yet still slightly soft. Leave to cool on the baking sheet for a few minutes, then transfer to a cooling rack to cool completely.

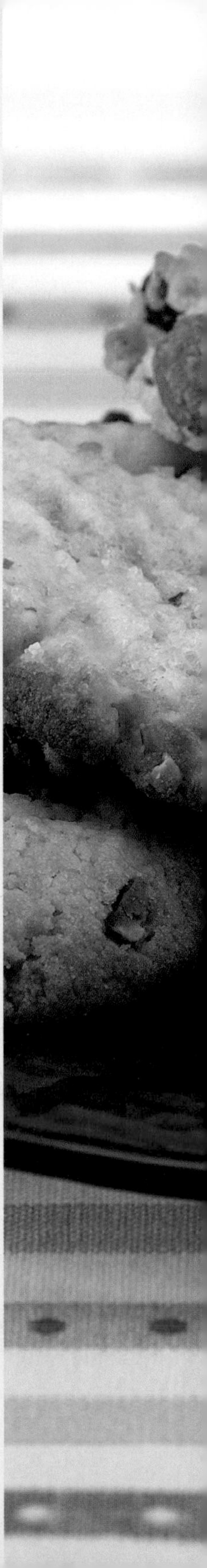

Makes 20–24 small squares
Prep time: 15 mins
Cook time: 35 mins plus cooling

225 g/8 oz plain flour
75 g/2³/₄ oz caster sugar
150 g/5¹/₂ oz cold unsalted butter,
diced

CARAMEL LAYER
125 g/4¹/₂ oz unsalted butter
125 g/4¹/₂ oz light soft brown sugar
1 x 397 g can condensed milk
a few drops of vanilla extract

CHOCOLATE TOPPING
200 g/7 oz dark or milk chocolate
1 tbsp vegetable oil

Millionaire's shortbread

1 Grease and base-line an 18 cm/7 in square cake tin,
5 cm/2 in deep. Preheat the oven to 180°C/350°F/Gas 4.

2 Mix together the flour and sugar in a large bowl. Rub in the
cold butter until it resembles breadcrumbs, then knead the
mixture to a smooth dough. Press the dough evenly into the
tin. Prick all over with a fork. Bake for 20–25 minutes until
light golden brown. Leave to cool.

3 For the caramel layer, melt the butter and sugar in a small
pan over a gentle heat. Add the condensed milk. Stirring
constantly, allow the mixture to come to a steady gentle simmer
for 5 minutes. Remove from the heat, beat in the vanilla extract
and pour over the shortbread. Leave to cool.

4 Melt the chocolate in a heatproof bowl set over a pan of
simmering water. Stir in the vegetable oil, then spread over
the cold caramel. Chill in the fridge until set. Cut into squares
to serve.

VARIATION
Stir a handful of raisins or sultanas into the caramel topping.

3

desserts & indulgences

Serves 8
Prep time: 25 mins plus freezing
Cook time: 20 mins

125 g/4½ oz butter
125 g/4½ oz caster sugar
2 eggs
75 g/2¾ oz self-raising flour
25 g/1 oz cocoa powder

FILLING
2 tbsp kirsch, Grand Marnier or
Tia Maria, to taste

450 g/1 lb ricotta cheese
2 tbsp icing sugar, to sweeten
120 ml/4 fl oz very strong cold black coffee
100 g/3½ oz dark chocolate (min. 70–75% cocoa solids) chopped
100 g/3½ oz white chocolate, chopped
50 g/1¾ oz toasted flaked almonds
50 g/1¾ oz glacé cherries, roughly chopped
½ x 397 g/14 oz can black cherries, drained and pitted
cocoa powder, to dust

Choc-cherry spectacular

1 You will need one 19 cm/7 in and one 20 cm/8 in round sandwich tin plus one 19 cm/7 in glass pudding bowl. Line the bowl with cling film. Preheat the oven to 190°C/375°F/Gas 5.

2 Cream the butter and sugar until light and fluffy. Beat in the eggs 1 at a time, then sift and fold in the flour and cocoa powder. Add a little milk if needed to make a soft, dropping consistency.

3 Divide the mixture between the 2 tins and level. Bake for 20–25 minutes or until risen and springy to the touch. Cool a little, then turn out. Roll out the larger sponge to make it a little thinner. Use this sponge while still warm to line the pudding bowl. Sprinkle over your chosen liqueur.

4 Mix together the ricotta and enough sugar to sweeten. Loosen with the coffee, then fold in the remaining ingredients. Spoon into the bowl, place the second sponge on top and press down firmly with a weighted dessert plate. Freeze for 3 hours, bringing out 1 hour before serving, dusted with cocoa powder.

Serves 8–10
Prep time: 40 mins plus chilling
Cook time: 20 mins

4 egg whites
250 g/9 oz caster sugar
1 tsp cornflour
1 tsp white wine vinegar
2 tsp coffee granules dissolved in
1 tbsp boiling water

FILLING
200 g/7 oz dark chocolate
(min. 70–75% cocoa solids),
broken into small pieces
600 ml/1 pt double cream
2 tbsp coffee liqueur or brandy
1 tbsp icing sugar
sifted cocoa powder, to decorate

Mocha mallow roulade

1 Line a 30 x 20 cm/12 x 8 in Swiss roll tin with baking parchment. Preheat the oven to 160°C/325°F/Gas 3.

2 Whisk the egg whites until stiff, then whisk in the caster sugar 1 tbsp at a time until stiff and shiny. Fold in the cornflour, vinegar and coffee, then spread gently into the tin. Bake for 20 minutes or until the surface is just crisp.

3 Leave to cool in the tin for a few minutes. Dust a piece of parchment paper slightly larger than the tin with icing sugar. Tip the meringue onto the paper, then ease away the lining.

4 Melt the chocolate in a heatproof bowl set over gently simmering water. Remove from the heat and leave to cool. Whip the cream and divide between 2 bowls. Reserve 5 tbsp of the chocolate, then fold the rest into 1 bowl of cream. Spread this over the roulade almost to the edges. Fold the liqueur and icing sugar into the other bowl and spread on top.

5 Starting from one short side, roll up the meringue. Place on a tray, seal side down, and refrigerate overnight to firm. To serve melt the reserved chocolate. Dust the roulade with cocoa powder, then drizzle over the chocolate.

Serves 6–8
Prep time: 20 mins
Cook time: 15–20 mins

50 g/1³/₄ oz cocoa powder
150 g/5 oz organic dried apricots, chopped
200 ml/7 fl oz boiling water
a few drops of vanilla extract
1 tsp bicarbonate of soda
75 g/2³/₄ oz unsalted butter

125 g/4¹/₂ oz light muscovado sugar
2 eggs
175 g/6 oz self-raising flour

CHOC-ORANGE SAUCE
175 g/6 oz soft brown sugar
75 g/2³/₄ oz unsalted butter
zest & juice of 1 orange
100 g/3¹/₂ oz dark chocolate (min. 50–55% cocoa solids)
150 ml/5 fl oz double cream

Chocolate icky sticky with choc-orange sauce

1 Lightly grease eight 150 ml/5 fl oz pudding basins and dust with cocoa powder. Preheat the oven to 190°C/375°F/Gas 5.

2 Put the apricots in a bowl and pour over the boiling water. Add the vanilla and bicarbonate of soda and leave to one side.

3 Cream the butter and sugar together in a mixing bowl until light and fluffy. Gradually beat in the eggs, then add the flour, the remaining cocoa powder and the apricot mixture. Mix well. At this stage the mixture is very sloppy.

4 Pour the mixture into the basins and bake for 15-20 minutes or until the tops are set and the puddings have risen and shrunk from the sides. Turn out of the basins onto individual serving plates.

5 Meanwhile put all the sauce ingredients in a pan and heat gently, stirring occasionally, until the sugar is dissolved. Pour over the puddings.

Serves 6–8
Prep time: 25 mins
Cook time: 45–55 mins

250 g/9 oz butter
50 g/1³/₄ oz demerara sugar
6 whole blanched almonds
3 pears, peeled, halved & cored
175 g/6 oz caster sugar
2 large eggs

125 g/4¹/₂ oz self-raising flour
2 tbsp cocoa powder
50 g/1³/₄ oz ground almonds
2 tbsp milk

MILK CHOCOLATE SAUCE
75 g/2³/₄ oz milk chocolate (min. 50–55% cocoa solids), broken in pieces
3 tbsp golden syrup
2 tbsp water

Chocolate & pear upside-down pudding

1 Grease and base-line a 25 cm/9 in deep, round, loose-bottomed cake tin. Preheat the oven to 180°C/350°F/Gas 4.

2 Melt 50 g/1³/₄ oz of the butter, mix with the demerara sugar and spread over the bottom of the cake tin.

3 Place an almond into each pear, then arrange the pears in the tin, cut side down and with stalk end toward the centre.

4 Cream the remaining butter with the caster sugar until light and fluffy. Beat in the eggs, 1 at a time, then fold in the flour, cocoa powder and ground almonds. If needed, add enough milk to form a soft dropping consistency. Spread the mixture evenly over the pears. Bake for 45–55 minutes or until the sponge springs back when lightly pressed.

5 To make the sauce, melt the chocolate with the syrup and water in a small heatproof bowl over a pan of simmering water, then beat until smooth. Turn the pudding out onto a serving dish, and pour over the warm chocolate sauce.

Makes 6
Prep time: 15 mins plus setting
Cook time: 14 mins

cocoa powder, for dusting

200 g/7 oz dark chocolate (min.50–55% cocoa solids), broken into pieces

150 g/5 oz butter, chopped + extra for greasing

100 g/3 1/2 oz caster sugar

3 eggs

3 egg yolks

1 tbsp dark rum (optional)

25 g/1 oz plain flour

whipped cream or icecream, to serve

Chocolate fondant

1 Butter six 150 ml/5 fl oz dariole moulds well. Preheat the oven to 200°C/400°F/Gas 6. Evenly coat the moulds with sifted cocoa powder, tapping off any excess. Place the moulds onto a baking sheet.

2 Gently heat together the chocolate, butter and sugar in a heatproof bowl set over but not touching simmering water. Once melted and the sugar no longer grainy, remove from the heat and beat until smooth.

3 Add the eggs and egg yolks, one at a time, beating until smooth and glossy. Add the rum if using and sift in the flour, folding through gently.

4 Divide the mixture evenly between the moulds and place in a fridge for at least 1 hour to set.

5 Cook for 14 minutes until risen and just setting on the surface. Leave to stand for 2 minutes before carefully turning out onto plates. Serve swiftly – with a generous dollop of whipped cream or vanilla ice cream.

Serves 6
Prep time: 25 mins plus chilling
Cook time: 20 mins

4 eggs
75 g/2¾ oz caster sugar
25 g/1 oz ground walnuts
25 g/1 oz cocoa powder
25 g/1 oz plain flour
1–2 firm bananas

rum, to taste
300 ml/10 fl oz double cream
1 tbsp icing sugar

TO DECORATE
150 ml/5 fl oz double cream
50 g/1¾ oz dark chocolate (min.
50–55% cocoa solids), melted and
cut into triangles, see page 11
2 tsp icing sugar

Chocolate, walnut & banana roulade

1 Line a 30 x 20 cm/12 x 8 in Swiss roll tin. Preheat the oven to 190°C/375°F/Gas 5.

2 Whisk the eggs and sugar in a large bowl until thick and creamy. Lightly fold in the walnuts, cocoa powder and flour. Spread the mixture gently and evenly into the tin. Cook for approximately 20 minutes or until the sponge is golden and springs back when pressed. Turn out onto a lightly floured kitchen paper, roll up and leave to cool.

3 Slice the bananas thinly, then sprinkle with a little rum. Whisk the cream and icing sugar until thick.

4 Neaten the edges of the sponge, then unroll and spread on the cream almost to the edges. Scatter on the bananas and re-roll. Wrap in cling-film and chill until ready to serve.

5 Whisk the double cream to soft peaks. Pipe the cream along the top of the roulade, decorate with the chocolate triangles and dust with icing sugar.

Serves 6
Prep time: 20 mins
Cook time: 10 mins

melted butter, for greasing
50 g/1¾ oz caster sugar + extra for dusting

175 g/6 oz dark chocolate (min. 50–55% cocoa solids) broken into pieces
3 tbsp double cream
4 egg yolks
5 egg whites
icing sugar, for dusting

Hot chocolate soufflé

1 You will need six 150 ml/5 fl oz ramekin dishes and one baking sheet. Preheat the oven to 200°C/400°F/Gas 6.

2 Place the baking sheet on the top shelf of the oven. Liberally brush the ramekin dishes with melted butter, sprinkle each with a teaspoon or so of the caster sugar, swirling to lightly coat, then tipping out excess.

3 Melt the chocolate and cream in a large heatproof bowl set over barely simmering water, cool, then whisk in the egg yolks.

4 Whisk the egg whites in another large clean bowl to soft peaks, then whisk in the remaining sugar, a little at a time until the egg whites are stiff. Whisk a spoonful into the chocolate mixture, then gently fold in the remaining egg whites.

5 Fill the ramekins, wipe the rims clean and run your thumb around the edges. This helps the soufflé rise evenly. Place the ramekins on the hot baking sheet and cook for 10–12 minutes or until risen and slightly wobbly.

6 Dust sieved icing sugar over the top, then serve straightaway.

Serves 8
Prep time: 30 mins
Cook time: 1–1½ hours

75 g/2¾ oz pistachio nuts, coarsely chopped
5 egg whites
250 g/9 oz caster sugar

100 g/3½ oz dark chocolate (min. 50–55% cocoa solids), chopped
100 g/3½ oz good quality white chocolate, chopped
100 g/3½ oz milk chocolate
450 ml/15 fl oz double cream
175 g/6 oz fresh raspberries
cocoa powder, for dusting

Triple chocolate pavlova

1 Line 2 baking sheets with baking parchment. Preheat the oven to 140°C/275°F/Gas 1. Draw a 23 cm/9 in circle on one sheet of parchment and a 15.5 cm/6 in circle on the other.

2 Dry-fry the nuts in a frying pan over a gentle heat. As soon as you smell a toasty aroma, remove from the heat to cool. Nuts burn very quickly!

3 Whisk the egg whites in a clean bowl until dry, then whisk in the sugar, a little at a time until glossy and stiff.

4 Gently fold in two-thirds of the nuts with the dark and white chocolate. Divide the meringue onto the parchment circles, spreading into peaked rounds. Bake for 1½ hours or until dry and the base sounds hollow when lightly tapped. Turn off the oven leaving the meringues to cool in the oven.

5 Meanwhile make some chocolate curls or shavings with the milk chocolate, see page 11.

6 To serve, lightly whip the cream and spread two-thirds over the large meringue. Scatter on half of the fruit, then top with the small meringue. Spread the remaining cream on top, then scatter over the remaining fruit, the chocolate shavings, a scattering of nuts and finally a dusting of cocoa powder.

Makes 6
Prep time: 20 mins plus overnight chilling

600 ml/1 pt whipping cream
a few drops of vanilla extract

100 g/4 oz dark chocolate (min. 70–75 % cocoa solids), broken into pieces
6 large egg yolks
1 tsp cornflour
50 g/1¾ oz caster sugar + extra for sprinkling

Chocolate crème brûlée

1 You will need six 150 ml/5 fl oz ramekins.

2 Pour the cream into a non-stick saucepan, stir in the vanilla and heat gently until the cream is scalding. Add the chocolate and whisk until melted and smooth.

3 Meanwhile in a large bowl use a wooden spoon to blend together the egg yolks, cornflour and caster sugar until just mixed but not frothy. Continue stirring whilst gradually pouring the hot chocolate cream onto the eggs.

4 Return the custard mix to the saucepan and constantly stir heat over a gentle heat until the custard thickens. Do not allow it to boil. Dip the wooden spoon in the custard to coat the back of it then run your finger through. If the custard forms a parting it is ready.

5 Strain the chocolate custard into a jug, then pour into the ramekins. Place on a tray and cool before covering and refrigerating for 5–6 hours and preferably overnight.

6 Take the ramekins out of the fridge 2 hours before serving. Sprinkle on a thin layer of caster sugar, then use the blowtorch in sweeping movements to melt and caramelize the sugar. Alternatively, place the ramekins on a baking sheet under a hot grill until the sugar caramelizes.

Serves 6
Prep time: 10 mins
Cook time: 45–50 mins

100 g/3½ oz plain flour
2 level tsp baking powder

50 g/1¾ oz cocoa powder
150 g/5 oz granulated sugar
150 ml/5 fl oz single cream
a few drops of vanilla extract
75 g/2¾ oz demerara sugar
350 ml/12 fl oz boiling water

Puddle pudding

1 Lightly grease a 1.4 l/2½ pt ovenproof dish. Preheat the oven to 160°C/325°F/Gas 3.

2 Sift the flour, baking powder and 2 tablespoons of the cocoa powder into a bowl, then whisk in the granulated sugar, cream and vanilla extract. Beat well to a smooth batter.

3 Pour into the dish. Mix together the remaining cocoa powder with the demerara sugar and sprinkle evenly over the surface. Pour on the boiling water.

4 Bake for 40–45 minutes or until risen, slightly moist but firm to the touch. Divide between warm bowls, making sure everyone gets a generous spoonful of the hidden hot chocolate sauce.

TIP
Delicious with cold pouring cream or vanilla ice cream.

4

tarts & pies

Serves 8–10
Prep time: 15 mins plus chilling
Cook time: 50–60 mins

50 g/1¾ oz butter, melted
200 g/7 oz pack chocolate-coated or plain digestive biscuits, crushed

FILLING
150 g/5½ oz dark chocolate (min. 70–75% cocoa solids)

700 g/1lb 8 oz mascarpone cheese
125 g/4½ oz light soft brown sugar
2 tbsp cornflour
3 eggs, beaten
mini chocolate eggs, to decorate

WHITE CHOCOLATE SAUCE
125 g/4½ oz good quality white chocolate
125 ml/4 fl oz double cream
15 g/½ oz butter

Baked cheesecake with white chocolate sauce

1 Base-line a 23 cm/9 in non-stick, spring-form cake tin. Preheat the oven to 180°C/350°F/Gas 4.

2 Melt the butter in a large bowl over a pan of barely simmering water. Stir in the crushed biscuits, then spread into the tin, pressing down evenly. Chill for 5 minutes.

3 Melt the dark chocolate in a small heatproof bowl set over the pan of barely simmering water. Stir until smooth, remove from heat and leave to cool a little.

4 In a large bowl, whisk together the mascarpone, sugar and cornflour until smooth. Whisk in the cooled chocolate and eggs. Spread over the biscuit base and level. Bake for 50–60 minutes. Turn off the oven and leave the door ajar until the cheesecake is completely cool. Decorate with mini eggs.

5 To make the sauce, place the white chocolate and cream in a small heatproof bowl set over a pan of simmering water. Heat until melted, then whisk in the butter.

Serves 8–10
Prep time: 15 mins plus chilling
Cook time: 50–60 mins

100 g/3½ oz butter
250 g/9 oz plain shortbread or
digestive biscuits, crushed

FILLING
175 g/6 oz white chocolate
375 g/13 oz cream cheese

75 g/2¾ oz caster sugar
a few drops vanilla extract
3 large eggs
200 ml/7 fl oz soured cream

TOPPING
75 g/2¾ oz caster sugar
150 ml/5 fl oz water
450 g/1 lb mixed summer berries
8–10 mint leaves, torn

White chocolate cheesecake

1 Base-line a 20 cm/8 in spring-form cake tin. Preheat the oven to 160°C/325°F/Gas 3.

2 Melt the butter in a bowl over a pan of barely simmering water. Stir in the biscuit crumbs, then spread into the tin, pressing down onto the base and sides. Chill for 5 minutes.

3 Melt the chocolate in a heatproof bowl over a pan of barely simmering water, stirring until smooth. Remove from the heat.

4 Whisk the cream cheese with the sugar and vanilla until smooth, then beat in the eggs, 1 at a time. Quickly stir the soured cream into the melted chocolate and add to the cream cheese mix, whisking until smooth. Pour over the biscuit base, level and bake for 50–60 minutes. Leave at room temperature for 1 hour, then chill until completely set.

5 For the topping, place the sugar and water in a pan and heat gently until dissolved; bring to the boil and simmer for a few minutes or until syrupy. Remove from the heat, then stir in the fruit and half the mint leaves. Leave to cool, then chill. Spoon over the cheesecake and decorate with remaining mint.

Serves 8–10
Prep time: 25 mins plus overnight soaking
Cook time: 33–45 mins

250 g/9 oz pitted ready-to-eat prunes, halved
3 tsp vanilla extract
175 g/6 oz butter
85 g/3 oz caster sugar

200 g/7 oz plain flour
50 g/1¾ oz cornflour

FILLING
100 g/3½ oz dark chocolate (min. 70–75% cocoa solids)
150 ml/5 fl oz double cream
2 tbsp caster sugar
250 g/9 oz mascarpone cheese
2 eggs, beaten

Dark chocolate, vanilla & prune tart

1 You will need a 23 cm/9 in deep fluted flan tin. Preheat the oven to 190°C/375°F/Gas 5.

2 Place the prunes in a bowl with the vanilla extract and 4 tbsp water. Stir to moisten thoroughly, then cover and leave in a cool place to soak overnight.

3 Cream the butter and sugar together, then work in both flours to a smooth firm dough. Place in the flan tin, pressing down evenly onto the base and sides. Chill for 15 minutes. Line the pastry case with greaseproof paper and fill with baking beans. Bake for 10–15 minutes, remove the beans and paper and bake for 3–5 minutes until just cooked. Reduce the oven temperature to 160°C/325°F/Gas 3.

4 Place the chocolate and cream in a heatproof bowl set over simmering water until the chocolate has just melted. Remove from the heat and whisk in the sugar, mascarpone and eggs.

5 Stir in the prunes and juices. Pour over the pastry case and bake for 20–25 minutes or until just set. Serve warm or chilled.

Makes 8
Prep time: 40 mins plus chilling
Cook time: 20 mins

250 g/9 oz plain flour
125 g/4½ oz salted butter, cubed
3 tbsp caster sugar

FILLING
400 ml/14 fl oz milk
1 vanilla pod, split lengthways
3 egg yolks
25 g/1 oz cornflour
200 g/7 oz white chocolate
2–3 tbsp redcurrant jelly
150 ml/5 fl oz whipping cream
225 g/8 oz fresh strawberries

Chocolate & strawberry tarts

1 You will need 8 x 9 cm/3½ in round fluted tartlet tins.
Preheat the oven to 200°C/400°F/Gas 6.

2 Rub the flour and butter together in a bowl until they
resemble breadcrumbs. Stir in the sugar; add 2–3 tbsp cold
water and work together to a soft dough. Chill for 30 minutes.

3 Gently heat the milk and vanilla pod in a pan until just
scalding. In a large bowl beat together the egg yolks and
cornflour. Strain on the milk whisking all the time. Discard
the pod. Return to the pan, break in half the white chocolate.
Stir constantly over a gentle heat until the chocolate has
melted and the custard thickened. Set aside until cool.

4 Cut the pastry into 6; roll each to circles large enough to
line the tins. Trim any excess. Line with paper and baking
beans; bake blind for 15 minutes. Remove the beans and paper
and bake for another 5 minutes. Transfer to a wire rack to cool.

5 Melt the remaining chocolate in a heatproof bowl set over
gently simmering water, then brush over the pastry cases. Melt
the redcurrant jelly. Whisk the cream to soft peaks, then fold
into the custard. Divide between the tarts, arrange the
strawberries on top and drizzle over the redcurrant jelly. Chill.

Serves 8
Prep time: 15 mins plus chilling
Cook time: 43–60 mins

175 g/6 oz butter
85 g/3 oz caster sugar
200 g/7 oz plain flour
50 g/1³/4 oz cornflour

FILLING
200 g/7 oz dark chocolate
(min. 50–55% cocoa solids)
125 g/4¹/2 oz unsalted butter
1 tbsp instant coffee dissolved in
1 tbsp boiling water
150 ml/5 fl oz single cream
175 g/6 oz dark soft brown sugar
3 eggs, beaten

Mississippi mud pie

1 You will need a 23cm/9 in deep fluted flan tin. Preheat the oven to 190°C/375°F/Gas 5.

2 Cream the butter and sugar together, then work in both flours to a smooth, firm dough. Press into the flan tin, lining it as evenly as possible. Chill for 15 minutes. Line the pastry case with greaseproof paper and fill with baking beans. Bake blind for 10–15 minutes, then remove the beans and paper and return to the oven for 3–5 minutes until just cooked. Reduce the oven temperature to 160°C/325°F/Gas 3.

3 Break the chocolate into a heatproof bowl set over gently simmering water, adding the butter and coffee. Stir until the chocolate has just melted. Remove from the heat and whisk in the cream, dark sugar and eggs.

4 Pour into the pastry base and return to the oven for 30–40 minutes until the filling is set. Serve at room temperature.

TIP
For an even richer filling, replace the dark soft brown sugar with muscovado sugar.

Serves 8
Prep time: 20 mins plus chilling

75 g/2³/4 oz butter
75 g/2³/4 oz demerara sugar
175 g/6 oz chocolate oat biscuits,
crushed

FILLING AND DECORATION
100 g/3¹/2 oz dark chocolate (min.
70–75% cocoa solids)

4 tbsp rum
3 leaves gelatine
1 tbsp instant coffee granules
dissolved in 5 tbsp boiling water
350 g/12 oz ricotta cheese
200 ml/7 fl oz whipping cream
3 eggs, separated
75 g/2³/4 oz caster sugar
8 chocolate truffles , see page 53
(optional) and chocolate shavings
cocoa powder, to dust

Mocha rum cheesecake

1 You will need a 20 cm/8 in non-stick, spring-form cake tin.

2 Melt the butter in a pan over a low heat. Stir in the sugar and crushed biscuits and mix well. Spread into the cake tin, pressing down evenly. Chill for 5 minutes.

3 Melt the chocolate in a small heatproof bowl set over a pan of barely simmering water, Stir in the rum, then remove from heat and leave to cool a little.

4 Soak the gelatine in a bowl of cold water for 5 minutes, then squeeze out the excess liquid, Place the coffee in a small bowl, add the gelatine and whisk until dissolved. In a large bowl, whisk together the ricotta cheese, cream, egg yolks and sugar until smooth. Whisk in the coffee mixture and the cooled chocolate.

5 Whisk the egg whites in a bowl until softly peaking. Whisk a spoonful into the cheese mixture, then gently fold in the rest. Pour onto the biscuit base and chill for 4–6 hours minimum. Run a palette knife around the edge of the tin, then release the spring clip and slide onto a serving plate. Decorate with truffles if liked and chocolate curls and dust with cocoa powder.

Recipe index

Apricot & white chocolate tray bake 16

Baked cheesecake with white chocolate sauce 84

Boston brownies 42

Choc-cherry spectacular 62

Chocolate & ginger parkin 26

Chocolate & pear upside-down pudding 68

Chocolate & strawberry tarts 90

Chocolate cheesecake swirls 44

Chocolate chip cookies 46

Chocolate crème brûlée 78

Chocolate cupcakes 40

Chocolate fondant 70

Chocolate icky sticky with choc-orange sauce 66

Chocolate kisses 48

Chocolate macaroons 50

Chocolate marble slice 18

Chocolate streusel cake 22

Chocolate, coconut & blueberry cereal bars 54

Chocolate, walnut & banana roulade 72

Dark chocolate, vanilla & prune tart 88

Five minute chocolate wonder 24

Fruit:
   Apricot & white chocolate tray bake 16
   Choc-cherry spectacular 62
   Chocolate & pear upside-down pudding 68
   Chocolate & strawberry tarts 90
   Chocolate icky sticky with choc-orange sauce 66
   Chocolate streusel cake 22

Chocolate, coconut & blueberry cereal bars 54

Chocolate, walnut & banana roulade 72

Dark chocolate, vanilla & prune tart 88

Spiced chocolate applesauce cake 28

White chocolate & orange drizzle cake 34

White chocolate cheesecake 86

White chocolate, cranberry & pistachio cookies 56

Ganache 21

Hot chocolate soufflé 74

Millionaire's shortbread 58

Mississippi mud pie 92

Mocha mallow roulade 64

Mocha rum cheesecake 94

Puddle pudding 80

Rocky chocolate truffles 52

Sauces:
   Choc-orange sauce 66
   Milk chocolate sauce 68
   White chocolate sauce 84

Smooth chocolate truffles 53

Spiced chocolate applesauce cake 28

Sunken gluten-free chocolate cake 36

The alternative Christmas chocolate cake 30

The ultimate chocolate cake 20

Triple chocolate pavlova 76

White chocolate & orange drizzle cake 34

White chocolate cheesecake 86

White chocolate, cranberry & pistachio cookies 56

ACKNOWLEDGEMENT

The author would like to thank the photographer, Michael Prior, for always going that extra mile – www.michaelpriorphotographer.com